Deepening Fiction

A Practical Guide for Intermediate and Advanced Writers

Sarah Stone
New College of California

Ron Nyren

New York San Francisco Boston
London Toronto Sydney Tokyo Singapore Madrid
Mexico City Munich Paris Cape Town Hong Kong Montreal

Managing Editor: Erika Berg
Executive Marketing Manager: Ann Stypuloski
Production Manager: Denise Phillip
Project Coordination, Text Design, and Electronic Page Makeup: Shepherd Incorporated
Cover Design Manager: John Callahan
Cover Designer: Maria Ilardi
Cover Photo: Joseph Cornell (1903–1972) American, "The hotel Eden" 1945, assemblage with music box, 38.3 × 39.7 × 12.1 cm. Purchased 1973. Photo © National Gallery of Canada, Ottawa
Manufacturing Buyer: Roy Pickering
Printer and Binder: Phoenix Color Corporation
Cover Printer: Phoenix Color Corporation

Library of Congress Cataloging-in-Publication Data

Stone, Sarah, 1961–
Deepening fiction : a practical guide for intermediate and advanced writers / Sarah Stone, Ron Nyren.
p. cm.
Includes bibliographical references and index.
ISBN 0-321-19537-X
1. Fiction—Authorship. 2. Short stories. I. Nyren, Ron. II. Title.

PN3355.S86 2005
808.3—dc22 2004053507

Please visit our website at http://www.ablongman.com

ISBN 0-321-19537-X

1 2 3 4 5 6 7 8 9 10—PHH—07 06 05 04

Brief Contents

Contents

Preface

The romantic image of the solitary writer persists in our culture—chopping wood outside a Montana cabin between chapters, writing stories on nights and weekends in a tiny eighth-floor walk-up in the Bronx, or filling handmade notebooks on a trans-Siberian train. Fiction writing is one of the least collaborative of the arts, unlike theater, dance, or music. At the same time, writers have always been in community with each other, sharing knowledge and support—the Japanese poets of the Edo period; the English Romantics; the habitués of Madame de Staël's salon; the poets, playwrights, and novelists of the Harlem Renaissance; the Beat writers. Today's writing classes, programs, and informal groups are a continuation of these traditions. The creative tensions that ran through those other literary groups—the conflicts between influence and originality, belonging and individual freedom, rivalry and friendship—also continue. We seek out advice on craft; we are suspicious of advice on craft; we test it, incorporate it, skew it, or reject it, sometimes in equal measure.

Deepening Fiction: A Practical Guide for Intermediate and Advanced Writers is intended to support the ongoing conversation of ideas about writing. We discuss ideas, our own and others', covering a range of intermediate and advanced writing issues. More experienced writers are ready to understand just how much writing *is* revision, how much we develop the shape and meaning of a story over the course of multiple drafts. Our goal is to help writers connect craft to a particular work they're wrestling with. *Deepening Fiction* addresses the "why" as well as the "what" and "how" of fiction writing, examining the artistic implications of different craft choices.

Approach

The connection between craft and creativity isn't always obvious, and we often behave as if they're at odds: plenty of creative writing advice tells us to shut the inner critic into a box until the first draft is done, to avoid letting the left side of the brain know what the right side is doing. And it's true that if we don't shut off the critic sometimes, we'll have a hard time completing our drafts.

The paradox is that it takes substantial knowledge of our craft to be original, to sweep readers into another world and leave them changed at the end of it. The long middle stretch of the writing apprenticeship—between the initial learning of the basic concepts and the production of meaningful, memorable works free of inconsistencies and clichés—can be a hard one. There are no "rules" for imaginative writing; the craft choices, it turns out, are infinite. It's one thing to learn the difference between scene and summary and quite another to figure out what parts of a particular story to render as scene, what as summary, and how these choices influence the story's meaning. As writers, we draw on the help of the community in order to find the approach that is uniquely our own.

We learn craft in order to forget it. Writers can use the exercises, craft discussions, and analyses in *Deepening Fiction* to increase their awareness of the possibilities of fiction-writing, acquiring knowledge and working methods to respond to the vague, uneasy feeling that something is wrong with a story. We would never suggest that writers spend the rest of their lives examining their point of view choices with the help of a chart or studying a story's every detail for its relation to the overall mood. We engage in these analyses just enough to allow us to master the concepts. Whenever we need to, we can return to a technical approach for help, but over the course of a lifetime, our story-making process becomes increasingly intuitive.

To develop writers' decision-making processes, we offer observations, questions, and examinations of the solutions other writers have found. We try to demystify the writing process at every stage. We intend *Deepening Fiction* to aid writers in discovering the purposes and subjects of their writing, as well as their place in the world, a place often at odds with mainstream values.

Lewis Hyde, in *The Gift: Imagination and the Erotic Life of Property,* writes about the struggle that artists, who exist in a "gift economy," come up against in our society's "market economy," which regards a work of art as a commodity for gain. He describes a gift not as a talent we make use of for our own purposes but as what we offer to the world:

> . . . whatever we have been given is supposed to be given away again, not kept. Or, if it is kept, something of similar value should move on in its stead, the way a billiard ball may stop when it sends another scurrying across the felt, its momentum transferred. You may keep your Christmas present, but it ceases to be a gift in the true sense unless you have given something else away. As it is passed along, the gift may be given back to the original donor, but this is not essential. In fact, it is better if the gift is not returned, but is given instead to some new, third party. The only essential is this: *the gift must always move.* There are other forms of property that stand still, that mark a boundary or resist momentum, but the gift keeps going.

Our lives as writers and teachers have led us away from the idea of the writer as a hermit engaged in solitary acts of genius. Hyde's remarks remind us that the gifts we have received must be shared if they are to help us thrive.

How the Book Is Organized

The book contains three sections: chapters on the elements of fiction, an anthology of stories, and a section on the writing processes and the writing life.

- In Part I, ten chapters reintroduce basic concepts and cover intermediate/advanced approaches to character, point of view, story structure, handling time in fiction, subject matter, setting and detail, research and societal context, style and dialogue, and revision. The chapters stand alone so instructors can use them in any order.

- In Part II, the anthology of 22 classic and contemporary stories, both realistic and experimental, provides examples by writers from a variety of backgrounds and nationalities. Analyses of these stories, and discussion questions in the chapters, help students learn to read *as writers*. For flexibility and easy reference, the text groups anthology stories together, rather than embedding them in the chapters.
- In Part III, discussions of the writing process and the writing life address the extraliterary issues key to developing a sustainable life as a writer: understanding the roles of talent and habit in a writer's development, overcoming writer's block, facing the thorny processes of rejection and publication, and unraveling the mythologies and realities of a writer's life. The aim of this section is to help serious writers persevere in their writing and understand their own place in the writing community.
- In addition to the dedicated revision chapter, each chapter addresses revision in relation to a specific craft topic, including examples of the revision process from well-known writers, some of them discussing their anthology stories. These different approaches emphasize the fundamental role of revision, both deep revision and line editing.
- Intermediate/advanced writing and reading exercises let students work, individually and in groups, with their previous writing and also generate new ideas in relation to each chapter's topic.
- Analyses of excerpts of published work, both anthology stories and additional selections, give context to illustrate aspects of craft, exploring how the author's choices relate to the story's overall aims. These examples enable writers to see that no effect exists for its own sake: all decisions affect the story as a whole.
- An extensive writer's glossary defines terms and key literary movements to save time and clarify concepts for classes with writers at different levels of skill and knowledge.
- Suggestions for further reading offer resources for intermediate/advanced writers, including additional anthologies, literary magazines, and books on the art and craft of writing, the writing life, and publishing.
- Quotes from writers, biographies of the writers in the anthology, story discussions, and the sections about writing processes all emphasize the connections between the act of writing and the resulting story.

Acknowledgments

Textbook writers, like fiction writers, exist as part of a community, and *Deepening Fiction* has benefited from the help of writers, teachers, and editors.

Our colleagues and cohorts at the University of Michigan, Ann Arbor; University of California, Berkeley; New College of California; and Stanford have taught us much of what we know: we are grateful for their wisdom, humor, and companionship. *Deepening Fiction* has had the good fortune to come into being under the guidance of Erika Berg, who has supported us at every step of the way, including assembling an invaluable group of reviewers. We appreciate Elisa Adams's helpful suggestions, Amy Freitag's meticulous copyediting, and the work of Ken Harrell, Michele Ryan, Michele Cronin, and Teresa Ward. Barbara Santoro has greatly assisted us throughout the process of bringing our words into print.

Fiction-writing instructors from around the country read various drafts of *Deepening Fiction* thoughtfully and responded with intelligent criticism and encouragement. Our thanks to Diana Abu-Jaber, Portland State University; Joseph Boyden, University of New Orleans; Michelle Herman, Ohio State University; Alyce Miller, Indiana University, Bloomington; Ruth Moose, University of North Carolina–Chapel Hill; Timothy Parrish, Southern Connecticut State University; Mike Raymond, Stetson University; Natalia Singer, St. Lawrence University; Cheryl Slean, University of Washington, and others who have chosen not to be named, but to whom we wish to express our gratitude. Susan Kenney, of Colby College, not only gave us extensive and insightful comments but annotated the entire manuscript, engaging us in conversation at every level. Lynna Williams, of Emerson College, has been a brilliant and challenging reader from the very first stages of this book. Ryan Harty, of Stanford University, extended a generous and encouraging reading of the book's early pages at a moment when it was much needed.

We appreciate the help of those who wrote their own biographies for this book—biographies aimed at encouraging rather than intimidating the writers who will be using the text—and those who helped with permissions. Our deep thanks to Andrea Barrett and Adam Johnson for writing descriptions of their stories' revision processes for this text, to ZZ Packer for the use of the beginning of one of her drafts of "Drinking Coffee Elsewhere," and to Daniel Orozco for his description of the revision process of "Orientation."

We are grateful to Charles Baxter for his guidance in writing and his belief in us: we would not have written this book without his encouragement. And we are grateful for Andrea Barrett's constant support, encouragement, generosity, and insight.

Our thanks to all of those who gave us their assistance, criticism, and advice and to all those writers whose words we have quoted. We want to express our gratitude to our teachers, our colleagues, and our students, for the many gifts they have given us. This book is for them, and for the community.

PART ONE

Intermediate and Advanced Approaches to Fiction-Writing

CHAPTER

1

Developing and Complicating Characters

(Anthology selections: "Drinking Coffee Elsewhere," "The Forest," and "Powder")

. . . a work of art is moral when you give integrity to all of the principal characters. You don't set any of your characters up as strawmen, or as foils, or as chess pieces; you give them all specific reasons for being the way they are, and then you follow and trace that. Even the objects in a fictional world are shot through with meaning and philosophical significance. So the moral fiction is a work of exploration, an intellectual adventure, an adventure of the spirit.

—Charles Johnson, interviewed in *The Book That Changed My Life*

GENERATING CHARACTERS

At any given moment in our lives, we may be involved in the stories of a dozen or more people: waiting to see if a close friend will be fired for mouthing off to her boss, hoping that the high school student we've been tutoring will get into college, worrying about a sister who's about to give birth to her fifth child, or learning that an ex-friend has been spreading our secrets all over town. This web of relationships is the ground from which we invent imaginary human beings or transform living ones into characters on the page.

Sometimes we develop a story idea from a newspaper headline or an overheard conversation. Sometimes we start from a real incident, but invent new appearances, histories, and personality quirks for our characters, as a way to free ourselves from the tyranny of real life and "what actually happened." Sometimes in a dream or daydream we get a vague image of people in a situation: we try to clarify this image by writing a story. Too often, though, no matter how we begin, we wind up with a set of names and details that stubbornly remain words on paper. What we need are ways of proceeding that will allow us, over the course of many drafts, to create characters who are surprising without being arbitrary and believable without being dull. Nothing is more essential to fiction-writing than this ability to make characters, which makes it all the more maddening when we feel that we aren't really understanding the people in our stories.

Often, we can't immediately see what has gone wrong. We've been told that our characters need to desire or fear something, and that these desires or fears then prompt the characters to take actions that have consequences for themselves and others, in the face of internal and external obstacles. And yet, a story can have all of this, but the characters remain semitransparent, not fully alive. As readers, we're aware of the story as a *made* thing, however well crafted, in which we never entirely lose ourselves.

What we want to get hold of is the particular, individual nature of a character, the way the complexities and contradictions seem to form a harmonious whole: the essence. These can include physical and emotional details, past choices and actions and the consequences these have had, and habitual ways of behaving. What is the constellation of images that occurs when we think of someone who's been important in our lives? Perhaps we recall the way he peered over his glasses when he was about to make a joke, the days he spent categorizing his mother's collection of jazz LPs, the clove cigarettes he smoked, his irritating refusal to lie to anyone, for any purpose. These separate details begin to cohere, to make sense together, to form a portrait.

Margot Livesey, in her essay "Mrs. Turpin Reads the Stars," gives us insight into deciding which facts are meaningful. After discussing approaches to character by Aristotle, E. M. Forster, and William Gass, she discovers "what brings a character to life for a reader" by analyzing this passage from Flannery O'Connor's "Revelation":

> The doctor's waiting room, which was very small, was almost full when the Turpins entered and Mrs. Turpin, who was very large, made it look even smaller by her presence. She stood looming at the head of the magazine table set in the center of it, a living demonstration that the room was inadequate and ridiculous. Her little bright black eyes took in all the patients as she sized up the seating situation. There was one vacant chair and a place on the sofa occupied by a blond child in a dirty blue romper who should have been told to move over and make room for the lady. He was five or six, but Mrs. Turpin saw at once that no one was going to tell him to move over.
>
> [Livesey then writes] . . . Mrs. Turpin has only a few physical attributes, her size, her little bright black eyes. She has a proper name; she has a ruling conception; she is an instrument of verbal organization and a source of verbal energy. She also, and I think we can glean this even from a few sentences, has what she *hasn't* been given; we amplify her size, we guess her wardrobe. From the moment Mrs. Turpin is introduced, in that beautifully cadenced first sentence, we know that her job is to make the world smaller; she marches into that waiting room and right out of it, into the reader's imagination. The crucial thing that brings Mrs. Turpin to life, though, is no single attribute or detail, no action or remark, but the overwhelming sense we get, as we read these lines, of how Mrs. Turpin regards herself and the world: her attitude.

> This seems to me the key to creating vivid and memorable characters. It is also, I think, the reason why doing so can prove such a tricky task. No amount of detail—eyes, teeth, hair, jobs, dreams, relationship to mother, history of dog ownership, bank balance—will avail unless it conveys attitude. Indeed long lists of detail without affect may simply make the task harder, for both reader and writer. What one needs are the right details, the so-called telling details, and what those details tell is attitude.

We ordinarily think of "attitude" in connection with a certain demanding in-your-face quality, but as used here it can be any set of actions, details, and characteristics that shows how the characters "regard [themselves] in the world." Characters, like real people, often reveal themselves most clearly in situations of pressure, when they're no longer bothering to wear their "game face." But our characteristic attitude shows in almost everything we do: in what we demand from or offer to the world. The idea of attitude helps us organize our details as we create and depict characters.

The approaches we describe in the following three sections—inhabiting a character, finding ways to represent that character, or coming up with more background—can be tried at any point in a story's drafting and revisions, not necessarily in the order we're presenting them. Our own experience of writing stories is that we frequently find ourselves baffled by the characters and ready to give up on the story (and, some days, on writing itself). Then, as we keep brooding about it, or as we deliberately try these approaches, we'll suddenly feel that we've found the answer. This feeling can lead to the delicious stage of exalted note-taking, followed by much more writing. A week or a month later, we'll realize that, although our changes may have helped, we still have more work to do. Like all aspects of fiction-writing, it's trial and error, more trial, more error: a messy process, but one that, repeated enough times, can result in characters who give the illusion of being real, complex, layered, and quirky human beings.

Inhabiting Characters

Whether our characters are major or minor, viewpoint or nonviewpoint, it helps to put ourselves in their shoes, to experience what it's like to be each of them. As we write successive drafts, we work to inhabit their bodies and history. The writer feels the twinge in one character's arthritic knee, flushes with shame as another blurts out a faux pas. It's most natural to inhabit our characters in the first-person point of view (POV), which is why first-person stories are often easiest and most vivid for us when we're beginning to write. Later on, we can accomplish this vividness in various viewpoints. We imaginatively move around the room to experience each character in the scene. After all, even minor characters are major to themselves. What is this person experiencing through the five senses, feeling about events, and understanding about the other characters? We may not put everything we discover into the story, but it will enrich our ability to describe each person's actions and gestures and may give us more perspective on our viewpoint characters.

If the story is showing us sensory details through a character's eyes, to what extent do the character's specific concerns influence the details that character perceives and how? For instance, a high-strung accountant called into the boss's office expecting to be fired might be examining the boss's desk for the telltale annual report, while a brash co-worker expecting a promotion might be expectantly checking out the fancy desk set and the luxury chair. Often sensory details can convey characters' states of mind with greater vividness and originality than direct reporting of their thoughts.

The more we are able to inhabit our characters, the more we will be able to give a reader vivid experiences of them. This paragraph from Melanie Rae Thon's "First, Body" demonstrates the combining of methods: she uses various kinds of information in a single paragraph, three pages into the story, during a sex scene, a natural time for the viewpoint character to be hyperaware of his own body and his lover's:

> She had narrow hips, a flat chest. He weighed more than twice what she did. He was too big for himself, always—born too big, grown too fast. Too big to cry. Too big to spill his milk. At four he looked six; at six, ten. Clumsy, big-footed ten. Slow, stupid ten. *Like living with a bear,* his mother said, something broken every day, her precious blown-glass ballerina crumbling in his hand, though he held her so gently, lifting her to the window to let the light pass through her. He had thick wrists, enormous thumbs. Even his eyebrows were bushy. *My monster.* Roxanne said the second night, *who made you this way?*

Thon give us a sense of his physical presence and appearance; his feelings about himself; some history; his mother's criticism of him; a remembered action—with its implication of the helpless inability to keep from destroying fragile things; and his lover's words about him. Six different aspects of the character—presented quickly and efficiently—and then we're back to the lovemaking and conversation. This works because we are so close to his thoughts, which Thon presents directly. Not "he felt bad that he was so big"—we're inside his experience. The sound of the short, balky sentences, like a large man in a small space, unable to take a full step, reflects the passage's meaning.

Sometimes one character's view of another tells us as much about the teller as the one observed. This method, whether through the observations of a first-person narrator or comments overheard in dialogue, allows us to learn something about both characters at once. Where an authorial commentary may focus our attention on the writer, a character's commentary focuses us on the characters themselves.

In Kazuo Ishiguro's *When We Were Orphans,* our first introduction to the very difficult character of Sarah Hemmings gives us enough physical detail to picture her, but is primarily a psychological portrait. We don't imagine her as a generic pretty young woman, but as a compelling and dangerous creature:

> . . . as it happened, that first time I saw her, I did not think her at all pretty. It is even possible I somehow sensed, there and then, at my first sight of her, those qualities which I have since discovered to be so significantly a part of her. What I saw was a small, rather elf-like young woman with dark, shoulder-length hair. Even though at that moment she was clearly wishing to charm the men she was talking to, I could see something about her smile that might in an instant turn it into a sneer. A slight crouch around her shoulders, like that of a bird of prey, gave her posture a suggestion of scheming. Above all, I noticed a certain quality around her eyes—a kind of severity, something ungenerously exacting, which I see now, in retrospect, was what more than anything else caused me to stare at her with such fascination that evening.

She has normal, even appealing qualities—is a "rather elf-like young woman," and yet the rest of the description is full of menace. The art here is in the skillful arrangement of details. If the description of her as "having a slight crouch about her shoulders, like that of a bird of prey" had directly followed the "elf-like," it would be too contradictory. And yet, by the time we get the second metaphor, we are ready for it because we have been told to expect contradictions, and were led from her attempt at charm to the possibility of a sneer. The combination of acute observation and unlikely juxtaposition of metaphors convinces us to see Sarah Hemmings as the narrator does initially. And, in the process, we learn more about the narrator himself: he is observant, judgmental, and attracted to the unusual and dangerous.

Our view as readers, like the narrator's, changes over the course of *When We Were Orphans*. We *experience* these characters, and we believe in them, but we never fully understand them. Psychological exploration is not the same as psychological explanation. The people we know operate in characteristic ways, but we can never completely understand them or predict precisely what they will do. As writers, we're looking to create characters who are individuals, not "typical" for their situation, but as unique as people in real life.

Representing Characters

At some point we have to put ourselves in the reader's shoes as well. To represent a character, we have an array of tools: characteristic dialogue and tone of voice, sensory details about the character's body and movement, the places the character frequents, the character's actions, the character's thoughts, the observations of other characters about this person, and narrative commentary. With a wide-ranging omniscient point of view, we can use any of these tools. With more restricted points of view, we have to choose details carefully in order to render characters seen only from the outside.

We have to decide which details will make the characters' individual essences coherent, vivid, and believable for the reader. Just because we have figured out that our character had a miserable experience in high school doesn't necessarily mean that this information goes into the story, not unless it's needed to help the reader make sense of the story's events.

In "Bookkeeping," Harold Brodkey shows us a woman, Annetje, seen through the eyes of a man, Avram, who finds her dangerously attractive. He notes her manner of dress and the shape of her body, and also comments on these aspects, coloring them with his opinions and desires:

> Abruptly the door opened, and there was Annetje. Bedraggled, uncombed, pale inside a tattered sweater and a heavy skirt that hung lopsidedly and was sliding lower on her hips. Annetje was one of those intensely seductive women who dress stylishly for the street and then relax at home inside shapeless old clothes, clothes they've perhaps had since college, or their first marriage—mementos of lost years, vanished fashions, and the emotions that went with the fashions.
>
> Annetje was very thin-waisted, with little cushionlike hips and thin, square shoulders, quite broad, and Avram was always aware of the small of her back; her shoulders and her hips were assertive: it was the small of her back which was private and where her vulnerability truly resided. His hands twitched, anxious to touch her there.

Through Avram's eyes, we see that Annetje doesn't take care of herself (she's "bedraggled"), and that despite her seductive power ("her shoulders and hips were assertive"), she's also fragile ("it was the small of her back which was private and where her vulnerability truly resided"). By focusing us unexpectedly on the detail of her back, Brodkey makes her physical and emotional presence palpable. Avram's generalization about intensely seductive women also expands the portrait beyond Annetje, to tell us something about the work that goes into dressing stylishly, the emotional cost of keeping up so furiously with the changing fashions of the present. Annetje is both distinctly imagined as an individual and yet representative of a larger human tendency, which makes her fragility even more compelling.

As an exercise in discovering how much character information our favorite writers include in a story—and how and when they introduce it—we might try going through a few pages (or an entire story, if we're feeling particularly desperate, ambitious, or in need of a task to help us procrastinate on our own writing) with different highlighters, choosing one color for a character's physical sensations or appearance, another for thoughts, another for background, another for objects or places that reveal important information about the character, another for the character's significant actions, another for characteristic phrases or expressions in the dialogue, and still another for direct comment by the narrator. This way we can see how the different methods are combined, how the character is initially presented to us, and what information is added later.

Character History/Background/Connections

Piling up too much information about a central character as soon as that person appears in the story tends to slow the action, diminish the mystery, and call attention to the writer rather than to the character. Still, we want our readers to know enough about the characters' genders, temperaments, races, classes, ages, and circumstances so that they are imagining characters similar to the ones we're imagining. Otherwise, readers may suddenly discover, halfway through the story, that they've been imagining a 60-year-old environmental activist with 3 children as a 16-year-old boy. A detail or two, presented indirectly in the course of describing events, will often give the idea, as in Tobias Wolff's "Powder":

> Just before Christmas my father took me skiing at Mount Baker. He'd had to fight for the privilege of my company, because my mother was still angry with him for sneaking me into a nightclub during his last visit, to see Thelonious Monk.

In two sentences, we know something about the age of the narrator—old enough for his father to sneak him into a nightclub, young enough for his mother to be angry about it; the class of the family—they can afford nightclubs and ski vacations; the family dynamic—the mother is a figure of authority to both the father and son, who clearly like to defy authority. We're located in the story's situation, without our narrator having to tell us his age, or that his parents fight frequently, or how much money they have.

Sometimes a writer does begin with history: Cynthia Ozick's story "The Suitcase" pulls off this tricky move, drawing us into the story before giving any dramatic scenes:

> Mr. Hencke, the father of the artist, was a German, an architect, and a traveler—not particularly in that order of importance. He had flown a Fokker for the Kaiser, but there was little of the pilot left in him: he had a rather commonplace military-like snap to his shoulders, especially when he was about to meet someone new. This was not because he had been in the fierce and rigid Air Force, but because he was clandestinely shy. His long grim face, with the mouth running across its lower hem like a slipped thread in a linen sack, was as pitted as a battlefield. Under a magnifying glass his skin would have shown moon-craters. As a boy he had had the smallpox. He lived in a big yellow-brick house in Virginia, and no longer thought of himself as a German. He did not have German thoughts, except in a certain recurring dream, in which he always rode naked on a saddleless horse, holding on to its black moist mane and crying "*Schneller, schneller.*"

Ozick weaves descriptions of Mr. Hencke's body in with the background information. Nearly every sentence contains a contradiction or two, which is part of what makes the opening complicated and intriguing. Ozick undermines details highlighting the remnants of his "fierce" military past—the Fokker he had flown, the "military-like snap of his shoulders," the face "as pitted as a battlefield"—with other details suggesting frailty—the shyness, the sewing metaphor for his mouth, the childhood smallpox. At the same time, by emphasizing both his quiet denial of his German past and the way it constantly pressures him through his dreams (not surprising, since the story takes place only 20 years after World War II), the author suggests his past still shadows everything about him. The effect is to set the reader up to wonder how these contradictory elements in his character will play out in his life. The information gives us context for later scenes and keeps us turning the pages.

Often writers wonder how to come up with convincing backgrounds for their characters, concerned that making lists of characters' hobbies, histories, or traumas may lead to arbitrary invention, unconnected to the artistic and structural needs of the story. Usually, if a surprising and necessary detail emerges, it's in the process of writing and rewriting, through a kind of attentive listening. This kind of detail, often produced by the writing mechanism after the writer has put in substantial time on a story, is more apt to relate to the plot, the subject matter, and the themes than an arbitrarily assigned favorite food or color. Allowing oneself to daydream about the characters and story while taking long walks, driving, or doing dishes is another way of leaving the mind open to sudden character discoveries.

On the other hand, for some writers, these lists may work, particularly if we have already written a draft or two or three of the story. Margot Livesey's ideas about "attitude" come into play here: the characteristic stances of characters show in their tastes, interests, hobbies, job history, pets, passions, peculiar habits, pet peeves, secret desires, vices, virtues, family background, favorite styles of clothing, habits of cooking and eating, religious and political convictions, and so on. Surprises here, ways that a character is complicated, and even somewhat contradictory—in the way that real people can be contradictory—help make the illusion of a three-dimensional human being.

We recommend approaching list-making in a dreamy, waiting mode, not "making things up," but listening for answers that come in their own time, full of false starts, in the time-wasting fashion so beloved of writing mechanisms everywhere. This is the opposite of efficiently coming up with a list of ten habits or tastes and busily applying them to the character. When we're rereading our stories, and perhaps adding information that we learned by list-making, we can bring our attention to what we're putting in and what we're leaving out, the amount and kind of background information. How do these choices serve the needs of the story? Does the information we include relate in some way to the story's themes or to the issues the characters struggle with? Will it affect the action or the relationships in the story?

STORY ANALYSIS AND QUESTIONS: "DRINKING COFFEE ELSEWHERE"

(Note: please read the story once before *you read the following analysis. Then, after you read the analysis, look at the story a second time, keeping the discussion questions in mind. You will get the most benefit out of this process*

if you mark specific passages in the story, take notes, and work through the questions in writing.)

ZZ Packer's "Drinking Coffee Elsewhere" demonstrates how to use a character's background to implicitly reveal motivation. The use of backstory here gives a sense of the narrator's whole life, without weighing down the forward progression of the story. The story's protagonist, Dina, is confronting an alien place, as well as feelings that make her alien to herself. She has set herself against the sociable, anti-intellectual values of her working-class black neighborhood to become a college student at Yale, only to find herself transformed, in this mostly white, elitist world, from "an honor-roll student" into someone "hard-bitten and recalcitrant." Her first resistance shows up in the orientation games:

> When it was my turn I said, "My name is Dina, and if I had to be any object, I guess I'd be a revolver." The sunlight dulled as if on cue. Clouds passed rapidly overhead, presaging rain. I don't know why I said it. Until that moment I'd been good in all the ways that were meant to matter. I was an honor-roll student—though I'd learned long ago not to mention it in the part of Baltimore where I lived. Suddenly I was hard-bitten and recalcitrant, the kind of kid who took pleasure in sticking pins into cats; the kind who chased down smart kids to spray them with Mace.

The first scene of the story gives us individual dialogue, physical description, background, the responses of other characters, and narrative commentary ("her hair was a shade of blond I'd only seen on Playboy covers.") Because we are seeing through Dina's eyes, the phrasing of the observations reveals her emotional state, both fragile and hostile, as well as information about her situation.

DISCUSSION QUESTIONS

1. What is it we hope might happen for Dina as the story goes on? What are we worried about? How are these hopes and worries the same as, or different from, what Dina herself hopes for or worries about?
2. When and how does Packer give us information about Dina's past? What seems to be left unspoken and why? What are the older Dina's purposes in telling this story?
3. How much information is given through dialogue and how much through direct reporting? How much of Dina's background is given through scene and how much through summary? What details are key in conveying both the facts and the emotional atmosphere of Dina's past?
4. How is the story about the boy with the nice shoes related to her experiences at Yale? How would the story be different without this episode from her past?

5. How does Packer use the title to illuminate Dina's motivations?
6. In what ways do the events of the story arise from Dina's character and history?

CONNECTING CHARACTER TO STORY

If, halfway through *Moby Dick,* Captain Ahab quit pursuing the white whale and enrolled in medical school, the whole thrust of the story's plot up to that point would strike the reader as irrelevant. Characters are part of the story as a whole, and must serve the needs of the fiction they inhabit, taking action based on these fears or desires, and then responding to the consequences of their choices. The characters' desires and fears can, of course, be understandable without being rational. If all people were flawlessly logical, wise, and kind, humans might not have the tradition of storytelling.

As we are writing, if we find ourselves asking, "What could happen next?" then we can look to the flaws and limitations of the character for clues. Mary Gaitskill's "A Romantic Weekend" shows how plot can arise from character:

> She was meeting a man she had recently and abruptly fallen in love with. She was in a state of ghastly anxiety. He was married, for one thing, to a Korean woman whom he described as the embodiment of all that was feminine and elegant. Not only that, but a psychic had told her that her relationship with him could cripple her emotionally for the rest of her life. On top of this, she was tormented by the feeling that she looked inadequate. Perhaps her body tilted too far forward as she walked, perhaps her jacket made her torso look bulky in contrast to her calves and ankles, which were probably skinny. She felt like an object unraveling in every direction. In anticipation of their meeting, she had not been able to sleep the night before; she had therefore eaten some amphetamines, and these had heightened her feeling of disintegration.

Beth is having an affair not just with a married man, but with a man who praises his wife in front of her; she seeks the advice of a psychic, rather than trusting her own judgment, and then ignores that advice. She has conflicting fears and desires: a desire for this love affair, and a fear of being emotionally crippled because of it. We know from the impossibility of the situation, from Beth's impulsive and anxious nature, and from the ominous images and language, that the meeting described in the first line will be the beginning of something disastrous.

When we find ourselves writing a draft that seems heavy on character description but light on plot, we can ask ourselves, what action or event could most test this person's particular personality? What does the character want most, and what happens if he or she pursues that desire? Or what tendency, when taken too far, might lead this person into a potentially dangerous or disruptive sequence of events?

Motivation and Action

What drives characters to take action? If the ghost of Hamlet's father had not demanded vengeance, Hamlet's subsequent actions would be as incomprehensible to the audience as they are to the other characters in the play. If Toni Morrison had not created for us such a vivid and terrible picture of slavery in *Beloved,* we would not understand why a woman would kill her children to keep them from being returned to this condition. If Alice Munro, in "The Turkey Season," did not give us such a minute picture of each character's habits and pruderies, we would not understand the explosion that results when sex, in the form of a swaggering and self-confident young man, enters the turkey barn. A horrifying discovery, a character's desire to change or escape an intolerable situation, a set of unfulfilled longings constrained by internal strictures—any of these can push people to change their lives or lead them into volatile situations.

It isn't always easy to make a character's desire as compelling to the reader as it is to the character. Suppose a character longs terribly for a lover, is being mistreated by a lover, or is trying to choose between two lovers. If we see that he's a charming, bright, socially adept fellow, beloved of men and women alike, we aren't apt to worry for him, or to keep reading, even if the prose is scintillating. We think, "Oh, he'll find someone as soon as he gets over this person." We've probably all had the experience of telling friends about a problem that seems a matter of life or death to us (a bad haircut the day before a prom or reunion), only to have them see it as minor. Later, when we're able to gain perspective, we realize they were right. Intense emotions do not necessarily correspond to true urgency.

A story will be more complicated if the reader's hopes and fears for the characters are not identical to the characters' hopes and fears for themselves. And one set of hopes and fears may turn into another, in a logical progression. In "The Aleph," Jorge Luis Borges presents a character whose frustrated longing leads to an otherwise inexplicable action that opens up the door to a new, even more impossible longing. After the death of Beatriz, the woman the narrator loves, he grieves to see new billboards go up, because they're evidence that the universe "was already growing away from her." But then, with "melancholy vanity," he decides to continue devoting himself to her: "I knew that more than once my futile devotion had exasperated her; now that she was dead, I could consecrate myself to her memory—without hope, but also without humiliation." This is not a love story in which the reader is expected to hope for a happy outcome. The narrator hopes to live up to his own image of himself and memorialize his love; we hope for him to come to his senses and to make a life for himself.

Every year, he visits Beatriz's father and her first cousin, despite the cool welcome and the cousin's endless disquisitions on life and poetry. As readers, we watch to see whether the narrator's devotion will be undermined by the cousin's pomposity. We also wonder whether the cousin is deliberately torturing the unsuccessful lover for pleasure or to drive him away. Now we're worried not only that he won't go away, but that he will awaken to his humiliating status and be crushed.

What happens, though it arises naturally from the story, is quite different than anything we might have predicted. In a Borges story, the desire for knowledge is often a driving passion. The cousin summons the narrator to view in his cellar "an Aleph . . . one of the points in space that contains all points . . . where . . . all the places of the world, seen from every angle, coexist." The narrator believes the cousin has gone mad, but agrees to come, motivated only by the desire to visit the photograph of Beatriz once again. To his surprise, the Aleph does seem to exist, and, for a dazzling page, the narrator is possessed, magnificently, of all knowledge. But when he emerges, the cousin's rudeness and arrogance sink in, and the narrator's motivation changes and produces in him a surprising response:

> "You did see it?" Carlos Argentino insisted anxiously. "See it clearly? In color and everything?"
>
> Instantly, I conceived my revenge. In the most kindly sort of way—manifestly pitying, nervous, evasive—I thanked Carlos Argentino Daneri for the hospitality of his cellar and urged him . . . to remove himself from the pernicious influences of the metropolis . . . I clasped him by both shoulders as I took my leave and told him again that the country—peace and quiet, you know—was the very best medicine one could take.

Here we see that the desire to strike at the cousin's pomposity has been building all along. The pleasure comes from seeing the narrator finally act out, his motivations complicated by the consequences of his annual visits. And yet the pleasure is mixed with pain—our hopes for him grew during the story, so his "triumph" is no longer enough; we wanted him, given a grand vision of the universe, to do something less petty.

Active and Passive Main Characters

Most fiction focuses on characters impelled by their desires to take certain actions in order to achieve what they want. These actions will have consequences—intended, unintended, or both. Much of the "gripping" quality of fiction comes from readers wondering what the character will do next and how things will turn out. If a story's main character is not actively participating in key dramatic actions, the reader may wonder why the story is focusing on this person. This is the problem of the passive main character—a role distinct from that of the peripheral narrator, who is not intended to be the center of the story. The passive main character seems central, but is only acted on by other characters, or only watches others behaving dramatically without engaging with them or challenging them.

Sometimes main characters are passive because they are based on the author—we sometimes protect characters like us from making mistakes. These stories are often sparked by some unusual event or events that "really happened" to us. Unfortunately, not all events that seem compelling in real life will automatically be compelling on the page, especially to readers who weren't there at the time. Passive main characters can also arise if the writer has not yet figured out what the character wants, or has not found a way to vividly convey the character's desire to the reader.

In revision, we have several ways to address the lethargy that passive main characters can bring to a story. Perhaps the character needs to have more responsibility or to make a mistake that has dramatic consequences. Or maybe the character's failure to stand up for his or her desires can have consequences, which then force the character to engage in dramatic actions to compensate. *Hamlet* is perhaps the most famous example of the disasters caused by the failure to act.

Sometimes sheer passivity can serve as an aggressive act in itself, the only way of resisting another character's insistence that the main character take some action. In general, it can be extremely difficult to make a passive main character work in a story, and sometimes the best course is to consider other, more dynamic characters in the story as potential main characters and viewpoint characters. Another possibility would be to combine the current main character with a more active one.

RELATING CHARACTERS TO EACH OTHER

Often writers consider each character as a separate unit, but characters in a story, even more than people in real life, exist only in relation to each other. Their relationships often provide the sense of the story's shape, its possibilities and limits. The characters may support or defeat each other; may have complementary or conflicting needs, world views, and desires; or may illuminate each other in the course of their interactions. One character may have qualities that another lacks, so that together they make up the functioning whole of the story. Thinking of characters in relation to each other gives us a way to understand character as a structural element. Then we can consider how characters might contrast or complement each other in ways that create movement in the story.

Charles Baxter calls the contrast between characters "counterpointed characterization." In his essay of the same title, he describes how the counterpointing of characters can replace a more traditional idea of conflict in which, as he writes, "One person wants something, another person wants something else, and conflict results. But this is not, I think, the way most stories actually work. Not everything is a contest. We're not always fighting our brothers for a share of the worldly goods. Many good stories have no antagonist at all." He gives us another way of imagining the relationships altogether:

> Plot often develops out of the tensions between characters, and in order to get that tension, the writer sometimes has to be a bit of a matchmaker, creating characters who counterpoint one another in ways that are fit for gossip . . . With counterpointed characterization, certain kinds of people are pushed together, people who bring out a crucial response to each other. A latent energy rises to the surface, the desire or secret previously forced down into psychic obscurity.
>
> It seems to be in the nature of plots to bring a truth or a desire up to the light, and it has often been the task of those who write fiction to expose elements that are kept secret in a personality, so that the mask over that personality (or any system) falls either temporarily or permanently. When the mask falls, something of value comes up. Masks are interesting partly for themselves and partly for *what* they mask. The reality behind the mask is like a shadow-creature rising to the bait: the tug of an unseen force, frightening and energetic.

As soon as we read these words, we begin to see counterpointed characterization everywhere. In Don DeLillo's story "The Angel Esmeralda," in *The Best American Stories 1995,* two nuns of very different temperament work in the war zone of the inner city Bronx. Edgar, older, more traditional and cynical, wearing latex gloves and thinking dark thoughts, contrasts with the contemporary, brisk, practical Gracie. The complexities of the characters and the differences in their responses to the Bronx, and to a miracle when it occurs, help drive the engine of the story.

In Manuel Puig's *Kiss of the Spider Woman,* told entirely in dialogue, the interaction of Valentin and Molina, one imprisoned for his sexuality and the other for his politics, forms a dance so complex that it resembles a tango. The intersection of their strengths and weaknesses both leads to the betrayal at the novel's center and gives that betrayal its emotional force.

One way of not turning every story into a hand-to-hand combat is to consider that the traditional notion of the protagonist and antagonist need not only apply to individual characters. The protagonist is the story's principal character—the leading actor, the home team (the word "protagonist" comes from the Greek word for competitor). The antagonist is the enemy or opposing force. If the story has an antagonist at all, it may well be a situation or group, like the police state in *Kiss of the Spider Woman,* or the crime-ridden city in "The Angel Esmeralda."

When examining our own stories for the interactions of characters, we look at what effect their personalities and actions have on others. How does one character shed light on another and what do we understand from their interactions? Do too many characters struggle with similar problems? Can these characters be changed or combined? If we're creating contrasting characters, are they so different that they risk becoming caricatures? How can we complicate them and find ways in which they overlap?

STORY ANALYSIS AND QUESTIONS: "THE FOREST"

(Note: please read the story once before *you read the following analysis. Then, after you read the analysis, look at the story a second time, keeping the discussion questions in mind. You will get the most benefit out of this process if you mark specific passages in the story, take notes, and work through the questions in writing.)*

Andrea Barrett's story "The Forest" shows us how two characters can have enough differences to set up an intriguing dynamic, and enough in common to make the emotional weight of their interactions believable. Krzysztof Wojciechowicz and Bianca Marburg try and fail to hold up the kind of masks described by Charles Baxter. Much of the tension and drama of the story, in fact, comes from the way they see through each other's masks, how much they know that the other wishes to keep secret.

Here are their initial evaluations of each other: Krzysztof sees Bianca as a "doll-like" woman, "amazingly young, amazingly smooth-skinned . . . . with her blond hair frizzing in all directions." Bianca sees Krzysztof as a "Polish émigré, physical-chemist turned theoretical structural-biologist, Cambridge-based multiply medaled old guy." We meet them at a scientist's party, where the differences in their status are highlighted, for them and for us:

> "Dr. Wojciechowicz?" she said, mangling his name as she steered him closer to the table. "Would you like a drink or something?"
>
> Reflexively, he corrected her pronunciation; then he shook his head and said, "Please. Call me Krzysztof. And you are Bianca, yes?" He could not help noticing that she had lovely breasts.
>
> "That's me," she agreed dryly. "Bianca the chauffeur, Rose's sister, *not* related to the famous Dr. Constance Humboldt. No one you need to pay attention to at all."
>
> "It's not . . ." he said. Of course he had insulted her. "It's just that I'm so tired, and I'm still jet-lagged, and. . . ."

The physicality of the two characters is counterpointed—he finds her physically attractive, she finds him distasteful. In some places, we learn about the same detail from their two opposing points of view. Krzysztof feels that "already the top of his head was burning; he was all alone and wished he had a hat. Was it possible these people meant to stay in the sun all afternoon?" And then on the next page, Bianca watches him: "Krzysztof raised his right hand and held it over his head, either feeling for hair that was no longer present or attempting to shade his array of freckles and liver spots from the burning sun." She walks away from him, unsympathetic at this point, but becoming aware of his outsider status: "entirely typical, she thought, gazing down at Krzysztof's sweaty pate. That Constance and Arnold and Herb and the others should fly this man across the ocean to hear about his work, then get so caught up in institute politics that they'd forget to talk to him at their party." And then the reason for her lack of sympathy for him becomes clear, as well as her awareness of something that he would hope she hadn't noticed: ". . . Had it not been for the lizardlike graze of his eyes across her chest, she might have felt sorry for him."

The physical details underline their differences, and help us to inhabit each of them in turn, but these characters also have a substantial amount in common, which is part of what makes the story so rich.

DISCUSSION QUESTIONS

1. In what ways is the physicality of Krzysztof and Bianca important to the reader's understanding of them? To the story?
2. What are the (many) ways in which these two are counterpointed/contrasting characters? What are their (many) similarities and areas of overlap?
3. What is it that each of them wants or fears? How do these desires/fears intersect with or illuminate each other? How do they give rise to the plot?
4. How does Barrett show us what each sees about the other, and what each misses?
5. What details does Barrett use to show how they are like or unlike the other scientists at the party? What do the characters and the story show us about the scientific process and the life of a scientist?

COMPLICATING CHARACTERS

The difference between the characters in our first and final drafts is often the difference between a cartoon and a multilayered oil painting. The cartoon contains the rough chalk outlines that we will paint over, adding colors, tones, the logic of light and shade. "Good" and "bad" characters develop quirks, virtues, motivations, and foibles that make them recognizable and memorable. The next few sections concentrate on those issues that come up again and again as we complicate our characters.

These range from the question of what makes characters sympathetic or unsympathetic, to ideas for moving away from simplistically drawn heroes, victims, and villains, to the ever-present problem of conveying emotional drama without giving way to melodrama or sentimentality. Although it's useful to have all of these in mind as part of our everyday context for writing, most of them are revision issues. As we're writing, we may be perfectly well aware that no human in the history of the world was ever so sweet and noble as our protagonist, or that the boss is perhaps a bit too much of a raving demon. We can change course as we go, adding complications in later scenes without having to go back to the beginning to rewrite, or we can just let it happen on the page, counting on our ability to deepen our characters in subsequent drafts.

Sympathetic and Unsympathetic Characters

Most of us want to be liked, and we may want our characters to be likeable too. But a world full of amiable, well-mannered people (or even charming rogues) is artificial, evading the true complexity and difficulty of life. Unlikable characters aren't easy to pull off either. Boring, rude, mean-spirited, pathetic, or disgusting people can end up repulsing readers. Robin Hemley discusses the problem of the unlikable character in his essay "Sympathy for the Devil: What to Do about Difficult Characters":

> I've found that I can be intrigued with characters without necessarily liking them. And it's certainly not important for me to identify with them. But I *must* feel sympathy for a character, and here I'm using the word "sympathy" not merely as a synonym for "like," but more in terms of "understanding." If we as writers understand our characters, even the unlikable ones, if we understand their motivations, and convey this understanding to the reader, then perhaps we will come to understand something more about the mysteries of human behavior and aspiration, not the givens we already grasp, not the people and borders we know well.

One way to create the possibility for sympathy is to show the consequences of a character's actions—how those actions affect their lives, what's lost, what's gained. Another possibility is to give characters a measure of awareness about their flaws (whether or not they are willing or able to correct them). Or we can arrange events so the reader sees that the character has at least the potential to choose good. If the story seems to imply the character has no free will, then the character is less likely to feel true to life.

Rethinking "Heroes," "Victims," and "Villains"

Portraying characters as heroes, victims, or villains takes finesse. A first-person narrator may lionize or demonize another character without raising a red flag. But if readers suspect the author adores or despises a character, they will likely feel suspicious of the story, as if the author is simply trying to disguise a personal vendetta or infatuation. Or if the author seems to be asking readers to feel sorry for a character, to see how badly others have treated him, readers will likely feel annoyed—and justly so.

This doesn't mean that all characters must be morally neutral, or that we must give each character an equal amount of good and bad traits. Heathcliff, Magwitch, Lady Macbeth, Emma Bovary, and Brother Jack express the destructive (or self-destructive) impulses most of us repress in our everyday lives. Hemley writes, "As Hannah Arendt said about the Nazis, it's dangerous for us to think of them as monsters. If we do, then they become apart from us. Evil, as she said, is banal, not extraordinary. What's extraordinary is the natural human inclination to look away from it, not to understand it in ourselves."

Because so much of literature requires us to look at the ordinariness of evil, and at our own complicities, heroes aren't necessarily protagonists, any more than villains are antagonists. In Shakespeare's play *Richard III,* Richard III is both villain and protagonist. Villains are characters who intend harm, while heroes are characters who succeed in doing good. (Victims just get beat up.) In deepening these characters, complications work better than contradictions, which can veer into the sentimental. An emotionally brutal salesman who collects Fabergé eggs may be more intriguing than one who volunteers with orphans on his day off.

Kate Braverman's "Tall Tales from the Mekong Delta" tells the story of a recovering addict putting her life back together. On her way to an Alcoholics Anonymous meeting, she meets Lenny, a scuzzy, ugly man with so much charisma that he begins drawing her back into her addictions. While he is certifiably a villain, his great complexity shows throughout the story, as it does in this dialogue, where he's explaining to the main character that he has been following her—"recon," he calls it:

> "In Nam. We called it recon. Fly over, get a lay of the land. Or stand behind some trees. Count the personnel. People look but they don't see. I'll tell you about it. Get coffee. You got an hour. Want to hear about Vietnam? I got stories. Choppers? I like choppers. You can take your time, aim. You can hit anything, even dogs. Some days we'd go out just aiming at dogs. Or the black market? Want to hear about that? Profiteering in smack? You're a writer, right? You like stories. I got some tall tales from the Mekong Delta for you, sweetheart. Knock your socks off. Come on." He reached out and touched her arm. "Later you can have your own war stories. I can be one of your tall tales. I can be the tallest."

His words capture his willingness to do harm ("Some days we'd go out just aiming at dogs"), but also his charisma (the rapid-fire phrases laced with offers and questions), his philosophical side ("People look but they don't see"), his enthusiasm ("I got some tall tales from the Mekong Delta for you, sweetheart"), and his almost touching, boyish boastfulness ("I can be one of your tall tales"). The knowledge of the war in his past helps the reader understand the tortured person behind the evil acts. Villainy is only one part of this complicated character, who we perceive as causing damage because he himself is so damaged.

It is even more difficult to write about "victims" without alienating readers' sympathies. If we just read the first line of Lydia Davis's "A Few Things Wrong with Me," we might jump to the conclusion that we're about to hear someone whine about being jilted—a victim story: "He said there were things about me that he hadn't liked from the very beginning." But the story begins veering off into unexpected directions, with a narrator who is unusually curious to parse the relationship's end and willing to view it dispassionately:

> It's easy to come to the wrong conclusions about people. I see now that all these past months I kept coming to the wrong conclusions about him. For example, when I thought he would be unkind to me, he was kind. Then when I thought he would be effusive he was merely polite. When I thought he would be annoyed to hear my voice on the telephone he was pleased. When I thought he'd turn against me because I had treated him rather coldly, he was more anxious than ever to be with me and went to great trouble and expense so that we could spend a little time together. Then when I made up my mind that he was the man for me, he suddenly called the whole thing off.

By repeating the phrase "when I thought," Davis emphasizes the narrator's ruminating nature rather than the extremity of her emotion. The information that the narrator had treated her lover coldly suggests both unusual honesty on her part and the possibility that she bears some responsibility for this breakup as well. If the narrator had simply ranted about the cruelty and whimsicality with which her former lover had treated her, it's less likely we'd be so drawn in. She is a jilted woman in love, but she is also more than that: she's a thoughtful, cerebral, wry person faced with the mystery of figuring out someone else—and herself as well. Her victimhood is a significant but small part of the story. When writing about someone who has been hurt, we rarely have to press the point home—instead, we can think of the story opening out from the hurt, using it to illuminate all corners of a character's life.

Portraying "good" people without resorting to using clichés is the most difficult of all. Often the key is in their flaws. The main subplot of Tolstoy's *Anna Karenina* focuses on the character of Levin, and the story of how he achieves a happy family life, cares for his desperately ill and difficult brother, and finds himself, his faith, and his work. He is at all times looking for the way to do good for the world (a deliberate counterpoint to the story of Anna, who gives way to her passionate impulses and loses everything). He wants for the "forty millions of the Slavic world" to be liberated. He attempts to see a larger reality, the question of "the relation to the Deity of all the various faiths of mankind," and he moves very far from his upbringing when he wonders, " 'Well, but the Jews, the Mohammedans, the Confucians, the Buddhists—what are they?' He asked himself the same question that had seemed dangerous to him. 'Can these hundreds of millions of people be deprived of the highest good, without which life has no meaning?' " We see him as philosophical because he addresses large questions: he is unusually open-minded about other religions for his time and is concerned for the millions, not only for himself.

But it's Levin's weaknesses that humanize him: his clumsiness in argument, his struggles with "impurity and unbelief." He also doesn't believe in his own goodness, which helps to make him sympathetic. A character who does good and is smug about doing good is no longer a "hero," but a comic or unsympathetic figure. And, most importantly, Tolstoy clearly understands Levin as a complicated and human character, avoiding the danger that writers sometimes fall into of presenting characters as role models. Using a story to teach moral lessons is a noble intention that never seems to work in practice. Instead readers, like anyone undergoing a moral lecture, start to look for a chance to escape.

Restraint in Writing Emotion

We also resist stories that seem to require us to feel specific emotions. In writing a particularly charged emotional scene, writers often make the mistake of turning the volume up too high, hoping to convey the characters' emotions by extravagant adjectives and dramatic descriptions of the feelings of those in the scene. For the reader, this high emotion creates the effect of coming into a room where someone is shouting: our natural impulse is to back out again. There's so much of the writer's emotion in the story that there's no room for the reader's own reactions.

Emotion can be most effectively conveyed in a less direct form: underwriting, rather than overwriting; understated metaphor; not trying to describe the emotional state itself, but instead closely observing the actions and perceptions of the characters. The response of one character whose world has just fallen apart will be quite different than another's.

In the main plot of *Anna Karenina,* Alexei Alexandrovich Karenin has his first suspicion that his wife Anna might be unfaithful after a party where she talks too much to Count Vronsky. Karenin chides Anna and she pretends not to know what he means:

> She looked at him so simply, so gaily, that no one who did not know her as her husband did could have noticed anything unnatural either in the sound or in the meaning of her words. But for him who knew her, who knew that when he went to bed five minutes late, she noticed it and asked the reason, who knew that she told him at once her every joy, happiness, or grief—for him it meant a great deal to see now that she did not want to notice his state or say a word about herself. He saw that the depth of her soul, formerly always open to him, was now closed to him. Moreover, by her tone he could tell that she was not embarrassed by it, but was as if saying directly to him: yes it's closed, and so it ought to be and will be in the future. He now felt the way a man would feel coming home and finding his house locked up. "But perhaps the key will still be found," thought Alexei Alexandrovich.

Most of this is quite plain, understated language, though it gives a very specific sense of their relationship. She used to notice something as small as when he went to bed five minutes late, and she used to tell him everything: we feel from these details the nature of their previous intimacy and her concern for him and trust in him. The one metaphor, the house locked against him, is a more powerful image of their separation than any amount of highly dramatized emotion. It's also appropriate because he feels that he owns her, that she, like the house, is a possession there for his comfort, so we feel both sympathy for and impatience with him. Tolstoy, who retains objectivity about his characters at all times, is letting us see Karenin's part in bringing about the oncoming tragedy.

Another example of skillful restraint is Bharati Mukherjee's story "The Management of Grief," told from the point of view of a woman who has lost her husband and two sons in the plane explosion that killed a substantial part of her community. Mukherjee focuses on the external details—what a person sees and does—rather than on the character's emotions. Mukherjee emphasizes the deadly numbing of grief. Mrs. Bhave is described as a "pillar" by a social worker, who tells her that she's "coping very well. All the people said, Mrs. Bhave is the strongest person of all."

The narrator answers her, " 'By the standards of the people you call hysterical, I am behaving very oddly and very badly, Miss Templeton.' I want to say to her, *I wish I could scream, starve, walk into Lake Ontario, jump from a bridge.* 'They would not see me as a model. I do not see myself as a model.' "

The very brief break into her thoughts, contrasting her apparently calm—drugged and shocked—exterior and the interior flash of pain, gives us her emotions very clearly. As does as the contrast between her and those who do weep—her neighbor who comes "stumbling and screaming across the lawn" in her bathrobe, a sailor who fished some of the bodies from the sea, a policeman who mistakenly thought he could help her identify the bodies of her still-missing children. Only the most minor cracks in this armor of calm show through, and when they do, they are all the more shocking. Mrs. Bhave mentions, offhandedly, "I haven't eaten in four days, haven't brushed my teeth." She runs to the edge of the sea, possessed by a sudden fantasy that her children may have escaped and be swimming home. Another time, she shouts at a customs official in India who is making them wait for a supervisor: " 'You bastard!' I scream at the man with the popping boils. Other passengers press close. 'You think we're smuggling contraband in those coffins!' " The rest of the story consists of her frozen efforts to help the other families, to find her way out of the maze. But these exact details will provoke more grief in the reader than any amount of high drama and wailing. We are pulled into the story; we imagine what it would be like to endure the loss.

STORY ANALYSIS AND QUESTIONS: "POWDER"

(Note: please read the story once before *you read the following analysis. Then, after you read the analysis, look at the story a second time, keeping the discussion questions in mind. You will get the most benefit out of this process if you mark specific passages in the story, take notes, and work through the questions in writing.)*

Tobias Wolff's "Powder" shows us how to create emotional restraint in the construction of a story, as well as in what the characters don't say to each other. This is a story of a drive home from a ski trip on a snowy Christmas eve. No accidents or immediate bad results occur, and yet the story hums with tension because of the relationship between the two characters and the shadow of future disasters. The charming and reckless father, "bankrupt of honor, flushed with certainty," could be a villain in less sure hands, and the anxious son, who "kept his clothes on numbered hangers to insure proper rotation . . . [and] bothered [his] teachers for homework assignments far ahead of their due dates so [he] could draw up schedules" could be an unsympathetic prig, but Wolff makes these characters engaging and complex.

Much of the power struggle between them shows through the subtext of the dialogue: "We passed a diner on our way out. 'You want some soup?' my father asked. I shook my head. 'Buck up,' he said. 'I'll get you there. Right, doctor?' I was supposed to say, 'Right, doctor,' but I didn't say anything."

By not playing along with his father, the narrator expresses his anxiety and accusation more memorably and realistically than if he'd simply said, "You screwed up." Later, when his father starts to admit they're in trouble, the boy becomes bolder: " 'We should have left before,' I said. 'Doctor.' " One word, part of the habitual game between father and son, has become a weapon.

DISCUSSION QUESTIONS

1. Where and how in the story do the power shifts take place?
2. What does Wolff show us about each character that makes him sympathetic or unsympathetic?
3. What roles do the other characters (on and offstage) play in their interactions?
4. What is the father's attitude? What is the son's attitude? What details does Wolff use to construct these attitudes? In what ways are they complementary or counterpointed?
5. Where and how does the narrative demonstrate emotional restraint?
6. What are we worried about as readers at the very beginning of the story? Does that change in the course of the story? How is the worry answered by the end?

REVISION: BRINGING CHARACTERS INTO FOCUS

Characters emerge over the course of several drafts, coming slowly into focus as we discover new facts about their histories, appearances, actions, and motivations. Meaning accrues slowly, a detail at a time, or through a sudden illumination that leads us to larger changes. In our first draft, we try to shut the inner critic in an imaginary closet and to abandon ourselves to the story, making intuitive decisions about which tools to use in constructing our characters.

In later drafts, we make more conscious decisions about how much and what kind of information to give based on the particular needs of the story. How important is the character to the story? (The more central the character, the more the reader needs to know.) How realistic and detailed is the story? (We need less character history and psychological exploration in a fable or minimalist story.) How much do we want the emphasis to be on character development and discovery, as opposed to the plot or the images/language? (The more character-centered the story, the more we work to inhabit and represent our people.)

We mentioned earlier the possibility of combining a passive main character with another, more active character. There are other reasons we may need to combine characters in revision. Sometimes the number of minor characters is so unwieldy readers can't keep track of them. We might cut two of the five children and give their lines to the remaining three, or combine two ex-lovers into a single character. Sometimes, even two active major characters may need to be combined, if their actions and goals are similar.

On the other hand, if the story's conflict is internal and we're having trouble finding dramatic outlets for it, we may need to split one character into two. In earlier drafts, John Cheever's well-known story "Goodbye My Brother" featured a narrator who was both critical of his family and proud of it. As Allan Gurganus points out in his introduction to the story in *You've Got to Read This,* in revision Cheever divided the character into two brothers, one critical, the other more optimistic. Their conflict could now be acted out in dramatic scenes with the rest of the family.

In revising our stories, we can flesh out attitude by imagining how our characters would describe themselves, and how that might be different from the ways other people would describe them. What choices have they made in their lives, and what have the consequences of these choices been? What physical characteristics, habits of speech, likes, dislikes, fears, desires, and actions express their ways of being in the world?

Our answers will influence the backgrounds that we invent for our characters, their motivations, and even the perspective that we, their creators, have on them. In this process we look for a balance between detachment and compassion. As Charles Johnson cautions us, we are not setting our characters up "as strawmen, or as foils, or as chess pieces." To discover our characters' attitudes is not the same thing as having attitudes about them; we're not sitting in judgment, but serving, as Chekhov wrote in one of his letters, as "impartial witnesses":

> In my opinion it is not the writer's job to solve such problems as God, pessimism, etc.; his job is merely to record who, under what conditions, said or thought what about God or pessimism. The artist is not meant to be a judge of his characters and what they say; his only job is to be an impartial witness . . . Drawing conclusions is up to the jury, that is, the readers. My only job is . . . to know how to distinguish important testimony from unimportant, to place my characters in the proper light and speak their language. To [a critic], the artist

who is a psychologist *must* figure things out because otherwise, why is he a psychologist? But I don't agree with him. It's about time that everyone who writes—especially genuine literary artists—admit that in this world you can't figure anything out.

The best way to separate our own motivation from that of our characters, or our desire to figure things out from the ability to tell the story, is to get good criticism and then to allow a story to sit for a while after we think it's "finished." Most of us want to be done with a story as soon as possible and get it in the mail. Writers' groups are useful in this, as in so many other ways; they can keep us from sending stories out before they're done, before we really know our characters. Once we've allowed our first, wild, rich draft to reveal its initial surprises and have begun to inhabit and understand our characters, then we can rely on our best critics to read our drafts. Our community of readers will let us know to what extent we've presented our characters vividly, made them surprising and believable, and created the illusion of humans who exist in their own right; rather than expressing our beliefs, paying back old scores, living the lives we haven't managed to, or simply proving our points.

CHARACTER EXERCISES

1. Become a researcher of different kinds of attitude. As secretly as possible, observe people under situations of pressure, where they're apt to reveal themselves. You can do this both with strangers—at a football game, a writers' conference, in a doctor's office—and with those you know—at work or at home. How do they seem to, as Margot Livesey describes it, "regard themselves and the world"? What is it that each person seems to demand from or offer to the world? How do you think they would describe themselves? How would other people describe them? What physical characteristics, habits of speech, likes, dislikes, fears, desires, and actions express their way of being in the world?
2. It can be easier to start a story if you're working with a world of characters you have already created. Choose a minor character from a previous story of yours, someone who interests you, but who you do not yet know well. Imagine the most baffling experience this character has had, or the most baffling action he or she has ever taken. Now write a series of scenes in which the actions, descriptions, objects in the room, and responses of other characters work together to convey this experience. Don't try to "explain" the character or actions. In these scenes, practice acting as Chekhov's "impartial witness" to events.
3. Choose a major character in a current story of yours who seems less developed, or more one-sided, than the other characters. Give this person two qualities, habits, or longings that seem to complicate what we already know. How might these qualities or habits relate to (or influence)

the central problem or conflict of the story? What actions does the character take because of these qualities, and what consequences do those actions have?

4. Go through a story and make a list of what dramatic (not symbolic or philosophical) functions each character serves. How does each affect the plot? Change one character into two separate characters, or combine two characters who seem to be filling the same function. What if someone's appearance or ideas or dominant mood changed dramatically? How would that affect the other characters and the story as a whole? Save your previous draft and let yourself experiment fearlessly with changing the people you have imagined in the story.
5. (This reading exercise can be done either individually or in a group.) How are characters made physically real to us in each of the stories you've read so far? What kinds of details did the author include, either of the characters' physical experiences or of their appearances and movements? Are these details presented in direct description or through another characters' eyes? How do the kinds of details used relate to a) the events of the story; b) the story's themes; and c) the characteristic style of the writer, whether maximalist, minimalist, bleak, humorous, distant, formal, chatty, surrealist, ironic, compassionate, quirky, inventive, or any combination of these?
6. (This reading exercise can be done either individually or in a group.) Look at character depiction in the stories you've read so far. Choose at least five sentences or paragraphs that vividly or engagingly create character through action, dialogue, commentary, or direct description. (Look for at least one example of each of these.) Consider some or all of the following questions as you discuss why and how these passages work: How does the writer keep the story's characters from being one-sided or developing into heroes or villains? What details subvert or add to the general impression? How does the way the narrator sees the character fit with either the narrative voice or the themes of the story? If you're doing this exercise in a group, go around the circle, with each person reading one example aloud in turn, until you have found an example for each question. When you read the example, explain what you've worked out about how and why these succeed, and how the character description fits the structure or nature of the story. This works best if group members have a chance to respond with their own ideas.

CHAPTER

2

Reintroducing Third-Person POVs

(Anthology selections: "The Niece," "Inferno I, 32," and "Gooseberries")

I had been trying to do the book [Legs] in a multiplicity of ways. I began thinking I would write it as a film-in-process, because the gangster had been such a charismatic presence in movies; I wanted to make a literary artifact in which the film would be a significant element. That became a silly gimmick. I tried to make it a surrealistic novel. I tried to pattern it totally on the Tibetan Book of the Dead; those chapters are pretty wild. The process of illumination left me with the Henry Jamesian wisdom that I really needed a point of view on this. I tried to write it from inside Diamond and it didn't work and I tried to write from outside Diamond with a chorus of voices and it didn't work. And then I discovered that if I used the lawyer who was in the book from the beginning as this intelligent presence who could look at Diamond and intersect with him at every level of his life, then I would be able to have a perspective on what was going on inside the man. So I did that and it made all the difference.

William Kennedy, *Paris Review* interview

THE CENTRALITY OF POV

It took William Kennedy six years of "a complicated and painful struggle" to find the viewpoint that showed him what *Legs,* his second novel, was about: until then he couldn't tell the story, even though he had the characters and situation. Although our first impulse in writing a story might come from a memory, an image, a line of dialogue, or an idea, it isn't until we find the viewpoint that we can make real progress. The story's revelations about the characters and the plot turns depend on the POV the writer has chosen. If we tell the story of Hansel and Gretel from the viewpoints of the children, the witch, the father, or the stepmother, we'll have not only different perspectives, but different events. In Hansel and Gretel's POV, we focus on the abandonment in the woods, the house made of sweets, the tricking of the witch, and the return home. In the witch's POV, though, Hansel and Gretel might be the last two of a long series of children: we might find out what adventures and disasters led to this predatory old age in a house made of sugar. The children's version might be a story about the triumph of resourceful innocence over various kinds of greed, including the stepmother's wish to have the father all to herself, the children's own desire to eat the house made of cake, and the witch's hunger for the children. The other, a much darker story, might show the descent of the witch from power to corruption.

When we first encounter the idea of POV, it seems we ought to be able to make rational decisions: close third person for this story, first person for that one. Sometimes, however, we may start writing a story in a POV without knowing what the implications are, or how it relates to our themes and subjects. We just "hear" the story in that POV: we are feeling our way towards some understanding about the story, and we need to have patience with our own writing process. Our first intuitions may well be right for reasons we don't yet understand: only time and revision will tell.

Eudora Welty, in *The Eye of the Story,* gives us a sense of the way that we can pay attention to the tangles in our growing story, reading it for clues to its possibilities:

> The story is a vision; while it's being written, all choices must be its choices, and as these multiply upon one another, their field is growing too . . . a growing maze of possibilities that the writer, far from being dismayed at his presence on unknown ground (which might frighten him as a critic) has learned to be grateful for, and excited by. The fiction writer has learned . . . that it is the very existence, the very multitude and clamor and threat and lure of *possibility* . . . that guide his story most delicately.

The more we examine the possible choices of POV, the more our choices branch into an overgrown cluster of shrubs and vines that we inch our way through, making new discoveries at every turn. Whose eyes are we looking through, and why? Do we want the intimacy of first person, the tight focus on first one and then another character of a rotating close third-person viewpoint, or the wide view of omniscience? Is the story being told just after it happened, or years later? Is the narrator presenting events through action, dialogue, and detail alone, or commenting on their significance? Are there limits to our perceptions, and, if so, what are they?

Real-World POV Decisions

Sometimes the viewpoint we choose, whether in our first draft or in revisions, arises from the relation of our past or current life to the character and story: our process as writers overlaps the process of the story. We might feel that our current story ought to be told in first person, but find ourselves using the third person, afraid that readers will identify the characters' actions and emotions as our own. Or perhaps we start off in first person because it's most comfortable, and it's not until we've written several drafts that we understand that the worldview of this particular story needs a wide scope. If we choose a rotating or omniscient third-person POV, we increase the number of scenes the reader can be present at and enlarge the vision of the world: each viewpoint character will notice different details, and the reader can be more directly engaged in a greater number of subplots. On the other hand, having more viewpoints risks a dispersal of attention, diluting the importance of each character or subplot.

Sometimes our life intrudes into the storytelling in ways that may either enrich or temporarily derail the story: if we're fighting with a parent, we might wind up telling our story from the mother's POV—even if the character is nothing like our real-life mother—as a way of trying to understand a different perspective. We may not even be fully aware of how the events and mood of our current experiences change the story, how they change our idea of the relative importance of different events, or alter our sympathies. Some of these emotions and experiences will turn out to have no place in the story, and will have to be edited out, ruthlessly, but others come as gifts that surprise us, energize our writing, and help give the story its power.

Meanwhile, we have to pick a viewpoint to begin writing, and though the POV may well change in revision, we need to give our instincts a chance: they may be giving us clues as to whose story this is, what matters, and why.

Complicating POV: Beyond First, Second, and Third

Fiction has an ability no other art form has—the ability to create an illusion of knowing an individual's (or several individuals') thoughts over time. Film can employ voiceovers, but even a voiceover doesn't give the reader the sensation of being inside someone's mind. In movie scripts, the term point of view is used to describe where the camera is looking from—"Jonathan's POV—exterior—day" or "From a child's POV, we see a woman hurrying out of the barn."

In fiction, we think of POV less as a camera, and more as a "narrative stance." POV is about where the narrator stands—in relation to the audience, herself, and to the events in the story. The narrator might be speaking directly to the reader, might be telling the story to another character, or might be musing in private. The narrator might be one of the characters in the story, major or minor, or the narrator might be an unidentified voice (usually, in this case, readers assume the author is telling the story).

The options we have in choosing our POV are sometimes presented as a set of rules, but the process is much more like that of a painter selecting from a palette of colors. To discuss POV in terms such as "first person," "second person," "third person limited," and "third person omniscient" is like discussing color only in terms of blue, red, and yellow. As with colors, the choices are infinitely more varied. Among blues, for example, a painter can choose from cobalt blue, cobalt blue deep, cobalt turquoise, aquamarine, Prussian blue, ultramarine blue, cerulean blue, and so on. The color the painter chooses depends on whether the painting is realistic or abstract, what time of day or mood the painting wants to suggest, and the balance of that blue with other colors.

ASPECTS OF THIRD-PERSON POV

We begin with third-person POV choices because, in our experience, this is the viewpoint that intermediate/advanced writers grapple with most urgently. Once we become aware of how much harder it is for a third-person narrative to sound natural and authoritative, we may gloomily conclude that we have no aptitude for it and should write in the first person for the rest of our lives. We may forget that we have much more practice with first person; we're used to inhabiting our own experience and describing it in journals, letters, and e-mails. But we can become comfortable with third person through practice, and can learn how to achieve effects in the third person not possible in first. In some ways, the third-person POVs are easier to examine in detail, because they don't raise questions about the narrator's role in events or the degree of reliability.

We have grouped aspects of third-person POV into a single chart below for easy reference. Each aspect is independent; the chart is meant to be read horizontally, not in columns. Each aspect is also a spectrum, as indicated by the arrows. For instance, with temporal distance, the possibilities are endless—a story's events might be taking place right now, two weeks ago, last year, three decades ago, or five centuries ago. The chart suggests an infinite number of possible POVs, each representing a different set of decisions on the six spectrums. After the chart, we will examine the spectrums in more detail. Later in the chapter, we use a number of examples from short passages and anthology stories to give a sense of the artistic effects of different choices.

The chart is an aid to revision, a way of examining our decisions, both deliberate and inadvertent. It is meant as a diagnostic tool to review our original POV decisions as we revise, rather than as a kit to build a POV in the first draft. If the POV in a story doesn't seem to be working, we might go through the chart and define how the story fits into each category. How well do our POV choices work together? Are there any places where we seem to be breaking our contract with the reader and suddenly changing the story's rules for no reason?

For clarity and ease of reference, we're using primarily anthology stories for examples. Even for those who haven't read the story, a glance at the first page or two will be enough to demonstrate the POV aspects we're discussing. Certain POV decisions often come in clusters: a story that gives us a character's sensory perceptions will usually, though not always, give us that character's thoughts. A story in which the narrator offers substantial commentary and opinions will usually, though not always, offer information or history that the characters don't necessarily know.

Number of Viewpoint Characters If readers are going to experience a story through more than one character's POV, it's generally a good idea to make the first switch within a page or two, so that the transition doesn't feel like a distracting mistake. Often, the thoughts and perceptions within any given paragraph (or several paragraphs in a row) will belong to a single character. Of the

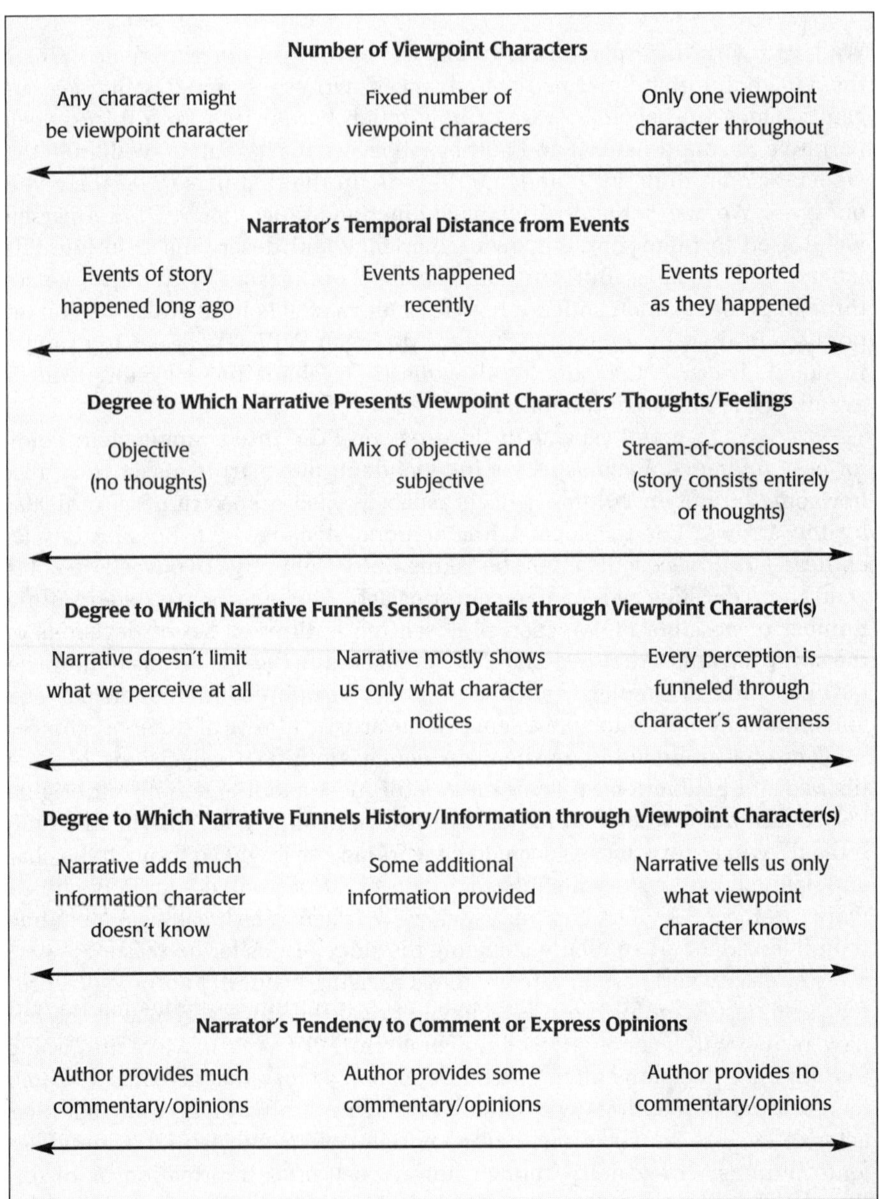

third-person stories in our anthology, "Civil Peace," "The Cures for Love," "The Niece," and "Pilgrims" present a single viewpoint. In "The Forest," the narrative moves back and forth between only two of the characters' POVs. In "The Rooster and the Dancing Girl," "Inferno I, 32," and "Gooseberries," the narrative can inhabit any character, depending on the focus of the story at that moment.

If a story gives only a single character's POV, it tends to focus the reader's attention on a change (or failure to change) in that character. If a story gives only two viewpoints, it tends to emphasize the relationship between the POV characters or some difference in their perceptions. A story with multiple viewpoints tends to highlight the relationships, differences in perceptions, surrounding community, philosophical ideas, or societal issues of the story. While a story in any POV *can* be about a change in a single character or about societal issues, a writer working against natural reading patterns must develop other elements very strongly to counterbalance a reader's assumptions.

Narrator's Temporal Distance from Events Most contemporary stories, and most of the third-person stories in the anthology, chronicle events that seem to have occurred not long before the telling of the story or in some unspecified recent time. If the events of the story happened long ago, the reader is likely to expect that the narrative will have a greater historical perspective, as Tolstoy does in *War and Peace,* with his analysis of the causes and events of the Napoleonic wars. Readers expect the least perspective from stories told in the present tense.

In "The Fence Party" and "Trauma Plate," for instance, events are reported as they happen, and the narrator knows no more about the future than the reader does. This makes for a tentative and dislocating reading experience, which, in both of these stories, is exactly right for the subject matter, mood, and events. Oddly enough, the present tense tends to feel less immediate than the more familiar past-tense story, partly because of this dislocation. We lose ourselves more easily in the past tense, which implies a future; the present tense keeps us on edge. Present tense, though, is just one possible tool to achieve this uncertainty. Other tools include unexpected events, alternate story structures, and surprising dialogue or observations.

Degree to Which Narrative Presents Viewpoint Characters' Thoughts/Feelings An objective story gives no thoughts or commentary, but only shows us what we might experience through the senses if we were in the room with the characters. Stories at the objective end of the spectrum resemble movies with no voiceovers, while stream-of-consciousness stories seem to consist entirely of the character's thoughts, in all their digressive glory. Neither extreme is common in contemporary fiction, but most stories fall closer to one end than the other, and many stories use objective or stream-of-consciousness passages for vividness and insight.

Of the anthology stories, "Pilgrims" achieves its effects primarily through objectivity; even the memories are usually offered in sensory terms. "The Niece," on the other hand, gives us an intimate view of the thoughts of the viewpoint character, Zeke. We are so close to Zeke's mind and experiences that sometimes the narrative slides smoothly into fragmentary thoughts that verge on stream-of-consciousness. Other third-person stories that give us the characters' thoughts and feelings in detail include "The Cures for Love," "The Fence Party," and "The Forest."

Degree to Which Narrative Funnels Sensory Details Through Viewpoint Character(s) Most contemporary North American short stories funnel sensory details through the viewpoint character or characters. In these stories, the reader does not experience anything that the POV character does not see, hear, smell, touch, or taste. In the third-person section of Adam Johnson's "Trauma Plate," for example, the narrative describes the landscape vividly through Jane's sensory experience of it: "There are bullet holes in the masonry between her and the old Godfather's, and she stops to twist her pinkie in the lead-traced pocks." Some stories or moments in stories emphasize the viewpoint character's sensory perceptions more than others.

Occasionally, stories will let readers perceive aspects of the world that the characters don't. In Yasunari Kawabata's "The Rooster and the Dancing Girl," the sensory details are not always connected to a specific character's experience: "[The rooster] began to fly well. Its wings were covered with dust and turned white. But it pecked at beans. . . ." None of the story's characters witness the rooster doing these things.

Degree to Which Narrative Funnels History/Information Through Viewpoint Character(s) In stories using close third-person POV, the narrative only gives us information through the viewpoint character's awareness. In "The Fence Party," we learn about Hart's purchase of his home through his memories, colored by his feelings and sensory perceptions: "He felt a sharp nostalgia when the door rocked open at the real estate agent's prodding to reveal the downy floor of the abandoned coop, with rays of light smoking in between the warped pine planks."

Stories that fall somewhere in the middle of the spectrum may give us history or information that the viewpoint character is probably aware of, though the information is not connected explicitly to the character's thoughts. In "The Silver Screen," Peter Ho Davies from time to time gives information directly to the reader: "In 1948, when Chin Peng, the chairman of the Malayan Politburo, authorized the first attacks on British plantation owners, the fourteenth branch of the Kuala Lumpur Communist Party went into the jungle along with five thousand other communist fighters." The characters (who are among the fighters) are not involved in conveying this information to the reader.

Many stories with an omniscient POV will tell the reader information that the viewpoint character doesn't necessarily know. This can include historical facts beyond the viewpoint character's knowledge, or even information about future events. For instance, early on in Ann Patchett's novel *Bel Canto,* terrorists take a roomful of people hostage, and the narrative reveals the following: "It was the unspoken belief of everyone who was familiar with the organization and with the host country that they were all as good as dead, when in fact it was the terrorists who would not survive the ordeal." This foreknowledge is essential to the book's structure, because we come to know the terrorists as people as the book progresses. Revealing the book's outcome keeps the reader from feeling betrayed when key characters suddenly die at the end. The information that is so reassuring in the beginning—that the terrorists will die—makes us more willing to read the book because we believe that the rest of the characters, those we initially care about, will be safe. Patchett, though, develops our compassion for the terrorists to such a degree that this foreshadowed end becomes heartbreaking. Even though we are told they will die, we begin to hope that they will be spared. Foreshadowing changes the narrative question from "What will happen?" to the more complicated "In exactly what way will things go so wrong?"

Narrator's Tendency to Comment or Express Opinions Except in metafiction, recent North American authors rarely express opinions about the events or address readers as if they were in the same room. Commentary was more prominent in nineteenth-century British novels, as in *Middlemarch,* or *Vanity Fair.* It went out of fashion until the 1960s, when metafictionists such as John Barth began using it with more ironic intent. Even stories with POVs that are omniscient in other ways—giving us additional historical background or access to various characters' thoughts—tend to refrain from direct addresses to the readers. Jorge Luis Borges does use authorial commentary sparingly, as in "Inferno I, 32," telling the reader "the machinery of the world is overly complex for the simplicity of men," an aphoristic phrase in keeping with the parable-like quality of the story. But by and large, contemporary fiction leaves readers to draw their own conclusions and make their own judgments. The POV choice we call "discerning third person," discussed below, is an exception—it generally gives readers information characters may not know, authorial commentary, and critical perspective, more than close third person does—though still without directly addressing the reader.

STORY ANALYSIS AND QUESTIONS: "THE NIECE"

(Note: please read the story once before *you read the following analysis. Then, after you read the analysis, look at the story a second time, keeping the discussion questions in mind. You will get the most benefit out of this process if you mark specific passages in the story, take notes, and work through the questions in writing.)*

In "The Niece," Margot Livesey shows how writers can have characters act in surprising ways, and still convince the reader that these actions are plausible and emotionally meaningful. The story also demonstrates the ways that a character who might inspire suspicion or judgment as an unreliable first-person narrator can instead earn our compassion and sympathy in close third. Here are the POV decisions the story makes, according to the chart: this story has only one viewpoint character; events have happened in the recent or undetermined past; the story presents a mix of objective and subjective observations, tending toward the subjective with a lot of the character's thoughts and feelings; every sensory perception is funneled through the viewpoint character's awareness; the narrator only tells us what the character knows; and there is no authorial commentary or opinion.

The narrator fully develops the viewpoint character, Zeke, without explicit commentary, while creating perspective on him, both through his thoughts and through the information he tells the niece about his life and history:

> ". . . but as soon as I stepped outside I worried that I'd left the gas on or the iron or the lights or I hadn't locked the door or I hadn't locked the window or I hadn't flushed the toilet or the cat's water bowl was empty or my mother was trying to phone. It didn't matter how often I checked, it didn't matter if I wrote down that I'd checked, I'd reach the street and have to go back. Remember in *Gulliver's Travels* when the Lilliputians tie him down? It was like that. Hundreds of strands of anxiety tugging me back. Soon it was easier not to try to get away."

The story has presented Zeke as such an outsider in society that it may surprise us that his problems are just an exaggeration of ordinary anxieties and the inability to read the emotions of others. Zeke's anxieties, however, have immobilized him. In this passage, where he's directly describing his compulsions, he's offering information, not asking for sympathy. In third-person passages that go more deeply into his experience, emotional events also appear informative, rather than as authorial attempts to manipulate the reader's emotions. Imagine in first person the moment when Zeke is remembering an interaction with his mother: "the day, six years earlier, that she turned her shiny blue eyes upon him and said, 'You'll end up in the loony bin if you carry on like this,' he had felt as if a pickaxe were aimed at the very center of his forehead."

In first person, this statement would seem exaggerated and melodramatic; in close third, we understand it as a description of just how key this moment was for Zeke, how much it embodied some of the reasons he has trouble with close relationships. It clarifies some of his later, otherwise difficult-to-understand interactions.

DISCUSSION QUESTIONS

1. What information or history do we learn through dialogue? Action? Exposition? How do these choices affect the story?
2. What images, details, and lines of dialogue make the niece (the non-viewpoint character) vivid and particular?
3. How would the story be different in the niece's POV? In an omniscient POV? What kinds of solutions might these POVs have required to retain the resonance of the ending?
4. How do we see both Zeke and the niece differently because we're looking through Zeke's eyes? Where might our evaluations differ from his, and how does Livesey guide our perceptions?

5. When and how does Livesey directly report Zeke's thoughts and experiences, and how does she move the narrative back to more general information?
6. What changes or doesn't change in Zeke over the course of the story? What details or incidents show us this?

VARIATIONS OF COMMON POV CHOICES

Some of the most-used combinations of POV choices are often referred to in shorthand terms. For example, an "omniscient narrator" usually describes a narrator who provides commentary and opinions, adds information the characters may not be aware of, tells the reader about the thoughts and feelings of a number of characters, and can describe events happening in any location. However, if we choose to write from an omniscient viewpoint, we still have a range of options. Some omniscient narrators may provide extra information, but no authorial opinions. Others may refrain from giving us characters' thoughts, while roaming through space and time freely.

We discuss four third-person POV choices below—objective, close third person, discerning third person, and omniscient—with explanations of the benefits and pitfalls of each and examples that show graceful ways of using these POVs.

Objective Narrators

An objective story has to rely on dialogue and description because it does not offer a window into a character's experience from the inside. M. T. Sharif's "The Letter Writer" shows us how to give a sense of the main character's personality through action and dialogue with no thoughts or interpretation:

> Amidst this melee, Haji crouched, observing the bustle with that yearning look of a camel upon cotton seeds. If shoppers snubbed him, if regulars slighted him, if the typist snatched a customer and settled down to punch his machine, Haji appealed to the store owners directly. "Brother vendors. Neighbor businessmen. I ask of you, is there room for more than one author in this square? Instruct your patrons to frequent my establishment."

In the first sentence of this excerpt, Haji observes the bustle around him, which might at first seem like a slip into his viewpoint. However, the phrase "with that yearning look of a camel upon cotton seeds" makes it clear we're seeing him from the outside. Next we see how others treat him, which Sharif describes with short phrases full of specific nouns and active verbs to keep the description lively. Then Haji's response reveals his character. His speech functions as an action, and will create reactions in turn over the course of the story. The pushiness and rhetorical flourishes of his dialogue show us who he is in a memorable way: we don't have to be told what he's like.

When we're using this kind of objective narrator in our own writing, we can, like Sharif, make sure that the dialogue and details convey the character and mood so that the reader isn't left wondering what the story's about and what the characters want. Our characters don't need to state all their feelings and beliefs directly, however. Character and emotion can be presented through the flavor and subtext of the dialogue, as in Mary Robison's story "Bud Parrot." Although we have no access to the character's thoughts, we gather that Bud is in love with Gail, who has just married his best friend Dean. He goes to visit them in their honeymoon suite on their wedding night:

> Bud, who had been standing by a low bureau that was covered with vases of flowers, poked his finger in the cellophane that covered a fruit basket. He took an apple from where it was nestled in green excelsior. "Hey, Dean," he said, "let's go for a little spin down the hall. Two minutes."
>
> "Dean's all settled in—with his robe and all," Gail said.

Bud is as close as we come to a viewpoint character in this story—the narrative follows him around, without revealing his thoughts. Instead, actions and dialogue show his character and emotions. In the above passage he invades the married couple's territory—their Eden. He pokes his finger into the untouched cellophane, and takes one of their apples while Gail's speech shows her trying to discourage him. The scene has more power because of the indirection of the dialogue. The very dangerous and potentially clichéd symbol of the apple works here because it is so meticulously observed and offered with such contemporary details (fruit basket, green excelsior) that we may not consciously notice the symbolism at all.

The objective viewpoint can be as mysterious and intriguing as it is in the above stories, but it runs the risk of appearing cold or withholding. This POV can be so mysterious that readers can't figure out why characters are doing what they're doing, or why it matters. The challenge for the writer is to make the actions and the dialogue revealing, but not stilted or unrealistic. Otherwise, readers may feel that if we're not going to be inside a character's mind, we lose some of the particular strength of fiction.

On the other hand, if the story has a compelling plot reason for hiding its characters' thoughts and feelings, this POV may be the right choice. Sharif's story is a contemporary fable, and the POV helps establish that magical distance. Robison's story makes the classic love triangle new again by not dwelling on emotions that we can easily imagine; instead, the narrative focuses the reader on how those emotions turn into action. If we're considering trying objective narration, another excellent example to study is Manuel Puig's *Kiss of the Spiderwoman,* which accomplishes all of its tasks through dialogue alone. The claustrophobia felt by the two men imprisoned together and their intricate processes of self-revelation, concealment, and betrayal support the novel's themes. The story's refusal to give either character's thoughts keeps us in the dark, just like the two men in their dark cell, who know so little about each other.

Close Third-Person POV (Third Person Limited)

This POV, one of the most common viewpoints in short stories, works well when one character's desires or trials form the center of the tale. Close third-person stories often cover a short, continuous period of time, as if we're spending a few hours or days with that character. Just as in first person, all of the story's perceptions are funneled through the character, whose beliefs, opinions, desires, judgments, and hopes color what we see. Close third person can be nearly, though not quite, as intimate as first person.

Writers often struggle over the choice between first and close third person. Third person may work best if there is no compelling reason for a character to tell us the tale, if the writer wants to distance the reader a little from the POV character, or if the distinctive voice of a character isn't an integral part of the story. This POV can also work well for stories that explore a particular person who is not self-aware enough to narrate his or her own story or is unable to take responsibility for his or her actions.

One of the questions writers often have about close third is how to inhabit the character's mind and experience without the distancing layer that Janet Burroway and John Gardner call "filtering" ("she wondered," "he noticed," "she remembered"—although the occasional uses of these may be needed to clarify a passage, in general, the less they're used, the better). Ann Cummins, in the second and third paragraphs of her story "Headhunter," shows how to let the reader see and feel the desert along with the viewpoint character, without filtering:

> She rolled down the window and let the air blow her hair. A white sign told her she was entering the largest antelope reserve in the United States. On the yellow caution signs the antelope had its front legs folded under it, very graceful in silhouette. There were blond rocks in the distance that could be animals wisely resting in the heat of the day. In places, the road had buckled and warped from the heat so the truck dipped and rose as it moved along.
>
> Without looking, she reached for the water bottle beside her and twisted off the lid. The water was warm. She shifted legs, using her left for the gas, resting her right on the passenger's side. The little shrunken head hanging from her key chain knocked against her thigh. When she was eight, her father threw a nickel into a carnival dish and won the head for her. He said, "Now you'll always have something uglier than you."

The clues that let us know we're inside the character are very subtle. Since Cummins has already established the close third-person POV in the first paragraph, "a white sign told her" is enough of a signal that we assume the whole paragraph to be in the woman's POV. Instead of desert clichés—cacti, sand—we get a particular and surprising image: the antelope reserve sign. Cummins doesn't continually remind us that the viewpoint character is feeling, noticing, or remembering. The reader automatically interprets "animals wisely resting in the heat" as the viewpoint character's perception, not an observation from an omniscient author who's perceiving something the character doesn't. Avoiding the unnecessary use of muffling words like "seemed," "sensed," "thought," "noticed," or "wondered" after establishing the POV helps make the prose more forceful and immediate, and places us inside the protagonist's experience.

Cummins moves us from the woman's physical experience of her surroundings (the sight and feeling of the hot landscape and warm drinking water) into her memories. The detail of the shrunken head knocking against her thigh helps us make the transition from what she's experiencing physically into a memory that sheds light on her relationship with her father.

Another essential skill is the ability to move smoothly into, and back out of, the direct reporting of a character's thoughts, while keeping those thoughts concise and specific. Nathan Englander does this, without using distracting italics, in "The Gilgul of Park Avenue":

> Charles Luger knew, if he knew anything at all, that a Yiddishe *neshama* was functioning inside him.
>
> He was not one to engage taxicab drivers in conversation, but such a thing as this he felt obligated to share. A New York story of the first order, like a woman giving birth in an elevator, or a hot dog vendor performing open-heart surgery with a pocketknife and a Bic pen. Was this not a rebirth in itself? It was something, he was sure. So he leaned forward in his seat, raised a fist, and knocked on the Plexiglas divider.

Englander moves very quickly from general information about the character, to a fragment that we can read as either reported or direct thinking ("A New York story of the first order"), full of lively, specific details. Next, he gives Luger's direct thought ("Was this not a rebirth in itself?"), then begins transitioning back out of the character's mind with the phrase "he was sure," and finally moves into an action. Part of the reason this works is the specificity of the thinking: we'd be more apt to notice the departure, and less interested, if Englander had written something abstract, like "Really, in New York all stories were grand, surprising—it was a city of strange miracles and everyday wonders." In early drafts, many of us tend to be abstract and to go on at length about a character's thoughts, staying too long in a character's head. When we go back into the passage, we see that we can cut much of what we've written, replace abstractions with specifics, and control the effect of the passage by concentrating on the central idea.

Sometimes, with a character who's limited in his ability to take responsibility for his emotions and actions, a third-person viewpoint lets us see him more clearly and feel more sympathetic towards him than if he were telling us the story himself. In Robert Stone's "Helping," the viewpoint character, Elliot, is a Vietnam veteran, a recovering alcoholic, and a counselor at a state hospital. Early on in the story, Stone introduces us to Blankenship, who comes to Elliot for counseling. Elliot judges his client harshly:

> Blankenship had red hair, a brutal face, and a sneaking manner. He was a sponger and petty thief whom Elliot had seen a number of times before.
>
> "I been having this dream," Blankenship announced loudly. His voice was not pleasant. His skin was unwholesome. Every time he got arrested the court sent him to the psychiatrists and the psychiatrists, who spoke little English, sent him to Elliot.

The description begins with physical details ("red hair") but quickly becomes shaded by adjectives indicating Elliot's opinion ("brutal face," "sneaking manner"). Because these judgments are simply stated rather than dramatically enacted (how is Blankenship's manner sneaking?), the reader begins to question Elliot's complete reliability. At the same time, we do get vivid images throughout the scene—"slack-jawed face," "Blankenship looked right and left like a dog surrendering eye contact," and "Blankenship sniffed and telescoped his neck," all of which have a persuasive power. Although we may agree with Elliot that Blankenship is an unsavory character, it's hard not to pity Blankenship, even though Elliot does not. And yet we feel sympathy for Elliot as well, for his emotional inabilities and frustrations. If a first-person narrator were to make such severe judgments about another character, we might resist these so firmly that the narrator would lose our sympathy altogether. The impartiality of third person—simply conveying a character's mindset—allows readers to be more objective as well.

Stone walks a fine line with point of view in this story, and at times it may seem that he is slipping into another character's mind:

> "Dreams are boring," Elliot told him.
>
> Blankenship was outraged. "Whaddaya mean?" he demanded.

It might seem as if the POV is shifting to include Blankenship's interior emotional state. But in context it's clear we're getting Elliot's observation of the emotion. Stone could have chosen to present a sensory detail that showed Blankenship's outrage to the reader, instead of "telling" us Blankenship's emotion. By choosing to give us Elliot's blunt, shorthand summaries of Blankenship's emotions instead, Stone increases our sense of Elliot's problems with compassion. Again, this wouldn't work if Stone didn't also give us images elsewhere. By judiciously choosing when to "tell" (always through Elliot's POV) and when to "show" (also always through Elliot's POV), Stone manages to render Blankenship vivid for the reader and reveal something about Elliot at the same time.

Discerning Third-Person POV (Third Person Flexible)

Discerning third-person POV has all the elements of close third person—the ability to inhabit the mind and body of the viewpoint character—but it also includes the ability to look at the character from the outside with more perspective and commentary. We call this "third person flexible" because it establishes the narrative voice as separate from the character's mind, and so the reader is not startled to receive either authorial commentary or information that the viewpoint character may not be thinking about. Discerning third person is different from an omniscient POV. We're still limiting our focus to a single character.

Discerning third person often allows for a mix of compassion and objectivity, since the narrative is examining the character, as well as presenting the character's experiences. This POV can also allow the story to cover a greater time period more easily than close third, jumping from one event to another across a span of time.

Ngugi wa Thiong'o, in "Minutes of Glory," uses discerning third person in a way that shows us why it might be useful for the narrative to have perspective on a character:

> Her name was Wanjiru. But she liked better her Christian one, Beatrice. It sounded more pure and more beautiful. Not that she was ugly; but she could not be called beautiful either. Her body, dark and full-fleshed, had the form, yes, but it was as if it waited to be filled by the spirit. She worked in beer halls where sons of women came to drown their inner lives in beer cans and froth. Nobody seemed to notice her. Except, perhaps, when a proprietor or an impatient customer called out her name, Beatrice; then other customers would raise their heads briefly, a few seconds, as if to behold the bearer of such a beautiful name, but not finding anybody there, they would resume their drinking, their ribald jokes, their laughter and play with the other serving girls. She was like a wounded bird in flight: a forced landing now and then but nevertheless wobbling from place to place so that she would variously be found in Alaska, Paradise, The Modern, Thome and other beer-halls all over Limuru. . . .

Because of the POV, the narrative question is, "Will Wanjiru find a way for her spirit to fill her body?" This is not a question that could be raised from the inside, since she herself doesn't seem to know what's missing. We feel concerned for her from the start without having to try to identify her problems from hints.

Discerning third may feel less immediate than close third, and if not skillfully handled, the narrative voice can be intrusive and irritating—the reader may begin to argue with the narrator's judgment, feel the author has created a "strawman," and be less intimately engaged with the story. In fact, this can be quite a difficult viewpoint to workshop in early drafts. Before the author has figured out exactly what commentary or perspective is necessary and why it fits the needs of the story, the commenting can appear to workshoppers as a common mistake: trying to explain a character's actions and feelings rather than embodying them through precise actions, dialogue, and detail. Part of what makes a discerning third-person POV work is restraint, using the kind of specific detail and concision that we employ with close third.

Degrees of Omniscience

Omniscience is the most authoritative and flexible of POVs, but generally the hardest to master. Within the framework of an omniscient POV, a writer has many choices. Some omniscient narrators inhabit each of their characters whenever they like; others limit themselves to a few. Some range over time, add historical information, and comment freely; others inhabit several characters, but without commentary.

Rotating close third person is a step along the way, although it is not yet full omniscience. The narrator sets up rules about whose mind we can inhabit and when. The order of rotation may be strongly patterned, or more freeform. In either case, different sections of the story—often separated by white space, titles, numbering, or chapter headings—each feature a different viewpoint character. We never get more than one viewpoint within a single passage or scene. Early on, the story or novel lets us know the rules: if we switch viewpoints after a section or a chapter, we expect to do so again in the next section. If the first couple of sections stay in a single viewpoint, we don't expect to leave that viewpoint without a very good reason.

When learning to use the omniscient POV, we struggle to establish how much information is enough, and when it becomes too much; how far back our omniscient narrative should stand from the characters; when to choose one person's viewpoint over another's; and how to gracefully make the transition between viewpoints.

Our choices depend on the needs of the story, but how do we know what the needs of a particular story might be? Once again, we turn to our bookcase for help. Toni Morrison, Jorge Luis Borges, and Anton Chekhov give us three very different approaches to the omniscient narrator. Morrison's *Song of Solomon* ranges gracefully through a multitude of viewpoints across an expanse of time. Borges's "Inferno I, 32" applies a large philosophical view to a very short story. Chekhov's "Gooseberries" moves the viewpoint among a small group of characters while keeping to a limited period of time and space and refraining from authorial commentary.

Because *Song of Solomon* is a novel, Toni Morrison has room to give us the large view and spend substantial time in the experience of several different characters. She begins the book with a dramatic event—an insurance agent attempting to fly—and, in her tour-de-force first chapter, tells us local history, looking at the lives of many of the town's occupants. We learn about "Not Doctor Street" and its history:

> Town maps registered the street as Mains Avenue, but the only colored doctor in the city had lived and died on that street, and when he moved there in 1896 his patients took to calling the street, which none of them lived in or near, Doctor Street. Later, when other Negroes moved there, and when the postal service became a popular means of transferring messages among them, envelopes from Louisiana, Virginia, Alabama, and Georgia began to arrive addressed to people at house numbers on Doctor Street. The post office workers returned these envelopes or passed them on to the Dead Letter Office. Then in 1918, when colored men were being drafted, a few gave their address at the recruitment office as Doctor Street. In that way, the name acquired a quasi-official status. But not for long.

This authoritative, Godlike narrator gives us, through the specificity of the details, a sense of the economic and racial implications of life in this time and place, with no direct comment or instruction to the reader. Before we ever meet the central characters, we have a dream-like and believable setting for their lives. The doctor's daughter and granddaughters accidentally spill velvet rose petals in the street, so that "the wind blew them about, up, down, and into small mounds of snow." But the poetry of this image is immediately linked to a hard reality: "Everyone knew the girls had spent hour after hour tracing, cutting, and stitching the costly velvet, and that Gerhardt's Department Store would be quick to reject any that were soiled."

The town ("everyone") is given to us as a group, creating the sense of a community so intertwined that their feelings can be reported on in a body. But the book dips into and explains the individual characters at length. Because of the omniscient opening of the novel, we accept this mix of general information, commentary, and movement from one character to another. We also gain a sense of individual lives in the context of their community and historical situation. After the book's opening scene, the narrative moves particularly into the birth of the child who will be the novel's most central character, and then back out to the community.

When writing a short story using an omniscient POV, we're going to have to make different choices than we would with a novel. We won't be able to spend long periods of time with a variety of characters, or to develop more than a few characters. The span of time is often shorter, and we have less room for digressions, whether in action or philosophy. And yet, even a short story can still create a sense of spaciousness, as in Borges's "Inferno I, 32."

STORY ANALYSIS AND QUESTIONS: "INFERNO I, 32"

(Note: please read the story once before *you read the following analysis. Then, after you read the analysis, look at the story a second time, keeping the discussion questions in mind. You will get the most benefit out of this process if you mark specific passages in the story, take notes, and work through the questions in writing.)*

Jorge Luis Borges's "Inferno I, 32" demonstrates the most omniscient POV possible, relying on all the components of complete omniscience: any character might be a viewpoint character, the narrative mixes objective and subjective observations, the narrative doesn't limit what the reader perceives, the narrative adds information the character doesn't know, and the author provides commentary and opinions. The events of the story also happened long ago, which adds to the feeling of distance. This fiction could not be told from any other POV, since it would be a completely different story if told solely from Dante's viewpoint, or even from the close third-person viewpoints of Dante and the leopard.

The omniscient viewpoint allows Borges to juxtapose two very different characters who undergo similar experiences. The title refers to Dante's great poem *Inferno,* with its tour of the seven circles of hell. In the first canto, the poet, lost in a dark and confusing forest and unable to find his way into hell, purgatory, or paradise, tries to climb a hill and sees a leopard: "Ed ecco, quasi al cominciar de l'erta,/una lonza leggiera e presta molto,/che di pel macolato era coverta;/e non mi si partia dinanzi al volto,/anzi 'mpediva tanto il mio cammino,/ch'i' fui per ritornar più volte vòlto," which translates roughly as "And behold—where the hill begins, a leopard—graceful and very quick, with a pelt all spotted—was always in my sight; it so blocked my way that I kept having to go back down." Knowing the original lines, with their sense of frustration, and of the impediment to ascension and understanding, helps clarify the fiction.

DISCUSSION QUESTIONS

1. How has Borges worked with the meaning of Dante's lines and transformed them in his story? What role does the POV play in this transformation?
2. How does Borges keep the commentary from being overly abstract or didactic?
3. How do the word "perhaps" and the phrase "Tradition holds that . . ." complicate the POV? How do they change the story?
4. What are the similarities and differences between the viewpoint characters? Between their situations?

EFFECTIVELY BREAKING POV RULES

Experience suggests that certain kinds of POV slips will distract the reader; most writers are warned about these when they begin learning the craft. Stories that shift viewpoints for no apparent reason break what John Gardner called "the vivid and continuous" dream of the story. If three-fourths of the story is in close third with one viewpoint character, but the POV then shifts to tell us what another character is thinking for a sentence or two, the reader will probably find that distracting, and even more so if this is the only dip into that particular POV. If a story begins with a narrator who gives us the thoughts of all the characters, but then becomes completely objective for six pages in the story's middle, the reader may feel cheated or confused. To avoid puzzling readers, the writer can revise the story to eliminate all subjective information, and make the narrative entirely objective. Or the writer may decide that this particular story would be more powerful if the narrator continued to provide some commentary on the characters throughout, to bind everything together.

On the other hand, writers who have spent any amount of time in workshop can turn into POV vigilantes. We wind up phrasing things awkwardly to avoid any appearance of the possibility that we might be in another point of view, or we make up odd rules as if we were choosing teams for volleyball. We might have decided that each character in a rotating or omniscient POV story must get exactly the same amount of room and number of pages. But why? Perhaps the story belongs more to one person than another. The only real rule is that *we can do anything we can get away with.* This means understanding the artistic requirements of our stories and not needlessly distracting the reader by either too much or too little craft. This also means finding extremely insightful manuscript readers who can let us know when we have successfully broken the rules, and when we still need to keep revising.

STORY ANALYSIS AND QUESTIONS: "GOOSEBERRIES"

(Note: please read the story once before *you read the following analysis. Then, after you read the analysis, look at the story a second time, keeping the discussion questions in mind. You will get the most benefit out of this process if you mark specific passages in the story, take notes, and work through the questions in writing.)*

In "Gooseberries," Chekhov illustrates how omniscience can be used with great restraint. He only shows us what's going on in his character's minds when necessary—he deploys these moments with great care, both to maintain narrative tension and to illustrate his themes. Throughout most of the story, he limits himself to describing what characters say and do. The opening paragraph has a far-reaching perspective that announces its omniscient POV:

> The whole sky had been overcast with rain-clouds from the early morning; it was a still day, not hot, but heavy, as it is in grey dull weather when the clouds have been hanging over the country for a long while, when one expects rain and it does not come. Ivan Ivanovitch, the veterinary surgeon, and Burkin, the high-school teacher, were already tired from walking, and the fields seemed to them endless. Far ahead of them they could just see the windmills of the village of Mironositskoe; on the right stretched a row of hillocks which disappeared in the distance behind the village, and they both knew that this was the bank of the river, that there were meadows, green willows, homesteads there, and that if one stood on one of the hillocks one could see from it the same vast plain, telegraph-wires, and a train which in the distance looked like a crawling caterpillar, and that in clear weather one could even see the town. Now, in still weather, when all nature seemed mild and dreamy, Ivan Ivanovitch and Burkin were filled with love of that countryside, and both thought how great, how beautiful a land it was.

The first sentence provides both history (what things had been like since morning) and context (weather). In the third sentence, Chekhov describes both Ivanovitch's and Burkin's states of mind using the third person plural (they're both tired, they both think the fields will never end). We see the countryside through their eyes, and see their mutual love for it. This POV choice establishes a unity of feeling between them—significant because by the end of the story, this unity will be broken.

Here are Chekhov's POV decisions defined according to the categories of the POV chart: any character might be a viewpoint character; the events happened in the recent or undetermined past; the story tends toward the objective side of the spectrum, with occasional information about the characters' thoughts and feelings; sensory details are funneled through the characters; the author does provide some history/information; and the narrative does not comment, express opinions, or judge the characters.

DISCUSSION QUESTIONS

1. When do the viewpoints switch from one character, or set of characters, to another? How does Chekhov let us know we've changed POVs? Why does he make each shift, and what changes because of it?
2. When and why does Chekhov use detail and action to convey information, and when does he give us the characters' thoughts and feelings?
3. What is the purpose and effect of the story-within-a-story? What is Ivanovitch's purpose in telling the story, and how does Chekhov let us know this? Does he seem to be a mouthpiece for Chekhov's ideas? Why or why not? What role do the different POVs play in this story?
4. How do the details of the last scene undercut or reinforce the effects of Ivanovitch's story? Why might Chekhov have ended "Gooseberries" this way?

5. What are the effects of each of Chekhov's POV decisions, and how do they shape the materials of the story?

REVISION: MAKING SUBTLE POV SHIFTS

Sometimes a problem that seems to be one of character or plot actually has to do with POV. When we realize this, we may take dramatic action, changing the POV from first to third, for example. Sometimes, however, instead of immediately pursuing a radical change, we might start with smaller changes. In some cases, just moving one step along the appropriate spectrum can make a problematic POV mesh with the story's intentions. We could make the story more objective, letting detail and action do the work. Or we could give the reader more of the viewpoint character's thoughts and experience. A narrative may paraphrase the viewpoint character's thoughts: "Sylvia decided to walk across the frozen pond, although she remembered her sister's earlier warning." Or it may give those thoughts directly: "Sylvia stepped onto the ice. Was it cracking underfoot? Should she keep going?" The first POV has more distance; the second is more intimate.

As an example of the large effect of small shifts in viewpoint, we can study two published versions of a story by Raymond Carver. In his later career, he published longer, richer versions of several of the stories that had appeared in his early short story collections (the early stories were apparently significantly edited). His story "The Bath," about parents whose son is hit by a car, appears in *What We Talk about When We Talk about Love.* The longer version, titled "A Small, Good Thing," is included in *Where I'm Calling From.* Both versions are in the third person, and in both, any character might be a viewpoint character, the events of the story seemed to have happened recently, and the narrator provides no commentary or opinions. But the degrees to which the narrative presents the viewpoint characters' thoughts/feelings and funnels sensory details, history, and information change in the second version. The first published version is so spare as to seem not only ominous but almost cold—for a close third-person POV, it's actually quite distant:

> The man drove home from the hospital. He drove the streets faster than he should. It had been a good life till now. There had been work, fatherhood, family. The man had been lucky and happy. But fear made him want a bath.
>
> He pulled into the driveway. He sat in the car trying to make his legs work. The child had been hit by a car and he was in the hospital, but he was going to be all right. The man got out of the car and went up to the door. The dog was barking and the telephone was ringing. It kept ringing while the man unlocked the door and felt the wall for the light switch.
>
> He picked up the receiver. He said, "I just got in the door!"

In the longer version, the POV is much more intimate. The characters are named; we know the details of what has made the man's life good; and we have his sensory experiences, the exact nature of his fears, and his attempt to rationalize these fears away:

> Howard drove home from the hospital. He took the wet, dark streets very fast, then caught himself and slowed down. Until now, his life had gone smoothly and to his satisfaction—college, marriage, another year of college for the advanced degree in business, a junior partnership in an investment firm. Fatherhood. He was happy and, so far, lucky—he knew that. His parents were still living, his brothers and his sister were established, his friends from college had gone out to take their places in the world. So far, he had kept away from any real harm, from those forces he knew existed and that could cripple or bring down a man if the luck went bad, if things suddenly turned. He pulled into the driveway and parked. His left leg began to tremble. He sat in the car for a minute and tried to deal with the present situation in a rational manner. Scotty had been hit by a car and was in the hospital, but he was going to be all right. Howard closed his eyes and ran his hand over his face. He got out of the car and went up to the front door. The dog was barking inside the house. The telephone rang and rang while he unlocked the door and fumbled for the light switch. He shouldn't have left the hospital, he shouldn't have. "Goddamn it!" he said. He picked up the receiver and said, "I just walked in the door!"

In this version, both the character and the story feel fully inhabited; the reader is inside the experience—the trembling left leg, the fumble for the light switch, Howard's very human conviction that leaving the hospital may have brought on disaster, and the slow nightmare of trying to get to the telephone as it rings and rings. His thought that Scotty has been hit by a car but will be all right, by the simple addition of Scotty's name, has been turned from indirect to direct reporting of his thoughts. The events and emotions seem to be unchanged, but the shorter version feels oblique and mannered. In the second version, we are thinking of Howard and Scotty, not about Carver. When we know them better, we are more moved by their situation.

As we reread our own stories, we can see how changing the POV would affect them. A close third-person approach might turn out to be ineffective for a particular story because the main character isn't aware of key information, and the author needs to step forward to provide the missing pieces. In rewriting, we can examine the story to see how close or how discerning that narrator is. If we're using authorial commentary, we can examine it to see how well the degree of commentary fits with the story's themes. Are the benefits from the commentary worth the sense of intrusion? Perhaps we need to add or subtract viewpoint characters, or to make sure that all of the viewpoint characters have their own separate concerns and issues. Is there a viewpoint we should be providing that isn't yet in the story? Will that character's action and dialogue suffice, or do we need the thoughts and perceptions as well?

In order to know whether a particular POV is the best choice for our story, we need to be aware not only of our material, but of our habitual weaknesses. We might avoid omniscience if we failed history, geography, and botany and are afraid of revealing the gaps in our knowledge. Or if we've been working on the same story for two years, we might rewrite it with the viewpoint rotating from character to character, imagining that otherwise our readers will be as bored by it as we are, when the real problems with the story have nothing to do with the POV. We might use the same POV over and over because we're used to it, or because it's currently fashionable and so appears in all the literary magazines. Perhaps every time we write in the first person, we sound as young and slangy as Holden Caulfield, or every time we write in the third person, we take on a pompous, antiquated tone. Every one of these difficulties can be worked through in revision, if the story requires a POV that pushes us past our previous limits.

POV EXERCISES

1. Pick a third-person story by one of your favorite authors. Rewrite the first three pages making subtle changes in the POV: recent versus long-ago, close versus distant, objective versus subjective, and so on. As far as possible, keep the author's voice and style, but consider what new information you might need to add, or what you would remove. Do you need more dialogue? Less? Different details? Should you start the story in a different place? This exercise can reveal new aspects of the story and the differences between POVs.
2. Choose one of your own third-person stories, a story for which you have at least one completed draft. What would you say the story is "about" at its deepest level? What is its POV? (Locate its exact "shade of blue" on the POV chart.) Write one or more pages of analysis of the POV of this story. What were the literary and personal reasons you chose that POV? Try analyzing the ways in which the POV is making the story stronger, and those in which the POV might be limiting the story. When you have finished this, make some notes for yourself about the changes you would have to make to put it in a different, but still logical, POV. What might your reasons be for making that change? What would the story lose? What would it gain? Try several versions of the first couple of paragraphs, in different points of view, thinking of the story's most urgent questions or issues. How do they relate to the POV?
3. Write a scene in close third person from the POV of someone you dislike. Imagine, though, that the narrative eye is that of the best friend of the character. What would that narrator see that you might not observe on your own? How would the narrator present the character's actions and dialogue? Write as if you loved the character.

Now revise the scene with a nonjudgmental stance, aware of strengths and weaknesses, but treating them as neutrally as you would the character's eye color or taste in breakfast cereals.

4. Using Borges as an example, write an omniscient short-short story that somehow embodies or makes specific a philosophical question. Don't try to answer the question or instruct the reader. Instead, use images and ideas that deepen the question.
5. (This reading exercise can be done either individually or in a group.) Examine a third-person story that you've read recently to determine whether it's close third person, discerning third person, or omniscient. If it's close third person, how intimate or distant is it? What are the specific passages in the story that reveal this POV? How is this POV choice related to the subjects and themes of the story, and what makes it an appropriate choice? Optional next step: choose a page from the story. Rewrite it in a different third-person POV. How does this change the mood and meaning of the story?

CHAPTER

3

The Uses of First and Second Person

(Anthology selections: "The Turkey Season" and "Trauma Plate")

Don't get me started on the challenges of doing this guy [the character Chen Pen in Monkey Hunting*]. He was so far removed from my own experience, sensibility, everything, that it took me forever to even approach his bloodstream. I first read an enormous amount about the period, in China as well as in Cuba, and I read an enormous amount of Chinese poetry and translation to capture the right sensibility and to find the right cultural references. Then I very gingerly began moving him through the world, but I was still seeing him from the outside and was not getting any sense of his internal life. Little by little, over several harrowing years, I kind of epidermally moved into the muscle tissue until I finally got into the bloodstream. At least that's what I hope I ultimately did, but it took a really long time, and I was fighting self-charges of fraud all along the way.*

Cristina García, *Atlantic Unbound* interview

STORIES THAT REQUIRE FIRST-PERSON NARRATORS

When we first begin writing stories, we often choose the first person, a voice that seems natural, since we're used to the word "I." We begin writing by posing as someone else. Later on, we notice all the possibilities of third person, and may turn against first person as a reaction. A number of situations, though, lend themselves naturally to first-person narration. Allowing a character to tell the story directly to the reader suggests that there is something about *the act of telling* that is urgent for the character: an important realization about a past or present situation, a need to figure out past events, or the desire to confess. This urge toward confession may be an atonement for past mistakes, a self-justification, or a correction of others' misinterpretations. The act of storytelling itself can be part of the subject matter of the story, and this will be altered by factors like the narrator's degree of reliability or the length of time between the story's events and the telling of them.

John Edgar Wideman, in his story "Weight," has a narrator driven by a need to communicate what he didn't say to, and about, his mother when she was alive. He's suffering from the pressure of undelivered words:

> I was scared, Mom. Scared every cotton picking day of my life I'd lose you. The fear a sing-song taunt like tinnitus ringing in my ear. No wonder I'm a little crazy. But don't get me wrong. Not your fault. I don't blame you for my morbid fears, my unhappiness. It's just that I should have confessed sooner, long, long ago, the size of my fear of losing you. I wish you'd heard me say the words. How fear made me keep my distance, hide how much I depended on your smile. The sunshine of your smiling laughter that could also send me silently screaming out the room in stories I never told you because you'd taught me as you'd been taught, not to say anything aloud I didn't want to come true. Nor say out loud the things I wished to come true. Doesn't leave a hell of a lot to say, does it. No wonder I'm tongue-tied, scared shitless.
>
> But would it be worth the risk, worth failing, if I could find words to tell our story and also keep us covered inside it, work us invisibly into the fret, the warp and woof of the story's design, safe there, connected there as words in perfect poems, the silver apples of the moon, golden apples of the sun, blue guitars.

Wideman's narrator operates from several of the motives we've described: he's coming to a realization, he's trying to understand the past, and he's confessing as a way of atoning for his behavior. The urgency of the style—the rush of the sentences and images—conveys the importance of this need to communicate.

First-person POV can also be a good choice for stories with central characters who are in some way highly eccentric: letting them tell their own stories may help them become more sympathetic, less prone to seem ridiculous. Robert Olen Butler's "Jealous Husband Returns in Form of Parrot" begins in this way:

> I never can quite say as much as I know. I look at other parrots and I wonder if it's the same for them, if somebody is trapped in each of them paying some kind of price for living their life in a certain way. For instance, 'Hello,' I say, and I'm sitting on a perch in a pet store in Houston and what I'm really thinking is Holy shit. It's you. And what's happened is I'm looking at my wife.

We're immediately pulled into the story, since like this parrot, we too are unable to quite say what we mean most of the time. We also wonder what kind of price he's paying, what he's done, who his wife is—a parrot, a woman?—and why he's so surprised to see her. By the end of the first paragraph, the writing has opened up our attention and sympathies to a character who might have seemed like a joke. And he *is* funny and absurd, this parrot narrator, but also touching: his story seriously engages the nature of jealousy and freedom.

If we imagine the story told in third person, we can see that we might have a hard time identifying with this wildly emotional bird. And yet, in first person, he may remind us, uncomfortably, of ourselves. The story is told in present tense, which does not allow the narrator the luxury of perspective—we see him trapped in the moment, just as he is trapped in the body of a bird.

Most experienced writers/teachers advise against writing from nonhuman POVs because we've so often seen it done just to shock or amuse, a story that never really develops. As Jerome Stern advises in *Making Shapely Fiction,* "Writers have, of course, written fine stories from various points of view—animate and inanimate, human and nonhuman—but that's just their starting premise. The question is what is achieved by the device." In other words, what makes this POV necessary to the deep purposes of the story? This question applies not only when we are writing from a nonhuman POV but from any POV far enough from our own experience to require research. Are we trying to be original for its own sake, or does something in the story require this POV?

ASPECTS OF FIRST-PERSON POV

The chart on the next page lists aspects of first-person POV. As with the third-person chart, each aspect is independent of the others—they should be read across, not down. Each aspect is also a spectrum, as indicated by the arrows. After the chart, we explain each aspect separately. Later in the chapter, we use examples from short passages and anthology stories to give a sense of the artistic effects of different choices.

A first-person voice may use a variety of combinations of the above possibilities. For example, a reliable, peripheral narrator tells another character a story about events in the very recent past, with almost no focus on his own thoughts or feelings, but only on the details and actions he has observed in the exterior world. Different choices produce different shades of closeness and distance for a reader. Subtle adjustments often occur in revision, though we may, occasionally, discover the precise combination the story needs the first time.

Sometimes we hear a character telling a story, without knowing what that character's reasons are. The reasons may emerge as we write, but if they don't become clearer after a draft or two, we might want to consider changing the POV.

Number of Viewpoint Characters The large majority of first-person stories have a single narrator. First-person short stories rarely have rotating narrators. When they do, they tend to be about the conflicting interpretations of events, as in Ryunosuke Akutagawa's "In a Grove" (the basis for the famous movie *Rashomon*), which consists entirely of the first-person testimonies of several witnesses to a murder, all of whom have wildly diverging accounts of what happened.

ASPECTS OF FIRST-PERSON POV

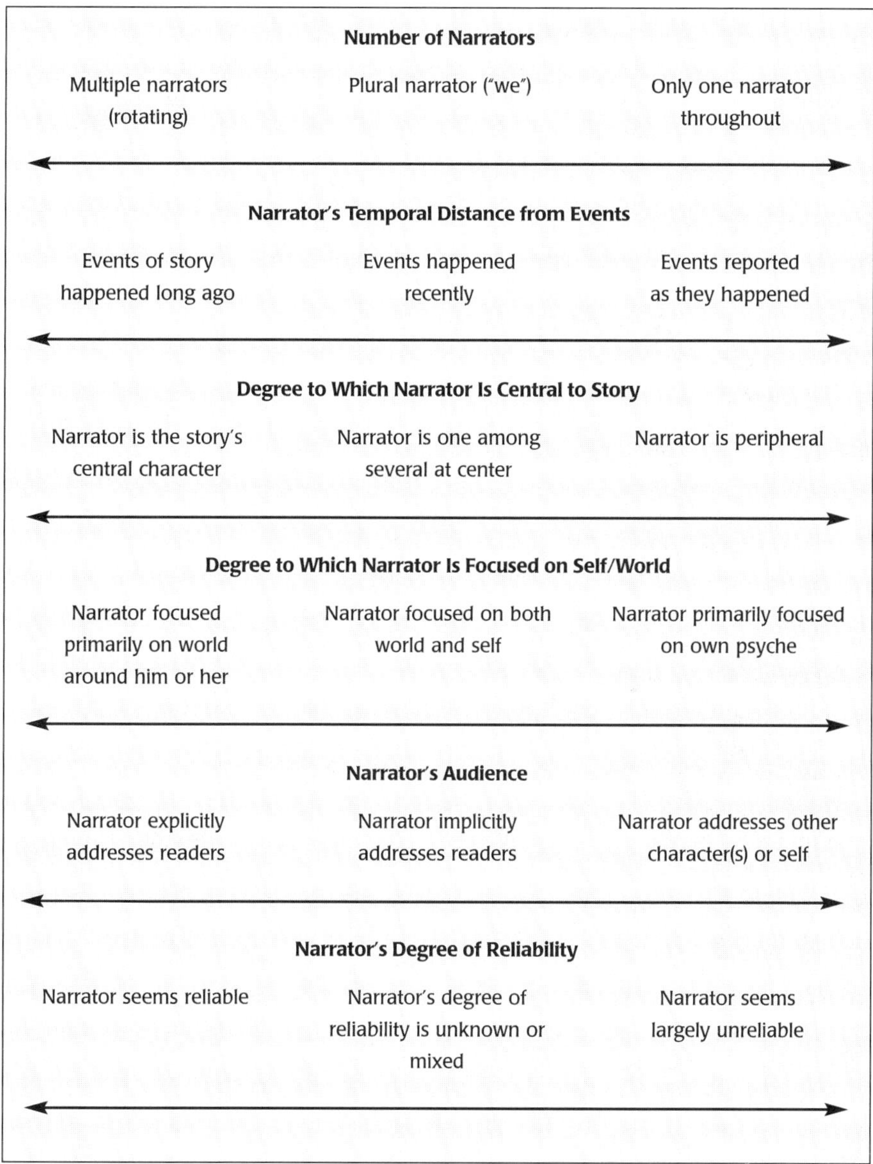

Number of Narrators
Multiple narrators (rotating)
Plural narrator ("we")
Only one narrator throughout
Narrator's Temporal Distance from Events
Events of story happened long ago
Events happened recently
Events reported as they happened
Degree to Which Narrator Is Central to Story
Narrator is the story's central character
Narrator is one among several at center
Narrator is peripheral
Degree to Which Narrator Is Focused on Self/World
Narrator focused primarily on world around him or her
Narrator focused on both world and self
Narrator primarily focused on own psyche
Narrator's Audience
Narrator explicitly addresses readers
Narrator implicitly addresses readers
Narrator addresses other character(s) or self
Narrator's Degree of Reliability
Narrator seems reliable
Narrator's degree of reliability is unknown or mixed
Narrator seems largely unreliable

The rotating first-person viewpoint is more common in novels, which offer more room for different narrators to give their perspectives and accounts of connected or overlapping events. Plural narrators are even more rare. In our anthology, "Father" is the only story with a plural narrator. Here, the use of a plural narrator focuses the reader on the father's relationship to the entire family, not just to one of his children.

Narrator's Temporal Distance from Events When using first-person narration, writers have to decide on the distance between the narrating self and the self to whom the story's events happen. If a lot of time has passed, the narrating self may see things the earlier self missed, or may interpret things differently. The narrator may be using the younger self as an object lesson, making reparations for past behavior, or figuring out the meaning of events that weren't clear at the time. This seems to be part of the motive behind "Drinking Coffee Elsewhere," "Turkey Season," and "The Eve of the Spirit Festival." The plural narrator of "Father" seems to be telling the story to atone for not having understood what was going on with the father.

Degree to Which Narrator Is Central to Story A narrator may be the story's central character, one among several characters central to the story, or peripheral. A narrator is central if the story primarily chronicles a change—or a dramatic resistance to change—in the narrator. (In some cases, if the narrator neither changes nor resists change, then the change may occur only in the reader's perception of the narrator over the course of the story. We discuss the role of change in more detail in Chapter 4.)

Sometimes a story's central character is not the best choice to narrate the story, because of a lack of awareness, perspective, or access to key information. Or if the subject matter is highly dramatic, then letting a central character tell a story may risk turning it into a melodrama or a litany of unrelieved misery. In these cases, a character on the periphery, watching the story's events but not as involved in them, can make a better narrator.

A peripheral narrator can either offer perspective on a group or serve as a stand-in for the reader. In *The Great Gatsby,* Nick Carraway comes in as an outsider to Gatsby's world, and so he gives the reader an entrée into a bewildering and complex society. The challenge of using a peripheral narrator is to ensure that this character is as vivid and believably human as the other characters, and is changed by the events in some way. Otherwise, the reader is likely to wonder why telling the story matters to the narrator. In the anthology stories "The Eve of the Spirit Festival," "Turkey Season," and "A Wagner Matinée," the narrators are relatively peripheral to dramatic events, but are definitely affected by the events. Narrators may also be one among several characters at the center of the story, as in "A Conversation with My Father," "DiGrasso: A Story of Odessa," "Car Crash While Hitchhiking," "Trauma Plate," and "Powder." These stories are either about the relationship between the narrator and the other characters, or as much about the other characters as about the narrator.

Degree to Which Narrator Is Focused on Self/World At one end of this spectrum, narrators are so focused on examining the world or other characters that we learn almost nothing about their inner life. At the opposite end, narrators concentrate so closely on their own psychology that we see very little of the world around them. Most first-person fiction lies somewhere in the middle of the spectrum. Even in a story with a narrative focused primarily on the psyche, as in "Photograph of Luisa," "Drinking Coffee Elsewhere," and "Car Crash While Hitchhiking," the narrators are aware of the world around them and describe it specifically. We get the sense, however, that the events and details have been assembled primarily for the purpose of examining the nature of the narrator's own actions, decisions, and motives. A more interior focus may be appropriate for a story about a narrator's trauma, as in these three stories. If we're writing a story with an internally focused narrator, the three can serve as models for how to create such a narrator without falling into an airless solipsism. In a more externally focused story, as in "DiGrasso," "Father," "Orientation," and "A Wagner Matinée," we get the sense that events and details have been selected and arranged to shed light on a community or another character. We may choose a more externally focused first-person narrator when we want to give the reader one character's view of events more intimately than a third-person narrator can.

If we compare the first page or so of "Photograph of Luisa," "Drinking Coffee Elsewhere," and "Car Crash While Hitchhiking" with the first few pages of "DiGrasso," "Father," "Orientation," or "A Wagner Matinée," we'll immediately see the difference. The focus affects when and how narrators introduce other characters, and how much they speculate on their own behavior versus that of others. In stories such as "Powder," "A Conversation with my Father," and "The Eve of the Spirit Festival," the narrators move their focus from internal to external and back again throughout the story.

Narrator's Audience Most first-person stories address the reader implicitly. "Drinking Coffee Elsewhere" opens with the sentence "Orientation games began the day I arrived at Yale from Baltimore." The narrator clearly isn't talking to herself, since she's delivering information she already knows. Unless something happens to convince us otherwise, we assume that the story is being told for the reader's benefit. In some stories, however, the writer chooses to have the narrator directly address the reader, as in "Photograph of Luisa" and "Car Crash While Hitchhiking." When Luisa says "I'm fooling you, hah, I'm not blind," we assume by "you" she means the reader, since she doesn't seem to be talking to another character. This kind of direct address is disorienting for the reader, which is an appropriate effect for both "Car Crash While Hitchhiking" and "Photograph of Luisa": in both stories the truth of what's happening is uncertain. Even in these two stories, the address to the reader is used sparingly, which makes it more effective. When overused, the technique can become mannered or intrusive.

Another approach is to have the narrator tell the story to a character. Such a story can consist of a dramatic monologue, in which one character is telling another a story about past events, as in Reginald McKnight's "Boot," which opens, "No, that's not what I'm saying. I'm not saying it's okay to lie. All I'm saying, Coburn, is—if you'll let me—is that there's lies you believe in, and lies you don't believe in." A variation on this approach is to have the story take place as the narrator is addressing another character, as in Daniel Orozco's "Orientation"—here, the monologue consists of a tour of the office. Monologues emphasize the spoken quality of stories; we "hear" the story as if we were in the room, eavesdropping.

In other stories, the narrator addresses the story to a character who is not present—an imagined listener. Usually in these stories, as in Andrea Barrett's "Theories of Rain," or Ryan Harty's "September," the narrator's yearning for the absent character is a significant aspect of the story. In "September," the narrator's longing is palpable: "I could almost picture you reaching up to open the blind, the light rolling over your body like a wave." If we want to emphasize the desire to connect to a character who is lost to the narrator, we might choose this form.

Narrator's Degree of Reliability An unreliable narrator creates a gap between the story the narrator tells and the story we see behind the narrator's version of the truth. Readers may believe that the events of a story are happening more or less the way the narrator describes them, without agreeing with the narrator's interpretation of those events. This doesn't necessarily mean that the narrator is a pathological liar. The narrator, like all humans, may simply miss important information about other people or about the situation of the story. In this case, some of the story's tension comes from our seeing and understanding what the narrator misinterprets or does not notice.

In the anthology, "Trauma Plate," "Photograph of Luisa," and "Car Crash While Hitchhiking" make use of this gap between what the narrator perceives and what we perceive. In "Orientation," we don't have any way to decide whether the narrator is reliable about the information he or she is reporting, and part of the story's drive comes from the readers both wondering what will be revealed next and not knowing how much to believe.

MOTIVES FOR TELLING THE STORY

When we tell stories in real life, we often describe what happened without examining our motives for doing so. In fiction, our first-person narrators may not always know why they're telling their stories either—but readers will expect the writer to know, and to make the motives apparent. Consciously or unconsciously, readers will be asking themselves certain questions: Why is this story urgent? Why has someone been moved to tell the story? What concerns does this narrator have? How does the telling of the story alter the narrator (or the readers' perception of the narrator) over the course of the story? (Not all narrators need to have epiphanies—"I realized my father had never loved my mother"—but the change in the narrator will be part of our experience of the story.) When writing and rewriting, we anticipate these questions and make sure that the story embodies answers to the above questions in some way.

Understanding the Past

Sometimes the need to come to terms with an inexplicable person or an overwhelming event provides the impulse that drives a narrator to reexamine the past. The opening paragraph of Ryan Harty's short story "What Can I Tell You About My Brother?" illustrates one way a writer can make the narrator's impulse for telling the story palpable, without being heavy-handed:

> On his first night home from marine boot camp, my brother killed Rob Dawson's German shepherd with a Phillips screwdriver. Rob was the captain of my football team at Arcadia High School. He was an all-league quarterback and a popular guy, and since the end of the summer he'd been seeing a girl named Jessica Lynn Armstrong, who'd gone out with my brother before he joined the marines. She and Victor had been together for a year and a half, and they'd been serious enough to talk about getting married after he finished boot camp. But during his tenth week of training, she called to say she was seeing Rob, and it must have made my brother crazy. He killed the dog in the backyard of the Dawsons' house, a three-story Spanish villa overlooking the whole sleeping valley. He left the body floating on the lighted blue pool, disappeared over a row of yuccas, and didn't come home until the next afternoon.

That the narrator begins the story with this horrific image suggests it haunts him as much as it haunts us when we read it. The phrase "it must have made my brother crazy" suggests he's attempting to understand the motives behind this act. When writing a story that begins with a dramatic act like this, our natural first-draft impulse might be to give backstory next, or to insert a flashback. But Harty chooses to have his narrator keep the story moving—the story advances to show us scenes that chronicle the consequences of Victor's action, rather than retreating to try to explain what provoked it.

Other stories that feature first-person narrators seeking to understand the past take a more reflective approach, focusing on the interior life. This is a difficult maneuver to pull off, and it's worth studying how a story like Doris Lessing's "How I Finally Lost My Heart" succeeds. The narrator, in trying to understand her romantic history, combines the expected with the unexpected—romantic truisms with a dispassionate and quirky analysis:

> It was just after I had had a lunch and a tea with two different men. My lunch partner I had lived with for (more or less) four and seven-twelfths years. When he left me for new pastures, I spent two years, or was it three, half-dead, and my heart was a stone, impossible to carry about, considering all the other things weighing on one. Then I slowly, and with difficulty, got free, because my heart cherished a thousand adhesions to my first love—though from another point of view he could be legitimately described as either my second *real* love (my father being the first) or my third (my brother intervening) . . .

> But if one were going to look at the thing from outside, without insight, he could be seen as (perhaps, I forget) the thirteenth, but to do that means disregarding the inner emotional truth. For we all know that those affairs or entanglements one has between *serious* loves, though they may number dozens and stretch over years, *don't really count.*

The lighthearted, matter-of-fact way in which she deliberately uses romantic pop song clichés—"my heart was a stone"—weaves through an obsessive, almost sociological attempt to quantify emotions with numbers, which continues throughout the story. If she reflected like this too long, the story would remain frustratingly abstract. However, while on the phone with a prospective lover, her troublesome heart actually leaves her body, literalizing the image: "There was my heart, a large red pulsing bleeding repulsive object, stuck to my fingers. What was I going to do? I sat down, lit a cigarette (with one hand, holding the matchbox between my knees), held my hand with the heart stuck on it over the side of the chair so that it could drip into a bucket, and considered." She spends the rest of the story trying to dispose of it. This surreal turn of events, concretely described, allows the story to break out of interior analysis into a scene without losing its focus on the nature of love. There is an emotional logic that keeps the surrealism from seeming arbitrary.

Applying Perspective

While some first-person narrators are mainly trying to understand past events, others are reevaluating their earlier selves and the people around them. These narrators are usually motivated by a feeling that they were gullible, at fault, or taken advantage of at some point in the past.

It can be easy when writing a first-person draft to simply lose ourselves in the narrator's experience of the events at hand. At some point, however, we have to make a decision—how much perspective does this person have on the events being narrated? In our own lives, as we look back on who we were in the past, we may disagree with opinions we once held. We may be ashamed of actions we were once proud of, or proud of actions that seemed humiliating at the time. We may doubt the accuracy of our memories and judgments. Even if we have narrators who do not explicitly comment on their past actions, their perspective may affect which incidents they choose to tell and what order they arrange them in.

Charles Dickens uses perspective to strong effect in *Great Expectations.* The first-person narrator, Pip, never gives his age, yet it's clear he is significantly older than he was at the time of the story's events; he constantly points out his younger self's moral weaknesses. In fact, this is part of the nature and purpose of the book—an offering to the past, a warning to others, and an expiation for his earlier snobbery and lack of gratitude. In the following passage, he has been elevated to a new social class by his mysterious benefactor. Joe, the blacksmith brother-in-law who raised him, comes for a visit, and the narrator castigates his younger self for his response to Joe's appearance:

> As to his shirt-collar, and his coat-collar, they were perplexing to reflect upon—insoluble mysteries both. Why should a man scrape himself to that extent, before he could consider himself full dressed? Why should he suppose it necessary to be purified by suffering for his holiday clothes? . . .
>
> I had neither the good sense nor the good feeling to know that this was all my fault, and that if I had been easier with Joe, Joe would have been easier with me. I felt impatient of him and out of temper with him; in which condition he heaped coals of fire on my head.

Dickens's use of this narrative distance works with the themes of the book, where so many characters, including Pip, are damaged or thrown off course by their delusions about what is possible for them in life. But Pip, at least, returns to a saner, humbler reality; the story of *Great Expectations* is the story of that journey. The older, more self-aware narrator can illuminate this journey for us. Because we know from the older voice that Pip *is* going to become less unbearable, we can stand the shame of watching his disloyalty and bad behavior.

Sometimes, the distance between older narrator and younger self can be tricky to navigate. Since the older narrator, of course, knows how the story turns out, it's essential to avoid the reader's suspicion that the writer is coyly withholding information. In *Great Expectations,* the young Pip does not know the source of his money until the end of the book. It would be possible to feel cheated by what the older narrator doesn't tell us, and yet we don't because, throughout the novel, the narrator never withholds information that the younger Pip learns, or conceals important scenes that Pip is involved in. We experience everything along with young Pip. Foreshadowing is another way to evade the charge of coyness, depending on the voice and nature of the narrator.

Narrators may have come to terms with the frailties of others, as Pip has, or their anger or pain may still be as strong as it was in the past. Louise Erdrich, in her story "Saint Marie," has a narrator who finds her younger self at fault (as Pip does). Marie, however, has equally strong words for the nuns who scarred her childhood. This kind of judging narrator can often make readers feel they're listening to a rant. Erdrich skillfully avoids this trap:

> I was ignorant. I was near age fourteen. The length of sky is just about the size of my ignorance. Pure and wide. And it was just that—the pure and wideness of my ignorance—that got me up the hill to Sacred Heart Convent and brought me back down alive. For maybe Jesus did not take my bait, but them Sisters tried to cram me right down whole.
>
> You ever see a walleye strike so bad the lure is practically out its back end before you reel it in? That is what they done with me. I don't like to make that low comparison, but I have seen a walleye do that once. And it's the same attempt as Sister Leopolda made to get me in her clutch.

Here, the narrator judges herself and the Sisters by using metaphors, which are more resonant and complex that if she simply said, "I was ignorant, and those nuns were greedy to get me." Describing the nuns as walleyes is more than just an unflattering comparison; it creates both a memorable image for the struggle between her and the nuns, and a way of thinking through the ways each party was culpable—she, for offering herself as bait, and the nuns, for their uncontrolled hunger. Erdrich lets the language and images do the work, rather than having the narrator describe her emotions in abstract terms.

Other first-person stories, however, will work best when the narrator does not have perspective on the former self. In Ha Jin's "The Bridegroom," which takes place in China, the first-person narrator tells the story of his son-in-law, Baowen, who is arrested under suspicion of being gay. The father-in-law struggles with, but fails to rise above, the traditional views of his culture. The narrating self seems to share both his past self's compassion and prejudice:

> We arrived at the hospital early in the afternoon. Baowen looked healthy, in good spirits. It seems that the bath had helped him. He was happy to see Beina and even cuddled her in my presence. He gave her two toffees; knowing I disliked candies, he didn't give me one. He poured a large mug of malted milk for both of us, since there was only one mug in the room. I didn't touch the milk, unsure whether homosexuality was communicable. I was glad to see that he treated his wife well. He took a genuine interest in what she said about their comrades in our factory, and now and then laughed heartily. What a wonderful husband he could have been if he were not sick.

The narrator does not distance himself from his judgments, not even in small ways by inserting a phrase such as "I thought" after some of the opinions. If Ha Jin had written the story so the narrator condemns his earlier self's prejudices, the story would be heavy-handed, a moral illustration of a political point. A literary author like Ha Jin can assume a contemporary, sophisticated audience for whom he doesn't need to underline his points. Ha Jin does, however, make sure that other characters in the story provide perspective—the narrator's own wife, his daughter Beina, and the doctor assigned to "treat" Baowen are all much more accepting than the narrator.

STORY ANALYSIS AND QUESTIONS: "THE TURKEY SEASON"

(Note: please read the story once before *you read the following analysis. Then, after you read the analysis, look at the story a second time, keeping the discussion questions in mind. You will get the most benefit out of this process if you mark specific passages in the story, take notes, and work through the questions in writing.)*

Alice Munro, in "The Turkey Season," shows us how to balance depiction and interpretation with a first-person narrator. This story can be fruitfully studied for its handling of not only point of view but also character and story structure—the way the narrator orders the events she tells us. The story features a single narrator; the events happened many years before the telling; the narrator is fairly peripheral to the story's main events; she is focused on both the world and herself; she is addressing the reader fairly directly, but still implicitly; and she seems to be reliable.

The challenge of writing first-person stories is to keep them from becoming so focused on the narrator's experiences and thoughts that these block readers' views of the other characters and the events. Munro avoids this by keeping a steady focus on the other characters' appearances and behaviors, colored by the narrator's guesses about their motivations:

> Gladys was not a fast gutter, though she must have been thorough; Herb would have talked to her otherwise. She never sang and certainly she never swore. I thought her rather old, though she was not as old as Lily and Marjorie; she must have been over thirty. She seemed offended by everything that went on and had the air of keeping plenty of bitter judgments to herself. I never tried to talk to her, but she spoke to me one day in the cold little washroom off the gutting shed. She was putting pancake makeup on her face. The color of the makeup was so distinct from the color of her skin that it was as if she were slapping orange paint over a whitewashed, bumpy wall.

The story gains urgency because we find out early on that the narrator is trying to learn from and function in a physical world in which she has always been clumsy. She seems to be reading the adult women around her for clues to what grown-up life might hold. This quest of hers makes details such as who sings and who does not, and how Gladys applies makeup, resonate with meaning. We see the purpose behind the selection of details, even as those details make the characters come to life. We're wondering what decisions and conclusions she'll make, and how this job will affect her.

DISCUSSION QUESTIONS

1. What makes the narrator the right character to tell this story? How would it be different if told by another character? By Gladys? Herb? Brian? Lily or Marjorie?
2. What changes does the narrator's younger self go through? What changes does the narrator seem to go through in the telling of the story?
3. How would you describe the narrator's attitude toward the turkey barn and the work she performs there? How does this attitude relate to or influence the way she sees her coworkers and the events of the story?

4. How would this story be different without the passages in which the narrator reflects on the meaning of events? How does Munro get this reflective material to work without bogging the story down?

THE VERSATILITY OF SECOND PERSON

Second person is the least frequently used POV in fiction. The danger of second person is that readers can feel ordered around, or grow tired of it. Sometimes it can seem like a gimmick. However, writers who find themselves drafting a story in the second person can choose among a surprisingly wide range of possible effects to support the story's meaning. The "Aspects of First-Person POV" chart can serve equally well for second person; there are, however, a few other considerations to keep in mind. When an "I" speaks to us, we imagine a specific person; when a narrator tells us about a "he" or "she," we also imagine specific people. "You," however, by its very nature is indeterminate.

Charles Johnson's "Moving Pictures" makes strong use of this indeterminacy, even though the "you" in the story is assigned particular traits and a particular history. The story is a short-short about someone who may or may not be a "semifamous" screenwriter, one who despises his work and suffers in his daily life. The first paragraph sets up the narrative strategy:

> You sit in the Neptune Theatre waiting for the thin, overhead lights to dim with a sense of respect, perhaps even reverence, for American movie houses are, as everyone knows, the new cathedrals, their stories better remembered than legends, totems, or mythologies, their directors more popular than novelists, more influential than saints—enough people, you've been told, have seen the James Bond adventures to fill the entire country of Argentina. Perhaps you have written this movie. Perhaps not. Regardless, you come to it as everyone does, as a seeker groping in the darkness for light, hoping something magical will be beamed from above, and no matter how bad this matinee is, or silly, something deep and maybe even too dangerous to talk loudly about will indeed happen to you and the others before this drama reels to its last transparent frame.

At first glance, the reader might think that the story could just as well begin "He sits in the Neptune Theatre. . . ." However, the "you" draws us in closer to identification with the narrator. The use of the word "perhaps" throws a curveball. We're in the realm of the hypothetical now. Are we supposed to read the "you" as a general stand-in for the reader, any reader? But then the "you" is assigned some specific traits: we learn that "you grew up in the '60s speeding on methadone" and that the protagonist has "a once-beautiful woman—or wife—a former model (local), college dancer, or semi-professional actress named Megan or Daphne . . ." a list which again blurs the exactness of the character's portrait, without being random.

The story makes use of a controlled ambiguity, drawing in the reader and describing everyday difficulties in the lives of moviemakers in order to demythologize them. We are invited to imagine ourselves in the narrator's position, and, because of this, the story short-circuits our usual glamorizing of Hollywood. If the story's POV were third person, no matter what we were told about the character's difficulties, we would be more likely to think of them as irrelevant next to money, status, and fame. But when we imagine ourselves suffering the bad marriages, the loss of the chance to do our own real and difficult writing, then the illusions we have about movies and the moviemaking life suddenly become clear.

Disguised First Person

Another reason to use second person is as a disguised first person—in these cases, it seems clear that a narrator is really speaking about him or herself, but is alienated from that self, or critical of it, and uses the second person to distance the current self from the self of the story. Lorrie Moore has used this technique to great effect in a number of her stories in the collection *Self Help.* She often uses the imperative, a verb form only possible with second-person. In this way, she mimics the advice-giving method of self-help books. Her story "How to Become a Writer" begins like this:

> First, try to be something, anything, else. A movie star/astronaut. A movie star/missionary. A movie star/kindergarten teacher. President of the World. Fail miserably. It is best if you fail at an early age—say, fourteen. Early, critical disillusionment is necessary so that at fifteen you can write long haiku sequences about thwarted desire. It is a pond, a cherry blossom, a wind brushing against a sparrow wing leaving for the mountain. Count the syllables. Show it to your mom. She is tough and practical. She has a son in Vietnam and a husband who may be having an affair. She believes in wearing brown because it hides spots. She'll look briefly at your writing, then back up at you with a face blank as a donut. She'll say: "How about emptying the dishwasher?" Look away. Shove the forks in the fork drawer. Accidentally break one of the freebie gas station glasses. This is the required pain and suffering. This is only for starters.

Although in self-help books the imperative is usually used to address an impersonal "you," Moore subverts this convention by making it clear midway through the paragraph that the "you" here is a specific individual, someone whose mother has a particular personality and situation. The second-person POV in the story emphasizes the critical distance between a young self, naive about what it takes to become a writer, and the all-too-aware narrating self. But the story also makes use of the identification of the reader; many of us who will read the story are also writers, and the story reminds us of our own struggles, making them amusing and letting us put them in perspective.

Direct Address and Second-Person Narrators

Second-person narrators aren't the same as the "you" of direct address. For example, Tillie Olsen's "I Stand Here Ironing" consists of a first-person monologue told to an unnamed "you": the "you" is a not a viewpoint character, undergoing the action, but someone listening to the story. Another direct-address story, Daniel Orozco's "Orientation," gives us an unnamed but distinctive narrator who provides a disorienting job orientation to an unnamed listener. This listener is a character, silently following along as the narrator gives an increasingly remarkable tour of the workplace. The reader is eavesdropping at one remove. We are reminded of all the strange events of our own work history, and the story is deliberately inviting these memories. The "you" is never given any specific traits or history, which helps our identification: in another world, it could be any of us learning which office machines we are not to touch and which of our co-workers are serial killers.

Sometimes the "you" who is a listener can blend into the "you" who is the viewpoint character. In "Graffiti," Julio Cortázar uses a first-person narrator to frame a second-person story, revealing how pliable this POV can be. We can understand more about second person, and about the possibilities of various POVs, by reading Adam Johnson's "Trauma Plate" and thinking about the choices he made in writing the story.

STORY ANALYSIS AND QUESTIONS: "TRAUMA PLATE"

(Note: please read the story once before *you read the following analysis. Then, after you read the analysis, look at the story a second time, keeping the discussion questions in mind. You will get the most benefit out of this process if you mark specific passages in the story, take notes, and work through the questions in writing.)*

In "Trauma Plate," Adam Johnson shows us how an inventive use of POV can be integral to a story's meaning. He separates the story into three sections—a first-person section in Bill's POV, a third-person section in Jane's POV, and a second-person section in Ruthie's POV. An examination of each section reveals how the author pulls off such a tricky maneuver in the span of a single short story, and what benefits the story gains as a result.

Readers generally aren't expecting a shift from first person to third person in a single story—"Trauma Plate" is the only story we know of, in fact, that uses first, second, and third person. The strategies the story uses to handle the transitions between each POV section, however, can also be applied to stories that use a rotating third-person POV.

Separating the POVs into three numbered sections is one way of providing a clear structure. Johnson also eases the way from the first section to the second by ending the first with five lines of nothing but dialogue—which by their very nature aren't filtered through any point of view—followed by the phrase "We both look up," which employs the first-person plural as a sort of bridge from Bill's POV to Jane's. By the time we reach section three, we're prepared to expect a change, so the author doesn't have to set us up as much. However, Ruthie's first paragraph discusses her mother, who we've just seen standing in the Body Armor Emporium, so there is a continuity of subject matter to help the story's flow. In addition, through all three POV shifts, the story remains in present tense, which provides unification. And none of the POVs involve authorial intrusion—in each section, we're firmly located in a character's viewpoint. The dystopia of the story is a world devoid of an authoritative, holistic vantage point.

DISCUSSION QUESTIONS

1. Why is each POV choice appropriate for its viewpoint character? How do the POV choices reflect each character's personality and life situation? What lines or details reveal these connections?
2. What kinds of information do we learn in each POV? How does Johnson include new information about the characters, their situation, and their world unobtrusively?
3. How would the story be different with a more traditional omniscient POV? What effect do the rotating POVs have on the story?
4. Why might Johnson have arranged the sections in the order he did? How would the story be different if it began with Jane or Ruthie and ended with Bill?
5. In what ways does Johnson let us know that the story is set in a future or alternate world? What details or events does he include to make this world comment on our own? How does he keep the story from being preachy?

REVISION: MAKING MAJOR POV CHANGES

There is much more involved in major POV changes than replacing "I" with "he" or "she." Consider the opening lines of *Moby Dick* translated directly from first person to third person: "Call him Ishmael. Some years ago—never mind how long precisely—having little or no money in his purse, and nothing particular to interest him on shore, he thought he would sail about a little and see the watery part of the world." In the first-person version, we might understand the apparent use of a pseudonym, the caginess about how long ago the events happened, the vagueness about how much money he had. The manner of telling gives us intriguing clues to the main character. Coming from a third-person authorial voice, however, it sounds oddly hostile, tells us nothing about the main character, and distracts from the story. If we change a story's viewpoint radically, it's best to rewrite the story from scratch, using our previous drafts only as a reference.

In the course of writing "Trauma Plate," Johnson found he needed to go into several viewpoints to tell the complete story. He rewrote sections in different POVs until he found the right one for each character. In his discussion of the changes the story went through, he shows us the thinking behind each of his POV choices:

> "Trauma Plate" began as an exercise. My writing mentor, Ron Carlson, and I were marveling at a story we'd just read by Stuart Dybek. The story, "Paper Lantern," hooks the reader with a casual mention of a time machine in the first paragraph. Then Dybek's story goes on to investigate passion, memory and nostalgia, until, in the end, the time machine returns. Carlson and I decided to try to employ a similar "hook" to engage the reader until they begin to care about the characters. Carlson wrote a brief story called "Asteroid Intervention," which features a giant laser in the opening, and I started "Trauma Plate" with a bulletproof vest rental store in the first line.
>
> The narrator of the first section, a father, thinks he's doing a public service by armoring his family and community; he doesn't see the price they've paid for accepting a life of fear. Whenever I have a character who doesn't understand his or her story, who is essentially deluded, I always use the first person. There's a double joy in that for readers: there's a surface story to enjoy, and then the one below that the reader knows to be true. The difference between the character's version and the reader's is the definition of dramatic irony.
>
> Thinking I'd written an exercise, I moved on to other projects, but that father's voice nagged me. He never woke up to his delusion, and I didn't want him to get away with accepting the violence in his society, even profiting from it, at the expense of his family. Yet this wasn't an epiphany kind of character. So I tried to tell the mother's story. I worked on her monologue twenty times but I just couldn't get her voice. She was too resigned to speak at all, let alone go confessing her troubles to a stranger. So I looked to fiction technique to help me. I switched the narrator to the third person, and when I began to tell this character's story for her, her hidden life simply poured onto the page.
>
> By the time I'd finished telling the mother's story, I was curious about the daughter. What would it be like to have parents so unaware and withdrawn? I wrote the daughter in first person and third, switching back and forth, over and over, but nothing worked. In the first person, the daughter sounded either posturing or confessional. She lacked the age and insight to tell her own story meaningfully, it seemed. And the third person made her character feel distant, like an object of study; the third person didn't capture the way, at fifteen, you're the center of your own universe.
>
> Again, a technical move saved the story, which came to life when I tried the second person. Anytime a character speaks with an "I," there's an awareness of an audience listening, and the narrator, like the rest of us, chooses her words carefully, so she doesn't sound sentimental or stuck up. But the second person is

> the private voice people use to talk to themselves inside their own heads. That unorchestrated, interior "you" is more intimate and truthful, and for the daughter at the end of "Trauma Plate," it was the only point of view that worked.

In revising our own stories, we can ask ourselves, which character has the most perspective on the events in my story? What advantage is there to giving us this wider view? Who among my characters is articulate? Writers are often charmed by the craft challenges of unreliable or limited narrators, but we need to think through whether this best serves the story. Why not give our stories the advantage of all of the intelligence and awareness we can muster? On the other hand, would the story's themes be served by choosing a less articulate character, or a character with no perspective? What issues in the story might genuinely be helped by these limits? And how much time has passed since the events of the story in relation to the time of the events? How does that affect the narrative?

The choice of a POV is far more complicated than we originally understand when we begin writing. Exploring POV's possibilities and limitations can be a lifelong process. Often our first instinct may be the best, for reasons we don't yet understand. Sometimes the POV needs a substantial change, sometimes only subtle adjustments. In POV, as in other aspects of the art and craft of writing, we need patience both with the story and with our own writing process.

POV EXERCISES

1. Take a first-person story that you've been having difficulty with. Instead of trying a completely different POV, like third person, experiment with some subtle shifts in one or two scenes. Try one scene with more observed sensory detail and fewer thoughts from the narrator. Try another version of the scene with more commentary instead of less. If the narrator is completely reliable, or completely unreliable, try moving more toward the middle of the spectrum. The narrator may still be essentially one or the other, but in a less overt way. Even if the POV is not the source of the difficulty, writers are apt to learn new things about the story and its characters in this process.
2. Sometimes using the same POV in story after story can lead writers to cover similar ground, even if the location or specific circumstances for each story differ. For instance, one writer might generally write stories with a first-person narrator who describes a time when he or she caught someone (a friend, family member, stranger) doing something wrong (stealing, lying, cheating), and the decisions the narrator had to make. Another writer might always use a detached, sarcastic authorial voice to tell stories in the third person, critically examining the characters' flawed attempts to rise above their circumstances. In either case, a different POV would influence both the events and the attitude of the

story. Look at your own stories, both completed and unfinished. Identify the POV choices for each of them, using the POV charts in this chapter and Chapter 2 as guides. Do you tend to gravitate toward a particular set of choices?

3. Choose one of your stories that uses your most typical POV choice. Rewrite the first few pages using POV choices you've never tried before. If you're intrigued, keep writing.
4. This time, start a brand new story, using POV choices that seem unfamiliar or difficult. What kinds of choices do you make about action, events, and character because of these different POV choices?
5. (This reading exercise can be done either individually or in a group.) Choose a published story you've read that has a POV that surprised you in some way. Using the appropriate POV chart, go through and name the writer's choices for each spectrum. What is it about the POV that was surprising to you? How does that POV fit with the story's subject, characters, and issues? Often when a story takes us off guard, we feel at first that the writer has made a mistake. We may find that it takes us several readings, and some serious thinking about the intentions of the writer, to discover how the story successfully challenges our expectations.

CHAPTER

4

Plot, Narrative Drive, and Alternative Story Structures

(Anthology selections: "Father," "Photograph of Luisa," and "Graffiti")

In the end, I say simply, a story should be about some change, large or small, in the universe of a person or people in a story. Generally, there is no story for me if all there is is another day in the life of the character, a day like all the others. To use a simple example, the whole point of something like "Humpty Dumpty" is that one day he falls off that wall and falls to pieces, after perhaps days or months or years of sitting there with nothing happening except time passing. He falls and all the powers of the King and his kingdom cannot put the thing together again.

—Edward P. Jones

RECLAIMING THE PLEASURES OF PLOT

The idea of "plot" doesn't have the best reputation among literary writers. Because so many thrillers and Hollywood movies are praised for their gripping stories, many writers of serious fiction prefer to think of their stories as character-driven, language-driven, image-driven, anything but plot-driven. They regret the necessity of plot, as E. M. Forster did in his *Aspects of the Novel:* "Yes—oh dear, yes—the novel tells a story. That is the fundamental aspect without which it could not exist. That is the highest factor, common to all novels, and I wish that it was not so, that it could be something different—melody, or perception of the truth, not this low atavistic form."

When we first begin to write, we often follow the dramatic and fairly predictable stories that we know from television and Hollywood: a batch of disasters ends in a marriage or in the death of most of the characters. It's not impossible to make great art this way (for example, *Hamlet* or *Romeo and Juliet*). But when we're starting out, we don't know how to wrestle familiar plot shapes into our own unique stories. Intermediate and advanced writers, in reaction against their beginning work, may renounce plot and action altogether in favor of a series of moments that reveal character but that never seem to add up to a definite shape or a meaningful experience.

If we allow the shape of our fiction to help create and express its meaning, we don't have to abandon the fierce and delicious pleasures of plotting. Usually, stories have a more or less organic pattern, like Gerard Manley Hopkins's idea of *inscape,* a poem's inherent structure and form, not imposed on it from the outside. We find our stories' patterns through reading the work of others, thinking about plot, fumbling through various drafts, and listening to criticism: in other words, through practice.

Classical Plot Structures

Because plot is so difficult—central to fiction and yet one of the last elements most of us typically master—we're repeating the common distinction between story and plot. "Story" tends to be used to describe the work as a whole. It's also used to describe what actually might be referred to more precisely as the "storyline": all the events in their chronological order. Plot is the meaningful arrangement of the key events, presented in such a way that the causality becomes clear—not just "what happened," but why and how the different events are connected. Understanding the difference between plot and storyline helps us in constructing and revising our stories. We begin to think of how one event gives rise to another, rather than just relating a string of unconnected incidents.

The plot of Shakespeare's *Much Ado About Nothing* could be expressed, in a very basic form, as follows: A man and woman, proud of their disdain for the opposite sex, are tricked by friends into falling in love with each other. Their ambivalent love, however, survives tests that their more romantic friends fail. United in their on-again, off-again courtship, they manage to expose an enemy's lies, in turn helping the friends who tricked them and arranging for happy marriages all around. Hero and Claudio, by playing a mischievous but good-hearted prank on their friends, help Benedick and Beatrice to become a team. Because of this, Benedick and Beatrice, in the end, are able to restore Hero and Claudio's happiness.

The storyline, though, is nothing more than a list of events: Don Pedro, Benedick, and Claudio return from the wars; Beatrice and Benedick taunt and torment each other; Claudio tells Benedick that he's in love with Hero and plans to marry her; Don Pedro agrees to help Claudio while Benedick tries to dissuade him from marriage, and so on. If we look at our own stories simply in terms of their storyline, they become a thicket of random happenings. One scene may be witty, another touching, but we don't know why they're there or what else might be needed.

In thinking about plot, we also need to consider story structure: how the story is built and what kinds of formal techniques are used to shape it. For instance, a story may alternate between segments of present action and flashback, or between three separate points of view, or it may have a relatively even distribution of climactic moments throughout its length.

Many of the ideas about plot that we use in teaching and learning fiction come from thinkers wrestling with the shapes of plays, not with short stories or novels. Writers still read the sternly authoritative guidelines Aristotle set out in his *Poetics*, in which he described epics and tragedies and the rules for each. Many writers also know some variation of the Freytag pyramid, which divides a story into five actions: exposition, complication, crisis, anticlimax, and resolution. Gustav Freytag originally came up with this structure in 1863 to describe certain five-act plays. We can understand this scheme by imagining a dramatic structure in which the first act lets us know about the characters and their situation (exposition); the second adds trouble and new information (complication); the third brings the situation to its highest, most explosive point (crisis); the fourth, the anticlimax, shows solutions and responses in a falling crescendo (in a tragedy, the reversal of fortunes of the protagonist); and the resolution wraps everything up, for good or ill.

Janet Burroway in *Writing Fiction: A Guide to Narrative Craft,* presents a modified version of Freytag's diagram in the form of an inverted check mark, a shape that more accurately reflects the relatively brief time modern fiction usually gives to resolving the tension of a story. Our own diagram, in the form of an asymmetrical triangle, builds on Aristotle's, Freytag's, and Burroway's ideas, along with those of novelist Susan Kenney. It features seven elements:

1. Ground situation—the story introduces readers to ongoing concerns at the moment they begin to change;
2. Complication or inception—the first actions produce reactions and additional elements come into the story;
3. Rising action—new actions and events increase the tension;
4. Crisis—the tension reaches its highest point;
5. Climax—the characters perform the most significant actions of the story in response to that peak of tension, thereby changing their own or each other's lives;
6. Falling action—the story shows the characters' responses to these changes;

Climax
Crisis
Rising action
Falling action
Complication
Ground situation
Resolution

7. Resolution or *denouement*—the story leaves its characters in their new ground situation, showing—explicitly or implicitly—either how they have changed or how they have definitively missed an opportunity for change.

Our diagram of plot structure shouldn't be understood as implying that all stories must gradually build toward a huge blowup of some kind. Many successful stories operate with events that are less literally dramatic than our triangle suggests. While apparently quiet on the surface, these events are dramatic in what they change or reveal; it may be more accurate to say that these stories intensify in meaning, rather than rise in action. Or a story might have two or more dramatic events, not necessarily arranged according to their degree of explosiveness—the most dramatic event may happen first, and subsequent events complicate it or push one of the characters to make a decision or significant change. A wife discovers her husband in bed with another woman, but stays with him for two more months until one night he refuses to do the dishes. The first event is more literally dramatic, but the second is the climax, the real turning point. Often in fiction, as in life, there's a delayed reaction.

Although diagrams can express certain fundamental, satisfying shapes of narrative, working with them too literally can be problematic for contemporary writers. When the authors of this book were students, we struggled with the various diagrams presented to us, tried to apply them to our own (at that point largely plotless) stories, gave it all up, and eventually worked our separate ways back to plot by more indirect means.

Students today have some of the same confusions we felt when we started to write (and that, alas, we still face—though less acutely—in the early drafts of each new piece of fiction). What is a ground situation? Should we show the characters being happy for a few pages before the trouble starts, to give a sense of how much they're about to lose? Does the ground situation need to have problems related to those that will form the center of the story or can it show a different set of concerns? Which of the story's actions are essential and "build" towards a climax, and which seem to be distractions? Do the crisis and the climax occur at the same time or separately? What if we want to have parallel stories, or three different climaxes, or some other structure altogether? How can we capture the richness of life in this kind of standard structure?

Instead of thinking of a story as a clear and singular set of events like a bull fight, which ends either with a goring or a sword thrust, we can think of a story as existing in layers. The more we clarify for ourselves what kinds of events are part of the plot and what kinds are part of the background, what narrative drive consists of, how to study a story to find the shape of its events, and how to tell a plot from a subplot, the more we are able to find our own forms.

Plots and Subplots

Novels and long stories have plenty of room for more than one plot, but even a fairly short story can have two or more, as long as they connect in some way and don't merely exist side by side. On the other hand, when writers first realize that they can add another plot, they often connect the different parts too tightly, so that the whole story begins to stagger under its symbolic weight. The plots need to be linked, but not chained together at the ankles. Denis Johnson, in "Car Crash While Hitchhiking," gives us two stories that refract light on each other: the narrator and his relationship with drugs and reality, and the fate of the people whose car he rides in. The plot and the subplot are not heavyhanded in their connections: the family in the accident haven't been taking drugs themselves, and the narrator doesn't make any decisions or have any epiphanies about his future based on what happens to them. But the wildness of the world the narrator lives in, his thrill-seeking and confrontations with reality (even with other people's disasters), and the life-and-death atmosphere of the medical environments connect the two plots. The ending of the story is startling because it reveals to us that what we thought was of lesser importance—the narrator's relationship with drugs and reality—is actually what the story is asking us to pay attention to.

In deciding which part of our story serves as the main plot and which as a subplot, we might consider a range of criteria: how much space each of the characters and their stories take up, what we care most urgently about, what the story seems to be "about" and who is affected by this, and even where the story begins and ends, though this is not an infallible guide. It's as if the author were taking a photograph of everyone in the story and had to choose what to focus on. What seems to be in the foreground, in sharp focus, and what seems less clear?

STORY ANALYSIS AND QUESTIONS: "FATHER"

(Note: please read the story once before *you read the following analysis. Then, after you read the analysis, look at the story a second time, keeping the discussion questions in mind. You will get the most benefit out of this process if you mark specific passages in the story, take notes, and work through the questions in writing.)*

John L'Heureux's "Father" is about art, death, and the psychological intricacies of family life and parent-child interactions. It also plays with the reality/fantasy line in other ways: "John," who teaches writing and is married to "Joan" who teaches English, is one of the central characters, but not the viewpoint character. The author is also John, who teaches writing, married to Joan, who teaches English. This move both does and does not invite us to read the story as an autobiography or as a commentary on the whole idea of autobiography, and yet the events are openly fantastic. The story lets us know early that it will not be bound by realistic conventions—important for any story altering the agreed-upon "rules" of realism—and yet the plot is a masterful, subtle example of classic structure. We can see the ground situation in the first paragraph.

> Long before he got sick, our father was down there in the cellar painting away. He had rigged up an easel for himself and suspended a couple naked light bulbs from a beam—to simulate northern light, he said—and he painted things from photographs and magazines and books. Later he painted things vaguely reminiscent of what he had seen on walks. At the beginning of the end he painted things nobody except himself had ever seen before. He claimed that his painting style simply evolved from representational to impressionistic to a kind of hard-edged expressionism of his own. But long before we understood what he was doing, our father began to escape from us. He was in the process of disappearing.

We know that the father is both gravely ill ("long before he got sick" and "at the beginning of the end"). We know that he is disappearing and that it somehow relates to his paintings, which "evolve" into something only he can understand. We know that this is a group point of view, a puzzled group. Then, in the next paragraph, the first complication appears, the beginning of the rising action:

> John, who is artistic, was the first to notice the hairline crack in each of the paintings. Our father was all done with his representational period. He had lined up a whole bunch of the things in the cellar, propped against the washer and dryer and the boiler and the old bikes. They were everywhere, stacked two and three deep, because he was having a sort of show, a retrospective as it were, for John and Joan who were visiting home from California where he teaches writing and she teaches English. John and Joan have no children. They don't go in for that sort of thing. Or perhaps they can't. In any case they were admiring the pictures generally, sometimes pointing out a special thing about one or another, and our father was standing by, very serious, as they assessed what they liked or disliked about his creations. All of a sudden John said, "Look at this. *Look* at this." He ran a long skinny finger down an invisible crack in a picture.

The crack, which will widen to a gap large enough for a man to pass through, is this first complication. In terms of John's role in the story, it's important that he's the one who notices the still "invisible" crack. Meanwhile, the father has finished his "representational" (realistic, fully a part of society's conventions and rules) period, in his paintings, as in his life, and is passing on to the next stage. The detritus of a life, including the old bicycles, surrounds him. It is possible to trace the development of the rest of the story through the rising action, crisis, climax, falling action, and resolution, and, in so doing, to think about the complexities of the experience the story provides.

DISCUSSION QUESTIONS

1. What are the events of the rising action?
2. What serves as the crisis, the point of highest tension?

3. What is the climax, where characters take action in response to that tension?
4. What is the falling action?
5. How does the story resolve?
6. How do the paintings serve as a central metaphor in this story? How does L'Heureux change and develop that metaphor over the course of the story? How does he let the reader know its meaning(s)?
7. What has changed for the rest of the characters in the story by the end?
8. In what ways does the story evade the melodrama and sentimentalism sometimes associated with stories about the deaths of close family members?

NARRATIVE DRIVE AND MEANING

For most writers, it takes a long time to understand the difference between storyline and plot, and to work out which events are significant to the plot and which are background or even irrelevant. In life, the "stories" we tell are often just anecdotes; they may strike our friends as funny, satisfying, or horrifying, but when we write them down, they don't feel complete. The people in our lives know us, and they often know the people we're talking about. They already care about what happens to us: if we are in danger of losing our job, they worry about us, or if Susan flirted heavily with us at a party, they know she's beautiful and we're interested in her, but also that she has a history of dumping her lovers after a month. Maybe our listener is also secretly interested in Susan, which adds an additional note of tension. Any anecdote we tell to those whose lives are intertwined with ours becomes part of an ongoing story we all share.

In fiction, though, it's the writer's job to get the reader to care about the characters and their actions, starting with the ground situation. The question we often hear in workshop is, "What's at stake in this story?" An annoying question to the writer, who may love the characters and feel the reader should naturally care what happens to them. As we mentioned in Chapter 1, there's a difference between what the characters care about (what the writer cares about) and what the reader cares about.

To achieve narrative drive—that sense of forward movement that keeps the reader turning pages—it's not enough for a character to have a desire, attempt to fulfill it, and be thwarted. The reader has to feel that something meaningful is at stake, and that subsequent events raise the stakes. What gives a story life-or-death urgency? The events don't have to be explicitly dramatic: Jonathan Franzen achieves phenomenal tension in *The Corrections*, a book where the fundamental narrative drive comes from the question of whether a group of adult children will give way to their parents and go home for Christmas. This is a story that could have been trivial or sentimental, except that Franzen's characters are so humiliatingly, touchingly realized. We see that the parents are much closer to death than the self-absorbed children have any idea of; we also see the pressures in the children's lives—their jobs or the survival of their marriages may depend on their missing this Christmas. We understand why the children are annoyed with, and ashamed of, their parents, but we want them to rise above it, to achieve the necessary level of adulthood before it's too late.

One way of considering how to achieve a sense of urgency is to think about sports. We tend to root for the home team or for the underdog. Human beings like success, but if a team has been successful for too long, especially if they seem to be getting above themselves, we then like to see them brought down. We like to watch someone winning against the odds, or we're sad when someone tries and fails, or we may understand that what looks like a failure in worldly terms can be a triumph of integrity or courage.

Writers, understanding this about human nature, often attempt to get sympathy for characters by putting them in a predicament and having a series of bad things happen to them, believing that the reader will then feel anxious on the characters' behalf. The key distinction we want to make here is between an underdog and a victim. No one wants to watch a boxing match in which one person simply gets hit in the face over and over. We may, however, be very interested in watching a small, fast boxer trying to beat the odds against a giant.

It doesn't help for the writer to tell us that characters are brave or that the odds are against them; we have to see this in action. In Thomas Mallon's *Bandbox,* Joe Harris is the editor in chief of a men's magazine. He's been given a year to bring this dying magazine back to life. He has put in so much work and imagination that the magazine takes off in a single business quarter. In fact, it's so successful that a rival magazine springs up, edited by Jimmy Gordon, a former protégé of Harris:

> Jimmy Gordon: who had brought in most of Harris's expensive new writers; who had three bad story ideas for every good one, but so many of each that, with Harris as a filter, every issue of *Bandbox* still abounded with first-rate stuff. Jimmy Gordon, who was now stealing not only Harris's formula but every keister not nailed down to the swivel chairs here on the fourteenth floor of the Graybar Building. He'd pried away three of his old writers, a photographer, and two production assistants, and had even made a run at Mrs. Zimmerman, the receptionist. But the real prize for Jimmy was Harris's readers and advertisers, whom he would surely keep wooing away if he managed, with stunts like this Leopold and Loeb picture, to undo the makeover of *Bandbox*. Things could turn around so quickly—hadn't Harris himself proved it?—that the older editor would be left with a shrunken subscriber base consisting chiefly of the perfumed boys you saw gazing at each other across the tables of the Jewel cafeteria.
>
> Hazel Snow buzzed Harris from the outer office.
>
> "It's a bad time!" he shouted.

If the magazine had been successful for years, or if Harris had inherited its success instead of getting there by hard work and imagination, we wouldn't care as much. On the other hand, if Harris had been a charming, handsome, hard-working, loyal, faithful, and obedient kind of guy, we would feel that the narrative was manipulating and instructing us, that we had stumbled into a formula where everything would turn out right and we were expected to feel gratified wish-fulfillment. But Harris is angry and drunk, and we're curious to see whether he's going to keep his territory or lose it, and what role his human flaws, and the flaws of his employees, will play in the outcome of the drama. We're interested, possibly despite ourselves, in Jimmy Gordon too. What will come of his erratic imagination without Harris to filter his ideas? Is he ungrateful or did he have some good reason for leaving?

Narrative drive has to do with creating a ground situation that arouses readers' sympathy and curiosity, raising questions, and then, as some of those are answered in the course of a story, raising new questions. Some of the questions will carry through the book until the end, but others are smaller, more immediate. By the time the story's events answer those questions or concerns, we know the characters better and their histories and actions create new questions and worries.

Forward and Backward Movement

The plot of a finished story takes into account the reader's experiences of it, both forward and backward. In both traditional and experimental fiction, the structure contains moments that drive the story forward, providing its narrative power. Whether dramatic events or interconnecting images, these build toward some shift in the story situation and/or the perceptions of the character or the reader. The backward experience, on the other hand, occurs after we have finished reading a story. We see the way the parts fit together, the connections and resonances.

What we are calling the forward experience is another way of referring to the narrative drive: it draws the reader to keep turning pages from start to finish. Consciously or unconsciously, the reader is asking a question or questions throughout: "What will happen next?" Or, "What intriguing experience am I learning more about?" Or, "What insights and/or perceptions are coming next?" With a vivid, well-made story, the reader is less likely to be conscious of these questions and more likely to experience unnamed feelings—a flash of worry for one character, a hope that another will get what she yearns for, a strong wish that a third character not get what he seeks. Some of these emotions will arise from the main plot, but sometimes a relevant side issue will keep us reading. We want to find out, as in Alice Munro's "Lichen," whether  the wife will keep her dignity and gracefulness intact when her ex-husband brings his new girlfriend to visit, but along the way we may be interested in what kinds of small disasters could come from the girlfriend's drug-impeded efforts to help get dinner on the table.

As soon as we finish reading a story, our minds consider it as a whole, and consciously or unconsciously we tend to ask questions such as, "Did it add up to something meaningful? How did all its elements fit together?" The backward experience is an appreciation of a story's final shape. When it works, whether the ending was happy, sad, or too complex to categorize, we feel a deep satisfaction. It's partly responsible for the great pleasure of rereading and analyzing a story that we've loved. A story, like a dream, can simply be experienced, but when we understand how it works and what it means, it unfolds for us in a new way.

As we're reading Grace Paley's "A Conversation With My Father," we may not stop to think of the parallels between the daughter sitting with her dying father and the mother who becomes a heroin addict to help her son but who is unable to help herself as he gets clean. What makes these parallels so satisfying—the ways the parent-child pairings fight, the judgments and love and helplessness—is that they are not exact. It's the storytelling daughter who has the responsibility and can't manage it—she's unable to convince her father of her hopeful vision and argues with him until he's taking nitroglycerin and turning up the oxygen tank. She has a clarity

in her storytelling that she can't act on in her life. The story is gripping in terms of its forward motion—what will happen to the addicted mother and son? What will happen to the dying father? But it is even more satisfying in retrospect, when we start to feel the shape of it, and how the parts work together.

Actual and Emotional Plots

Much of the strength of the backward movement of the story comes from the resolutions and interconnections of the actual and emotional plots. What appears to be a subplot may actually be the emotional underpinnings or changes of the main plot. Elizabeth McCracken, in a talk at the Napa Valley Writer's Conference in 1999, discussed the idea of the "actual plot" versus the "emotional plot." As soon as we hear these terms, they make sense—the actual plot consists of the events of the story, linked by causality, and the emotional plot consists of the underlying changes in the characters or our understanding of their situation. Sometimes events lead to a change in the characters' circumstances, but sometimes what the story accomplishes is an emotional shift or a revelation of what may have been there all along.

As an example, we might think of a story in which a scholarly man who has been revered by his family comes home to the estate that his previous wife's brother, Vanya, and his niece, the scholar's daughter, have been managing. The scholar has health difficulties and a beautiful, bored young wife. The daughter asks her stepmother to broach the topic of her love for her father's doctor, a visionary who drinks, but the doctor has become smitten by the stepmother, and Vanya catches them in what appears to be an affair. Because he's also in love with the stepmother and wretched in his life, Vanya explodes, and the scholar and his wife leave. That's the actual plot of Chekhov's play *Uncle Vanya*, more or less.

The emotional plot, on the other hand, has to do with people who have spent their lives sacrificing for others and for causes, who are now overcome by a dry spell: they no longer believe in the work they've done. The young wife's bored, destructive, unhappy beauty contrasts with the plain, generous solidity of her stepdaughter. The center of the emotional plot is the efforts of various characters to come to terms with this struggle over beauty and true worth, to find meaning where it has been lost. The two plots come together at the moment when Uncle Vanya, in despair over the waste of his life and his desire for his brother-in-law's new wife, first chases his brother-in-law, firing shots, and then utters one of the most beautiful, heartrending long monologues in the history of the theater. In the end, Uncle Vanya and his niece, the scholar's daughter, see no alternative but to return to their work, without the hope and belief that formerly made it seem worthwhile. We feel grief over their sense of futility, and yet a pleasure in the reassertion of duty and self-sacrifice.

Sometimes the actual and emotional plots will have overlapping climaxes, but sometimes they may occur at separate times, which complicates the structure interestingly, as in the following story.

STORY ANALYSIS AND QUESTIONS: "PHOTOGRAPH OF LUISA"

(Note: please read the story once before *you read the following analysis. Then, after you read the analysis, look at the story a second time, keeping the discussion questions in mind. You will get the most benefit out of this process if you mark specific passages in the story, take notes, and work through the questions in writing.)*

In "Photograph of Luisa," Melissa Pritchard has created a literary mystery in which we can examine forward and backward movement and actual and emotional plot. The question "What are these people going to do?" (forward) is not as key as "What happened to create this situation?" (backward). As we read, we're trying to figure it out, picking up clues. We slowly come to understand Luisa's circumstances, and it's only then that we begin to ask a second question, "What could free Luisa from her mother's angry grief and her own self-blame?"

When Luisa tells us, "Mr. Sanchez even left me a shotgun, but I don't remember how to use it. Have you ever held a rifle every which way and then put it away for good?" we have a vaguely uneasy feeling. She seems too young to have handled a shotgun, and why did she put it away for good? Does this have anything to do with the fact that she used to wonder whether her mother would "punish [her] forever"? And, if so, why does she no longer wonder this? But it's only as we finish the story that everything comes together, and we understand even the narrator's mysterious opening need to color the white postcard with red crayon before sending it out into the world.

The story's mysterious opening could be frustrating if it weren't for the grace of the writing and the vividness of the imagery. If Luisa started with a rambling and abstract soliloquy, we wouldn't be brought into the story the way we are by the ghost town, the smeared postcard, the notion of the rattlesnake killer and the people who did not have money for him last time, the mother on the porch, and the old movie set. The combination of the strong voice of the piece and the arresting sense of place make us trust that the writer will not lead us on a wild goose chase, but will allow us to experience both the mystery and some resolution.

DISCUSSION QUESTIONS

1. When do we first suspect what Luisa's mother is blaming her for? When do we know for sure? How does Pritchard set up and answer the mystery?
2. What are the first indications of the actual plot? What lines or events direct our attention to the key events?
3. What are the first indications of the emotional plot? Where and how do the actual and emotional plots intersect?
4. How does Pritchard build the momentum of both the backward and forward movements in the story? In rereading this story, stop at each paragraph to identify the question it raises in the reader's mind. Is the question about what will happen next or is it about the characters' pasts?
5. What questions from previous paragraphs are answered in whole or in part as we continue through the story? Why does the narrator make us wait for information? What makes the strategy of withholding information work for this particular story?

ADVANCING PLOT THROUGH DIALOGUE AND EXPOSITION

In Chapter 9, we look at the rhythm and language of dialogue, and at the ways that dialogue can help reveal character and subtext. Here we want to focus on ways that dialogue can advance the plot or reveal background without becoming heavy-handed in its exposition, i.e., "I haven't seen you in three-and-a-half years, Michael. Not since just after Uncle Joe crashed his car, and all his children came to live with me."

Of course, first-rate dialogue is always accomplishing two or three tasks at once—revealing character and moving the plot forward, for instance. Or, as Janet Burroway describes in *Writing Fiction: A Guide to Narrative Craft,* dialogue can "set the mood . . . reveal the past . . . change the relationship . . ." and so on. She writes, "If a significant detail must both call up a sensory image and *mean,* then the character's words, which presumably mean something, should simultaneously suggest image, personality, or emotion."

In ZZ Packer's "Drinking Coffee Elsewhere," Dina and Heidi, who have become close friends, begin sleeping together, though not having sex. This exchange of dialogue is the beginning of a scene that takes place not long before Heidi comes out as a lesbian:

> Heidi started sleeping at my place. Sometimes she slept on the floor; sometimes we slept sardinelike, my feet at her head, until she claimed that my feet were "taunting" her. When we finally slept head to head, she said, "Much better." She was so close I could smell her toothpaste. "I like your hair," she told me, touching it through the darkness. "You should wear it out more often."
>
> "White people always say that about black people's hair. The worse it looks, the more they say they like it."
>
> I'd expected her to disagree, but she kept touching my hair, her hands passing through it till my scalp tingled. When she began to touch the hair around the edge of my face, I felt myself quake. Her fingertips stopped for a moment, as if checking my pulse, then resumed.

Their subterranean argument advances the plot—we see that Heidi is now aware of their attraction, and Dina is resisting her own response to Heidi. Packer uses subtext to make the conflict compelling. It would be pallid and obvious if Heidi had said, "You know, I think I'm falling in love with you," and Dina had responded, "That makes me very uncomfortable." Instead, they appear to be having a discussion about Dina's hair. Heidi can't express her desire directly but can touch Dina when praising her hair. And, since Heidi hasn't said anything Dina can respond to, Dina replies, "White people always say that about black people's hair. . . . " She has firmly set a boundary—they are no longer Heidi and Dina, but a white person and a black person; furthermore, Heidi has joined the category of *white people who don't understand and who praise the wrong thing.* The description of Dina's feelings, as usual at odds with her words, further complicates the dialogue.

We don't necessarily have to use dialogue in an expository fashion to advance the plot. We can take a cue from Packer and create discussions that appear on the surface to be about something else entirely. In this way, we can ratchet up the tension so that the reader is worrying about that character—as we worry here, about whether Dina is ever going to be able to drop her defenses. The dialogue shows Dina closer to real intimacy than we've ever seen her before. She's still defended and yet not in an undeveloped, two-dimensional fashion. This dialogue also shows the development of Heidi's character—she is much braver than when we first met her. As a result, her coming out will make emotional sense; we're being prepared for that action. (When readers say, "This action doesn't yet seem earned," they often mean that the story hasn't fully laid the groundwork, and so the action seems surprising or unbelievable.)

Alice Munro's "Turkey Season" provides an example of dialogue that gives substantial background information without slowing the story unnecessarily or having the characters speak in forced ways:

> Marjorie and Lily talked about marriage. They did not have much good to say about it, in spite of their feeling that it was a state nobody should be allowed to stay out of. Marjorie said that shortly after her marriage she had gone into the woodshed with the intention of swallowing Paris green.
>
> "I'd have done it," she said. "But the man came along in the grocery truck and I had to go out and buy the groceries. This was when we lived on the farm."
>
> Her husband was cruel to her in those days, but later he suffered an accident—he rolled the tractor and was so badly hurt he would be an invalid all his life. They moved to town, and Marjorie was the boss now.
>
> "He starts to sulk the other night and say he don't want his supper. Well, I just picked up his wrist and held it. He was scared I was going to twist his arm. He could see I'd do it. So I say, 'You *what?*' And he says, 'I'll eat it.'"
>
> They talked about their father. He was a man of the old school. . . .

Most of the exposition is delivered here by summary—only a few key, memorable remarks are picked out to stand alone, usually unaccompanied even by the responses of other characters. Because of this strategy, the story covers, in two pages, ground that could require twenty pages if we listened to the characters talking back and forth, expressing commiseration and making shocked noises.

Beginning writers are often steered away from writing passages of exposition and summary, which can often seem dull or irrelevant. Munro's example, however, is full of lively, vivid detail—these women's stories are worth telling in themselves. And the reader's experience is complicated because we're seeing through our narrator's eyes, and at the same time watching her to see what ideas about adulthood and marriage she is drawing from the encounter.

We can complicate the dialogue we write by thinking about which characters are listening to it, and what it's revealing to them. We can add subtle details that show the listener's response—as Munro does, with the phrase "They did not have much good to say about [marriage] in spite of their feeling that it was a state nobody should be allowed to stay out of." The narrator is making a judgment here that seems justified by what we see and hear of her co-workers.

The dialogue above advances the emotional plot of Munro's story more than it advances the actual plot. In the actual plot, Gladys has hysterics and Brian gets run off. In the emotional plot, we see our narrator adapting to a very different world than the one she's used to, and this dialogue is implicitly expressing some of the rules of that world.

PLOT IN LITERARY AND GENRE WRITING

If reading a story is like taking a trip, then the literary novel or story is adventure travel: we don't know when and how we'll eat or sleep, we have only a glimmer of where we're going, and we usually end up dirty, startled, disillusioned, or exhilarated. We're hitchhiking, backpacking, taking the third-class local train, and getting to know the countryside. In the end, we know both ourselves and the world better; we've grown and changed in the process. The genre novel, on the other hand, is like a package tour. We don't expect to have our view of the world unsettled. What we want is a cruise with all the expenses paid ahead of time, umbrella drinks by the pool, and a good floorshow in the evenings. Genres are all about the pleasures of the familiar.

Some writers believe that gorgeous, sophisticated language is what distinguishes literary writing from genre work. However, this idea leaves out great writers who work in a plain style. Others believe that genre writing doesn't examine human nature or create complex characters. This theory doesn't hold up if we consider first-rate genre writing: the mysteries of P. D. James and Sara Paretsky, or the romances of Georgette Heyer and Fiona Hill, for example. Bad genre writing does tend toward clichéd language, obvious plots, and cardboard characters, but bad literary writing has its own flaws.

We suggest that the difference between literary and genre writing has to do with story structure. By the end of the murder mystery, the killer will be identified. By the end of the romance novel, the couple will be locked in a clinch that can never be dulled by quotidian life. The characters play fairly predictable roles in order to insure that the story behaves in predictable ways: the familiarity of the form is what provides the satisfaction.

Speculative fiction is often considered genre writing. Yet literary authors as diverse as Jorge Luis Borges, Italo Calvino, Ursula K. Le Guin, and Doris Lessing (in her *Canopus in Argos: Archives* series) can all be found, at least occasionally, stocked in the science fiction and fantasy sections of bookstores and libraries. Some fantasy writers would disagree, but in many ways, the terms "science fiction" and "fantasy" seem to be marketing categories rather than true genres, although they apply to the space operas and sword-and-sorcery books that do operate by the standard rules of the package tour.

If writers are the tour guides for readers, then it's useful while learning the tour guide profession to go on adventure travel trips first, even if we know we want to lead package tours. If we want to create our own package tour, we'll create something richer and more distinctive if we choose from all the experiences available. Otherwise, we're reduced to choosing elements from other tour guides' package tours.

It's often possible to tell when a mystery or a science fiction writer has been reading primarily other mystery or science fiction writers. A certain sameness creeps in, similar ways of using language or describing character—even though these conventions have nothing inherently to do with the pleasures of the genre that readers are seeking. It's just as possible to tell when a contemporary American literary writer has been consuming nothing but contemporary American literary writing. We are what we eat.

ALTERNATE AND EXPERIMENTAL STRUCTURES

Experimental structures may be perfect for playful stories, as well as for stories whose material is just too painful to approach directly. The devices of numbering sections, reversing chronological order, moving randomly in time via white space jump cuts, or organizing a story by images or the repetition of phrases all provide alternatives to linear narratives. Sometimes the best way to tell a story is just to make it as transparent and straightforward as possible. At other times, though, the material may be so difficult that a chronological structure would be melodramatic. Or we need to cover so much time and space, or so many characters, that we want to try other ways of organizing our information. Sometimes a story comes to us in images or flashes, and we want to reproduce that; or we want to hold up certain ideas for consideration, reflecting on them from one angle and then another.

Nonlinear Story Structures

A sectioned story may use numbers or titles to separate discrete passages, whether long or short, that in some way shed light on each other. When this kind of story is unfinished or unsuccessful, the pieces feel random, the story doesn't come together as a whole, and readers may feel as if it's trying too hard to be clever. When it does succeed, it can create a discovery-filled experience for the reader. Some writers use fairly long sections—a page or two—and others may have sections as brief as a paragraph. Donald Barthelme has a number of nonlinear sectioned stories, like "The Genius," that are worth looking at as examples of this form. Sara Pritchard, in *Crackpots,* uses a wild and exhilarating range of poetic experiments in form and language, including the sectioned story.

William Gass's "In the Heart of the Heart of the Country" is the story of a place and the people in it, along with one set of piercing memories. Some of the sections are titled, in order, from the beginning, "A Place," "Weather," "My House," "A Person," "Wires," "The Church," "My House," "Politics," "People," "Vital Data," "Education," "Business," "My House," "This Place and Body," and so on. The form gives the story a chance to range widely and to recreate the scattered quality of thought and memory. The shape of the story suits the material:

A Place

So I have sailed the seas and come . . .

to B . . .

a small town fastened to a field in Indiana. Twice there have been twelve hundred people here to answer to the census. The town is outstandingly neat

> and shady, and always puts its best side to the highway. On one lawn there's even a wood or plastic iron deer.
>
> You can reach us by crossing a creek. In the spring the lawns are green, the forsythia is singing, and even the railroad that guts the town has straight bright rails which hum when the train is coming, and the train itself has a welcome horning sound.
>
> Down the back streets the asphalt crumbles into gravel. There's Westbrook's, with the geraniums, Horsefall's, Mott's. The sidewalk shatters. Gravel dust rises like breath behind the wagons. And I am in retirement from love.
>
> **Weather**
>
> In the Midwest, around the lower Lakes, the sky in the winter is heavy and close, and it is a rare day, a day to remark on, when the sky lifts and allows the heart up. I'm keeping count, and as I write this page, it is eleven days since I have seen the sun.

The quality of associative rather than linear thinking is poetic—instead of having it explained to us how and why the speaker is retired from love, we move from the idea of love to weather, and then later to "My House." It doesn't seem like an arbitrary jump because we are being offered information primarily about a place, rather than about a person. On the other hand, there's just enough information about the person to awaken our interest in the story. The endings of each of the sections are worth studying to see how Gass, a highly literary writer, still uses "hooks" that pull the reader forward. A hook arouses our interest and curiosity, as here, where we wonder why the narrator is in retirement from love. We need the story to refer to love or this retirement again—which it does—but because this passage is identifying itself as poetry, in language, as well as in logic, we don't need it tidily resolved. Narrative tension in linear and nonlinear stories often arises from intriguing unanswered questions or worries, but readers want to feel the question is addressed in some way, not just brought up and then abandoned. The disruption of linearity can increase tension as we move around in time, change points of view, and switch subjects. One plot line leaves us hanging, just long enough for us to hold the idea in the back of our minds and wait for its reappearance.

The Gass story is also held together by the originality and poetry of its images and verbs: the railroad that "guts the town" with its "straight bright rails," the train which has "a welcome horning sound," and the gravel dust that "rises like breath." In a more conventional story, the near rhyme of "straight bright," and the metaphors for the railroad and gravel dust could border on being too rich, too obtrusive. But this story invites us into a fiction that operates by different laws and asks us to slow down, even to read it aloud, when it's at its best.

A sectioned story, of course, may not be poetic: the language may be clear and straightforward, and the juxtapositions of pieces funny or unsettling. Sections are one way to bring together a number of wildly disparate times in a character's life or the experience of several different people—if they are somehow related by an event, theme, or image. We don't have to know, before we start writing, what the links are. We might invent various pieces and move them around until we start to suspect what the subject and nature of the story might be. Then we can write and rewrite the pieces in light of our discoveries.

Image as Structure

The crayoned postcards and drawings in "Photograph of Luisa," Emily's hair in "The Eve of the Spirit Festival," and the different bulletproof vests in "Trauma Plate" are successful uses of recurring imagery, linking events across time, or ideas and feelings from one character to another. The bulletproof vests and their trauma plates also serve as a central metaphor for the different ways the characters protect or expose their hearts (their emotions). All these stories are organized primarily by traditional chronologies, but it's also possible to move around in time using images or repetitive language as locating devices.

In organizing a story by means of its recurring concepts, metaphors, or imagery, we need to think of how these elements build, just as when we organize by action. The image needs to change in some meaningful way over the course of the story, acquiring weight and depth.

One of the best-known of the stories that use repetition and image as an organizing principle is Tim O'Brien's "Things They Carried." O'Brien organizes the story not in chronological order, or as a linear narration interrupted by flashbacks, but in a regular, alternating pattern of storytelling and lists. The detailed lists itemize for us what Lieutenant Jimmy Cross and the members of his platoon carry with them during the Vietnam War. Here too the weights are both literal and metaphorical. The pattern is not obtrusive because the theme of carrying extends through the storytelling segments as well, and these segments are full of recurring imagery, as repetitive and jumbled as the men's traumatic memories.

In the beginning of the story, what the men carry is largely physical:

> The things they carried were largely determined by necessity. Among the necessities or near-necessities were P-38 can openers, pocket knives, heat tabs, wristwatches, dog tags, mosquito repellent, chewing gum, candy, cigarettes, salt tablets, packets of Kool-Aid, lighters, matches, sewing kits, Military Payment Certificates, C rations, and two or three canteens of water.

In the middle of this passage, in the middle of a long list of who carries what, comes the sentence, "Ted Lavender, who was scared, carried tranquilizers until he was shot in the head outside the village of Than Khe in mid-April." The story's central tragic event is mentioned for the first time as part of the list, in a seemingly casual way. The memories are told differently and give us new insight each time they appear, and they are followed by long, convincing, specific lists: "What they carried was partly a function of rank, partly of field specialty," ". . . they carried whatever presented itself, or whatever seemed appropriate as a means of killing or staying alive," "What they carried varied by mission."

As the story progresses, it starts to chronicle the weight of the intangibles they carry:

> They carried all the emotional baggage of men who might die. Grief, terror, love, longing—these were intangibles, but the intangibles had their own mass and specific gravity, they had tangible weight. They carried shameful memories. They carried the common secret of cowardice barely restrained, the instinct to run or freeze or hide, and in many respects this was heaviest burden of all, for it could never be put down, it required perfect balance and perfect posture.

By the time the story shows us what portions of his humanity Lieutenant Cross has had to shed—or thinks he has had to shed—for his own survival and that of his men, we have come to feel the heaviness of men at war.

When revising a story of our own that uses recurring images or motifs as an organizing structure, we can work to make sure that the recurring elements accomplish something new dramatically each time, and that they expand or take on more weight for the reader as the story progresses.

STORY ANALYSIS AND QUESTIONS: "GRAFFITI"

(Note: please read the story once before *you read the following analysis. Then, after you read the analysis, look at the story a second time, keeping the discussion questions in mind. You will get the most benefit out of this process if you mark specific passages in the story, take notes, and work through the questions in writing.)*

Julio Cortázar's "Graffiti" provides an example of images that form part of the structural element of the story, without substituting for meaning or dramatic tension. The story lacks many of the conventional elements of fiction, such as dialogue and scenes in which the main characters interact directly with each other. It's structured around a conversation that takes place solely via graffiti writing.

The images of the graffiti become more clearly described and more fully developed in the course of the story. In the first paragraph, the graffiti is referred to only as "the sketch" and not described. Next we learn the messages are not political. The first actual description appears in the third paragraph, and is as abstract as the sketch itself: "the profile of a bird or two entwined figures." These suggest images of freedom and love in the totalitarian world of the story. It's worth tracing the progress of the graffiti: how they're described and how they develop throughout the story.

What provides the narrative tension in the story is the increasingly risky behavior of the two graffiti writers, and their narrow escapes from the patrols. The story doesn't overload the graffiti images by making them carry the weight of meaning—they don't substitute for the events that make us see the effects of totalitarianism. Instead, they illuminate and comment on events.

DISCUSSION QUESTIONS

1. What is the story's actual plot, and what is the emotional plot? Where and how do they intersect?
2. Where is the story's climax or climaxes?
3. How would the story be different if the encounter with the patrol were dramatized more fully and we knew details about individual policemen?
4. Does the imagery of the graffiti function as a central metaphor in the story? Why or why not?
5. The story ends with a surprising twist that changes the way we perceive the story. How and why does this twist work without seeming like a "trick ending?"
6. What takes the place of the more usual elements of dialogue, physical description, and background information? What makes the story vivid?

REVISION: HOW STRUCTURE EMERGES THROUGH MULTIPLE REVISIONS

When we're writing first drafts, we're usually just meeting our characters and getting our first hints as to what they may be up to: we've rarely found the story's real structure. Once we have a draft and have put it aside for a week or so, we can go back into it as detectives of our own work. We might try reading through and highlighting or making a check mark by those moments or events that seem to genuinely matter, making notes about ways of leading up to these moments.

A good first step is to think about the story as a whole: does it chronicle a significant change in at least one character's life? In other words, what is the difference between life at the beginning of the story and life at the end? What was at stake, and how was it resolved? Or if a significant change doesn't occur, how will the reader's perceptions of the character shift significantly by the end of the story? What does the lack of change mean in the characters' lives? Even in a nontraditional story, something needs to *happen,* though it may be no more than a shift in the reader's perceptions. After thinking about these questions, we may need to push our characters to take more risks, to reveal themselves more deeply in their actions; or we may need to raise the stakes.

Next, we can consider how the arrangement of scenes and events contributes to the overall meaning of the story. Even in the age of computers, it makes sense to print out a copy of the story, cut the scenes apart, and try physically moving them around, changing the order. What's happening in each scene? What events lead to what other events? How? What might we need to add for the story to make sense? Are there pieces that, however interesting in themselves, do not contribute to the story's overall meaning, and could be successfully deleted? Within each scene, what change takes place? How are the characters or situation different at the end of the scene than they were at the beginning? Is anything taking place only in people's heads that we could rewrite so it plays out through interactions between people, or through actions the characters take in the world?

In terms of the narrative drive, we can ask questions both about the story as a whole and about each individual scene: "What is the reader hoping for?" and/or "What is the reader worried about?" These will sometimes, but not always, be the same things the characters are hoping for or worried about. A character may be hoping to get more money out of his father, while we the readers are hoping that he will look after his father in some way instead of taking advantage of him. Or another character may be worried about whether or not his romantic relationship will work out, but we see him as an attractive and engaging person who doesn't have much in common with the woman he's with and who will happily find someone else. We don't necessarily identify with characters' desires and fears—our experience as a reader is often more like watching our friends go through troubles, although without being able to offer advice or help.

Once we have a rough draft of a story, we can start thinking about the reader's forward and backward experiences. We can't predict what every reader will make of it—what draws one reader will repel others—but we can imagine a group of fairly intelligent readers, in general predisposed to like the kind of stories we want to tell. Recognizing that they have many demands on their time and things on their minds, we can read our own story through these imaginary people's eyes. This process of imagining the reader's experience can give us useful distance on the characters and events, as long as we don't get carried away and begin to damage our story in the hopes of pleasing the reader.

A story might provide a strong forward experience, but a weak backward experience. In this case, although we're turning pages rapidly, drawn from line to line, scene to scene, after we've finished the story, we wonder what all the fuss was about. Did the events really warrant all those pages? Or do we have unanswered questions: "Why was that stranger in Mary's bathtub in the second scene, and what did he have to do with the story?" "What difference did it make that Arthur was musing about the role of fate in his life, when it didn't seem related to the rest of the story?"

The opposite may also be true: if an unfinished story is too weak on the forward experience, the readers may have to drag themselves through it. Many readers may manage only a few pages before giving up and never find out that the story makes a great deal of sense by the end, adding up to something of profound significance.

Another useful technique is to outline what we have so far, writing short descriptions of each key scene. When we have an outline written, we can *see* the story as a whole, even at a glance. For novels, outlining is even more helpful. Some writers outline (specifically or vaguely) beforehand, change as they write, and update their outlines (which may be several pages long) frequently. It's a way of keeping hold of a great slithering mass of prose, of keeping track of days and months, of remembering what happens in each plot or subplot. Outlines in chart form, colored pens to highlight different plot elements, wall graphs showing the relationship of characters or their family trees: all of these can be useful tools. The initial outline can be as simple as a few notes about what might happen for each character or it can be as elaborate as pages of notes for each chapter. Some writers don't outline at all but just charge in; others want to feel some sense of structure, however illusory.

Either cutting a story apart or outlining it helps us to see its shape in a new way, so that we take nothing for granted in our revision. Writing a plot summary is another way of clarifying the important events and the ways in which they connect.

PLOT AND STRUCTURE EXERCISES

1. Think of a story that you haven't yet been able to revise successfully. Write a long paragraph that summarizes the entire plot (very hard to do, but useful both artistically and practically). If you don't have the ending or the plot doesn't work, that's fine. Think through the structures of the plots of a couple of your favorite short stories. What changes during the story? Where are the key moments that build to that change (the climaxes)? In what order does the story deliver its events and information?

   Now look at your own plot again. (Some of the knowledge of our plot needs to emerge over the course of multiple revisions, but sometimes we can jump start it.) What changes for the characters, or what shifts occur in the reader's perception of the characters? Is anything taking place in people's heads that could instead be dramatized in dialogue or actions the characters take in the world? Make notes on what might be different, giving yourself complete freedom to brainstorm. Write scenes for each of the possibilities that intrigue you and see what they have to teach you about your story.
2. Write out a chronological timeline of the events in your story. Does it make sense to tell it in this order? Experiment with turning some of the events into backstory or flashback. Then try starting the story at an earlier or later moment in the timeline. How does that change the narrative questions the story might raise in readers' minds?
3. Write a story organized by images—choose three images that strongly appeal to you. You're most apt to get images that relate to the story if you daydream about the story for a while and let various images appear.

(Don't try to analyze what they mean, or to pick images that seem thematically appropriate: just let the writing mechanism come up with whatever it pleases.)

Allow these images to appear throughout the story, changing as they go. The story can be told chronologically, or in numbered or named sections, or using jump cuts and white space, with the images organizing the material, as they do in "The Things They Carried." Try this with a story you've already written (save the old version as a backup first), or write a new one for the purpose. Put it aside for a few days, then reread it. Are the images changing and developing over the course of the story, so that they take on meaning? Do they carry just enough symbolic weight without overwhelming the rest of the story? Is there an image that serves as a central metaphor? The images won't substitute for meaningful events, but will have enough presence to illuminate them.

4. Write a story in sections. Either start with moments from a traditional and linear story you have already written, or write different sections and then move them around to see what order works best.
5. (This reading exercise can be done either individually or in a group.) Choose one of the stories you've read so far. Identify the actual plot—the events in the order in which they are presented. Then identify the emotional plot. How do the two intersect? Where is/are the climax(es) of the story? What is the resolution of the actual plot? Of the emotional plot? ("The Niece" and "The Forest" work very well for this exercise, though it can be done with any story.)
6. (This reading exercise can be done either individually or in a group.) In "Father," what do the narrating voices think and feel about their father? About their mother? About John and Joan? How do they feel about the events of the story? What specific lines or words let us know these thoughts, feelings, and attitudes? If there are places where the thoughts, feelings, and attitudes seem ambiguous, how did L'Heureux create this ambiguity? What is the artistic effect? In what ways does the presence of the authorial figure (the character whose name and life circumstances seem to reflect the author's) affect the story?

CHAPTER

5

Time in Fiction

Scene, Summary, Flashbacks, Backstory, and Transitions

(Anthology selections: "The Eve of the Spirit Festival" and "The Rooster and the Dancing Girl")

Crowding is what Keats meant when he told poets to "load every rift with ore." It's what we mean when we exhort ourselves to avoid flabby language and clichés, never to use ten vague words when two will do, always to seek the vivid phrase, the exact word. By crowding I mean also keeping the story full, always full of what's happening in it; keeping it moving, not slacking and wandering into irrelevancies: keeping it interconnected with itself, rich with echoes forward and backward. Vivid, exact, concrete, accurate, dense, rich: these adjectives describe the prose that is crowded with sensations, meanings, and implications.

But leaping is just as important. What you leap over is what you leave out. And what you leave out is infinitely more than what you leave in. There's got to be white space around the word, silence around the voice. Listing is not describing. Only the relevant belongs. Some say God is in the details: some say the Devil is in the details. Both are correct.

—Ursula K. Le Guin, *Steering the Craft: Exercises and Discussions on Story Writing for the Lone Navigator or the Mutinous Crew*

SETTING THE STORY'S TIME SPAN

Ursula K. Le Guin, in her discussion of "crowding" and "leaping," gives us a sense of fictional time as infinitely malleable: we have the power to decide what to describe, how much detail to include, what to leave out, and how much of the story to tell. The first step is to set the overall time span, to decide whether we're covering a day, a month, a single car trip, or—far more rarely—several years. We can easily fall into unthinking habits—every one of our stories takes place over the course of a single week or a single season—so we need to pay attention in revision to the choices we've made and the reasons for them. Our decisions about time affect the shape and themes of the story. The length of the period of time covered and the events depicted in full scenes let the reader know what's important in the story.

By looking at the beginnings of a pair of stories, we can analyze why they start where they do and how the beginning relates to the story's time span as a whole. Both stories cover brief spans of time, but use backstory and summary in a way that makes readers understand the characters' lives. We have a sense of the depth of time, even in these relatively short stories.

The present action of Junot Díaz's "Ysrael" covers a couple of days. The story opens with the narrator's older brother's decision to go see Ysrael, a boy with a damaged face:

> We were on our way to the colmado for an errand, a beer for my tío, when Rafa stood still and tilted his head, as if listening to a message I couldn't hear, something beamed in from afar. We were close to the colmado; you could hear the music and the gentle clop of drunken voices. I was nine that summer, but my brother was twelve, and he was the one who wanted to see Ysrael, who looked out towards Barbacoa and said, We should pay that kid a visit.
>
> —Junot Díaz, "Ysrael"

Díaz organizes the story into numbered sections—the above paragraph is the entire first scene. The next two sections, much longer than the first, rely on backstory and summary to give a sense of the violence and dislocation of the boys' lives in the city. Halfway through the third section the narrative moves back to the present, and focuses almost entirely on the events of the afternoon they visit Ysrael (with the exception of one short numbered section containing a flashback to the year before). The story's time span starts when they make the decision to see Ysrael, and ends with an explosion of violence and an escape. Because of the information the backstory provides, we understand the circumstances that lead to the violence and how this incident relates to the rest of their lives. Even the backstory is full of scene and half-scenes, rich with dialogue and sensory details.

Stuart Dybek's "We Didn't" is told mostly in summary, with one major scene and several partial scenes containing brief passages of dialogue. The story's time span covers a summer and fall—the story opens with a summary of the two characters' habitual actions over the summer:

> We didn't in the light; we didn't in darkness. We didn't in the fresh-cut summer grass or in the mounds of autumn leaves or on the snow where moonlight threw down our shadows. We didn't in your room on the canopy bed you slept in, the bed you'd slept in as a child, or in the backseat of my father's rusted Rambler, which smelled of the smoked chubs and kielbasa he delivered on weekends from my Uncle Vincent's meat market. We didn't in your mother's Buick Eight, where a rosary twined the rearview mirror like a beaded, black snake with silver, cruciform fangs.
>
> —Stuart Dybek, "We Didn't"

After two more paragraphs, Dybek presents the story's major scene, which takes place one evening on the beach at the end of summer. During this scene everything changes between the two characters, but without the summary we wouldn't understand the full emotional impact of the event that permanently keeps them from ever having sex. Although the story then goes on to summarize what happens afterward over the course of the fall, Dybek ends the story by returning to that evening at the beach, resuming where he left off. The structure shows how that one brief moment crystallized the emotions of a significant period in the narrator's life. In "Ysrael," the very short time period echoes the explosive nature of events; in "We Didn't," the summary of months passing conveys a cumulative sense of frustration. In both cases the time period reinforces the story's themes and tone.

In our own stories, we may want to cover a long span, using summary to quickly move across the time between major scenes or to fill in missing information. Or we may want to chronicle just a short period of time, perhaps using summary or backstory to illuminate its significance. The success or failure of these strategies will depend on our mastery of scene and summary.

SCENE AND SUMMARY IN DRAFT AND REVISION

Our first impulses in handling time may tend heavily toward either scene or summary. The proportion of scene and summary is part of the voice, the characteristic fingerprint, of each writer. Decisions about scene and summary—like those about character, story, style, and subject matter—vary not only from story to story and writer to writer, but also from country to country, and historical period to historical period. A writer who is reading and rereading classic novels, and also exploring contemporary writing from all over the world, will be aware of a far greater array of choices about scene and summary than a writer who reads only contemporary fiction from a single country.

In the United States, not too long ago, historical background and narrative commentary had become anathema. Everything was told in scenes: all we knew about the characters came from physical detail, dialogue, and action. We had the sense of being right there in the room with the characters at all times, with the narrator as transparent as glass. Madison Smartt Bell has suggested that this tendency arose because scene is so much easier to write than summary and because, in what he calls the "Skinner shock box" of the workshop, we all got "check marks" for our scenes and criticism for our summaries. Now, on the other hand, contemporary American fiction has such a lively strain of stories and novels with ebullient background detail and hands-on narrators summarizing events and commenting on everything, including their characters, that this approach may well have become the current dominant mode. The fashions keep changing. It's up to each of us to find a balance between the extremes of ignoring the work of our contemporaries and having our own ideas and style overwhelmed by it.

Sometimes when we're writing a first draft, we need to write through every moment of what happens, in order to "live" the scene and make it real for ourselves. Or we rush along with long passages of summary, just getting the people and events down on the page, not stopping to observe what they say, whether there's cornbread in the oven or a traffic accident in the street below, a skunk under the front porch or a younger sister listening in on the extension.

In revision, we fiddle with the proportion of scene and summary. When we have some event important enough to be dramatized in detail, we need to decide, as we're revising, just how much of it the reader needs to be present for. What period of time does the story cover, and do we need more or less to give it its full power? We decide which events or background we're offering briefly, in a summary, and which deserve a scene; how long a given scene should be; and whether a few lines of dialogue and a few details—a half-scene—would be enough or whether we want to give the reader a chance to luxuriate in being part of these events.

Action, Description, and Dialogue

Creative writing teachers often spend a lot of time encouraging writers to slow down, to move away from an emphasis on action or theorizing, and toward observing the details of the moment, to balance sensory details, characters' thoughts, and dialogue. In our scenes, we work out how to observe specific, surprising details with all our senses, inhabiting the story. This means avoiding the natural temptation to rush over *what happens* in order to get on with explaining it. We let readers linger in a scene, in what feels like real time.

Scenes chronicle an extended period of time (usually measured in minutes) and often occur in a single location (the kitchen, the inside of a moving bus, the side of Mount Everest). We see the actions, hear the dialogue, and (depending on the POV) may overhear characters' thoughts. Beginning writers sometimes use scenes merely to give a sense of the texture of daily life, but a scene usually depicts some change in the characters' lives or relationships and advances the story. The shift can be dramatic (at the beginning of the scene, Malcolm and Julia are friends; by the end, they aren't speaking to each other) or subtle (at the beginning of the scene, Malcolm will do anything Julia asks; by the end Malcolm begins to resist her requests).

Activity alone is no guarantee we've written a complete scene: cars can crash, characters can punch each other, and a blimp can crash into the house they live in, all without necessarily changing whatever is truly at stake for the characters or for us as readers. And a scene in which a man does nothing more than show up for a job interview—after he's previously missed several—can signal a huge shift in attitude.

When we revise, we may find that long strings of events we portrayed as scenes can actually be condensed into a quick summary. If nothing has changed, or the way things change is not significant, we may be able to write,

"Mercedes spent the entire day arguing fruitlessly with her mother over the amount of the donation" or "Over the next month, Allen trained the dog not to bite members of the family."

The change in a scene can occur in the surface events and relationships, or in the subtext. How characters behave and the way in which things happen are as important as what happens. Every action and every spoken sentence reveal something about the characters, and often about the subtext: the meaning behind or beneath the surface. (We discuss subtext in more detail in terms of plot in Chapter 4 and in terms of dialogue in Chapter 9.)

One useful way to become more accomplished at scenes is to sit down with a pile of our favorite stories and observe how scenes start and what period of time they cover, as well as how to get from scene to summary and back again. What is the balance of action, description, and dialogue in different scenes and with different writers? Donald Barthelme might have scenes that are almost entirely dialogue, while Julian Barnes might have scenes that lean heavily toward description, and Ana Lydia Vega might move the scene forward with substantial action. Writers tend to have particular strengths but may, consciously or unconsciously, vary their focus depending on the needs of a particular scene or story.

To push our limits, we change our usual balance. We might get our characters to talk much more than usual, or much less. We might have them tear up a letter or hide their bottle of bourbon under the couch or perform some other action instead of standing around talking. We might give a more lush sense of the physical world by adding description that enhances character or tone. The key to deepening our fiction, rather than making arbitrary changes, is to return to our sense of the heart of the story. We look for changes that reveal to us, and to the reader, what might otherwise be muffled or obscured.

Compelling Summaries

We need summary to provide background, to rapidly cover the passing of a significant chunk of time, to describe repeated events ("every Wednesday Evan would haul his cello up the steep hill to Mr. Whitaker's house, even when it snowed"), or to give information that doesn't need to be dramatized. An effective summary can set up or ask questions, introduce a mystery, or move us gracefully through hours or years when nothing much is happening to our characters. Summary can be so fascinating and particular that the readers don't even realize they've left the scene.

In "First Marriage," Joan Silber uses summary that covers a long period of time, gives information about the characters, creates setting, adds to the dramatic tension, and introduces an object (a bathtub) that will be important in the plot. The narrator has just married an occasional lover, as a favor, to get him a green card:

> We were quarrelsome in the weeks after the wedding. Terry had—still has—the habit of holding forth, of airing his opinions without quarter. On his side, he

> hated the way I was always talking about him on the phone to my friends; he was not fooled by code names. All the same we both got caught up in making improvements on the loft—we had some hippie electrician rig up a battery electric line, we partitioned studios for both of us, and in the bathroom (where I had been bathing one part at a time in an industrial sink) we brought in an old oil drum to use for a tub. You climbed the ladder over the side and sat on a stool under a hose, like a swimmer under a waterfall. We were quite proud of having devised this. We painted it with Rustoleum, and Terry put plants around it. Twenty years later it was still our bathtub. I'd had no idea.
>
> Terry almost left, years ago, with someone even younger than I was, but then he didn't. Now he's too old to go anywhere. His conversation is the same as it's always been—literally the same, I know these stories—except that he's more blustery, more like an old Brit. His voice is thicker and scratchier, and he gets winded on long walks. We walk around the city a lot, still.
>
> This summer, on a walk to a friend's house, we ran into the woman Terry almost ran off with.

This summary, in a couple of paragraphs, crosses twenty years and gives a deep, rich picture of this relationship by the juxtaposition of details: the things that annoy the couple about each other, the ways they have worked together to improve their studio, and the fact that, despite the distance between them, they still listen to each other's stories and take walks together. Even though we're being told how the characters feel, it comes to us in specifics: we can imagine her code names, and we have an image of him holding forth. The details about fixing up the bathroom, too, make this feel as if it were a scene, although it's summary.

Sara Pritchard's story "The Very Beautiful Sad Elegy for Bambi's Dead Mother" covers seven years in thirteen pages, largely through summary:

> Locked in the bathroom at 41 Cherry Street after morning half-day kindergarten, while your father is out working for Atlas Powder Company, your sister Albertine and your brother Mason at school, and your mother doing laundry or teaching piano lessons downstairs, you spend many happy hours laying crayons out on the radiator and watching them melt, tap dancing on the tile floor while singing the McGuire Sisters' "Sugartime" or Burl Ives's "Big Rock Candy Mountain," playing Albertine's flutophone (which she keeps hidden in a Buster Brown shoebox under the bed and that you are forbidden to touch), eating Vicks VapoRub out of the jar with your finger, sipping Cheracol cough syrup, watching St. Joseph's aspirin for children dissolve on your tongue, taking your clothes off and examining every square inch of your body with your mother's hand mirror, shaving the hair off your arms with your father's Gillette razor, or standing on the bright red bench, staring into the medicine cabinet mirror on the opposite wall and repeating endlessly your favorite phrase in many different voices, pronunciations, variations, accents, and volumes:

Yellow Velvet.
YEL-LOH VEL-VET!
yel-LOW vel-VET.
YEL-low **VEL-**vet
YEL-low vel-**VET**
VELVET YELLOW
VELLOW YELVET
YellowyVellowysmellowyVELVET
yellowvelvetyellowvelvetyellowvelvet
YALLLLLOUH VALL-VETTTT!

None of this is scene—this is all habitual action and even habitual speech. It's the vivid invention of the details that creates for us this remarkable character in her 1950s childhood. A dull summary that gave us the same information might read, "I was (or else "she was"—second person doesn't seem to go with this new summary style) an inventive and adventurous child who could have used more supervision. I enjoyed being alone and was very interested in words. Most of my family was out of the house every day, but I locked myself in the bathroom and played very happily." This character, Ruby Jean, is going to be in trouble and in love with words her whole life—and the "happy hours laying crayons out on the radiator and watching them melt" or the experiments with the medicines and the razor give us a quick and vivid picture of the kinds of chances she takes, and her blithe indifference to consequences. So the summary not only has strong specific images, but also adds to the narrative drive as we wait to see what kinds of trouble she will get herself into.

Once we've written our own summaries, we can go back over them to see how we can include specific details, surprising observations, and a subtle continuation of the story's purposes. If the reader notices what we're doing, then we've probably overdone it. But if we retain the voice and mood of the story, even when giving information, a summary can draw the reader along without feeling like an interruption.

Summary Within Scenes

Usually writers talk about summary as a bridge between different scenes. But summary can fast-forward us through less essential moments. When we write our first drafts, we might write down every line of dialogue, noting what the characters are doing at each moment. Then later we read it over and find a lull—a period of time within the scene when nothing dramatically significant is happening. In some cases, we need to rewrite the events. But sometimes all that we need to do is use summary *inside* the scene. For instance, in the following selection from Akhil Sharma's "Cosmopolitan," Gopal Maurya and his neighbor Helen Shaw have gone to bed together for the first time. The author has just spent several necessary pages giving us a scene that tracks each awkward interaction as they get to know each other, in exchanges such as this:

> "Your house was two stories?"
>
> "Yes. And my room was on the second floor. Tell me about yourself."
>
> "I am the third of five brothers. We grew up in a small, poor village. I got my first pair of shoes when I left high school." As Gopal was telling her the story, he remembered how he used to make Gitu feel lazy with stories of his childhood, and his voice fell. "Everybody was like us, so I never thought of myself as poor."

In the next paragraph, Sharma uses two sentences of summary to condense the rest of their conversation until we come to a moment in the dialogue that gives essential information:

> They talked this way for half an hour, with Gopal asking most of the questions and trying to discover where Mrs. Shaw was vulnerable and how this vulnerability made him attractive to her. Although she answered his questions candidly, Gopal could not find the unhappy childhood or the trauma of an abandoned wife that might explain the urgency of this moment in bed. "I was planning to leave my husband," she explained casually. "He was crazy. Almost literally. He thought he was going to be a captain of industry or a senator. He wasn't registered to vote. He knew nothing about business. Once, he invested almost everything we had in a hydroponic farm in Southampton. With him I was always scared of being poor. He used to spend two hundred dollars a week on lottery tickets, and he would save the old tickets in shoeboxes in the garage. . . . "

We can use summary like this both to speed through the undramatic moments of a scene, and also to give insight into a character's overall intentions, as Sharma does here with Gopal's desire to discover Mrs. Shaw's vulnerabilities. We are listening over his shoulder: because he wants to hear where she is vulnerable, we begin listening to see what *he* might discover. This adds a layer between the story and the readers, one that doesn't exist between the characters.

In looking at our own work, we might ask ourselves whether our scene starts with the interesting part of what's happening, or whether it spends too much time in establishing mood, location, and the number of people involved and their relationship. Can we move more swiftly and elegantly into the part that matters? How does the length of the scene signal the importance—in terms of character growth or plot development—of the events it covers? How can we make the change between scene and summary without distracting the reader?

Abdulrazak Gurnah's "Escort" begins with a two and a half page scene between the narrator, who now lives in England and is back in East Africa on business, and the taxi driver who drops him at his hotel. This taxi driver, who will pay an increasingly key role in the story, utters spiteful speeches about the need to come home. He represents an emotional threat to the narrator that we feel from the very beginning of the story.

To deliver information, at the end of the scene, Gurnah moves from dialogue to summary as the driver finishes speaking:

> "The name is Salim. I'm always there by the Post Office taxi-rank. Come by any time."
>
> I had found the hotel by chance. The Immigration Officer had explained that he could not give me an entry permit unless I gave an address in the country on my form. He said this apologetically, because after seeing the place of birth on my passport he had spoken enthusiastically about Zanzibar, where he too had relatives. He showed me a list of hotels—*Whichever you like,* he said. *You don't have to stay there. Just for the form.* So I picked one, and when I found a cab outside the airport it was the only name I could remember. Its inaccessibility, and the intimidating silence of the loco-yard and warehouses outside working hours, suited me as it meant that no one came to visit me, as they might have done if I had been staying in one of the glittery palaces on the other side of town with their casinos and pool-side combos.
>
> So it was a surprise to have the receptionist ring the following evening to announce a visitor. It was Salim, of course.

This passage of summary slides us out of one scene and into the next, making a smooth transition, while offering apparently irrelevant details about the hotel—far away and plain—that actually tell us quite a bit. Although this could be considered a homecoming, the narrator doesn't want pleasure and glitter, doesn't want to see anyone, just wants his visit to pass unremarked. The details of the summary establish place for us, allow the narrator to be essentially stranded with Salim, and convey our narrator's alienation from Africa and his old life.

STORY ANALYSIS AND QUESTIONS: "THE EVE OF THE SPIRIT FESTIVAL"

(Note: please read the story once before *you read the following analysis. Then, after you read the analysis, look at the story a second time, keeping the discussion questions in mind. You will get the most benefit out of this process if you mark specific passages in the story, take notes, and work through the questions in writing.)*

In "The Eve of the Spirit Festival," Lan Samantha Chang uses a mixture of scene and summary to cover a long period of time with clarity and economy. The opening scene contains just enough summary and background to let us know how old our narrator Claudia and her sister Emily are, as well as that they've just come from their mother's funeral. This story has a conflict of judgment about what happened in the recent past: Emily disagrees with her parents' decision to avoid an operation, but Claudia secretly thinks they were right. The scene shows the family dynamic as Emily begins to openly blame their father:

"You told me she would get better," I heard her say. "Now you're burning paper money for her ghost. What good will that do?"

"I am sorry," Baba said.

"I don't care."

Her voice burned. I squirmed beneath her hand, but she wouldn't let me look. It was something between her and Baba. I watched his black wingtip shoes retreat to the door. When he had gone, Emily let go of me. I set up and looked at her; something had changed. Not in the lovely outlines of her face—our mother's face—but in her eyes, shadow-black, lost in unforgiveness.

They say the dead return to us. But we never saw our mother again, though we kept a kind of emptiness waiting in case she might come back. I listened always, seeking her voice, the lost thread of a conversation I'd been too young to have with her. I did not dare to mention her to Emily. Since I could remember, my sister had kept her most powerful feelings private, sealed away. She rarely mentioned our mother, and soon my memories faded. I could not picture her. I saw only Emily's angry face, the late sun streaking red through her dark hair.

After the traditional forty-nine day mourning period, Baba did not set foot in the Buddhist temple.

This story covers decades, moving sometimes swiftly and sometimes slowly. In some of the story's passages, we know what time we have moved to immediately—but here the sections are linked by the images of Emily's angry face. We watch to see how the interactions between the three of them play out for the rest of the story. The first time, we read the story because we're worried about the children. Later, when we begin to look at it technically, we can explore Chang's decisions. As a beginning, we might consider the following questions.

DISCUSSION QUESTIONS

1. Of the six sections of the story, which start with summary and which take us directly into the scenes? Why?
2. How do the scenes vary in length, and what is the effect of these variations?
3. How does Chang make her summaries vivid?
4. When Emily says, "It's Baba's fault," Chang reveals Claudia's opinion in backstory rather than in dialogue. Why might Chang have chosen this approach and how does it affect our reading?
5. Why does the story begin after their mother's death?
6. How does Chang signal the passage of time? What phrases or details does she use?
7. What changes during the time period of the story, and why does Chang choose these particular events to show change?

MOVING THROUGH TIME

We need techniques that will help us move from one important or compelling moment to another: from childhood to adulthood, without needing to pass through middle school and the teens; from one afternoon to another afternoon two years later, in which some experience clarifies or complicates the events of the first afternoon; from one character's POV to another's; from the present to the past and back again; even from one room to another without having to open and close every door. We can make these transitions either through language or the use of white space. And then we have another decision to make: how much of the past do we include in a story? Do we create a scene to let the reader live through a past memory along with the character? Or do we bring up the past through dialogue, a character's memory, or direct narration?

White Space and Transitional Phrases

In her essay "Time and Order: The Art of Sequencing," Lan Samantha Chang describes the manipulation of time and the art of the transition:

> A writer who studies sequencing is concerned with some of the most basic and essential elements of storytelling: selection, order, the passage of time, and the creation of narrative . . . When a writer sets a moment, when she writes in a certain tense, and when she strings two scenes together by using narrative, she draws upon her power, as the storyteller, to manipulate time. For example, two scenes, separated by a brief transition, a description, or a summary, hang together because the writer has decided that they should, because she is making a choice. The writer has brought the reader to a place where the laws of time have disappeared and have been replaced by story time, with its own laws, where a moment can take pages to explain, but where a year, or ten, might pass in a flicker of white space. Italo Calvino, in his essay "On Quickness," writes, "Sicilian storytellers use the formula *'lu cuntu nun metti tempu'* (time takes no time in a story) when they want to leave out links or indicate gaps of months or even years."

Two of the most common ways to make these transitions across time, from one scene to another, are white space (an extra double space between paragraphs) and transitional phrases ("The next day," "Two years later," "By the time they got home," and so on.) Another common move is to repeat a word, image, or idea from one paragraph to the next. Or the writer might name a specific incident that clearly comes some time later. The challenge is deciding which kind of approach to use for each transition. We can develop our transition skills through intuition, practice, and studying the techniques of other writers, paying attention to their handling of time. Using primarily transitional phrases generally creates a more dense, linear feeling to a story. Using primarily white space can emphasize the "leaping" quality of a story and so help the reader cross great swaths of time, shifts in POV, or emotional distance.

We can see the inconspicuous use of a range of transition techniques in the following passage from Peter Turchi's "Night, Truck, Two Lights Burning," in which an adult narrator tells about the time when his childhood broke apart. Throughout, the narrator presents the briefest flashes of moments from his later life in a way that serves as a complicated version of a frame for the childhood story. The following two transitions move from one specific moment to a general description; then to another specific moment, not long after the first; and finally to nighttime, perhaps that night or soon after:

> My mother arrived two days later, in my father's pickup truck. We had made a sign for the door—Welcome Home—but that didn't appear to register. Even before she went inside, I understood that the pizza we had watched the pizza man spin almost to the ceiling, the cupcakes for dessert, and the grocery store flowers my father had arranged in a beer bottle on the tiny countertop would not be sufficient to create, for my mother, a mood of celebration.
>
> The trailer park was not a park, as I had imagined, but a series of crude terraces cut into the side of a steep clay hill, with a gravel road up the middle and a security light at the top of a telephone pole. There were twelve trailers, six on each side, and the way they were placed on the hill, one above the other, meant nearly everyone could look down into someone else's kitchen, living room, and bedroom. The most desirable spots were the two at the top, which were relatively private—though none of the trailers could have been more than twenty feet from its neighbor—and had the best view of the woods across the road. Our trailer was at the very bottom, which meant, my mother said as she stood in the doorway, not unbuttoning her coat, Everyone could see in. A modest woman, she sewed our curtains closed.
>
> I woke to a strange sound. Not a dog, not a cat . . . There had been talk of bears, and I hoped to see one in exactly those circumstances: from under the covers, safe inside our trailer. When I heard the sound again, and understood what I heard, it became a glowing ember, a warm promise.

The white spaces prepare the reader to expect a transition of some sort; Turchi keeps it smooth by the logic of the transition. In the first sentence, the narrator's mother is unhappy; in the second sentence, the narrator shows us what it is about the park that makes her unhappy. At the end of the second paragraph she sews the curtains closed, and the mention of curtains makes a natural transition to prepare us for the leap into nighttime. The use of white space makes these transitions more poetic than laborious, reproducing the associative quality of memory so important in the story.

In "Sonny's Blues," James Baldwin vaults through time using both white space and transitional phrases, from a conversation between the narrator and his mother to a conversation with his brother that takes place much later.

> "I won't forget," I said. "Don't you worry, I won't forget. I won't let nothing happen to Sonny."
>
> My mother smiled as though she were amused at something she saw in my face. Then, "You may not be able to stop nothing from happening. But you got to let him know you's *there.*"
>
> Two days later I was married, and then I was gone. And I had a lot of things on my mind and I pretty well forgot my promise to Mama until I got shipped home on a special furlough for her funeral.
>
> And, after the funeral, with just Sonny and me alone in the empty kitchen, I tried to find out something about him.
>
> "What do you want to do?" I asked him.
>
> "I'm going to be a musician," he said.

The first sentence of the second paragraph takes us a short way into the future ("Two days"). In the next sentence we move much further, located not by time, but by event, by the mother's death. A story like "Sonny's Blues," which covers a long stretch of relationship, with all its ups and downs, has to choose the key moments to focus on. The white space serves to emphasize the size of the shift in time and emotions, and the transitional phrases specify exactly what those time periods are. The "two days" conveys how short a time it was before the narrator was gone, and then the information that he was shipped home for his mother's funeral lets us know how much had changed before he came back.

Flashbacks and Backstory

Every character has a history. And when we're writing or rewriting a story, we are always confronted with two questions: how much should we reveal to the reader about events that happened before the story's events, and in what form should we reveal that information?

The answer to the first question depends partly on the story's needs (how much information is necessary for the reader to make sense of current events?) and partly on the writer. Writers like Alice Munro, John Edgar Wideman, and Nicholas Delbanco often weave in a good deal about what happened to characters before the events of the story—sometimes long before. Other writers keep their focus tightly on the present and the recent past and tend to spend less time exploring how people got the way they are. Writers like Frederick Barthelme, Mary Robison, and Sandra Cisneros often take this approach.

Probably most writers find themselves falling into one camp or another over time, rather than making a conscious choice early in their writing careers.

The approach that feels natural to us will depend on our philosophy of human character and on the kind of fiction that we have always been most drawn to reading. It can strengthen our writing, however, to push ourselves from time to time to write a story using an approach we are less accustomed to.

Backstory—the events that happened before the time period of the story—can be revealed through summary, dialogue, or scenes that drop us into the past: flashbacks. A flashback is always in the POV of the rest of the story. In a first-person story, a flashback is a memory that occurs to the narrator in the process of telling the story. It's usually triggered by some event or remark. This is also true in a close third-person story. In a more omniscient or distant third-person story, the narrator may choose some other way to link the main and back stories.

Alice Munro's "Oh, What Avails," which begins in the present tense and then moves into the past, is an example of how a story retains its POV. The first POV signal doesn't necessarily have to be in the first line, depending on the distance of the story, as long as it appears in time to keep readers from being disoriented. Here's a paragraph from early in the story, leading into the first flashback:

> On the table, under the fan, the two women have spread out cards and are telling their fortunes. They talk and laugh in a way that Joan finds tantalizing, conspiratorial. Morris is lying on the floor, writing in a notebook. He is writing down how many copies of *New Liberty* magazine he sold that week, and who has paid and who still owes money. He is a solid-looking boy of about fifteen, jovial but reserved, wearing glasses with one dark lens.
>
> When Morris was four years old, he was roaming around in the long grass at the foot of the yard, near the creek, and he tripped over a rake that had been left lying there, prongs up. He tripped, he fell on the prongs, his brow and eyelid were badly cut and his eyeball was grazed. As long as Joan can remember—she was a baby when it happened—he has had a scar, and been blind in one eye, and worn glasses with a smoky lens.

Here the third person is filtered through the POV of Morris's sister, Joan, but with some authorial distance: we enter only Joan's thoughts, but the author also gives us some descriptions directly, without filtering everything through what we know Joan is seeing and hearing. The transition from present to past uses the physical image of Morris's glasses as the "hinge" between the two time periods. If the story were in a more close third-person POV, the flashback section might have begun with "As long as Joan can remember. . . . " or with the moment when Joan first heard the story for herself.

Writers sometimes overuse flashbacks. If a writer moves into flashback too early in the story, or spends too much time in the past, the reader may become impatient, wanting to return to present time. Substantial flashbacks will usually only work if it's clear that the past story is the urgent one, and that the later events, which tend to be minimally presented, exist primarily as context. It's very rare to have a successful story with large amounts of flashback. Usually, this is a story that should actually start much earlier. Or else the backstory could be presented in much more abbreviated form, as a brief memory or a couple of lines of dialogue. (Too heavy a reliance on flashback is different from having two interwoven storylines, one past and one present. There we're switching between stories, not constantly halted in our forward movement by the insertion of scenic memories or informative detail.) In the process of questioning the story, we may find structural changes we can make, or we may become more aware of our story's deeper shape and purposes.

When we're writing a story and have a flashback that doesn't seem to fit smoothly, we can examine other writers' stories to see how the flashbacks are begun and ended, and how the writer connects them to the main story. What makes them work? What range of strategies does each writer use? In addition to white space and transitional phrases, changes in verb tense help control the movement to the past and back again, signaling the reader that we've changed times.

If the story is in the present tense ("She hurries past the McDougal's house . . .") then the flashbacks and backstory should be given in the simple past ("When she was 12, she spent almost every afternoon playing with Sally McDougal").

If the story is told in the past tense ("she hurried past . . ."), then flashbacks and backstory should be given in the past perfect ("She had never really liked Sally, but . . ."). If the flashback or backstory is longer than a few sentences, we drop the "had" and use the simple past for the rest of the flashback. Long flashbacks in the past perfect—bristling with "had's"—distract readers; we don't need to keep saying "had" once the move into the past has been established.

To make sure readers don't get lost, it's good to signal the return to the story's present with some detail or action that's clearly part of that time period.

If we decide we don't need a full flashback, we can leak the past into the story's main line of events either in scene or in summary. Characters can refer to the past in dialogue, describing events or arguing about different memories of the same thing:

> "So," she said, folding the sandpaper onto the sanding block, "is decorating the family business? Or your heart's desire?"
>
> "Neither." He was longing to ask about her, so he offered himself up, a pound of apples, a fistful of bananas. "My father was a greengrocer in Brighton. Got up at four every day, except Sunday, to buy the food and veg. Then he worked until seven at night, hauling sacks of potatoes and chatting up housewives."
>
> —Margot Livesey, "The Niece"

The narrator can dip into a character's memory:

> This is a careless spirit Jane had forgotten. As she sees them whisper, she remembers that time before Bill, and tries to read her daughter's lips. Ruthie rubs

> her forehead against the jut of this boy's cheekbone, whispering, and Jane almost thinks she can make it out—*let's make a break for Texas,* her daughter might be saying, and *I want my Monte Carlo back,* Jane thinks. She imagines a car she will never see again, enters it under maroon T-tops, feels the rocking slosh of dual fuel tanks, smells the leather, hears the spark plugs crackle to life, and swivels in custom seats to see it all disappear behind her.
>
> —Adam Johnson, "Trauma Plate"

Depending on the POV, the narrator might simply tell the reader about the past, without the medium of a character's memory.

> No one knows how badly Hart wanted this house on the river. Not Caro, and not Kevin, Hart's 15-year-old son, who read his father's emotions with uncanny and troubling accuracy. But Caro and Kevin would never have suspected Hart of such single-mindedness, though in fact he was intent on having the house as soon as he saw it, from the intaglio Moorish Cross on the granite threshold, through each of the quiet, cobwebbed rooms, to the chicken coop on the slope.
>
> —Elizabeth Tallent, "The Fence Party"

The techniques we use to move our characters through time will depend on the narrative voice, the size of the time periods we have to cover, our sense of the importance of different events in the story, our literary or cultural background, and even the story's degree of realism.

STORY ANALYSIS AND QUESTIONS: "THE ROOSTER AND THE DANCING GIRL"

(Note: please read the story once before *you read the following analysis. Then, after you read the analysis, look at the story a second time, keeping the discussion questions in mind. You will get the most benefit out of this process if you mark specific passages in the story, take notes, and work through the questions in writing.)*

In "The Rooster and the Dancing Girl," Yasunari Kawabata's impressionist, elliptical style and handling of time create a distinct variation from some of the more realistic stories in the anthology. This story has a strong sense of time, but no backstory or flashbacks, only forward progression.

Kawabata marks time not only from day to day—with some dramatic jumps—but also from rooster to rooster as the symbolic meanings of the bird change and deepen. He economically sets up transitions between scenes, often throwing us into the middle of a scene with a line of dialogue. Although sometimes he begins with a clear marker of time ("At the dancing girl's house, twenty chicks had hatched"), in other sections the time locator appears several lines down, adding to the disorienting effect of the story.

The following questions provide a chance to consider Kawabata's story in more detail, including the ways he shows change through a series of short scenes containing similar elements:

DISCUSSION QUESTIONS

1. Where are we in time at various points in the story, and how does Kawabata show us time, both directly and indirectly?
2. How does Kawabata present the changes in the dancing girl's attitude toward the roosters?
3. What does "great" seem to mean to the girl at different points in the story? How does it change over time?
4. What material or transitions might Kawabata have included if this were a story in the realist tradition?
5. What kind of backstory would we expect if this were a contemporary American short story?

REVISION: EXPERIMENTING WITH TIME

Most stories, as we've been told over and over, cover a brief period—a day, a week, a moment of time. It's hard to do justice to years of life in a story, just as it's hard to introduce a large number of characters. Some wonderful stories, though, cover large stretches of time, including James Baldwin's "Sonny's Blues," Lars Gustafsson's "Greatness Strikes Where It Pleases," Alice Munro's "Carried Away," and William Trevor's "Torridge."

By the time we have reached a more intermediate or advanced level, it's time to go ahead and break some "rules," to take risks, to allow ourselves to take on challenges that we fear are too much for us. We can experiment with changing the time period covered in our stories. Allowing ourselves to take on a long timeline in a story is a great way to push against our limits. If the story fails, it doesn't matter. We know we'll write other stories, that some stories are bound to fail, and that we can examine those stories for what we've learned and what we can then apply to other stories. We may even be able to revise the story, days, months, or years later, so that it works after all.

It can help, after the first pleasurable reading of a published story we admire, to examine it with an eye to seeing how much time it covers, how long before the key action the story begins, what the balance of scene and summary is, how the writer makes any necessary jumps across time, and how the writer gives us information about the characters' pasts.

All this work and analysis then frees the wilder, less logical part of our mind to experiment, just as the laborious day-to-day work we do on the story prepares our mind for sudden inventions. In the passage below, Andrea Barrett describes how a key piece of backstory came to her as an unexpected gift after a long period of working on "The Forest":

> "The Forest" was completed (I thought) in the summer of 1995, accepted for publication in *Ploughshares* in July, 1996, and published the following winter. By then, after working at it on and off since early 1994, it seemed cast in stone. Over a dozen or so revisions Krzysztof's background had developed and changed, his mother had emerged more clearly, the scene at the party had expanded, contracted, and then expanded again, the appearance of the deer was more deftly described, and the dialogue throughout had become a little less lumpy. The images that had started the story—the doll-shaped lanterns at the beginning, and the vision of Krzysztof calmly blowing his bubbles into molecular forms—had remained almost unchanged throughout. Equally fixed, I'd always felt, were Bianca and Rose Marburg and their relationship to each other. While I might tinker with what they said and did to each other, I thought I understood what they meant.
>
> Then I went back to the story again during 2001, when I saw how it might fit into the other stories that were joining to form *Servants of the Map*. As I began to understand the relationships between the stories more clearly, I realized that I needed to add to "The Forest" something that would bring into its world physical relics from other stories, while also reminding us of Suky, the Marburg sisters' mother. I wrote the passage swiftly (unusual, for me), realizing only later that, in addressing what had seemed like a purely mechanical problem, I had also, finally, gotten at an essential element of the girls' relationship, which is their different attitude toward the past and its relics.
>
> The new material I wedged between what, in the *Ploughshares* version, were once contiguous sentences: "Rose has a little apartment above the garage of one of those estates," and "It used to be the gardener's quarters." To someone who doesn't write, cracking open a story like this—breaking a passage in half to insert a long new passage—might seem strange, inorganic. But writers know that this is one of the ways fiction grows, wings unexpectedly sprouting off the main body, and by now I hope for this and have learned to wait for it. It happens, if it happens at all, only after I've done everything I know how to do. But the knowledge that I may be granted a surprising gift even after I've set the story aside as "done" is one of the reasons I tend to hold onto my stories for so long. The late gifts, when they do come, tend to be the best.

When we look again at the story, we see what important information this small section of backstory provides about the characters. This kind of gift enriches a story far beyond the amount of actual room it occupies on the page. When we have worked and worked on a story, sometimes writing relatively easily and sometimes driving ourselves up a wall with frustration, the story becomes part of our dreaming imagination, and its deeper truths surface unexpectedly.

TIME EXERCISES

1. Write a short or short-short story that has a paragraph for each year of a character's life. Decide which events are important enough to include, and how they'll be linked. Connect the sections through recurring images, events that share a similar theme, or a particular set of changes in the character and/or that character's friends and family.
2. Make copies of two or three stories you admire, from authors with quite varied styles. Go through them with different colors of pen and mark the scenes, the half-scenes, and the passages of summary. Where in the story do they occur? How long are they? Are they separate or intermingled? What functions of plot or character development do they serve? What transitions has the writer used? If the proportions of scene and summary vary, what effect does that have on your reading of the story? How might each author have chosen a strategy? Choose a scene and try rewriting it as summary, and then choose some summary and try rewriting it as a scene. This exercise is not for the purpose of trying to form rules about the proportions of scene and summary, but just to develop awareness of some of their possibilities.
3. Select one of your own stories that moves too quickly or too slowly. Experiment with turning some scenes into summary and vice versa. Try expanding the climactic scene and/or giving more information through summary. See where backstory, in summary or flashback, could enrich the story.
4. (This exercise can be done either individually or in a group.) Find one relatively minor scene and one climactic scene from a story you've read. Read each of these aloud to get a sense of the amount of time and detail spent on them. Why do they start where they do? What kind of information or detail does the climactic scene include that the less important scene omits? What do you notice about each?

CHAPTER

6

Discovering the Story's Subject

Material and Subject Matter

(Anthology selections: "A Wagner Matinee" and "Car Crash While Hitchhiking")

I listened to their stories [Australian prisoners of war interviewed on the radio] four or five years before I wrote The Great World. *A lot of what I put into the book, aside from details that I heard then, were things that I picked up from those men's voices. Imagination doesn't mean making things up; it means being able to understand things from the inside, emotions, events, and experiences that you haven't actually been through but that you will have experienced by the time you've got them onto the page.*

—David Malouf, *The Kenyon Review* interview

WAYS FOR WRITERS TO IDENTIFY THEIR OWN MATERIAL

A writer's material evolves over time: someone who begins with stories about her brother's hidden schizophrenia might, later on, write about other discrepancies between her characters' personas or public personalities and their inner lives. Another writer might set his first stories in Paris, Madrid, and Tokyo; it's not until he moves to the other side of the country that he can write stories that take place in his hometown.

When we talk about a writer's material, we usually mean the ideas, places, relationships, and situations that show up, in different forms, over the course of a writer's work. Each story, though, will have its own individual subject matter: its circumstances, location, and emotional and psychological explorations. A writer might write repeatedly about troubled romantic relationships and the struggles of artists (ongoing material). Over time, that writer might create one story about Botticelli burning his own paintings, and another about the efforts of a contemporary printmaker to extricate herself from her ongoing sexual relationship with her ex-husband (subject matter).

Subject matter can be murky ground—so much a part of the writer's private territory that we feel leery about questioning it. Outside the official meeting space, some members of a workshop agree that the subject matter—a job crisis in a Seattle airplane manufacturing facility—feels unconvincing or that the characters seem to have no lives or interests beyond themselves. But during the workshop, the group spends its discussion time on less risky questions of story tense or descriptive detail. We can't tell each other what to write, but we need to be able to raise questions about fundamental materials, our own and others.

Some writers luck into their material right away. Others may even publish several books before they feel that their fiction connects to their deepest preoccupations. Until then, their work can seem imitative or have a false shimmer, but no emotional depth. Still other writers run through their initial material after a number of stories and feel that their ability to write is now exhausted. One possible result is temporary writer's block. If possible, it's best to relax and let ourselves play with writing as we wait for our next subject(s) to emerge. This play can include wild experimentation in subject and form, as well as trying out subjects that interest us as readers, but that we've never written about.

When we're starting out, the most familiar subject matter may be our current experiences, which feel both urgent and authentic, like a recent blow-up with a roommate. Another common starting point is our own childhood. A third approach is to try writing about people and events we have no direct experience with, because our own lives strike us as tedious or not imaginative enough. We don't always notice the riches in our own sphere of attention: a job we had at a fast food restaurant, a set of wildly eccentric relatives, or a fascination with the worlds of quilting, salsa dancing, or football.

The more we write, the more we realize the dangers and strengths of any approach. Stories that come too directly from our lives sometimes strike readers as unshaped, anecdotal, and primarily of interest to those who were involved in the original events. The writer may still be too close to the events to make much sense of them or to be able to change "what really happened." Stories that focus on childhood may excessively limit the viewpoint character's awareness or vocabulary, seeming mannered or tiresome. Stories that come from worlds and times the writer has no experience with may feel inauthentic and off the mark. On the other hand, we can address any of these story problems in revision, through reshaping, restructuring, researching, and getting feedback. We need to be aware of the pitfalls, but to put aside that knowledge in our first drafts, to take the risk of writing messy, exploratory work.

Our native gifts can't function in a void. Our imagination needs the outside world: adventures; jobs and organizations; history, science, anthropology, and philosophy; plays, musical or dance performances; and travel—even if it's only attentive walks or visits to well-known local sights. (Television doesn't work as imaginative food; however good the show may be, as a source of "experience" it comes out oddly flattened on the page, producing clichés in plot, language, and character.)

Reading fiction also feeds the imagination. When we find the writers who are our literary family, they give us permission to write about what matters to us. Anne Tyler, in her essay "Still Just Writing," describes this moment of recognition:

> I spent my adolescence planning to be an artist, not a writer. After all, books had to be about major events, and none had ever happened to me. All I knew were tobacco workers, stringing the leaves I handed them and talking up a storm. Then I found a book of Eudora Welty's short stories in the high school library. She was writing about Edna Earle, who was so slow-witted she could sit all day just pondering how the tail of the *C* got through the loop of the *L* on the Coca-Cola sign. Why, I knew Edna Earle. You mean you could *write* about such people? I have always meant to send Eudora Welty a thank-you note, but I imagine she would find it a little strange.

Like Tyler, some of us may find our true subject matter close to home. If we moved a lot as a child or had a difficult relationship with stepsiblings, this kind of experience may show up either directly or indirectly: stories about moving or stories about rivalries in the workplace that draw on the dynamics of our stepfamily. Others of us may find our materials in history, biography, mythology, or invented worlds.

Repetition and Variation in a Writer's Material

Some writers spend most of their careers working with particular subject matters, whether in terms of the relationships and feelings or the characters' locations and circumstances. Reading a number of story collections or novels by the same author will show us how they do or do not avoid writing stories that feel like repeats of their other work. Lorrie Moore frequently writes about romantic relationships and the difficulties between men and women. What keeps this from feeling repetitious is the inventiveness of her language, and the way she looks for the uniqueness, rather than the ordinariness, of each situation. Peter Carey's novels tend to examine the damaging effects of one country's colonization of another, but the books vary wildly—the main characters of each book have distinct backgrounds (one is an outlaw, one is a priest's son, one is a theatrical performer . . .) and the place and time is different from story to story (nineteenth-century England, a futuristic fictional country, the Australian outback).

Amy Tan writes often about different aspects of the struggle between mothers and daughters, the misunderstandings between first-generation immigrants to the United States and their American children, ambition, and terrible losses. Her strength in creating individual characters gives her the ability to provide a sense of meaning and context. In her story "Two Kinds," the ostensible subject matter is a young girl's resistance to her mother's attempts to turn her into a piano prodigy. Tan enlarges the story by means of the background information she includes early in the story:

> America was where all my mother's hopes lay. She had come here in 1949 after losing everything in China: her mother and father, her family home, her first husband, and two daughters, twin baby girls. But she never looked back with regret. There were so many ways for things to get better.

Tan shows us not only the hopefulness but also the extreme poverty of the family—they get their haircuts from a student at a beauty training school, and the mother trades housecleaning services for piano lessons from a deaf piano teacher. The mother's desperation to turn her daughter into a prodigy gains weight in the face of these complications, and the daughter's resistance is heartbreaking as well as understandable. When we're working on our own stories, we can look for similar opportunities to provide context that enlarges a story beyond the simple chronicling of emotion. Maybe what we need is a paragraph of background that provides a sense of who these people are and what their history has been. Or perhaps we need some concrete sense of their societal context, the life going on all around the characters and the ways it influences both the characters and the action of the story.

In "Two Kinds," we see that the mother hopes for a better life for her child, even as we see that the child experiences her mother's attempts as an invasion of individuality. It would be simplistic to refer to this dynamic as simply an example of "the generation gap." It touches on the generation gap (applicable to all cultures everywhere), it touches on issues of cultural assimilation (issues immigrants struggle with everywhere), but it also derives from a particular, urgent family history.

The context isn't just dutifully pasted in to instruct us. Tan incorporates it into the drama later on when the daughter finally bursts out:

> "Then I wish I wasn't your daughter. I wish you weren't my mother," I shouted. As I said these things I got scared. I felt like worms and toads and slimy things were crawling out of my chest, but it also felt good, as if this awful side of me had surfaced, at last.
>
> "Too late to change this," said my mother shrilly.
>
> And I could sense her anger rising to its breaking point. I wanted to see it spill over. And that's when I remembered the babies she had lost in China, the ones we never talked about. "Then I wish I'd never been born!" I shouted. "I wish I were dead! Like them."

Our own characters may not have such dramatic pasts, but a key event in the characters' history, even if it is less tragic, can still help provide a story with a larger context, incorporated into the action or dialogue of the story.

As long as we keep pushing toward the deep originality and uniqueness of each character in each situation, we needn't be afraid of coming back to the same subject matter when we're not through with it. Only we know when we've started to go stale and need to move on. All that our helpful critics can tell us is whether or not we're continuing to expand and deepen our approach.

The Difference Between a Subject and a "Theme"

The themes we learned about in high school were something like "the child's need to establish her independence" or "the plight of the family farm." If we're writing an essay about a work of fiction we've read, we would probably be able to name its theme in an arguable thesis sentence: "Toni Morrison's *Song of Solomon,* a contemporary *bildungsroman,* delineates the construction of liminal narratives that revivify Homi Bhabha's 'primordial polarities.' " It may be true, partly true, or totally absurd, but its reductiveness is almost invariably annoying to the work's author; a story is far more than a dressed-up central idea.

Since we often learn about theme in literature classes, we may attempt to work backwards from theme, as if the story were a kind of code for what we really mean. Some writers do make successful stories by beginning with a central idea and then fleshing it out. But even they develop their ideas in an experiential way, rather than making their fiction illustrate some moral or maxim.

Milan Kundera, talking about *The Unbearable Lightness of Being* in his essay "Dialogue on the Art of the Novel," gives a sense of the role ideas can play in the writing process:

> What lies beyond the so-called psychological novel? Or, put another way: What is the nonpsychological means to apprehend the self? To apprehend the self in my novels means to grasp the essence of its existential problem. To grasp its *existential code.* As I was writing *The Unbearable Lightness of Being,* I realized that the code of this or that character is made up of certain key words. For Tereza: body, soul, vertigo, weakness, idyll, Paradise. For Tomas: lightness, weight. In the part called "Words Misunderstood," I examine the existential codes of Franz and Sabina by analyzing a number of words: woman, fidelity, betrayal, music, darkness, light, parades, beauty, country, cemetery, strength. Each of these words has a different meaning in the other person's existential code. Of course, the existential code is not examined *in abstracto;* it reveals itself progressively in the action, in the situations.

The concerns Kundera names above are part of his material; he combines and analyzes them with a fiercely intelligent energy, so that the framework of his fiction can be said to be as much philosophical as dramatic or psychological.

Psychological and Situational Subject Matters

When someone asks us what a story is about, we often describe the character(s) and the main action: "It's about a middle-aged woman who runs away from her family" or "it's about a family of pig farmers who inherit a castle in

Ireland." These descriptions don't actually address the story's deeper subject matter. We divide subject matter into two main elements. The first is the situational subject matter, the circumstances of the story: an artists' colony in a San Francisco warehouse; a small family farm in Nebraska; or a high school in New York in the 1960s. Situational subject matter includes the setting, the historical moment of the events, the social and cultural conditions of that moment, and the particular social structure of the group in the story.

The second kind of subject matter is the psychological material, the human drama: mothers who aren't there for their children, love triangles, or the difficulty of understanding the world by scientific means. A story about a middle-aged woman who runs away might be about a struggle between duty and pleasure, for example, or it might be about the discovery of mortality. The story of the pig farmers might be a satire on class, if the local gentry rejects the family; or of the effects of greed, if the family begins to quarrel over their new riches. It could be a study of the differences between desire and reality. A dozen different possibilities are available for each of these premises. This is the true "aboutness" of the story, and it arises from the story's situational materials, rather than being imposed on them.

We can see this difference between situational and psychological subject matters by thinking about the ways directors set productions of various Shakespeare plays in different time periods and locations. Despite the alterations in costumes, settings, and political structures, the basic human drama, the psychological material, remains the same. *Hamlet* set in 1920s Chicago is still recognizably *Hamlet,* even if the father becomes a mob boss—Hamlet's mentor—and the uncle becomes a rival who has murdered the boss and taken over his woman.

Part of what gives a story its power occurs in the overlap between the two kinds of subject matter: the situation provokes feelings and actions. *Hamlet* can easily be set among a group of gangsters because it's a life-and-death story about affiliation, loyalty, power, indecision, and betrayal. We can imagine rival gangs ready to move in as the characters we're watching destroy themselves and each other. On the other hand, *Hamlet* would likely lose its characteristic power if it were set among the members of a garden club preparing for a big floral exhibition. The tension between the size of the psychological drama and the cheerful coziness of the situation is so incongruous as to become comical.

Even when there's a match between the size of the psychological issues and the setting, the situation changes the psychology and actions, as we can see from examining the opening paragraph of Reginald McKnight's story "The Kind of Light That Shines on Texas":

> I never liked Marvin Pruitt. Never liked him, never knew him, even though there were only three of us in the class. Three black kids. In our school there were fourteen classrooms of thirty-odd white kids (in '66, they considered Chicanos provisionally white) and three or four black kids. Primary school in primary col-

> ors. Neat division. Alphabetized. They didn't stick us in the back, or arrange us by degrees of hue, apartheidlike. This was real integration, a ten-to-one ratio as tidy as upper-class landscaping. If it all worked, you could have ten white kids all to yourself. They could talk to you, get the feel of you, scrutinize you bone deep if they wanted to. They seldom wanted to, and that was fine with me for two reasons. The first was that their scrutiny was irritating. How do you comb your hair—why do you comb your hair—may I please touch your hair—were the kinds of questions they asked. This is no way to feel at home. The second reason was Marvin. He embarrassed me. He smelled bad, was at least two grades behind, was hostile, dark skinned, homely, close-mouthed. I feared him for his size, pitied him for his dress, watched him all the time. Marveled at him, mystified, astonished, uneasy.

The situational material places us in a mixed-race Texas classroom in the 1960s. The psychological material consists of cowardice, bravery, betrayal, and internalized racism. The situational material shapes the psychological—in the classroom setting, the racism is extremely open, and the children are vulnerable, just beginning to face the implications of the prejudices that surround them. As an experiment, we could imagine the psychological material playing out with different situational materials—for instance, a contemporary advertising agency with only three employees who are black, giving rise to an entirely different set of dynamics.

The beginning of the story expresses the distance between the narrator and one of his fellow black classmates, and his discomfort, shown by direct statement ("I never liked Marvin Pruitt") and in the details of the ways he observes Marvin. We could describe the central idea in this way: "The children's marginalization damages their ability to accept themselves and each other." The drama arises from the story's circumstances and setting, rather than being somehow located there by accident.

STORY ANALYSIS AND QUESTIONS: "A WAGNER MATINEE"

(Note: please read the story once before *you read the following analysis. Then, after you read the analysis, look at the story a second time, keeping the discussion questions in mind. You will get the most benefit out of this process if you mark specific passages in the story, take notes, and work through the questions in writing.)*

The subject matter of Willa Cather's "A Wagner Matinee" may seem unpromising: a man's old aunt comes to visit him in the city; they watch a performance together; he observes her as she experiences the music. The situational subject matter of this story is not inherently dramatic, and neither are the events. But because Cather has a strong connection to her material and the people she writes about, she makes us understand their entire lives through this one afternoon. The situational subject matter is mundane, but the psychological subject matter is dramatic.

The power of the story depends very much on our knowledge of the rest of the characters' lives. The man was a boy in the countryside, and the aunt who raised him loved music, but her marriage and her life have been too plain and hard to feed her artistic side. The tragedy here comes from a type of dutiful self-sacrifice no longer part of most people's ethos or current experience. For us, the story serves as a window into the values and assumptions of another time.

Cather uses specific details to make vivid for us the depth of the aunt's loss. The image of hands recurs throughout, beginning with the second paragraph when a letter from his aunt brings back the narrator's childhood:

> I felt suddenly a stranger to all the present conditions of my existence, wholly ill at ease and out of place amid the familiar surroundings of my study. I became, in short, the gangling farm boy my aunt had known, scourged with chilblains and bashfulness, my hands cracked and sore from the corn husking. I felt the knuckles of my thumb tentatively, as though they were raw again. I sat again before her parlor organ, fumbling the scales with my stiff, red hands, while she, beside me, made canvas mittens for the huskers.

Later on, the aunt touches the narrator's sleeve at the concert's start and then twists her fingers in her lap:

> . . . her fingers worked mechanically upon her black dress, as though, of themselves, they were recalling the piano score they had once played. Poor old hands! They had been stretched and twisted into mere tentacles to hold and lift and knead with; the palms unduly swollen, the fingers bent and knotted—on one of them a thin, worn band that had once been a wedding ring. As I pressed and gently quieted one of those groping hands I remembered with quivering eyelids their services for me in other days.

The hands serve as an objective correlative for everything she's given up. They have been transformed from instruments for producing beauty to tools of simple utility (elsewhere in the story her cuticles are described as resembling "a sort of flexible leather," enhancing our sense of their mechanical nature). The state of her hands shows that this transformation has become permanent over time. For the narrator, who was able to leave farm life young, the damage was reversible—his hands are no longer raw. The contrast between the nephew's and the aunt's situations also makes the story more poignant.

DISCUSSION QUESTIONS

1. What details show us the complexities of the aunt's character? What kinds of emotions do you think Cather wants us to feel about her? Which passages create these effects and how do they do it?

2. What would you say is the theme of the story? The subject matter? What is the psychological subject matter and what is the situational subject matter? How do they intersect?
3. Would you say this is a sentimental story? If so, what lines or details make it seem sentimental? If not, what prevents it from being sentimental?
4. Does Cather enlarge the story's context beyond one woman and the consequences of her decision? If not, what limits the story? If so, how does she do it?

TAKING RISKS WITH SUBJECT MATTER

We think of "risky" subject matter as that which might offend some readers: outrageous sexual situations, religious blasphemy, vividly described bodily fluids appearing at unfortunate times and places, or unfashionable politics. But almost any subject matter contains risks. Readers can find certain subjects to be mundane, cliché, sentimental, melodramatic, or unbelievable. Some instructors or classes try to offer rules that prevent this: no stories from the POV of animals or inanimate objects; no love stories; no divorces or breakups; no dying family members; no roommate stories; no alcoholism, drugs, or abuse; and no vampires or aliens. And perhaps it's true that beginning writers would do well to avoid these subjects, if they can. But for any rule we make, we can come up with brilliant examples of how that subject has been handled so well as to become surprisingly touching or thought-provoking.

The key in choosing any kind of subject matter is to follow our *own* interests, the pricklings of the imagination, rather than an idea about what someone else might find interesting, acceptable, or shocking. People are always telling each other what to write about and how to do it, which is a little like instructing someone who to fall in love with. Some writers, anxious for approval or success, may listen to the voices from outside, or to their ideas of what the marketplace might want, and so go astray. To resist this requires a continual setting aside of worldly goals. Only then do we wind up making the kind of writing that readers become passionate about (better to have even a few passionate readers than many indifferent readers). We can't trick ourselves into this freedom by pretending not to care; we have to genuinely give ourselves
to write anything at all. It can help to imagine, whi
will ever see the story, or at least will never see it in
The following four sections look at examples of
matter, their likely pitfalls, and some possible soluti

Ordinary Subject Matter: Beyond the Trivial

Some writers' true material is naturally dramatic. They write honestly and movingly about the death of a child, or resistance and endurance in the face of a repressive political régime, or a life of such aching poverty that it threatens to destroy a family. Other writers may feel their life experiences haven't furnished them with the right raw material; if they try to write stories based on events that happened to other people, just because they seem more dramatic or more like the stories they read in anthologies, the writing is apt to have an artificial feeling. They may try to write about parents losing a child in a car accident and find the story lifeless, the emotions remote. This is another time to resist the impulses that would seem to make a story more publishable, and instead to persist in discovering our own interests, following them until they become so clear and vivid that they find their audience. The question is how ordinary events, if those are what we want to write about, can reveal their inherent interest.

Suppose we find ourselves writing about a birthday party at which a child doesn't get the present he longed for. The risk we run with the subject matter is that we (or the reader) may feel either that the child is spoiled or that this is an ordinary moment that doesn't need memorializing in a short story. But perhaps the boy's disappointment is subtly related to a more consequential failure—the father's inability to keep a job or the town's losing bid to become the site of a large factory that would have pumped money into a weak economy. The emotions of disappointment are no longer the focus of the story, but a vehicle for conveying larger concerns. As beginning writers, we may have sharpened our skills in expressing emotion with vivid sensory details. At the intermediate stage, we're able to see how these emotions can serve as one of several elements in a story, allowing us to create complicated fiction that reveals people's lives.

Gina Berriault's story "The Birthday Party" charges the ordinary with significance. The story concerns a boy whose mother has just returned from staying away all night, having said she wouldn't come back. He is not the guest of honor at the party, but an acquaintance. Still, the party is a chance to lay claim to his mother's attention, to help him in negotiating ordinary life, which has become terrible and uncertain:

> "Who's going to take me to Molly's party?"
>
> "I'll take you," she said. "Grandma's going early, and it's out of her way to pick you up anyway. But, my God, it's not until two.
>
> "We've got to buy a present," he said, afraid that nothing would be attended to from now on, that everything would be neglected; using the party to urge her to look after him again, to distract him again, and engage him again.

The narrator gives us the "aboutness" of the story very explicitly here. We see the boy's anxiety expressed in his nagging of his mother, and his panic described. We see her chafing at his fear—in the next paragraph she calls him "the champion anxiety hound." If the whole story had this level of direct information, it would be too abstract, but Berriault reinforces the mood and brings it to life through the details she uses, like her description of the birthday girl opening her presents:

> Molly, under her canopy, lifted the presents one by one up from the ribbons and rustling papers. Each time she swung to the side to take a present from a cart, or clapped her hands, her long hair bounced against her back. The children nearest her, himself among them, fingered the gifts piling up before her—a long bow and a leather quiver of arrows; a small doll with a bald head and three wigs, dyed red and yellow and black, each like a puff of cocoon silk; a lifelike poodle dog of dark gray wool; a white petticoat with blue ribbons intertwined in it, for which she kissed her grandmother, whose restless hands rested for that moment on the wrapping papers she was folding. The transistor radio she turned on at once, and the tiny, crackling voices of the singers went on and on under the tissue paper and other presents.

Using a range of sensory details, this scene creates simultaneous feelings of abundance and uneasiness. All the presents are reasonable ones, and yet there is something subtly off about many of them: the antiquated weapons; the bald doll, suggesting illness and yet possessing luxurious wigs; the dog which is lifelike but not alive; the strange little voices muffled by the paper and presents. The ordinariness of the petticoat keeps the oddness of the other details from being too marked. Molly has piles of presents, even from children not at the party, and the narrator tells us, "There was such a profusion of gifts that it seemed to him the reason for the party was more than that the day was her birthday. The party, he felt, was to take care of any crying to come." This story is about the terrible vulnerability we can experience through our need for others; a birthday party (the ultimate celebration of an individual life) is a suitable, ironic situation.

The decision about how much of the psychological subject matter of the story can be explicit will depend very much on the intentions, skill, and style of the writer. In Berriault's story, the outright statements might be too much without the sensory details, and the details might be too overwhelming or too hard to "read" without some commentary that lets us understand the nature of the potential disaster we fear.

Some of the stories in the anthology that handle "everyday" material in a way that shows its possibilities and strength include "Di Grasso: A Tale of Odessa," "The Cures for Love," "A Wagner Matinee," "The Turkey Season," and "Drinking Coffee Elsewhere."

Dramatic Subject Matter: Power vs. Sentiment

Highly dramatic subjects include mortal illness, death, accidents, war, revolutions, violence, and shocking betrayals. If the story's intent is to provoke either tears or happy sighs from the reader, then it risks becoming sentimental or maudlin. Often what works best is to complicate the subject, not to look for the expected or typical image or psychological reaction but for something more intricate and individual. This means engaging readers' minds, as well as their emotions. It may mean finding an edge of humor or it may mean observing characters' actions, dialogue, and thoughts so exactly that the emphasis is on the readers' understanding rather than on the grief or horror.

By taking a complicated approach, the writer seems to be saying, "Look how human beings feel and behave under these extreme circumstances," not "Did you ever see anything more disgusting/awful?" When we read or write about overtly dramatic subjects, we're trying to understand what human beings go through, to make sense of our own past tragedies, or to expand our awareness of other people's lives. In order to be true to our job of representing and making sense of the world, sometimes we have to figure out how to face those parts of life we wish didn't exist. Facing mortality is different from wallowing in the pornography of gossip or the narcissistic thrill of imagining ourselves the victims of terrible circumstances.

The narrator of Alice Munro's "Miles City, Montana" undergoes the horror of having her three-and-a-half-year-old daughter nearly drown in a swimming pool. She realizes the children are gone, runs for the pool, understands that the lifeguard is taken up with her boyfriend, calls out to her six-year-old at the edge of the pool, sees the "cluster of pink ruffles" in the water, then sees her husband climbing the fence, and finally runs through the corridors to the pool and her rescued child, all in three pages of closely observed detail that render the shock, surreal clarity, and helpless rage of a crisis moment. The narrator's mental state shows both in the collection of details and the careful observation of emotions, as when she calls to her older daughter, Cynthia:

> "Cynthia!" I had to call twice before she knew where my voice was coming from. "Cynthia! Where's Meg?"
>
> It always seems to me, when I recall this scene, that Cynthia turns very gracefully toward me, then turns all around in the water—making me think of a ballerina on point—and spreads her arms in a gesture of the stage. "Dis-ap-peared!"
>
> Cynthia was naturally graceful, and she did take dancing lessons, so these movements may have been as I described. She did say "Disappeared" after looking all around the pool, but the strangely artificial style of speech and gesture, the lack of urgency, is more likely my invention. The fear I felt instantly when I couldn't see Meg—even while I was telling myself she must be in the shallow water—must have made Cynthia's movements seem unbearably slow and inappropriate to me, and the tone in which she could say "Disappeared" before the implications struck her (or was she covering, at once, some ever-ready guilt?) was heard by me as quite exquisitely, monstrously self-possessed.

Later, the narrator does imagine what might have happened, in detail, from shipping the coffin to taking sedatives to imagining how she and her husband would have reproached themselves. This horrified rehearsing of what might have happened is probably inevitable, but she has the self-awareness to have complicated feelings even about this: "There's something trashy about this kind of imagining, isn't there? Something shameful. Laying your finger on the wire to get the safe shock, feeling a bit of what it's like, then pulling back."

There are other ways to acknowledge the dangers of writing about this kind of material; maybe the narrator is not self-aware, but the story makes it clear that the author is. Maybe some element of humor or the peculiar allows the material to be dramatic without being self-dramatizing.

Some of the stories in the anthology that successfully handle highly dramatic material include "Civil Peace," "The Forest," "The Eve of the Spirit Festival," "Graffiti," "Trauma Plate," "Car Crash While Hitchhiking," "The Niece," "Pilgrims," and "Photograph of Luisa." "The Fence Party" and "Powder" have potentially highly dramatic events that result primarily in emotional changes, rather than tragic consequences.

Transgressive Subject Matter: Crossing Boundaries

Transgressive fiction takes on subjects its society considers taboo. In 1899, Kate Chopin's *Awakening* was transgressive. The novel is about an artist who loves her children but is so stifled by domesticity and the failures of love that she walks into the sea. At the time, the book aroused tremendous controversy: it challenged a Victorian ideal in which women are primarily designed for motherhood and service. It showed a sympathetic character, not a monster but someone disastrously ill-suited to the only roles available to her; she wanted a life in which she could have both love and work. The book raised an unpleasant awareness of topics and ideas that no one wanted to face at the time.

Transgression has to do not just with the subject the writer chooses but with the attitude toward the subject or the arrangement of the facts. If the author seems to be condemning the character for defying conventions, then the fiction can't be considered transgressive. In Tolstoy's great *Anna Karenina,* Anna's death under a train seems like the natural consequence of the adultery and willfulness that excluded her from her society.

Adultery and women's desire for freedom are no longer taboo in today's mainstream society. Actually, very few things are taboo anymore. As a result, transgressive fiction has moved to the extreme edges of imaginable human ideas and behavior. Kevin Canty's "Pretty Judy" is the story of an adolescent boy who begins an obsessive sexual affair with a retarded neighbor. Kathy Acker's *Don Quixote,* a thought-provoking book, sometimes wonderfully readable and sometimes repulsing, is the story of a masochistic woman named Don Quixote who goes on a polyamorous quest for love. The texts within the text include dreams, poetry—in English and Latin, "Texts of War for Those who Live in Silence," and scraps of newspaper clippings. The book has abortion, a brothel in which Don Quixote loves the madam who beats her, political rants, sudden changes in form, and conversations between Don Quixote and her dog, as well as between Nixon and the Angel of Death. A selection of Nixon's rant gives an idea of one approach to the contemporary transgressive:

> "I'll tell you about this country. That is I'll tell you why I support nuclear weaponry. I, Richard Nixon, support nuclear weaponry because. This cunt

> stinks. No wonder I have to work with the Mafia. Bitches never get enough. . . . America is now a piece of diarrhea, no, of wormy shit in the flux and flow of the music of the Third World. Rape America the Cunt! (I do. Yay.) Give her revomited puke to drink so that you, even you, can see with your very own eyes that she doesn't know the difference between one kind of puke and another. America: our land of liberty. What is liberty?" Nixon pulled its wad of bills out of its pocket.

If we're pulled to try writing at the extreme edges, we need to examine our own motives. Alienating straitlaced readers is only a side effect of transgressive fiction, not the main point. What gives strong transgressive fiction its sense of meaning is a feeling of *what* is being transgressed against and why. *Don Quixote* is, among other things, a philosophical work about gender, violence, the nature of love, and the ways texts influence our lives. It offers a Hobbesian view of reality and a mirror of political life, in which the shock exists not for its own sake but to break open our received views of reality and to make us enter into radical ways of thinking. Here, as in any other kind of fiction, the lecture hall can get old quickly: if we, as writers, think we're far more interesting and radical than our readers, or that we need to educate them, our fiction will annoy readers rather than encouraging them to enter with us into a difficult journey. The transgressive isn't as shocking to the literate world as it once was. Mainstream publications praise Acker highly—Tom LeClair's *New York Times* review said, "Scarified sensibility, subversive intellect, and predatory wit make her a writer like no other I know," and *Esquire* wrote, "The best of punk writers, she has an unmistakable voice that's brash, feisty, sexy, and smart."

Many stories do transgress, at least somewhat, in one way or another, against current conventions. Stories in the anthology that contain particularly transgressive images and elements include "Car Crash While Hitchhiking" and "Trauma Plate."

Nonrealistic Subject Matter: The Literary Fantastic

Realist fiction works to create an illusion that the events being chronicled could very likely have happened in the world as we know it. The rules of physics apply just as they do in reality—if the character throws a baseball high in the air, it will come down. Depending on the era and the cultural background, different readers will have different opinions about what is realistic. Most of our ideas about realism come originally from the nineteenth century: *Middlemarch, Madame Bovary, War and Peace,* and Chekhov's stories. In general conversation, we describe a realist story as one that tends to follow a linear pattern, with logical events, reasonable motives—whether explained or not—and details of daily life. Realism can be defined most of all by what it does not include: ghosts or supernatural beings, magic, enormous coincidences, unexplained leaps in time and space, or other worlds.

An "experimental" story, in contrast, may be challenging and unexpected in language and format—written all in verbs or without any verbs, so condensed as to be almost poetry, divided into segments or made into a one-of-a-kind singular form—and yet fairly realistic in subject matter. It may be a wildly interesting take on a failing marriage or a misunderstanding between mother and daughter, and the language and form give us new insight into these familiar situations.

Sometimes the subject matter itself leaves the bounds of what we commonly agree is plausible in daily life. Among the nonrealistic approaches described in the glossary, the following approaches tend to subvert standard conventions about subject matter: absurdism; the dreamlike/surreal; metafiction; fantasy; science fiction; and magical realism. Some stories combine approaches.

Still another nonrealistic approach is to revise some form of literary tradition—fairy tales, biblical stories, myths, or even canonical literary works. Writers may change the source text until it is almost unrecognizable, or else play very explicitly with, or against, the original. Successful stories in this vein usually combine the situational material of the old stories with a new or reconsidered psychological subject matter. John Barth's *Chimera* is a three-part reflection on the stories we tell ourselves and each other. The characters of Dunyazade (Scheherazade's little sister), a middle-aged Perseus, and Bellerophon each show a different facet of the relationship between myth and reality. All three are aware of their mythological roles, as when Bellerophon, the tamer of Pegasus, learns all the elements of the Hero's Story, constantly checking himself against the mythic heroes of the past. As he says, "By imitating perfectly the Pattern of Mythic Heroism, I'd become, not a mythic hero, but a perfect Reset. . . ." The book is a metafictional commentary on mythology itself and on our mythologizing of our own lives.

Tanith Lee's "When the Clock Strikes" gives us a Cinderella (unnamed, but we recognize her through subverted traditional details) who has become a powerful witch practicing dark magic, luring the prince as a way of revenging herself against his family. By using a story we know well and turning it on its head, Lee challenges our assumptions about the perfect heroine.

The reworking of plot lines, characters, and situations from earlier literary works, mythology, fables, fairy stories, and wisdom tales is not a recent invention. Shakespeare, one of the most famous reworkers, drew very directly on traditions and on the work of others, but his borrowings are far more naked and direct than we consider allowable today. These days, when writers are careful about each other's intellectual property rights, we refrain from working with characters or plots not in the public domain. And, even then, writers like Peter Carey in *Jack Maggs* or Kathy Acker in *Don Quixote* don't merely reuse another writer's material; they transform and acknowledge well-known characters so that the origin of the material is clear. The new work becomes a conversation with the old work, with the reader as a silent participant. The cheerful piracy of some online communities doesn't translate to the realm of substantive fiction, where such liberty would be not only legally dubious but an invasion of a writer's right to his or her own imaginative world.

One of the thorniest problems in writing nonrealistic fiction is how to avoid making the stories seem arbitrary. If anything can happen, then why would any of it matter? The nonrealistic stories that work best tend to refer back to or comment on the reality we know, exaggerating certain aspects of life while still providing a sense that there's some kind of logic at work. The strangeness of the situational subject matter provides a vehicle for the psychological subject matter, rather than displacing it.

Vivid sensory details are key to drawing the reader in. For instance, Franz Kafka's dreamlike story "The Metamorphosis" backs up its famous first line with concrete imagery:

> As Gregor Samsa awoke one morning from uneasy dreams he found himself transformed in his bed into a gigantic insect. He was lying on his hard, as it were armor-plated, back and when he lifted his head a little he could see his domelike brown belly divided into stiff arched segments on top of which the bed quilt could hardly keep in position and was about to slide off completely. His numerous legs, which were pitifully thin compared to the rest of his bulk, waved helplessly before his eyes.

The "domelike brown belly divided into stiff arched segments" helps the reader clearly imagine the creature Samsa has become. That the bed quilt is about to slide off is a wonderful grace note: when we're describing unreal occurrences, we can use details of this kind of domestic ordinariness, placed next to the fantastic, to make everything more convincing. Within the next few pages we learn that Samsa is a traveling salesman who hates traveling and is always afraid of being fired. That he's turned into an insect doesn't seem so strange after all, given his scuttling, fearful personality. If Samsa had awakened to find himself transformed into a box of facial tissue, the scenario would have been just as strange, but not particularly moving.

Even the anarchic impulses of absurdist fiction aren't pointless. By thumbing their noses at rationality, absurdist writers critique systems that try to enforce one point of view. In Stalin's repressive regime in Russia, absurdist writers were arrested for their fiction and poetry because they supposedly distracted the people from the cause of building socialism. One of those writers, Daniil Kharms, wrote stories that captured the senselessness of the violence and totalitarianism during and after the Russian Revolution. Often his stories had a satirical edge, as in the beginning of "Rebellion":

> —Drink vinegar, gentlemen—said Shuyev.
>
> No one gave him any reply.
>
> —Gentlemen!—shouted Shuyev—I propose to you the drinking of vinegar!
>
> Makronov got up from his armchair and said:—I welcome Shuyev's idea. Let's drink vinegar.
>
> Rastopyakin said:—I shall not be drinking vinegar.

> At this point a silence set in and everyone began to look at Shuyev. Shuyev sat stony-faced. It was not clear what he was thinking.

The seriousness with which everyone considers drinking vinegar isn't psychologically realistic on the surface, but in the context of a government that demands everyone toe the line it becomes a sharp commentary.

Magical realism is set in a recognizably ordinary world, in which fantastic events are treated nonchalantly, as if part of everyday life. In Thaisa Frank's story "A Brief History of Camouflage," a woman begins sewing clothes for herself that match the living room armchair in color and pattern. When she sits in the chair dressed like this, her husband can't see her:

> She felt vaguely guilty about what she'd done, but she was curious about what he was like when he was alone. So she began to wear the matching outfit and sit in the chair without telling him. She discovered that his private face was sad and his eyes seemed more transparent. Usually he read, but sometimes he spoke out loud, saying things like: What? or: I didn't want to do that. Once he delivered an angry monologue about a bar of soap she'd allowed to disintegrate in the sink. I can't live this way, he said. You never do what I ask. She decided she would try to be more careful.

This story of a woman who gradually disappears from her husband's life in order to observe him becomes chilling. The husband's monologue about the bar of soap, as trivial as it seems, grounds the story in familiar reality and tells us something about the state of their relationship. The story is ultimately less about a clever ability to camouflage oneself in a house than it is about the distance that can grow in marriage, about the strangeness of living in houses full of inanimate objects, and about the tradeoff between observation and experience.

This is the paradox of nonrealistic fiction: to be memorable, it needs to have something to do with the real struggles of life, and yet it also needs to accurately convey the strangeness of living in the world. Nonrealistic fiction is one way of putting us in touch with the uncomfortable truth that life is not, ultimately, as rational as we like to think it is. When we're experimenting with writing in nonrealistic ways, we can put down anything we imagine: it would be too inhibiting and artificial to try to figure out what it all means in the first draft. In revision, we begin to understand the story and to bring the elements together. But even in a rough draft, if our intention is to keep *telling the truth,* no matter how absurd or fantastic it may be, we increase the odds of making meaningful fiction.

In the anthology, stories that could be considered to have elements of the literary fantastic include "Inferno I, 32," "The Cures for Love," "The Eve of the Spirit Festival," "Trauma Plate," "Father," and "Orientation."

STORY ANALYSIS AND QUESTIONS: "CAR CRASH WHILE HITCHHIKING"

(Note: please read the story once before *you read the following analysis. Then, after you read the analysis, look at the story a second time, keeping the discussion questions in mind. You will get the most benefit out of this process if you mark specific passages in the story, take notes, and work through the questions in writing.)*

"Car Crash While Hitchhiking" is a story that is at once realistic—car crashes are all too common—and fantastic in its language, images, unexpected emotions, perceptions, and time sense. The highly dramatic situational subject matter includes stormy weather, a dark night, a fatal car accident, and drugs. What lifts the story beyond sensationalism is the way in which Johnson handles its psychological subject matter, which has to do with mortality, the desire to seek out intense experiences, the evasion of responsibility that comes with such experiences, and the difficulty of knowing what is real. Because we know that the narrator has taken amphetamines, bourbon, and hashish, we have an explanation for the more fantastic details. We believe that he perceives everything he reports, but we don't know what an "objective" observer would see. The narrator has a tortured relationship with reality that is far more complicated than mere thrill-seeking, and his responses are never what we might have expected. We see this as he observes a dying man:

> The man hanging out of the wrecked car was still alive as I passed, and I stopped, grown a little more used to the idea now of how really badly broken he was, and made sure there was nothing I could do. He was snoring loudly and rudely. His blood bubbled out of his mouth with every breath. He wouldn't be taking many more. I knew that, but he didn't, and therefore I looked down into the great pity of a person's life on this earth. I don't mean that we all end up dead, that's not the great pity. I mean that he couldn't tell me what he was dreaming, and I couldn't tell him what was real.

The narrator isn't feeling the expected emotions. Instead, he has a complicated, original set of thoughts and feelings that can't be reduced to simple platitudes. On the one hand, he is looking to see if there is anything he can do, and, on the other, he thinks of "the great pity of a person's life on this earth." We might expect him to feel pity—but this isn't the pity we were expecting. It isn't the imminent death of the man that troubles the narrator, but the ways in which they are unable to reach each other, and the elusiveness of reality.

DISCUSSION QUESTIONS

1. In which passages in the story does Johnson's narrator most explicitly address the story's psychological subject matter? Do these moments

seem heavy-handed? Why or why not? How would the story be different without these passages?

2. What specific details, events, thoughts, or lines of dialogue make the story seem realistic? Which make it fantastic?
3. How is the narrative constructed, and what moments work as the story's climaxes?
4. What role does the wife play, and how does this change over the course of the story? How does this relate to the psychological subject matter?
5. Johnson could have ended with "I've gone looking for that feeling everywhere." How would that have changed the story? What is the effect of the final scene?

REVISION: DISCOVERING THE STORY'S TRUE SUBJECT

Our own material may strike us as shameful—our preoccupation with drugs, our perverse sexuality, or our hatred of our younger brother. Or we may fear that our stories are trivial. What interests us, we think, cannot possibly interest anyone else. Who cares about our baseball games? Our sister's worries about not being beautiful? The time we lost the milk money? Is this a subject worth writing about?

Even a writer as assured as Willa Cather turned away from her own material in search of something more "exciting." In her afterword for Cather's *Troll Garden,* Katherine Anne Porter shows us how Cather realized that her passion was for the Midwest she knew so well, not the seemingly exotic world of London:

> The scene, London, was strange and delightful to her; she was trying to make a novel out of some interesting people in what seemed to her exotic situations, instead of out of something she really knew about with more than the top of her mind. "London is supposed to be more engaging than, let us say, Gopher Prairie," she remarks, "even if the writer knows Gopher Prairie very well and London very casually."
>
> She realized at once that *Alexander's Bridge* was a mistake, her wrong turning, which could not be retraced too instantly and entirely. It was a very pretty success, and could have been her finish, except that she happened to be Willa Cather. For years she still found people who liked that book, but they couldn't fool her. She knew what she had done. So she left New York and went to Arizona for six months, not for repentance but for refreshment, and found there a source that was to refresh her for years to come.

When we talk about the true subject matter of a story, we're getting at what writers sometimes describe as "the heart of the story"—the hot spot where the writing turns electric. This is sometimes apparent to us, and usually to our good readers—though not necessarily to everyone who happens to pick up a story. Once we've written the story and set it aside for a week or two, we can see that what we thought it was about may only be the first step: the true psychological subject matter of the story emerged as we were working on it.

Suppose a story started for us with an imagined situation: the narrator has rented a room to a new roommate he has not yet met. The roommate has not shown up for a couple of weeks, and instead his former girlfriend gets the apartment's number and calls the narrator. As we're working on the story, it seems that the story will be about a love triangle, as an affair develops between the narrator and the woman. Through the course of various drafts, however, we may find it becomes more a story about absence, and the fear of being valued for arbitrary circumstances instead of for our unique selves. The first draft, or two, or four, may have strong traces of our original idea, so that the whole story seems muddled. Eventually, though, if we identify the hot spots, we begin to remove those details and episodes that still point to our first impulse, and clarify and strengthen the events and images that suit what the story has turned into. The hot spots—the areas where the story comes alive and is full of energy and interest—are likely to be those that fascinate us, that scare us, or that we don't want to explore. They may show characters behaving strangely or badly, trying to behave well and failing, or succeeding at something in a way that costs them or those around them more than it should.

Ways of identifying these hot spots include waiting a couple of weeks and rereading the story, reading it aloud to someone, and, most of all, giving it to a writing group or workshop. Not everyone will agree on the hot spots, but the discussion will reveal some of what we haven't seen about the story. We may feel, when someone suggests an element be taken out or changed, a reluctant agreement—we hoped we'd gotten away with that, but we secretly knew we hadn't. Or we may feel the loud, gut-level *NO* that lets us know this element, incident, or character is essential for us, and what we need to do is to find a way to make it essential for the reader as well. Sometimes this means getting rid of other sections or characters and rewriting, even expanding, the part that our readers didn't, at first, understand.

It's normal to be embarrassed by or uncomfortable about our subject matter—we cannot help revealing our essential concerns in our stories, no matter how far they are from being autobiographical. We have to be braver in writing than we ever imagined as beginners. Once workshop and, later, reviewers, hold us up to ourselves, we have to find the place in our minds that can take in criticism and responses and make use of them, still retaining a calm, humorous, firm sense of the legitimacy of our own work and impulses.

SUBJECT MATTER EXERCISES

1. Make a list of ten jobs or volunteer activities. These can be jobs you've held yourself, or that people close to you have held, if you've spent enough time in their workplace to know it well. Once you've made the list, choose some job that taught you *what it means to work for a living.* Now put your pen to the paper, and, without stopping to evaluate, write everything you can think of about this job. Where were you? What were you doing? What did the place look, sound, and smell like? What were the details of the tasks and duties you accomplished? What were the spoken and unspoken expectations that you had to meet? Who was there with you? What did they say or do? What were their tasks and duties? What incidents took place as part of this job? Give yourself at least a half an hour for the freewrite.

   When you're done, put your freewrite aside for an hour or a day. After you've established a little distance, you can think about ways of transforming this material into a story. What kinds of issues, conflicts, desires, or fears arose in this situation? Could some actual incident be the basis for a story? (A set of interactions that you observed is easier to have perspective on than one in which you were centrally involved.) Could you make up an incident to happen in the context of this job? The style of the story can be experimental, poetic, realistic, chronologically straightforward, or fragmented: you might try more than one approach before you find the one that feels right for this material.

2. Make a list of ten hobbies you've pursued, both the "official" kind of hobby, like stamp collecting, whale watching, or trading baseball cards, and the unofficial kinds of habits/hobbies. Think of where these activities take place. Comic book stores? Observatories? The broken tree root in the field behind the elementary school? Used car lots at midnight? Now choose one of your hobbies, and continue with a freewrite as in Exercise 1. When you come back to it, ask yourself, "What's exciting about this memory? What scares me? What am I ashamed of? Who behaved strangely or badly there?"

3. Each morning, as soon as you wake up, write down everything you can remember about the dreams you had the night before, no matter how fragmentary. After two weeks, go back through your entries and note where the dreams take place and what kinds of conflicts or problems they deal with. Are there issues that show up more than once? Are there issues you would never have thought of as subject matter for a story, but that seem pressing and urgent to your subconscious? Write a story that draws on the emotional content of a dream. The story need not be dreamlike at all—you may get more mileage by translating the conflict or issues to a realistic story.

4. Pick your favorite fairy story or wisdom tale. What most interests you about it? Try rewriting it, setting it in a different time and place, and making whatever changes in the characters' lives and thoughts seem to be required by the alteration. For inspiration, try reading Tanith Lee's "Cinderella," Robert Coover's *Pinocchio in Venice,* or Angela Carter's *Bloody Chamber and Other Stories,* which transforms, among others, the tales of Beauty and the Beast and Puss in Boots.
5. Pick a situation you have written about before and come back to it. You might look at your previous version of the story, but without letting yourself be limited by it. What kinds of fantastic events might happen in this situation, if anything at all were possible? How would these events be related to the circumstances they arose from? Take all the brakes off your imagination and see what develops.

CHAPTER

7

Macrosetting, Microsetting, and Detail

(Anthology selections: "The Fence Party" and "Pilgrims")

It is by the nature of itself that fiction is all bound up in the local. The internal reason for that is surely that feelings *are bound up in place. The human mind is a mass of associations—associations more poetic even than actual. I say, "The Yorkshire Moors," and you will say,* "Wuthering Heights"*. . . . The truth is, fiction depends for its life on place. Location is the crossroads of circumstance, the proving ground of "What happened? Who's here? Who's coming?"—and that is the heart's field. . . .*

Being shown how to locate, to place, any account is what does most toward making *us believe it, not merely allowing us to, may the account be the facts or a lie; and that is where place in fiction comes in. Fiction is a lie. Never in its inside thoughts, always in its outside dress.*

—Eudora Welty, "Place in Fiction," *The Eye of the Story*

RESEEING FAMILIAR SETTINGS

Eudora Welty reminds us that "*feelings* are bound up in place," but in our own lives we sometimes take these feelings for granted—we automatically avoid the third-floor lavatory because it's depressingly dark, we barely notice that we made an extra left turn to avoid driving past our ex-lover's house. When writing, however, we try to consciously tune in to these feelings in ourselves and others, taking note of what different landscapes mean to different people.

In our first drafts, much of the action may take place in the characters' minds or through dialogue. Even if we have a vague feeling that they're in the living room or a moving car, we tend not to observe these surroundings too closely. We're paying attention to the human interactions, as we do in life. To really, deeply, see our surroundings requires that we stop the constant, feverish planning, inventing, remembering, and worrying that for most people is the normal state of daily life. Instead, we have to let our eyes move very slowly over each birch tree, pile of books, fringed floor lamp, water fountain, or glassy high-rise, as slowly as if we were touching them instead of looking at them. What are the shapes of these objects? It can help to try to draw them, or to keep a writer's journal in which, day after day, we describe in detail something we have seen, heard, smelled, touched, and even tasted. The more senses the better; if we spend an entire page describing one thing, before we even begin to explore its history or associations, we will really come to know it. Of course, we're not going to put a two-page description of a fork into a short story, unless we're doing something highly experimental, but the practice can be valuable. Out of two pages of description of a fork—or a bedroom, café, or town hall—a single unexpected detail may emerge, one we might not have noticed if we'd hastily put down our first, obvious impression.

It also helps to think more closely about what we mean by setting, including the wider context in which a story takes place. For the purposes of discussion, we can divide setting into macrosetting, microsetting, and detail.

MACROSETTING, MICROSETTING, AND DETAIL

Macrosetting provides the context for a work of fiction, starting with the place and time: Medieval Rome, a farm community in South Dakota in the 1930s, contemporary San Francisco, or Bali in 1980. Macrosetting also includes all the elements that give a sense of the larger world of the story, including the historical, political, artistic, scientific, moral, biographical, or religious background, as well as indicators of characters' status, occupation, and class. Not all these aspects will be explicit or visible in every work of fiction, but the more of them the author is aware of, the more substantial the story will feel.

Microsetting is the immediate surroundings within which each scene takes place: the nave of a cathedral, the farm's front porch, the field behind the high school, or an outdoor market. In fiction, we need to know where events are happening at any given moment, to avoid the humming gray feeling of not really being anywhere, as if we had lost our sense of gravity and direction and were floating in a mist. A story without a strong sense of location is a kind of purgatory, very occasionally employed deliberately to good effect, but much more often stumbled into from a mistaken feeling that nowhere is more universal than somewhere.

Detail refers to the particular elements that collectively make up the setting. It includes all sensory information about the place, including smells, sounds, colors, textures, tastes, temperatures, objects, and weather. Descriptions of details is a big part of what makes the world of the story come alive. Although brilliant description won't substitute for strong, believable characters and a functioning story structure, without some sense of location and physicality, the story will feel flat and "made-up." Detail is to setting what gesture is to action—it's what makes the kitchen not just any kitchen, but the kitchen of a man who has hung fifteen copper pots along one wall, organized according to size, just above the signed photograph of Julia Child in a gilt frame.

Much of the work of understanding either macrosetting or microsetting takes place in revision: from revisiting settings, to library research, to thinking through the background, to imagining the furnishings. In the first draft, we're just getting down on paper as much of the people and story as we can. It's in subsequent drafts that we restructure, enrich, and develop what we're discovering.

ESSENTIAL AND ARBITRARY SETTINGS

If we're not in the habit of thinking about place, it may seem to us that all that really matters is the people and what they do, and that "setting" is set decoration, a little local color added to our story to give it a feeling of reality. In fact, a combination of our own overfamiliarity with the places we come from and the often homogenizing influence of television may keep us from realizing just how much a particular group of people are part of their own particular place, and how much that place influences the actions they take. A Cormac McCarthy rancher can't be dropped into Virginia Woolf's London without creating chaos. Some writers play against the disruption caused by moving people out of their natural environments, like T. C. Boyle in "I Dated Jane Austen." Before we turn to the first page, we may already be delighted by Boyle's cleverness and our own imaginings of the possible incongruities. For most stories, though, it makes sense to consider—without stereotyping—how times and places form our characters, and what kinds of stories occur in those times and places. An essential setting informs the plot and characters, instead of serving, arbitrarily, as background.

Beginners tend to leave out the setting or to use details that have nothing to do with the characters and story; this is understandable, when there's so much to wrestle with just to get any story down on paper. More advanced writers have to determine how to balance the necessity for detail with their own particular styles: how much setting is too little and how much is overkill for a particular writer or story?

Maximalist Settings

Maximalist settings, with an overflowing abundance of information and detail, can seem gratuitous and excessive or richly evocative. In our own writing, we can ask, why does the reader need to know this? What does it contribute to the story? How can we make the setting essential to the action and meaning of the story?

In the following excerpt from *Grand Ambition,* Lisa Michaels gives us a vivid description of a river, a boat, and the objects in that boat. Because Glen and Bessie are embarking on a dangerous rapid-running trip for their 1928 honeymoon, the river and boat serve almost as characters in the story: the river their antagonist, the boat their protector. Before the scene of their embarkation, we've already had a scene in Glen's father's point of view letting us know they've disappeared. We don't know what's happened to them, which gives every detail—of the river, the boat, and their possessions—drama or poignancy:

> [Bessie] sat on the bare box springs in the center of the boat, while Glen stood on a cross plank, working the long sweeps. They were plowing through a caramel river—thick, with a greasy sheen. It ran flat and smooth to the banks, which were bare and just high enough to block the views on either side. A deep ditch, really. A canal. Within it, the boat looked rather substantial: a flat-bottomed barge the size of a peddler's wagon, piled with supplies. A box stove, a .30-30 rifle, two cartons of bullets, crates of canned peaches and tomatoes and beans, rope and blankets. Bessie kept her things wrapped in oilskin: a box camera, twenty-seven dollars in a beaded purse—a sentimental object, frivolous for any occasion ahead—pencils, charcoal, a sketchbook, and blank diary.

The river has a dangerous, almost snakelike quality, "greasy," something you wouldn't want to fall into. The boat fits almost too tightly into its space. The practicality of the couple—the food and blankets, the slightly ominous number of bullets—contrasts with the "frivolous" objects Bessie has with her. They're just useful enough—money and drawing materials—to make them plausible, touching without being sentimental. It's not as if she'd brought her old doll with her. Nothing here is decorative; every sentence provides key information.

Tom Barbash's novel *The Last Good Chance* is also very much about place: Jack Lambeau, a rising, ambitious urban planner, returns to his hometown to revive it. Not long before the scene described below, we've seen Jack's brother, Harris, dumping toxic waste in the countryside at night; one of his co-workers poisoned; and Harris forced into a series of attempts to hide the body. Jack keeps himself from being too aware of the shady side of his celebrated project, which makes the details of his pleasure in being home, instead of in "rank" New York, and his fierce aesthetic displeasure at those who ruin towns when trying to preserve them, both fascinating and ironic:

> With a warm buzz in his head Jack left Turner and headed toward the old harbor parking lot where he'd left his car. New York had been greener, and more beautiful than it had the right to, but he'd willfully focused on what he hadn't liked there, the sardined streets, the rank smells, the thin ribbons of sky, and wondered how you could expect to live on that. The temperature had dropped while they were inside Tuck's, but it was still fine to run in. He didn't want a corporate-crap seaport any more than Tuck did. That was one of his fears, his pet peeves, the towns Turner was referring to and the cheesy stunts they came up with to bring in tourists—water worlds, wax museums, the biggest ball of twine, but most of all some conspicuously contrived historical section, filled with fake

> history, some slightly sad depiction of historical ambiance, shop and restaurant employees dressed like escapees from old musicals at the community playhouse and speaking in bad brogues and fake regional dialects, treating all who come before them like children. When you tried to preserve a town's history, you always ran the risk of missing your mark and preserving merely the history of kitsch and bad taste. It was everywhere.

We may agree with Jack in his condemnation of towns turned into amusement parks, but our emotions are likely to be complex: horror at the consequences of his actions, anger or frustration with him for his blindness, amusement at his wit, depression at the commercialization of beautiful old places, and sympathy for his desire to make something beautiful (and to be recognized for doing so). These complicated emotions, and our desire for him to wake up and start paying attention, add an electrical charge to the descriptions. The dramatic irony and the narrative's detachment keep us from feeling as if the author has abandoned the story to make a point about preservation.

Minimalist Settings

Other authors take a minimalist approach to setting. The stories of Haruki Murakami often have a fable-like quality, and his descriptions are almost as spare as those in any Japanese fable. In his story "Thailand," Satsuki, a divorced Japanese thyroid specialist, meets Nimit, a Thai limousine driver-guide who misses the deceased Norwegian gem dealer he chauffeured for 33 years. Even though Satsuki is a newcomer to Thailand, Murakami doesn't describe the city until five pages in:

> Together, they passed through Bangkok's vulgar, noisy, polluted streets. The traffic crawled along, people cursed each other, and the sound of car horns tore through the atmosphere like an air-raid siren. Plus, there were elephants lumbering down the street—and not just one or two of them. What were elephants doing in a city like this? she asked Nimit.
>
> "Their owners bring them from the country," he explained. "They used to use them for logging, but there was not enough work for them to survive that way. They brought their animals to the city to make money doing tricks for tourists. Now there are far too many elephants here, and that makes things very difficult for the city people. Sometimes an elephant will panic and run amok. Just the other day, a great many automobiles were damaged that way. The police try to put a stop to it, of course, but they cannot confiscate the elephants from their keepers. There would be no place to put them if they did, and the cost of feeding them would be enormous. All they can do is leave them alone."

Murakami gives us only three sentences of description, and fairly short ones at that—just enough to give us an impression of the daily chaos of the streets, and to introduce the elephants so Nimit can tell us about their history. The image of those elephants—displaced, vulnerable, dangerous—resonates with the themes of displacement, loneliness, and loss that run throughout the story. As in a fable, meaning is conveyed almost entirely through action and dialogue; description and detail play only a minor role.

Vendela Vida's novel *And Now You Can Go* also employs a minimalist approach to description. Early in the book Ellis, the first-person narrator, a young woman in New York, is accosted by a man with a gun. Sitting under a bench with him, terrified, she becomes hyperaware of her surroundings:, "I can suddenly smell the trees we're sitting under." She notices that the man is wearing Armani glasses and thinks, *"I am going to be killed by a man wearing Giorgio Armani glasses."* A true urban dweller, she doesn't seem to know what kind of trees she's sitting under or what they smell like, but she's alert to brand names, even—or especially—in her state of shock. Through much of the novel, she notices isolated details in a dreamy way, as if she were living behind glass, physically unharmed after escaping the gunman but psychologically dislodged. The often distanced, nonspecific, or absent descriptions of setting make sense for this narrator. The few, telling details she notices give the story a hypnotic quality. Later in the story, upset over a breakup, she decides to water the plants:

> It's Tuesday, which means it's plant-watering day. I rejoice in having remembered this: it's a sign that things are back in order, on schedule. I dump out the contents of the wastebasket in the bathroom. I notice that my roommate is an excessive flosser. I fill the wastebasket with water from the kitchen sink. Above the faucet is a notice from Susan:
>
> *Please heed my wishes*
> *And do the dishes!!*
>
> We have three plants. I start watering the one in my bedroom, the squat one with curving leaves, like extended tongues. I can't remember how much water it needs and so I pour and pour until it's leaking out of the bottom. I mop up the spill with a clean, unmatched sock.

The description of her mopping up the excess water with a mismatched sock effectively (and hilariously) undercuts her claim that things are back in order. We also notice that she doesn't go on to do the dishes. The details of the setting—the leaves like tongues reaching out to her repulsively, the plant with its mysterious water needs, the sock as unmatched as she is—convey her isolation. Here is a character who is displaced, rather than victimized; the chaos of the surroundings contradicts her denial that she's in trouble.

STORY ANALYSIS AND QUESTIONS: "THE FENCE PARTY"

(Note: please read the story once before *you read the following analysis. Then, after you read the analysis, look at the story a second time, keeping the discussion questions in mind. You will get the most benefit out of this process*

if you mark specific passages in the story, take notes, and work through the questions in writing.)

Elizabeth Tallent's "Fence Party" could be used to study character, point of view, the delicate handling of potentially melodramatic subject matter, and language or imagery. In this case, we're looking at the story to learn about ways of making an everyday place—a house by a river during a garden party—vivid and unique. Tallent uses substantial descriptions of place that both remind us of the relationships between the characters and prepare us for the plot's climax:

> Caro is standing on the reedy bank, out of earshot, stripping a willow twig and letting the leaves wing down into the current, fast with snowmelt. Beside her, an elderly guest in baggy trousers scans the river for teal with Caro's binoculars; Caro must have told him what to search for. It's a good thing that in bird-watching Caro has found something she likes. Hart hadn't known how she would handle the solitude of the house in the gorge. He teaches mathematics three days a week, fifty miles each way, and those nights it's easiest for him to sleep on the couch in his office. But in the intense, close Dominguez clan of brothers, sisters, godparents, and cousins, no one is ever by himself, and at first Caro was frightened of the house's remoteness—of the way that up and down the canyon at night there were no lights that were not stars. Lately, though, Hart has almost ceased to worry about her. Last month when the river began to rise, she spent the days dragging and stacking sandbags into a wall that now protects the house, tapering away along the lawn's undercut, somewhat treacherous bank. Because they were meant to hold wheat for famine relief, the hundreds of dun sandbags had DONATED BY THE PEOPLE OF THE U.S.A. printed on them, and, for longshoremen, USE NO HOOKS. Caro had even been in the paper—a grainy, dramatic photograph of a young woman, her arms streaked with mud, fortifying her house against the rising Rio Grande.

Every phrase of description here evokes both the lonely situation of the house, and the isolation of the relationships within the house. In some ways, every member of Hart's family is as remote from the others as the house is from other human beings. The swiftness of the current gives us a sense of the river's danger. Caro's successful heroism during the rising of river serves as a contrast to Hart's later attempt to save Kevin.

DISCUSSION QUESTIONS

1. How does the house figure into the relationships among the characters in the story? What details give us a sense of the house, and how do they work?
2. What aspects of setting are you surprised to see included or left out? How is the party described in relation to the setting?
3. What relationships do each of the characters have to the river, and where and how do we see these relationships played out?

4. What changes for each of the characters in the story, and how are these changes related to the setting?
5. What effect do the descriptions have on the overall mood of the story?

THE POSSIBILITIES OF DETAIL

As we reread a draft, we see that some elements contribute to the story's overall feeling or theme, and others do not, or may even contradict the overall feeling. This contradiction can be good, if intentional. In general, we want to strive toward a unity of effect, but not a one-note, uncomplicated effect. If the protagonist's girlfriend leaves him for a rival, his dog runs away, the bank where he works lays him off, and the washing machine eats his socks, all on the same day, then the story will seem overdetermined or broadly comic. A balance between unity of effect and the unpredictability of real life is likely to work best. Sometimes, as in the following passage from Eileen Pollack's *Paradise, New York,* it can be achieved through the voice that reports the details:

> If God had found a reason to take a snapshot of Paradise, it would have shown Main Street to be the trunk of an evergreen, roads sprouting like boughs so ragged and droopy the whole thing resembled a Christmas tree left by the curb. Once, fifty resorts had decorated the branches of Paradise. Now, the remains clung to the roads like cracked, fading baubles. That December afternoon in 1978, as I drove with my mother to our family's hotel, I counted nine victims of Jewish lightning, the freakish force that strikes only vacant resorts with no chance for profit except from insurance. ("Hey Solly, I was upset to hear about your fire." "Shh!" whispers Sol, "it's not until tomorrow.") Patches of snow drifted over charred beams; the chimneys had fallen and lay in jutted curves like black spinal columns.

The setting is bleak, with charred beams, falling chimneys, and faded resorts. But the writing is humorous and engaging, presenting us with the image of God as a tourist in Paradise and slipping in a vaudeville joke. We unconsciously feel the intriguing tension between how well the narrator knows the place she grew up and how distant she seems to feel from it—a Jewish girl using a Christmas metaphor to describe her old town. As readers, we have enough detail to convince us of the decay of the town, and we're curious about how the town got this way and how it's going to affect our engaged but distanced narrator.

Point of View and Detail

In some ways, the challenge of re-envisioning setting is really a POV challenge. We are seeing the world anew because we look through a character's eyes. No detail is vivid in a vacuum—by figuring out our characters' attitudes toward the landscapes, job sites, and houses they move in, we make setting come to life more powerfully than if we simply try to come up with metaphors that are striking in and of themselves. Even when we have an omniscient narrator, who may have opinions that differ from those of the characters, we benefit from imagining what each character sees and feels.

We can see the influence of POV on setting most easily in a first-person story. In Beth Nugent's "City of Boys," the setting is New York City. The girl who narrates the story has come there from Fairborn, Ohio to escape the presence of her mother—and to find the teenage boys and young men who seem to fill the city:

> I watch them on the street corners, huddled under their puddles of blue smoke. They are as nervous as insects, always some part of their bodies in useless, agitated motion, a foot tapping, a jaw clenching, a finger drawing circles against a thigh, eyes in restless programmed movement as they watch women pass—they look from breasts to face to legs to breasts. They are never still and they twitch and jump when I walk by, but I still want them. I want them in the back seats of their cars; I want them under the bridge where the river meets the rocks in a slick slide of stone; I want them in the back rows of theaters and under the bushes and benches in the park.

Countless writers have described New York City, but Nugent's version is fresh because the narrator's specific attitudes and desires color it. This passage doesn't have what we might think of when we first think of setting—Nugent doesn't describe towering skyscrapers, pigeons, neon signs, or traffic jams. The setting, for the narrator, consists of men. When she mentions inanimate objects—the bridge, the theater, the benches—they're in relation to her desire.

In a third-person story, the details of the setting are also affected by the POV. Characters go to particular places because of their situations or emotional state, and, once there, they notice certain details and interpret them according to their own moods and temperaments. In Eudora Welty's "No Place for You, My Love," two strangers meet in New Orleans one warm Sunday afternoon, go for a drive together, and increasingly, silently, struggle against a desire that could turn their lives inside out. Halfway through the story, they find themselves standing by a body of water at sunset:

> There was a touch at her arm—his, accidental.
>
> "We're at the jumping-off place," he said.
>
> She laughed, having thought his hand was a bat, while her eyes rushed downward toward a great pale drift of water hyacinths—still partly open, flushed and yet moonlit, level with her feet—through which paths of water for the boats had been hacked. She drew her hands up to her face under the brim of her hat; her own cheeks felt like the hyacinths to her, all her skin still full of too much light and sky, exposed. The harsh vesper bell was ringing.

Here Welty uses an aspect of the setting to illuminate her character, who identifies with the flushed, exposed hyacinths. The image might seem sentimental (especially with the light of the moon), if not balanced by those paths ominously hacked through the water and the harsh vesper bell. When we're describing setting, we have the opportunity to stay true to the complexity of emotions. We might also notice the difference between the sheer numbers of people in Beth Nugent's city—where everyone is looking or being looked at—and the largely deserted environment that Welty's characters find themselves in. Different concentrations of people create different effects on characters and plots.

The more we imagine the setting around our characters, picturing what they see and experience, the more we come to understand the different and possibly conflicting emotions the characters may be feeling.

Symbolic Detail

The challenge of description is to choose details that provide information about the people and the situation, without overdoing it so that every single item in the story becomes symbolic. Symbolism is especially a danger with the weather: rain storms during arguments, clouds gathering to provide a note of suspense. In the category of things that can easily be overdone, maraschino cherries and symbolic weather top the list. Note that the excerpt from Pollack's *Paradise, New York,* above, mentions snow on the ground, appropriate for December, but the author does not have a blizzard fall on the charred remains of the burned resorts as the narrator arrives home; it would be too much.

Nugent's "City of Boys" shows desire and longing through the symbolic details in the description of the interiors, like the one-room apartment where the narrator lives with her lover, an older woman:

> Sometimes I wake up to see her leaning on her thin knees against the wall that is stripped down to expose the rough brick beneath the plaster. I dream that she prays to keep me, but I am afraid that it is something else she prays for, a beginning, or an end, or something I don't know about. She came to bed once and laid her face against my breast, and I felt the imprint of the brick in the tender skin of her forehead.
>
> She herself is not particularly religious, although the apartment is littered with the scraps of saints—holy relics of one sort or another: a strand of hair from the Christ child, a bit of fingernail from Saint Paul, a shred of the Virgin's robe. They are left over from Tito, who collected holy relics the way some people collect lucky pennies or matchbooks, as a kind of hedge against some inarticulated sense of disaster.

The setting here is spare but clearly imagined. The wall marks the narrator's lover, as if she's been hit in the forehead by a brick—which subtly readies us for the emotional blow the narrator will inflict on her later in the story. The room is also littered with "scraps" that would be meaningful to someone else, but for these two, they're no protection against the disasters of desire. For the two characters, the objects are a reminder of previous lovers and an overriding anxiety. For the reader, these objects may have a different resonance. When we're revising and focusing on the selection of the right details for our own stories, we can sort through the array of possibilities by considering how objects might be meaningful to our characters, how they reflect the characters' urgent needs or emotionally charged histories, and how they may strike the reader.

STORY ANALYSIS AND QUESTIONS: "PILGRIMS"

(Note: please read the story once before *you read the following analysis. Then, after you read the analysis, look at the story a second time, keeping the discussion questions in mind. You will get the most benefit out of this process if you mark specific passages in the story, take notes, and work through the questions in writing.)*

Julie Orringer's "Pilgrims" is a powerful example of how writers can effectively use details to carry symbolic weight and establish a mood—in this case, a mood of quiet desperation and menace. The story is written in a distanced third-person point of view: every perception is funneled through Ella's awareness, but the story does not offer authorial commentary or opinions or tell us what Ella is thinking. As readers, though we might not stop to think about the details, we can feel how they create the world and mood of the story. After reading the story once for the reader's experience, we can go through it again as writers to see how the individual objects and observations combine to give us a vivid picture of the enchanted, nightmare world taking over the children's lives, and how these details provide an eerie, tangible substitute for more abstract thoughts or emotions. Some of the details directly convey the disorder, exposure, and insecurity of the children's situation:

> In the upstairs hallway, toys and kids' shoes were strewn across the floor, and crumpled pants and shirts and dresses lay in a musty-smelling heap. Two naked Barbies sprawled in a frying pan. A record player sat in the middle of the hall, its vacant turntable spinning. Ella stepped over the cord and went into the first room, a small room with a sleeping bag on the bare mattress ticking. In a cage on the nightstand, a white rat scrabbled at a cardboard tube. A finger-painted sign above the bed said CLARIES ROOM. [Ella's] mother's cough rose again from down the hall, and she turned and ran toward the sound.

Everything here is out of order, sometimes in ways we might expect from a house in which the mother has died—no one is picking up or doing the laundry—and sometimes with an exact, memorable detail like the vulnerable, naked Barbies in a frying pan, as if they were about to be cooked. The pet rat "scrabbled at a cardboard tube"—even the verb sounds desperate—and the tube, presumably for sleep and shelter, is impermanent, makeshift. The record player is empty but still spinning. Everything here builds to a particular, freshly observed sense of loss and nightmare. The sound of Ella's own mother's illness, floating over this in the form of her cough, adds another note of desperation: if Ella loses her mother, as Clarie has lost hers, this kind of scene could take over her own home.

In later passages, the details give us a sense of the world the adults live in:

> Hands deep in the pockets of her velvet dress, Ella wandered through the echoing hall into a room lined from floor to ceiling with books. Many of the titles were in other languages, some even written in different alphabets. She recognized *D'Aulaires' Book of Greek Myths* and *The Riverside Shakespeare* and *Grimm's Fairy Tales.* Scattered around on small tables and decorative stands were tiny human figurines with animal heads: horse-man, giraffe-man, panther-man. On one table sat an Egyptian beetle made of milky green stone, and beside him a real beetle, shiny as metal, who flew at Ella's face when she reached to touch his shell. She batted him away with the back of her hand.

Orringer here uses details as symbols, but with a delicate touch. In Egyptian culture, the beetle is a symbol of resurrection, but the story does not provide this information—by having Ella remember that she learned this at school, for example. The writer trusts the reader to catch the connection and is willing, if necessary, to have us miss some of the symbolism. We still feel the weight of the objects, whether or not we know what they mean. If all the objects in a paragraph had been symbols of resurrection or death, the passage would have been heavy-handed. Instead Orringer gives us animal-headed figurines, which seem of a piece with the books of fairy tales and the beetle, but not directly representative of anything in particular. At the end, a beetle that appears to be part of the collection of objects suddenly turns out to be alive and flies into Ella's face, which adds a menacing, surreal edge, and at the same time plays a role in the plot by drawing Ella's attention to the glass of red water.

In our own stories, we can look for ways to calibrate our use of detail similarly to convey meaning clearly but subtly. It may take a fair amount of revision, adding and subtracting objects and sensory images, to achieve this. If one of those figurines had had the head of a jackal, for instance, we would have instantly thought of Anubis, the Egyptian god of death, which would have been too much.

DISCUSSION QUESTIONS

1. Which details in "Pilgrims" convey the parents' states of mind? Which details convey the children's states of mind?

2. Which incidents, details, and remarks cause the characters to cry? Why these?
3. How and where are details used to convey information to the reader without relying on authorial explanation or a character's thoughts?
4. What would you expect to be explained that isn't? What is the effect of the story's lack of explanations?
5. How do the different stages of the ending work? How do they fit with the rest of the story?

REVISION: INHABITING PLACES

Place is at the core of the story, not an irrelevant, arbitrary add-on. In revision, we are probably not going to change the macrosetting, to decide a story originally set in a suburb of Tucson, Arizona, should take place in Venice instead. Radical adjustments in microsetting, however, can be quite helpful in revision. We may decide that the story's climactic confrontation between a son and mother will be more intense and have more consequences if it is set in the local diner (in front of the community) than in the family living room with no onlookers. For thematic reasons, we may change the setting of a story's opening from a generic street to a gymnasium, if the story concentrates heavily on physical bodies.

Sometimes, conversation and actions can be simply transposed from one setting to another during revision, only requiring some changes in the descriptive passages. At other times, the new setting will give the characters more to do and may end up inspiring changes in the action.

Some places are claustrophobic by nature (an elevator or a phone booth), others convey emptiness (a deserted football field at night). Some carry taboos that augment the tension or raise the stakes (a mother screaming at her child in the middle of a packed church service reads differently than the same event in a moving car).

The macrosetting is also worth paying attention to, for it can expand the story and give it depth and resonance. In a first draft we are simply trying to imagine as best we can what the characters are doing. In revision, we think about how the events of the story might be influenced by the larger context of the place where they occur. One way we can enlarge our vision of the place is to return, if possible, to take notes for an hour or two. A hasty note-taking trip will mean seeing the obvious, but if we spend real time, we'll see details we have previously overlooked. Another research method is to visit the library or the Internet (that fount of information and misinformation, which needs triple-checking before we include anything as a fact). What aspects of our setting are we overlooking? What new information expands our understanding? What does the detail we're using *mean* in terms of the characters and their story?

Flannery O'Connor in her essay "Writing Short Stories" in *Mysteries and Manners,* wrote very firmly about the importance of detail in making our fictional world seem real:

> Fiction operates through the senses, and I think one reason that people find it so difficult to write stories is that they forget how much time and patience is required to convince through the senses. No reader who doesn't actually experience, who isn't made to feel, the story is going to believe anything the fiction writer merely tells him. The first and most obvious characteristic of fiction is that it deals with reality and what can be seen, heard, smelt, tasted, and touched. . . . for the fiction writer, judgment begins in the details he sees and how he sees them.
>
> Fiction writers who are not concerned with these concrete details are guilty of what Henry James called "weak specification." The eye will glide over their words while the attention goes to sleep. Ford Madox Ford taught that you couldn't have a man appear long enough to sell a newspaper in a story unless you put him there with enough detail to make the reader see him.

O'Connor, who suffered a great deal physically and could be quite sharp-tongued, attributed all the "uncontained" thought and unspecified emotions in beginning stories to students being interested only in their own thoughts and emotions, not in the story's action. She attributed this to laziness or being "highfalutin."

Professional writers like O'Connor may forget just how hard it is to master the creation of meaningful detail in literary fiction. Other kinds of writing take much less out of us. We might write ten pages of our thoughts, emotions, and speculations in a journal or letter and go happily about our business. We might vaguely imagine a fictional room, assign some funny or typical details (an apron hanging on a refrigerator hook, a set of windup teeth on a desk), and feel that the whole business of writing is a lot of fun. Quite a few best-sellers give the impression that the writer was having fun while writing but was not deeply engaged, and we're not deeply engaged either. If we read much of a book like this, we may increasingly find ourselves feeling unsatisfied or annoyed: the writer, we feel, is not *telling the truth.* Creating a detailed, integral, meaningful (but not overdone) setting is phenomenally hard work. We may be left drained and exhausted after even a half-hour or hour of a session in which we work our way all the way down into the core of the story. Once in that writing state, we no longer seem to be "making things up," but actually reporting on the events and places in another world, working hard to shape them in the telling. And yet, for writers, these trips down into the core are satisfying and addictive. The good news is that, with regular practice, we can usually get down into that core faster and stay there longer, coming back up with more and better information about our ch[illegible] their surroundings.

SETTING EXERCISES

1. Go back to a place where you've set a story you'd like to rework. Spend at least an hour and a half with a notebook, observing the details of what you see, hear, feel, and smell. If you feel you're done after half an hour, keep going. The point of this exercise is what you discover after you have observed all the obvious facts about this place. You might follow this up with a trip to the library to see what, if anything, you can find out about the history of this place and its surroundings.

    When you're done, save your previous draft so that you can feel free to experiment, then begin working your new details into the story. How do they change the characters and the meaning? Do they inspire new actions and events? Let yourself experiment, without feeling bound by your earlier ideas about the story's events and themes. Your original story may simply be enriched by the new details, or it may change dramatically as you learn more about its possibilities.
2. Make a list of ten places you have traveled to, near or far (Israel, Japan, a tree house, the corner store). Now put your pen to the paper, and, without stopping to evaluate, write everything you can think of about one of these places. Where were you? What were you doing? What did the place look, sound, smell like? What objects or sights did you see? What incidents did you observe or overhear? Who was there with you? What did they say or do? Give yourself at least a half an hour for the freewrite.

    When you're done, put it aside for an hour or a day. After you've established a little distance, you can think about ways of using this as the setting for a story. What went wrong on these trips? What might have gone wrong, even if it worked out in real life? How did the people involved react—or how might they have reacted—to problems? The style of the story can be experimental, poetic, realistic, chronologically straightforward, or fragmented. You might try more than one approach before you find the one that feels right for this particular material.
3. Make a list of every place that has ever frightened you. Choose one, and continue as in Exercise 2.
4. Make a list of every place where you have felt safe and happy. Choose one, and continue as in Exercise 2.
5. Think of a place you love and know well. Write down all the elements that make this place what it is—the objects, the sense of space, and the people or lack of people. Are there aspects you have mixed or negative feelings about? Write a brief scene about a character who enters the

space for the first time and finds it disappointing, or has conflicted feelings about it, or likes it for very different reasons than you do. This may spark ideas as to where this person is in his or her life, and what recent events may have influenced these attitudes.

6. (This exercise can be done either individually or in a group.) Choose three stories you've read and look through them for indicators of setting. How do the settings relate to the themes and subject matter of the stories? What details establish each setting? How do these details shed light on the characters, create mood, or work symbolically?

CHAPTER

8

Society, Culture, and Context: Research and the Imagination

(Anthology selections: "Orientation," "Di Grasso: A Tale of Odessa," and "Civil Peace")

Often for a story, I will do enough research to write a couple of novels, and for a novel I'll do enough research to have written an encyclopedia. . . . It's very easy to succumb to the impulse to stuff all that research in the book. I do stuff too much into my early drafts, and a lot of the process of my later drafts is to take it out chunk by chunk, painfully and kicking and screaming the whole time, realizing I'm interested in this or that fact, but nobody else is. I do this until finally all that's left is a sort of whiff of the original or a kind of distilled particle of what was a great vat of research. But in the end fiction is about the characters, the image, the language, the poetry, the sound; it isn't about information. The information has to be distilled down to let us focus on what's really going on with the people.

Having said this, I'm not always successful. Sometimes it's my editor in the last drafts or one of my dear friends and readers who says, "You know, maybe these six pages about how dew is formed could be one page." And of course having started out with thirty pages on how dew is formed I'm very reluctant. But I always have to let it go in the end.

—Andrea Barrett, *Atlantic Unbound* interview

CREATING CONTEXT

If we're describing a place, a work process, or a community—the New York gallery world, a Watsonville vegetable-packing factory, or an eighteenth-century monastery—it matters that we get it right. Readers who know the subject will be distracted by careless invention. Even readers who don't know the subject can tell if the writer has done the necessary research; without it, the story will have a thin, unbelievable quality. When we're drawing on situations we've lived through, research can fill gaps in our memory, enlarge our perspective, and make our stories richer. Sometimes, though, as Andrea Barrett reminds us, we fall in love with the facts we discover or we want to put in all our research to show how much work we've done. Then we need to begin cutting. But even if we wind up condensing 30 pages of information into a single page, the knowledge we've acquired informs and permeates the story.

By connecting our characters' struggles to the challenges that society as a whole faces, we raise the stakes in our plots and make our characters more three-dimensional. We see characters in relation to their world, not just to each other and to their own immediate desires. Possibilities for enlarging the context of a story include the issues, situations, language, and details of work and leisure; art, science, and other fields of inquiry; history, biography, and depictions of other cultures; and politics and religion. We've grouped these elements into categories according to the challenges they raise when writers attempt to incorporate them into fiction. When writing about work or leisure, we need to discover how to keep the context from being merely decorative. How does the nature of the characters' pursuits give rise to, or change, the story? History, biography, and the depiction of other cultures pose the same challenge and also require us to figure out how to locate readers in relation to past events or potentially unfamiliar places. How much research do we include and how can we blend it into events? And with politics and religion, we consider how much to conceal or expose our beliefs, as well as the difference between presenting a reality and arguing for it. How do we depict characters' political or religious lives without turning our stories into tracts or diatribes?

When we're writing a story that draws on our own experiences and is set in fairly recent times, we can read microfiches of newspapers from that period—what were people reading and thinking about? What was happening in the culture at large that might relate to the events of the story, serve as a counterpoint to them, illuminate them, or connect them to larger issues?

Sometimes the balance for the story we're working on may lean heavily toward the inclusion of information. Don DeLillo and Jonathan Franzen work this way. Both of them, however, are primarily novelists rather than short story writers and thus have room for extended passages of information and background. Most short stories, though not all, will incorporate information and depict processes in ways that move more swiftly.

For our own writing, we might think of the forms, procedures, rules, and ideas that come from our work lives, our artistic or leisure pursuits, and the surrounding culture. Which of these might be fruitfully adopted as a form for fiction? What kinds of characters or content would arise from this use of context? How do the processes interact with the story's dramatic movement? What different kinds of setting or circumstance can we imagine, invent, or make use of?

Using Research to Enlarge Subject Matter

As writers become more experienced, they often wind up using research substantially in the writing process. Beginning writers sometimes interpret the advice to "write about what you know" in too limited a fashion; some of our most essential material may come from our obsessions with the world around us, rather than our life circumstances. The question is how to expand what we know, to make our subjects accurate and convincing. We happen to read a series of books about horse racing, or Polish politics, or WWI psychiatric clinics, and the more we learn, the more we respond by imagining a few invented or transposed people in this particular circumstance. Maybe while growing up we read every book we could find on the Wright Brothers or about the Egyptians and their beliefs about the dead. If we eventually find ourselves writing directly about these subjects, we can supplement our earlier haphazard reading with more formal, primary research.

Some writers do research for weeks or months before beginning a story, letting the form, nature, and characters of the story arise from their discoveries. The potential pitfall of this approach is that the writer may use research as a way of procrastinating, or can be stifled by the research, feeling more like a historian than a writer of fiction. Other writers rely on their background knowledge and write first: then they know exactly what it is they don't know. John Fowles has said that he wrote the entire first draft of *The French Lieutenant's Woman,* set in nineteenth-century England, before he began his research. The pitfall of this approach can be that the writer may invent such inaccurate attitudes and details that rewriting becomes a great struggle. For a writer who already has a substantial background knowledge of the subject, as Fowles did, this approach tends to work better. Many writers do some initial research and then begin writing, stopping to do more research only when they find they can't go forward without more facts.

Work and Leisure

Workplaces provide a natural source of conflict and tension. Even if characters love their jobs, they probably struggle with bosses, office politics, funding difficulties, or unruly clients. Writers can use work or leisure activities to provide narrative structure, as in a story that unfolds during a neighborhood croquet game, beginning with the setting up of the wickets and ending with the final showdown between the last two players. Or writers can show how these pursuits change the way characters feel and behave, as in a story documenting the tensions of a small group of restaurant employees working in close quarters. We often show our most devious, unrestrained, or baffling behavior in endeavors like work and play that bring out desires for power and connection, fears for survival, and the need to control our circumstances. Very often, human nature collides with the rules, spoken and unspoken, of a particular endeavor.

In "Pet Fly," Walter Mosley depicts a recent college graduate with a degree in political science who stumbles into a real-life maze of sexual and racial politics in his first office job. The story takes place in a Wall Street office; the narrator is Rufus Coombs, a young black interoffice mail courier who develops a crush on a white coworker and is subsequently accused of sexual harassment. Mosley delineates the complicated lines of power and fear—both racial and hierarchical—throughout. The characters consistently act believably but unpredictably, in ways that subvert or complicate the official standards of behavior corporate life demands. In the passage below, the narrator is brought into the office of the company's vice president, Averill, who has on his desk both Rufus's resume and the pink sexual harassment form:

> Averill looked down at his desk. "This does not compute."
>
> "What?"
>
> He patted the white page. "This says that you're a college graduate, magna cum laude in political science, that you came here to be a professional trainee." He patted the pink sheet. "This says that you're an interoffice-mail courier who harasses secretaries in the mortgage department."
>
> Averill reached into his vest pocket and came out with an open package of cigarettes. At orientation they'd told us that there was absolutely no smoking anywhere in the building, but he took one out anyway. He lit up and took a deep drag, holding the smoke in his lungs for a long time before exhaling.
>
> "Is there something wrong with you?" he asked.

Neither the resume nor the sexual harassment form come close to describing the directionless, genial, daydreamy Rufus we've gotten to know over the course of the story, but they're all that the vice president has to go on in this large company. So much of the story is about who gets to break what rules and how, about discovering what the spoken and unspoken rules are, and about power and powerlessness. Like Mosley, we can move beyond decorative details of the working world to examine its issues and situations.

Because work lives are often stressful, people expect leisure time to be the opposite—calm, fun, and easy. But when we're on vacation or playing as part of a team, we may find ourselves clashing over personal issues, meeting unexpected setbacks, competing, or lost at sea—literally or figuratively. In Margaret Atwood's "A Travel Piece," a bored travel writer on her way to an idyllic vacation spot finds herself stranded on a life boat with other passengers after a crash. In Amy Tan's *The Joy Luck Club,* the narrator joins the mah jong club her recently deceased mother founded and learns the often-tragic stories of the lives of her mother's friends.

Context becomes a structural rather than a decorative element in stories like Daniel Orozco's "Orientation." The work situation isn't an incidental detail—like a person's height or favorite kind of pie; it's essential to the story's themes and the characters' lives. These people would have entirely different problems in a different job. Orozco's discussion of the revision process for this story (in Chapter 10, under "Structural Revision") gives an idea of how the subject matter of the story shaped its form, characterization, and narrative movement.

STORY ANALYSIS AND QUESTIONS: "ORIENTATION"

(<u>Note</u>: please read the story once before *you read the following analysis. Then, after you read the analysis, look at the story a second time, keeping the discussion questions in mind. You will get the most benefit out of this process if you mark specific passages in the story, take notes, and work through the questions in writing.)*

In Daniel Orozco's "Orientation," the societal context and the story are inextricably and memorably intertwined. This story, in the form of a tour, opens a window into a world where no one has a truly private life, exposing the banal details of the working world: the photocopier, the kitchenette, and the office supplies cabinet. The tension here is between the uniformity of the business world, with the increasing numbers of rules required by the close proximity of the employees, and the eruptions of wild individuality. Like "Pet Fly," "Orientation" presents a nightmarish view of the working world. But while "Pet Fly" uses a plot-oriented, realistic approach to draw the reader in, "Orientation" does so with a surreal touch, keeping the reader at a slight distance with its mysterious narrator and obsessive cataloging of details.

This is a first-person story, one narrator's dramatic monologue addressed to an unidentified listener. The narrator's instructions suggest many details of the setting; the story also uses repetition to give some details greater resonance. For instance, when we first learn that John LaFountaine occasionally uses the women's restroom, it comes across as comic:

> John LaFountaine, who sits over there, uses the women's room occasionally. He says it is accidental. We know better, but we let it pass. John LaFountaine is harmless, his forays into the forbidden territory of the women's room simply a benign thrill, a faint blip on the dull flat line of his life.

Later the narrator tells us about the apparently sunny Gwendolyn Stich, with her passions for collecting penguin knickknacks, bringing pastry and doughnuts for everyone, and organizing office parties:

> Gwendolyn Stich's door is always open to all of us. She will always lend an ear, and put in a good word for you; she will always give you a hand, or the shirt off her back, or a shoulder to cry on. Because her door is always open, she hides and cries in a stall in the women's room. And John LaFountaine—who, enthralled when a woman enters, sits quietly in his stall with his knees to his chest—John LaFountaine has heard her vomiting in there. We have come upon Gwendolyn Stich huddled in the stairwell, shivering in the updraft, sipping a Diet Mr. Pibb and hugging her knees.

The new detail about John LaFountaine echoes and builds on the earlier one, connecting the two passages and also changing the implications:

what was once a childish trespass is now a real boundary violation—the discovery of a coworker's private misery. In this office, though, there is no privacy of any kind.

DISCUSSION QUESTIONS

1. Why is the monologue form appropriate? How is the writer's experience and/or research apparent in the details? How does Orozco reveal the setting/context without overwhelming the reader?
2. At what point does the world of this office begin to seem threatening or alarming? What is our first clue that something is amiss? How is it introduced? How is it followed up?
3. How does Orozco connect the different lives and stories? How do they reinforce or subvert each other?
4. What power structures does the story depict?
5. How and when does Orozco use repetition to create tension and/or humor? What kinds of moods does the story create? How do they intersect or collide?
6. Where does the story associate objects or people with danger or loss? How do these associations connect to or complicate the themes of the story?

Art, Science, and Other Fields of Inquiry

Stories about art and science may have similarities to those about work, as they chronicle the efforts of artists or scientists to investigate the world and add to their respective traditions. Writers examining the lives of artists and scientists may be intrigued by the ways people conceive of the world, by the particular ideas they are exploring, by the human costs of artistic and scientific lives, or by the nature of the artistic or scientific processes themselves.

In *The Bug,* Ellen Ullman shows both the beauty and the difficulty that programmers experience in writing code and inventing virtual "life." In *Nuns and Soldiers,* Iris Murdoch creates a wide array of characters (a pair of hard-scrabble artists, a nun who's just left the convent, a rich woman, and a "count"—actually a government official) wrestling not only with philosophical issues and family, money, and love problems but also with their work. In the collection of short stories *Troll Garden,* Willa Cather presents a series of artists at different levels of ability and commitment, self-awareness and self-delusion.

Our society tends to romanticize those who make art or carry out scientific processes; they have almost a shamanic status. A whole set of myths and stereotypes has sprung up: mad scientists, tortured artists, geniuses who effortlessly paint masterpieces, researchers so buried in abstract ideas that they fail to see the danger their work will do, and playwrights so poor they have to burn their own pages for heat.

We can avoid the romantic clichés about artists and scientists by acknowledging everyday details and events in their lives, and by reading biographies to get a better sense of the varied and complicated personalities who are drawn to these fields. We might also look for the particular peculiarities of our characters, rather than assigning them a generically heroic or tortured persona.

Stacey D'Erasmo, in *A Seahorse Year,* gives a realistic view of an artist through a close examination of her particular artistic concerns:

> Marina dots the tip of the branch. It's okay. Today the tree is okay, not so bad, she won't have to scrape it off and start again. Probably. . . .
>
> For instance, this tree that she's been making for the last seven years: it hasn't been that well-received, but she has persevered for reasons she can't quite explain. She's made the tree big; she's made the tree small; she's made the tree in oil, watercolor, gouache, collage, tinfoil, Polaroid, and acrylic; she's repeated identical trees in suspiciously regular rows on a single canvas; once she made an entire forest of trees from fabric remnants. This is a tree in oil, dense and telegraphic. She might have to scrape it off after all. There's another tree, a tree she can see clearly in her mind's eye, that will not fail, as this one suddenly seems in imminent danger of doing. . . . When she first drew it as a child in Los Angeles, it was a tree she had never seen, except in a dream. In the dream, it was the most beautiful tree in the world. She woke up needing to draw it. That was all she knew. In many ways, she thinks it may be all she still knows. She begins on another branch, with guarded hope.

D'Erasmo focuses on Marina's painting in a way that gives a sense of the slow accretion of artistic ideas, the work of wrestling them into being. This is the artist as worker, not the artist as inspired madwoman.

Sometimes a character's involvement with art or science can symbolically reflect the dramatic situation, if the symbolism is handled delicately. Cornelia Nixon's *Angels Go Naked,* a "novel-in-stories," shows the work and love/family lives of Margy, a violinist, and Webster, an oceanic microbiologist who is ambivalent about the idea of becoming a father. The beginning of the following scene gives a sense of how Webster's work relates to his situation and concerns:

> He made a lab table out of a door and squeezed it into the dining room. He taped his field notes on *Aurelia* around the walls. The last year in Bolinas, he had noticed something odd about the jellyfish. He could always find their early plankton forms along the reef, the ones that looked like many-legged worms or plant-like polyps rooted to a rock. But no matter how often he searched, he rarely found the final two stages. They had to break free first as swimming stars, to reach the final transformation, when they grew legs and bent them back, turned inside out to form the bell-shaped bodies they would keep. Only then did they gain sex, grow up to spawn.
>
> Why were they stalling out instead as eunuch polyps? It could be a form of birth control. Animals knew when to keep their numbers down . . .

The narrative then shows his ideas and discoveries about the effects of temperature differences on the jellyfish. The jellyfish, like the character, are having difficulty in reaching the stage at which they can reproduce themselves, although in the biologist's case, the problem is emotional. Because the actual reason for the jellyfish's difficulties in spawning has no direct relation to Webster's life, the symbolism functions in a slantwise, inconspicuous fashion. If there were a direct correlation on every level between his problems and those of the jellyfish, the scene would seem overdetermined. But we are willing to believe that his preoccupation with fatherhood may have influenced his interest in jellyfish reproduction, since our work concerns often do reflect our lives. The thoroughness of the research and the specificity of the supporting details also ground the scene in reality.

Sometimes writers will incorporate the structures of art or science into a work: a story about artists that functions as a collage of words; or fiction that, like Whitney Otto's *A Collection of Beauties at the Height of Their Popularity,* draws on specific artistic works. Otto has structured the linked stories of her novel around a series of Japanese woodblock prints, reproducing and describing each one, then following it with a story that loosely echoes its themes and images and the sensual, evanescent Floating World.

Donald Barthelme's story "The Explanation" is not about the lives of scientists, but uses a scientific form—a quirky, mock-scientific interview that may be sociological or psychological or both. Barthelme allows the subject to create the structure: he incorporates information and processes that seem familiar, but then transforms them into something unexpected, juxtaposing the official question-and-answer format with absurd but meaningful content.

At the story's beginning and at various places in the text a large black square is inserted, without captions. Here is the opening that follows the first box:

> Q: Do you believe that this machine could be helpful in changing the government?
>
> A: Changing the government . . .
>
> Q: Making it more responsive to the needs of the people?
>
> A: I don't know what it is. What does it do?
>
> Q: Well, look at it.
>
> [Another black square]
>
> A: It offers no clues.
>
> Q: It has a certain . . . reticence.
>
> A: I don't know what it does.
>
> Q: A lack of confidence in the machine?
>
> Q: Is the novel dead?
>
> A: Oh yes. Very much so.

The story goes on, always in this format, to suggest that the interviewee comes to interpret the squares as photographs, and even to describe events taking place in them and the associations they call up. At one point, the lack of ordinary setting is explicitly acknowledged:

Q: Are you bored with the question-and-answer form?
A: I am bored with it but I realize that it permits many valuable omissions: what kind of day it is, what I'm wearing, what I'm thinking. That's a very considerable advantage, I would say.
Q: I believe in it.

The story's context is not the physical surroundings, but apparently unconnected facts and images—error messages, the purity of Maoism, the death of the bicycle—linked as part of a ludicrously offbeat bureaucratic approach to research.

Some stories about art or science focus on artists or scientists; others draw on the ideas or the experience of art and science, like Susan Vreeland's *Girl in Hyacinth Blue,* A. S. Byatt's *Matisse Stories* and *Possession,* and Mary Robison's "An Amateur's Guide to the Night." In some Isaac Babel stories, part of the context or drama comes from characters responding to art, like the translator in "Guy de Maupassant" or the ticket scalpers in "Di Grasso: A Tale of Odessa."

STORY ANALYSIS AND QUESTIONS: "DI GRASSO: A TALE OF ODESSA"

(Note: please read the story once before *you read the following analysis. Then, after you read the analysis, look at the story a second time, keeping the discussion questions in mind. You will get the most benefit out of this process if you mark specific passages in the story, take notes, and work through the questions in writing.)*

In "Di Grasso: A Tale of Odessa," Isaac Babel shows us the impact of the work of art on those who view it, rather than focusing on the artist's process. Babel weaves the context—in this case, the theater—into the lives and fortunes of the characters, making it part of the shape and structure of the story, but not substituting it for the human drama. Babel begins the story at a high-stakes moment in the history of the Italian Opera in Odessa, Russia:

> Taking a lead from the critics on the local paper, our impresario decided not to import Anselmi and Tito Ruffo as guest artistes but to make do with a good stock company. For this he was sorely punished; he went bankrupt, and we with him. We were promised Chaliapin to straighten out our affairs, but Chaliapin wanted three thousand a performance; so instead we had the Sicilian tragedian Di Grasso with his troupe. They arrived at the hotel in peasant carts crammed with children, cats, cages in which Italian birds hopped and skipped. Casting an eye over this gypsy crew, Nick Schwarz opined:
>
> "Children, this stuff won't sell."

A writer using a strong outside element like a play has to consider how much it will dominate the "main" story. Babel doesn't rely on the Sicilian folk drama's plot to provide narrative momentum—in fact, the narrator disparages the play as commonplace. Instead, the story invites the reader to worry about the fortunes of the theater and its ticket scalpers, one of whom is the narrator. In addition, the slightly odd behavior of the shepherd in Act I ("he twisted his head this way and that like a startled bird") maintains the tension throughout the six paragraphs summarizing the play's inconsequential plot, until finally the drama explodes in a cathartic moment of bloody melodrama.

As crude as Di Grasso's methods are, the villagers' reaction—buying tickets at five times face value—shows how starved they are for what the theater can give them. Throughout the story, Babel reveals theater's transcendent power and its perverse relationship to the commonplace nature of everyday life.

DISCUSSION QUESTIONS

1. Why might Babel have made his two main characters ticket scalpers, rather than a theatrical impresario and a box office ticket taker? How would the story be different if Nick Schwarz and the narrator were official employees of the theater?
2. What details does Babel use to give us a sense of the nature of the theater and its power?
3. Why does Babel wait so long to introduce the element of the pawned watch? How would the story be different if the reader learned about it early on?
4. How does the episode of the watch and Madame Schwarz relate to Di Grasso's play thematically? How does it relate structurally? How does it relate emotionally?
5. How does the theatrical context lead to or illuminate the ending of the story?

History, Biography, and Other Cultures

If we write stories set in the past, we have to decide whether to invent the characters or to use people who actually lived—or some mixture of real and invented characters. If we set a story in a culture or place we haven't grown up in or lived in extensively, we have to decide how much to draw on research.

When writing about actual historical people, writers take on the task of imaginatively reexperiencing a life or part of a life, in order to understand something about it. Several approaches are possible. Penelope Fitzgerald makes the eighteenth-century German poet Novalis the central character of her novel *Blue Flower.* Robert Olen Butler, in his short story "A Good Scent from a Strange Mountain," invents a character who chronicles his friendship with Ho Chi Minh, using lesser-known events from the life of the man who became famous as the communist leader of North Vietnam. Raymond Carver wrote a story called "Errand" about the death of Chekhov, inspired by reading a biography. Carver was interested in and baffled by Chekhov's doctor's decision to order champagne when the great writer lay on his deathbed. Carver writes, "As much as anything, I needed to figure out how to breathe life into actions that were merely suggested or not given moment in the biographical telling." "Errand" includes brief excerpts from memoirs and letters of historical figures, but the character whose experience the reader most fully inhabits is a fictional hotel servant who delivers the champagne.

Alice Munro's "Meneseteung" shows us yet another possibility for drawing on biographical information. Set in the 1800s, the story discusses a poet as if she had really lived, although she is an invention based on women in similar situations.

When writing about other times and places, we have to decide how much background information to give the reader, and in what way. We can directly provide the reader with background, which gives us one kind of freedom and artistic effect, or we can write as if the reader already knows the information, which may give the story a more intimate feeling.

Peter Ho Davies in "The Silver Screen" tells us the time and place very directly in the first paragraph:

> From the end of the Second World War until the outbreak of the insurgency in 1948, the fourteenth Kuala Lumpur branch of the Malayan Communist Party held its meetings in the Savoy Cinema on Brickfields Street.
>
> The owner of the cinema, Mr. Ming, had joined the party during the Japanese occupation. In those days he had cycled to work at his father's rubber plantation on the outskirts of the town. Every morning he would join the line of workers and schoolchildren in front of the Japanese sentry at Pudu jail. They would all dismount at a respectful distance from the sentry, wheel their bicycles to his post, bow, wheel them on, and remount at an equally respectful distance beyond. All this under the eyes of the severed heads lined up along the walls of the jail.

Davies also conveys the—to us—surreal combination of great courtesy and horror, through the exact detail of the polite dismounting underneath the severed heads. We understand not only *when* all this is happening, but also the atmosphere of the time.

In contrast, Andrea Barrett's "Birds with No Feet" uses the indirect method. The opening identifies the date for us but concentrates on the main character's thoughts and feelings:

> *[Fire—1853]*
>
> There was no breeze that night. The sea, lit by the full moon, shone smooth and silver; the Southern Cross turned above the ship and below it squid slipped invisibly through the depths. Between sky and sea lay Alec Carrière, sprawled like a starfish in his hammock and imagining how the treasures packed in the holds were about to change his life.

> Beetles and butterflies and spiders and moths, bird skins and snakeskins and bones: these were what he'd collected along the Amazon and then guarded against the omnivorous ants. Mr. Barton, his agent back home in Philadelphia, had sold Alec's first specimens for a good price, and Alec expected this shipment would finally set him free to pursue his studies in peace. He was a few months shy of twenty-one, and dreaming a young man's dreams.

Unlike the narrator in the Davies passage, this narrator could well be talking to a contemporary of Alec, describing the circumstances to someone who needs no explanation of their meaning. Davies's omniscient narrator insists on the difference in the time period—"At the end of the Second World War" and "In those days," while Barrett's narrator writes "the ship" and "his agent back home" as if we would know what kind of ship he was apt to be on, or that collector-scientists had agents to sell their specimens. Her narrator gives us enough information that we can understand the implications of the story situation, but in a way that's appropriate to the flexible third-person POV. The effects of these two stories are different because of their narrative stances toward time: one is history and is presented as such; the other puts us *inside* a historical moment.

Before writing about places outside the country (or countries) that we're most familiar with, we need to think through our degree of relationship to the culture we are writing about, since readers certainly will. We have a different relationship to a place depending on whether we were born there, whether our parents or grandparents emigrated from there, whether we've spent a couple of years there or a week's vacation once when we were 14, or whether we have never been there but are relying on books we've read. This last approach is hard to recommend, since people who have lived in the place are likely to find the experience thin or unconvincing, and the writer will be hard pressed to create a vivid setting without plagiarizing from other writers.

Outsiders to a culture often inadvertently create characters whose basic values and ideas reflect those of their own culture rather than the one at hand, thereby making the work unrealistic. We can ask ourselves certain questions before venturing into this territory: What is the difference between appropriation and a justifiable attempt to imagine different lives? Have our life circumstances plunged us into the middle of the issues of the community we're writing about, giving us an urgent connection? How can we do justice to the experience of people from cultures other than our own? How can we ensure that the story's psychological subject matter is appropriate to the situational subject matter of that culture?

For those who feel called to write about cultures other than their own, one successful approach can be to tell stories from the point of view of a character who is also an outsider, looking in at the community. The attempt to understand the differences, similarities, and gaps between the cultures becomes part of what the story is about.

When writing about members of a marginalized or oppressed group that we're not part of, we have even more issues to consider. Some people believe these stories are so important that any writer, regardless of background, has the right to tell them, if they do so with sensitivity and conscientiousness. Other people, however, feel that only members of a particular oppressed group have the right to tell stories arising from that experience. Outsiders, they argue, can't truly understand these experiences, or are illegitimately borrowing the stories for their own gain because they are more dramatic than tales drawn from a life of privilege and relative comfort. These issues continue to inspire heated debates, with writers of all ethnicities and sexual orientations on both sides of the argument.

Religion and Politics

Beginning writers often have a beautifully idealistic desire to use their fiction to bring about greater social justice through the depiction of an ideal world or to convince readers of the happiness and peace that come through surrendering their lives to God. If an environmental activist finds love and success by dedicating his life to saving the world, then even if the writer or characters don't specifically argue for their viewpoints, readers will feel the author is presenting the activist as an example to follow.

In all our years of reading, and even writing, this kind of well-meaning story, we have never yet seen one that had its intended effect. Nonfiction, if the arguments are strong and well supported, may persuade readers. Fiction, on the other hand, if it influences readers' beliefs and behavior, does so subtly, by enlarging people's understanding and therefore their compassion and perspective. It can successfully show humans struggling in political or religious situations. But if the story tries to argue for particular views, or if the events and characters seem to serve as propaganda, it usually becomes lifeless and unreal, and readers feel resistant. Using fiction to make political or religious points is like trying to mow the lawn with a sewing machine; you will only flatten the lawn, and you'll ruin the sewing machine in the process.

Nonetheless, writers have succeeded in showing the effects of religion and politics, those key elements of human life. To tell the story, we have to decide on our approach: detached or partisan. Flannery O'Connor's fiction falls into the latter category. Even though O'Connor doesn't lecture her readers, her religious beliefs are detectable. However, her characters feel so true to life—showing the ways people damn themselves—that readers who don't share her religious faith find her writing compelling. She avoids oversimplifying or falsifying what it's like to be human, beset by temptation and egotism.

Lynna Williams takes a detached approach to religion in her story "Personal Testimony," in which the story's narrator, "twelve and a criminal," writes "personal testimonies" for the senior boys to deliver at evening worship services. Like O'Connor, Williams gives us a complex, multidimensional look at the characters' beliefs and actions. The narrator's engaging voice and the exact details of the camp she knows so well make us insiders to the world of the story:

> The last night of church camp, 1963, and I am sitting in the front row of the junior mixed-voice choir looking out on the crowd in the big sanctuary tent. The tent glows, green and white and unexpected, in the Oklahoma night; our choir director, Dr. Bledsoe, has schooled us in the sudden crescendos needed to compete with the sounds cars make when their drivers cut the corner after a night at the bars on Highway 10 and see the tent rising out of the plain for the first time. The tent is new to Faith Camp this year, a gift to God and the Southern Baptist Convention from the owner of a small circus who repented, and then retired, in nearby Oklahoma City. It is widely rumored among the campers that Mr. Talliferro came to Jesus late in life, after having what my mother would call Life Experiences. Now he walks through camp with the unfailing good humor of a man who, after years of begging hardscrabble farmers to forsake their fields for an afternoon of elephants and acrobats, has finally found a real draw: his weekly talks to the senior boys on "Sin and the Circus" incorporate a standing-room-only question-and-answer period, and no one ever leaves early.

We get a mix of practicality and religion from the very beginning—the choir director teaches techniques for coping with the incursion of the outside world in the form of the noise of passing cars. The suggestion of showmanship and the connection between the boys' testimonies and the circus lay the groundwork for the story to come. The story neither pushes a particular viewpoint nor condemns all religions. We don't know the author's beliefs—they are beside the point. The narrator, however, has a complicated and realistic mixture of belief, doubt, self-dramatizing fantasy, and altruism. She herself is planning to have "Life Experiences" and then repent later, and we both hope for her to get away with it and worry about the inevitable trouble to come.

Theresa Hak Kyung Cha's *Dictee* is a political story, passionately partisan. It takes the form of a collage, weaving photos and calligraphy into a narrative that contains a variety of materials—

Narrative:

> She calls the name Jeanne d'Arc three times.
> She calls the name Ahn Joong Kun five times.

Historical documents:

> We are informed that a bad fight took place about eight miles from Su-won on Sunday, September 12th.

A poetic fragmented rant:

> To the other nations who are not witnesses, who are not subject to the same oppressions, they cannot know. Unfathomable the words, the terminology: enemy,

> atrocities, conquest, betrayal, invasion, destruction. They exist only in the larger perception of History's recording, that affirmed, admittedly and unmistakably, one enemy nation has disregarded the humanity of another. Not physical enough. Not to the very flesh and bone, to the core, to the mark, to the point where it is necessary to intervene, even if to invent anew, expressions, for *this* experience, for this *outcome,* that does not cease to continue.

Cha's example seems to contradict our suggestions that subtlety works best—she exposes her political beliefs fiercely and openly. But—and this is key—the story is more than a rant. The piece as a whole contains many voices. Because of the collage form, we never know what to expect. Pure rant, whether we agree or not, tells us what we already know. A story can tell us what we don't know by making a fable—as Eugene Ionesco does in his play *Rhinoceros*—by using collage like Cha, or by making a strong, unexpected storyline that keeps us engaged with the lives and actions of the characters.

Examples of political fiction range from Doris Lessing's *Children of Violence* series, with her detached and observant sympathy for the communists in Southern Africa and London, to Alice Walker's poetic partisanship in "Everyday Use." Writers can also indirectly make points through a depiction of a complex political reality, as Chinua Achebe does in much of his work, including his story "Civil Peace."

STORY ANALYSIS AND QUESTIONS: "CIVIL PEACE"

(Note: please read the story once before *you read the following analysis. Then, after you read the analysis, look at the story a second time, keeping the discussion questions in mind. You will get the most benefit out of this process if you mark specific passages in the story, take notes, and work through the questions in writing.)*

Though the characters in Chinua Achebe's "Civil Peace" are not engaged politically as far as we can tell, the story reminds us of the ways in which everyone's life is affected by larger-scale politics. The narrator details the sufferings of the main character, Jonathan, almost as if they were caused by a series of natural disasters, rather than by humans. The issues of victimization and villainy that we discuss in relationship to character in Chapter 1 appear here in other guises, and it's worth thinking through who plays what role and how Achebe complicates these roles for us.

The setting, a Nigerian village, shows the aftereffects of a civil war. The story connects readers to national events by concentrating very particularly on the life of one person. The story tells us almost nothing about which entities fought the war or why, but it vividly portrays the chaos and damage through Jonathan's day-to-day recouping of his life.

The tone of the story, the plot's unexpected turns, and what the narrator chooses to focus on or ignore combine to raise for the reader the question of who this character is, and how he is shaped by his setting and circumstances:

> Jonathan Iwegbu counted himself extra-ordinarily lucky. 'Happy survival!' meant so much more to him than just a current fashion of greeting old friends in the first hazy days of peace. It went deep to his heart. He had come out of the war with five inestimable blessings—his head, his wife Maria's head and the heads of three out of their four children. As a bonus he also had his old bicycle—a miracle too but naturally not to be compared to the safety of five human heads.
>
> The bicycle had a little history of its own.

This is a startling opening—in Jonathan's position, most of us would not describe ourselves as lucky. The POV throughout the story is a very close third-person, offering Jonathan's feelings and opinions to us without mediation or commentary—the story often includes exclamations and rhetorical questions on Jonathan's behalf. As a result, when the narrator immediately begins to concentrate on the bicycle, rather than on the memories of what—and who—Jonathan's lost, we see what Jonathan is choosing to focus on. This gives us a strong sense of who Jonathan is. The societal context is ever-present, but the physical setting is sparely described and focused on necessity:

> His children picked mangoes near the military cemetery and sold them to soldiers' wives for a few pennies—real pennies this time—and his wife started making breakfast akara balls for neighbors in a hurry to start life again. With his family earnings he took his bicycle to the villages around and bought fresh palm-wine which he mixed generously in his rooms with the water which had recently started running again in the public tap down the road, and opened up a bar for soldiers and other lucky people with good money.

From this description of action, we can picture where and how the family lives, who in this postwar society has money, and something about the scenery that surrounds them. Given the characters' urgent need to survive in this particular set of circumstances, it would be a bizarre luxury for the story to stop and describe in detail the trees along the road. The only tree we need to know about is the mango tree, since it provides food and money. The kind of information in a story needs to be appropriate to the story's mood, subject, and purposes. The details are also part of the action.

When our readers tell us we need a stronger sense of setting, they might mean more physical description of the landscape, a stronger sense of the objects in the interiors; or they might mean that the story needs societal context, pertinent details of the sociopolitical surroundings. We can directly connect this material to the plot, the point of view, and the lives of the characters, as Achebe does.

DISCUSSION QUESTIONS

1. Where and how does Achebe connect the personal events of Jonathan's days to the larger context of the civil war?
2. How would the story be different if Achebe had described in detail the political struggles and history behind the civil war? What is the effect of his not including this?
3. Ordinarily, contemporary writers avoid having characters speak in dialect, which can seem patronizing or off-putting to today's readers. How does the pidgin work here? What is its effect? How does it work with the other language used in the story?
4. What role is played by the detailed accounts of the money Jonathan receives or pays?
5. In what other areas is Achebe extremely precise and detailed? What elements does he choose to leave vague? What do we understand about Jonathan's life and situation as a result?
6. What points does the story seem to be making? How does Achebe keep it from being didactic?

REVISION: CONTEXTUALIZING THE STORY

In "How Stories Take Place in a Place," from *The Passionate, Accurate Story: Making Your Heart's Truth into Literature,* Carol Bly challenges us to consider including in our stories the past of a place, our worries about its future, and the "sociological periphery":

> Noting the periphery of a place gives the story characters dignity as members of a wider community. . . .
>
> We can thank Virginia Woolf [in *Three Guineas*] for forcing writers never to allow themselves the illusion that all human society is not connected. Of course, the idea of all of human society being interdependent is dear to biologists, feminists, social workers, and physicists, and it has always been upheld by the best of the serious writers, but it is not always dear to literary critics.
>
> Nor, to the best of my knowledge, are short-story writers regularly taught to ask, as they lay out the later drafts of their story,
>
> Where are the *others* who live around the edges of this?
>
> What is the landscape around the edges of your protagonists' properties?
>
> Who or which animals are in the *other* laboratories and offices?
>
> Every field of work, even literature, offers its own reasons for letting its practitioners be self-centered. It is cozy to be self-centered—comparatively painless. Pain avoidance is a *major* human psychological activity.

Occasionally the kinds of questions Bly asks occur to us spontaneously as we're writing a first draft, and produce surprising effects and sidelines.

hough, as she acknowledges, these questions are more useful during , freeing us to get the first draft on paper without being blocked by ical mind. We suffocate our stories if we constantly consult a mental ch ist too early in the creative process.

The more writers wrestle with incorporating research, the more the ideas and the issues become part of the story's themes and advance the plot; they become essential, structural elements. When deciding what material to include during writing and revision, we can ask ourselves, what is the effect of this fact on events? How does enlarging the context enhance the story? How does it illuminate or resonate with the characters' desires and actions?

SOCIETY, CULTURE, AND CONTEXT EXERCISES

1. Choose a place or time you've read about that made you want to read and learn more. Do some research at the library or on the Internet until you have a more palpable sense of this setting. Now, setting aside your research for the moment (you'll return to it later), do a freewrite about this place/time. Allow yourself to remember any fact that struck you, invent characters, inhabit historical people (you can work on historical accuracy later), and follow the story wherever it takes you. Give yourself an uninterrupted, uncensored, unworried half hour to write without stopping to critique yourself.

   A few hours or days after you finish your freewrite, reread it, looking for clues. What issues or images might give rise to potentially dramatic situations? What conflicts are characteristic of this time and place, and how might they develop into events? What questions do you have about the people of this place/time and their problems and choices? From these hints and questions, write the first pages or draft of a story.

2. Return to a story of yours that needs revision. Write a few paragraphs describing some intersection between one of the main character's lives and the larger context—perhaps detailing the character's challenges at work, or political concerns, or involvement with some issue or activity in the local community, or one of the other topics suggested in the discussion of context in this chapter. How might this aspect of the character's life influence the story's action, or complicate the readers' sense of who this person is? Look for places in the story where references to the larger context might be smoothly interlaced. The additions may require changing the plot in small or large ways.

3. Read any newspaper front to back, looking for hints of strange or intriguing stories. Rather than focusing on heroic or sensational material or the police record, think about large-scale stories as well as more intimate ones. (Did a member of Congress vote in some completely unexpected fashion? What power struggles and alliances does that reflect? How did it happen? What might the result be?) Watch out with this exercise for

anything "heartwarming" or for the "isn't that awful?" story. Instead, investigate complicated, peculiar, and layered events. You can do research before, during, or after your first draft, to make the context accurate.

4. Visit an art museum and study the works there. What calls to you? What repels or puzzles you? Make some notes, both about the pieces themselves and about the artists. Then read about the artists—visiting the library or checking university or museum Web sites, which are more likely to offer accurate information than most of the sites on the great hodgepodge of the Web. Is there any event from the lives of these artists that fascinates, baffles, or disturbs you? Write a scene about this event as biography. Now write another scene, as invention, changing the incident and making up your own artist(s). How did the artist come to be in this situation? What happened next? Make it into a story. Don't worry if your art world seems unconvincing in the first draft—if you find yourself connecting with the material, you can take an art class, read more, and gradually make the story convincing.
5. (This reading exercise can be done either individually or in a group.) Choose a story from the anthology and go through it looking for the events, details, and references that provide context. Does the context include art, science, work, play, history, other cultures, religion, and/or politics? Do money, status, or social class make a difference to the story? How does the context enhance the plot or structure of the story? What effect does it have on events? How does it enlarge your view of the characters? How does it relate to the story's themes?

CHAPTER

9

Style and Dialogue

(Anthology selections: "The Cures for Love" and "A Conversation with My Father")

I decided I needed to get "serious" and that meant realism . . . directly from life with no exaggeration. That was really an unfortunate choice because I had no skill whatsoever in that, and no spontaneous attraction to that kind of writing . . . I had the sense that . . . there was something weak about honoring my natural inclinations . . . I wrote some silly little Dr. Seuss poems . . . just trying to be entertaining, and those seemed to have more life in them than anything I'd written in the previous five years. You know Junot Diaz has this theory about how writers come out of a background where language is power? In his case, as an immigrant who could speak English, that was the powerful thing. In my neighborhood back in Chicago it was humor . . . I just knew I had something to say, but I hadn't been able to do it. The stuff I'd been writing looked like it was written by somebody else. So I took the gloves off and decided to do everything I could to do something that wasn't derivative and hackneyed. I had so much fun with that, and I couldn't deny that there was something in it, more energy and honesty than anything I'd written in years.

—George Saunders, Salon.com interview

THE WRITER'S STYLE

A writer can't help but develop an individual style over time, just through the process of writing, rewriting, reading, and trying to get the sentences right. We learn to slow down our revision, to take two hours to go over a couple of paragraphs or a page instead of racing through until we're "finished." We see how a series of small changes can add up to a surprisingly large effect. This process of learning to pay attention to our words can have some pitfalls. As we're learning we might, as George Saunders did initially, fall heavily under the spell of a writer whose style is very different from our own. Or, concerned about sounding too much like someone else, we might work hard to develop an elaborate, quirky style in a quest for originality. Then again, we might avoid anything remotely fancy or literary-sounding in a quest for honesty and transparency.

To avoid unconsciously imitating one writer's voice, we can read a wide variety of fiction, and we can also practice conscious imitation as an exercise, thoroughly digesting what we love (or hate) about a writer's style. By embracing rather than running from influence, we can extend our natural range. When we imitate an author's sentences, we might find ourselves analyzing motive more, or adding more detail about character than we have before, or describing action more specifically.

Writing instructors are usually careful to remind writers not to spend too much energy tinkering with language before addressing the larger questions of structure and character that may require massive reconfiguring of a story. Most advice about sentences, however, teaches us how to make our writing less awkward, but not how to make it wonderful.

Intention is the essential element. Who do we secretly picture reading these sentences? Are we thinking only about demonstrating our brilliance to workshop mates, editors, reviewers, or contest judges? Are we toning down the vocabulary solely to reach an imagined audience of millions? Or have we separated our more anxious, self-aggrandizing fantasies from the work itself? To fully develop the style of a piece, we need to look at it in terms of word choice, tone and vision, figurative language, and sentence and paragraph work.

Word Choice

Thesauruses are full of synonyms, none of which have exactly the same effect: "He ran down the hill," "He scrambled down the slope," and "He descended the gradient" all technically mean the same thing, but the second example makes the runner sound more out of control than in the first one, while the third variation comes across as stiff and unwieldy. The sounds of the words we choose, and their histories, have a powerful influence on the way readers imagine the story we're telling.

English is a grab bag of words from different cultures and times. Although it has its roots in the Germanic Anglo-Saxon language, over the centuries it has lifted words from many others, primarily Greek, Latin, and Latin-based languages like French, Spanish, and Italian. In England, Latin and Greek were historically the language of the highly educated class, and as a result, words with Anglo-Saxon roots ("kick," "door," "sing"—often one syllable long) still tend to sound more direct, more physical to us, while words with Latin and Greek origins ("accelerate," "splendid," "polymorphism"—often multisyllabic) tend to strike us as more abstract and intellectual. The following passage from Richard Bausch's "The Man Who Knew Belle Starr" shows a stylistic effect created by relying more heavily on Anglo-Saxon words:

> Mcrae thought he knew what might happen when the gas ran out: she would make him push the car to the side of the road, and then she would walk him back into the cactus and brush there, and when they were far enough from the road, she would shoot him. He knew this as if she had spelled it all out, and he

> began again to try for the cunning he would need. "Belle," he said. "Why don't we lay low for a few days in Albuquerque?"

For this story about a young ex-convict caught in a life-or-death circumstance, the short, plain words make sense. The word "cunning" suggests an almost animal craftiness; "intelligence" would have seemed more abstract and less suited to Mcrae's perilous situation. The clause "then she would walk him back into the cactus and brush there" crackles with hard consonants, mostly c's and b's, which provide an appropriate soundtrack for the danger Mcrae imagines. The clauses of the first sentence build on each other until the most significant one, "she would shoot him," which comes last for emphasis. If Bausch had ended the sentence ". . . and she would shoot him when they were far enough from the road," it would be just as correct grammatically, but not nearly as dramatic. Although the writing is highly readable, it's crafted with meticulous thoroughness. This kind of "plain" style, when carried out at this high a level, is just as labor-intensive as more elaborate prose.

In "Eisenheim the Illusionist," Steven Millhauser makes very different word choices, in keeping with the time period the story is set in and the subject matter:

> In the last years of the nineteenth century, when the empire of the Hapsburgs was nearing the end of its long dissolution, the art of magic flourished as never before. In obscure villages of Moravia and Galicia, from the Istrian Peninsula to the mists of Bukovina, bearded and black-caped magicians in market squares astonished townspeople by drawing streams of dazzling silk handkerchiefs from empty paper cones, removing billiard balls from children's ears, and throwing into the air decks of cards that assumed the shapes of fountains, snakes, and angels before returning to the hand . . . It was the age of levitation and decapitations, of ghostly apparitions and sudden vanishings, as if the tottering empire were revealing through the medium of its magicians its secret desire for annihilation.

The much higher percentage of Latinate words—"dissolution," "flourished," "obscure," "levitation," "decapitations," "apparitions," and "annihilation"—gives the narrative voice a more distanced, formal, and intellectual feel. Note, however, that Millhauser still relies on Anglo-Saxon words to give concrete details that make the abstractions vivid: "drawing," "streams," "dazzling," "balls," "decks," and "snakes," for example. If he had written "extracting rivulets of scintillating silk textiles from vacant paper cones," the effect would have been over the top.

The sound of words—both individually and in concert with each other—matters too. The phrase "drawing streams of dazzling silk handkerchiefs from empty paper cones" gains some of its power from the way the consonants, particularly the d's and s's, reinforce and play against each other. Substitute the word "bright" for "dazzling," and the sentence loses some of its sonic pizzazz.

It's easy to become overly abstract when relying on Latinate words, but that's not to say we should avoid them. We should use them only when artistically appropriate, never to try to make ourselves sound more intelligent and our story more "serious." If we use obscure words like "eructation" and "sudorific" in order to show off, the intention will show through, and our readers will be less apt to continue.

We don't have to take courses in Latin, Greek, and Old English in order to figure out how to choose the best words. The more we read, the more we pick up on the connotations that different words have. Beginning writers may choose more formal words, unconsciously reaching for the kind of literary authority we tend to associate with this kind of language. As we develop, we find ways to use a more contemporary voice, unless we're actually writing historical fiction, and even the style of a writer like Millhauser could not be mistaken for the styles of the past.

Tone and Vision

Vision is the writer's worldview, which colors everything in the story. Tone is the way the writer expresses that worldview. A writer's, or narrator's, habitual attitude about the world gives the work its characteristic flavor: cynicism or hopefulness, boredom or excitement, humor or bleakness, or some specific combination of any of these. Paying attention to our own vision can help us avoid being sideswiped by the influence of another writer's voice.

We can see, from a couple of examples, the way that tone and vision work together to create two writers' very particular voices. From the very first lines of Sherman Alexie's "This is What It Means to Say Phoenix, Arizona," we can hear both the narrator's cynical political awareness and a genuine concern for the viewpoint character:

> Just after Victor lost his job at the Bureau of Indian Affairs, he also found out that his father had died of a heart attack in Phoenix, Arizona. Victor hadn't seen his father in a few years, had only talked to him on the telephone once or twice, but there still was a genetic pain, which was as real and immediate as a broken bone. Victor didn't have any money. Who does have money on a reservation, except the cigarette and fireworks salespeople? His father had a savings account waiting to be claimed, but Victor needed to find a way to get from Spokane to Phoenix. Victor's mother was just as poor as he was, and the rest of the family didn't have any use at all for him. So Victor called the tribal council.

The rhetorical question, "Who does have money on a reservation, except the cigarette and fireworks salespeople?" indirectly accuses the salespeople of profiting at the expense of others. The phrase "the rest of his family didn't have any use at all for him" uses blunt, almost flippant language to sum up complex emotional terrain. The overall effect is to express a cynical weariness. At the same time, the story does convey compassion toward Victor. The metaphor "as real and immediate as a broken bone" makes Victor's pain vivid, rather than diminishing its importance. The tension between cynicism and compassion, along with the energy of the language, give us a sense of Alexie's voice.

The tone of the opening of Carolyn See's *Golden Days* is very different:

> Once, I remember, in an entirely different world, I'd interviewed that East Coast photographer who made a good living taking pictures of people as they jumped. He asked if he could take a picture of me, and I jumped! I put everything into it! I took a look outside of his white studio into the grimy New York streets below; I thought of how I'd jumped from a ratty house with a tired mom, past two husbands, one sad, one mad; hopscotched with kids and lovers and ended up—here? In *New York!* I sized up the directions of the room, tried to find east. I started out from there, ran a maximum of ten heavy steps, and jumped—not far, not far enough by a long shot—and came down hard.
>
> The photographer winced. "Try it again," he said.
>
> So I went back to the far corner, ran, defied gravity, jumped. This time I held up my arms, held up my chin, grinned. His camera clicked. "That's it."
>
> "*That's it?*"
>
> "You only have one jump in you," he said. (I found out later he said it to everybody.)

The narrator's voice here is defiant, funny, sad, and inviting. The way the sentences jump from thought to thought shows us a mind with no pretense, experiencing the kind of freedom that George Saunders found when he no longer tried to write according to the "rules" of realism. The narrator in See's passage is on an urgent mission: to teach the art of survival. Both the long and the short sentences create an impression of compressed time and speed, primarily by means of what they leave out. The thumbnail description of her two husbands—"one sad, one mad"—is both humorous in its rhyming and rueful in its content. The passage lets us know that the narrator has been through too much not to have fun, and that if she only has one jump in her, she's going to make it a good one. Like Alexie, See has worked with the rhythm, word choice, and mood to create a tone appropriate to the story's vision of the world.

Figurative Language

Figurative language, an essential part of poetry, can bring some of poetry's compression and vividness to fiction. Metaphors and similes are both ways to compare one thing to something else. The best metaphors and similes usually mark a similarity that we might not have noticed before, but which seems surprising and right once we hear it. They startle us into seeing the world freshly. In a simile, the comparison is made obvious by the words "like" or "as." With a metaphor, the comparison is only implied. If the things being compared are too similar or too often linked, the metaphor will go flat ("His teeth were pearls," "puppy love," etc.). If the things being compared are too dissimilar, the metaphor may seem arbitrary, confusing, or comical ("Her heart was a bicycle wheel").

Metaphors and similes are like raisins in spice cake: they add surprise, interest, and variation when used in the right amount, but, if overdone, the eaters (or readers) may be so distracted by them that they wish to start picking them out with a fork and leaving them by the side of the plate.

Edie Meidav's novel *The Far Field* gracefully incorporates both metaphors and similes in a variety of ways. When the protagonist, Henry, sees the palm trees of Ceylon for the first time, Meidav describes them through his eyes: "They flocked up a slope, tentpoles for a canopy of . . . green . . ." Meidav uses metaphor to compare trunks to poles, and leaves to the canopy of the tent: we make the connection instantly. Later, Henry is thirsty: "His palate is dry as road dust." Here simile is more appropriate than metaphor: "His palate is road dust" would be confusing. Readers need the word "dry" here to make the connection so they don't need to stop and figure out what the similarity is.

Sometimes a metaphor is contained in a single word, creating a highly poetic effect. Henry is in a fever: "When he thought he heard his friend pacing about outside he called out and heard nothing but the hiss of sulfured water and the answering spasm of night insects." A spasm is literally a muscular contraction, but here Meidav uses the word to suggest the jerky movements of the insects, trusting the reader to make the connection. Because the image is so vivid and tangible, readers can grasp it at once. Carrying this poetic compression even further, Meidav occasionally uses metaphors as verbs, as when she draws on the branching qualities of veins: ". . . a swamp drift of vapors had made the African cliffs vein into a mirage of faces." Metaphors work best when they are appropriate to the world of the characters, and when the connection is not too tenuous or far-fetched. All of the metaphors and similes here fit with the mood and subject: they have to do with travel (tents, road dust, physical discomfort, and the presence of many unknown faces). The figures of speech reflect the hallucinogenic sense of fever hanging over Henry.

Some plainspoken writers shy away from metaphor altogether because they think of it as belonging to the poets or to more language-driven fiction writers. But even character-driven fiction has a place for metaphor. In *Anna Karenina,* Karenin has his first suspicion that his wife Anna might be unfaithful when she talks too much to Count Vronsky at a party. Karenin chides Anna and she pretends not to know what he means:

> She looked at him so simply, so gaily, that no one who did not know her as her husband did could have noticed anything unnatural either in the sound or in the meaning of her words. But for him who knew her, who knew that when he went to bed five minutes late, she noticed it and asked the reason, who knew that she told him at once her every joy, happiness, or grief—for him it meant a great deal

> to see now that she did not want to notice his state or say a word about herself. He saw that the depth of her soul, formerly always open to him, was now closed to him. Moreover, by her tone he could tell that she was not embarrassed by it, but was as if saying directly to him: yes it's closed, and so it ought to be and will be in the future. He now felt the way a man would feel coming home and finding his house locked up. "But perhaps the key will still be found," thought Alexei Alexandrovich.

Most of the language here is quite plain, though it gives a very specific sense of their relationship. The one metaphor, the house locked against him, is a more powerful image of their separation than any amount of highly dramatized emotion. It's also appropriate because he feels that he owns her, that she, like the house, is a possession there for his comfort, so we feel both sympathy for and impatience with him. He has a part in bringing about the tragedy that's about to befall both of them.

If Tolstoy had said that Karenin felt as if his threshing machine had stopped working, we would be completely distracted. For one thing, Karenin is not an agricultural man—he lives his life indoors. For another, we can see how a marriage can be like a home, but, up until that point at least, it hadn't been much like a threshing machine. And we might start wondering—were the Russians as apt to use threshing machines as the British? Didn't the serfs do most of the work? We might even, depending on our temperament, put down the book and begin wandering around the Internet looking for answers.

Unlike metaphors and similes, which have a one-to-one correlation with the objects or situations they capture, symbols have multiple meanings and associations. They usually convey archetypal, collectively shared meanings (sun, moon, money, ocean, night). It can be tricky to either employ or undercut the familiar meanings: though sometimes we succeed, at other times we distract the reader if the symbol is heavy-handed or overused. Readers may not get the full impact of a subtle symbol until they finish the story; understanding the way a story works on a symbolic level can be one of the pleasures of the backward experience of reading a story.

Sentence and Paragraph Work

Compare the following two versions of the same paragraph (it might be a good idea to read them aloud):

1.

> The abandoned house was two doors from Henry's. Anyone could see that it wore cinderblock bandages over the windows and doorway. Henry imagined that it looked like a mummy with blanked eyes and stilled howling mouth. He noticed that the blasted yard had no gate or fence. The stoop was barren too. It didn't have a rail. Henry wondered if someone had taken the ironwork for scrap.

> The mummy house was a flat surface with no windows. It made a high wall for wallball games. A spaldeen was bounced high against a wall by a thrower. The spaldeen was then caught by a catcher. The catcher stood in the field of the street. He zipped between cars to make the catch.

2.

> Two doors from Henry's was the abandoned house. It wore cinderblock bandages over the windows and doorway like a mummy with blanked eyes and stilled howling mouth, and had a blasted yard with no fence or gate. The stoop was barren too, no rail. Possibly someone had taken the ironwork for scrap. The mummy house was a flat surface with no windows, so it made a high wall for wallball, a game where a spaldeen was bounced high against the wall by a thrower and caught by a catcher standing in the field of the street, zipping between cars to make the catch.

The second paragraph is from Jonathan Lethem's *Fortress of Solitude.* The first paragraph is our version, rewritten (with apologies to Lethem) to show many of the common faults of writers' early drafts; the choppy series of sentences demonstrates just how effective Lethem's more complex structures are. Both versions contain the same vivid details, and both present the same information in roughly the same order. But in the first example, most of the sentences have the same structures, which gives the passage a thunking, repetitive rhythm, and makes it hard for the reader to know which details are most significant. The paragraph is like a subdivision full of identical houses, offering no landmarks to give us our bearings.

The second version eliminates repetition, avoids excessive use of the word "to be," and has much more variety in its sentence structures. But the sentences aren't put together differently just for the sake of novelty. Lethem structures the sentences to show how certain details relate to each other, to emphasize other details, and to create a rhythm that flows with the naturalness of speech. The long second sentence collects almost all of the physical description of the house, from the cinderblocks to the lack of a fence or gate. The metaphor for the doorway—"stilled howling mouth"—is now in the middle of a sentence, where it calls less attention to itself than it would at the end—whatever is placed at the end of the sentence tends to gain extra emphasis, something this dramatic metaphor doesn't need. The third and fourth sentences are shorter than the second, and simpler—they each have just one subject and one verb. Their brevity provides some breathing room between two longer sentences. They also both concentrate on just one detail—the stoop—to focus the reader's attention. The fifth sentence, the longest of all, shows the relation of the house to the games the children play. The description of wallball is collected in a subordinate clause ("where a spaldeen was bounced high . . ."); this description, extensive as it is, is less important than the first part of the sentence. Subordinating conjunctions like "where," "after," "unless," "while," "because," "that," and "if" make it clear that whatever comes after them is additional information, not the main point.

Although Lethem's writing is rich with detail, it's also concise, with no wasted words. Lethem has avoided excessive passive constructions. He's chosen active and specific verbs and nouns, pared away any excesses of detail that would obscure rather than reveal the scene, and eliminated unnecessary repetition. The directness of the POV avoids what John Gardner and Janet Burroway call filtering. Burroway quotes Gardner as describing this as "the needless filtering of the image through some observing consciousness. The amateur writes: 'Turning, she noticed two snakes fighting in among the rocks.' Compare: 'She turned. In among the rocks, two snakes were fighting. . . .' Generally speaking—though no laws are absolute in fiction—vividness urges that almost every occurrence of such phrases as 'she noticed' and 'she saw' be suppressed in favor of direct presentation of the thing seen."

Filtering can plague the first drafts of writers at any stage. It creates problems of excessive distance: the scene remains flat rather than coming to life in a reader's mind, as Lethem's does.

We have heard some writers say that a series of short sentences creates a feeling of speed, because we move quickly from one sentence to the next. According to this way of thinking, a long sentence slows the reader. But there's no simple rule to apply here. Everything depends on the rhythms involved, the word choices, and the variations in sentence structure. Long sentences can move swiftly and sleekly, carrying the reader downstream, like the second sentence of Lethem's paragraph. And a chain of short sentences can slow the pace very deliberately.

Sometimes, though, a long sentence does create a sense of suspension. The opening of Maxine Clair's story "The Great War" gets much of its power from a combination of the sensory details it uses and the rhythm of the paragraph.

> It is dusk. You could say that every time Pearlean has come out to sit on her front porch, every time she has sat in the flamingo-pink glider that, with every rocking glide, squawks from its warp of metal on metal, every time she has brought her comb and brush and sat in the glider combing her just-washed hair, every evening that she has painted her toenails pink on the porch while she watched the children play hopscotch, every single evening after ironing tablecloths and pinafores all day, after laying white shirts out on the table to sprinkle and roll like white jelly rolls to be ironed and on hangers all turned the same way by six o'clock when cars drive up and collect the blouses and skirts, the white shirts with not too much starch and, Lord no, no blueing, no bleach—all those evenings after all those days, you could say that she has been waiting.

The short, flat, declarative sentence, followed by an unusually long sentence, creates a contrast that not only sounds aesthetically pleasing but also suits the subject matter. The key verb that makes the second sentence grammatically complete (waiting) is placed at the very end. We're not just being told that she's waiting; we experience it for ourselves as we wait for the end of the sentence. In the second sentence, the words themselves are short and plain, but the effect is lyrical because Clair orchestrates them into a complex, rhythmic arrangement. This opening reveals the character and her world, and, at the same time, gives the reader the question that takes us to the next paragraph: what is Pearlean waiting for?

We can read our sentences aloud to see how they fit the pace and themes of the story. When we're varying the lengths of our sentences in a paragraph, which are we making shorter, which longer, and why? If we have several long sentences in a row, should we use the occasional short sentence to provide breathing space? Is there information that should be collected into a single sentence? Repetition we can eliminate? A detail or event that we want to emphasize with its own short sentence? How can we highlight the most important information? Which are the most important words, and what happens if we place them at the beginning or the end of the sentence or paragraph?

STORY ANALYSIS AND QUESTIONS: "THE CURES FOR LOVE"

(Note: please read the story once before *you read the following analysis. Then, after you read the analysis, look at the story a second time, keeping the discussion questions in mind. You will get the most benefit out of this process if you mark specific passages in the story, take notes, and work through the questions in writing.)*

Charles Baxter controls the tone of "The Cures for Love" with his word choice and use of figurative language. A young woman left by her lover, in an extreme of pain, begins to find her way out of it by reading Ovid and taking an unlikely bus trip to the airport, where she meets an old friend whom she has forgotten. From the beginning, the language is full of surprises:

> On the day he left her for good, she put on one of his caps. It fit snugly over her light brown hair. The cap had the manufacturer's name of his pickup truck embossed above the visor in gold letters. She wore the cap backward, the way he once had, while she cooked dinner. Then she kept it on in her bath that evening. When she leaned back in the tub, the visor hitting the tiles, she could smell his sweat from the inside of the headband, even over the smell of the soap. His sweat had always smelled like freshly broiled whitefish.

We don't even know her name yet. We know she's been left by a lover, that he's apparently walked out on her before, that she wants to be close to him despite everything, that she has "light brown hair." The way we inhabit the moment with her is through her senses, not only sight and touch, but smell—"his sweat had always smelled like freshly broiled whitefish." This kind of unexpected detail and the matter-of-fact tone are more enticing than a long description of Kit's feelings of grief and desperation would have been.

Baxter also uses both narrative commentary and metaphorical language to convey the pain that Kit feels in the days that follow, replacing emotional excess with an intensity of language:

> Her cat now yowled around five-thirty, at exactly the time when he used to come home. She—the cat—had fallen for him the moment she'd seen him, rushing over to him, squirming on her back in his lap, declawed paws waving in the air. The guy had had a gift, a tiny genius for relentless charm, that caused anything—women, men, cats, trees for all she knew—to fall in love with him, and not calmly, either, but at the upper frequencies.
>
> Her clocks ached. Time had congealed. For the last two days, knowing he would go, she had tried to be busy. She had tried reading books, for example. They couldn't preoccupy her. They were just somebody's thoughts. Her wounded imagination included him and herself, but only those two, bone hurtling against bone.

One way to show rather than simply tell about Kit's relationship would have been to dramatize it, providing scenes of Kit and her boyfriend interacting. But since this story focuses on Kit's state of mind after the breakup, Baxter chooses another way to be specific—he conveys the distinct flavor of the relationship metaphorically.

The narrative commentary on the guy's charm can be read as Kit's thoughts. The cat's behavior serves as a metaphor for Kit's—the first two sentences give a vivid image of the helpless, undignified stance she takes in relation to her boyfriend. Even the paws are declawed, a metaphor for Kit's weakness and inability to defend herself emotionally. The next sentence illustrates the power of creatively chosen adjectives: the man's genius for charm is "tiny," and his charm is "relentless," two surprising words that show Kit acknowledging his ability while also expressing anger and contempt for it. The paragraph might have ended "and not calmly, either, but wildly." But Baxter chooses a subtle metaphor, "at the upper frequencies," which vividly describes the piercing, jangling quality of that love, and also echoes and reinforces the "yowl" at the beginning of the paragraph. The sensory detail and metaphor create an almost physical sense of how the pain of loss can be like a high-pitched, inescapable noise.

DISCUSSION QUESTIONS

1. What other metaphors does Baxter use in the story, and how do they work with the themes and subject of the story?
2. Where and how does Baxter use plain language and how does it affect your reading of the metaphors?
3. How does the poetry affect the mood and tone of the story?
4. Which words or phrases are particular to Ovid, which to Kit, and which to the narrative voice?

5. How is the language of the dialogue in the story like or unlike the language of Kit's thoughts? What effect does the dialogue have on the story?

DIALOGUE AND SUBTEXT

People say one thing but mean another—either consciously or unconsciously. People misunderstand or ignore what someone else has said, they digress, their words say one thing and their tone of voice or body language says another, they make remarks that surprise even themselves. Of course, in real life we do sometimes say, "Can you hand me that hammer?" and mean nothing more than that. But fictional dialogue is most effective when it captures the tangle of meaning that arises when language gets away from people. By studying both real-life and fictional dialogue, we can train ourselves to become masters of this tangle. In good fictional dialogue, the digressions from meaning give us information that advances the plot, reveals more about our characters and their relationships with each other, and complicates the rhythm and prevailing emotions of the scene.

Subtext—everything the characters are *not* saying—gives dialogue much of its weight and depth. In our early drafts, our characters tend to say exactly what they mean, respond to each other directly, and discuss all their problems and fears openly. In later drafts, much of the meaning moves underground so that we have a sense of the history and secrets of each character. The range of possible subtexts to conversations is as wide as the range of characters and their concerns. Some characters, unable or unwilling to state their meaning directly, intend that the person they're speaking to will perceive the subtext. They may want to express an idea or feeling without having to take responsibility. They may want to pick a fight while appearing innocent of bad intentions (they say, "Isn't it freezing in here?" but they mean, "You don't care about anyone's comfort but your own, and you've opened all the windows again, even though it's 30 degrees outside.") Or they may not be fully aware of their own thoughts and motivations. Examples of subtext include the conversation about hair between Heidi and Dina in "Drinking Coffee Elsewhere" (see Chapter 4, "Advancing Plot through Dialogue and Exposition") and the excerpts from Chitra Banerjee Divakaruni and Grace Paley later in this chapter.

Apart from its functionality, dialogue can offer the reader a sheer physical pleasure. Dialogue opens up the page, lets light and air into huge blocks of text, allows us to feel present in the scene, and provides a break from the author's voice. A writer can keep the dialogue at about the same level of formality as the narrative voice, or can mix vernacular dialogue with poetic description and philosophizing, like William Kennedy in *Ironweed:*

> "What the hell you workin' out now?" Francis asked.
>
> "The worms," Rudy said. "How many worms you get in a truckload of dirt."

> "You countin' 'em?"
>
> "Hundred and eight so far," said Rudy.
>
> "Dizzy bedbug," said Francis.
>
> When the truck was fully loaded Francis and Rudy climbed atop the dirt and the driver rode them to a slope where a score of graves of the freshly dead sent up the smell of sweet putrescence, the incense of unearned mortality and interrupted dreams. The driver, who seemed inured to such odors, parked as close to the new graves as possible and Rudy and Francis then carried shovelfuls of dirt to the dead while the driver dozed in the truck.

The Latinate words—"sweet putrescence," "the incense of unearned mortality," and "inured"—seem as natural here as the affectionate, loopy, naturalistic dialogue. They work in combination with the exact details—the image of Rudy and Francis with their dirt and the driver dozing. The description doesn't try too hard: we don't need to get a lot of detail about how the dirt looks. It's the style that surprises us, and convinces us with its authority.

Dialogue Rhythms and Styles

Even when we're reading silently, we *hear* dialogue inside our heads: the staccato of an argument or series of commands; the slow, spare discussions that arise out of intimacy; the chattering or the painful silences when people avoid saying what they mean. To give an idea of the range of dialogue styles, we've selected two passages, one spare and realistic by Chitra Banerjee Divakaruni, the other rich and stylized by Don DeLillo. Reading the passages aloud is a good way to hear the differences.

In "The Lives of Strangers," Chitra Banerjee Divakaruni tells the story of Leela, who's traveling in a group through her parents' homeland—India—for the first time. She begins to make friends with a woman the other travelers see as bad luck, which fascinates Leela because she's come through a period in her own life so hard that she attempted suicide, though her family doesn't know this. As the women lie awake, talking about Mrs. Das, the subtext of their conversation has everything to do with the contagion of bad luck, though no one says so directly:

> The talk starts at the end of the first day's trek. In one of the women's tents, where Leela lies among pilgrims who huddle in blankets and nurse aching muscles, a voice rises from the dark.
>
> "Do you know, Mrs. Das's bedroll didn't get to the camp. They can't figure out what happened—the guides swear they tied it onto a mule this morning—"
>
> "That's right," responds another voice. "I heard them complaining because they had to scrounge around in their own packs to find her some blankets."

> In the anonymous darkness, the voices take on cruel, choric tones. They release suspicion into the close air like bacteria, ready to multiply wherever they touch down.
>
> "It's like that time on the train, remember, when she was the only one who got food poisoning—"
>
> "Yes, yes—"
>
> "I wonder what will happen next—"
>
> "As long as it doesn't affect us—"
>
> "How can you be sure? Maybe next time it will—"
>
> "I hate to be selfish, but I wish she wasn't here with us at all—"
>
> "Me, too—"

The rhythm of their talk is naturalistic, or apparently naturalistic. They don't finish sentences; they interrupt each other. And yet, the dialogue is highly crafted to give this illusion of actual speech, which in real life would be much messier, more repetitive, and more long-winded.

In Don DeLillo's *White Noise,* the characters create a different kind of choir: not naturalistic, but stylized, the voices not so much differentiated as intertwined, part of one patterned whole. DeLillo depicts a family full of stepbrothers and stepsisters, six of them in the car with the narrator and his wife Babette, driving to the mall. One child tries to entrap her mother into admitting something about Dylar, the mysterious pill she's taking, which leads them into discussing Dakar, coasts, surfer movies, tidal waves that one daughter says are called "origamis," and so on. There is an inherent pleasure for readers in eavesdropping on a conversation, even if we don't immediately understand every reference the characters make. We are sharing in the family intimacy. About halfway through the conversation, the characters begin to try to educate each other about camels:

> "What is it camels store in their humps?" Babette said. "Food or water? I could never get that straight."
>
> "There are one-hump camels and two-hump camels," Heinrich told her. "So it depends which kind you're talking about."
>
> "Are you telling me a two-hump camel stores food in one hump and water in the other?"
>
> "The important thing about camels," he said, "is that camel meat is considered a delicacy."
>
> "I thought that was alligator meat," Denise said.
>
> "Who introduced the camel to America?" Babette said. "They had them out west for a while to carry supplies to coolies who were building the great railroads that met at Ogden, Utah. I remember my history exams."
>
> "Are you sure you're not talking about llamas?" Heinrich said.
>
> "The llamas stayed in Peru," Denise said. "Peru has the llama, the vicuña and one other animal. Bolivia has tin. Chile has copper and iron."
>
> "I'll give anyone in this car five dollars," Heinrich said, "if they can name the population of Bolivia."

> "Bolivians," my daughter said.
>
> The family is the cradle of the world's misinformation. There must be something in family life that generates factual error. Overcloseness, the noise and heat of being. Perhaps something even deeper, like the need to survive.

This last paragraph is the beginning of a long speculation on fact, family units, magic, and "the orthodoxy of the clan." Part of the delight of this passage comes from the assumptions it makes about our intelligence as readers: even before we're told we're getting misinformation, the deadpan ludicrousness of some of the information—the earnest way they speculate on the camels' humps—allows us to become insiders in what may or may not be a joke. The uneasiness comes from our not being sure—none of the characters laughs, grins, or gives any other sign of finding themselves clever and their conversation unusual. We have a sense of texture, of people living in the world, and of the calmness of their misinformation.

DeLillo uses minimal dialogue tags to show who is speaking, and Divakaruni uses none, which creates a rhythmic, back-and-forth exchange. But for some passages of dialogue, writers will make a point of describing characters' tones or the gestures they make as they speak. When a line of dialogue could be read two different ways, it helps to indicate what the character is doing, or give their tone of voice or facial expression.

Dialogue Tags and Accompanying Actions

We've all been trained not to write sentences like "'That's a wretched thing to say,' he shouted angrily," and "'You're too good to me,' she simpered girlishly." Of course there's no need to use adverbs to repeat the point of a line of dialogue. And too many vivid verbs (she wailed, he gasped, he expostulated, she ejaculated, he screeched) shove the reader right out of the story. As we move along in our writing, we also stop having our characters do the dishes in every single scene or roll pencils between their fingers, meaningless actions that break up the dialogue but add nothing to our understanding of the scene. Still, we want to avoid getting so careful that our prose goes lifeless on us. Sometimes we want long stretches of unadorned dialogue; sometimes we want to hear the characters' thoughts, sometimes we want to know what they're doing. And sometimes we even want some verb besides "said" or "asked," as in the following examples.

From Amy Hempel's "In the Cemetery Where Al Jolson Is Buried," told by a narrator whose best friend is in the hospital, dying:

> "Bring me something back," she says. "Anything from the beach. Or the gift shop. Taste is no object."
>
> The doctor slowly draws the curtain around the bed.
>
> "Wait!" she cries.
>
> I look in at her.

> "Anything," she says, "except a magazine subscription."
> The doctor turns away.
> I watch her mouth laugh.

In Tommaso Landolfi's "Gogol's Wife," a "biographer" of Gogol tells us, as a contribution to Gogol studies, about the supposed mad passion of the genius for an inflatable wife:

> After a certain time Nikolai Vassilevitch seemed to pluck up courage. He burst into tears, but somehow they were more manly tears. He wrung his hands again, seized mine in his, and walked up and down, muttering: "That's enough! We can't have any more of this. This is an unheard of thing. How can such a thing be happening to me? How can a man be expected to put up with *this*?"
>
> He then leapt furiously upon the pump, the existence of which he seemed just to have remembered, and, with it in his hand, dashed like a whirlwind to Caracas. He inserted the tube in her anus and began to inflate her. . . . Weeping the while, he shouted like one possessed: "Oh, how I love her, how I love her, my poor, poor darling! . . . But she's going to burst! Unhappy Caracas, most pitiable of God's creatures! But die she must!"

In our own writing, we might try—if we have nothing but unadorned "said" and "asked"—the occasional unexpected adverb or more descriptive dialogue tag. Any time we're working on our own dialogue, it makes sense to find five or six examples of writers whose dialogue we admire and to read one scene after another aloud, noting the rhythms, the kind of information conveyed and when and how, the pauses, the tags or lack of tags. And then we read our own dialogue aloud, listening to the rhythms, watching for excessive repetition, eliminating lines that don't work, and examining our use of action and gesture. Depending on our intentions, we make sure that each of our characters has a distinctive and separate voice, or else that all the voices work together to form a coherent stylized pattern.

STORY ANALYSIS AND QUESTIONS: "A CONVERSATION WITH MY FATHER"

(<u>Note</u>: please read the story once before *you read the following analysis. Then, after you read the analysis, look at the story a second time, keeping the discussion questions in mind. You will get the most benefit out of this process if you mark specific passages in the story, take notes, and work through the questions in writing.)*

Grace Paley's dialogue in "A Conversation with My Father" creates a strong subtext for the story through individual voices, each with their own rhythms and concerns. Late in the story, we begin to see that the argument about narrative expresses the two characters' views of the world and the father's concern for his daughter:

> "Poor woman. Poor girl, to be born in a time of fools, to live among fools. The end. The end. You were right to put that down. The end."
>
> I didn't want to argue, but I had to say, "Well, it is not necessarily the end, Pa."
>
> "Yes," he said, "what a tragedy. The end of a person."
>
> "No, Pa," I begged him. "It doesn't have to be. She's only about forty. She could be a hundred different things in this world as time goes on. A teacher or a social worker. An ex-junkie! Sometimes it's better than having a master's in education."
>
> "Jokes," he said. "As a writer that's your main trouble. You don't want to recognize it. Tragedy! Plain tragedy! Historical tragedy! No hope. The end."
>
> "Oh, Pa," I said. "She could change."
>
> "In your own life too, you have to look it in the face." He took a couple of nitroglycerin. "Turn to five," he said, pointing to the dial on the oxygen tank. He inserted the tubes into his nostrils and breathed deep. He closed his eyes and said, "No."

The father, dying, is afraid for his daughter, who he sees as foolishly optimistic, unworldly, and playing around with stories about people sitting in trees (a reference to Paley's famous "Faith in a Tree"). How will she survive the world when he's gone? But the closest he comes to actually saying this is, "In your own life, too, you have to look it in the face." The rest is implied in his remarks about her fictional character.

Paley differentiates the voices of these two characters as clearly as she does their views. The father uses a common Russian Jewish syntax, shared by many for whom Yiddish is a first language. He frequently inverts his sentences ("As a writer that's your main trouble.") He also uses frequent short fragments for dramatic emphasis. The daughter's speech still has the flavor of the language she grew up with, but her dialogue is more American, the inversions and fragments less pronounced. The words she uses when she switches to storytelling mode are different from her usual speech, but still recognizably her own.

DISCUSSION QUESTIONS

1. Where in the story does the dialogue express connection between the characters?
2. Where does the dialogue express conflict? What different kinds of conflict do the characters experience, and how do the words they use show this?
3. How does Paley vary the rhythms of the sentences and paragraphs? When does she use long or short sentences and how do her choices relate to the meaning of those sentences? When and how does she use dialogue tags, tone, or gestures?

4. Which words or phrases seem key to the story's effects?
5. How and why is the story-within-a-story different in tone and rhythm from the main story?

REVISION: LINE EDITING

When we revise, if we sink back into the world we're making, then we can focus on refining word choice, tone, figurative language, sentence and paragraph structures, and dialogue. We can fit these elements to the themes and mood of the story. The following is an earlier version of the opening of ZZ Packer's story, "Drinking Coffee Elsewhere." To keep other writers from getting discouraged, we want to point out that this is *not* a first draft, but one far enough along that it's already strong and vivid. The character of Dina is fairly well-established, as is her rebelliousness at Yale. The changes in the version that appeared in *The New Yorker,* and later in the eponymously titled collection of Packer's stories, are subtle ones. Here is the draft version, followed by a detailed examination of some of the changes and their effects, and finally the opening paragraphs of the published story, for easy reference:

> Outside the library, girls wore denim cut-offs and tank tops, their brown legs smooth-looking and sexy in that metropolitan sunlight. "You not fast and nasty and loose like them girls who be shakin' their rumps on the street," Miss Gloria, the Enoch Pratt librarian told me, then chucked her chin toward the library windows. A row of hair salons lined the street across from the library, and when high-school dismissed, girls would troop to the hairdressers and come out hours later: a flash of neon nails, coiffs the color and sheen of patent leather, curls that bounced with each step toward the bus stop. I watched them with envy, with longing. Miss Gloria went on to shake her head in slow disapproving arcs at these other girls, clicking her teeth like castanets. "Uhn uhn uhn," was all she had left to say about those girls. "You go on to college and get out of Baltimore. Don't let these boys around here sweet-talk you. Next thing you know, you'll have so many babies crying and spitting and pooping you'll think you'd opened a nursery."
>
> Miss Gloria had five sons of her own, and though she raised them well enough, two of them were in prison. The third had left on a Wednesday afternoon, never to be seen again. The two youngest sons lived with her although they themselves had children Miss Gloria had rescued from cocker-spaniel-like hyperactivity, popsicle juice dripping from their mouths. She didn't play around, and she'd turned these grandkids into children who sat through church service like respectable brown statuettes. They helped out at the library shelving books, and if they ran when walking was in order, or forgot to say "ma'am" or "sir" to their elders, Miss Gloria shot them a look which meant they'd get a royal ass-whupping when they got home.

> But Miss Gloria could never guess that I often imagined myself as one of her grandchildren. I wished I could say, "Me, too. Take me in, too," but whenever I checked out books, she always looked at me with the proud, glinting eyes of someone taking in the sight of a finished product. When I'd gotten the acceptance letter from Yale, she was the first to hear the news.
>
> I got on a plane for the first time, took a taxi to Yale's Old Campus, put away the luggage Miss Gloria had given me, and before I knew it, I was back outside, right in the middle of old faux-Gothic buildings. You couldn't walk a step without hearing some carillon or other, they were chiming all around me, their notes annoyingly ancient and whimsical. I was sure whoever was in charge hid them in the branches of trees the way supermarkets rigged up Muzak speakers behind the cantaloupes.
>
> Before the orientation games began, groups of freshmen milled about like throngs of penguins at an Antarctic social. In my group, the Freshman counselor made everyone play a game called Trust. The idea of Trust, as far as I could tell, was that you could learn to trust your fellow students if you simply had the faith to fall backwards and wait for four scrawny former high-school geniuses to catch you, just as your head threatened to crack open on the slate sidewalk.
>
> "No way," I said to the Playboy blonde counselor. The white boys waited for me to fall back, holding their arms out for me, sincerely, gallantly, forming a sort of stretcher of shaky ladder rungs. I shook my head. "No fucking way."
>
> "It's all cool, it's all cool," the counselor said, her palms facing me as though she were backing away from a growling dog. She pulled me aside and amicably explained, once again, that it "was cool" if I didn't want to play this game, that I was my own person and needed my own space.
>
> "Sister," she said, not sounding nearly as street-wise as she'd wanted to, but like one nun addressing another, "you don't have to play this game." Then she whispered in my ear, spy-to-spy, "As a person of color, you shouldn't have to fit into any white, patriarchal system."
>
> "Well," I said, "it's a bit too late for that."
>
> The counselor looked at me with what could have been consternation or confusion or both, and I was quickly shuffled off to another quadrant of Old Campus where a different game was being played. In this game, you had to wait your turn in a circle to tell what you would be, had you the chance to be any object you wanted.

We've included the entire previous opening because it allows us to consider how the opening sets up the story. In contrast to the final version's opening, what does this opening suggest the story will be about? What role do we think Miss Gloria will play in the story? How do we see Dina differently in this version of the story because of her relationship to Miss Gloria? How does the neighborhood's response to Dina differ from that in the published version?

In the following passage, we look at the line-editing changes—the added, subtracted, and rearranged words and sentences. (We want to note that this is not the result of a single session of rewriting, but the cumulative effect of a number of small changes made to the final drafts.) Our analysis follows the passage. The additions are marked in bold and the deletions lined through.

> ~~Before the~~ **O**rientation games began **the day I arrived at Yale from Baltimore.**~~, groups of freshmen milled about like throngs of penguins at an Antarctic social.~~ In my group, **we played heady, frustrating games for smart people. One game appeared to be charades reinterpreted by existentialists; another involved listening to rocks. Then** ~~the~~ **a freshman counselor made everyone play** ~~a game called~~ Trust. The idea ~~of Trust, as far as I could tell,~~ was that ~~you could learn to trust your fellow students~~ if you ~~simply~~ had the faith to fall backward and wait for four scrawny former high-school geniuses to catch you, just ~~as~~ **before** your head ~~threatened to crack open~~ **cracked on** the slate sidewalk, **then you might learn to trust your fellow students. Russian roulette sounded like a better way to go.**
>
> "No way," I said ~~to the Playboy blonde counselor~~. The white boys waited for me to fall ~~back~~, holding their arms out for me, sincerely, gallantly.~~, forming a sort of stretcher of shaky ladder rungs. I shook my head.~~ "No fucking way."
>
> "It's all cool, it's all cool," the counselor said.~~, her palms facing me as~~ **Her hair was a shade of blond I'd seen only on Playboy covers, and she raised her hands as** though ~~she were~~ backing away from a growling dog. ~~She pulled me aside and amicably explained, once again, that it "was cool" if I didn't want to play this game, that I was my own person and needed my own space.~~ "Sister," she said, ~~not sounding nearly as street wise as she'd wanted to, but like one nun addressing another,~~ **in an I'm-down-with-the-struggle voice,** "you don't have to play this game. ~~." Then she whispered in my ear, spy-to-spy, "~~As a person of color, you shouldn't have to fit into any white, patriarchal system."
>
> ~~"Well,"~~ I said, "It's a bit too late for that."
>
> ~~The counselor looked at me with what could have been consternation or confusion or both, and I was quickly shuffled off to another quadrant of Old Campus where a different game was being played.~~ In ~~this~~ **the next** game, ~~you~~ **all I** had to **do was** wait ~~your turn~~ in a circle **until it was my turn** to ~~tell what you would be, had you the chance to be any object you wanted.~~ **say what inanimate object I wanted to be.**

The story now begins at Yale, with the disorienting "orientation games." In the draft version, Packer used a number of figures of speech, all vivid and engaging in themselves, but they become more effective when she pares them down. The first image of the freshmen as "throngs of penguins at an Antarctic social" was witty, sophisticated, and observant. But the tone was too lighthearted and comic for the mood of the story. The simile made the first image of black and white (those penguins, who are black and white at the same time) amusing instead of painful. Also, this view of the students requires a level of detachment that Dina, lost and angry, doesn't have.

Instead, Packer adds the information that the students play "heady, frustrating games," an observation that conveys Dina's state of mind. Packer then backs up this statement with a couple of specific examples, reported in a way that shows both Dina's level of education (she can imagine how the existentialists would play charades) and her disdain. The reordering of the sentence about waiting for "four scrawny former high-school geniuses to catch you" puts the idea of trusting one's fellow students at the end of the sentence, where it has the strongest impact. The final sentence of the paragraph adds a note that is tough both in emotion (a preference for Russian roulette over this game) and in sound—the hard gutturals of the g, d's, and t's.

The second paragraph has been stripped clean—notice the difference between the boys waiting for Dina to "fall back" and waiting for her to "fall." The second usage carries the implications of all the ways she could fall or fail at this university, and a sense of how little she can trust her fellow students. The words "Playboy blond counselor" are also eliminated; it's so condensed an image that a reader might have to stop and figure it out. Instead, Packer has clarified the image and included it in the paragraph underneath. The memorable image of Dina as a growling dog remains—of all the figurative language of the earlier draft, this one most accurately conveys the emotional tone of the story, reflects Dina's sense of her relationships with the people at Yale, and fits with the scene. Since we can actually imagine a growling dog in New Haven, unlike a flock of penguins, the simile doesn't make us stop in the same way: it seems realistic, while the penguins were almost surreal. In the final draft, Packer eliminated the last sentence of the earlier version of this paragraph, which undercut its power and repeated earlier information.

The next paragraph has wonderful dialogue that tells us about both speaker and listener: "Sister, you don't have to play this game. As a person of color, you shouldn't have to fit into any white, patriarchal system." The counselor attempts to be supportive and instead winds up making an unintended racist assumption about Dina's reasons for disliking the games, confirming Dina's fears. In the earlier version of the paragraph, the painful humor of this is somewhat diluted by two conflicting metaphors—the nuns and the spies. In the final version, both of these have been cut, and "not sounding nearly as streetwise as she'd wanted to" is replaced with the much more powerful "an I'm-down-with-the-struggle-voice." The new phrasing has Dina's trademark ferocious humor and assumes the reader will be able to infer that the counselor isn't too streetwise.

The "well" disappears from the beginning of the next paragraph—by this draft, Dina is less diffident, more fierce. And then the counselor's reaction, which isn't completely unexpected and doesn't affect the story, disappears. Removing the sentence helps clarify that she's not an important character. The rest of the changes in this paragraph cut an unnecessary location change, smooth the phrasing, and maintain a consistent POV.

Packer's generosity in sharing this portion of one of her drafts makes it possible for us to see the large effects of line editing. We suggest rereading the entire opening scene of the finished story to see how Packer establishes the character, the tensions of Dina's situation, and our hopes and worries for Dina. Why does this story begin on Dina's first day at Yale, rather than with her childhood, or when she meets Heidi, or in Dr. Raeburn's office? How would these possible beginnings change the story? What words or phrases establish the voice and the character? What draws us into the story and makes us keep reading?

Look at the opening paragraphs, without the markings, as they appeared in the final published version: elegant, specific, electric, gripping, and alarming:

> Orientation games began the day I arrived at Yale from Baltimore. In my group we played heady, frustrating games for smart people. One game appeared to be charades reinterpreted by existentialists; another involved listening to rocks. Then a freshman counselor made everyone play Trust. The idea was that if you had the faith to fall backward and wait for four scrawny former high school geniuses to catch you, just before your head cracked on the slate sidewalk, then you might learn to trust your fellow students. Russian roulette sounded like a better way to go.
>
> "No way," I said. The white boys were waiting for me to fall, holding their arms out for me, sincerely, gallantly. "No fucking way."

Many of the images and sentences were already in the earlier version, but their effect was muffled until the writing was edited and tightened. For another example of line editing, see the revision section at the end of Chapter 2, where we examine two different versions of a Raymond Carver story. The best writers work and rework their writing the way Packer does here, changing a paragraph or a sentence as many as twenty times until it looks and sounds exactly right, and until every part of it fits with the overall meaning of the story.

STYLE AND DIALOGUE EXERCISES

1. Copy out a paragraph from one of your favorite stories by another writer. Read it aloud. Then choose a paragraph from a story of your own, one with a similar subject matter and mood. Rewrite your paragraph in the style of the writer you've chosen. Pay attention to sentence length, the sound of the words, the kinds of nouns and verbs used, the tone, and the simplicity or elaborateness of both words and sentences.
2. Find a paragraph by an author whose style feels alien to your own—much more spare or more dense with detail; ironic or earnest; poetic or plain. Using the sentence structures of the paragraph as a model, write your own paragraph that describes a completely different scene drawn from your own experience or imagination. Follow the style and rhythm of your model, but don't worry about exactly replicating the sentences. Come as close as you can without straining. Try this exercise using a paragraph that describes setting, and then another paragraph that describes a character's interior experience. The purpose of this exercise is to stretch your range by opening up your options. In the end, you'll

write in your own style, but find ways of developing that style while still being true to yourself.

3. Every day for a week, make up three metaphors or similes and record them in your writer's journal or image notebook. They can be metaphors for situations, people, events, or objects in your own life or in your characters' lives. See how far you can push the metaphors and similes, and then how subtle you can make them. Have some of them be single words—verbs or nouns—and others several sentences long.
4. Read a passage of dialogue from one of your stories aloud to a friend, using no dialogue tags or gestures. Can your listener tell, just from the speech patterns, rhythms, subjects discussed, and attitudes, which character is speaking? If not, rewrite the passage to more clearly differentiate your characters' voices.
5. Take a story of yours that hasn't been working and invent secrets for two of the main characters, secrets that would mean trouble if anyone discovered them. (Each character should have his or her own secret to keep the exercise from becoming schematic.) How could these secrets change or complicate the plot of your story? Create a scene, with action, dialogue, and descriptive details, in which one of the characters communicates his or her secret to the other without discussing it directly. The conversation appears to be about another subject entirely, but by the end, the reader knows that the first character has told the secret, that the second character understands it, and that they are each aware of what they now both know.
6. (This reading exercise can be done either individually or in a group.) Choose a sentence from one of the stories that you've read recently, one that you admire, perhaps one that breaks some rules. What is it that you admire about the sentence? What does it do well? Now look at a paragraph that you admire, and the way the sentences work together. Where and how does the writer vary the length? What kinds of details or phrasing make this paragraph work?

CHAPTER

10

Revision: Beginnings, Middles, and Endings

(Anthology selections: Beginnings from "Pilgrims," "Orientation," and "A Conversation with My Father"; Endings from "Powder," "The Cures for Love," and "The Turkey Season.")

We start with a blank: a world of possibility. Even that, though, is only a *beginning, as opposed to* the *beginning, as there are many kinds of blanks . . . Words can never be a simple reflection of life. Our very limited set of symbols, the letters of our alphabet, are forced to translate all the unspeakable data of our senses, all of our thoughts, and all of our emotions.*

This is why it is important for all of us realists, damned by that word conventional, *to remember, always, that we have chosen a particular projection—one that seems to us to minimize distortion and to speak powerfully.* This is our choice. *And to simply learn how others have done it, to pick up the graph paper and begin plotting our lines, limits us from the start. Realism, like every other artistic endeavor, fails when it becomes an exercise in filling in the blanks. Realism succeeds when the author remembers to question his or her assumptions. Why do we represent dialogue the way we do? Why are smells so often absent? What is the relation of chronology to the way we think? What are we doing when we imagine a character's consciousness, the flow of thoughts through her head—and then render them on the page in some particular order, in a particular syntax? How are we manipulating the data? To what ends?*

The same holds true for surrealists, experimentalists, modernists, postmodernists, and romantics, hopeless or otherwise. All *of our approaches are possible projections.*

—Peter Turchi, "The Writer as Cartographer"

THE WRITING ROOM

Peter Turchi reminds us that we are establishing a new reality with each story. In revising, as in writing, we have to go back to the beginning and start as if we've never written before. When we lapse into feeling accomplished or professional, as if we know what we're doing, we go off track. Revision starts with questioning the story, our writing processes, and the nature of our projections. After the initial questioning, the decision about how to incorporate revision into the writing process is as individual as the question of how to write at all. Some writers tear through a whole first draft—perhaps in mercifully incomprehensible handwriting or even at a computer with the screen turned off—and don't revise until that draft is finished. They may turn out draft after draft, the first few unbearably bad, the later ones coming slowly into focus. Others, or the same writers at a different time or stage, write a few sentences, revise them, then move forward, finish a scene, and immediately begin reworking again, making their sentences perfect as they go, inching their way along.

Many writers or teachers will recommend their own way of working, and it's worth trying options we haven't considered before. But we have to find our own way, just as we have to learn for ourselves whether we do our best writing in the morning or at night, on a yellow legal pad or a computer, in a café surrounded by people or in a room by ourselves with the door shut.

Just realizing that we have to try different ways of writing (and that our usual methods may not work for some particular story) can free us up to experiment. For experienced writers, writing first drafts, despite the excitements of initial ideas, is like running across the frozen tundra in shorts and a tank top, or wrestling alligators in hundred-degree heat. Revision, however, offers the delight of making connections, *reseeing* relationships and incidents, learning the fierce pleasure of throwing out dozens of pages (this usually follows mind-numbing pain, caused by either reading the pages over or receiving criticism that shows us just how much work we still have ahead of us).

In revision, we run into certain dangers, as Jerome Stern points out in *Making Shapely Fiction:*

> Some writers get hung up on first-draft ideas, as if to abandon any one is to betray some primal creative impulse. "If I wrote it, it must be important." Other writers are too quick to cut their freshest passages. "Oh, that part's too weird." But it's the thoughtful shaping of these impulses that creates art. Fear of making decisions or an oversolicitous, doting fondness for your prose paralyzes your work. And it's a lack of trust in their individual vision that makes writers take out the best parts.

One way to return to the heart of the story, to revise from *inside* rather than mechanically, is to imagine the story as already existing in a room in our minds. Inside, we see, hear, and live in the story's world: we can both take notes on events and shape them. There is no separation between writer and characters, writer and story. We *become* the events in that room.

The hard part is getting there. Daily work—even an hour, every day—is more likely to make the barrier between us and the writing room permeable, a thin curtain we can slip through. Sometimes, even when we've been writing consistently, there's a brick wall in front of us, with no door visible, and we sit outside, cursing. This is less apt to happen, though, if we give ourselves the chance to walk into the room on a regular basis.

If we write our first drafts in this room but then regard revision as a separate process, in which we sit outside the room trying to "fix" what we've made, our revision is artificial, a lumpish mess. We may feel the balky, recalcitrant story in front of us is our enemy—the enemy of the perfect idea we had in mind; the enemy that keeps us from moving on to a new story; the enemy that shows us our own weaknesses and makes us despair. It helps to regard revision as a creative process—a way to reenter the writing room and focus even more closely on the people and events we've imagined.

Giving and Receiving Criticism: The Workshop

No writer gets better without criticism. Criticizing others is also one of the best ways to develop our own eye; as we help others, we help ourselves. Helpful, supportive, intelligently stringent workshops and writers' groups allow writers to make quantum leaps in their writing.

In this book, we've tried to avoid absolute pronouncements, since so much depends on the individual circumstances of a writer and story. But we stand behind these statements. Workshops, sometimes painful, often criticized, and full of pitfalls, are still the best way we know for writers to improve. In our own and our students' writing, we've seen huge transformations come from this laborious and sometimes bewildering process. Workshops, though, can go wrong and can leave writers with temporary or permanent writer's block. Both the workshop and the writers need to understand the mechanisms by which unfinished stories are read.

Some workshop methods protect the imagination better than others. Workshops can become damaging if the participants let their natural irritation at an unfinished story get out of hand. The writer whose story has been critiqued experiences this irritation as a personal attack and a sign that the story is an unfixable disaster and the writer has no talent: we all retain criticism far longer than praise.

This damage is less apt to happen in workshops where no one is allowed to praise or criticize until the group has thoroughly named and explored the intentions of the work. What is the piece trying to do? What does it seem to be about? What changes during the course of the story? What connections and correlations exist between incidents and characters? What kind of aesthetic or writerly tradition is it located in? These questions allow the writer to feel heard and also force workshop participants to put aside their own tastes and assumptions in order to explore the nature and possibilities of the story. This process almost always increases a reader's sympathies, as well as the usefulness of any subsequent criticism.

The next stage of this kind of workshop is detailed, honest praise of those aspects of the story that are already working or that seem to be illuminating the intent. Even the strongest writer, who has been praised for every other story, needs to hear what is working about each one.

It's only after the group has spent some time understanding and praising the story that criticism becomes useful. Even then, specific questions are often less insulting and more helpful than statements. "The character of the mother is totally annoying" is hurtful without being informative. A more exact response might be to ask, "Is there some detail about the mother's character, or some information about her background, that would help us see why she won't visit her son in the hospital?"

For a writer to become objective about criticism, it helps to understand the way readers respond to unfinished work. Certain common early-draft maneuvers will often annoy a workshop, as when the writer is trying to make a point—and many of us are in early drafts—using the story's characters as object lessons. As readers, we don't want to be expected to feel sorry for the characters. Another common and provoking stumbling block is an excessive presence of the author, which may arise from the natural exuberance of writers learning to play with words, not yet confident that their voices will naturally emerge if they focus on making the story come alive for the reader.

As workshoppers, we have to get past our initial irritability before we write our comments. We have to guard against the intrusion of personal tastes, our own insecurities or jealousies, and remarks that refer to the writer's personality or history, real or imagined. If the writer being workshopped has previously given us a critique that we felt was hurtful or inadequate in some way, we're much better off if we assume it was unintentional. No matter what happened in the past, we approach each new story with our best, good-faith effort.

As the one being workshopped, we have to quell our tendency to take the comments of others personally. It is completely unnatural, but absolutely necessary, for us to learn to nod, take notes, and, at the end, smile and say—no matter what anyone has said in the course of a workshop—"That was very helpful. Thank you very much." Defending our story, explaining what we meant to say, or impugning the motives of our critics makes us look foolish and turns off the flow of potentially useful criticism. The writer might contribute an occasional question, either in the middle or at the end of the workshop, if it's not a disguised defense of the story: "No one has said anything about the pacing. I was worried that the story slows down too much in the middle. Was that a problem?" Otherwise, it's up to the writer, often with the help of a workshop buddy who can clarify what people said, to sort it all out in revision.

Ways of Reentering a Story

After a story of ours has been critiqued, we see it in a new, unflattering light and have to work to return to a sense of hope and possibility in revision. Trying to incorporate every comment and please each one of our critics will fix errors, but usually produce a lifeless work. Ignoring everyone's comments limits the story in other ways and is a waste of the workshop gifts. One successful approach is to write out, immediately after the workshop or critique, a summary of the points and questions that struck us, incorporating our own speculations, ideas, answers, and notes. Then we might put both our own summary and the comments aside for a couple of weeks before we begin to revise.

Sometimes we'll be so excited by a set of criticisms that we immediately start to rework a story, which is fine as long as we save a copy of the earlier version and the critiques. We don't have to wait to start revising, but it's still a good idea to reread the critiques to see what we might have missed. Sometimes our first rewrite will make a story worse. Solving one problem often creates new ones. This is a normal part of the process, the lurching back and forth that takes us in a zigzag towards a finished story.

Instead of trying to cure our story of the disease of imperfection, we approach it, once again, as a whole. Are there places where the story feels false or invented? Does anything seem illogical? Emotionally implausible? What is this story *about*? Where does it make the hair stand up on our necks? Sometimes we have an insight, a psychological understanding, into the story's connections, an off-the-cuff thematic analysis: "The story is really about the ways he's paralyzed by a belief in his own insignificance. That's why he writes those love notes in invisible ink, and never even mails them. And that's why he lost his job!" The danger of these little epiphanies about our stories is that they can be reductive if we then force the whole story to march in lockstep with the theme. On the other hand, they can be useful if they help us identify connections that we still need to make for the reader, or entire episodes that need to be changed or struck out.

After we've been receiving criticism for a while, we begin to have a sense of our own habitual strengths and weaknesses in early drafts. Rather than despairing because we don't feel we're getting better, or blaming ourselves because we've made the same mistakes we made last time, we forgive ourselves for the imperfections, and we think about the procedures we used in revising previous stories.

Over time we develop more extensive and useful tools for addressing particular first-draft mistakes. A writer who tends to start with abstract first drafts, full of philosophizing, grand ideas, and very little action or detail, might ask, what objects are in the room? What actions could embody the conflicts/emotions in the story? Are there places in the first draft where my thoughts and opinions replace action and storytelling? Are there any places where I'm making a point rather than letting characters be themselves? A writer who usually starts with images and beautiful language, without much sense of the characters and their motivations, might ask, what's at stake for the characters at this point in their lives? Why do they do what they do? Which images and events exist for their own sake, and which are integral to the story, advancing the plot?

Whether we start revising right away or wait, we need to find a way to get back inside the story, to work from inside the writing room. Writers will try all kinds of techniques to become part of the story again, from reading it over until it starts to become alive, to messing with a few sentences to see if that brings us back, to putting it aside and starting over from memory. Sometimes it works to re-edit all of the pages from the day before. Sometimes it works to sit quietly at our desk with eyes closed, imagining the scene we're about to write until we feel an irresistible impulse to begin writing.

STRUCTURAL REVISION

In earlier chapters we discuss revision in relation to specific aspects of fiction writing. But in real-world revising, writers don't tend to go through a story and revise the characters first, then the POV, then the plot, then the style—revising happens at many levels at once. Changing the nature of the characters influences their behavior and action; changing the events of a story changes the characters and themes. These changes start during the initial drafting of a story, so that it may be hard to tell where one draft ends, and another begins.

Beginning writers often find themselves unwilling to make substantial changes: they will tinker with the words or move sentences, but they haven't yet learned to step back and reimagine the story in large ways. Deep, structural revision can involve reshuffling scenes, reordering paragraphs, taking out entire plot elements and characters and adding others, and letting the story begin or end in new places. It takes time to learn how to make changes this large without throwing out the entire story.

Here is part of an account of how Daniel Orozco came to write, and rewrite, "Orientation," and the way in which his plot and characters changed because of his desire to depict a contemporary work environment. His description shows how he reconceived the structure and purposes of the story:

> It was, for the most part, very tedious work with very nice people about whom I knew very little. Near the tail end of my clerical career there . . . I became reacquainted with the work of Chekhov. It struck me then—and it does still—that no other writer has been so adept at portraying the vagaries of unrequited love with such humane and unremitting clarity. So I set out to write a contemporary Chekhovian love story about an office romance. I wrote several versions of the story, all bad, and all proving the futility, I think, of trying to "do Chekhov."
>
> [Orozco then describes being a full-time student and also working as a temp in a place where . . .] If you craned your neck and stood on your toes from anywhere in the hallway, there would come into view an expanse of cubicles that receded toward a horizon of shatterproof floor-to-ceiling windows, through which could be seen the shatterproof floor-to-ceiling windows of other downtown office buildings.
>
> About six months later, I had to turn in a story for a workshop. I wanted to tackle that office romance again (*sans* the Neo-Chekhovian pretensions), and when I recalled that rat maze image from the 12th floor . . . the voice of a narra-

> tor came to me. As I worked on the first few drafts, the voice embodied itself as an omniscient guide, orienting a new employee to the workings of the office, conducting an initiate through the topography of the cubicles and of the lives contained therein. The unrequited-love story I had originally intended to write is gone . . . sort of. With every revision I made—adding and deleting characters, shuffling scenes and episodes, playing with the rhythms of language—the story became less and less about any particular one of its characters, and more about *all* of them, a kind of collective love story, perhaps, assembled and told by an all-knowing narrator—part gossip, part guide—whose litany of intimate knowledge reveals much more about the vagaries of love and loneliness than any of us might care to know.

For Orozco, everything about the story remained open to rethinking and re-envisioning. Rather than letting the story become fixed in form at some early-draft stage, or sticking to his own first ideas about what the story might be, he let the story itself lead him through revision. Sometimes we find the images and hints that lead us from one draft to another; sometimes our readers and workshop help us discover the areas where the story comes alive. With each revision, we relinquish both the work we've done and the ideas that we had in the last stage. For additional commentaries on the revision process, see the end of Chapter 3 (Adam Johnson on the deep, structural revisions to POV in "Trauma Plate") and the end of Chapter 5 (Andrea Barrett on the late gifts that came through repeated revision of "The Forest"). For examples of line editing, see the ends of Chapters 2 and 9 (Raymond Carver's two different endings to "The Bath"/"A Small, Good Thing" and ZZ Packer's revisions to the beginning of "Drinking Coffee Elsewhere").

As we become more practiced as writers, we learn to examine the story as objectively as if it had been written by someone else. We no longer spend energy on self-questioning or embarrassment, but calmly (reasonably calmly) separate out the story's elements and rework them. Everyone's drafts are awful—that's just how it is. But we can improve them miraculously, first through deep revision and later through line editing.

BEGINNINGS

Beginnings and endings are two of the hardest aspects of fiction to discuss in any systematic way, because they're so dependent on the needs of a particular story. The story may start or end with an image, dialogue, action, summary, description, or some combination of these, but the knowledge of these different types of beginnings and endings doesn't begin to give a sense of the possibilities. The beginning of a story almost always introduces the ground situation and very often adds the first complication (we discuss and define these terms in Chapter 4). When the story starts *in medias res,* we often learn about the ground situation through backstory or by implication.

The decision of *where* in the story to start is usually arrived at by trial and error. Meg Files, in *Write from Life,* gives us a metaphor for story beginnings:

> A story on the page is like a house where a party is going on. The reader enters the story by opening the front door (no knocking necessary). The party is already in progress. Nobody introduces the new guest. The partiers are too far gone already. There's a drunk in the kitchen, an argument in the living room, a pair kissing in a bedroom. The reader begins by stepping into the middle of the story, at a critical point perhaps, just before the neighbors' complaints bring the police pounding on the door.
>
> As we begin writing a story, we don't know what all is going to happen or who is going to show up, so we get started however we can. We spend three pages making canapés and cleaning house. And that's okay. Later though, we delete those pages and find the true beginning.

Often writers feel that they have to show the ground situation of a story at length—the opening conditions and their tensions: the happy family about to be visited by disaster, the dancer before her injury, the doctor who has not yet lost his reputation, the entire background. Story writers who fall into this can spend pages explaining and setting up; novelists will sometimes produce as many as eight chapters of background in their early drafts before anything actually happens. Reading other stories can help us to determine how to give the minimum of background before getting on with events. (We discuss the timing of openings in more detail in Chapter 5.)

Some stories do take a little time to set up the ground situation. This approach tends to be most successful when the situation is already unstable or full of interesting tensions. If the doctor is happily practicing medicine, we don't need much of that. If, however, he's begun drinking and canceling appointments, this is already part of the action.

Once we've written enough drafts of a story that we think we know what it's about, we can look at how the narrative is moving and ask the following questions from a reader's perspective: What expectations does the beginning raise in us? How does it engage us? What questions do we have about the people or situation, and how are they answered by the time we finish reading the story? What is it that we hope for, are worried about, or are so curious about that we keep reading? How are these hopes, worries, or questions augmented or subverted in the course of the story? What moments, images, and events give a sense of growing meaning or building towards change?

The Creative Beginning and the Literal Beginning

There are two kinds of beginnings and endings for each story, the creative and the literal. The creative beginning is the initial impulse that sparks the story and gets us started putting words on the page, while the literal beginning consists of the final draft's first sentence, paragraph, or scene. And the same is true of endings: the creative ending is our first inspiration for completing the story, while the literal ending consists of the final draft's last paragraphs or pages that close the arc of the story (however open-ended that closing may be). Sometimes our creative beginning matches up with the literal beginning, and the first words we write on the story become the opening lines. Or the final paragraph is the last piece we write. More often, the first scene we write ends up somewhere in the middle of the story or in the recycling bin; our first attempt at an ending goes awry and needs several replacements before we find a satisfactory one.

Therefore, the first "beginning" we write is rarely the final beginning of a story, just as the final "ending" of that first draft is likely to be changed, moved, or eliminated. Until we've identified the story's plot, we can't know where it begins or ends: revision is a process of shaping both the storyline (what happens) and the plot (how we *structure* the telling of what happens) until they resonate with each other.

Too often, however, we hold onto the original beginning or ending through many drafts because we associate it with the *feeling* of beginning or ending. To realize the story's full potential, we have to separate the needs of the plot from the excitement of coming up with a first line and the satisfaction of bringing events to a close.

Setting Up the Story

The opening of a story teaches readers how to interpret what is to come. What's happening in the world of this story? What kinds of promises does the language make? Who are the characters? What viewpoint(s) are we looking through, and what kind of narrator do we have as a guide? How close or distant is that narrator? How much commentary, detail, and information does the narrator provide? What tone or mood does the story set? Is the story preparing the reader to be anxious, amused, saddened, mystified, or enlightened? What kinds of information are introduced, and how might the facts or ideas play themselves out by the end? Will the story move quickly or take a more meditative, exploratory pace? What interests us in this story? Why?

Readers assume that the beginning is making implicit promises about the kind of characters and experiences the story is going to offer. If after a few paragraphs a story that appears to be a realistic psychological examination of sibling rivalry suddenly turns into an absurdist love story, readers are likely to feel angry, even betrayed. Few experiences are more disappointing than a story that suggests it will give us one thing and then arbitrarily delivers something unrelated, a story that fails to grapple with the issues it raises. When we are revising our stories, we can look at the beginning to see what promises it's making to the reader. If the rest of the story doesn't deliver on that promise, then no matter how brilliant and engaging the beginning may be, we either have to write a new beginning, ruthlessly revise the one we have, or change the rest of the story.

STORY ANALYSIS AND QUESTIONS: THREE BEGINNINGS

(If you have not yet read "Pilgrims," "Orientation," and "A Conversation with My Father," we suggest reading them before *the analysis and questions to get the clearest sense of how the beginnings set up the rest of the story. For this chapter, we are departing from our previous method of presenting a single anthology story. Instead we present analyses of three separate beginnings, followed by discussion questions for all three stories.)*

In "Pilgrims," Julie Orringer establishes both the POV and the characters swiftly and subtly. Please reread from "It was Thanksgiving Day and hot, because this was New Orleans; they were driving uptown to have dinner with strangers" to "And now they were going to have dinner with people they had never met, people who ate seaweed and brown rice every day of their lives."

This beginning, about a page long, establishes the ground situation: the mother has cancer, the children are terrified, the parents don't seem to understand the effects of the illness on the children, and all their lives have changed in various small and large ways. The beginning also introduces the first complication: the holiday to be spent among strangers who will take them further into this nightmare world.

We know that we're in Ella's POV from the second sentence—her experience of the loose tooth—and from the following paragraphs, which give us her memories of her mother's chemotherapy and of her secret, frightened alliance with her brother. This is a close third-person narrator with only one viewpoint character; the events of the story happened at some undetermined time in the past, though they feel very immediate; we have the character's physical sensations and observations, but very little of her thoughts; the narrator funnels all the sensory details, history, and information through the character; and the narrator never comments directly on the story.

Orringer establishes the characters primarily through the action, largely revealed in flashback: the parents inflict suffering on their children with the best, most misguided intent, and the children turn to each other for help. The story uses detail to let us know that the family still keeps up appearances: Ella's velvet dress, her mother's jade beads and hat to cover her baldness, and Ben's elaborate costume.

Although there's no clear break or scene change at the end of the beginning, it nonetheless forms a complete movement—from the introduction of the characters to the paragraphs of incident and history that establish their situation and relationships, then back to the present with "And now . . ." which reminds us that they're going to visit strangers. The transitions are smooth—we only realize that the beginning ends here by studying it closely. All the themes of the story show themselves in this beginning. Even the title, "Pilgrims," not only refers to Ben's costume and to Thanksgiving, but also lets us know that this family is going on a hard journey to a new world in which they will encounter strangers with an entirely different set of values and assumptions.

In Daniel Orozco's "Orientation," the mood is ominous and humorous at the same time. The mood of a beginning not only tells us something about the characters' situation, but also prepares us for the kind of emotional climate we're in for. If the mood sounds only one note over and over—suggesting nothing but hopelessness, for example—the reader may feel locked into a world of limited possibilities, and lose interest. Complex moods might have elements of both tragedy and comedy, or an angry edge as well as a note of compassion. Please reread from "Those are the offices and these are the cubicles" through "If you make an emergency phone call without asking, you may be let go."

In this story, the first-person narrator addresses the story to another character and reports events as they happen. The reader is not given access to the narrator's thoughts and feelings (except those which he or she speaks out loud). The narrator is one among several at the center of events, and is focused primarily on the world around him or her. We remain eerily unsure of this narrator's degree of reliability.

What sets up a mood is not only the language, but also the pacing and the substance. For example, beginning with several lines of short dialogue—instructions, in this case—can affect the mood differently than starting with a paragraph describing the setting. In this story, we quickly learn we're not going to linger over characters' history, physical appearance, or psychological quirks.

"Orientation" sets up its situation by implication in the very first paragraph. By the end of twelve fairly quick sentences, we know that a speaker is orienting a new employee, that we can expect emergencies, and that there's something very strange about this office. It seems ordinary enough—cubicles, voicemail, supervisors—except for the oddness of some of the instructions. Why don't they answer the phone? How can this place be so inhuman that one must go through two layers of bureaucracy to make an emergency phone call? Why the immediate threat that the listener may be, for the least infraction, "let go"? All the story's surprises unfold from these conditions. The title lets us know what's happening, ironically—nothing could be more disorienting than this introduction. The warnings and remarks about emergencies and being let go add to the ominous mood; the sheer uncertainties of the statements, and the juxtaposition of the ordinary and bizarre, create the humor. Using a combination of the surreal and the mundane, Orozco comments on our contemporary workplaces.

In various places, particularly Chapter 4, we've discussed the key role beginnings play in creating readers' expectations. What is the story about?

What's the nature of this world? What do we hope for or worry about for the characters? What kind of experience does the story promise? How do we know what will be important? In "A Conversation with My Father," Grace Paley lets us know from the beginning that although mortality is central to the story, we're going to approach the subject indirectly. Please reread from "My father is eighty-six years old" through "'Just recognizable people and then write down what happened to them next.'"

Sometimes writers keep back information out of the fear that being too clear about the story's territory will be dull or off-putting. We may be afraid that we'll somehow lose the power of mystery that we hold over the reader. But the mystery of "what the hell is going on here?" is actually a much less interesting mystery than the kind of specific narrative question that Paley establishes.

The question is not whether or not the father will die; he's clearly at the end of his life. What the story takes on is the nature of the narratives we tell ourselves and each other—how they make us despair or hope. In the first two paragraphs, the father undercuts his daughter's metaphor about his heart. This disagreement, and his request for a "simple story," sets up a narrative question: what is a simple story, and is it still possible to tell one? Since this is very nearly a dying request, the stakes are high. Storytelling is revealed as an essential task, important enough to matter at the end of life. From this opening, we expect the story to grapple with the nature of storytelling and the nature of truth in a life-or-death context, and it does, both in the "real" story of the father and daughter and the "invented" story of the mother and son.

That opening metaphor is so grand that, marvelous as it is, it risks sounding overwritten or sentimental. But the narrative immediately undercuts these dangers by having the father refuse to be seen sentimentally. This story is quite postmodern and complex, but it manages to give us the deep pleasures of human interaction and narrative drive, exactly what the father is asking his daughter to do.

DISCUSSION QUESTIONS

1. "Pilgrims," "Orientation," and "A Conversation with My Father" each could have started at different moments in their respective time sequences. Where else might each one have started? How would this have changed the meaning or mood of the story?
2. Which words or phrases establish the POV in each story?
3. How are the characters introduced? What are our first clues to their personalities and concerns?
4. What different moods do the openings contain? What words or phrases show these moods?
5. What makes each opening intriguing? What keeps us reading? What expectations do we have for each story?

MIDDLES

The middle of the story includes the complications, rising action, crisis, climax, and usually the falling action (all discussed in Chapter 4). The issues that arise as we rework the middle of a story have to do with sustaining emotional logic, complicating tone, and making sure that we're developing the characters and plot, rather than repeating the same information in different words.

If the father in John L'Heureux's "Father" is going to disappear into his canvas by the end of the story, what steps along the way will create conditions under which this could seem possible? What actions does he take? What details does the story reveal? How does each new piece of information or event build the action? What more do we learn about the characters and situation as the story continues? The story has both a practical and an emotional logic.

The same issues of tone and mood that we discussed in terms of beginnings still apply. Some details or events will subvert the prevailing tone, complicating it. Even in a bleak story there may be notes of sweetness or humor; a more comic story may occasionally include a hint of grief or terror.

Pacing remains important in the middle of the story. Does each scene intensify the conflict or possibility of connection? Which are the key turning points? What does each scene add to the story? We look for scenes or exposition that seem extraneous, that don't build. Can two scenes be combined? If we were to cut a particular scene, would the story be noticeably less comprehensible, moving, or memorable?

ENDINGS

In revising, we look back to see if our ending makes good on the implicit promises we made to the reader in the beginning. In a first draft we can get carried away, writing a beautiful, dramatic ending that may not have much to do with the story. The alternate danger is writing an ending that delivers exactly what the beginning promises and nothing more—for instance, at the beginning of the story, a couple seems on the verge of breaking up, and by the end of the story they *have* broken up, in a predictable fashion. Satisfying endings usually provide unexpected but logical turns of events and emotions. Of course, we can include events and changes that seem inevitable from the start, *if* the story brings them about in an unexpected way, with the recognizable complexity and messiness of human life.

The ending consists of the entire final movement of the story, often the last two to three pages, not simply the last paragraph. The ending chronicles the events and interactions that close down the brief moment of the story—the resolution and occasionally the falling action. This closing may not resolve the conflicts or obstacles of the story, but it usually intensifies or alters them. In writing and revising, we have to listen to each story to find its own particular ending. If we're unsure how to end the story, or if our original idea for an ending falls apart, we can go back through our story to look for clues and new possibilities.

It can be useful to read the last page or so of 15 stories in a row (not necessarily all by contemporary writers of the same nationality) to get a sense of the many possibilities for ending a story. When does each ending seem to start? How long does it last? Does the story end with dialogue, summary, an image, an epiphany, an action or event, or some combination of these? How does the strategy of the ending fit with the scene, tone, and events of the story? How does the tone or mood of the ending reflect that of the beginning, or how has it been altered? What is resolved or concluded by the end? How does the ending arise or evolve from the story? What does the story choose to leave unresolved? If something is left unresolved, does the story provide the reader with a sense of how it might be resolved in the future, or is it totally unknowable? What about this particular ending is surprising? In what way does it seem inevitable? How does it fit with the logic of the characters' natures and previous actions? How does it seem to satisfy the expectations the story raises?

Inevitable Surprises

When we're writing the end of a first draft, we often come up with banal solutions to dramatic problems. Then, in revision, we see we've been too obvious, too clichéd; so we replace the ending with something vividly weird or head-scratchingly obscure. The next step is to find a third solution, one that is neither predictable nor unnecessarily off-the-wall.

A discussion of classic plot, derived from the structure of plays, may give us the idea that a story is headed towards an ascent/redemption ending (as in a comedy) or a descent/disaster ending (as in a tragedy). Writers can spend a lot of time arguing about which view is more true to life. We may even let our fears get in the way: we want our mother to stop telling us our stories are too depressing to read or we think literary readers won't take our story seriously if the ending isn't bleak enough. But the happy/sad dichotomy is misleading: sometimes the main character is better off in some ways, and worse off in others, or perhaps some characters are in a better position, and others in a worse position than they were at the story's beginning. Characters may be better off materially, but worse off spiritually, or vice versa. Some stories are like a drive through bizarre terrain that brings the characters to a new and unexpected location in their lives: this new state is neither better nor worse, but the trip was illuminating. Sometimes we know from the beginning, because the story has told us so, that we're headed for disaster, and our question is "how did things go so wrong?" And sometimes the story is an investigation that brings the reader closer and closer to the heart of a mystery.

What makes an ending so difficult is that it needs to be logical and arise from the story, and yet it shouldn't be something that the reader could have made up just by knowing the beginning. A great story ending gives us something of the same sensation that we might get by going into a forest on a cloudy day, climbing over rocks and tree roots, and then, unexpectedly, coming out into a flood of light. Whether an ending is "happy" or "sad" is irrelevant. Literary endings can almost never be characterized so simply. It's that sensation of the unexpected in the expected that makes readers feel larger and more open to the world when they finish a story than when they started it.

For a writer to come up with such an ending takes time and involves many balls of crumpled paper, or small files on the computer labeled "Father coming home ending" or "Kite at park ending." We can't solve for an ending as if it were an algebraic equation: "x = y," "the kite equals Bob's lost youth." Successful subtle endings often have several layers—more than one thing going on at the same time—so no one object or action has to carry all the weight of the ending.

STORY ANALYSIS AND QUESTIONS: THREE ENDINGS

(If you have not yet read "Powder," "The Cures for Love," and "The Turkey Season," please read them before *the analysis and questions. In this section, we discuss the crises and climaxes of the stories as well as the endings, so the discussions will be much less useful without a knowledge of the story. For this chapter, we are departing from our previous method of presenting a single anthology story. Instead we present analyses of three separate endings, followed by discussion questions for all three stories.)*

The beginning of Tobias Wolff's "Powder" sets us up to worry that the father and son won't get home, and that there will be some sort of blow-up between them. Please reread from "'Okay then. What are my strong points?'" through "'you haven't driven.'" We could imagine an ending in which the connection between father and son is broken, and the son decides he will never again be trapped in his father's plans. Instead, this ending gives us a marvelous sense of surrender—an enlarged but unsentimental view of both characters. The process of the surrender is echoed by the physical action, the downhill slide of the car across powder. This ending gives us a chance to consider the difference between a satisfying ending and one that wraps everything up neatly.

The crisis of this story, when the tension reaches its highest point, comes when the state trooper stops the car and orders them to turn back. The son expresses his anger at the father, obliquely, and the father makes the decision to go home despite the trooper's order. He coerces his son first into agreeing and then into helping him move the sawhorses. This is the climax, the characters' most significant actions in response to the crisis. One of the pleasures of this story is that it physically enacts its own dramatic shape: the falling action commences with the downhill drive. On the drive, the son finally listens to his father.

The ending starts with the beginning of the son's surrender. "'Okay then. What are my strong points?'" he asks, and with this question he opens himself up to the glory of his father: "rumpled, kind, bankrupt of honor." The narrator lets us know that their successful return doesn't permanently save the marriage, and we don't believe that what happens here will substantially change either of their characters. Our final impressions of the characters in "Powder" reinforce and deepen our first impressions. It's not a "happy" ending, just an exhilarating one. The narrator has taken on a little of his father's freedom and power, as he sees his father in a new light.

One side effect of workshop is that writers can be nervous about making assertions someone might disagree with, or including images and events that don't immediately reveal their meaning. The ending of Charles Baxter's "Cures for Love" is an argument for allowing a little mystery in a story.

Please reread from "When she awoke, at the sound of the air brakes" through "watching the way the orange was reflected in that one lens." The mystery and oddness of this ending is essential to its success. Nothing is harder to write about than recovery or happiness: grandparents playing with their children, lovers lying on the beach, family picnics—all these have been co-opted by soft-focus posters, advertising, and certain magazine stories. Charles Baxter, however, has convincingly depicted complicatedly happy love in serious novels: *The Feast of Love* and *Saul and Patsy.* In "The Cures for Love," he gives us a contemporary literary ending that depicts not happiness, but the lifting of unhappiness. It's almost never a good idea to spell out or underline a story's emotions for a reader, and this story avoids that temptation.

The crisis of the story comes when Kit—holding the mustard-and-relish-smeared Ovid—meets the woman who she "ought to" remember; the climax comes when Kit turns on "the Caroline person" and announces that she doesn't remember her at all. She does so later on, however, in the short paragraph that begins the falling action, which continues through her bus ride. If Kit found love or redemption at the airport, the ending would be too sweet. But she behaves badly to her old friend and, in so doing, gives herself a taste of freedom from the distant past she hardly remembers. By implication, the story suggests that someday she will be free of her current heartbreak. It's a moment of sentimental education: she discovers (though neither she nor the story spell this out) that it's possible to forget someone who meant everything to you at one time.

An ending that gives us a rediscovery of meaning may not work, as writer Michael Pritchett points out, if the author tries to push the character too fast through all the stages of recovery. One of the ways "The Cures for Love" succeeds is by letting us just start to feel the changing of Kit's emotional state in the falling action, her knowledge that "all right" is "approaching her, somewhere off there in the distance." Baxter hasn't saved up all the changes for the final moment. And even at the end, Kit doesn't attain happiness. She merely moves outside her state of self-absorbed misery to *see* the remarkable and peculiar world around her. The hard-edged humor and dreamy logic of Ovid's speech segue into a waking dream—not a wish-fulfillment dream, but one in which the damaged inhabitants and their curses are so interesting that a person can forget to be unhappy.

Alice Munro's "Turkey Season" takes both reader and character on a strange journey that leads to a greater understanding of human behavior. Many writers, not trusting the effect of their work, will attempt to spell out the exact nature of the trip and the destination, with an explicit statement of what the character has learned. A reader may feel a little bored or insulted by not being allowed to do some share of the work. Other writers may give us so little information that the events seem unconnected or meaningless; nothing helps us understand what has changed for the character or what kind of experience we've had in reading the story.

As writers, we have to refrain from underlining the point, even if that means our reader won't have the exact experience we had in mind. In "The Turkey Season," the narrator has become part of something by the end of the story, but what has she become part of? What is it that she and we have come to sense about thwarted or misdirected desire, about yearning and reality?

The crisis and the climax of the story come so close together that they're almost indistinguishable: in fact, the narrator isn't even present for the crisis—when Brian somehow shocks or insults Gladys. The narrator arrives at work just as Morgan is cursing Brian and chasing him with a cleaver. The underlying simmer of sex has erupted, but no one will discuss it, and this becomes the falling action: the hints that replace the conversation they never have.

Please reread from "I have a picture of the Turkey Barn crew . . ." through "So we sang." The ending, the final movement of the story, is several pages long. We're in the new, changed ground situation. Brian is gone, and the narrator is sorting out what happened. The actions of the other turkey gutters make it clear that she is one of them—at least for the moment, no longer the intellectual outsider.

The emotional plot—in which the narrator is exposed to and changed by the adult world—has been fulfilled. Whether or not we stop to analyze the story, we're both unsettled by the events and satisfied by the feeling that comes from vicariously learning to navigate an unfamiliar world. How does Munro convey all of this subtle material? It may take more than one rereading to understand why the musing in the final pages—such a dangerous tactic—is successful in this case.

The songs that Lily and Marjorie discuss and then sing in the final paragraphs are neither arbitrary nor overly obvious, but very consciously chosen by the author. Munro has layered the final lines of dialogue with history and subtext. The characters themselves seem to have some idea of the relationship of the songs to their own circumstances—Munro allows her characters dignity, complexity, and self-awareness.

DISCUSSION QUESTIONS

1. What roles do image, dialogue, summary, or actions and events play in each of these endings?
2. What are our final impressions of the characters? In what way are they different from our first impressions?
3. What are the different moods of the ending?
4. What about these endings is surprising? In what way do the endings fulfill the expectations and answer the questions raised by the stories' beginnings?

COMMON PITFALLS IN BEGINNINGS AND ENDINGS

Instructors often mention that beginning a story with an alarm clock going off or ending with a surprise or trick like "it was all a dream" is not only clichéd but usually a violation of the requirements of our own individual story. As Jerome Stern says, "Who wants to read a whole story just for a punch line . . .?" And extended descriptions of the setting or weather, or long passages of abstract musing by the author usually feel like scaffolding that hasn't been taken down. As readers, we know how dull it can be to read either a long explanation or the description of desperately ordinary events that seem to have no dramatic justification for being in the story. In other cases, a writer stuck for an ending may have the main character commit suicide, wanting to dramatize the completeness of a descent. When revising, we may discover a more original solution, in which something else ends or at least significantly changes. It's not the character who needs to die, but some aspect of his or her life. Or maybe the story could end with images or conversations that suggest loss, in ways that grow out of the characterizations and events.

In an attempt to avoid melodramatic endings, intermediate and advanced writers can sometimes fall into more subtle traps: images that don't seem to mean anything, cryptic dialogue, mysterious beginnings and abrupt endings, dramatic actions that seem to come out of nowhere, or philosophical ramblings that feel like the author's attempt to have the story make a point. Sometimes writers try to telegraph their meanings with paragraphs that hastily sum up a situation: these appear at the transitions of scenes and sections as well as at beginnings and endings of stories.

Our knowledge of the difficulty of getting stories published, or our desire to impress a workshop, teacher, or editor, may lead us into showy displays that focus attention on the writer instead of the story, like the example of a beginning below:

> *September, October, November, December, January, February, March, April, May.* Benjamin James stood under the slick jets of his jerry-rigged shower, weeping,

> water cascading off his ears and dripping down the ends of his mustache, over his chest, belly, arthritic left knee. Loneliness encased him, a corroded glass bubble. *Every year, a whole new life sentence.*

There's an old adage: once dressed, take off one accessory. We can apply this to the beginning of a story by taking out as many adjectives, adverbs, and moments of rumination as we can stand to. Although this beginning has some vivid details, such as the arthritic left knee, and shows an enthusiasm for language, the alliteration, excessive adjectives, and self-conscious verbs, in combination with the strong emotion, make this beginning less inviting than it could be. It's as if the reader had come into a room where someone was already shouting.

This beginning also shows a misunderstanding of the advice to begin in medias res, in the middle of events. This doesn't mean starting when the character is in a highly emotional state, but starting at the moment when something is beginning to unravel, letting the reader experience, at the same time as the character, the events that provoke the emotions. Even then, this is one of those opportunities for emotional restraint: the more dramatic or emotional the situation, the less the story needs to insist on it.

Another possible trap is that, terrified of being obvious, we may go out of our way to avoid having the characters behave in identifiably human ways: we refuse to let them have a love affair, pursue a desire, or do anything at all, and we obscure both their actions and their motivations. In the following example, it's very difficult to tell what is happening or who the characters are:

> She had not seen him in a long time. The box gave off a tinny odor when she opened it. "Cynthia," her mother said, sliding the dictionary off the shelf, "come here a moment and help me with the clock." For years the family had had a man come and tune the piano every six weeks, even though she had not played it since she was a child.
>
> "They are not for you," he had whispered.

The air of mystery that opens the story—who has she not seen, what's in the box—could be promising, but the story goes too far, piling on the mystery. We don't know why her mother is sliding a dictionary off the shelf, what's with the clock or the piano, or who whispered to her and what was not for her. The opening promises a distractingly coy story, determined to keep the reader off balance at the expense of meaning.

Also, not every aspect of the story needs to make it into the first paragraph. The example above attempts to introduce too many characters and incidents all at once. In addition, we could ground the reader with a few more sensory details, identifying the characters and saving some mysteries for later in the opening pages.

Here are some strategies for revising beginnings:

We can examine the beginning to see how it sets up the world of the story. How do the particular details bring it to life? What does it give the reader to hope for, to worry about, or to be curious to see more of? Does it subtly and elegantly provide the contextual information to compel the reader to "read forward"?

We can cut a story apart by paragraphs, holding each one up to see if it would make an exciting or intriguing beginning. Sometimes we can move a later passage up to the beginning, rearrange some of the other pieces, and substantially trim exposition and setup. This strategy can also be used for endings: could the story end in a flashback or with some unexpected but telling scene between two characters?

If we have a story with a slow beginning, we can try starting with a character in the middle of a significant action, possibly related to something he or she is doing later in the story.

When it comes to endings, it's usually a good idea not to introduce important new information that turns the ending into a surprise, as if the short story were a Gilbert and Sullivan operetta ("One moment! Let me tell you who they are! They are no members of the common throng; they are all nobleman who have gone wrong!") In the nineteenth century, readers expected these kinds of endings more often, but now it seems like a betrayal of the relationship between the writer and the reader.

Other common pitfalls include a puzzling final image, a psychological insight that feels predictable, or a cryptic ending that just trails off. In genre fiction, we expect to know the identity of the murderer or watch the lovers united by the end. In literary fiction however, we don't want to see, halfway through the story, an epiphany heading toward us like an oncoming train ("he realized then how much he resembled his father").

The example below tries the strategy of ending with an image:

> "All through," he said. Joseph the Thecodont, missing his children. In his mind he could still hear the sound of Suzanne's voice describing her party, the bursts of laughter, her faraway delight. He rested against the warm railing at cliff's edge where he could watch waves breaking on the beach below. The water had nearly reached its high mark, his mussels hidden until the next ebb tide. *Postelsia* palms, broken loose from their rocks, floating over the mussels in a tangle of kelp and detritus, moved in and out as sunlight scattered, blindingly, across the hard green of the water's surface.

An image can often be a good way to end a story, but these floating palms are both too symbolic and not clear enough. This last paragraph is full of a vaguely portentous, elegiac quality. It uses clichés—"faraway delight" and the "blinding" sunlight—to symbolically express a character's epiphany.

This next ending, also portentous and elegiac in its own way, has a musing first-person narrator trying to tie up all the strands of the story:

> I still have the photographs. I never look at them. I thought I would burn them. I ought to burn them. I'm thirty years old now, and there's only the usual chance

> that I will die by some accident any time soon, but whenever I do, somec could certainly stumble across the portfolio, jammed underneath some blankets in my attic. And yet, if I burned them, they would cling to my memory. Everything that has vanished from my life has taken up home in my head and will not let me go. But those photographs, those photographs that I scrutinized as if to memorize for all time, they are not inside my head. My mind slides away from recalling them. Though I do not say I don't want to recall them. Perhaps the images are in Mr. Croy's head, wherever he is, and I hope they haunt him, I hope all that grainy, pale, naked flesh haunts him.

The repetitions and contradictions, the high emotion, become unintentionally comic, the opposite of the effect the writer seems to be intending. The story is working overtime to express its emotions. Like the first ending example, this one is trying to accomplish in a few lines a meaning that needs to be worked out in the course of the story's actions.

Here are some strategies for revising endings:

We can examine our story to see when the ending actually starts. Is the last paragraph trying to do too much work? Can the concluding events begin earlier? Could the ending be a page or two instead of a paragraph? We can try writing out full scenes of two or three other possible endings to a story, making sure that each directly results from the climax, and that each either picks up a different theme or image of the story or skips sideways from the main events into an unexpected corner. Rather than sketching out these alternate endings, we can write each one as if it really mattered, as if it were *the* ending—letting our inner writing mechanism surprise us.

Or we might take a story ending that doesn't seem to be working and write what happens *after* that ending, continuing for two or three pages. How does the new ending change the experience of "reading backwards"? What does it reveal about the story?

We usually need to revise up to and beyond the point where we're sick of the story. Sometimes we put it aside for a while. It can take months of listening to and reworking a story until we feel sure we have it right. And then, after we put it aside for a while and come back to it, we usually discover that we need to revise it again. It's worth it, when we get the ending that transfigures the story.

REVISION EXERCISES

1. Write a two-paragraph synopsis of what happens in one of your stories, including only the major events. Now write a two-sentence statement of what you think your story is about. Try writing two alternative short synopses—in each one, make one or two significant (but not arbitrary) changes to the characters or the events of the original story. What makes either your original or your alternative versions show the "aboutness" of the story more clearly?

2. If anyone has made a suggestion or criticism in workshop that inspired a loud and clear "NO" inside you, that may be a clue to finding the heart of your story. What is it about your story that feels nonnegotiable to you? Change or cut some other element to make what's clear to you clear to the reader as well, and to prevent possible misreadings.
3. In a group, describe to each other what really matters to you about your own story. People are allowed to ask for clarifications, but not to make critiques. Repeat the process a second time, each person having the chance to refine or expand on what they said the first time. If your first response described what made the story personally important to you, think about what might make the story matter to someone who doesn't have the same personal investment.
4. Examine the characters in your story, major and minor. Consider the story without each one. Could a character's actions or dialogue be appropriately assigned to another character without diminishing the story? Sometimes two underdeveloped characters, when combined, form a complex character. On the other hand, if much of the story chronicles an internal struggle within a main character, consider what would happen if you split that person into two characters. Dramatize the struggle in scenes between these characters. Look for ways to keep each one complicated, representing more than an ideological position.
5. Cut your story into pieces—literally, with scissors. Each piece should consist of an entire scene, or an extended flashback, or an entire passage of stand-alone description or summary. Arrange the pieces randomly, or in alphabetical order according to the first letter of the piece, so that you are able to study them away from their original context. Consider each piece as the opening of the story—which one would most likely draw you in, if you were a reader leafing through a literary journal or story collection? Once you have chosen the beginning, try placing the pieces in different orders until you find one that tells the story most smoothly. In some cases, you may find yourself cutting up individual scenes as well, restructuring the order of events. Which pieces seem most vivid? Which seem most emotionally charged? Are there pieces that could be removed entirely, replaced by a brief line here or there?
6. Choose any story you've written and revised extensively, one that seems finished. Imagine that the editor of your favorite magazine has called up and said, "I'll take it, if you can make it 20 percent shorter." See if you can meet the challenge without harming the story.
7. (This reading exercise can be done either individually or in a group.) Examine the beginnings of a number of the stories you've read in the anthology. What is the ground situation? Where does the story begin and what seems to be the end of that beginning? What narrative questions does it raise? What are we hoping for or worried about? What is our first impression of the characters? How is that impression created?

In what way does the author establish the POV for us? What are the moods of this beginning, and what words, details, action, images, or dialogue create those moods?

8. (This reading exercise can be done either individually or in a group.) Examine the endings of a number of the stories you've read from the anthology. When does each ending seem to start? What signals that the story is now in its ending? How long does each ending last? Which stories end with dialogue, summary, an image, an epiphany, an action or event, or some combination of these? How does the strategy of the ending fit with the scene, tone, and events of the story? What about this particular ending is surprising? In what way does it seem inevitable? How does it seem to satisfy the expectations the story raises?

PART TWO

Anthology of Stories

Civil Peace

Chinua Achebe

Jonathan Iwegbu counted himself extra-ordinarily lucky. 'Happy survival!' meant so much more to him than just a current fashion of greeting old friends in the first hazy days of peace. It went deep to his heart. He had come out of the war with five inestimable blessings—his head, his wife Maria's head and the heads of three out of their four children. As a bonus he also had his old bicycle—a miracle too but naturally not to be compared to the safety of five human heads.

The bicycle had a little history of its own. One day at the height of the war it was commandeered 'for urgent military action'. Hard as its loss would have been to him he would still have let it go without a thought had he not had some doubts about the genuineness of the officer. It wasn't his disreputable rags, nor the toes peeping out of one blue and one brown canvas shoe, nor yet the two stars of his rank done obviously in a hurry in biro, that troubled Jonathan; many good and heroic soldiers looked the same or worse. It was rather a certain lack of grip and firmness in his manner. So Jonathan, suspecting he might be amenable to influence, rummaged in his raffia bag and produced the two pounds with which he had been going to buy firewood which his wife, Maria, retailed to camp officials for extra stock-fish and corn meal, and got his bicycle back. That night he buried it in the little clearing in the bush where the dead of the camp, including his own youngest son, were buried. When he dug it up again a year later after the surrender all it needed was a little palm-oil greasing. 'Nothing puzzles God,' he said in wonder.

He put it to immediate use as a taxi and accumulated a small pile of Biafran money ferrying camp officials and their families across the four-mile stretch to the nearest tarred road. His standard charge per trip was six pounds and those who had the money were only glad to be rid of some of it in this way. At the end of a fortnight he had made a small fortune of one hundred and fifteen pounds.

Then he made the journey to Enugu and found another miracle waiting for him. It was unbelievable. He rubbed his eyes and looked again and it was still standing there before him. But, needless to say, even that monumental blessing must be accounted also totally inferior to the five heads in the family. This newest miracle was his little house in Ogui Overside. Indeed nothing puzzles God! Only two houses away a huge concrete edifice some wealthy contractor had put up just before the war was a mountain of rubble. And here was Jonathan's little zinc house of no regrets built with mud blocks quite intact! Of course the doors and windows were missing and five sheets off the roof. But what was that? And anyhow he had returned to Enugu early enough to pick up bits of old zinc and wood and soggy sheets of cardboard lying around the neighbourhood before thousands more came out of their forest holes looking for the same things. He got a destitute carpenter with one old hammer, a blunt plane and a few bent and rusty nails in his tool bag to turn this assortment of wood, paper and metal into door and window shutters for five Nigerian shillings or fifty Biafran pounds. He paid the pounds, and moved in with his overjoyed family carrying five heads on their shoulders.

His children picked mangoes near the military cemetery and sold them to soldiers' wives for a few pennies—real pennies this time—and his wife started making breakfast akara balls for neighbours in a hurry to start life again. With his family earnings he took his bicycle to the villages around and bought fresh palm-wine which he mixed generously in his rooms with the water which had recently started running again in the public tap down the road, and opened up a bar for soldiers and other lucky people with good money.

At first he went daily, then every other day and finally once a week, to the offices of the Coal Corporation where he used to be a miner, to find out what was what. The only thing he did find out in the end was that that little house of his was even a greater blessing than he had thought. Some of his fellow ex-miners who had nowhere to return at the end of the day's waiting just slept outside the doors of the offices and cooked what meal they could scrounge together in Bournvita tins. As the weeks lengthened and still nobody could say what was what Jonathan discontinued his weekly visits altogether and faced his palm-wine bar.

But nothing puzzles God. Came the day of the windfall when after five days of endless scuffles in queues and counterqueues in the sun outside the Treasury he had twenty pounds counted into his palms as ex-gratia award for the rebel money he had turned in. It was like Christmas for him and for many others like him when the payments began. They called it (since few could manage its proper official name) *egg-rasher.*

As soon as the pound notes were placed in his palm Jonathan simply closed it tight over them and buried fist and money inside his trouser pocket. He had to be extra careful because he had seen a man a couple of days earlier collapse into near-madness in an instant before that oceanic crowd because no sooner had he got his twenty pounds than some heartless ruffian picked it off him. Though it was not right that a man in such an extremity of agony should be blamed yet many in the queues that day were able to remark quietly at the victim's carelessness, especially after he pulled out the innards of his pocket and revealed a hole in it big enough to pass a thief's head. But of course he had insisted that the money had been in the other pocket, pulling it out too to show its comparative wholeness. So one had to be careful.

Jonathan soon transferred the money to his left hand and pocket so as to leave his right free for shaking hands should the need arise, though by fixing his gaze at such an elevation as to miss all approaching human faces he made sure that the need did not arise, until he got home.

He was normally a heavy sleeper but that night he heard all the neighbourhood noises die down one after another. Even the night watchman who knocked the hour on some metal somewhere in the distance had fallen silent after knocking one o'clock. That must have been the last thought in Jonathan's mind before he was finally carried away himself. He couldn't have been gone for long, though, when he was violently awakened again.

'Who is knocking?' whispered his wife lying beside him on the floor.

'I don't know,' he whispered back breathlessly.

The second time the knocking came it was so loud and imperious that the rickety old door could have fallen down.

'Who is knocking?' he asked them, his voice parched and trembling.

'Na tief-man and him people,' came the cool reply. 'Make you hopen de door.' This was followed by the heaviest knocking of all.

Maria was the first to raise the alarm, then he followed and all their children.

'Police-o! Thieves-o! Neighbours-o! Police-o! We are lost! We are dead! Neighbours, are you asleep? Wake up! Police-o!'

This went on for a long time and then stopped suddenly. Perhaps they had scared the thief away. There was total silence. But only for a short while.

'You done finish?' asked the voice outside. 'Make we help you small. Oya, everybody!'

'Police-o! Tief-man-so! Neighbours-o! we done loss-o! Police-o! . . .'

There were at least five other voices besides the leader's.

Jonathan and his family were now completely paralysed by terror. Maria and the children sobbed inaudibly like lost souls. Jonathan groaned continuously.

The silence that followed the thieves' alarm vibrated horribly. Jonathan all but begged their leader to speak again and be done with it.

'My frien,' said he at long last, 'we don try our best for call dem but I tink say dem all done sleep-o . . . So wetin we go do now? Sometaim you wan call soja? Or you wan make we call dem for you? Soja better pass police. No be so?'

'Na so!' replied his men. Jonathan thought he heard even more voices now than before and groaned heavily. His legs were sagging under him and his throat felt like sandpaper.

'My frien, why you no de talk again. I de ask you say you wan make we call soja?'

'No'.

'Awrighto. Now make we talk business. We no be bad tief. We no like for make trouble. Trouble done finish. War done finish and all the katakata wey de for inside. No Civil War again. This time na Civil Peace. No be so?'

'Na so!' answered the horrible chorus.

'What do you want from me? I am a poor man. Everything I had went with this war. Why do you come to me? You know people who have money. We . . .'

'Awright! We know say you no get plenty money. But we sef no get even anini. So derefore make you open dis window and give us one hundred pound and we go commot. Orderwise we de come for inside now to show you guitar-boy like dis . . .'

A volley of automatic fire rang through the sky. Maria and the children began to weep aloud again.

'Ah, missisi de cry again. No need for dat. We done talk say we na good tief. We just take our small money and go nwayorly. No molest. Abi we de molest?'

'At all!' sang the chorus.

'My friends,' began Jonathan hoarsely. 'I hear what you say and I thank you. If I had one hundred pounds . . .'

'Lookia my frien, no be play we come play for your house. If we make mistake and step for inside you no go like am-o. So derefore . . .'

'To God who made me; if you come inside and find one hundred pounds, take it and shoot me and shoot my wife and children. I swear to God. The only money I have in this life is this twenty-pounds *egg-rasher* they gave me today . . .'

'Ok. Time de go. Make you open dis window and bring the twenty pound. We go manage am like dat.'

There were now loud murmurs of dissent among the chorus: 'Na lie de man de lie; e get plenty money . . . Make we go inside and search properly well . . . Wetin be twenty pound? . . .'

'Shurrup!' rang the leader's voice like a lone shot in the sky and silenced the murmuring at once. 'Are you dere? Bring the money quick!'

'I am coming,' said Jonathan fumbling in the darkness with the key of the small wooden box he kept by his side on the mat.

At the first sign of light as neighbours and others assembled to commiserate with him he was already strapping his five-gallon demijohn to his bicycle carrier and his wife, sweating in the open fire, was turning over akara balls in a wide clay bowl of boiling oil. In the corner his eldest son was rinsing out dregs of yesterday's palm-wine from old beer bottles.

'I count it as nothing,' he told his sympathizers, his eyes on the rope he was tying. 'What is *egg-rasher?* Did I depend on it last week? Or is it greater than other things that went with the war? I say, let *egg-rasher* perish in the flames! Let it go where everything else has gone. Nothing puzzles God.'

Di Grasso: A Tale of Odessa

Isaac Babel

I was fourteen, and of the undauntable fellowship of dealers in theater tickets. My boss was a tricky customer with a permanently screwed-up eye and enormous silky handle bars; Nick Schwarz was his name. I came under his sway in that unhappy year when the Italian Opera flopped in Odessa. Taking a lead from the critics on the local paper, our impresario decided not to import Anselmi and Tito Ruffo as guest artistes but to make do with a good stock company. For this he was sorely punished; he went bankrupt, and we with him. We were promised Chaliapin to straighten out our affairs, but Chaliapin wanted three thousand a performance; so instead we had the Sicilian tragedian Di Grasso with his troupe. They arrived at the hotel in peasant carts crammed with children, cats, cages in which Italian birds hopped and skipped. Casting an eye over this gypsy crew, Nick Schwarz opined:

"Children, this stuff won't sell."

When he had settled in, the tragedian made his way to the market with a bag. In the evening he arrived at the theater with another bag. Hardly fifty people had turned up. We tried selling tickets at half-price, but there were no takers.

That evening they staged a Sicilian folk drama, a tale as commonplace as the change from night to day and vice versa. The daughter of a rich peasant pledges her troth to a shepherd. She is faithful to him till one day there drives out from the city a young slicker in a velvet waistcoat. Passing the time of day with the new arrival, the maiden giggled in all the wrong places and fell silent when she shouldn't have. As he listened to them, the shepherd twisted his head this way and that like a startled bird. During the whole of the first act he kept flattening himself against walls, dashing off somewhere, his pants flapping, and on his return gazing wildly about.

"This stuff stinks," said Nick Schwarz in the intermission. "Only place it might go down is some dump like Kremenchug."

The intermission was designed to give the maiden time to grow ripe for betrayal. In the second act we just couldn't recognize her: she behaved insufferably, her thoughts were clearly elsewhere, and she lost no time in handing the shepherd back his ring. Thereupon he led her over to a poverty-stricken but brightly painted image of the Holy Virgin, and said in his Sicilian patois:

"Signora," said he in a low voice, turning away, "the Holy Virgin desires you to give me a hearing. To Giovanni, the fellow from the city, the Holy Virgin will grant as many women as he can cope with; but I need none save you. The Virgin Mary, our stainless intercessor, will tell you exactly the same thing if you ask Her."

The maiden stood with her back to the painted wooden image. As she listened she kept impatiently tapping her foot.

In the third act Giovanni, the city slicker, met his fate. He was having a shave at the village barber's, his powerful male legs thrust out all over the front of the stage. Beneath the Sicilian sun the pleats in his waistcoat gleamed. The scene represented a village fair. In a far corner stood the shepherd; silent he stood there amid the carefree crowd. First he hung his head; then he raised it, and beneath the weight of his attentive and burning gaze Giovanni started stirring and fidgeting in his barber chair, till pushing the barber aside he leaped to his feet. In a voice shaking with passion he demanded that the policeman should remove from the village square all persons of a gloomy and suspicious aspect. The shepherd—the part was played by Di Grasso himself—stood there lost in thought; then he gave a smile, soared into the air, sailed across the stage, plunged down on Giovanni's shoulders, and having bitten through the latter's throat, began, growling and squinting, to suck blood from the wound. Giovanni collapsed, and the curtain, falling noiselessly and full of menace, hid from us killed and killer. Waiting for no more, we dashed to the box office in Theater Lane, which was to open next day, Nick Schwarz beating the rest by a short neck. Came the dawn, and with it the *Odessa News* informed the few people who had been at the theater that they had seen the most remarkable actor of the century.

On this visit Di Grasso played *King Lear, Othello, Civil Death,* Turgenev's *The Parasite,* confirming with every word and every gesture that there is more justice in outbursts of noble passion than in all the joyless rules that run the world.

Tickets for these shows were snapped up at five times face value. Scouting round for ticket-traders, would-be purchasers found them at the inn, yelling their heads off, purple, vomiting a harmless sacrilege.

A pink and dusty sultriness was injected into Theater Lane. Shopkeepers in felt slippers bore green bottles of wine and barrels of olives out onto the pavement. In tubs outside the shops macaroni seethed in foaming water, and the steam from it melted in the distant skies. Old women in men's boots dealt in seashells and souvenirs, pursuing hesitant purchasers with loud cries. Moneyed Jews with beards parted down the middle and combed to either side would drive up to the Northern Hotel and tap discreetly on the doors of fat women with raven hair and little mustaches, Di Grasso's actresses. All were happy in Theater Lane; all, that is, save for one person. I was that person. In those days catastrophe was approaching me: at any moment my father might miss the watch I had taken without his permission and pawned to Nick Schwarz. Having had the gold turnip long enough to get used to it, and being a man who replaced tea as his morning drink by Bessarabian wine, Nick Schwarz, even with his money back, could still not bring himself to return the watch to me. Such was his character. And my father's character differed in no wise from his. Hemmed in by these two characters, I sorrowfully watched other people enjoying themselves. Nothing remained for me but to run away to Constantinople. I had made all the arrangements with the second engineer of the S.S. *Duke of Kent,* but before embarking on the deep I decided to say goodbye to Di Grasso. For the last time he was playing the shepherd who is swung aloft by an incomprehensible power. In the audience were all the Italian colony, with the bald but shapely consul at their head. There were fidgety Greeks and bearded externs with their gaze fastened fanatically upon some point invisible to all other mortals; there was the long-armed Utochkin. Nick Schwarz had even brought his missis, in a violet shawl with a fringe; a woman with all the makings of a grenadier she was, stretching right out to the steppes, and with a sleepy little crumpled face at the far end. When the curtain fell this face was drenched in tears.

"Now you see what love means," she said to Nick as they were leaving the theater.

Stomping ponderously, Madam Schwarz moved along Langeron Street; tears rolled from her fishlike eyes, and the shawl with the fringe shuddered on her obese shoulders. Dragging her mannish soles, rocking her head, she reckoned up, in a voice that made the street re-echo, the women who got on well with their husbands.

"'Ducky' they're called by their husbands; 'sweetypie' they're called . . ."

The cowed Nick walked along by his wife, quietly blowing on his silky mustaches. From force of habit I followed on behind, sobbing. During a momentary pause Madam Schwarz heard my sobs and turned around.

"See here," she said to her husband, her fisheyes agoggle, "may I not die a beautiful death if you don't give the boy his watch back!"

Nick froze, mouth agape; then came to and, giving me a vicious pinch, thrust the watch at me sideways.

"What can I expect of him," the coarse and tear-muffled voice of Madam Schwarz wailed disconsolately as it moved off into the distance, "what can I expect but beastliness today and beastliness tomorrow? I ask you, how long is a woman supposed to put up with it?"

They reached the corner and turned into Pushkin Street. I stood there clutching the watch, alone; and suddenly, with a distinctness such as I had never before experienced, I saw the columns of the Municipal Building soaring up into the heights, the gas-lit foliage of the boulevard, Pushkin's bronze head touched by the dim gleam of the moon; saw for the first time the things surrounding me as they really were: frozen in silence and ineffably beautiful.

Translated by Walter Morison

The Forest

Andrea Barrett

Later the squat white cylinders with their delicate indentations would be revealed as a species of lantern. But when Krzysztof Wojciechowicz first glimpsed them, dotted among the azaleas and rhododendrons and magnolias surrounding Constance Humboldt's kidney-shaped swimming pool, he saw them as dolls. The indentations cut the frosted tubes like waists, a third of the way down; the swellings above and below reminded him of bodices and rounded skirts. Perhaps he viewed the lanterns this way because the girls guiding him down the flagstone steps and across the patio were themselves so doll-like. Amazingly young, amazingly smooth-skinned. Sisters, they'd said. The tiny dark-haired one who'd appeared in the hotel lobby was Rose; the round-cheeked one driving the battered van, with her blond hair frizzing in all directions, was Bianca. Already he'd been clumsy with them.

"You are . . . are you Dr. Humboldt's daughters?" he'd asked. The sun was so bright, his eyes were so tired, the jumble of buildings and traffic so confusing. The step up to the van's back seat was too high for him, but neither girl noticed him struggling.

The small one, Rose, had laughed at his question. "We're not related to Constance," she'd said. "I'm a postdoctoral fellow at the institute." The blond one, who called to mind his own mother sixty years earlier, pulled out of the hotel driveway too fast and said nothing during the short drive to the Humboldts' house. He feared he'd hurt her feelings. For the last decade or so, he'd been subject to these embarrassing misidentifications, taking young scientists for children or servants when he met them out of context. They all dressed so casually, especially in this country; their faces were so unmarked—how could anyone tell them from the young people who chauffeured him about or offered trays of canapes at parties? But these girls he should have known, he'd probably met them earlier. Now, as he stepped down into the enormous back garden and moved toward the long table spread with food and drink, the girl called after a flower veered toward a crowd gathered by the pool and left him with the girl he'd affronted.

"Dr. Wojciechowicz?" she said, mangling his name as she steered him closer to the table. "Would you like a drink or something?"

Reflexively he corrected her pronunciation; then he shook his head and said, "Please. Call me Krzysztof. And you are Bianca, yes?" He could not help noticing that she had lovely breasts.

"That's me," she agreed dryly. "Bianca the chauffeur, Rose's sister, *not* related to the famous Dr. Constance Humboldt. No one you need to pay attention to at all."

"It's not . . ." he said. Of course he had insulted her. "It's just that I'm so tired, and I'm still jet-lagged, and . . ."

Could he ask her where he was without sounding senile? Somewhere north of Philadelphia, he thought; but he knew this generally, not specifically. When he'd arrived two days ago, his body still on London time, he had fallen asleep during the long, noisy drive from the airport. Since then he'd had no clear sense of his location. He woke in a room that looked like any other; each morning a different stranger appeared and drove him to the institute. Other strangers shuttled him from laboratory to laboratory, talking at length about their research projects and then moving him from laboratory to cafeteria to auditorium to laboratory, from lobby to restaurant and back to his hotel. The talk he'd given was the same talk he'd been giving for years; he had met perhaps thirty fellow scientists and could remember only a handful of their names. All of them seemed to be gathered here, baring too much skin to the early July sun. Saturday, he thought. Also some holiday seemed to be looming.

"Do forgive me," he said. "The foibles of the elderly."

"How old *are* you?"

Her smile was charming and he forgave her rude question. "I am seventy-nine years of age," he said. "Easy to remember—I was born in 1900, I am always as old as the century."

"Foibles forgiven." She—*Bianca,* he thought. *Bianca*—held out her hand in that strange boyish way of American women. Meanwhile she was looking over his shoulders, as if hoping to find someone to rescue her. "Bianca Marburg, not quite twenty-two but I'm very old for my age."

"You're in college?"

She tossed her hair impatiently. "Not *now.* My sister and I were dreadful little prodigies—in college at sixteen, out at nineteen, right into graduate school. Rose already has her Ph.D.—how else do you think she'd have a postdoc here?"

Would he never say the right thing to this bristly girl? "So then you . . . what is the project you are working on?" Americans, he'd been reminded these last two days, were always eager to talk about themselves.

"So then *I*—I should be in graduate school, and I was until two months ago but I dropped out, it was seeming stupid to me. Unlike my so-successful sister Rose, *I* am at loose ends."

She moved a bowl of salad closer to a platter of sliced bread draped with a cloth, then moved it back again. "Which is why I'm driving you around. Why I'm here. I'm sort of between places, you know? I got a temp job typing for an Iraqi biophysicist—see the short guy near the volleyball net? He hired me because I can spell 'vacuum.' I'm staying with my sister until I get enough money together to move. I might go to Alaska."

"That's nice," Krzysztof said helplessly.

"Oh, please," she said. "You don't have to pretend to be interested. Go talk to the other famous people. Constance collects them, they're everywhere."

She huffed off—furious, he saw. At him? In the battered leather bag that hung from his shoulder he felt the bottle he'd carried across the ocean as a special gift for his hostess. But his hostess was nowhere to be seen, and no one moved toward him from either the pool or the round tables with their mushroomlike umbrellas. Already the top of his head was burning; he was all alone and wished he had a hat. Was it possible these people meant to stay in the sun all afternoon?

Bianca made a brisk circuit through the backyard, looking for someplace to settle down. There was Rose, leaning attentively toward Constance's camel-faced husband, Roger, and listening to him as if she were interested. Entirely typical, Bianca thought; Rose submitted herself to Roger's monologues as a way of pleasing Constance, who was her advisor. Constance herself was holding court from a elegant lawn chair beneath an umbrella, surrounded by graduate students and postdocs—but Bianca couldn't bear the way Constance patronized her, and she steered wide of this group. She considered joining the two students Constance employed, who were trotting up and down the steps bearing pitchers of iced tea and lemonade; at last week's reception, though, Constance had rebuked her for distracting the help. The knot of protein chemists at the volleyball net beckoned, Rick and Wen-li and Diego stripped of their shirts and gleaming in the sun, but she'd slept with Diego after that reception, and now they weren't speaking. Perhaps Vivek and Anisha, easing themselves into the shallow end of the pool just as Jocelyn, already cannonball-shaped, curled her arms around her legs and launched herself into the deep end with a splash?

No, no, no. Vivek was charming but Jocelyn, impossible Jocelyn, was already whaling down on her young squire. Everywhere Bianca looked there was laughter, chatter, the display of flesh—much of it, Bianca thought, better left hidden—flirtation and bragging and boredom. A standard holiday-weekend party, except that all of these people were scientists, and many were famous, while she was neither. And had, as Rose reminded her constantly, no one to blame for this but herself.

Off by the fragrant mock orange tree, she spotted the institute's two resident Nobel laureates side by side, looming over the scene in dark pants and long-sleeved shirts. She drifted their way, curious to see if they were clashing yet. Arnold puffed and plucked at his waistband; Herb snorted and rolled his eyes: but they were smiling, these were still playful attacks. Last week, during Winifred's seminar on the isozymes of alpha-amylase, she'd watched the pair shred Winifred in their boastful crossfire. Arnold, sitting to her left, had favored her with a smile.

"Nice to see you gentlemen again," Bianca said.

The men stared at her blankly, Arnold's left foot tapping at the smooth green grass.

"Bianca Marburg," she reminded them.

"From Jocelyn's lab?" Arnold said now.

"Rose Marburg's sister," she said, grinning stupidly.

Herb frowned, still unable to place her. "Didn't I see you . . . were you *typing?* For Fu'ad?"

She held her hands up like claws and typed the air. *"C'est moi,"* she said. What was she doing here?

"Ah," Arnold said. "You must be helping Constance out. It's a lovely party, isn't it? So well organized. Constance really amazes me, the way she can do this sort of thing and still keep that big lab working. . . . "

"But that last pair of papers," Herb said. "Really."

Bianca fled. From the corner of her eye she saw the man she'd driven here, that Polish émigré, physical-chemist turned theoretical structural-biologist, Cambridge-based multiply medaled old guy, standing all alone by the bamboo fountain, watching the water arc from the stem to the pool. Pleasing Constance inadvertently, she thought; Constance fancied her home as a place conducive to contemplation and great ideas. Krzysztof raised his right hand and held it over his head, either feeling for hair that was no longer present or attempting to shade his array of freckles and liver spots from the burning sun.

Quickly Bianca traversed the yard and the patio, slipped through the glass doors and across the kitchen, and ran upstairs to the third and smallest bathroom. The door closed behind her with expensive precision: a Mercedes door, a jewel-box door. On the vanity was a vase with a Zen-like twist of grapevine and a single yellow orchid. She opened the window and lit up a joint. Entirely typical, she thought, gazing down at Krzysztof's sweaty pate. That Constance and Arnold and Herb and the others should fly this man across the ocean to hear about his work, then get so caught up in institute politics that they'd forget to talk to him at their party. Had it not been for the lizardlike graze of his eyes across her chest, she might have felt sorry for him.

Krzysztof crouched down by the rock-rimmed basin and touched a blade of grass to the water, dimpling the surface and thinking about van der Waals forces even as Constance rushed to his side, burbling and babbling and asking if he was ill. When he assured her that he was fine, she asked about Cambridge, and then if he'd like a swim—but of course not, he should come sit here; he knew everyone, didn't he? She helped him into a long, low, elaborately curved chair, webbed with canvas that trapped him as securely as a fishnet. She couldn't have meant to let him languish there; that would have been rude, she was never rude. She must not have known that he couldn't rise from this snare unaided. Nor could she have known, as the faces bent toward him politely for a moment and then turned back to their animated conversations about meetings he hadn't attended, squabbles among colleagues he didn't know, that he'd forgotten almost all their names and was incapable of attaching those he did remember to the appropriate faces and research problems.

The sun had moved, was moving, so that first his knees, then his thighs and crotch were uncomfortably roasted. This was the throne room, he saw. This cluster of chairs, perched where an adrenal gland would be if the pool were really a kidney: himself and Constance, Arnold, Herb, Jocelyn, and Sundralingam. All the senior scientists. Directly across the pool the junior researchers stood in tight circles, occasionally glancing his way; the postdocs and students were gathered at the farthest end of the pool, where a group of bare-torsoed, highly muscled young men tended a grill that sent up disturbing smoky columns.

He made columns in his mind: faces, names, research projects. Then he tried and failed to match up the lists. The girl named Rose walked by and smiled at him. Although he smiled back eagerly she continued to walk, past him and between a pair of those low white cylinders standing among the glossy mounds of hosta like dolls in a dark wood. He knew he'd fallen asleep only when his own sudden, deep-throated snore woke him.

The sun had dropped and the sky had turned a remarkable violet-blue; perhaps it was seven o'clock. A few people still swam in the pool, but most were out, and mostly dressed, and the smell of roasting fowl filled the air. On the patio people milled around the grill and the table with paper plates in their hands. Bottles of wine, bottles of beer, dripping glasses, ice; he was, he realized, very thirsty. And past embarrassment, although the chairs near him were empty now, as if he'd driven everyone away. Somehow he was not surprised, when he rolled sideways in an unsuccessful attempt to pull himself from his lounge chair, to see Bianca, cross-legged on the grass, watching over him.

"Have a nice nap?" she asked.

"Lovely," he replied. She seemed happy now; what had he missed? "But you know I *cannot* get up from this thing."

The hand she held out was not enough. "If you would," he said, "just put your hands under my arms and lift . . ."

Effortlessly she hauled him to his feet. "You want to go over toward the tables?"

"Not just yet. I'll sit here for a minute." This time he chose a straight metal chair with a scallop-shell back. He sat gingerly, then more firmly. A fine chair, he'd be able to rise himself.

"I'll get you some food."

He sniffed the air, repelled by the odor of charred flesh. "Get something for yourself," he said. "Maybe I'll eat later. But I'm terribly thirsty—do you suppose you could bring me something cold? Some water?" He remembered, then, the bottle in his bag. "And if you could find two small empty glasses, as well," he said. "I have a treat to share with you."

When she returned he gulped gratefully at the cool water. "Do you like vodka?" he asked.

"Me? I'll drink anything."

He reached into his leather satchel and took out the bottle he'd meant to give Constance. In return, Bianca held out two paper cups, printed with blue and green daisies. "The best I could do."

"Good enough." He held up the heavy bottle, showing her the blade of grass floating blissfully inside. *"Zubrowka,"* he said. "Bison vodka, very special. It's flavored with the grass upon which the bison feed in the Bialowieza Forest, where my family is from. A friend brings it to me from Poland when he visits, and I brought it here from Cambridge."

"Cool," she said. "Should I get some ice?"

"Never," he said, shuddering. "We drink this neat, always." He poured two shots and handed her one. "Drink it all in one gulp—*do dna.* To the bottom."

"Bottoms up," Bianca said. Together they tossed the shots down. Almost immediately he felt better. Bianca choked and shook her head, her pale hair flying in all directions. He forbade himself to look at her smooth neck or the legs emerging, like horses from the gate, from her white shorts. He focused on her nose and reminded himself that women her age saw men like him as trolls. Even ten years ago, the occasional women with whom he'd forgotten himself had let him know this, and cruelly. How was it he still felt these impulses, then? That the picture of himself he carried inside had not caught up to his crumpled body?

"Take a sip of water," he said.

"It *burns!*"

"Of course. But isn't it delicious?" He refilled the ridiculous cups and they drank again. She had spirit, he thought. This time she hardly choked at all. He tried to imagine her as the granddaughter of one of his oldest friends, himself as an elderly uncle.

"Delicious," she agreed. "It's like drinking a meadow. Again?"

"Why not?"

Around the left lobe of the kidney came Rose, a platter of chicken in her hand. She seemed simultaneously to smile at him and glare at her sister, who was caught with the paper cup still at her lips. Was that a glare? He couldn't figure out what was going on between them.

"Welcome," he said. And then, reluctant to lose Bianca's undivided attention, "Will you join us?"

"I can't just now," Rose said. "But Constance wants to know if you'd like to come over to the patio and have something to eat." She thrust the platter toward his face. "The chicken's great."

"Maybe later."

"Bianca?"

"No," Bianca said firmly; she seemed to be rejecting more than just the food. The sisters glared at each other for a minute—*children,* Krzysztof thought; then remembered Bianca's earlier word. *No, prodigies. All grown up*—before Rose made a clicking sound with her tongue and walked away.

Her mouth tasted of meadows and trees, Bianca thought. As if she'd been turned into a creature with hooves, suavely grazing in a dappled glade. The joint she'd smoked earlier was still with her but barely, palely; this warmth in her veins, this taste in her mouth, were from the splendid bison vodka. And this man, whom at first she'd felt saddled with and longed to escape, was some sort of magician. Now it seemed like good fortune that everyone else had abandoned him to her care. They rose from their chairs, on their way to join the crowd and examine the platters of food. But the voices on the patio seemed terribly loud and someone was shrieking with laughter, a sound like metal beating metal. Chased away, they drifted toward the Japanese fountain tucked in the shrubbery, where Krzysztof had earlier crouched until Constance captured him.

"Isn't this pretty?" he asked, and she agreed. Ferns surrounded one side of the fountain, lacy and strongly scented.

She peered down into the basin and said, "We could just sit here for a bit."

"We could," he agreed. His smile distracted her from the odd way his lower lids sagged, exposing their pale inner membranes. "If you wouldn't mind lowering me down on this rock."

This time she knew just how to fit her hands into his armpits. "So what is it you do, exactly?" she asked. When he hesitated, she said, "I did a couple of years of graduate work in biochemistry, you know. It's not like I can't understand."

"I know that," he said. "But I'm more or less retired now."

"What about before?"

His whole long life as a scientist stretched behind him, inexplicable to the young. He tried to skim over it quickly. "In Kraków," he said, "where I went to university, I was trained as a physical chemist specializing in polymers. I went to England, just before the Second World War"—he looked at her open, earnest face, and skipped over all that painful history, all those desperate choices—"and after I'd been there a little while I was recruited to work on a secret project to develop artificial rubber. Then I studied alpha helices and similar structures in polymers, and then did some fiber-diffraction work on proteins. Once I gave up running a lab I started doing more theoretical work. Thought experiments. Do you know much thermodynamics?"

"Enough to get by," she said. "But it's not my strong point."

"I like to think about the thermodynamics of surfaces, and the folding of globular proteins. The buried residues inside the assembly and all the rest. There are a set of equations—"

But Bianca shook her head. "Your bad luck," she said. "I'm probably the only person here who can't follow your math."

"I can show you something," he said. "Something that will make you understand at once."

"Yes?" she said. She was, she realized, wonderfully, happily drunk. Her companion reached into his magic bag once more.

"More vodka?" she said. "I could do another shot."

The paper cups were soft-edged and crumpled now, but he straightened them and filled them before delving again in his capacious bag. Sometimes, when he traveled to foreign countries, his audiences were so diverse that he had to bring the level of his standard lecture down a notch, use visual aids so the biologists could grasp what he was saying as well as the biochemists and biophysicists. Here at the institute, where the staff prided themselves on their mathematical sophistication, he hadn't had to use the toys he always carried. But now his hand found the coil of copper wire and the little plastic bottle.

"Perhaps," he said, "if there was a way we could get a bowl of water?"

Bianca pointed at the basin just below them. "Right here."

Had he not had so much *zubrowka* he might have considered more closely the relationship between the limpid water in the basin and the tiny stream trickling from the hollow bamboo. But he looked at the small pool and the eager, beautiful girl beside him, and without further thought he opened the bottle and poured some solution into the basin. From the wire he quickly fashioned several simple polygons. "Watch," he said.

The voices from the patio faded, the ferns waved gently, her vision narrowed until she saw only his hands, the basin, the rocks where they sat. He dipped a wire shape in the basin and blew a large bubble; then another, which he fastened to the first. More wire forms, more bubbles, more joinings—and before her, trembling gently in the air, rose a complicated structure supported by almost nothing.

"See where the faces join?" he said. "Those shapes the film makes as the faces join other faces?" He launched into an explanation of molecular interactions that seemed simplistic to him, incomprehensible to her. "You see," he said, "what a clear visual demonstration this is of the nature of surface tension. I stumbled on this some years ago, blowing soap bubbles for a friend's grandchildren."

"That was soap?" she said. "What you put in the water?"

"Not exactly—the film it makes isn't sturdy enough. There's glycerine in here, some other things. . . . " He added two more bubbles to his airy construction.

There was a theory behind all this, Bianca knew. An idea that this growing structure of soap film and wire exemplified; at this rarefied gathering, only she was incapable of grasping what he was trying to explain. Yet as she sat in the blue air, the bubble structure elongating while he expounded on his ideas, she felt almost purely happy. Soon she'd have to leave this place. Although she was closer to Rose than to anyone else in the world, so close they sometimes seemed to share a soul, they couldn't seem to get along now. At night, lying in Rose's tiny apartment, she could feel the fierceness of Rose's desire that she go back to school and continue the work they'd shared since their father gave them their first chemistry set. Or, if she refused to do that, that she leave Rose alone. Coming here had been a bad mistake.

Soon her whole life would change. But at that moment, sitting on the rocks with Krzysztof, she felt as if he'd led her to a castle from which she'd been barred, opened the front door with a flourish and then gaily flung open other doors one by one. The rooms were filled with sunlight and treasure. And although they were rooms she'd given up, rooms that from now on would belong to Rose and not her, this moment of remembering that they existed comforted her like balm.

She said, "I had a grandfather who did wonderful tricks. Maybe not as good as this but still, you would have liked him. He was from your part of the world, I think. I mean the part where you came from originally."

"He was Polish?" Krzysztof said eagerly. That she equated him with her grandfather was something he wouldn't think about now. "You have Polish blood?"

"Sort of," she said. "Not exactly. I'm not sure. Our grandfather's name was Leo Marburg, and the story in our family goes that he had a German name but was born and raised in Poland, near some big forest somewhere. Or maybe it was Lithuania. But somehow he ended up in the Ukraine, trying to establish vineyards there just before the revolution. And then—this is all confused, my mother told me these stories when I was little—he came to New York, and he worked as a janitor until he got sick and had to go live in the mountains. When he got better he found a job with one of the big wineries on the Finger Lakes."

"What are Finger Lakes?"

"Some long skinny lakes all next to each other, out in western New York, where I grew up. The glaciers made them. It's a good place to grow grapes. When he'd saved enough money he bought some land of his own, and established the winery that my father still runs. I know a lot about making wine. Grandpa Leo was still alive when Rose and I were tiny, and he used to bring us down into the corner of the cellar where he had his lab and show us all sorts of apparatus. The smells—it was like an alchemist's cave."

It was astounding, Krzysztof thought. What she left out, what she didn't seem to know. That Leo might have been hardly older than him, if he were still alive; what did it mean, that he'd made his way here, worked as a laborer but then reestablished himself and his real life?

"So was he German, really?" he asked. "Or Russian, or Polish . . . ?"

"I don't know," she admitted. "He died when I was five or so, before I could ask him anything. Most of what I know about him my mother told me, and she died when Rose and I were still girls. I don't know much history, I guess. My own or anyone else's."

How could she tell him about her mother, whom she still missed every day? And talked with, sometimes, although this was another point over which she and Rose quarreled bitterly. She felt a sudden sharp longing for her sister and craned her head toward the crowd behind her, but Rose, who was talking with Vivek, had her back to them. "It's because of Grandpa Leo," Bianca said, "that I studied biochemistry in the first place. Because of him and my father and the winery."

"But you stopped," Krzysztof said. "Why was that?"

She couldn't explain this to Rose, or even to herself: how could she explain it to him? The argument she and Rose had had, when they were working together on one of the papers that grew out of Rose's thesis—how bitter that had been. At its root was a small kinetics experiment that Rose interpreted one way, she herself another.

"It's so . . . *pushy,*" she said. The easy excuse, and at least partially true. "Science, I mean. At least at this level. When I started I thought it was something people did communally. Everyone digging their own small corner of the field, so that in the end the field would flower—I didn't know it got so vicious. So competitive. I hate all this hustling for money and priority and equipment. Actually," she said, "I hate these *people.* A lot of them. I really do."

"We're not very inspiring in groups," Krzysztof said. He pulled his hands apart and dropped the wire forms, disrupting the bubbles so that suddenly he held nothing, only air. Science was a business now, and sometimes he could hardly bear it himself. Yet he could remember the excitement of his youth, that sense of clarity and vision; it was this, in part, that had pulled him from Kraków to Cambridge. But not only this.

"Your grandfather," he said. "If what you remember about his youth was true, our families might have come from the same place. In northeastern Poland is this huge forest—the forest where the bison live, where this vodka comes from. That might have been the forest your mother meant in her stories."

"Do you think?"

"It's possible," he said, and he repeated the name he'd told her earlier: *Bialowieza*. Bianca tried to say it herself. "It's a beautiful place."

"And there are bison there? Now?"

"There are," he said. "It is partly because of my own mother that they still exist." The whole story swirled before him, beautiful and shapely and sad, but just as it came together in his mind Bianca leapt up from her seat and held out her hands.

"I could show you something," she said. "Something really beautiful, that you'll never see if we stay here. You probably think this country is ugly, all you ever see are airports and highways and scientists. Do you want to get out of here for a while? We'd only be gone an hour, and you could tell me about the bison on the way."

"I don't want to be rude."

"I promise you, no one will notice. I'll have you back so soon they'll never know you're gone."

No one had approached them this last half hour; the other guests had taken root, on the grass and the steps and the chairs, and were eating and drinking busily, arguing and laughing and thrusting their chins at each other. But a threat loomed, in the person of the woman—the wife of Arnold?—standing closest to them. Although she was chattering with a postdoc she was sending glances Krzysztof's way, which made him shudder. He'd been stuck with her, at an earlier dinner, while she explained the chemistry of what made things sticky, but not too sticky: something to do with those small yellow paper squares that now littered all other sheets of paper, and on which his colleagues scribbled curt notes. She might sidle over if he and Bianca continued to sit by this fountain.

He held out his arms to Bianca. "If you would?" Just then all the cylinders in the shrubberies flared at once, casting a warm light on the paths and the pool and the patio—yes, of course they were lanterns, not dolls. Expensive, tasteful lanterns, meant to look faintly oriental.

"My pleasure," she said. She raised him and held her finger to her lips in a gesture of silence. Then, to his delight, she led him through the ferns and azaleas until they disappeared around the side of the house, unseen by anyone. Krzysztof was too pleased by their cunning escape to tell Bianca how badly he needed to urinate.

They drove toward the glorious red horizon, as if chasing the vanished sun. Although the road was narrow and twisted, almost like an English road, Bianca drove very fast. Krzysztof clutched the dash at first, but then relaxed; what was left of his hair rose in the wind, tugging at his scalp like a lover's hands and distracting him from the pressure in his bladder.

"Is there any of that vodka left?" Bianca asked.

He handed her the bottle and watched as she held it to her lips. "So," she said. "Tell me about those bison."

He stuck one hand through the open window, letting it cut into the rushing breeze; then tilted it slightly and let the air push his arm up. "I was born and raised in Kraków," he said. Had he told her that already? "But my mother grew up in the country, in this forest where perhaps your grandfather was from. It is so beautiful, you can't imagine—the last bit of primeval forest in Europe, the trees have never been cut. There are owls there, and roe deer and storks and bears. And it was the last place where the wild bison, the *zubre,* lived. When my mother was young the Russians controlled that part of Poland and the forest was the tsar's private hunting preserve."

"Your mother was Russian?"

"No—*Polish.* Defiantly, absolutely Polish." He almost stopped here, overwhelmed by the complexities of Polish history. But it wasn't important, he skipped it all; it was not Bianca's fault that she knew nothing and that, if he were to hand her a map, she couldn't place Poland more than vaguely. "After she married my father they moved to Kraków—he was an organic chemist, he taught at the university. During the First World War he was conscripted into the Austrian army and disappeared. We don't even know where he died. So it was just my mother and me after that. Later, when I started university myself, we heard stories about how the German armies trapped in the forest during the war's last winter ate the *zubre* after they'd finished off the lynx and wild boars and weasels. There were only a thousand or so of them left in the world. The forests had been cleared everywhere else in Europe and rich people had been hunting them for centuries. Then those German soldiers ate all the rest. What could they do? They were freezing and starving, and they butchered the *zubre* with their artillery. This made my mother bitter. Her father had been a forester, and she'd grown up watching the bison grazing on buttercups under the oaks."

Bianca interrupted him—he seemed old again, he was wandering. And crossing and uncrossing his legs like a little boy who had to pee. Was a bison the same as a buffalo?

"This is Meadowbrook," she said, gesturing at the gigantic houses and formal gardens tucked back from the road they whizzed along. "Isn't that a ridiculous name? Rose has a little apartment above the garage of one of these estates."

A tiny space, further cramped by mounds of books and papers and useless things—that was her sister, Bianca thought, trailing a whole life's garbage everywhere. From apartment to apartment Rose had toted relics of their mother: old clothes, mismatched earrings, broken dishes. A faded green book, which Suky had used to study mosses. A big wad of old letters and another, much older book, bound in flaking brown leather: antique geology, bent to prove God's role in the creation of the world. When Bianca, in a cleaning frenzy, had tried to throw it out, Rose had seized it and pointed to the handsome pictures. Engravings of fossils, stony fish and oysters and ferns—and wasn't the inscription inside the front cover marvelous? Unmoved, Bianca had examined the spidery handwriting:

> I do this day, June 4, 1888, bequeath this most valuable book to my dear friend—to be by her kept all of her life—I also trust that she with her very brilliant mind may find great instruction therein, and that through her, the good contained herein may be spread far and wide.
> Farewell—
> Yours devotedly—
> Susan A. Snead

Who was Susan Snead? Who wrote that book, where had it come from? Suky's aunts might have known, but they were gone and had taken Suky's history with them. Now no one, not even their father, knew anything anymore—or so Rose had shouted at Bianca, wrapping the book in a sheet of paper and tucking it back in the corner. Someone has to save *something,* Rose had said.

The truth, Bianca thought, was that Rose kept the book simply because she'd found it in Suky's closet. That clinging to the past was the single most irritating thing about her. Why hang on to useless relics, when life was all about moving quickly, shedding the inessential?

"What did you say?" Krzysztof asked.

Had she spoken? "It used to be the gardener's quarters," Bianca said, gesturing vaguely in the direction of the apartment. "Over there, near that big stone house."

He ducked his head to see over her shoulder. Whatever house she'd pointed out had vanished. Suddenly she slowed and turned the van down a narrow lane between two stone pillars. "Almost here," she said.

He hurried on with his story, sensing that time was short. He skipped everything personal, all his struggles between the two great wars. He skipped the strange evolution of his mother's heart, the way she'd left him alone in Kraków and returned to the forest of her youth, yearning to rebuild what had been destroyed. The way she'd turned in disgust from his work, from every kind of science but forestry.

"The bison were gone by the end of the war," he said. "Almost extinct. But a Polish forester started trying to reestablish a breeding stock, and my mother moved back to the Bialowieza to help him. There were a few in a zoo in Stockholm, and some in zoos in Hamburg and Berlin. A few more had survived the war in the south of Poland. And my mother and this man, they brought some females from that little group to the forest, and borrowed bulls from the zoos, and they started a breeding program. From them come all the

European bison left in the world. There are several thousand of them now—because of my mother, you see? My own mother."

They were in a forest of sorts right now—the lane grew narrower and turned into a dirt track, and trees brushed the side of the van. When they emerged into a small clearing, Bianca stopped the van without saying a word in response to his tale.

"I run here," she said. "Almost every night. It's a park, this place. But no one comes here, I never see any people. I like to run just before dark." For a second he pictured her pounding down the dirt paths. She came around to his side of the van and helped him down the awkward step.

"It's beautiful," he said. Why had he been telling her that story? The forest, his mother, the starving soldiers; the bison, so huge and wild, just barely rescued from oblivion. That part ended happily. The rest, which he would never tell Bianca, did not: the German army had overrun the forest in a matter of weeks. Then it had passed to the Russians, then back to the Germans; swastikas had flown from the roofs. The resident Jews had been slaughtered under those ancient oaks, and the farmers and foresters had been deported. His mother had disappeared. And all the while he'd been safe in England, unable to persuade her to join him. Unable to save her, or anyone. In test tubes he'd grown chains of molecules, searching for something that might be turned into tires for planes and jeeps.

"It's a park now, that forest," he said, unable to let the story go. Then the pressure in his bladder grew unbearable and he said, "Would you excuse me for a minute?" He stepped behind an oak and into a thorny tangle, disappearing in the brambles. Behind him, Bianca was puzzled and then amused as she heard the long splatter of liquid on leaves, a pause, more splatter, a sigh. The sigh was one of pleasure; even this simple act was no longer reliable, and Krzysztof felt such relief as his urine flowed over the greenery that he was hardly embarrassed when he emerged and Bianca gently pointed out the bit of shirttail emerging from his fly like a tongue.

After he tidied himself, Bianca led him across a muddy field and into the trees at the far edge of the clearing. The sky had turned a smoky violet gray, truly dusk, all traces of red disappeared, and with it the color of the leaves and Bianca's hair.

"No bison here," she said cheerfully. "But I think we made it just in time. This whole area—I hate this area, it's one giant suburb. This is the only bit of real woods left for miles. But something kept eating everything Rose planted in her garden, and when I started jogging here I found out what it was. Be quiet now."

He was. He was exhausted, remarkably drained, the vodka swirling through his veins. The marzipanlike taste of the bison grass; was it that flavor the secretive, lumbering creatures had craved as they grazed? The only time he'd visited his mother in the forest, just before he left for England, she'd fed him a dish of wild mushrooms, wild garlic, and reindeer, washed down with this vodka. He'd tried to persuade her that war was inevitable. Her hair was gray by then, she no longer looked anything like Bianca. She lived in a low dark hut by herself and said she'd rather die than leave her home again.

A deer appeared in the clearing. He blinked his eyes; it hadn't been there, and then it was. Bianca inhaled sharply. "Oh," she whispered. "We made it just in time." He blinked again: four deer, then eleven, then seventeen. They came out of the trees and stood in the gathering darkness, looking calmly at each other and at the sky. How beautiful they were. He squeezed Bianca's hand, which was unaccountably folded within his own.

She stood very still. Night after night, during these unsettled weeks, she'd left Rose's apartment and their difficult quarrels, slipped on her running shoes, and sped down the long driveway, past the houses of the wealthy, across the busy suburban road, and into this park. Almost every night she was rewarded with this vision. She could hear her mother's voice then, as if the deer were transmitting it: *The good contained herein may spread far and wide.* The deer seemed unafraid of her and often stayed for half an hour. Tonight they were edgy, though. Their tails twitched and their ears rotated like tiny radar dishes; their heads came up suddenly and pointed toward the place where Bianca and Krzysztof were hidden. They were nothing like bison. They were dainty and delicate-footed, completely at home here and yet out of place beyond the confines of this small haven. Still she couldn't figure out either how or when they crossed the bustling road between the park and Rose's apartment, to browse on the lettuce and peas.

She didn't have to tell Krzysztof not to speak; he stood like a tree, wonderfully still and silent. But his face gleamed, she saw. As if he'd been sprayed with water; was he crying? Suddenly one doe leapt straight up, turned in the air, and then bounded away. The others quickly followed. Darkness had fallen, the show was over.

"You okay?" she whispered.

"Fine," he said. "That was *lovely.* Thank you."

"My pleasure."

She slipped an arm beneath his elbow to guide him back through the muddy part of the field, but he shook her off. He was restored, he was himself. He strode firmly over the ruts. "It's hard to believe there's a place like this so close to the congestion," he said.

She was behind him, unable to make out his words. "What?" she said.

He turned his head over his shoulder to repeat his comment. As he did so his right foot plunged into a deep hole. For a moment he tottered between safety and harm, almost in balance, almost all right. Then he tipped and tilted and was down in the mud, looking up at the first stars.

In the emergency room, the nurses and residents were impatient. No one seemed able to sort out Krzysztof's health insurance situation: what were these British papers and cards, this little folder marked *Traveler's Insurance?* Then there was the vodka on his breath, and Bianca's storm of hysterical tears; for some minutes the possibility of calling the police was raised. X-rays, blood tests, embarrassing questions: "Are you his girlfriend?" one nurse said. From Bianca's shocked rebuttal, Krzysztof understood that, as he'd feared, she'd never seen him, not for one moment, as an actual man. Almost he was tempted to tell her how clearly, and in what detail, he'd imagined her naked. She sat in an orange plastic chair and sobbed while he was wheeled in and out of rooms, his veiny white legs exposed in the most humiliating fashion. And this exposure was what distressed him most, although several friends had met their deaths through just such casual falls. Somehow the possibility of actual bodily harm had not occurred to him as he lay calmly regarding the stars from the muddy field.

"The ankle's not broken," a young doctor finally said. "But it's badly sprained."

"So he's all right?" Bianca kept saying. "He's all *right?"* Unable to calm herself, she sat as if paralyzed while the doctors drew a curtain around Krzysztof and went to work.

Krzysztof emerged with his lower leg encased in two rigid plastic forms, each lined with a green plastic air-filled pod. Velcro straps clamped the shells around him, as if his ankle were an oyster. A boy young enough to be his grandson had given him two large pills in a white pleated cup, which resembled in miniature the nurse's cap worn by a woman he'd loved during the war; the woman's name had vanished, as had the pain, and his entire body felt blissful. Bianca carried the crutches, and a sheaf of instructions and bills. She opened the van's side door and tried to help as two men lifted Krzysztof from the wheelchair and draped him along the back seat.

All the way back to Constance's house Bianca drove slowly, avoiding potholes and sudden swerves. "Are you all right?" she asked every few minutes. "Is this hurting you?"

Drowsily he said, "I have not felt so good in years." Actually this long narrow seat was more comfortable than the vast bed in his hotel. The jacket Bianca had folded into a pillow beneath his head smelled of her; the whole van was scented with her presence. On the floor, just below his face, he saw nylon shoes with flared lumpy soles, socks and shirts and reeds and a bird's nest, a canvas sack and a withered orange. Behind his seat was a mat and a sleeping bag. "Do you sleep in here?" he asked.

"I have—but not these last weeks. I'm so sorry, I never meant—I can't *believe* this happened."

"My fault," he said. "Entirely. You mustn't blame yourself."

"Everyone else will," she said bitterly. "Everyone."

Should she bring him straight back to his hotel? But she had to stop at Constance's house, let Constance and the others decide what was best for him. Perhaps Constance would want to have him stay with her. It was past eleven, they'd been gone for hours; and although she'd had plenty of time to call from the hospital, the phone had seemed impossibly far away. Now the only honest thing to do was to show up, with her guilty burden, and admit to everyone what had happened. Behind her, Krzysztof was humming.

"Talk to me," he said. "It's lonely back here. All I can see is the back of your head."

"Those bison," she said. "Are they anything like our buffalo?"

"Similar," he said. "But bigger. Shaggy in the same way, though."

"I heard this thing once," she said. "From a friend of my mother's, who used to visit the winery when Rose and I were little girls. He was some kind of naturalist, I think he studied beetles. Once he said, I think he said, that the buffalo out West had almost gone extinct, but then some guy made a buffalo refuge in Montana and stocked it with animals from the Bronx Zoo. Like your mother did, you see?" For a minute her own mother's face hovered in the air.

The van slowed and made a broad gentle curve—Constance's circular driveway, Krzysztof guessed. "In Polish," he said dreamily, "the word for beetle is *chrzaszcz.*"

Bianca tried to repeat the word, mashing together the string of consonants in a way he found very sweet. How pleasing that after all she'd paid attention to his stories. Their slow progress through the afternoon and evening had culminated properly among the deer, and all of it had been worthwhile.

"We're here," she said. "Boy, this is going to be *awful*—just wait for a minute, I'll tell everyone what's going on and we'll see what to do."

She turned and touched his head, preparing to face her sister.

"Don't worry," he said gently. "I'll tell everyone I asked you to take me for a drive. I had a lovely evening, you know. I'm very glad to have met you."

Neither of them knew that out back, beyond the rubble of the party, large sturdy bubbles had been forming for hours at the lip of the bamboo fountain, to the mystification of everyone. They did not see the bubbles, nor the inside of the house, because Rose and Constance came flying out the front door to greet the van. Terrified, Bianca saw. And then, as she prepared the first of many explanations, the first clumsy attempt at the story she'd tell for years, with increasing humor and a kind of self-deprecation actually meant to charm in the most shameful way, she saw their faces change: that was rage she saw, they were enraged.

In an instant she'd thrown the van into gear again and stomped on the gas. Krzysztof said, "Where . . . ?" and as they lurched back onto the road, leaving behind Constance and Rose and the fountain and the lanterns, the squabbling scientists, the whole world of science, she said, "Back to your hotel, you need to be in your own bed."

Back, Krzysztof thought. Back to the airport, back to England, back across the ocean and Europe toward home; back to the groves of Bialowieza, where his mother might once have crossed paths with Bianca's grandfather. Might have escaped, like him; might have survived and adopted another name and life during all the years when, in the absence of family or friends, her only son shuttled between his laboratory and his little flat and the rooms of the women who one by one had tried and failed to comfort him. Back and back and back and back. Where had his life gone?

He thought *back* but Bianca, her foot heavy on the accelerator, thought *away.* From Rose, their mother, their entire past, books and papers and stories and sorrows: let it sink into the ocean. She had her wallet and her sleeping bag and her running shoes and her van; and she drove as if this were the point from which the rest of her life might begin.

The Cures for Love

Charles Baxter

On the day he left her for good, she put on one of his caps. It fit snugly over her light brown hair. The cap had the manufacturer's name of his pickup truck embossed above the visor in gold letters. She wore the cap backward, the way he once had, while she cooked dinner. Then she kept it on in her bath that evening. When she leaned back in the tub, the visor hitting the tiles, she could smell his sweat from the inside of the headband, even over the smell of the soap. His sweat had always smelled like freshly broiled whitefish.

What he owned, he took. Except for the cap, he hadn't left much else behind in the apartment. He had what he thought was a soulful indifference to material possessions, so he didn't bother saving them. It hadn't occurred to her until later that she might be one of those possessions. He had liked having things—quality durable goods—around for a little while, she thought bitterly, and then he enthusiastically threw them all out. They were there one day—his leather vest, his golf clubs—and then they were gone. She had borrowed one of his gray tee-shirts months ago to wear to bed when she had had a cold, and she still had it, a gray tee in her bottom dresser drawer. But she had accidentally washed it, and she couldn't smell him on the fabric anymore, not a trace of him.

Her cat now yowled around five-thirty, at exactly the time when he used to come home. She—the cat—had fallen for him the moment she'd seen him, rushing over to him, squirming on her back in his lap, declawed paws waving in the air. The guy had had a gift, a tiny genius for relentless charm, that caused anything—women, men, cats, trees for all she knew—to fall in love with him, and not calmly, either, but at the upper frequencies.

Her clocks ached. Time had congealed. For the last two days, knowing he would go, she had tried to be busy. She had tried reading books, for example. They couldn't preoccupy her. They were just somebody's thoughts. Her wounded imagination included him and herself, but only those two, bone hurtling against bone.

She was not a romantic and did not like the word *romance.* They hadn't had a romance, the two of them. Nothing soft or tender, like that. They had just, well, driven into each other like reckless drivers at an intersection, neither one wanting to yield the right-of-way. She was a classicist recently out of graduate school, and for a job she taught Latin and Greek in a Chicago private school, and she understood from her reading of Thucydides and Catullus and Sophocles and Sappho, among others, how people actually fought, and what happened when they actually fell in love and were genuinely and almost immediately incompatible. The old guys told the truth, she believed, about love and warfare, the peculiar combination of attraction and hatred existing together. They had told the truth before Christianity put civilization into a dream world.

After she got out of the bathtub, she put herself into bed without drying herself off first. She removed the baseball cap and rolled around under the covers, dampening the sheets. *It's like this,* she said to herself.

She thought of herself as "she." At home she narrated her actions to herself as she performed them: "Now she is watering the plants." "Now she is feeding the cat." "Now she is staring off into space." "Now she is calling her friend Ticia, who is not at home. She will not leave a message on Ticia's machine. She doesn't do that."

She stood naked in front of the mirror. She thought: I am the sexiest woman who can read Latin and Greek in the state of Illinois. She surveyed her legs and her face, which he had praised many times. I look great and feel like shit and that's that.

The next morning she made breakfast but couldn't eat it. She hated it that she had gotten into this situation, loaded down with humiliating feelings. She wouldn't tell anyone. Pushing the scrambled eggs around on the plate, making a mess of them, the buttered wheat toast, and the strawberry jam, her head down on her arm, she fell into speculation: *Okay, yes, right, it's a mistake to think that infatuation has anything to do with personality, or personal tastes. You don't, uh,* decide *about any of this, do you?* she asked herself, half-forming the words on her lips. Love puts anyone in a state outside the realm of thought, like one of those Eleusinian cults where no one ever gets permission to speak of the mysteries. When you're not looking, your mouth gets taped shut. You fall in love with someone not because he's nice to you or can read your mind but because, when he kisses you, your knees weaken, or because you can't stop looking at his skin or at the way his legs, inside his jeans, shape the fabric. His breath meets your breath, and the two breaths either intermingle and create a charge or they don't. Personality comes later; *personality,* she thought, reaching for the copy of Ovid that was about to fall off the table, *is the consolation prize of middle age.*

She put the breakfast dishes in the sink. She turned on the radio and noticed after five minutes that she hadn't listened to any of it. She snapped it off and glanced angrily in the direction of the bedroom, where all this trouble had started.

She and he had ridden each other in that bed. She glowered at it, framed in the doorway of the bedroom, sun pouring in the east window and across the yellow bedspread. They had a style, but, well, yes, almost everyone had a style. For starters, they took their time. Nothing for the manuals, nothing for the record books. But the point wasn't the lovemaking, not exactly. What they did started with sex but ended somewhere else. She believed that the sex they had together invoked the old gods, just invited them right in, until, boom, there they were. She wondered over the way the spirit-gods, the ones she lonesomely believed in, descended over them and surrounded them and briefly made them feel like gods themselves. She felt huge and powerful, together with him. It was archaic, this descent, and pleasantly scary. They both felt it happening; at least he said he did. The difference was that, after a while, he didn't care about the descent of the old gods or the spirits or whatever the hell he thought they were. He was from Arizona, and he had a taste for deserts and heat and golf and emptiness. Perhaps that explained it.

He had once blindfolded her with her silk bathrobe belt during their lovemaking and she had still felt the spirit coming down. Blindfolded, she could see it more clearly than ever.

Ovid. At the breakfast table she held onto the book that had almost fallen to the floor. Ovid: an urbane know-it-all with a taste for taking inventories. She had seldom enjoyed reading Ovid. He had a masculine smirking cynicism, and then its opposite, self-pity, which she found offensive.

And this was the *Remedia amoris,* a book she couldn't remember studying in graduate school or anywhere else. The remedies for love. She hadn't realized she even owned it. It was in the back of her edition of the *Ars amatoria.* Funny how books put themselves into your hands when they wanted you to read them.

Because spring had hit Chicago, and sunlight had given this particular Saturday morning a light fever, and because her black mood was making her soul sore, she decided to get on the Chicago Transit Authority bus and read Ovid while she rode to the suburbs and back. Absentmindedly, she found herself crying while she stood at the corner bus stop, next to the graffitied shelter, waiting. She was grateful that no one looked at her.

After the bus arrived in a jovial roar of diesel fumes and she got on, she found a seat near a smudgy semi-clean window. The noise was therapeutic, and the absence on the bus of businessmen with their golf magazines relieved her. No one on this bus on Saturday morning had a clue about how to conduct a life. She gazed at the tattered jackets and gummy spotted clothes of the other passengers. No one with a serious relationship with money rode a bus like this at such a time. It was the fuck-up express. Hollow and stoned and vacant-eyed people like herself sat there, men who worked in carwashes, women who worked in diners. They looked as if their rights to their own sufferings had already been revoked months ago.

Over the terrible clatter, trees in blossom rushed past, dogwood, and lilacs, and like that. The blossoms seemed every bit as noisy as the bus. She shook her head and glanced down at her book.

Scripta cave relegas blandae servata puellae:
  Constantis animos scripta relecta movent.
Omnia pone feros (pones invitus) in ignes
  Et dic 'ardoris sit rogus iste mei.'

Oh, right. Yeah. Burn the love letters? Throw them all in the flames? And then announce, "This is the pyre of my love"? Hey, thanks a lot. What love letters? He hadn't left any love letters, just this cap—she was still wearing it—with "Chevy" embossed on it in gold.

Quisquis amas, loca sola nocent: loca sola caveto;
Quo fugis? in populo tutior esse potes.
Non tibi secretis (augent secreta furores)
Est opus; auxilio turba futura tibi est.

Riding the CTA bus, and now glimpsing Lake Michigan through a canyon of buildings, she felt herself stepping into an emotional lull, the eye of the storm that had been knocking her around. In the storm's eye, everyone spoke Latin. The case endings and the declensions and Ovid's I-know-it-all syntax and tone remained absolutely stable, however, no matter what the subject was. They were like formulas recited from a comfortable sofa by a banker who had never made a dangerous investment. The urbanity and the calm of the poem clawed at her. She decided to translate the four lines so that they sounded heartbroken and absentminded, jostled around in the aisles.

The lonely places
are the worst. I tell you,
when you're heart-
sick, go
where the pushing and shoving
crowd gives you
some nerve. Don't be
alone, up in your
burning room, burning—
trust me:
get knocked
down in public,
you'll be helped up.

All right: so it was a free translation. So what? She scribbled it on the back of a deposit slip from the Harris Bank and put it into her purse. She wouldn't do any more translating just now. Any advice blew unwelcome winds into her. Especially advice from Ovid.

Now they were just north of the Loop. This time, when she looked out of the window, she saw an apartment building on fire: firetrucks flamesroof waterlights crowdsbluesky smokesmoke. There, and gone just that rapidly. Suffering, too, probably, experienced by someone, but not immediately visible, not from here, at forty miles per hour. She thought: *Well, that's corny, an apartment fire as seen from a bus. Nothing to do about that one.* Quickly she smelled smoke, and then, just as quickly, it was gone. To herself, she grinned without realizing what she was doing. Then she looked around. No one had seen her smile. She had always liked fires. She felt ashamed of herself, but momentarily cheerful.

She found herself in Evanston, got out, and took the return bus back. She had observed too much of the lake on the way. Lake Michigan was at its most decorative and bourgeois in the northern suburbs: whitecaps, blue water, waves lapping the shore, abjectly picturesque.

By afternoon she was sitting in O'Hare Airport, at gate 23A, the waiting area for a flight to Memphis. She wasn't going to Memphis—she didn't have a ticket to anywhere—and she wasn't about to meet anyone, but she had decided to take Ovid's advice to go where the crowds were, for the tonic effect. She had always liked the anonymity of airports anyway. A businessman carrying a laptop computer and whose face had a WASPy nondescript pudgy blankness fueled by liquor and avarice was raising his voice at the gate agent, an African-American woman. Men like that raised their voices and made demands as a way of life; it was as automatic and as thoughtless as cement turning and slopping around inside a cement mixer. "I don't think you understand the situation," he was saying. He had a standby ticket but had not been in the gate area when they had called his name, and now, the plane being full, he would have to take a later flight. "You have no understanding of my predicament here. Who is your superior?" His wingtip shoes were scuffed, and his suit was tailored one size too small for him, so that it bulged at the waist. He had combed strands of hair across his sizable bald spot. His forehead was damp with sweat, and his nose sported broken capillaries. He was not quite first class. She decided to eat a chili dog and find another gate to sit in. Walking away, she heard the gate agent saying, "I'm sorry, sir. I'm sorry."

You couldn't eat a chili dog in this airport sitting down. It was not permitted. You had to stand at the plastic counter of Here's Mr. Chili, trying not to spill on the polyester guy reading *USA Today,* your volume of Publius Ovidius Naso next to you, your napkin in your other hand, thinking about Ovid's exile to the fringe of the Roman empire, to Tomis, where, broken in spirit, solitary, he wrote the *Tristia,* some of the saddest poems written by anyone anywhere, but a—what?—male sadness about being far from where the action was. There was no action in Tomis, no glamour, no togas—just peasants and plenty of mud labor. On the opposite side of Here's Mr. Chili was another gate where post-frightened passengers were scurrying out of the plane from Minneapolis. A woman in jeans and carrying a backpack fell into the arms of her boyfriend. They had started to kiss, the way people do in airports, in that depressing public style, all hands and tongues. And over here a chunky Scandinavian grandma was grasping her grandchildren in her arms like ships tied up tightly to a dock. You should go where people are happy, Ovid was saying. You should witness the high visibility of joy. You should believe. In . . . ?

Si quis amas nec vis, facito contagia vites
Right, right: "If you don't
  want to love,
    don't expose yourself to
the sight
      of love, the contagion."

Evening would be coming on soon; she had to get back.

She was feeling a bit light-headed, the effect of the additives in the chili dog: the Red concourse of O'Hare, with its glacially smooth floors and reflecting surfaces, was, at the hour before twilight, the scariest manmade place she'd ever seen. *This airport is really manmade,* she thought, *they don't get more manmade than this.* Of course, she had seen it a hundred times before, she just hadn't bothered looking. If something hadn't been hammered or fired, it wasn't in this airport. Stone, metal, and glass, like the hyperextended surfaces of eternity, across which insect-people moved, briefly, trying before time ran out to find a designated anthill. Here was a gate for Phoenix. There was a gate for Raleigh-Durham. One locale was pretty much like another. People made a big deal of their own geographical differences to give themselves specific details to talk about. Los Angeles, Cedar Rapids, Duluth. What did it matter where anyone lived—Rome, Chicago, or Romania? All she really wanted was to be in the same room with her as-of-yesterday ex. Just being around him had made her happy. It was horrible but true. She had loved him so much it gave her the creeps. He wasn't worthy of her love but so what. Maybe, she thought, she should start doing an inventory of her faults, you know, figure the whole thing out—scars, bad habits, phrases she had used that he hadn't liked. Then she could do an inventory of his faults. She felt some ketchup under her shoe and let herself fall.

She looked up.

Hands gripped her. Random sounds of sympathy. "Hey, lady, are you all right?" "Can you stand?" "Do you need some help?" A man, a woman, a second man: Ovid's public brigade of first-aiders held her, clutched at her where she had sprawled sort of deliberately, here in the Red concourse. Expressions of fake concern like faces painted on flesh-colored balloons lowered themselves to her level. "I just slipped." "You're okay, you're fine?" "Yes." She felt her breast being brushed against, not totally and completely unpleasantly. It felt like the memory of a touch rather than a touch itself, no desire in it, no nothing. There: She was up. Upright. And dragging herself off, Ovid under her arm, to the bus back to the Loop and her apartment. Falling in the airport and being lifted up: okay, so it happened as predicted, but it didn't make you feel wonderful. Comfortably numb was more like it. She dropped the *Remedia amoris* into a trash bin. Then she thought, uh oh, big mistake, maybe the advice is all wrong but at least he wants to cheer me up, who else wants to do that? She reached her hand into the trash bin and, looking like a wino grasping for return bottles, she pulled out her soiled book, smeared with mustard and relish.

"Kit?"

A voice.

"Yes?" She turned around. She faced an expression of pleased surprise, on a woman she couldn't remember ever seeing before.

"It's me. Caroline."

"Caroline?" As if she recognized her. Which she didn't. At all.

"What a coincidence! This is too amazing! What are you doing here?"

"I'm, um, I was here. Seeing someone off. You know. To . . . ah, Seattle."

"Seattle." The Caroline-person nodded, in a, well, professional way, one of those therapeutic nods. Her hair had a spiky thickness, like straw or hay. Maybe Caroline would mention the traffic in Seattle. The ferries? Puget Sound? "What's that?" She pointed at the haplessly soiled book.

"Oh, this?" Kit shrugged. "Ovid."

More nodding. Blondish hair spiked here and there, arrows pointing at the ceiling and the light fixtures and the arrival-and-departure screens. The Caroline-person carried—no, actually pulled on wheels—a tan suitcase, and she wore a business suit, account executive attire, a little gold pin in the shape of the Greek lambda on her lapel. Not a very pretty pin, but maybe a clue: lambda, lambda, now what would that . . . possibly mean? Suitcase: This woman *didn't* live here in Chicago. Or else she *did*.

"You were always reading, Kit. All that Greek and Latin!" She stepped back and surveyed. "You look simply fabulous! With the cap? Such a cute retro look, it's so street-smart, like . . . who's that actress?"

"Yeah, well, I have to . . . it's nice to see you, Caroline, but I'm headed back to the Loop, it's late, and I have to—"

"—Is your car here?" A hand wave: Caroline-person wedding ring: tasteful diamond of course, that's the way it goes in the Midwest, wedding rings everyfuckingwhere.

"Uh, no, we took, I mean, he and I took the taxi out." Somehow it seemed important to repeat that. "We took a taxi."

"Great! I'll give you a ride back. I'll take you to your place. I'll drop you right at the doorstep. Would you like some company? Come on!"

She felt her elbow being touched.

Down the long corridors of O'Hare Airport shaped like the ever-ballooning hallways of eternity, the Caroline-person pulled her suitcase, its tiny wheels humming behind her high-heeled businesslike stride; and easily keeping up in her jogging shoes, in which she jogged when the mood struck her, Kit tried to remember where on this planet, and in this life, she'd met this person. Graduate school? College? She wasn't a parent of one of her students, that was certain. *You were always reading.* Must've been college. "It's been so long," the woman was saying. "Must be . . . what?" They edged out of the way of a beeping handicap cart.

Kit shook her head as if equally exasperated by their mutual ignorance.

"Well, I don't know either," Caroline-person said. "So, who'd you see off?"

"What?"

"To Seattle."

"Oh," Kit said.

"Something the matter?"

"It was Billy," Kit said. "It was Billy I put on the plane."

"Kit," she said, "I haven't seen you in years. Who's this Billy?" She gave her a sly girlish smile. "Must be somebody special."

Kit nodded. "Yeah. Must be."

"Oh," Caroline said, "you can tell me."

"Actually, I can't."

"Why not?"

"Oh, I'd just rather not."

A smile took over Caroline's face like the moon taking over the sun during an eclipse. "But you can. You can tell me."

"No, I can't."

"Why?"

"Because I don't remember you, Caroline. I don't remember the first thing about you. I know a person's not supposed to admit that, but it's been a bad couple of days, and I just don't know who you are. Probably we went to college together or something, classics majors and all that, but I can't remember." They had stopped near a Buick display, and Kit wondered for a moment how the GM people got the car, a large midnight blue Roadmaster, into the airport. People rushed past them and around them. "I don't remember you at all."

"You're kidding," the woman said.

"No," Kit said, "I'm not. I can't remember seeing you before."

The woman who said her name was Caroline put her hand on her forehead and stared at Kit with a what-have-we-here? shocked look. Kit knew she was supposed to feel humiliated and embarrassed, but instead she felt shiny and new and fine for the first time all day. She didn't like to be tactless, but that seemed to be the direction, at least right now, this weekend, where her freedom lay. She'd been so good for so long, she thought, so loving and sweet and agreeable, and look where it had gotten her. "You're telling me," the woman said, "that you don't remember our—"

"—Stop," Kit said. "Don't tell me."

"Wait. You don't even want to be reminded? You're . . . but why? Now I'm offended," the woman told her. "Let's start over. Let's begin again. Kit, I feel very hurt."

"I know," Kit said. "It's been a really strange afternoon."

"I just don't think . . ." the woman said, but then she was unable to finish the sentence. "Our ride into the city . . ."

"Oh, that's all right," Kit said. "I couldn't take up your offer. I'll ride the bus back. They have good buses here," she added.

"No," she said. "Go with me."

"I can't, Caroline. I don't remember you. We're strangers."

"Well, uh, goodbye then," the woman muttered. "You certainly have changed."

"I certainly have. But I'm almost never like this. It's Billy who did this to me." She gazed in Caroline's direction. "And my vocabulary," she said, not quite knowing what she meant. But she liked it, so she repeated it. "My vocabulary did this to me."

"It's that bad?" the woman said.

Standing by the Buick Roadmaster in O'Hare Airport, where she had gone for no good reason except that she could not stand to be alone in her apartment, she felt, for about ten seconds, tiny and scaled-down, like a model person in a model airport as viewed from above, and she reached out and balanced herself on the driver's side door handle and then shook her head and closed her eyes. If she accepted compassion from this woman, there would be nothing left of her in the morning. Sympathy would give her chills and fever, and she would start shaking, and the shaking would move her out of the hurricane's eye into the hurricane itself, and it would batter her, and then wear her away to the zero. Nothing in life had ever hurt her more than sympathy.

"I have to go now," Kit said, turning away. She walked fast, and then ran, in the opposite direction.

Of course I remember you. We were both in a calculus class. We had hamburgers after the class sometimes in the college greasy spoon, and we talked about boys and the future and your dog at home, Brutus, in New Buffalo, Minnesota, where your mother bred cairn terriers. In the backyard there was fencing for a kennel, and that's where Brutus stayed. He sometimes climbed to the top of his little pile of stones to survey what there was to survey of the fields around your house. He barked at hawks and skunks. Thunderstorms scared him, and he was so lazy, he hated to take walks. When he was inside, he'd hide under the bed, where he thought no one could see him, with his telltale leash visible, trailing out on the bedroom floor. You told that story back then. You were pretty in those days. You still are. You wear a pin in the shape of the Greek letter lambda and a diamond wedding ring. In those days, I recited poetry. I can remember you. I just can't do it in front of you. I can't remember you when you're there.

She gazed out the window of the bus. She didn't feel all right but she could feel all right approaching her, somewhere off there in the distance.

She had felt it lifting when she had said his name was Billy. It wasn't Billy. It was Ben. Billy hadn't left her; Ben had. There never had been a Billy, but maybe now there was. She was saying goodbye to him; he wasn't saying goodbye to her. She turned on the overhead light as the bus sped through Des Plaines, and she tried to read some Ovid, but she immediately dozed off.

Roaring through the traffic on the Kennedy Expressway, the bus lurched and rocked, and Kit's head on the headrest turned from side to side, an irregular rhythm, but a rhythm all the same: enjambments, caesuras, stophes.

My darling girl, (he said, thinner
than she'd ever thought he'd be,
mostly bald, a few sprout curls,
and sad-but-cheerful, certainly,
Roman and wryly unfeminist, unhumanist,
unliving), child of gall and wormwood (he pointed his
thin malnourished finger at her,
soil inside the nail),
what on earth
brought you to that unlikely place?
An airport! Didn't I tell you,
clearly,
to shun such spots? A city park on a warm
Sunday afternoon wouldn't be as bad. People fall
into one another's arms out there all the time.
Hundreds of them! (He seemed exasperated.)
Thank you (he said)
for reading me, but for the sake
of your own well-being, don't go there
again without a ticket. It seems
you have found me out. (He
shrugged.) Advice? I don't have any
worth passing on. It's easier
to give advice when you're alive
than when you're not,
and besides, I swore it off. Oh I liked
what you did with Caroline, the lambda-girl
who wears that pin because her husband
gave it to her on her birthday,
March twenty-first—now that
I'm dead, I know everything
but it does me not a particle of good—
but naturally she thinks it has no
special meaning, and that's the way
she conducts her life. Him, too. He
bought it at a jewelry store next to a shoe
shop in the mall at 2 p.m.
March 13, a Thursday—but I digress—
and the salesgirl,
cute thing, hair done in a short cut
style, flirted with him
showing him no mercy,
touching his coat sleeve,
thin wool, because she was on commission. Her
name was

Eleanor, she had green eyes.
The pin cost him $175, plus tax.
She took him, I mean, took him for a ride,
as you would say,
then went out for coffee. By herself, that is,
thinking of her true
and best beloved, Claire, an obstetrician
with lovely hands. I always did admire
Sapphic love. But I'm
still digressing. (He smirked.)

The distant failed humor of the dead.
Our timing's bad,
the jokes are dusty,
and we can't concentrate
on just
one thing. I'm as interested
in Eleanor as I am
in you. Lambda. Who cares? Lambda: I suppose
I mean, I *know,*
he thought the eleventh letter, that uncompleted triangle,
looked like his wife's legs. Look:
I can't help it,
I'm—what is the word?—salacious, that's
the way I always was,
the bard of breasts and puberty, I was
exiled for it, I turned to powder
six feet under all the topsoil
in Romania. Sweetheart, what on earth
are you *doing* on
this bus? Wake up, kiddo, that guy
Ben is gone, good riddance
is my verdict from two thousand
years ago, to you.
Listen: I have a present for you.

He took her hand.
His hand didn't feel like much,
it felt like water when you're reaching
down for a stone or shell
under the water, something you don't
have, but want, and your fingers
strain toward it.
Here, he said, this is the one stunt
I can do: look up, sweetie, check out
this:
(he raised his arm in ceremony)

See? he said proudly. It's raining.
I made it rain. I can do that.
The rain is falling, only
it's not water, it's
this other thing. It's the other thing
that's raining, soaking you. Goodbye.

When she awoke, at the sound of the air brakes, the bus driver announced that they had arrived at their first stop, the Palmer House. It wasn't quite her stop, but Kit decided to get out. The driver stood at the curb as the passengers stepped down, and the streetlight gave his cap an odd bluish glow. His teeth were so discolored they looked like pencil erasers. He asked her if she had any luggage, and Kit said, no, she hadn't brought any luggage with her.

The El clattered overhead. She was in front of a restaurant with thick glass windows. On the other side of the glass, a man with a soiled unpressed tie was talking and eating prime rib. On the sidewalk, just down the block, under an orange neon light, an old woman was shouting curses at the moon and Mayor Daley. She wore a paper hat and her glasses had only one lens in them, on the left side, and her curses were so interesting, so incoherently articulate, uttered in that voice, which was like sandpaper worried across a brick, that Kit forgot that she was supposed to be unhappy, she was listening so hard, and watching the way the orange was reflected in that one lens.

Inferno I, 32

Jorge Luis Borges

In the final years of the twelfth century, from twilight of dawn to twilight of dusk, a leopard looked upon some wooden planks, some vertical iron bars, men and women who were always different, a thick wall and, perhaps, a stone trough filled with dry leaves. The leopard did not know, could not know, that what he craved was love and cruelty and the hot pleasure of rending and the odor of a deer on the wind; and yet something within the animal choked him and something rebelled, and God spoke to him in a dream: *You live and will die in this prison, so that a man I know may look at you a certain number of times and not forget you and put your figure and your symbol in a poem which has its precise place in the scheme of the universe. You suffer captivity, but you will have furnished a word to the poem.* In the dream, God enlightened the rough beast, so that the leopard understood God's reasons and accepted his destiny; and yet, when he awoke, he felt merely an obscure resignation, a gallant ignorance, for the machinery of the world is overly complex for the simplicity of a wild beast.

Years later, Dante lay dying in Ravenna, as little justified and as much alone as any other man. In a dream, God revealed to him the secret purpose of his life and labor; in wonderment, Dante knew at last who he was and what he was and he blessed his bitter days. Tradition holds that on awakening he felt he had received and then lost something infinite, something he could not recuperate, or even glimpse, for the machinery of the world is overly complex for the simplicity of men.

Translated by Anthony Kerrigan

A Wagner Matinee

Willa Cather

I received one morning a letter, written in pale ink on glassy, blue-lined notepaper, and bearing the postmark of a little Nebraska village. This communication, worn and rubbed, looking as though it had been carried for some days in a coat pocket that was none too clean, was from my Uncle Howard and informed me that his wife had been left a small legacy by a bachelor relative who had recently died, and that it would be necessary for her to go to Boston to attend to the settling of the estate. He requested me to meet her at the station and render her whatever services might be necessary. On examining the date indicated as that of her arrival I found it no later than tomorrow. He had characteristically delayed writing until, had I been away from home for a day, I must have missed the good woman altogether.

The name of my Aunt Georgiana called up not alone her own figure, at once pathetic and grotesque, but opened before my feet a gulf of recollection so wide and deep that, as the letter dropped from my hand, I felt suddenly a stranger to all the present conditions of my existence, wholly ill at ease and out of place amid the familiar surroundings of my study. I became, in short, the gangling farm boy my aunt had known, scourged with chilblains and bashfulness, my hands cracked and sore from the corn husking. I felt the knuckles of my thumb tentatively, as though they were raw again. I sat again before her parlor organ, fumbling the scales with my stiff, red hands, while she, beside me, made canvas mittens for the huskers.

The next morning, after preparing my landlady somewhat, I set out for the station. When the train arrived I had some difficulty in finding my aunt. She was the last of the passengers to alight, and it was not until I got her into the carriage that she seemed really to recognize me. She had come all the way in a day coach; her linen duster had become black with soot, and her black bonnet gray with dust, during the journey. When we arrived at my boardinghouse the landlady put her to bed at once and I did not see her again until the next morning.

Whatever shock Mrs. Springer experienced at my aunt's appearance she considerately concealed. As for myself, I saw my aunt's misshapen figure with that feeling of awe and respect with which we behold explorers who have left their ears and fingers north of Franz Josef Land, or their health somewhere along the Upper Congo. My Aunt Georgiana had been a music teacher at the Boston Conservatory, somewhere back in the latter sixties. One summer, while visiting in the little village among the Green Mountains where her ancestors had dwelt for generations, she had kindled the callow fancy of the most idle and shiftless of all the village lads, and had conceived for this Howard Carpenter one of those extravagant passions which a handsome country boy of twenty-one sometimes inspires in an angular, spectacled woman of thirty. When she returned to her duties in Boston Howard followed her, and the upshot of this inexplicable infatuation was that she eloped with him, eluding the reproaches of her family and the criticisms of her friends by going with him to the Nebraska frontier. Carpenter, who, of course, had no money, had taken a homestead in Red Willow County, fifty miles from the railroad. There they had measured off their quarter section themselves by driving across the prairie in a wagon, to the wheel of which they had tied a red cotton handkerchief, and counting off its revolutions. They built a dugout in the red hillside, one of those cave dwellings whose inmates so often reverted to primitive conditions. Their water they got from the lagoons where the buffalo drank, and their slender stock of provisions was always at the mercy of bands of roving Indians. For thirty years my aunt had not been further than fifty miles from the homestead.

But Mrs. Springer knew nothing of all this, and must have been considerably shocked at what was left of my kinswoman. Beneath the soiled linen duster which, on her arrival, was the most conspicuous feature of her costume, she wore a black stuff dress, whose ornamentation showed that she had surrendered herself unquestioningly into the hands of a country dressmaker. My poor aunt's figure, however, would have presented astonishing difficulties to any dressmaker. Originally stooped, her shoulders were now almost bent together over her sunken chest. She wore no stays, and her gown, which trailed unevenly behind, rose in a sort of peak over her abdomen. She wore ill-fitting false teeth, and her skin was as yellow as a Mongolian's from constant exposure to a pitiless wind and to the alkaline water which hardens the most transparent cuticle into a sort of flexible leather.

I owed to this woman most of the good that ever came my way in my boyhood, and had a reverential affection for her. During the years when I was riding herd for my uncle, my aunt, after cooking the three meals—the first of which was ready at six o'clock in the morning—and putting the six children to bed, would often stand until midnight at her ironing board, with me at the kitchen table beside her, hearing me recite Latin declensions and conjugations, gently shaking me when my drowsy head sank down over a page of irregular verbs. It was to her, at her ironing or mending, that I read my first Shakespeare, and her old textbook on mythology was the first that ever came into my empty hands. She taught me my scales and exercises, too—on the little parlor organ, which her husband had bought her after fifteen years, during which she had not so much as seen any instrument, but an accordion that belonged to one of the Norwegian farmhands. She would sit beside me by the hour, darning and counting while I struggled with the "Joyous Farmer," but she seldom talked to me about music, and I understood why. She was a pious woman; she had the consolations of religion and, to her at least, her martyrdom was not wholly sordid. Once when I had been doggedly beating out some easy passages from an old score of *Euryanthe* I had found among her music books, she came up to me and, putting her hands over my eyes, gently drew my head back upon her shoulder, saying tremulously, "Don't love it so well, Clark, or it may be taken from you. Oh, dear boy, pray that whatever your sacrifice may be, it be not that."

When my aunt appeared on the morning after her arrival she was still in a semisomnambulant state. She seemed not to realize that she was in the city where she had spent her youth, the place longed for hungrily half a lifetime. She had been so wretchedly train-sick throughout the journey that she had no recollection of anything but her discomfort, and, to all intents and purposes, there were but a few hours of nightmare between the farm in Red Willow County and my study on Newbury Street. I had planned a little pleasure for her that afternoon, to repay her for some of the glorious moments she had given me when we used to milk together in the straw-thatched cow-shed and she, because I was more than usually tired, or because her husband had spoken sharply to me, would tell me of the spendid performance of the *Huguenots* she had seen in Paris, in her youth. At two o'clock the Symphony Orchestra was to give a Wagner program, and I intended to take my aunt; though, as I conversed with her I grew doubtful about her enjoyment of it. Indeed, for her own sake, I could only wish her taste for such things quite dead, and the long struggle mercifully ended at last. I suggested our visiting the Conservatory and the Common before lunch, but she seemed altogether too timid to wish to venture out. She questioned me absently about various changes in the city, but she was chiefly concerned that she had forgotten to leave instructions about feeding half-skimmed milk to a certain weakling calf, "old Maggie's calf, you know, Clark," she explained, evidently having forgotten how long I had been away. She was further troubled because she had neglected to tell her daughter about the freshly opened kit of mackerel in the cellar, which would spoil if it were not used directly.

I asked her whether she had ever heard any of the Wagnerian operas and found that she had not, though she was perfectly familiar with their respective situations, and had once possessed the piano score of *The Flying Dutchman.* I began to think it would have been best to get her back to Red Willow County without waking her, and regretted having suggested the concert.

From the time we entered the concert hall, however, she was a trifle less passive and inert, and for the first time seemed to perceive her surroundings. I had felt some trepidation lest she might become aware of the absurdities of her attire, or might experience some painful embarrassment at stepping suddenly into the world to which she had been dead for a quarter of a century. But, again, I found how superficially I had judged her. She sat looking about her with eyes as impersonal, almost as stony, as those with which the granite Rameses in a museum watches the froth and fret that ebbs and flows about his pedestal—separated from it by the lonely stretch of centuries. I have seen this same aloofness in old miners who drift into the Brown Hotel at Denver, their pockets full of bullion, their linen soiled, their haggard faces unshaven; standing in the thronged corridors as solitary as though they were still in a frozen camp on the Yukon, conscious that certain experiences have isolated them from their fellows by a gulf no haberdasher could bridge.

We sat at the extreme left of the first balcony, facing the arc of our own and the balcony above us, veritable hanging gardens, brilliant as tulip beds. The matinee audience was made up chiefly of women. One lost the contour of faces and figures—indeed, any effect of line whatever—and there was only the color of bodices past counting, the shimmer of fabrics soft and firm, silky and sheer: red mauve, pink, blue, lilac, purple, ecru, rose, yellow, cream, and white, all the colors that an impressionist finds in a sunlit landscape, with here and there the dead shadow of a frock coat. My Aunt Georgiana regarded them as though they had been so many daubs of tube-paint on a palette.

When the musicians came out and took their places, she gave a little stir of anticipation and looked with quickening interest down over the rail at that invariable grouping, perhaps the first wholly familiar thing that had greeted her eye since she had left old Maggie and her weakling calf. I could feel how all those details sank into her soul, for I had not forgotten how they had sunk into mine when I came fresh from plowing forever and forever between green aisles of corn, where, as in a treadmill, one might walk from daybreak to dusk without perceiving a shadow of change. The clean profiles of the musicians, the gloss of their linen, the dull black of their coats, the beloved shapes of the instruments, the patches of yellow light thrown by the green-shaded lamps on the smooth, varnished bellies of the cellos and the bass viols in the rear, the restless, wind-tossed forest of fiddle necks and bows—I recalled how, in the first orchestra I had ever heard, those long bow strokes seemed to draw the heart out of me, as a conjurer's stick reels out yards of paper ribbon from a hat.

The first number was the *Tannhauser* overture. When the horns drew out the first strain of the Pilgrim's chorus my Aunt Georgiana clutched my coat sleeve. Then it was I first realized that for her this broke a silence of thirty years; the inconceivable silence of the plains. With the battle between the two motives, with the frenzy of the Venusberg theme and its ripping of strings, there came to me an overwhelming sense of the waste and wear we are so powerless to combat; and I saw again the tall, naked house on the prairie, black and grim as a wooden fortress; the black pond where I had learned to swim, its margin pitted with sun-dried cattle tracks; the rain-gullied clay banks about the naked house, the four dwarf ash seedlings where the dishcloths were always hung to dry before the kitchen door. The world there was the flat world of the ancients; to the east, a cornfield that stretched to daybreak; to the west, a corral that reached to sunset; between, the conquests of peace, dearer bought than those of war.

The overture closed; my aunt released my coat sleeve, but she said nothing. She sat staring at the orchestra through a dullness of thirty years, through the films made little by little by each of the three hundred and sixty-five days in every one of them. What, I wondered, did she get from it? She had been a good pianist in her day I knew, and her musical education had been broader than that of most music teachers of a quarter of a century ago. She had often told me of Mozart's operas and Meyerbeer's, and I could remember hearing her sing, years ago, certain melodies of Verdi's. When I had fallen ill with a fever in her house she used to sit by my cot in the evening—when the cool, night wind blew in through the faded mosquito netting tacked over the window, and I lay watching a certain bright star that burned red above the cornfield—and sing "Home to our mountains, O, let us return!" in a way fit to break the heart of a Vermont boy near dead of homesickness already.

I watched her closely through the prelude to *Tristan and Isolde,* trying vainly to conjecture what that seething turmoil of strings and winds might mean to her, but she sat mutely staring at the violin bows that drove obliquely downward, like the pelting streaks of rain in a summer shower. Had this music any message for her? Had she enough left to at all comprehend this power which had kindled the world since she had left it? I was in a fever of curiosity, but Aunt Georgiana sat silent upon her peak in Darien. She preserved this utter immobility throughout the number from *The Flying Dutchman,* though her fingers worked mechanically upon her black dress, as though, of themselves, they were recalling the piano score they had once played. Poor old hands! They had been stretched and twisted into mere tentacles to hold and lift and knead with; the palms unduly swollen, the fingers bent and knotted—on one of them a thin, worn band that had once been a wedding ring. As I pressed and gently quieted one of those groping hands I remembered with quivering eyelids their services for me in other days.

Soon after the tenor began the "Prize Song," I heard a quick drawn breath and turned to my aunt. Her eyes were closed, but the tears were glistening on her cheeks, and I think, in a moment more, they were in my eyes as well. It never really died, then—the soul that can suffer so excruciatingly and so interminably; it withers to the outward eye only; like that strange moss which can lie on a dusty shelf half a century and yet, if placed in water, grows green again. She wept so throughout the development and elaboration of the melody.

During the intermission before the second half of the concert, I questioned my aunt and found that the "Prize Song" was not new to her. Some years before there had drifted to the farm in Red Willow County a young German, a tramp cowpuncher, who had sung the chorus at Bayreuth, when he was a boy, along with the other peasant boys and girls. Of a Sunday morning he used to sit on his gingham-sheeted bed in the hands' bedroom which opened off the kitchen, cleaning the leather of his boots and saddle, singing the "Prize Song," while my aunt went about her work in the kitchen. She had hovered about him until she had prevailed upon him to join the country church, though his sole fitness for this step, insofar as I could gather, lay in his boyish face and his possession of this divine melody. Shortly afterward he had gone to town on the Fourth of July, been drunk for several days, lost his money at a faro table, ridden a saddled Texan steer on a bet, and disappeared with a fractured collarbone. All this my aunt told me huskily, wanderingly, as though she were talking in the weak lapses of illness.

"Well, we have come to better things than the old *Trovatore* at any rate, Aunt Georgie?" I queried, with a well-meant effort at jocularity.

Her lip quivered and she hastily put her handkerchief up to her mouth. From behind it she murmured, "And you have been hearing this ever since you left me, Clark?" Her question was the gentlest and saddest of reproaches.

The second half of the program consisted of four numbers from the *Ring,* and closed with Siegfried's funeral march. My aunt wept quietly, but almost continuously, as a shallow vessel overflows in a rainstorm. From time to time her dim eyes looked up at the lights which studded the ceiling, burning softly under their dull glass globes; doubtless they were stars in truth to her. I was still perplexed as to what measure of musical comprehension was left to her, she who had heard nothing but the singing of gospel hymns at Methodist services in the square frame schoolhouse on Section Thirteen for so many years. I was wholly unable to gauge how much of it had been dissolved in soapsuds, or worked into bread, or milked into the bottom of a pail.

The deluge of sound poured on and on; I never knew what she found in the shining current of it; I never knew how far it bore her, or past what happy islands. From the trembling of her face I could well believe that before the last numbers she had been carried out where the myriad graves are, into the gray, nameless burying grounds of the sea; or into some world of death vaster yet, where, from the beginning of the world, hope has lain down with hope and dream with dream and, renouncing, slept.

The concert was over; the people filed out of the hall chattering and laughing, glad to relax and find the living level again, but my kinswoman made no effort to rise. The harpist slipped its green felt cover over his instrument; the flute players shook the water from their mouthpieces; the men of the orchestra went out one by one, leaving the stage to the chairs and music stands, empty as a winter cornfield.

I spoke to my aunt. She burst into tears and sobbed pleadingly. "I don't want to go, Clark, I don't want to go!"

I understood. For her, just outside the door of the concert hall, lay the black pond with the cattle-tracked bluffs; the tall, unpainted house, with weather-curled boards; naked as a tower, the crook-backed ash seedlings where the dishcloths hung to dry; the gaunt, molting turkeys picking up refuse about the kitchen door.

The Eve of the Spirit Festival

Lan Samantha Chang

After the Buddhist ceremony, when our mother's spirit had been chanted to a safe passage and her body cremated, Emily and I sat silently on our living room carpet. She held me in her arms; her long hair stuck to our wet faces. We sat as stiffly as temple gods, except for the angry thump of my sister's heart against my cheek.

Finally she spoke. "It's Baba's fault," she said. "The American doctors would have fixed her."

I was six years old—I only knew that our father and mother had decided against an operation. And I had privately agreed, imagining the doctors tearing a hole in her body. As I thought of this, I felt a sudden sob pass through me.

"Don't cry, Baby," Emily whispered. "You're okay." I felt my tears dry to salt, my throat lock shut.

Then our father walked into the room.

He and Emily had grown close in the past few months. Emily was eleven, old enough to come along on his trips to the hospital. I had often stood in the neighbor's window and watched them leave for visiting hours, Emily's mittened hand tucked into his.

But now my sister refused to acknowledge him. She pushed the back of my head to turn me away from him also.

"First daughter—" he began.

"Go away, Baba," Emily said. Her voice shook. The evening sun glowed garnet red through the dark tent of her hair.

"You told me she would get better," I heard her say. "Now you're burning paper money for her ghost. What good will that do?"

"I am sorry," Baba said.

"I don't care."

Her voice burned. I squirmed beneath her hand, but she wouldn't let me look. It was something between her and Baba. I watched his black wingtip shoes retreat to the door. When he had gone, Emily let go of me. I sat up and looked at her; something had changed. Not in the lovely outlines of her face—our mother's face—but in her eyes, shadow-black, lost in unforgiveness.

They say the dead return to us. But we never saw our mother again, though we kept a kind of emptiness waiting in case she might come back. I listened always, seeking her voice, the lost thread of a conversation I'd been too young to have with her. I did not dare mention her to Emily. Since I could remember, my sister had kept her most powerful feelings private, sealed away. She rarely mentioned our mother, and soon my memories faded. I could not picture her. I saw only Emily's angry face, the late sun streaking red through her dark hair.

After the traditional forty-nine day mourning period, Baba did not set foot in the Buddhist temple. It was as if he had listened to Emily: what good did it do? Instead he focused on earthly ambitions, his research at the lab.

At that time he aspired beyond the position of lab instructor to the rank of associate professor, and he often invited his American colleagues over for "drinks." Emily and I were recruited to help with the preparations and serving. As we went about our tasks, we would sometimes catch a glimpse of our father, standing in the corner, watching the American men and studying to become one.

But he couldn't get it right—our parties had an air of cultural confusion. We served potato chips on laquered trays; Chinese landscapes bumped against watercolors of the Statue of Liberty, the Empire State Building.

Nor were Emily or I capable of helping him. I was still a child, and Emily said she did not care. Since my mother's death, she had rejected anything he held dear. She refused to study chemistry and spoke in American slang. Her rebellion puzzled me, it seemed so vehement and so arbitrary.

Now she stalked through the living room, platform shoes thudding on the carpet. "I hate this," she said, fiercely ripping another rag from a pair of old pajama bottoms. "Entertaining these jerks is a waste of time."

Some chemists from Texas were visiting his department and he had invited them over for cocktails.

"I can finish it," I said. "You just need to do the parts I can't reach."

"It's not the dusting," she said. "It's the way he acts around them. 'Herro, herro! Hi Blad, hi Warry! Let me take your coat! Howsa Giants game?' " she mimicked, in a voice that made me wince, a voice alive with cruelty and pain. "If he were smart he wouldn't invite people over on football afternoons in the first place."

"What do you mean?" I asked, startled. Brad Delmonte was our father's boss. I had noticed Baba reading the sports pages that morning—something he rarely did.

"Oh, forget it," Emily said. I felt as if she and I were utterly separate. Then she smiled. "You've got oil on your glasses, Claudia."

Baba walked in carrying two bottles of wine. "They should arrive in half an hour," he said, looking at his watch. "They won't be early. Americans are never early."

Emily looked away. "I'm going to Jodie's house," she said.

Baba frowned and straightened his tie. "I want you to stay while they're here. We might need something from the kitchen."

"Claudia can get it for them."

"She's barely tall enough to reach the cabinets."

Emily stood and clenched her dustcloth. "I don't care," she said. "I hate meeting the people you have over."

"They're successful American scientists. You'd be better off with them instead of running around with your teenage friends, these sloppy kids, these rich white kids who dress like beggars."

"You're nuts, Dad," Emily said—she had begun addressing him the way an American child does. "You're nuts if you think these bosses of yours are ever going to do anything for you or any of us." And she threw her dust-cloth, hard, into our New York Giants wastebasket.

"Speak to me with respect."

"You don't deserve it!"

"You are staying in this apartment! That is an order!"

"I wish you'd died instead of Mama!" Emily cried. She darted past our father, her long braid flying behind her. He stared at her, his expression oddly slack, the way it had been in the weeks after the funeral. He stepped toward her, reached hesitantly at her flying braid, but she turned and saw him, cried out as if he had struck her, and ran out of the room. His hands dropped to his sides.

Emily refused to leave our bedroom. Otherwise that party was like so many others. The guests arrived late and left early. They talked about buying new cars and the Dallas Cowboys. I served pretzels and salted nuts.

Baba walked around emptying ashtrays and refilling drinks. I noticed that the other men also wore vests and ties, but that the uniform looked somehow different on my slighter, darker father.

"Cute little daughter you have there," said Baba's boss. He was a large bearded smoker with a sandy voice. He didn't bend down to look at me or the ashtray that I raised toward his big square hand.

I went into our room and found Emily sitting on one of our unmade twin beds. It was dusk. Through the window I could see that the dull winter sun had almost disappeared. I sat next to her on the bed. Until that day, I think, it was Emily who took care of me and not the other way around.

After a minute, she spoke. "I'm going to leave," she said. "As soon as I turn eighteen, I'm going to leave home and never come back!" She burst into tears. I reached for her shoulder but her thin, heaving body frightened me. She seemed too grown up to be comforted. I thought about the breasts swelling beneath her sweater. Her body had become a foreign place.

Perhaps Emily had warned me that she would someday leave in order to start me off on my own. I found myself avoiding her, as though her impending desertion would matter less if I deserted her first. I discovered a place to hide while she and my father fought, in the living room behind a painted screen. I would read a novel or look out the window. Sometimes they forgot about me—from the next room I would hear one of them break off an argument and say, "Where did Claudia go?" "I don't know," the other would reply. After a silence, they would start again.

One of these fights stands out in my memory. I must have been ten or eleven years old. It was the fourteenth day of the seventh lunar month: the eve of Guijie, the Chinese Spirit Festival, when the living are required to appease and provide for the ghosts of their ancestors. To the believing, the earth was thick with gathering spirits; it was safest to stay indoors and burn incense.

I seldom thought about the Chinese calendar, but every year on Guijie I wondered about my mother's ghost. Where was it? Would it still recognize me? How would I know when I saw it? I wanted to ask Baba, but I didn't dare. Baba had an odd attitude toward Guijie. On one hand, he had eschewed all Chinese customs since my mother's death. He was a scientist, he said; he scorned the traditional tales of unsatisfied spirits roaming the earth.

But I cannot remember a time when I was not made aware, in some way, of Guijie's fluctuating lunar date. That year the eve of the Spirit Festival fell on a Thursday, usually his night out with the men from his department. Emily and I waited for him to leave but he sat on the couch, calmly reading the *New York Times*.

I finished drying the dishes. Emily began to fidget. She had a date that night and had counted on my father's absence. She spent half an hour washing and combing her hair, trying to make up her mind. Finally she asked me to give her a trim. I knew she'd decided to go out.

"Just a little," she said. "The ends are scraggly." We spread some newspapers on the living room floor. Emily stood in the middle of the papers with her hair combed down her back, thick and glossy, black as ink. It hadn't really been cut since she was born. Since my mother's death I had taken over the task of giving it a periodic touch-up.

I hovered behind her with the shears, searching for the scraggly ends, but there were none.

My father looked up from his newspaper. "What are you doing that for? You can't go out tonight," he said.

"I have a date!"

My father put down his newspaper. I threw the shears onto a chair and fled to my refuge behind the screen.

Through a slit over the hinge I caught a glimpse of Emily near the foyer, slender in her denim jacket, her black hair flooding down her back, her delicate features contorted with anger. My father's hair was disheveled, his hands clenched at his sides. The newspapers had scattered over the floor.

"Dressing up in boys' clothes, with paint on your face—"

"This is nothing! My going out on a few dates is nothing! You don't know what you're talking about!"

"Don't shout." My father shook his finger. "The neighbors will hear you."

"Goddammit, Dad!" Her voice rose to a shriek. She stamped her feet to make the most noise possible.

"What happened to you?" he cried. "You used to be so much like her. Look at you—"

Though I'd covered my ears I could hear my sister's wail echo off the walls. The door slammed, and her footfalls vanished down the stairs.

Things were quiet for a minute. Then I heard my father walk toward my corner. My heart thumped with fear—usually he let me alone. I had to look up when I heard him move the screen away. He knelt down next to me. His hair was streaked with gray, and his glasses needed cleaning.

"What are you doing?" he asked.

I shook my head, nothing.

After a minute I asked him, "Is Guijie why you didn't go play bridge tonight, Baba?"

"No, Claudia," he said. He always called me by my American name. This formality, I thought, was an indication of how distant he felt from me. "I stopped playing bridge last week."

"Why?" We both looked toward the window, where beyond our reflections the Hudson River flowed.

"It's not important," he said.

"Okay."

But he didn't leave. "I'm getting old," he said after a moment. "Someone ten years younger was just promoted over me. I'm not going to try to keep up with them anymore."

It was the closest he had ever come to confiding in me. After a few more minutes he stood up and went into the kitchen. The newspapers rustled under his feet. For almost half an hour I heard him fumbling through the kitchen cabinets, looking for something he'd probably put there years ago. Eventually he came out, carrying a small brass urn and some matches. When Emily returned home after midnight, the apartment still smelled of the incense he had burned to protect her while she was gone.

I tried to be a good daughter. I stayed in every night and wore no make-up, I studied hard and got all A's, I did not leave home but went to college at NYU, right down the street. Jealously I guarded my small allotment of praise, clutching it like a pocket of precious stones. Emily snuck out of the apartment late at night; she wore high-heeled sandals with patched blue jeans; she twisted her long hair into graceful, complex loops and braids that belied respectability. She smelled of lipstick and perfume. Nothing I could ever achieve would equal my sister's misbehavior.

When Emily turned eighteen and did leave home, a part of my father disappeared. I wondered sometimes: where did it go? Did she take it with her? What secret charm had she carried with her as she vanished down the tunnel to the jet that would take her to college in California, steadily and without looking back, while my father and I watched silently from the window at the gate? The apartment afterwards became quite still—it was only the two of us, mourning and dreaming through pale-blue winter afternoons and silent evenings.

Emily called me, usually late at night after my father had gone to sleep. She sent me pictures of herself and people I didn't know, smiling on the sunny Berkeley campus. Sometimes after my father and I ate our simple meals or TV dinners I would go into our old room, where I had kept both of our twin beds, and take out Emily's pictures, trying to imagine what she must have been feeling, studying her expression and her swinging hair. But I always stared the longest at a postcard she'd sent me one winter break from northern New Mexico, a professional photo of a powerful, vast blue sky over faraway pink and sandy-beige mesas. The clarity and cleanness fascinated me. In a place like that, I thought, there would be nothing to search for, no reason to hide.

After college she went to work at a bank in San Francisco. I saw her once when she flew to Manhattan on business. She skipped a meeting to have lunch with me. She wore an elegant gray suit and had pinned up her hair.

"How's Dad?" she asked. I looked around, slightly alarmed. We were sitting in a bistro on the East Side, but I somehow thought he might overhear us.

"He's okay," I said. "We don't talk very much. Why don't you come home and see him?"

Emily stared at her water glass. "I don't think so."

"He misses you."

"I know. I don't want to hear about it."

"You hardly ever call him."

"There's nothing we can talk about. Don't tell him you saw me, promise?"

"Okay."

During my junior year at NYU, my father suffered a stroke. He was fifty-nine years old, and he was still working as a lab instructor in the chemistry department. One evening in early fall I came home from a class and found him on the floor, near the kitchen telephone. He was wearing his usual vest and tie. I called the hospital and sat down next to him. His wire-rimmed glasses lay on the floor a foot away. One-half of his face was frozen, the other half lined with sudden age and pain.

"They said they'll be right here," I said. "It won't be very long." I couldn't tell how much he understood. I smoothed his vest and straightened his tie. I folded his glasses. I knew he wouldn't like it if the ambulance workers saw him in a state of dishevelment. "I'm sure they'll be here soon," I said.

We waited. Then I noticed he was trying to tell me something. A line of spittle ran from the left side of his mouth. I leaned closer. After a while I made out his words: "Tell Emily," he said.

The ambulance arrived as I picked up the telephone to call California. That evening, at the hospital, what was remaining of my father left the earth.

Emily insisted that we not hold a Buddhist cremation ceremony. "I never want to think about that stuff again," she said. "Plus, all of his friends are Americans. I don't know who would come, except for us." She had reached New York the morning after his death. Her eyes were vague and her fingernails bitten down.

On the third day we scattered his ashes in the river. Afterward we held a small memorial service for his friends from work. We didn't talk much as we straightened the living room and dusted the furniture. It took almost three hours. The place was a mess. We hadn't had a party in years.

It was a warm cloudy afternoon, and the Hudson looked dull and sluggish from the living room window. I noticed that although she had not wanted a Buddhist ceremony, Emily had dressed in black and white according to Chinese mourning custom. I had asked the department secretary to put up a sign on the bulletin board. Eleven people came; they drank five bottles of wine. Two of his Chinese students stood in the corner, eating cheese and crackers.

Brad Delmonte, paunchy and no longer smoking, attached himself to Emily. "I remember you when you were just a little girl," I heard him say as I walked by with the extra crackers.

"I don't remember you," she said.

"You're still a cute little thing." She bumped his arm, and he spilled his drink.

Afterward we sat on the couch and surveyed the cluttered coffee table. It was past seven but we didn't talk about dinner.

"I'm glad they came," I said.

"I hate them." Emily looked at her fingernails. "I don't know whom I hate more: them, or him—for taking it."

"It doesn't matter anymore," I said.

"I suppose."

We watched the room grow dark.

"Do you know what?" Emily said. "It's the eve of the fifteenth day of the seventh lunar month."

"How do you know?" During college I had grown completely unaware of the lunar calendar.

"One of those chemistry nerds from Taiwan told me this afternoon."

I wanted to laugh, but instead I felt myself make a strange whimpering sound, squeezed out from my tight and hollow chest.

"Remember the time Dad and I had that big fight?" she said. "You know that now, in my grown-up life, I don't fight with anyone? I never had problems with anybody except him."

"No one cared about you as much as he did," I said.

"I don't want to hear about it." She twisted the end of her long braid. "He was a pain, and you know it. He got so strict after Mama died. It wasn't all my fault."

"I'm sorry," I said. But I was so angry with her that I felt my face turn red, my cheeks tingle in the dark. She'd considered our father a nerd as well, had squandered his love with such thoughtlessness that I could scarcely breathe to think about it. It seemed impossibly unfair that she had memories of my mother as well. Carefully I waited for my feelings to go away. Emily, I thought, was all I had.

But as I sat, a vision distilled before my eyes: the soft baked shades, the great blue sky of New Mexico. I realized that after graduation I could go wherever I wanted. A rusty door swung open and filled my mind with sweet freedom, fearful coolness.

"Let's do something," I said.

"What do you mean?"

"I want to do something."

"What did we used to do?" Emily looked down at the lock of hair in her hand. "Wait, I know."

We found newspapers and spread them on the floor. We turned on the lamps and moved the coffee table out of the way, brought the wineglasses to the sink. Emily went to the bathroom, and I searched for the shears a long time before I found them in the kitchen. I glimpsed the incense urn in a cabinet and quickly shut the door. When I returned to the living room it smelled of shampoo. Emily stood in the middle of the papers with her wet hair down her back, staring at herself in the reflection from the window. The lamplight cast circles under her eyes.

"I had a dream last night," she said. "I was walking down the street. I felt a tug. He was trying to reach me, trying to pull my hair."

"Just a trim?" I asked.

"No," she said. "Why don't you cut it."

"What do you mean?" I snipped a two-inch lock off the side.

Emily looked down at the hair on the newspapers. "I'm serious," she said. "Cut my hair. I want to see two feet of hair on the floor."

"Emily, you don't know what you're saying," I said. But a pleasurable, weightless feeling had come over me. I placed the scissors at the nape of her neck. "How about it?" I asked, and my voice sounded low and odd.

"I don't care." An echo of the past. I cut. The shears went *snack.* A long black lock of hair hit the newspapers by my feet.

The Chinese say that our hair and our bodies are given to us from our ancestors, gifts that should not be tampered with. My mother herself had never done this. But after the first few moments I enjoyed myself, pressing the thick black locks through the shears, heavy against my thumb. Emily's hair slipped to the floor around us, rich and beautiful, lying in long graceful arcs over my shoes. She stood perfectly still, staring out the window. The Hudson River flowed behind our reflections, bearing my father's ashes through the night.

When I was finished, the back of her neck gleamed clean and white under a precise shining cap. "You missed your calling," Emily said. "You want me to do yours?"

My hair, browner and scragglier, had never been past my shoulders. I had always kept it short, figuring the ancestors wouldn't be offended by my tampering with a lesser gift. "No," I said. "But you should take a shower. Some of those small bits will probably itch."

"It's already ten o'clock. We should go to sleep soon anyway." Satisfied, she glanced at the mirror in the foyer. "I look like a completely different person," she said. She left to take her shower. I wrapped up her hair in the newspapers and went into the kitchen. I stood next to the sink for a long time before throwing the bundle away.

The past sees through all attempts at disguise. That night I was awakened by my sister's scream. I gasped and stiffened, grabbing a handful of blanket.

"Claudia," Emily cried from the other bed. "Claudia, wake up!"

"What is it?"

"I saw Baba." She hadn't called our father Baba in years. "Over there, by the door. Did you see him?"

"No," I said. "I didn't see anything." My bones felt frozen in place. After a moment I opened my eyes. The full moon shone through the window, bathing our room in silver and shadow. I heard my sister sob and then fall silent. I looked carefully at the door, but I noticed nothing.

Then I understood that his ghost would never visit me. I was, one might say, the lucky daughter. But I lay awake until morning, waiting; part of me is waiting still.

Gooseberries

Anton Chekhov

The whole sky had been overcast with rain-clouds from early morning; it was a still day, not hot, but heavy, as it is in grey dull weather when the clouds have been hanging over the country for a long while, when one expects rain and it does not come. Ivan Ivanovitch, the veterinary surgeon, and Burkin, the high-school teacher, were already tired from walking, and the fields seemed to them endless. Far ahead of them they could just see the windmills of the village of Mironositskoe; on the right stretched a row of hillocks which disappeared in the distance behind the village, and they both knew that this was the bank of the river, that there were meadows, green willows, homesteads there, and that if one stood on one of the hillocks one could see from it the same vast plain, telegraph-wires, and a train which in the distance looked like a crawling caterpillar, and that in clear weather one could even see the town. Now, in still weather, when all nature seemed mild and dreamy, Ivan Ivanovitch and Burkin were filled with love of that countryside, and both thought how great, how beautiful a land it was.

"Last time we were in Prokofy's barn," said Burkin, "you were about to tell me a story."

"Yes; I meant to tell you about my brother."

Ivan Ivanovitch heaved a deep sigh and lighted a pipe to begin to tell his story, but just at that moment the rain began. And five minutes later heavy rain came down, covering the sky, and it was hard to tell when it would be over. Ivan Ivanovitch and Burkin stopped in hesitation; the dogs, already drenched, stood with their tails between their legs gazing at them feelingly.

"We must take shelter somewhere," said Burkin. "Let us go to Alehin's; it's close by."

"Come along."

They turned aside and walked through mown fields, sometimes going straight forward, sometimes turning to the right, till they came out on the road. Soon they saw poplars, a garden, then the red roofs of barns; there was a gleam of the river, and the view opened on to a broad expanse of water with a windmill and a white bath-house: this was Sofino, where Alehin lived.

The watermill was at work, drowning the sound of the rain; the dam was shaking. Here wet horses with drooping heads were standing near their carts, and men were walking about covered with sacks. It was damp, muddy, and desolate; the water looked cold and malignant. Ivan Ivanovitch and Burkin were already conscious of a feeling of wetness, messiness, and discomfort all over; their feet were heavy with mud, and when, crossing the dam, they went up to the barns, they were silent, as though they were angry with one another.

In one of the barns there was the sound of a winnowing machine, the door was open, and clouds of dust were coming from it. In the doorway was standing Alehin himself, a man of forty, tall and stout, with long hair, more like a professor or an artist than a landowner. He had on a white shirt that badly needed washing, a rope for a belt, drawers instead of trousers, and his boots, too, were plastered up with mud and straw. His eyes and nose were black with dust. He recognized Ivan Ivanovitch and Burkin, and was apparently much delighted to see them.

"Go into the house, gentlemen," he said, smiling; "I'll come directly, this minute."

It was a big two-storeyed house. Alehin lived in the lower storey, with arched ceilings and little windows, where the bailiffs had once lived; here everything was plain, and there was a smell of rye bread, cheap vodka, and harness. He went upstairs into the best rooms only on rare occasions, when visitors came. Ivan Ivanovitch and Burkin were met in the house by a maid-servant, a young woman so beautiful that they both stood still and looked at one another.

"You can't imagine how delighted I am to see you, my friends," said Alehin, going into the hall with them. "It is a surprise! Pelagea," he said, addressing the girl, "give our visitors something to change into. And, by the way, I will change too. Only I must first go and wash, for I almost think I have not washed since spring. Wouldn't you like to come into the bath-house? and meanwhile they will get things ready here."

Beautiful Pelagea, looking so refined and soft, brought them towels and soap, and Alehin went to the bath-house with his guests.

"It's a long time since I had a wash," he said, undressing. "I have got a nice bath-house, as you see—my father built it—but I somehow never have time to wash."

He sat down on the steps and soaped his long hair and his neck, and the water round him turned brown.

"Yes, I must say," said Ivan Ivanovitch meaningly, looking at his head.

"It's a long time since I washed . . ." said Alehin with embarrassment, giving himself a second soaping, and the water near him turned dark blue, like ink.

Ivan Ivanovitch went outside, plunged into the water with a loud splash, and swam in the rain, flinging his arms out wide. He stirred the water into waves which set the white lilies bobbing up and down; he swam to the very middle of the millpond and dived, and came up a minute later in another place, and swam on, and kept on diving, trying to touch the bottom.

"Oh, my goodness!" he repeated continually, enjoying himself thoroughly. "Oh, my goodness!" He swam to the mill, talked to the peasants there, then returned and lay on his back in the middle of the pond, turning his face to the rain. Burkin and Alehin were dressed and ready to go, but he still went on swimming and diving. "Oh, my goodness! . . ." he said. "Oh, Lord, have mercy on me! . . ."

"That's enough!" Burkin shouted to him.

They went back to the house. And only when the lamp was lighted in the big drawing-room upstairs, and Burkin and Ivan Ivanovitch, attired in silk dressing-gowns and warm slippers, were sitting in arm-chairs; and Alehin, washed and combed, in a new coat, was walking about the drawing-room, evidently enjoying the feeling of warmth, cleanliness, dry clothes, and light shoes; and when lovely Pelagea, stepping noiselessly on the carpet and smiling softly, handed tea and jam on a tray—only then Ivan Ivanovitch began on his story, and it seemed as though not only Burkin and Alehin were listening, but also the ladies, young and old, and the officers who looked down upon them sternly and calmly from their gold frames.

"There are two of us brothers," he began—"I, Ivan Ivanovitch, and my brother, Nikolay Ivanovitch, two years younger. I went in for a learned profession and became a veterinary surgeon, while Nikolay sat in a government office from the time he was nineteen. Our father, Tchimsha-Himalaisky, was a kantonist, but he rose to be an officer and left us a little estate and the rank of nobility. After his death the little estate went in debts and legal expenses; but, anyway, we had spent our childhood running wild in the country. Like peasant children, we passed our days and nights in the fields and the woods, looked after horses, stripped the bark off the trees, fished, and so on. . . . And, you know, whoever has once in his life caught perch or has seen the migrating of the thrushes in autumn, watched how they float in flocks over the village on bright, cool days, he will never be a real townsman, and will have a yearning for freedom to the day of his death. My brother was miserable in the government office. Years passed by, and he went on sitting in the same place, went on writing the same papers and thinking of one and the same thing—how to get into the country. And this yearning by degrees passed into a definite desire, into a dream of buying himself a little farm somewhere on the banks of a river or a lake.

"He was a gentle, good-natured fellow, and I was fond of him, but I never sympathized with this desire to shut himself up for the rest of his life in a little farm of his own. It's the correct thing to say that a man needs no more than six feet of earth. But six feet is what a corpse needs, not a man. And they say, too, now, that if our intellectual classes are attracted to the land and yearn for a farm, it's a good thing. But these farms are just the same as six feet of earth. To retreat from town, from the struggle, from the bustle of life, to retreat and bury oneself in one's farm—it's not life, it's egoism, laziness, it's monasticism of a sort, but monasticism without good works. A man does not need six feet of earth or a farm, but the whole globe, all nature, where he can have room to display all the qualities and peculiarities of his free spirit.

"My brother Nikolay, sitting in his government office, dreamed of how he would eat his own cabbages, which would fill the whole yard with such a savoury smell, take his meals on the green grass, sleep in the sun, sit for whole hours on the seat by the gate gazing at the fields and the forest. Gardening books and the agricultural hints in calendars were his delight, his favourite spiritual sustenance; he enjoyed reading newspapers, too, but the only things he read in them were the advertisements of so many acres of arable land and a grass meadow with farm-houses and buildings, a river, a garden, a mill and millponds, for sale. And his imagination pictured the garden-paths, flowers and fruit, starling cotes, the carp in the pond, and all that sort of thing, you know. These imaginary pictures were of different kinds according to the advertisements which he came across, but for some reason in every one of them he had always to have gooseberries. He could not imagine a homestead, he could not picture an idyllic nook, without gooseberries.

" 'Country life has its conveniences,' he would sometimes say. 'You sit on the verandah and you drink tea, while your ducks swim on the pond, there is a delicious smell everywhere, and . . . and the gooseberries are growing.'

"He used to draw a map of his property, and in every map there were the same things—(a) house for the family, (b) servants' quarters, (c) kitchen-garden, (d) gooseberry-bushes. He lived parsimoniously, was frugal in food and drink, his clothes were beyond description; he looked like a beggar, but kept on saving and putting money in the bank. He grew fearfully avaricious. I did not like to look at him, and I used to give him something and send him presents for Christmas and Easter, but he used to save that too. Once a man is absorbed by an idea there is no doing anything with him.

"Years passed: he was transferred to another province. He was over forty, and he was still reading the advertisements in the papers and saving up. Then I heard he was married. Still with the same object of buying a farm and having gooseberries, he married an elderly and ugly widow without a trace of feeling for her, simply because she had filthy lucre. He went on living frugally after marrying her, and kept her short of food, while he put her money in the bank in his name.

"Her first husband had been a postmaster, and with him she was accustomed to pies and home-made wines, while with her second husband she did not get enough black bread; she began to pine away with this sort of life, and three years later she gave up her soul to God. And I need hardly say that my brother never for one moment imagined that he was responsible for her death. Money, like vodka, makes a man queer. In our town there was a merchant who, before he died, ordered a plateful of honey and ate up all his money and lottery tickets with the honey, so that no one might get the benefit of it. While I was inspecting cattle at a railway-station, a cattle-dealer fell under an engine and had his leg cut off. We carried him into the waiting-room, the blood was flowing—it was a horrible thing—and he kept asking them to look for his leg and was very much worried about it; there were twenty roubles in the boot on the leg that had been cut off, and he was afraid they would be lost."

"That's a story from a different opera," said Burkin.

"After his wife's death," Ivan Ivanovitch went on, after thinking for half a minute, "my brother began looking out for an estate for himself. Of course, you may look about for five years and yet end by making a mistake, and buying something quite different from what you have dreamed of. My brother Nikolay bought through an agent a mortgaged estate of three hundred and thirty acres, with a house for the family, with servants' quarters, with a park, but with no orchard, no gooseberry-bushes, and no duck-pond; there was a river, but the water in it was the colour of coffee, because on one side of the estate there was a brickyard and on the other a factory for burning bones. But Nikolay Ivanovitch did not grieve much; he ordered twenty gooseberry-bushes, planted them, and began living as a country gentleman.

"Last year I went to pay him a visit. I thought I would go and see what it was like. In his letters my brother called his estate 'Tchumbaroklov Waste, alias Himalaiskoe.' I reached 'alias Himalaiskoe' in the afternoon. It was hot. Everywhere there were ditches, fences, hedges, fir-trees planted in rows, and there was no knowing how to get to the yard, where to put one's horse. I went up to the house, and was met by a fat red dog that looked like a pig. It wanted to bark, but it was too lazy. The cook, a fat, barefooted woman, came out of the kitchen, and she, too, looked like a pig, and said that her master was resting after dinner. I went in to see my brother. He was sitting up in bed with a quilt over his legs; he had grown older, fatter, wrinkled; his cheeks, his nose, and his mouth all stuck out—he looked as though he might begin grunting into the quilt at any moment.

"We embraced each other, and shed tears of joy and of sadness at the thought that we had once been young and now were both grey-headed and near the grave. He dressed, and led me out to show me the estate.

" 'Well, how are you getting on here?' I asked.

" 'Oh, all right, thank God; I am getting on very well.'

"He was no more a poor timid clerk, but a real landowner, a gentleman. He was already accustomed to it, had grown used to it, and liked it. He ate a great deal, went to the bath-house, was growing stout, was already at law with the village commune and both factories, and was very much offended when the peasants did not call him 'Your Honour.' And he concerned himself with the salvation of his soul in a substantial, gentlemanly manner, and performed deeds of charity, not simply, but with an air of consequence. And what deeds of charity! He treated the peasants for every sort of disease with soda and castor oil, and on his name-day had a thanksgiving service in the middle of the village, and then treated the peasants to a gallon of vodka—he thought that was the thing to do. Oh, those horrible gallons of vodka! One day the fat landowner hauls the peasants up before the district captain for trespass, and next day, in honour of a holiday, treats them to a gallon of vodka, and they drink and shout 'Hurrah!' and when they are drunk bow down to his feet. A change of life for the better, and being well-fed and idle develop in a Russian the most insolent self-conceit. Nikolay Ivanovitch, who at one time in the government office was afraid to have any views of his own, now could say nothing that was not gospel truth, and uttered such truths in the tone of a prime minister. 'Education is essential, but for the peasants it is premature.' 'Corporal punishment is harmful as a rule, but in some cases it is necessary and there is nothing to take its place.'

" 'I know the peasants and understand how to treat them,' he would say. 'The peasants like me. I need only to hold up my little finger and the peasants will do anything I like.'

"And all this, observe, was uttered with a wise, benevolent smile. He repeated twenty times over 'We noblemen,' 'I as a noble'; obviously he did not remember that our grandfather was a peasant, and our father a soldier. Even our surname Tchimsha-Himalaisky, in reality so incongruous, seemed to him now melodious, distinguished, and very agreeable.

"But the point just now is not he, but myself. I want to tell you about the change that took place in me during the brief hours I spent at his country place. In the evening, when we were drinking tea, the cook put on the table a plateful of gooseberries. They were not bought, but his own gooseberries, gathered for the first time since the bushes were planted. Nikolay Ivanovitch laughed and looked for a minute in silence at the gooseberries, with tears in his eyes; he could not speak for excitement. Then he put one gooseberry in his mouth, looked at me with the triumph of a child who has at last received his favourite toy, and said:

" 'How delicious!'

"And he ate them greedily, continually repeating, 'Ah, how delicious! Do taste them!'

"They were sour and unripe, but, as Pushkin says:

" 'Dearer to us the falsehood that exalts
Than hosts of baser truths.'

"I saw a happy man whose cherished dream was so obviously fulfilled, who had attained his object in life, who had gained what he wanted, who was satisfied with his fate and himself. There is always, for some reason, an element of sadness mingled with my thoughts of human happiness, and, on this occasion, at the sight of a happy man I was overcome by an oppressive feeling that was close upon despair. It was particularly oppressive at night. A bed was made up for me in the room next to my brother's bedroom, and I could hear that he was awake, and that he kept getting up and going to the plate of gooseberries and taking one. I reflected how many satisfied, happy people there really are! What a suffocating force it is! You look at life: the insolence and idleness of the strong, the ignorance and brutishness of the weak, incredible poverty all about us, overcrowding, degeneration, drunkenness, hypocrisy, lying. . . . Yet all is calm and stillness in the houses and in the streets; of the fifty thousand living in a town, there is not one who would cry out, who would give vent to his indignation aloud. We see the people going to market for provisions, eating by day, sleeping by night, talking their silly nonsense, getting married, growing old, serenely escorting their dead to the cemetery; but we do not see and we do not hear those who suffer, and what is terrible in life goes on somewhere behind the scenes. . . . Everything is quiet and peaceful, and nothing protests but mute statistics: so many people gone out of their minds, so many gallons of vodka drunk, so many children dead from malnutrition. . . . And this order of things is evidently necessary; evidently the happy man only feels at ease because the unhappy bear their burdens in silence, and without that silence happiness would be impossible. It's a case of general hypnotism. There ought to be behind the door of every happy, contented man someone standing with a hammer continually reminding him with a tap that there are unhappy people; that however happy he may be, life will show him her laws sooner or later, trouble will come for him—disease, poverty, losses, and no one will see or hear, just as now he neither sees nor hears others. But there is no man with a hammer; the happy man lives at his ease, and trivial daily cares faintly agitate him like the wind in the aspen-tree—and all goes well.

"That night I realized that I, too, was happy and contented," Ivan Ivanovitch went on, getting up. "I, too, at dinner and at the hunt liked to lay down the law on life and religion, and the way to manage the peasantry. I, too, used to say that science was light, that culture was essential, but for the simple people reading and writing was enough for the time. Freedom is a blessing, I used to say; we can no more do without it than without air, but we must wait a little. Yes, I used to talk like that, and now I ask, 'For what reason are we to wait?' " asked Ivan Ivanovitch, looking angrily at Burkin. "Why wait, I ask you? What grounds have we for waiting? I shall be told, it can't be done all at once; every idea takes shape in life gradually, in its due time. But who is it says that? Where is the proof that it's right? You will fall back upon the natural order of things, the uniformity of phenomena; but is there order and uniformity in the fact that I, a living, thinking man, stand over a chasm and wait for it to close of itself, or to fill up with mud at the very time when perhaps I might leap over it or build a bridge across it? And again, wait for the sake of what? Wait till there's no strength to live? And meanwhile one must live, and one wants to live!

"I went away from my brother's early in the morning, and ever since then it has been unbearable for me to be in town. I am oppressed by its peace and quiet; I am afraid to look at the windows, for there is no spectacle more painful to me now than the sight of a happy family sitting round the table drinking tea. I am old and am not fit for the struggle; I am not even capable of hatred; I can only grieve inwardly, feel irritated and vexed; but at night my head is hot from the rush of ideas, and I cannot sleep. . . . Ah, if I were young!"

Ivan Ivanovitch walked backwards and forwards in excitement, and repeated: "If I were young!"

He suddenly went up to Alehin and began pressing first one of his hands and then the other.

"Pavel Konstantinovitch," he said in an imploring voice, "don't be calm and contented, don't let yourself be put to sleep! While you are young, strong, confident, be not weary in well-doing! There is no happiness, and there ought not to be; but if there is a meaning and an object in life, that meaning and object is not our happiness, but something greater and more rational. Do good!"

And all this Ivan Ivanovitch said with a pitiful, imploring smile, as though he were asking him a personal favour.

Then all three sat in arm-chairs at different ends of the drawing-room and were silent. Ivan Ivanovitch's story had not satisfied either Burkin or Alehin. When the generals and ladies gazed down from their gilt frames, looking in the dusk as though they were alive, it was dreary to listen to the story of the poor clerk who ate gooseberries. They felt inclined, for some reason, to talk about elegant people, about women. And their sitting in the drawing-room where everything—the chandeliers in their covers, the arm-chairs, and the carpet under their feet—reminded them that those very people who were now looking down from their frames had once moved about, sat, drunk tea in this room, and the fact that lovely Pelagea was moving noiselessly about was better than any story.

Alehin was fearfully sleepy; he had got up early, before three o'clock in the morning, to look after his work, and now his eyes were closing; but he was afraid his visitors might tell some interesting story after he had gone, and he lingered on. He did not go into the question whether what Ivan Ivanovitch had just said was right and true. His visitors did not talk of groats, nor of hay, nor of tar, but of something that had no direct bearing on his life, and he was glad and wanted them to go on.

"It's bed-time, though," said Burkin, getting up. "Allow me to wish you good-night."

Alehin said good-night and went downstairs to his own domain, while the visitors remained upstairs. They were both taken for the night to a big room where there stood two old wooden beds decorated with carvings, and in the corner was an ivory crucifix. The big cool beds, which had been made by the lovely Pelagea, smelt agreeably of clean linen.

Ivan Ivanovitch undressed in silence and got into bed.

"Lord forgive us sinners!" he said, and put his head under the quilt.

His pipe lying on the table smelt strongly of stale tobacco, and Burkin could not sleep for a long while, and kept wondering where the oppressive smell came from.

The rain was pattering on the window-panes all night.

Translated by Constance Garnett

Graffiti

Julio Cortázar

To Antoni Tàpies

So many things begin and perhaps end as a game, I suppose that it amused you to find the sketch beside yours, you attributed it to chance or a whim and only the second time did you realize that it was intentional and then you looked at it slowly, you even came back later to look at it again, taking the usual precautions: the street at its most solitary moment, no patrol wagon on neighboring corners, approaching with indifference and never looking at the graffiti face-on but from the other sidewalk or diagonally, feigning interest in the shop window alongside, going away immediately.

Your own game had begun out of boredom, it wasn't really a protest against the state of things in the city, the curfew, the menacing prohibition against putting up posters or writing on walls. It simply amused you to make sketches with colored chalk (you didn't like the term graffiti, so art critic-like) and from time to time to come and look at them and even, with a little luck, to be a spectator to the arrival of the municipal truck and the useless insults of the workers as they erased the sketches. It didn't matter to them that they weren't political sketches, the prohibition covered everything, and if some child had dared draw a house or a dog it would have been erased in just the same way in the midst of curses and threats. In the city people no longer knew too well which side fear was really on; maybe that's why you overcame yours and every so often picked the time and place just right for making a sketch.

You never ran any risk because you knew how to choose well, and in the time that passed until the cleaning trucks arrived something opened up for you like a very clean space where there was almost room for hope. Looking at your sketch from a distance you could see people casting a glance at it as they passed, no one stopped, of course, but no one failed to look at the sketch, sometimes a quick abstract composition in two colors, the profile of a bird or two entwined figures. Just one time you wrote a phrase, in black chalk: *It hurts me too.* It didn't last two hours, and that time the police themselves made it disappear. Afterward you went on only making sketches.

When the other one appeared next to yours you were almost afraid, suddenly the danger had become double, someone like you had been moved to have some fun on the brink of imprisonment or something worse, and that someone, as if it were of no small importance, was a woman. You couldn't prove it yourself, but there was something different and better than the most obvious proofs: a trace, a predilection for warm colors, an aura. Probably since you walked alone you were imagining it out of compensation; you admired her, you were afraid for her, you hoped it was the only time, you almost gave yourself away when she drew a sketch alongside another one of yours, an urge to laugh, to stay right there as if the police were blind or idiots.

A different time began, at once stealthier, more beautiful and more threatening. Shirking your job you would go out at odd moments in hopes of surprising her. For your sketches you chose those streets that you could cover in a single quick passage; you came back at dawn, at dusk, at three o'clock in the morning. It was a time of unbearable contradiction, the deception of finding a new sketch of hers beside one of yours and the street empty, and that of not finding anything and feeling the street even more empty. One night you saw her first sketch all by itself; she'd done it in red and blue chalk on a garage door, taking advantage of the worm-eaten wood and the nail heads. It was more than ever she—the design, the colors—but you also felt that that sketch had meaning as an appeal or question, a way of calling you. You came back at dawn, after the patrols had thinned out in their mute sweep, and on the rest of the door you sketched a quick seascape with sails and breakwaters; if he didn't look at it closely a person might have said it was a play of random lines, but she would know how to look at it. That night you barely escaped a pair of policemen, in your apartment you drank glass after glass of gin and you talked to her, you told her everything that came into your mouth, like a different sketch made with sound, another harbor with sails, you pictured her as dark and silent, you chose lips and breasts for her, you loved her a little.

Almost immediately it occurred to you that she would be looking for an answer, that she would return to her sketch the way you were returning now to yours, and even though the danger had become so much greater since the attacks at the market, you dared go up to the garage, walk around the block, drink endless beers at the café on the corner. It was absurd because she wouldn't stop after seeing your sketch, any one of the many women coming and going might be her. At dawn on the second day you chose a gray wall and sketched a white triangle surrounded by splotches like oak leaves; from the same café on the corner you could see the wall (they'd already cleaned off the garage door and a patrol, furious, kept coming back), at dusk you withdrew a little, but choosing different lookout points, moving from one place to another, making small purchases in the shops so as not to draw too much attention. It was already dark night when you heard the sirens and the spotlights swept your eyes. There was a confused crowding by the wall, you ran, in the face of all good sense, and all that helped you was the good luck to have a car turn the corner and put on its brakes when the driver saw the patrol wagon, its bulk protected you and you saw the struggle, black hair pulled by gloved hands, the kicks and the screams, the cut-off glimpse of blue slacks before they threw her into the wagon and took her away.

Much later (it was horrible trembling like that, it was horrible to think that it had happened because of your sketch on the gray wall) you mingled with other people and managed to see an outline in blue, the traces of that orange color that was like her name or her mouth, her there in that truncated sketch that the police had erased before taking her away, enough remained to understand that she had tried to answer your triangle with another figure, a circle or maybe a spiral, a form full and beautiful, something like a yes or an always or a now.

You knew it quite well, you'd had more than enough time to imagine the details of what was happening at the main barracks; in the city everything like that oozed out little by little, people were aware of the fate of prisoners, and if sometimes they got to see one or another of them again, they would have preferred not seeing them, just as the majority were lost in the silence that no one dared break. You knew it only too well, that night the gin wouldn't help you except to make you bite your hands with impotence, cry, crush the pieces of colored chalk with your feet before submerging yourself in drunkenness.

Yes, but the days passed and you no longer knew how to live in any other way. You began to leave your work again to walk about the streets, to look fleetingly at the walls and the doors where you and she had sketched. Everything clean, everything clear; nothing, not even a flower sketched by the innocence of a schoolboy who steals a piece of chalk in class and can't resist the pleasure of using it. Nor could you resist, and a month later you got up at dawn and went back to the street with the garage. There were no patrols, the walls were perfectly clean; a cat looked at you cautiously from a doorway when you took out your chalk and in the same place, there where she had left her sketch, you filled the boards with a green shout, a red flame of recognition and love, you wrapped your sketch in an oval that was also your mouth and hers and hope. The footsteps at the corner threw you into a felt-footed run, to the refuge of a pile of empty boxes; a staggering drunk approached humming, he tried to kick the cat and fell face down at the foot of the sketch. You went away slowly, safe now, and with the first sun you slept as you hadn't slept for a long time.

That same morning you looked from a distance: they hadn't erased it yet. You went back at noon: almost inconceivably it was still there. The agitation in the suburbs (you'd heard the news reports) had taken the urban patrols away from their routine; at dusk you went back to see that a lot of people had been seeing it all through the day. You waited until three in the morning to go back, the street was empty and dark. From a distance you made out the other sketch, only you could have distinguished it, so small, above and to the left of yours. You went over with a feeling that was thirst and horror at the same time; you saw the orange oval and the violet splotches where a swollen face seemed to leap out, a hanging eye, a mouth smashed with fists. I know, I know, but what else could I have sketched for you? What message would have made any sense now? In some way I had to say farewell to you and at the same time ask you to continue. I had to leave you something before going back to my refuge where there was no mirror anymore, only a hollow to hide in until the end in the most complete darkness, remembering so many things and sometimes, as I had imagined your life, imagining that you were making other sketches, that you were going out at night to make other sketches.

Translated by Gregory Rabassa

Trauma Plate

Adam Johnson

I

The Body Armor Emporium opened down the street a few months back, and I tell you, it's killing mom-and-pop bulletproof vest rental shops like ours. We've tried all the gimmicks: two-for-one rentals, the VIP card, a night drop. But the end is near, and lately we have taken to bringing the VCR with us to the shop, where we sit around watching old movies.

Lakeview was supposed to expand our way, but receded toward the interstate, and here we are, in an abandoned strip mall, next to the closed-down Double Drive In where Jane and I spent our youth. After Kmart moved out, most of the stores followed, leaving only us, a Godfather's Pizza, and a store, I swear, that sells nothing but purified water and ice. It is afternoon, near the time when Ruthie gets out of school, and behind the counter, Jane and I face forty acres of empty parking spaces while watching *Blue Hawaii.*

I am inspecting the vests—again—for wear and tear, a real time killer, and the way Jane sighs when Elvis scoops the orphan kid into the Jeep tells me this movie may make her cry. "When's he going to dive off that cliff?" I ask.

"That's *Fun in Acapulco,*" Jane says. "We used to have it on Beta." She sets down her design pad. "God, remember Beta?"

"Jesus, we were kids," I say, though I feel it, the failed rightness of Betamax smiling at us from the past.

"I loved Betamax," she says.

I only rented one vest yesterday, and doubtful I'll rent another today, await its safe return. There aren't many customers like Mrs. Espers anymore. She's a widow and only rents vests to attend a support group that meets near the airport. The airpark's only a medium on threat potential, but I always send her out armed with my best: thirty-six-layer Kevlar, German made, with lace side panels and a removable titanium trauma plate that slides into a Velcro pocket over the heart the size of a love letter. The Kevlar will field a .45 hit, but it's the trauma plate that will knock down a twelve-gauge slug and leave it sizzling in your pant cuff. I wear a lighter, two-panel model, while Jane goes for the Cadillac—a fourteen-hundred-dollar field vest with over-shoulders and a combat collar. *It's like a day-long bear hug,* she says. *It feels that safe.* She hasn't worn a bra in three years.

The State Fair is two weeks away, which is usually our busiest season, so Jane's working on a new designer line we think may turn things around. Everyone's heard the reports of trouble the State Fair has caused other places: clown killings in Omaha, that Midway shootout in Columbus, 4-H snipers in Fargo.

Her custom work started with the training vest she made for Ruthie, our fourteen-year-old. It was my idea, really, but Jane's the artist. The frame's actually a small men's, with the bottom ring of Kevlar removed, so it's like a bulletproof bolero, an extra set of ribs really. The whole lower GI tract is exposed, but fashion, comfort, anything to get the kids to wear their vests these days. Last week I had Jane line a backpack with Kevlar, which I think will rent because it not only saves important gear, but protects the upper spine in a quick exit. Next I want to toy with a Kevlar baby carrier, but the problem as I see it will be making a rig that's stiff enough to support the kid, yet loose enough to move full-speed in. We'll see.

Through the windows, there's a Volvo crossing the huge lot, and I can tell by the way it ignores the lane markings that it's not the kind of person who cares about the dangers of tainted water and stray bullets. The car veers toward Godfather's Pizza, almost aiming for the potholes, and Jane sniffles as Elvis hulas with the wide-eyed orphan at the beach party. "Remember Ruthie at that age?" I ask.

"You bet," Jane says.

"Let's have another baby."

"Sure," she answers, but she's only half listening. She really gets into these movies.

After Elvis is over, Jane makes iced teas while I drag two chairs out into the parking lot so we can enjoy some of the coming evening's cool. We bring the cordless phone, lean back in the chairs, and point our feet toward sunset. This time of day brings a certain relief because even in September, a good vest is like an oven.

There is a freedom that comes with doom, and lately we use our large lot to play Frisbee in the evening or football in the near-dark, with Ruthie always outrunning one of us for the long bomb. Some nights the Filipinos who own the water store drift out under the awnings to watch us. They wipe their brows with apron ends and seem to wonder what kind of place this America is.

Honestly, I've lost most of my spirit in the fight against the Emporium. When we opened, we were cutting edge, we were thinking franchise. Our customers were middle class, people like us; they still wanted to believe but understood that, hey, once in a while you needed a little insurance. Their lives were normal, but nobody went out on New Years without a vest. To buy a vest ten years ago was to admit defeat, to say *what's out there* isn't just knocking at the door—it's upstairs, using your toothbrush, saying good morning to your wife.

As the sun sinks lower, we watch the first pizza delivery boys of the evening zoom off in their compact cars, and it's a sight that hurts to see. These are high-school kids, most of them too poor to afford or too young to appreciate the value of a vest. I mean, they're going out there every night *as is,* which makes them all the more alluring to Ruth.

People used to make excuses when they came in to rent a vest—*vacationing in Mexico, weekend in the city, reception at a Ramada Inn, flying Delta.* Now they're haggling over expired rent-nine-get-one-free coupons. Now they're going to the Emporium to buy sixteen-layer Taiwanese knockoffs for three hundred bucks. The Emporium is 24-hours, something I'm philosophically against: you should see the tattoos on some of those guys coming out of there at 3:00 A.M. These days people are making the investment. They're admitting the world's a dangerous place.

Across the parking lot, we see Ruth pedaling toward us. She's wearing a one-piece red Speedo, her training vest, and the Kevlar backpack. Her hair is still wet from freshmen swim practice. She meanders over, awkward on a Schwinn she is now too big for, and pedaling big, easy loops around us, announces that she's an outcast. "Only dorks wear their vests to school," she says. "You're killing my scene."

It feels good though, the open-endedness of the day, the last light on my feet, being the center of my daughter's universe for a few minutes. Ruth pedals then coasts, pedals then coasts, the buzz of her wheel bearings filling the gaps in our afternoon, and I almost forget about the Emporium.

Later, after Jane leaves to find Ruthie and take her home for the evening, I'm sitting in the shop when Mrs. Espers comes in. She looks a little down, is holding the vest like it's made of burlap and I know the feeling: it's been one of those days for me too.

"How was the support group?" I ask as I fill out her receipt.

"I've crossed the line," she says.

"How's that?"

"I'm not afraid of flying anymore."

I'm not sure what this means in terms of her group, of whether she'll no longer be needing my services, but you know, I say, "Great, congratulations."

"I'm not afraid of anything," she says with a certain formality.

"Wow, good, good."

She pauses at the sight of her held-out receipt and shakes her head no. "I'm sorry, Bill, but I've made the decision."

She says this and leaves, and I'm left thinking she's decided to go to the Emporium to make the purchase. I figure some flying counselor talked her into the idea of permenant protection, but it is when I go to throw her vest atop the "in" stack, when I remove the titanium trauma plate, that I know she will never wear a vest again. The shiny titanium is lead-streaked, and as I rub my thumb in the indention some bullet has made, I can still feel her body heat on it.

I float out into the parking lot and watch her red taillights disappear into the night, and know that she's right, she's free, that nobody gets shot in the heart twice. I stand in a handicapped parking spot, rubbing the titanium, and I lean against the old shopping cart bin. The faint laughter of distant gunfire comes from the direction of the rail yard, and I look at the lighted windows of the few shops left in the mall, but can only see the darkened stores between them. In my hands, the bright titanium reflects the stars my fourteen-year-old already knows by heart, but I no longer have it in me to look up, to lift my head to the place of our dreams, Jane's and mine, when we were eighteen.

I wander the mall, waiting for my wife to return, something that takes longer and longer these days. She gets a little melancholy now and then, needs a little space to herself, and I understand; these are hard times we're living in. Leaving the shop wide open, I head for Godfather's. But when I get there, I'm confused because I see my daughter through the window, the girl my wife said she was taking home.

Ruth is leaned up against an ancient Donkey Kong machine, talking to a delivery boy on a backward chair. She is wearing her training vest with nothing on under, you can tell, and this boy stares at the exposed plane of her stomach. She has her cheek against the side of the video game, chatting about something, while the boy subtly marvels at how the fine hairs around her navel hum pink in the neon beer light, and I am roaring through the door. I walk right up to my daughter and thump her trauma plate to hear the squish of a cigarette pack and the crack of a CD case. Out of the pocket that should cover her heart forever, I pull Aerosmith and menthols.

I grab her by the wrist. "Where's your protection?"

"Jesus, Dad," she says and starts to dig in the backpack at her feet.

The pizza boy looks like he's about to pipe in, and I wheel on him, "Your parents don't love you."

"Dad, nobody wears their vests to school. I'm a total outcast."

This is my daughter. This is the age she is at.

Jane eventually returns, finds me watching *Cool Hand Luke* in the dark store, and neither of us says anything. She puts her hands on the counter when she comes in and I ask no questions about where she's been. I place my hands on hers, stroke the backs of her fingers, and then turn out the lights, closing up shop a little early.

Lately we have taken to cruising late at night under the guise of R&D. We'll pull the tarp off the '72 Monte Carlo her mom left us, the car Jane used to run wild in. It has the optional swivel passenger seat, black leather, that can turn 180 degrees. We grab the foam cooler and Jane swivels the seat all the way around so her feet are on the backseat and her head reclines to the dash, so she can watch me drive her wherever she wants to go. We'll glide by the boarded-up Ice Plant where we once drank on summer nights, feet dangling off the loading ramps. We prowl past by the Roadhouse with our lights off and count the Ninja motorcycles lined up out front. The cemetery these days is fenced and locked and a security guard cruises the old stadium in a golf cart, but we circle nonetheless.

Midnight finds us rolling through the waves of the old Double Drive In, the gravel crunching under our tires, the Monte Carlo's trunk bottoming out like it used to, and all the broken glass, beer caps, and bullet casings now sparkle like stars.

We park and sit on the warm, ticking car hood and look off at the Emporium across the street. We have his-and-hers binoculars, 7X40s from her father on our tenth anniversary, and we sit here, side by side in the dark, as we check out their customers. We train our lenses at the bright displays. Jane rolls her focus in and out.

"Is that Fred Sayles?" she asks. "By the baby armor."

I focus in on him fondling the competition's goods. "That son of a bitch."

"Remember the night he streaked through the second feature?"

"We all turned on our headlights. *The Day the Earth Stood Still,* right?"

"Plan Nine From Outer Space," she says. "Remember window speakers?"

"Remember high-point beer."

"Nash seats."

"Trunkloads."

"Keys left in the ignition."

"Mars Invades."

We both look up.

II

It is a moment near the end of things, a point at which, seated in a lawn chair amid the vast emptiness of a Kmart parking lot, Jane is forced to reflect. Her husband is giving driving lessons to her daughter, who loops circles around Jane in the old Caprice they are now reduced to driving. The circles are big and slow, impending as Jane's thoughts, which come to focus on the notion that Ruthie's sixteen, and Bill should have taught her this a year ago.

The Caprice stops, backs up, parallel parks between a pair of worn yellow lines somehow chosen from the thousands in front of the closed-down discounter. It's just like Bill, she thinks, to worry about lines when there's not another car for miles. Jane lifts her hand and the sun disappears. In this brief shade she notices the moon, too, is up there.

Check your mirrors, she can hear Bill say, even from here, as he trains her daughter to always, always be on the lookout. But Jane knows Ruthie's come to be on intimate terms with her blind spot. It's one of the few things they share these days.

Behind her their small rental store is empty. These days, the final ones, he has a VCR running all day in the shop. Over her shoulder she can hear the melancholic coo of *Jailhouse Rock*—Bill's choice today—and it feels like it is their whole history looming behind them: the mom-and-pop store, those liberal-arts dreams, their own *let's put on a barn dance* notion of being their own bosses, here, in a strip mall. She has the cordless phone with her, but it doesn't ring, has not in *we don't talk about how long,* and Jane reclines some in the heat, points her feet toward the horizon.

Look out, Bill yells, *you just hit a Volvo,* and slaps the dash for effect, leaving Ruthie momentarily breathless: she swivels her head to see the chrome and glass she must have missed, but there is only forty acres of empty parking.

The sun swoops low, Ruthie pedals off to junior-varsity swim practice, and *no,* Jane says, not *The Treasure of Sierra Madre* again. On the counter before them are two dozen bulletproof vests frayed to the point that they wouldn't stop slingshots and sixty or seventy videos Bill got cheap when the Video-Utopia store closed three stores down. *And here's where we are,* Jane thinks, between a Chapter 11 pizza joint and a store that has made the switch from water to spirits. *This is the place we are at,* around the corner from the drive-in theater where she and Bill spent their youth, a place she won't even look at because these days, even worse than hope, nostalgia is her enemy.

Bill shrugs his shoulders, lights a menthol, and pops in *Viva Las Vegas,* as if Elvis can soothe her anymore, as if Elvis wasn't 187,000 miles away.

Jane begins to toy with the register, hitting *no sale, no sale,* a sound she knows can wound him. But Bill's busy doing "R&D," as he calls it. First he thought bulletproof teen wear would save the business, and he made Ruthie wear a "training" vest to school for two years to drum up business. Now she won't take the vest off for her life.

His ongoing obsession is a bulletproof baby carrier, something he's reworked twenty times, and if there's anything that offends Jane more than the grandeur of his optimism, it's the notion of wanting to make infants bulletproof, of fusing the two ideas into the same breath. The whole idea is fatally flawed, she knows as she teases the few remaining twenties in the register. It's not what's out there you need to look out for, but what's closer, what's making your cereal crackle, what's tinkering in the garage, or crashing all around like unseen cars.

Bill tugs the straps of his Kevlar carrier, trying to simulate every force that could come between a mother and child. Then he begins stuffing the carrier with videotapes—Clint Eastwood, Annette Funicello, Benji—until, he seems to decide, the carrier takes on the mass and weight of a small person, and he is off on tonight's R&D, running laps around the abandoned drive-in to gauge the carrier's give and take, its ability to cradle a baby at full speed.

Now that he is gone, Jane unfastens the chest-crushing vest, and it smolders off her with all that body heat. She pinches the sticky shirt from her side, runs her hand underneath, over creases in the skin she knows are red. She wakes up some nights, thinking the oven has been left on. She can feel the coils glowing downstairs, but she won't go check, she won't give it that. Now she pulls the twenties, tens, and fives from the till, *for safety's sake,* she thinks, so she can feel the lightweight cash in her pocket.

Wandering, she strolls along the grit-worn sidewalk, stares at stars through holes in the Kmart awning. This way it all looks black up there, the occasional star the rarity. There are bullet holes in the masonry between her and the old Godfather's, and she stops to twist her pinkie in the lead-traced pocks. Mr. Ortiz, the Filipino who owns the liquor store, has started keeping a gun in his register, she's sure. She hasn't seen it, but there's a weight in the cash drawer that nearly pulls the register off the counter when he makes a sale.

There was a day when she was scared of guns, when the vest store seemed like the right idea, a public service even. *Jesus,* they had really said that to each other. Though she has never touched a gun, she's confident now she could heft one pretty handily, squeeze off a few rounds, rest it warm against her cheek and smell the breech.

Where the masonry meets glass, she thinks she gets a glimpse of him reflected out there, an aberration in the dark lot. Behind her, she's sure it's his arms glinting, racing nearly invisible in a sheen of black Kevlar. But she does not turn to be sure.

At the pizza joint, she sees through the window her daughter stretched across the empty bartop, drafting two beers into Styrofoam cups. Ruthie's hair is still wet from JV swim, and she wears loose-hanging jeans over her red Speedo. Now she's got her trauma plate pulled out and is using it as a lipstick mirror, drinking between applications. This is something Jane has never before seen, Ruthie so loose with her trauma plate, and this makes Jane stop outside and stare.

There is a boy, one of those big Ortiz kids it looks like, and he and Ruthie are drinking hard and fast together. Jane looks at them for some time through the soap paint on the window, an interstellar pizza scene. Ruthie laughs, they drink, something is said to her, and she punches him hard. He thumps her back, *there,* in the chest, and then she's holding him again, cupping his chin in the open throat of her palms, the Vulcan oven glowing behind them. She holds him, they dance three slow steps, he spins her. They drink, they laugh, they box each other's ears, they drink again, laughing till fine mists of beer shoot pink from their mouths in the neon light.

This is a careless spirit Jane has forgotten. As she sees them whisper, she remembers a time before Bill, and tries to read her daughter's lips. Ruthie rubs her forehead against the jut of this boy's cheekbone, whispering, and Jane almost thinks she can make it out—*let's make a break for Texas,* her daughter might be saying, and *I want my Monte Carlo back,* Jane thinks. She imagines a car she will never see again, enters it under maroon T-tops, feels the rocking slosh of dual fuel tanks, smells the leather, hears the spark plugs crackle to life, and swivels in custom seats to see it all disappear behind her.

Later, after she has dropped Ruthie off at home, Jane steers the Caprice the long way back to the shop, where she will wait out the last hour with Bill before closing. He will want to make love tonight, she knows—Westerns always do that to him, especially *The Treasure of Sierra Madre*—and that's okay with her. But there's one stop she needs to make.

She slowly eases past the Body Armor Emporium, and just getting caught in its gallery lights is enough to draw her in. She's been here before, enough times it would kill Bill to know. Inside, the lights are of the brightest variety, the walls white, expansive, always that smell like aspirin coming off the rows and rows of black nylon vests. Jane could care less about every vest in the world, but she runs her fingers down whole groves of them because unlike her husband, she feels safe in the arms of the enemy.

There is a tall man, older, with close-cropped gray hair and no-fooling shoulders he seems almost embarrassed of—a by-product of the joy of exertion—

and he beckons her into the fitting mirrors where she sees herself in satellite view, from three different angles. For a moment, there are no blind spots and she is at ease. This man takes her measurements quietly, as he has done many times before—humming and storing numbers in his head—the little green tape zipping under his thumbnail as he circles the wings of her pelvis and cliff dives down to her pant cuffs. He is calm, confident, placing his hand warm on her sternum to demonstrate where the trauma plate will be. She closes her eyes, remembering a time when she still believed, feels his fingers measuring over, under the cups of her breasts—Jane inhaling—for the purchase she will never make.

III

Let's say you're seventeen. Your mom checked out a while ago. Some nights she just disappears, the Caprice peeling out in front of the family rental store, and maybe you'll see her near morning, standing out there in the parking lot, buzzed, taking potshots at the giant drive-in screens two miles away.

Your old man's a little whacked-out too. Let's say you're crashed out with Hector, both of you sleeping in the Home Improvement section of Kmart, his hand over the nylon vest he again tried to remove tonight, and even though you quit the team, you're dreaming you're swimming the butterfly. *Stroke stroke, dig dig,* Mr. Halverson is yelling in the dream but you can go no faster. Hector is swimming under you, upside-down, telling you *use your back, your chest, put your shoulders into it,* but it is useless because these are the parts of you that are always, always off limits.

So you're sleeping, 3:00 A.M. say, when your dad rents a vest to some punk who uses it to rob the Filipino drug store two doors down, and after, Mr. Ortiz, Hector's dad, stands waving his Colt .45 and saying he's going to put a hole in your old man big as a mantel clock. And there is your father, facing him in a vast black parking lot, wearing an Israeli *alz-hesjhad* forty-eight-layer combat field vest and he's shouting *come on, come on and get some.* You watch this scene with Hector from the bankrupt pizza place, both of you curious if his dad will shoot your dad, and Hector tells you he's heard there's a smell when the hot bullet melts the nylon on its way toward Kevlar. *Like a cross between Tanqueray gin and burning hair,* he says, *a green-black gum.* You remember that Canis Major was wheeling overhead that night.

Let's say that Pluto's gone, that the little planet swings wide one day and never comes back. Your varsity swim coach is also your Advanced Placement Astronomy teacher, and in AP Astronomy, the boys never stop because yours are the only breasts that are a mystery to them. It's a game they play, rapping on your titanium trauma plate when they pass in the hall, though you know the spirit of their fingers goes deeper, and you learn to put your arms up in anticipation. In class, the sun and earth are two white dots, while Pluto's historical orbit, as Mr. Halverson calls it, races away with his running chalk line across four blackboards. Sometimes he lectures directly to the Kevlar outline of your chest. These boys have never seen Pluto, have never reached for it across a black sky, but they moan and wring their hands, as if they can feel its loss, just out of reach, as Mr. Halverson's orbit line comes to a halt at the end of the black slate.

There's nothing out there but starlight and locomotion, Halverson tells you at night swim practice. You think about this for five thousand yards, back-stroking through the blue lanes, the steam rising off your arms to the batter-black sky.

And this is what you come home wet to, the place where you grew up: a hole in the wall behind a Dumpster that opens into the dust-flashing cavern of a closed-down Kmart. Here is where you learn to drive at thirteen, racing rusty carts full tilt through Automotive. Among the smashed racks of Entertainment is where Hector always waits for you. You first kiss in the room above, with mirrors that are really windows, lookouts over a discount wasteland. Through the ductwork, you can hear the nonstop static of your old man's stupid movies. You hear him joking through the vent, endlessly joking. *Always take a bomb with you when you fly on an airplane,* he says to a rare customer, *it's safer, because the odds of there being two bombs on board are astronomical.*

You've slept with seven boys in here, *making love,* they call it, for your sake, but you know better. Through the hole, into the dark Kmart, they come, and you are waiting for them. But none ever fingers your ribs, strokes your shoulders, handles that hollow under your heart because every time one starts to tug on those Velcro straps you are in terror. That is your event horizon, Mr. Halverson calls it at swim practice, the speed beyond which you can no longer safely swim without changing your form, the point at which you must let yourself be taken by your own current. *Safety is your enemy,* he likes to say, and you know he's right. In your own Kmart you're safe, vested, with thirty-six layers of Kevlar to help you take a boy's weight on top of you. But in a Speedo, wet, leaning over the starting block, dripping on the spring-board, it's like being naked under floodlights, unshouldered and alone. That's what made you break the school record in the 400 Individual Medley last month—the arm-throwing terror of being vestless before the shouts of those who want the most from you. You took your little trophy—a golden girl, hands up, chest out—and quit the team.

Karen Coles, whose locker is above yours, is seeing Mr. Halverson. Everybody knows since she crashed his Volvo last week. But only you've seen the notes that have floated through the cracks into your locker, only you know that she veered on purpose, that she was testing what was between them when she crossed the centerline, that she was saying I love you even as the airbags blew in their faces.

Your father is different since Mr. Ortiz fired those warning shots in the parking lot that night. He tries to be even more happy-go-lucky, but there is a nervous edge to it, and you know that he is the one on the lookout now. He has bought a gun, a little silver number, your mom calls it, and she stores it under her end of the counter. You remember the excuse he gave, leaning down to you at fourteen: *it's for that one bullet, that one well-intended bullet, and after that the odds say you're good.* This is the line that made you cinch your Velcro straps and wonder if you'd hear the bullet coming. But now you wonder if deep down, your old man isn't disappointed Mr. Ortiz didn't shoot for the heart. At home, you turn the oven on before climbing into bed.

It is the last of the warm days, the end of the semester nearing, one more till you graduate, and Mr. Halverson has saved the best for last: black holes. For now, the black and the hole do not seem to concern him. It is a thing called the event horizon he describes, the line beyond which light is forever drawn in, and you know this is going to be his *big metaphor for life,* his contribution toward bettering your future, a lecture, you can tell, he has made before. He draws a big, easy circle on the board and asks everyone to reflect a moment on the point of no return. But you know it is a mistake to call it that because nothing ever returns, really. Orbits are only historical. You like the swim-team explanation better: call it a line beyond which you can expect only a change in form and high rates of speed, a point of sudden inevitability. You lean back in your desk, your foot looping big, easily drawing his attention, and with a rift in his breathing, he returns his lecture to an institutional mode, comparing the point of no return to drugs and dropouts, to the joys of college learning and beyond. *And we all know what happens in the black hole,* he concludes, but his heart is no longer in it. You know those airbags were his event horizon.

In bed, at night, you sweat. You dream in shades of pink and green of gin and burning hair. In the morning, you, your mom, your dad, all eat breakfast in boxer shorts and bulletproof vests. Dad has a VCR set up on the table and watches *Clambake!* while your mom stares at her cereal.

You had been thinking about it this way: there's a ring around the thing that draws you near—the palms of Hector's hands, say, or your reflection in Halverson's glasses—and to cross that line is to be taken, swept, changed. But today you see it different. Today, standing in the empty AP classroom, not wanting to believe the rumors that Halverson's fired, packed up in his rental car and gone, you wonder where is your event horizon, where is the line beyond which something will forever be drawn to you. His handwriting is still on the blackboard. *Binary star homework due Tuesday,* is all it says, and he can't be gone, he can't be. Stupidly waiting under the Styrofoam-coat hanger model of the solar system you reach up and set it in motion. But the hand-colored planets swing too smoothly it seems to you, too safely Halverson would say, and plucking Pluto from the mix sets the model wildly spinning.

So it's not just anybody waiting for you in the Kmart after school, not just some boy grabbing you by the vest straps and pulling you to him, but Hector. It's Hector's drugstore heart thumping next to yours, Hector's letterman chest against yours, Hector's dive team hips gaining on yours and you want to believe, you want.

Hector has his father's gun, you your mother's, and you will ask the boy you love to break the plate guarding your heart. Hector has a Monte Carlo and you've seen the movie *Bullitt* enough times in your dad's shop that there's a California road map in your head as clear as the grooves around Steve McQueen's eyes, deep as the veins in Hector's arms, but it is not enough. The line must be crossed. He's ten feet from you, a parking space away. You hand him your mother's silver little number. It will knock you down, you know, there will be that smell, but soon there will be no more vests, no more fears, only Hector's fingers on the bruise he's made, on your sternum, and the line will be crossed, the event set in motion, at the highest of speeds.

Car Crash While Hitchhiking

Denis Johnson

A salesman who shared his liquor and steered while sleeping . . . A Cherokee filled with bourbon . . . A VW no more than a bubble of hashish fumes, captained by a college student . . .

And a family from Marshalltown who headonned and killed forever a man driving west out of Bethany, Missouri . . .

. . . I rose up sopping wet from sleeping under the pouring rain, and something less than conscious, thanks to the first three of the people I've already named—the salesman and the Indian and the student—all of whom had given me drugs. At the head of the entrance ramp I waited without hope of a ride. What was the point, even, of rolling up my sleeping bag when I was too wet to be let into anybody's car? I draped it around me like a cape. The downpour raked the asphalt and gurgled in the ruts. My thoughts zoomed pitifully. The travelling salesman had fed me pills that made the linings of my veins feel scraped out. My jaw ached. I knew every raindrop by its name. I sensed everything before it happened. I knew a certain Oldsmobile would stop for me even before it slowed, and by the sweet voices of the family inside it I knew we'd have an accident in the storm.

I didn't care. They said they'd take me all the way.

The man and the wife put the little girl up front with them and left the baby in back with me and my dripping bedroll. "I'm not taking you anywhere very fast," the man said. "I've got my wife and babies here, that's why."

You are the ones, I thought. And I piled my sleeping bag against the left-hand door and slept across it, not caring whether I lived or died. The baby slept free on the seat beside me. He was about nine months old.

. . . But before any of this, that afternoon, the salesman and I had swept down into Kansas City in his luxury car. We'd developed a dangerous cynical camaraderie beginning in Texas, where he'd taken me on. We ate up his bottle of amphetamines, and every so often we pulled off the Interstate and bought another pint of Canadian Club and a sack of ice. His car had cylindrical glass holders attached to either door and a white, leathery interior. He said he'd take me home to stay overnight with his family, but first he wanted to stop and see a woman he knew.

Under Midwestern clouds like great grey brains we left the superhighway with a drifting sensation and entered Kansas City's rush hour with a sensation of running aground. As soon as we slowed down, all the magic of travelling together burned away. He went on and on about his girlfriend. "I like this girl, I think I love this girl—but I've got two kids and a wife, and there's certain obligations there. And on top of everything else, I love my wife. I'm gifted with love. I love my kids. I love all my relatives." As he kept on, I felt jilted and sad: "I have a boat, a little sixteen-footer. I have two cars. There's room in the back yard for a swimming pool." He found his girlfriend at work. She ran a furniture store, and I lost him there.

The clouds stayed the same until night. Then, in the dark, I didn't see the storm gathering. The driver of the Volkswagen, a college man, the one who stoked my head with all the hashish, let me out beyond the city limits just as it began to rain. Never mind the speed I'd been taking, I was too overcome to stand up. I lay out in the grass off the exit ramp and woke in the middle of a puddle that had filled up around me.

And later, as I've said, I slept in the back seat while the Oldsmobile—the family from Marshalltown—splashed along through the rain. And yet I dreamed I was looking right through my eyelids, and my pulse marked off the seconds of time. The Interstate through western Missouri was, in that era, nothing more than a two-way road, most of it. When a semi truck came toward us and passed going the other way, we were lost in a blinding spray and a warfare of noises such as you get being towed through an automatic car wash. The wipers stood up and lay down across the windshield without much effect. I was exhausted, and after an hour I slept more deeply.

I'd known all along exactly what was going to happen. But the man and his wife woke me up later, denying it viciously.

"Oh—*no!*"

"NO!"

I was thrown against the back of their seat so hard that it broke. I commenced bouncing back and forth. A liquid which I knew right away was human blood flew around the car and rained down on my head. When it was over I was in the back seat again, just as I had been. I rose up and looked around. Our headlights had gone out. The radiator was hissing steadily. Beyond that, I didn't hear a thing. As far as I could tell, I was the only one conscious. As my eyes adjusted I saw that the baby was lying on its back beside me as if nothing had happened. Its eyes were open and it was feeling its cheeks with its little hands.

In a minute the driver, who'd been slumped over the wheel, sat up and peered at us. His face was smashed and dark with blood. It made my teeth hurt to look at him—but when he spoke, it didn't sound as if any of his teeth were broken.

"What happened?"

"We had a wreck," he said.

"The baby's okay," I said, although I had no idea how the baby was.

He turned to his wife.

"Janice," he said. "Janice, Janice!"

"Is she okay?"

"She's dead!" he said, shaking her angrily.

"No, she's not." I was ready to deny everything myself now.

Their little girl was alive, but knocked out. She whimpered in her sleep. But the man went on shaking his wife.

"Janice!" he hollered.

His wife moaned.

"She's not dead," I said, clambering from the car and running away.

"She won't wake up," I heard him say.

I was standing out here in the night, with the baby, for some reason, in my arms. It must have still been raining, but I remember nothing about the weather. We'd collided with another car on what I now perceived was a two-lane bridge. The water beneath us was invisible in the dark.

Moving toward the other car I began to hear rasping, metallic snores. Somebody was flung halfway out the passenger door, which was open, in the posture of one hanging from a trapeze by his ankles. The car had been broadsided, smashed so flat that no room was left inside it even for this person's legs, to say nothing of a driver or any other passengers. I just walked right on past.

Headlights were coming from far off. I made for the head of the bridge, waving them to a stop with one arm and clutching the baby to my shoulder with the other.

It was a big semi, grinding its gears as it decelerated. The driver rolled down his window and I shouted up at him, "There's a wreck. Go for help."

"I can't turn around here," he said.

He let me and the baby up on the passenger side, and we just sat there in the cab, looking at the wreckage in his headlights.

"Is everybody dead?" he asked.

"I can't tell who is and who isn't," I admitted.

He poured himself a cup of coffee from a thermos and switched off all but his parking lights.

"What time is it?"

"Oh, it's around quarter after three," he said.

By his manner he seemed to endorse the idea of not doing anything about this. I was relieved and tearful. I'd thought something was required of me, but I hadn't wanted to find out what it was.

When another car showed coming in the opposite direction, I thought I should talk to them. "Can you keep the baby?" I asked the truck driver.

"You'd better hang on to him," the driver said. "It's a boy, isn't it?"

"Well, I think so," I said.

The man hanging out of the wrecked car was still alive as I passed, and I stopped, grown a little more used to the idea now of how really badly broken he was, and made sure there was nothing I could do. He was snoring loudly and rudely. His blood bubbled out of his mouth with every breath. He wouldn't be taking many more. I knew that, but he didn't, and therefore I looked down into the great pity of a person's life on this earth. I don't mean that we all end up dead, that's not the great pity. I mean that he couldn't tell me what he was dreaming, and I couldn't tell him what was real.

Before too long there were cars backed up for a ways at either end of the bridge, and headlights giving a night-game atmosphere to the steaming rubble, and ambulances and cop cars nudging through so that the air pulsed with color. I didn't talk to anyone. My secret was that in this short while I had gone from being the president of this tragedy to being a faceless onlooker at a gory wreck. At some point an officer learned that I was one of the passengers, and took my statement. I don't remember any of this, except that he told me, "Put out your cigarette." We paused in our conversation to watch the dying man being loaded into the ambulance. He was still alive, still dreaming obscenely. The blood ran off him in strings. His knees jerked and his head rattled.

There was nothing wrong with me, and I hadn't seen anything, but the policeman had to question me and take me to the hospital anyway. The word came over his car radio that the man was now dead, just as we came under the awning of the emergency-room entrance.

I stood in a tiled corridor with my wet sleeping bag bunched against the wall beside me, talking to a man from the local funeral home.

The doctor stopped to tell me I'd better have an X-ray.

"No."

"Now would be the time. If something turns up later . . ."

"There's nothing wrong with me."

Down the hall came the wife. She was glorious, burning. She didn't know yet that her husband was dead. We knew. That's what gave her such power over us. The doctor took her into a room with a desk at the end of the hall, and from under the closed door a slab of brilliance radiated as if, by some stupendous process, diamonds were being incinerated in there. What a pair of lungs! She shrieked as I imagined an eagle would shriek. It felt wonderful to be alive to hear it! I've gone looking for that feeling everywhere.

"There's nothing wrong with me"—I'm surprised I let those words out. But it's always been my tendency to lie to doctors, as if good health consisted only of the ability to fool them.

Some years later, one time when I was admitted to the Detox at Seattle General Hospital, I took the same tack.

"Are you hearing unusual sounds or voices?" the doctor asked.

"Help us, oh God, it hurts," the boxes of cotton screamed.

"Not exactly," I said.

"Not exactly," he said. "Now, what does that mean."

"I'm not ready to go into all that," I said. A yellow bird fluttered close to my face, and my muscles grabbed. Now I was flopping like a fish. When I squeezed shut my eyes, hot tears exploded from the sockets. When I opened them, I was on my stomach.

"How did the room get so white?" I asked.

A beautiful nurse was touching my skin. "These are vitamins," she said, and drove the needle in.

It was raining. Gigantic ferns leaned over us. The forest drifted down a hill. I could hear a creek rushing down among rocks. And you, you ridiculous people, you expect me to help you.

The Rooster and the Dancing Girl

Yasunari Kawabata

Of course, the dancing girl hated it—carrying a rooster under her arm—no matter how late at night it was.

The dancing girl was not raising chickens. Her mother was raising them.

If the girl were to become a great dancer, perhaps her mother would no longer raise chickens.

"They're doing gymnastics naked on top of the roof."

Her mother was taken aback.

"Not just one or two. There are forty or fifty. Just like at a girls' school. Naked . . . well, their legs are."

The spring light overflowed from the concrete rooftop. The dancing girls felt their arms and legs stretching like young bamboo shoots.

"Even in elementary school they don't do gymnastics on the ground anymore."

The girl's mother had come to the door of the dressing room to see her daughter.

"The rooster crowed in the night. That's why I came. I thought something had happened to you."

Her mother waited outside until rehearsal was over.

"Starting tomorrow, I'm going to dance naked in front of an audience." She had not told her mother before. "There was a strange man here. The dressing room bath was right by where you were waiting. Someone said there was a man who stood there vacantly watching for an hour—even though the window was up high and made of frosted glass. He couldn't even see a shadow. They said he just watched the drops that formed on the glass as they ran down the window."

"No wonder the rooster crowed at night."

There was a custom of discarding roosters that crowed at night to the deity Kannon of Asakusa. By doing so, they say you could avoid calamity.

Evidently the chickens that lived among the Kannon's pigeons were all faithful prophets for their masters.

The dancing girl went home once the next evening, then went back to Asakusa, crossing Kototoi from Honjo. She was carrying a rooster wrapped in cloth under her arm.

She untied the bundle in front of the Kannon. As soon as the rooster touched the ground, it flapped its wings and hurried away.

"Chickens are real idiots."

She felt pity for the rooster, which was probably cowering in the shadows. She looked for it but could not find it.

Then the dancing girl recalled that she had been told to pray.

"Kannon, did you once dance long ago?" She bowed her head. When she looked up again, she was startled.

She gazed at the high branches of a gingko tree and saw four or five chickens roosting there.

"I wonder how that rooster is doing."

On the way to the theater, the dancing girl stopped in front of the Kannon.

The rooster she had delivered the day before began to approach her. Blushing, the girl fled. The rooster chased after her.

The people in the park stared, their mouths gaping open as the rooster chased the girl.

Day by day the rooster became a wild bird among the crowds of people in the park.

It began to fly well. Its wings were covered with dust and turned white. But it pecked at beans alongside the pigeons with the nonchalance of an Asakusa delinquent and swaggered about on top of the offertory chest of the deity.

The dancing girl never tried to pass in front of the Kannon again.

Even if she *had* passed by, the rooster had forgotten her.

At the dancing girl's house, twenty chicks had hatched.

"It's probably not an ill omen for chicks to peep at night."

"For humans, you know, it's only natural for a child to cry at night."

"It's strange for an adult to cry at night."

The dancing girl spoke these trivial words; still, she had begun to feel that they had meaning.

She often walked with boys who were students. It seems that dancing girls who were not particularly great sometimes walked with students.

When she got home, her mother said, "I wonder what can be the matter. A rooster crowed at night again. You go pray to the Kannon."

The dancing girl felt she had been discovered, but she smiled. "Twenty chicks have hatched, so maybe the rooster's crowing means it's all right for me to walk with twenty men. That would be enough for one lifetime."

But she was mistaken. The rooster's prophecy was not about walking with students.

A strange man followed the dancing girl as she carried the rooster in a bundle under her arm. But because of the rooster, the girl was more embarrassed than afraid. Then the timid girl—that's right—we should shout to warn her.

A dancing girl carrying a rooster was certainly a bizarre sight. The man surely thought this would be convenient.

"Young lady, wouldn't you like to take part in a fine money-making plan with me? I search through the trash can every day at the theater where you dance—not to pick up scraps or anything like that. The trash is full of love letters addressed to the dancers, ones that they've thrown away."

"Oh?"

"You catch what I'm getting at, don't you? We could use those letters to get a little money from the men who were fools enough to send them. If I had someone in the dance hall who would assist me, it would make the work that much easier."

The dancing girl tried to run away. The man grabbed her. Without thinking, the girl pushed his face to the side with her right hand—the hand that held the rooster.

She shoved the bundle, rooster and all, into the man's face. The rooster flapped its wings. How could he stand it?

The man fled, screaming. He did not know it was the rooster.

The next morning, when the girl tried to walk in front of the Kannon, wouldn't you know it but the rooster from the previous night was there and came running to her feet. She stifled a laugh, but this time she did not run away. She left quietly.

As soon as she entered the dressing room, she said, "Everyone, please take care of your letters. Let's not throw them in the trash can. And let's send a notice to the other theaters—to protect public morals."

Of course, with this, perhaps she *would* become a great dancing girl.

Translated by J. Martin Holman

Father

John L'Heureux

Long before he got sick, our father was down there in the cellar painting away. He had rigged up an easel for himself and suspended a couple naked light bulbs from a beam—to simulate northern light, he said—and he painted things from photographs and magazines and books. Later he painted things vaguely reminiscent of what he had seen on walks. At the beginning of the end he painted things nobody except himself had ever seen before. He claimed that his painting style simply evolved from representational to impressionistic to a kind of hard-edged expressionism of his own. But long before we understood what he was doing, our father had begun to escape from us. He was in the process of disappearing.

John, who is artistic, was the first to notice the hairline crack in each of the paintings. Our father was all done with his representational period. He had lined up a whole bunch of the things in the cellar, propped against the washer and dryer and the boiler and the old bikes. They were everywhere, stacked two and three deep, because he was having a sort of show, a retrospective as it were, for John and Joan who were visiting home from California where he teaches writing and she teaches English. John and Joan have no children. They don't go in for that sort of thing. Or perhaps they can't. In any case they were admiring the pictures generally, sometimes pointing out a special thing about one or another, and our father was standing by, very serious, as they assessed what they liked or disliked about his creations. All of a sudden John said, "Look at this. *Look* at this." He ran a long skinny finger down an invisible crack in a picture. And then in another. And in another.

At the time our father just stood there, not doddering yet, not even a little bit dingy, just smiling as if he were getting some secret pleasure out of John's discovery. There's no telling just how much he was planning or how much he was deceiving us at that point; he was still in his impressionistic period. But there was no question that John was right: there was this line, wiggly sometimes and at other times jagged like a bolt of lightning and at all times almost invisible. It ran down the center of the painting as if it were a warning or a threat or a prophecy.

"A theme," John said. "A recurrent theme, as if your impression of the world reflected the primal fall or as if you saw that it might all come apart at any minute."

We laughed at that because it sounded so important, and our father laughed, and then we all went upstairs for a drink and dinner.

Not long after this he moved into his expressionist period, where people seemed less than whole and things no longer looked like what they were. He used a lot of dark colors in this period, though some had a grim brilliance that made us look at them, and look again. Huge rocks began to appear in his paintings, boulders practically, hovering in the air as if they might fall out of the picture any minute and crush us. And those cracks down the center began to get bigger. We could see them clearly now, even from a few feet off. Everything was distorted. What he was expressing wasn't very nice, even in the abstract.

Later when our father was diagnosed as Parkinson's, and well advanced too, he went on heavy doses of L-dopa that controlled the shaking and allowed him to continue to paint. That seemed fine, because it kept him occupied and out of our mother's way. He was deteriorating fast. And he was driving her crazy with things like putting the kettle on while she was out for groceries and forgetting it until it melted down flat to the burner. "He could have burned the house down," she would scream, while he flinched at the sound, "he could have burned himself to death," and then she would cry and scream and cry some more, until she had enough strength to go on. We were less patient with her than we should have been because we just didn't know how bad off our father was or what it was like for her to never have a quiet thought, midnight or morning, for years as she took care of him. When she finished her scene, our father would dodder on down the stairs and paint away. It was very near the end.

He had been in his expressionist period for quite a while when John and Joan came to visit again. They stayed in the house for a week with our father and mother and got a close look at the way things were. At first John was horrified at what had happened to our father physically: the stumble when he tried to walk, the wandering mind, the uncompleted sentence. And at our mother who seemed half-lunatic.

On the first morning, for instance, at breakfast time, she was shuffling in her bunny slippers from the stove to the table and all of a sudden she stopped dead. She let out a long scream and pulled her hair back from her temples, wailing, "Oh God, oh God, *now* you see what I have to put up with." John pushed away from the table and ran to her and said, "What? What is it?" And she cried out, in tears, in despair, "I already *stirred* his orange juice. I try to save him. I try. I try." John looked over at our father, who was clinking the glass as he tried to stir the orange juice with a fork, and he looked down at our mother, who was sobbing helplessly against his chest, and he looked over at Joan, who was looking the way Joan does, which we have frankly never figured out, and he said, "Something has to be done here. But what? What?"

After breakfast John took a look at the new paintings and, as he admitted later, he should have noticed how things were. Each picture had a thousand different fractures but there was something new; in the center, a kind of dark cave opened up into the canvas. "You could hide there," John said. "You could disappear forever." The newest painting stood unfinished on the easel, the same dark colors with their odd brilliance, the same fractures, fissures, cracks, but in the middle where that dark cave should be, there was empty canvas. Our father had left an absence in the center of things, for later.

The days that week were very long, John said. Our mother slept sometimes but mostly she raved like a madwoman, in desperation and devotion to our father, who merely sat, silent, or went for slow slow painful walks with John. The days were all right and the evenings were all right but at night our father was impossible. Sitting with them in the living room, like old times, he would nod and smile and make a little rambling comment now and then, but when they wanted to help him to bed, they found he had become nearly paralyzed. His limbs would not bend, they were like stone, and John and Joan together could barely move him. But they had method. They would pry him from his chair, pulling and pushing until they got him upright, and then they staggered him between them to his bed. He was bones only, but he was heavy beyond belief. Our mother would scuffle around saying, "See? Do you see?" and run ahead to ready the pillows, to pull down the sheet and blankets the way he liked, then "Do you see?" It took an hour to get him into bed.

"This is not the worst of it," our mother said. "You don't know. He pees in the wastebasket. He does. In the night he gets afraid of the toilet. So help me God." John laughed and our mother laughed and said, "I'm not crazy yet, I guess, because I still know it's funny . . . in a way. And once he's up, you never know what he'll do. He'll boil water and burn us down or go out on the street in the middle of the night—he's done it more than once—and there's no one who cares or who can help. . . ."

She stopped then because our father suddenly appeared from bed, stood smiling at the door, and moved across the room to his favorite chair, walking easily now, his limbs unstuck. "Oh no," she said, "don't let him sit. He'll fall asleep and we'll never get him up." And she was right. In less than a minute he slumped down into sleep and they had to go through it all again: prying him from the chair, getting him upright, staggering him down the hall to his bed. It was exhausting. It was frightening.

"How is this possible?" John said. "He was stiff as a board and out like a light, and it took an hour to get him into bed, and then minutes later he appears as if he's all set for a jaunt in the country. This isn't possible."

Our mother laughed this time, with bitterness and gratitude that someone saw at last what it was like, but before they could even get a drink and try to recover, there he was again. She ran ahead to do the pillows, but she was seventy-six and nearly done herself, and as they were staggering him to bed, she came apart, and shouted, "Bastard life, what kind of bastard life is this? I want out, I want out, I want out," but there was no way out, and she knew it, so she hurled herself into the hall closet, and tore the clothes from hangers and threw the hangers on the floor and, screaming, crouched there in a wretched corner, screaming still. Our father, paralyzed and dumb, snapped out of it and said to Joan, "That poor woman, that poor woman," and tears came as he said, "she'll die."

The next morning when our father went downstairs to paint, John made arrangements for a Home, and then he called us to our father's house and gave a speech. Our mother cowered in a chair.

"We must not deceive ourselves," he said. "We are sentencing our father to death. Because he is old and dotty and frail and cannot be responsible for wandering or peeing in the night, we say yes, this is impossible, he must have specialized care. But what we are *really* saying is: we cannot cope with this, so we must put him away. And he defies us, our pretensions and excuses and our lies." John teaches writing. He stands like a professor, wringing his hands as if that way he could squeeze the instincts out of them. "He defies us," John said, "by being, now and then, shockingly rational and sane and simple. One minute, we think he's lost it. The next, with his words and with his smile and with his knowing acceptance of this impossible situation, he tells us that we are putting out of our sight and our concern a living, feeling, suffering human person—who is *my* father and *your* father and *your* husband—and on and on until we can never forget and, if we are honest, never forgive ourselves. Something must be done here. But what? What?"

Thus, it was settled. Our father would be put in a Home and our mother would be saved, in a sense, and we would all live with what had to be done.

John went downstairs to get him, to tell him how it was, to break the hard news. And then we all went down. But our father was not there.

The paintings were there, spread around the cellar, the huge boulders in them ready to fall on us, the fractured surfaces, the dark caves. But our father was not there. He was gone.

His last canvas stood on the easel, finished now but unlike any of the others. In the center where there should have been a cave, there was the door our father had gone through. The door stood open to a silver night. He had disappeared. He had escaped, leaving us with all our business incomplete, our goodness, understanding.

In the end our father painted clear untroubled air and, quicker than our love, he entered it.

The Niece

Margot Livesey

He had replaced five light bulbs that day, and by late afternoon he couldn't help anticipating the soft ping of the element flying apart whenever he reached for a switch. The third time—the fixture on the landing—the thought zigzagged across his mind that these little explosions were a sign, like the two dogs he had come across in the autumn, greyhound and bulldog, locked together on the grassy slope of the local park. He had given them a wide berth; still, he'd felt responsible on the bus the next day when a man had turned puce and slid to the floor. By the fifth light, though, he had given up on superstition and was blaming London Electricity. Some irregularity in the current, some unexpected surge, was slaughtering the bulbs.

The Barrows were away, at a conference in Latvia, which was why the decorating was being done now, but they were the sort of people who kept spares—he could tell from their orderly supplies of toilet paper and condiments—just not in any place he could find. Meanwhile, he gradually emptied the upstairs rooms, slipping the bulbs from bedside lights and desk lamps. Next time he went to the shops, he'd pick up a pack and add it to his bill under "Miscellaneous."

Later, of course, the little zaps made perfect sense. But when the doorbell rang Zeke set aside the wallpaper steamer without a shard of premonition. Often, if he was up a ladder, he didn't answer the knocks and rings of late afternoon—after all, they were never for him—but now the pallor of the sky, the flashes of light and dark, the weariness of working alone all conspired to make even the prospect of rebuffing a double-glazing salesman, or a greasy-haired collector for Oxfam, a pleasure. Last Friday, in a similar mood, he'd found a chap on the doorstep, thin as a junkie, pretending to be blind. He had the dark glasses, the white cane, the fluttery stuff with the hands. "You're a painter," the man had said, sniffing slightly. Zeke had ended up giving him fifty pence.

"But how do you know he was a con man?" his mother had asked that night on the phone. "People compensate."

"I was looking out of the window and I saw him in the street, checking the 'A to Z.' "

"Barmy," his mother said, but there was a note of admiration in her voice, as if a fake blind man might be closer to her ideal son than a conscientious decorator.

Now the door swung open and a woman, no collecting tin, no clipboard, filled his vision. He hadn't replaced the bulb in the hall yet, and in the dim light her features took a few seconds to assemble. He made out abrupt dark eyebrows above a substantial nose and plump, glistening lips, as if the inside of her mouth had flowed alarmingly onto the outside.

For a moment, Zeke was baffled. Then he went through the steps he'd learned from the poster at the clinic. Eyes wide, a glimpse of teeth, corners of the mouth turning up rather than down: usually these indicated a smile that could, he knew, mean anger but more often meant friendliness. Yes, she was smiling, although not necessarily at him. Her expression had clearly been prepared in advance, but Zeke admired the way she held her face steady at the sight of him, and of his work clothes. His jeans and shirt were so paint-spattered as to be almost a separate entity.

"Good afternoon." She stretched out her hand and, seeing his, white with Spackle, faltered, neither withdrawing nor completing the gesture.

"Hi," he said, hating the single, stupid syllable. She was tall for a woman, his height save for the doorstep, and dimly familiar, though not as herself. As she began to speak, he realized who she reminded him of: the bust of Beethoven on his father's piano. Something about the expansiveness of her features, the way her tawny hair sprang back from her forehead.

"I'm the niece," she said.

Her breath streamed toward him, a chilly plume, carrying more words, perhaps an entire sentence, which Zeke lost as he blinked away Beethoven. "I'm the decorator," he said. "The Barrows are away."

"But they told you I would be here," she said with no hint of a question.

She stooped to pick up the large black suitcases on either side of her, and as she straightened he saw that she was pregnant. She stepped past him—the word "pushed" came to mind—and set the cases, gently, at the foot of the stairs. "Where are you working?"

He nodded toward the living room. She stood in the empty doorway—the door was at the strippers—surveying the room. Under the influence of her attention, Zeke saw again what his work had revealed: the ragged plaster painted not a single color but in pale bands of blue and brown, gray and yellow, the work of some unknown artist. In the middle of the floor the furniture was piled up and draped in dust sheets, like some ungainly prehistoric animal.

"Groovy," she said. "We should do a mural—hunting and fishing, golfing and shopping."

"I don't think your aunt and uncle . . ." Then he caught himself: humor. That had always been tricky for him. Even the question about the hen crossing the road could make him pause. "I told them it was a big job. You never know what you'll find when you strip off the paper. And Emmanuel, the guy who helps me, did his back in."

"How?" she said.

"What?"

"How"—she patted the small of her back—"did he bugger up his back?"

"Reaching for a corner. Snooker, not painting." In the bare space, their voices took on burly undertones. Hers was deep, anyway. As for his, Zeke wasn't sure. He had read that humans hear their own voices through the jaw, not the air; every time a tooth is lost or filled, the timbre changes.

"Aren't they due back this week?" she said.

"The nineteenth, they told me."

Finally she shrugged off her coat, revealing a dark-green dress. The heating was on full blast, not his bill, and the house was as snug as a tea cozy. She retreated to sling her coat over the banister and then came back into the room with that greedy, pushing motion. As she turned, he saw again, silhouetted against the window, her belly. Who would have expected the whey-faced Barrows to have a niece like this? And older than he'd thought, he saw now, as the light caught the little line like an exclamation mark between her eyebrows.

"Don't let me stop you," she said, her nose, her lavish mouth, bearing down, "working."

A sentence appeared in Zeke's head: *I'd like to tie you to the bed.* How did that get there, inside his brain, about this woman?

"I was taking a break," he said. "Anyway."

He was no longer certain that she was ugly, only that he wanted to keep looking to make sure. But in the empty room he didn't dare. This must be why people had furniture: not just for comfort but, like clothing, for camouflage. And why interrogation and torture were traditionally carried out in sparsely furnished spaces.

"When I was fifteen," she said, and her tone was such that he couldn't tell if she was talking to him or to herself, "my parents let me paint my room. We were a family—this probably sounds absurd—who never painted anything. First I wrote on the wall the things I wanted to be rid of: hypocrisy, mother, father, brother. Then I slapped on the paint, deep purple."

"Did it work?"

Her head swivelled in his direction, and he had the sense of being seen at last. "Not," she exhaled, "entirely. But I did like the feeling of making my mark. Do you ever get the glums?"

"No," he said. And then the word seemed to leap from his larynx: "Sometimes." To his own stupefaction, he imagined telling her the whole deformed story, the one his mother wanted to wrap in euphemisms, like offal in newspaper, and chuck in the dustbin. "Why 'brother'?" he asked.

"I have one." Her eyebrows dashed together. "In America, maybe." She seized a wallpaper brush and fingered the gluey bristles. "Years ago, I was hitching near Oxford, and a polystyrene salesman picked me up. The back seat of his car was full of those nice white containers, all different sizes. It started to rain, bucketing down, the windscreen wipers going lickety-split, and he said, 'Do you ever think of killing yourself?' His voice was so casual, I was sure I'd misunderstood, like you just now. I said, 'Sometimes.' "

Zeke blinked again rapidly.

"Then he asked if I'd read 'Steppenwolf.' I said yes, though to be honest I wasn't sure. It's one of those books that were in the ether for a while. I looked over at this porky, red-faced, middle-aged bloke and his eyes were brimming. 'I have,' he said. 'Every day I think of it. There's always the razor and the knife.' "

She set aside the brush and flicked a roll of lining paper. "Are you taking off the paper just to put it on again?"

The Barrows, her aunt and uncle, had asked that, too. He explained about the old houses of London, how the walls were held up by wood-chip paper. When you removed it, the best way to get a smooth finish was to put on lining paper and paint over that.

"Cup of tea?" he suggested, and, cursing himself, backed out of the room. Once, maybe twice a year, he had something that resembled a conversation, something that wasn't about fish fingers or the telly or who was effing whom. And, idiotically, he bolted. Blind rejection was one thing. To be seen, then dismissed, was quite another. He might hate his mother's mealymouthed phrases—Oh, Zeke's just under the weather—but the day, six years earlier, that she turned her shiny blue eyes upon him and said, "You'll end up in the loony bin if you carry on like this," he had felt as if a pickaxe were aimed at the very center of his forehead.

Afraid to return to the living room, he hovered beside the kettle. Give me another surge, he thought, winging his request to the head office. He heard a sound from the hall, one thud followed by another.

"Did I scare you?"

Seeing her stocking feet, he understood not only the noises he'd just heard but those that came most nights through his bedroom ceiling: one shoe, two shoes.

"Which side are you on?" he said.

"Roundheads or cavaliers? Arsenal or Chelsea? Flat earth or solar system?"

"Mr. or Mrs. Barrow." He pushed a mug of tea toward her. "Whose niece are you?"

"Mr.'s—can't you tell?" Her eyelids grew wide and her chin rose, as if defying him not to notice the similarity. "Maybe I could take Emmanuel's place."

Bewildered, Zeke stared at her feet, not broad like her hands but long and slender in dark-purple hose. Was this humor, too?

"He's not around," she said. She sounded so definite that for a moment Zeke wondered if she somehow knew Emmanuel. Then he remembered that he was the one who had told her about him, the snooker and the bad back. "Perhaps I could lend a hand."

"You?"

She gave a hoot. "I'm not offering to spend twelve hours a day up a ladder, but some things are easier with two people, like folding sheets."

I am, Zeke thought, profoundly boring, a notion not contradicted by her announcement that she was going to check out the sleeping arrangements. Heels striking the floor, she carried her tea upstairs.

Normally he quit at five, but today he kept pressing Spackle into even the smallest cracks until close to six-thirty. Then, in the face of an unbroken silence from above, he admitted defeat. He tidied his tools in the way that his old boss Ferdinand had taught him. The two of them had been united in their meticulous attitude toward objects and their hesitation toward people. "You know, they say the brain has pathways," Ferdinand had said. "Mine are covered with sand." Zeke washed his hands, and called the news of his departure, wanly, up the stairs.

"Wait." There she was on the landing. "Are you coming tomorrow? When?" Her face was once again indistinguishable.

"I aim for eight," he told her. "Shall I bring up your suitcases?"

"No."

The word hit him with such force that he grabbed the banister. He was still wondering what he'd done wrong when she added, at more normal volume, "Thanks. I need the keys." She swam down the stairs, stopping on the last one, hand outstretched. He should have guessed then, from the way her eyes fastened on his, that something was awry, that she wasn't on good terms with her aunt and uncle or that Ms. F.—weren't all fetuses female at first?—was a problematic guest, but the warmth of her breath, the lilt of her perfume, expunged rational thought. Helpless, he laid the keys in her palm.

"Will you be up to let me in?" he said.

"Up with the lark." She made a flapping motion with one hand. "Up with the milkman."

"Are you all right?" he found himself asking.

"There's always the razor and the knife," she said softly. Then—he pictured all the buses in London rising an inch into the air—she leaned forward and pressed her lips to his cheek.

The next morning, Zeke rang the bell, knocked, tried the knob. The door stayed resolutely shut, the windows adamantly blank. He even bent down and called, foolishly, through the letter box, "Hello, it's me. Zeke." By the end of five minutes, he was holding on to himself, like a kite on a gusty day. He fished around in his pockets, his bag, and was rewarded with an unmistakable vision of his mobile phone, lying on the floor beside his bed. As he walked to the corner, he counted the fag ends on the pavement, some crushed, some whole, to keep himself from floating away: seven, eight, eleven. Twice he had to stop and retrace his steps to make sure he hadn't missed one. Look down, he thought, not up. In the forecourt of the underground station, he found a free phone and, trying not to think of all the hands, the mouths, that had touched it, he picked up the receiver and dialled the Barrows' number. The answering machine clicked on with Mr. Barrow's brief, nasal message. She's popped out for a paper, he told himself, she's taking a bath. Walking back, he forgot the cigarettes and placed his feet, carefully, in the middle of each paving stone.

At the house, nothing had changed. He knocked, rang, shouted again, before climbing in through the living-room window. He had opened it the day before while using the steamer and, in the excitement of her arrival, had neglected his usual security measures. Now the ease with which the sash slid up made him feel stricken; he had left her at the mercy of any passing lunatic or thief.

Inside, he began to tiptoe toward the hall, then, reconsidering, attempted his normal gait. "Hello. Anyone home?"

He turned things on: kettle, radio, lights. No flash and zap today. He made the obligatory cup of tea and set to work. But after ten minutes of sanding he couldn't bear it. The possibility that she was gone bounded into his head and ricocheted around. And he didn't even know her name. He laid the sandpaper aside and, wiping his powdery hands on his jeans, climbed the stairs.

He had reconnoitered the first day he had the house to himself—he always did, flitting through bedrooms, checking wardrobes and drawers, cupboards and desks. It wasn't what Emmanuel thought—snooping for kinky underwear or helpful pills—but the way he coped with strange houses; he picked out a hiding place. Sometimes, when he felt particularly shaky, he even stored provisions there: a bottle of water, a packet of biscuits. Here, at the Barrows', he'd chosen the pedestal desk in the study. With his knees drawn up, he fit almost perfectly into the dark U.

Now he moved from one light-bulb-less room to another. In the master bedroom, the tattered floral wallpaper made his teeth ache. As did the disorder that seemed, mysteriously, to have worsened since his last visit. The drawers of the dressing table were half-open and several of the photographs on top lay face down. In the study, next to the desk, the row of machines—computer, printer, fax, even a photocopier—winked at him with little red or green lights. Mrs. Barrow worked at home, she'd explained, editing textbooks. Last, their son—Sean's? Seth's?—old room. She had mentioned him at their first meeting, only to be cut off by her husband in a tone that suggested the boy was already halfway to hell in a handcart. Zeke knew that his mother had for several months reacted to his name in a similar fashion.

Had he ever been so glad to see a suitcase? The larger of the two lay open at the foot of the bed. Not meaning to snoop, he stared at the contents. Almost half the case was filled with small, multicolored boxes of the kind used for earrings and necklaces; the remainder was occupied by two camera cases, a portable CD player, a clock, and a pair of silver candlesticks. For a moment, Zeke was tempted to count the boxes, each so orderly and distinct. Then he stepped over to the bed and knelt to bury his face in the pillow. Here she was, and here.

The scrape of the front door hurled him to his feet. "Hello," he called, starting down the stairs.

She was in the hall, levering off her boots, heel to toe. "I went to get us fried-egg sandwiches." She flourished a paper bag.

"I broke in," he offered.

"Brilliant," she said, handing him the bag. In the kitchen he set out plates, salt and pepper, sheets of paper towel. He had had his usual bowl of cereal only an hour ago; but now, following her example, he ate ravenously. She was wearing a faded blue sweatshirt, the sleeves rolled up, the hem stretched tight. How far along was she, he wondered, trying to recall Emmanuel's sister's configuration at various stages. Six months, maybe seven.

Watching her pepper the egg, he realized that he had dreamed about her the night before.

Only a fragment remained: she was winching a metal bucket, brimming with water, out of a well. But before he could tell her about it she was talking again, describing her stint as an office cleaner when she'd eaten a fried-egg sandwich every day. "We were meant to start at six. Instead we'd come in at eight-thirty, spray Lysol around, and sit down to our sannies. When the suits arrived at nine, they assumed we were taking a well-earned break after hours of work." She licked her lips, first lower, then upper, in a glistening circle. "So what are we doing today? Putting up paper?"

He began to stammer. He was making good progress. Besides, her aunt and uncle were paying him a fair wage.

"I'm serious," she said. "I need something to take my mind off things."

At the time, he assumed a covert reference to Ms. F. Later, when he went back and scrutinized her every utterance, it became one of those mysterious manhole covers, briefly raised over the sewer of secrecy.

Before he could voice any further objections—the dust, the fumes—she had spotted a pair of overalls hanging on the back door, and the next thing he knew she had scrambled into them and was demonstrating how well they fit; her belly split the front like a chestnut its shell. "Come on," she said. "I bet you're paid by the job, not the hour."

At first he was embarrassed telling a woman, older than him by perhaps a decade, what to do, but she turned out to be much more biddable than Emmanuel. As they finished the sanding, he on the ladder, she on foot, she lobbed questions in his direction, and despite her careless manner he sensed that she was, in fact, listening to his answers. Whereas the doctors, to a man and woman, as soon as he opened his mouth, had focussed on pencil sharpeners, radiators, doorknobs. They were paid—not enough, not by him—to barely feign attention, scribble a couple of notes, and, as quickly as possible, write a prescription that would propel him, thank God, out of their offices. But this woman, with her fierce brow, her chapped knuckles, for whatever reason, actually seemed interested.

"So," she said, folding the sandpaper onto the sanding block, "is decorating the family business? Or your heart's desire?"

"Neither." He was longing to ask about her, so he offered himself up, a pound of apples, a fistful of bananas. "My father was a greengrocer in Brighton. Got up at four every day, except Sunday, to buy the fruit and veg. Then he worked until seven at night, hauling sacks of potatoes and chatting up housewives."

"Did you live near the sea?" she asked.

"Not far. If I stood on my bed on tiptoe, there was a tiny triangle of water." He had done this precisely once, dismayed at what the maneuver had revealed. Now he climbed down the ladder, moved it four feet, climbed back up, and started on the next stretch of cornice.

"I used to think," she said, "that life would make sense if I could see the sea every day."

"Not for me. A street makes sense, a house makes sense, but the sea just goes on and on: wave, wave, wave. I couldn't wait to get away. We were ten when we moved." Even the absent-minded doctors had caught these sorts of slips. "Do you see yourself as two people?" a man with a wedge-shaped head had asked, gleefully. Barely one, he had thought but not said. She tapped her sandpaper and said nothing.

In London, Highbury, his father had a new shop, bigger and busier. "I used to help, evenings, Saturdays. Lovely tomatoes. Nice, juicy oranges. Then one day one of our regulars, Mrs. Oma, said, 'When you're the boss,' and suddenly I understood why my father was always pounding away at me about what to order, how to price stuff. I started to pay attention in school, do my homework. It drove him mad. 'Do you want to be a dreamer all your life,' he used to say, 'head stuck in a book?' "

"Careful," she said.

Beneath his savage sanding the ladder swayed like a sapling in the wind. He couldn't tell the story without jumping back into that old, hopeless arena. Over fresh sandpaper, he admitted that he had studied accounting at university. "I wanted to do anthropology—I'd read a book about the rain-forest tribes of Papua, New Guinea—but I didn't have the nerve. I needed to know that I was heading toward a job."

She didn't ask the obvious question, which, as they began to measure and cut the lining paper, enabled him to answer it. The day after his final exams, he couldn't leave the house.

"The people I shared with had all gone away, and I'd been looking forward to having the place to myself. But as soon as I stepped outside I worried that I'd left the gas on or the iron or the lights or I hadn't locked the door or I hadn't locked the window or I hadn't flushed the toilet or the cat's water bowl was empty or my mother was trying to phone. It didn't matter how often I checked, it didn't matter if I wrote down that I'd checked, I'd reach the street and have to go back. Remember in 'Gulliver's Travels' when the Lilliputians tie him down? It was like that. Hundreds of strands of anxiety tugging me back. Soon it was easier not to try to get away."

He slid the scissors through the paper, enjoying the smooth mutter of the blades. "When I got better, I knew I couldn't be an accountant. I liked numbers, but I couldn't cope with the people on the other end of them. One of our neighbors did odd jobs, so I started helping him." A strip of paper released from the roll curled back on itself and fell to the floor; he began on the next. "Ferdinand is—" He stopped, searching for the word that would embody his friend, then gave up. "I felt O.K. with him, and, gradually, he wanted to retire, so I took over the business."

"Your dad must have gone nuts."

A hot, dry wind blew through the room. Zeke dropped the scissors. "Break," he said.

He started to ask questions, the same ones she'd asked him—where she grew up, what her mum and dad did; after all these hours it seemed too late to ask her name. "You know," she said, "when you reach a certain age people don't ask what your parents do. They ask what you do."

But, without waiting, she went on. "My mother, after years as a bored housewife, runs a glorified junk shop. She invents amazing provenances for her goods: this hot-water bottle warmed the feet of Marie Antoinette; Dr. Johnson dipped his pen in this very inkwell. My father used to be a schoolteacher. Now he's a chancer. He'll bet on anything: horses, dogs, which of his children will go to rack and ruin first. He's the kind of person who tells everyone else in the cinema to shut up and then chats away for the rest of the film. I take after both of them."

"Do you mean that?" Zeke said.

She stopped and looked at him, eyes flickering. "Yes and no. You know how it is. You make every effort not to be like your parents and then you catch yourself tying your shoelaces in exactly the fussy way that your mother does. Or, even worse, doing something you don't really want to do—leaving a huge tip after a bad meal—just to be different from them."

She didn't mention Ms. F., nor did he. Every so often, Zeke would catch himself wondering whether she really existed. Then he would turn around—or her mother would—and there she was.

At lunchtime, she opened a tin of tomato soup and he made cheese sandwiches. They worked on through the darkening afternoon. Oughtn't she to take a rest? he asked. They could finish the lining paper tomorrow. But she shrugged off the suggestion. The street lights came on, buzzy amber splodges, and in the houses opposite curtains were drawn. He bungled the last piece of paper, an awkward corner, then bungled it again. "If at first you don't succeed," she chanted from the foot of the ladder, "try, try, and try again. That was my English teacher's favorite saying: Robert the Bruce and his stupid spider."

Two years ago, even one, he might have presumed himself the spider, vermin to be trampled underfoot; today he recognized encouragement. He mounted the ladder once again and, while she described the Scottish king, hiding in a cave, drawing inspiration from the arachnid's repeated efforts to anchor its web, he smoothed the top of the paper into place and, slowly descending, pressed the seams together.

Now what? he thought, glancing around the neatly papered room. Dismissal?

"Can you make a fire," she said, "while I forage?"

"A fire?" He saw himself soaking the dust sheets with petrol, the *whoompf* of flame engulfing the mute furniture. But then she pointed at the fireplace, the grate messy with cinders. Investigation proved that the Barrows had supplies. He rolled newspapers, added kindling, fire lighter, and coal, tasks he hadn't performed since leaving drafty Brighton. Meanwhile, from the kitchen came various sounds, some recognizable, some not. When he went in, she was at the stove, stirring a saucepan. "Frozen lasagna," she announced. "Tinned spinach, fresh carrots. There's beer in the cupboard under the stairs."

"Thanks. I think I'll have some Ribena."

"Don't you drink?"

"Not often. It makes me . . ." He hesitated between "weird" and "stupid" and eventually chose the latter.

"Not so stupid you don't know it." She reached for a glass, and he saw the froth of beer. Stop, he wanted to say. Ms. F. doesn't deserve to start life with a hangover. But before he could think of a polite way, or indeed any way, to voice his concern she was shouting, "Fuck, fuck."

He watched in amazement as she grabbed the saucepan and banged it against the stove, once, twice. Carrots flew.

And then he was in the hall. He had seen her wet lips stretched wide, her eyes starting out of her head, not gestures that had appeared on the poster but, combined with the shouting, fairly unequivocal. In the living room he bent to tend the fire, fighting the desire to climb out of the window and never come back. The first flare of the kindling had died down and the coals were glowing dully when he heard her footsteps.

"Sorry. I got a little carried away."

He could feel her standing behind him. Don't touch me, he thought. *Do.*

"I take my cooking seriously," she said. "Even if it is just tins. What makes you angry?"

You drinking beer, Emmanuel being a wanker, my life. Using the tongs, he moved a knob of coal an inch to the right, an inch to the left.

"If I promise to be quiet, will you come back and keep me company?"

She walked away, not waiting for an answer, and he thought of all the tiny motions—the vertebrae one after another sliding against each other, the hip joints swivelling in their sockets, the tarsals and metatarsals flexing and straightening—that make up departure. Yet the most mysterious motion, the one that couldn't be named or diagrammed, was what spilled a mood into a room. How he knew, with absolute certainty, that she wasn't taking his answer for granted, but simply leaving him alone to figure it out.

As he sat back down at the kitchen table, she was peering into the oven. "Is there a reason," she said, "for upstairs to be plunged in Stygian gloom?"

He told her about the five light bulbs of the day before. "Interesting." She turned, cheeks flushed from anger or the oven, to face him. "I'm O.K. with appliances, usually. But I can't wear a watch for more than a day or two before it goes haywire. Apparently, I make my own electricity."

They ate off a card table in front of the fire in the freshly papered room. She had found candles in the cutlery drawer, and in their light the ladder cast a hangman's shadow. They talked about computers, and whether a person could ever really disappear, and if life was better in Papua, New Guinea. She told a story about her grandfather, who had fought in the First World War.

Then, at last, she spoke about herself, but almost, Zeke noticed, as if she were talking about another person. Well, that was something he understood. He often felt as if the events in his life, the things people claimed he'd said and done, were really part of a stranger's story. His biology teacher at school had explained that the cells in the body are replaced every seven years. No wonder we don't always feel like our old selves.

"Once, years ago, I had a friend. She was the opposite of me: tiny, neat, ferociously ironic. We shared an office at my first real job, and three or four nights a week we'd go out for a drink after work. I couldn't get enough of her company."

He watched her lips, her eyes, her cheeks, the muscles of her throat and her forehead, and fewer and fewer of her words reached him. But when her story was done, the candles guttering, the fire dying, her face wore an expression that he understood. He took her hand. "You did what you could," he said, and squeezed her palm against his own. The effort of consolation made him bold.

Her face changed inexplicably, the light in her eyes leaping and fading. Had he done something wrong? Then he understood. With his free hand, he snuffed the flames.

She rose to her feet, the whole magnificent swell of her, pulled him to his feet, and led him up the stairs. "Help me," she said, presenting the overalls. Soon she was naked, ample and unabashed. Beside her Zeke felt pallid, sticklike. Can this be happening? he thought. Then she was pulling back the covers, and he was lost. Ms. F., fully acknowledged, never mentioned, lay between them.

Hours, days, weeks later she said, "I have to tell you something." For a moment she was silent, and he pictured, in the darkness, her eyebrows drawing together. "I'm no more Mr. Barrow's niece than I am a cavalier." She made a little rasping sound. "Actually, I've never laid eyes on either of the Barrows. A friend told me that the house was empty and I needed somewhere to go."

Even as she spoke, he was counting their contiguous places—thighs, hips, elbows, shoulders, floating ribs, biceps, calves—and wherever they touched he felt the slight tingling of her electricity.

"It's not fair," he had told his mother one day after school. "I can't lie like the other boys."

"Everyone lies," she had said. "You're just a slow learner."

Now he remembered how her face had changed when he asked whose niece she was.

"I knew that," he said slowly.

"And don't you wonder who I am? What I'm doing here? You saw what was in my suitcase, didn't you?"

He searched high and low, the spiral of his right ear, the knotted place behind the left temple, the hollow where his skull met his spine, the airy lattice inside his forehead, but he couldn't find a trace of wondering. The Barrows had insurance. Let her take whatever she needed for herself, and for Ms. F. What he did find, regrettable but obdurate, was his old fear of the unfamiliar.

"I have to go home," he said. "I'm sorry. It's not you. I just can't handle strange houses."

She touched his cheek.

The next morning, Zeke knocked only once before setting aside the fried-egg sandwiches—he'd asked for brown bread in an effort to offset last night's beer—and sliding the blade of his penknife under the snib of the side window. He left the bag of sandwiches on the kitchen table and climbed the stairs, hoping to find her still in bed, hoping to slip in beside her and bring as many of his current cells as possible into proximity with hers. And this time, he thought, however stupid, however embarrassing, he would ask her name.

The bed was unmade, empty and cold to the touch, the suitcases gone. At the foot of the bed the rug was rolled up and, spread-eagle on the bare wooden boards, lay the overalls, neatly buttoned, arms and legs wide, like an empty person. Only when Zeke tried to pick them up did he discover the three-inch nails that skewered the collar, pinned the cuffs and ankles to the floor.

The Turkey Season

Alice Munro

To Joe Radford

When I was fourteen I got a job at the Turkey Barn for the Christmas season. I was still too young to get a job working in a store or as a part-time waitress; I was also too nervous.

I was a turkey gutter. The other people who worked at the Turkey Barn were Lily and Marjorie and Gladys, who were also gutters; Irene and Henry, who were pluckers; Herb Abbott, the foreman, who superintended the whole operation and filled in wherever he was needed. Morgan Elliott was the owner and boss. He and his son, Morgy, did the killing.

Morgy I knew from school. I thought him stupid and despicable and was uneasy about having to consider him in a new and possibly superior guise, as the boss's son. But his father treated him so roughly, yelling and swearing at him, that he seemed no more than the lowest of the workers. The other person related to the boss was Gladys. She was his sister, and in her case there did seem to be some privilege of position. She worked slowly and went home if she was not feeling well, and was not friendly to Lily and Marjorie, although she was, a little, to me. She had come back to live with Morgan and his family after working for many years in Toronto, in a bank. This was not the sort of job she was used to. Lily and Marjorie, talking about her when she wasn't there, said she had had a nervous breakdown. They said Morgan made her work in the Turkey Barn to pay for her keep. They also said, with no worry about the contradiction, that she had taken the job because she was after a man, and that the man was Herb Abbott.

All I could see when I closed my eyes, the first few nights after working there, was turkeys. I saw them hanging upside down, plucked and stiffened, pale and cold, with the heads and necks limp, the eyes and nostrils clotted with dark blood; the remaining bits of feathers—those dark and bloody, too—seemed to form a crown. I saw them not with aversion but with a sense of endless work to be done.

Herb Abbott showed me what to do. You put the turkey down on the table and cut its head off with a cleaver. Then you took the loose skin around the neck and stripped it back to reveal the crop, nestled in the cleft between the gullet and the windpipe.

"Feel the gravel," said Herb encouragingly. He made me close my fingers around the crop. Then he showed me how to work my hand down behind it to cut it out, and the gullet and windpipe as well. He used shears to cut the vertebrae.

"Scrunch, scrunch," he said soothingly. "Now, put your hand in."

leathly cold in there, in the turkey's dark insides.

r bone splinters."

ously in the dark, I had to pull the connecting tissues loose.

Herb turned the bird over and flexed each leg. "Knees up, ... Now." He took a heavy knife and placed it directly on the knee knuckle joints and cut off the shank.

"Have a look at the worms."

Pearly-white strings, pulled out of the shank, were creeping about on their own.

"That's just the tendons shrinking. Now comes the nice part!"

He slit the bird at its bottom end, letting out a rotten smell.

"Are you educated?"

I did not know what to say.

"What's that smell?"

"Hydrogen sulfide."

"Educated," said Herb, sighing. "All right. Work your fingers around and get the guts loose. Easy. Easy. Keep your fingers together. Keep the palm inwards. Feel the ribs with the back of your hand. Feel the guts fit into your palm. Feel that? Keep going. Break the strings—as many as you can. Keep going. Feel a hard lump? That's the gizzard. Feel a soft lump? That's the heart. O.K.? O.K. Get your fingers around the gizzard. Easy. Start pulling this way. That's right. That's right. Start to pull her out."

It was not easy at all. I wasn't even sure what I had was the gizzard. My hand was full of cold pulp.

"Pull," he said, and I brought out a glistening, liverish mass.

"Got it. There's the lights. You know what they are? Lungs. There's the heart. There's the gizzard. There's the gall. Now, you don't ever want to break that gall inside or it will taste the entire turkey." Tactfully, he scraped out what I had missed, including the testicles, which were like a pair of white grapes.

"Nice pair of earrings," Herb said.

Herb Abbott was a tall, firm, plump man. His hair was dark and thin, combined straight back from a widow's peak, and his eyes seemed to be slightly slanted, so that he looked like a pale Chinese or like pictures of the Devil, except that he was smooth-faced and benign. Whatever he did around the Turkey Barn—gutting, as he was now, or loading the truck, or hanging the carcasses—was done with efficient, economical movements, quickly and buoyantly. "Notice about Herb—he always walks like he had a boat moving underneath him," Marjorie said, and it was true. Herb worked on the lake boats, during the season, as a cook. Then he worked for Morgan until after Christmas. The rest of the time he helped around the poolroom, making hamburgers, sweeping up, stopping fights before they got started. That was where he lived; he had a room above the poolroom on the main street.

In all the operations at the Turkey Barn it seemed to be Herb who had the efficiency and honor of the business continually on his mind; it was he who kept everything under control. Seeing him in the yard talking to Morgan, who was a thick, short man, red in the face, an unpredictable bully, you would be sure that it was Herb who was the boss and Morgan the hired help. But it was not so.

If I had not had Herb to show me, I don't think I could have learned turkey gutting at all. I was clumsy with my hands and had been shamed for it so often that the least show of impatience on the part of the person instructing me could have brought on a dithering paralysis. I could not stand to be watched by anybody but Herb. Particularly, I couldn't stand to be watched by Lily and Marjorie, two middle-aged sisters, who were very fast and thorough and competitive gutters. They sang at their work and talked abusively and intimately to the turkey carcasses.

"Don't you nick me, you old bugger!"

"Aren't you the old crap factory!"

I had never heard women talk like that.

Gladys was not a fast gutter, though she must have been thorough; Herb would have talked to her otherwise. She never sang and certainly she never swore. I thought her rather old, though she was not as old as Lily and Marjorie; she must have been over thirty. She seemed offended by everything that went on and had the air of keeping plenty of bitter judgments to herself. I never tried to talk to her, but she spoke to me one day in the cold little washroom off the gutting shed. She was putting pancake makeup on her face. The color of the makeup was so distinct from the color of her skin that it was as if she were slapping orange paint over a whitewashed, bumpy wall.

She asked me if my hair was naturally curly.

I said yes.

"You don't have to get a permanent?"

"No."

"You're lucky. I have to do mine up every night. The chemicals in my system won't allow me to get a permanent."

There are different ways women have of talking about their looks. Some women make it clear that what they do to keep themselves up is for the sake of sex, for men. Others, like Gladys, make the job out to be a kind of housekeeping, whose very difficulties they pride themselves on. Gladys was genteel. I could see her in the bank, in a navy-blue dress with the kind of detachable white collar you can wash at night. She would be grumpy and correct.

Another time, she spoke to me about her periods, which were profuse and painful. She wanted to know about mine. There was an uneasy, prudish, agitated expression on her face. I was saved by Irene, who was using the toilet and called out, "Do like me, and you'll be rid of all your problems for a while." Irene was only a few years older than I was, but she was recently—tardily—married, and heavily pregnant.

Gladys ignored her, running cold water on her hands. The hands of all of us were red and sore-looking from the work. "I can't use that soap. If I use it, I break out in a rash," Gladys said. "If I bring my own soap in here, I can't afford to have other people using it, because I pay a lot for it—it's a special anti-allergy soap."

I think the idea that Lily and Marjorie promoted—that Gladys was after Herb Abbott—sprang from their belief that single people ought to be teased and embarrassed whenever possible, and from their interest in Herb, which led to the feeling that somebody ought to be after him. They wondered about him. What they wondered was: How can a man want so little? No wife, no family, no house. The details of his daily life, the small preferences, were of interest. Where had he been brought up? (Here and there and all over.) How far had he gone in school? (Far enough.) Where was his girlfriend? (Never tell.) Did he drink coffee or tea if he got the choice? (Coffee.)

When they talked about Gladys's being after him they must have really wanted to talk about sex—what he wanted and what he got. They must have felt a voluptuous curiosity about him, as I did. He aroused this feeling by being circumspect and not making the jokes some men did, and at the same time by not being squeamish or gentlemanly. Some men, showing me the testicles from the turkey, would have acted as if the very existence of testicles were somehow a bad joke on me, something a girl could be taunted about; another sort of man would have been embarrassed and would have thought he had to protect me from embarrassment. A man who didn't seem to feel one way or the other was an oddity—as much to older women, probably, as to me. But what was so welcome to me may have been disturbing to them. They wanted to jolt him. They even wanted Gladys to jolt him, if she could.

There wasn't any idea then—at least in Logan, Ontario, in the late forties—about homosexuality's going beyond very narrow confines. Women, certainly, believed in its rarity and in definite boundaries. There were homosexuals in town, and we knew who they were: an elegant, light-voiced, wavy-haired paperhanger who called himself an interior decorator; the minister's widow's fat, spoiled only son, who went so far as to enter baking contests and had crocheted a tablecloth; a hypochondriacal church organist and music teacher who kept the choir and his pupils in line with screaming tantrums. Once the label was fixed, there was a good deal of tolerance for these people, and their talents for decorating, for crocheting, and for music were appreciated—especially by women. "The poor fellow," they said. "He doesn't do any harm." They really seemed to believe—the women did—that it was the penchant for baking or music that was the determining factor, and that it was this activity that made the man what he was—not any other detours he might take, or wish to take. A desire to play the violin would be taken as more a deviation from manliness than would a wish to shun women. Indeed, the idea was that any manly man would wish to shun women but most of them were caught off guard, and for good.

I don't want to go into the question of whether Herb was homosexual or not, because the definition is of no use to me. I think that probably he was, but maybe he was not. (Even considering what happened later, I think that.) He is not a puzzle so arbitrarily solved.

The other plucker, who worked with Irene, was Henry Streets, a neighbor of ours. There was nothing remarkable about him except that he was eighty-six years old and still, as he said of himself, a devil for work. He had whiskey in his thermos, and drank it from time to time through the day. It was Henry who had said to me, in our kitchen, "You ought to get yourself a job at the Turkey Barn. They need another gutter." Then my father said at once, "Not her, Henry. She's got ten thumbs," and Henry said he was just joking—it was dirty work. But I was already determined to try it—I had a great need to be successful in a job like this. I was almost in the condition of a grownup person who is ashamed of never having learned to read, so much did I feel my ineptness at manual work. Work, to everybody I knew, meant doing things I was no good at doing, and work was what people prided themselves on and measured each other by. (It goes without saying that the things I was good at, like schoolwork, were suspect or held in plain contempt.) So it was a surprise and then a triumph for me not to get fired, and to be able to turn out clean turkeys at a rate that was not disgraceful. I don't know if I really understood how much Herb Abbott was responsible for this, but he would sometimes say, "Good girl," or pat my waist and say, "You're getting to be a good gutter—you'll go a long ways in the world," and when I felt his quick, kind touch through the heavy sweater and bloody smock I wore, I felt my face glow and I wanted to lean back against him as he stood behind me. I wanted to rest my head against his wide, fleshy shoulder. When I went to sleep at night, lying on my side, I would rub my cheek against the pillow and think of that as Herb's shoulder.

I was interested in how he talked to Gladys, how he looked at her or noticed her. This interest was not jealousy. I think I wanted something to happen with them. I quivered in curious expectation, as Lily and Marjorie did. We all wanted to see the flicker of sexuality in him, hear it in his voice, not because we thought it would make him seem more like other men but because we knew that with him it would be entirely different. He was kinder and more patient than most women, and as stern and remote, in some ways, as any man. We wanted to see how he could be moved.

If Gladys wanted this, too, she didn't give any signs of it. It is impossible for me to tell with women like her whether they are as thick and deadly as they seem, not wanting anything much but opportunities for irritation and contempt, or if they are all choked up with gloomy fires and useless passions.

Marjorie and Lily talked about marriage. They did not have much good to say about it, in spite of their feeling that it was a state nobody should be allowed to stay out of. Marjorie said that shortly after her marriage she had gone into the woodshed with the intention of swallowing Paris green.

"I'd have done it," she said. "But the man came along in the grocery truck and I had to go out and buy the groceries. This was when we lived on the farm."

Her husband was cruel to her in those days, but later he suffered an accident—he rolled the tractor and was so badly hurt he would be an invalid all his life. They moved to town, and Marjorie was the boss now.

"He starts to sulk the other night and say he don't want his supper. Well, I just picked up his wrist and held it. He was scared I was going to twist his arm. He could see I'd do it. So I say, 'You *what*?' And he says, 'I'll eat it.' "

They talked about their father. He was a man of the old school. He had a noose in the woodshed (not the Paris green woodshed—this would be an earlier one, on another farm), and when they got on his nerves he used to line them up and threaten to hang them. Lily, who was the younger, would shake till she fell down. This same father had arranged to marry Marjorie off to a crony of his when she was just sixteen. That was the husband who had driven her to the Paris green. Their father did it because he wanted to be sure she wouldn't get into trouble.

"Hot blood," Lily said.

I was horrified, and asked, "Why didn't you run away?"

"His word was law," Marjorie said.

They said that was what was the matter with kids nowadays—it was the kids that ruled the roost. A father's word should be law. They brought up their own kids strictly, and none had turned out bad yet. When Marjorie's son wet the bed she threatened to cut off his dingy with the butcher knife. That cured him.

They said ninety per cent of the young girls nowadays drank, and swore, and took it lying down. They did not have daughters, but if they did and caught them at anything like that they would beat them raw. Irene, they said, used to go to the hockey games with her ski pants slit and nothing under them, for convenience in the snowdrifts afterward. Terrible.

I wanted to point out some contradictions. Marjorie and Lily themselves drank and swore, and what was so wonderful about the strong will of a father who would insure you a lifetime of unhappiness? (What I did not see was that Marjorie and Lily were not unhappy altogether—could not be, because of their sense of consequence, their pride and style.) I could be enraged then at the lack of logic in most adults' talk—the way they held to their pronouncements no matter what evidence might be presented to them. How could these women's hands be so gifted, so delicate and clever—for I knew they would be as good at dozens of other jobs as they were at gutting; they would be good at quilting and darning and painting and papering and kneading dough and setting out seedlings—and their thinking so slapdash, clumsy, infuriating?

Lily said she never let her husband come near her if he had been drinking. Marjorie said since the time she nearly died with a hemorrhage she never let her husband come near her, period. Lily said quickly that it was only when he'd been drinking that he tried anything. I could see that it was a matter of pride not to let your husband come near you, but I couldn't quite believe that "come near" meant "have sex." The idea of Marjorie and Lily being sought out for such purposes seemed grotesque. They had bad teeth, their stomachs sagged, their faces were dull and spotty. I decided to take "come near" literally.

The two weeks before Christmas was a frantic time at the Turkey Barn. I began to go in for an hour before school as well as after school and on weekends. In the morning, when I walked to work, the street lights would still be on and the morning stars shining. There was the Turkey Barn, on the edge of a white field, with a row of big pine trees behind it, and always, no matter how cold and still it was, these trees were lifting their branches and sighing and straining. It seems unlikely that on my way to the Turkey Barn, for an hour of gutting turkeys, I should have experienced such a sense of promise and at the same time of perfect, impenetrable mystery in the universe, but I did. Herb had something to do with that, and so did the cold snap—the series of hard, clear mornings. The truth is, such feelings weren't hard to come by then. I would get them but not know how they were to be connected with anything in real life.

One morning at the Turkey Barn there was a new gutter. This was a boy eighteen or nineteen years old, a stranger named Brian. It seemed he was a relative, or perhaps just a friend, of Herb Abbott's. He was staying with Herb. He had worked on a lake boat last summer. He said he had got sick of it, though, and quit.

What he said was, "Yeah, fuckin' boats, I got sick of that."

Language at the Turkey Barn was coarse and free, but this was one word never heard there. And Brian's use of it seemed not careless but flaunting, mixing insult and provocation. Perhaps it was his general style that made it so. He had amazing good looks: taffy hair, bright-blue eyes, ruddy skin, well-shaped body—the sort of good looks nobody disagrees about for a moment. But a single, relentless notion had got such a hold on him that he could not keep from turning all his assets into parody. His mouth was wet-looking and slightly open most of the time, his eyes were half shut, his expression a hopeful leer, his movements indolent, exaggerated, inviting. Perhaps if he had been put on a stage with a microphone and a guitar and let grunt and howl and wriggle and excite, he would have seemed a true celebrant. Lacking a stage, he was unconvincing. After a while he seemed just like somebody with a bad case of hiccups—his insistent sexuality was that monotonous and meaningless.

If he had toned down a bit, Marjorie and Lily would probably have enjoyed him. They could have kept up a game of telling him to shut his filthy mouth and keep his hands to himself. As it was, they said they were sick of him, and meant it. Once, Marjorie took up her gutting knife. "Keep your distance," she said. "I mean from me and my sister and that kid."

She did not tell him to keep his distance from Gladys, because Gladys wasn't there at the time and Marjorie would probably not have felt like protecting her anyway. But it was Gladys Brian particularly liked to bother. She would throw down her knife and go into the washroom and stay there ten minutes and come out with a stony face. She didn't say she was sick anymore and go home, the way she used to. Marjorie said Morgan was mad at Gladys for sponging and she couldn't get away with it any longer.

Gladys said to me, "I can't stand that kind of thing. I can't stand people mentioning that kind of thing and that kind of—gestures. It makes me sick to my stomach."

I believed her. She was terribly white. But why, in that case, did she not complain to Morgan? Perhaps relations between them were too uneasy, perhaps she could not bring herself to repeat or describe such things. Why did none of us complain—if not to Morgan, at least to Herb? I never thought of it. Brian seemed just something to put up with, like the freezing cold in the gutting shed and the smell of blood and waste. When Marjorie and Lily did threaten to complain, it was about Brian's laziness.

He was not a good gutter. He said his hands were too big. So Herb took him off gutting, told him he was to sweep and clean up, make packages of giblets, and help load the truck. This meant that he did not have to be in any one place or doing any one job at a given time, so much of the time he did nothing. He would start sweeping up, leave that and mop the tables, leave that and have a cigarette, lounge against the table bothering us until Herb called him to help load. Herb was very busy now and spent a lot of time making deliveries, so it was possible he did not know the extent of Brian's idleness.

"I don't know why Herb don't fire you," Marjorie said. "I guess the answer is he don't want you hanging around sponging on him, with no place to go."

"I know where to go," said Brian.

"Keep your sloppy mouth shut," said Marjorie. "I pity Herb. Getting saddled."

On the last school day before Christmas we got out early in the afternoon. I went home and changed my clothes and came into work at about three o'clock. Nobody was working. Everybody was in the gutting shed, where Morgan Elliott was swinging a cleaver over the gutting table and yelling. I couldn't make out what the yelling was about, and thought someone must have made a terrible mistake in his work; perhaps it had been me. Then I saw Brian on the other side of the table, looking very sulky and mean, and standing well back. The sexual leer was not altogether gone from his face, but it was flattened out and mixed with a look of impotent bad temper and some fear. That's it, I thought; Brian is getting fired for being so sloppy and lazy. Even when I made out Morgan saying "pervert" and "filthy" and "maniac," I still thought that was what was happening. Marjorie and Lily, and even brassy Irene, were standing around with downcast, rather pious looks, such as children get when somebody is suffering a terrible bawling out at school. Only old Henry seemed able to keep a cautious grin on his face. Gladys was not to be seen. Herb was standing closer to Morgan than anybody else. He was not interfering but was keeping an eye on the cleaver. Morgy was blubbering, though he didn't seem to be in any immediate danger.

Morgan was yelling at Brian to get out. "And out of this town—I mean it—and don't you wait till tomorrow if you still want your arse in one piece! Out!" he shouted, and the cleaver swung dramatically towards the door. Brian started in that direction but, whether he meant to or not, he made a swaggering, taunting motion of the buttocks. This made Morgan break into a roar and run after him, swinging the cleaver in a stagy way. Brian ran, and Morgan ran after him, and Irene screamed and grabbed her stomach. Morgan was too heavy to run any distance and probably could not have thrown the cleaver very far, either. Herb watched from the doorway. Soon Morgan came back and flung the cleaver down on the table.

"All back to work! No more gawking around here! You don't get paid for gawking! What are you getting under way at?" he said, with a hard look at Irene.

"Nothing," Irene said meekly.

"If you're getting under way get out of here."

"I'm not."

"All right, then!"

We got to work. Herb took off his blood-smeared smock and put on his jacket and went off, probably to see that Brian got ready to go on the supper-time bus. He did not say a word. Morgan and his son went out to the yard, and Irene and Henry went back to the adjoining shed, where they did the plucking, working knee-deep in the feathers Brian was supposed to keep swept up.

"Where's Gladys?" I said softly.

"Recuperating," said Marjorie. She, too, spoke in a quieter voice than usual, and "recuperating" was not the sort of word she and Lily normally used. It was a word to be used about Gladys, with a mocking intent.

They didn't want to talk about what had happened, because they were afraid Morgan might come in and catch them at it and fire them. Good workers as they were, they were afraid of that. Besides, they hadn't seen anything. They must have been annoyed that they hadn't. All I ever found out was that Brian had either done something or shown something to Gladys as she came out of the washroom and she had started screaming and having hysterics.

Now she'll likely be laid up with another nervous breakdown, they said. And he'll be on his way out of town. And good riddance, they said, to both of them.

I have a picture of the Turkey Barn crew taken on Christmas Eve. It was taken with a flash camera that was someone's Christmas extravagance. I think it was Irene's. But Herb Abbott must have been the one who took the picture. He was the one who could be trusted to know or to learn immediately how to manage anything new, and flash cameras were fairly new at the time. The picture was taken about ten o'clock on Christmas Eve, after Herb and Morgy had come back from making the last delivery and we had washed off the gutting table and swept and mopped the cement floor. We had taken off our bloody smocks and heavy sweaters and gone into the little room called the lunchroom, where there was a table and a heater. We still wore our working clothes: overalls and shirts. The men wore caps and the women kerchiefs, tied in the wartime style. I am stout and cheerful and comradely in the picture, transformed into someone I don't ever remember being or pretending to be. I look years older than fourteen. Irene is the only one who has taken off her kerchief, freeing her long red hair. She peers out from it with a meek, sluttish, inviting look, which would match her reputation but is not like any look of hers I remember. Yes, it must have been her camera; she is posing for it, with that look, more deliberately than anyone else is. Marjorie and Lily are smiling, true to form, but their smiles are sour and reckless. With their hair hidden, and such figures as they have bundled up, they look like a couple of tough and jovial but testy workmen. Their kerchiefs look misplaced; caps would be better. Henry is in high spirits, glad to be part of the work force, grinning and looking twenty years younger than his age. Then Morgy, with his hangdog look, not trusting the occasion's bounty, and Morgan very flushed and bosslike and satisfied. He has just given each of us our bonus turkey. Each of these turkeys has a leg or a wing missing, or a malformation of some kind, so none of them are salable at the full price. But Morgan has been at pains to tell us that you often get the best meat off the gimpy ones, and he has shown us that he's taking one home himself.

We are all holding mugs or large, thick china cups, which contain not the usual tea but rye whiskey. Morgan and Henry have been drinking since suppertime. Marjorie and Lily say they only want a little, and only take it at all because it's Christmas Eve and they are dead on their feet. Irene says she's dead on her feet as well but that doesn't mean she only wants a little. Herb has poured quite generously not just for her but for Lily and Marjorie, too, and they do not object. He has measured mine and Morgy's out at the same time, very stingily, and poured in Coca-Cola. This is the first drink I have ever had, and as a result I will believe for years that rye-and-Coca-Cola is a standard sort of drink and will always ask for it, until I notice that few other people drink it and that it makes me sick. I didn't get sick that Christmas Eve, though; Herb had not given me enough. Except for an odd taste, and my own feeling of consequence, it was like drinking Coca-Cola.

I don't need Herb in the picture to remember what he looked like. That is, if he looked like himself, as he did all the time at the Turkey Barn and the few times I saw him on the street—as he did all the times in my life when I saw him except one.

The time he looked somewhat unlike himself was when Morgan was cursing out Brian and, later, when Brian had run off down the road. What was this different look? I've tried to remember, because I studied it hard at the time. It wasn't much different. His face looked softer and heavier then, and if you had to describe the expression on it you would have to say it was an expression of shame. But what would he be ashamed of? Ashamed of Brian, for the way he had behaved? Surely that would be late in the day; when had Brian ever behaved otherwise? Ashamed of Morgan, for carrying on so ferociously and theatrically? Or of himself, because he was famous for nipping fights and displays of this sort in the bud and hadn't been able to do it here? Would he be ashamed that he hadn't stood up for Brian? Would he have expected himself to do that, to stand up for Brian?

All this was what I wondered at the time. Later, when I knew more, at least about sex, I decided that Brian was Herb's lover, and that Gladys really was trying to get attention from Herb, and that that was why Brian had humiliated her—with or without Herb's connivance and consent. Isn't it true that people like Herb—dignified, secretive, honorable people—will often choose somebody like Brian, will waste their helpless love on some vicious, silly person who is not even evil, or a monster, but just some importunate nuisance? I decided that Herb, with all his gentleness and carefulness, was avenging himself on us all—not just on Gladys but on us all—with Brian, and that what he was feeling when I studied his face must have been a savage and gleeful scorn. But embarrassment as well—embarrassment for Brian and for himself and for Gladys, and to some degree for all of us. Shame for all of us—that is what I thought then.

Later still, I backed off from this explanation. I got to a stage of backing off from the things I couldn't really know. It's enough for me now just to think of Herb's face with that peculiar, stricken look; to think of Brian monkeying in the shade of Herb's dignity; to think of my own mystified concentration on Herb, my need to catch him out, if I could ever get the chance, and then move in and stay close to him. How attractive, how delectable, the prospect of intimacy is, with the very person who will never grant it. I can still feel the pull of a man like that, of his promising and refusing. I would still like to know things. Never mind facts. Never mind theories, either.

When I finished my drink I wanted to say something to Herb. I stood beside him and waited for a moment when he was not listening to or talking with anyone else and when the increasingly rowdy conversation of the others would cover what I had to say.

"I'm sorry your friend had to go away."

"That's all right."

Herb spoke kindly and with amusement, and so shut me off from any further right to look at or speak about his life. He knew what I was up to. He must have known it before, with lots of women. He knew how to deal with it.

Lily had a little more whiskey in her mug and told how she and her best girlfriend (dead now, of liver trouble) had dressed up as men one time and gone into the men's side of the beer parlor, the side where it said "Men Only," because they wanted to see what it was like. They sat in a corner drinking beer and keeping their eyes and ears open, and nobody looked twice or thought a thing about them, but soon a problem arose.

"Where were we going to go? If we went around to the other side and anybody seen us going into the ladies', they would scream bloody murder. And if we went into the men's somebody'd be sure to notice we didn't do it the right way. Meanwhile the beer was going through us like a bugger!"

"What you don't do when you're young!" Marjorie said.

Several people gave me and Morgy advice. They told us to enjoy ourselves while we could. They told us to stay out of trouble. They said they had all been young once. Herb said we were a good crew and had done a good job but he didn't want to get in bad with any of the women's husbands by keeping them there too late. Marjorie and Lily expressed indifference to their husbands, but Irene announced that she loved hers and that it was not true that he had been dragged back from Detroit to marry her, no matter what people said. Henry said it was a good life if you didn't weaken. Morgan said he wished us all the most sincere Merry Christmas.

When we came out of the Turkey Barn it was snowing. Lily said it was like a Christmas card, and so it was, with the snow whirling around the street lights in town and around the colored lights people had put up outside their doorways. Morgan was giving Henry and Irene a ride home in the truck, acknowledging age and pregnancy and Christmas. Morgy took a shortcut through the field, and Herb walked off by himself, head down and hands in his pockets, rolling slightly, as if he were on the deck of a lake boat. Marjorie and Lily linked arms with me as if we were old comrades.

"Let's sing," Lily said. "What'll we sing?"

" 'We Three Kings'?" said Marjorie. " 'We Three Turkey Gutters'?"

" 'I'm Dreaming of a White Christmas.' "

"Why dream? You got it!"

So we sang.

Orientation

Daniel Orozco

Those are the offices and these are the cubicles. That's my cubicle there, and this is your cubicle. This is your phone. Never answer your phone. Let the Voicemail System answer it. This is your Voicemail System Manual. There are no personal phone calls allowed. We do, however, allow for emergencies. If you must make an emergency phone call, ask your supervisor first. If you can't find your supervisor, ask Phillip Spiers, who sits over there. He'll check with Clarissa Nicks, who sits over there. If you make an emergency phone call without asking, you may be let go.

These are your IN and OUT boxes. All the forms in your IN box must be logged in by the date shown in the upper left-hand corner, initialed by you in the upper right-hand corner, and distributed to the Processing Analyst whose name is numerically coded in the lower left-hand corner. The lower right-hand corner is left blank. Here's your Processing Analyst Numerical Code Index. And here's your Forms Processing Procedures Manual.

You must pace your work. What do I mean? I'm glad you asked that. We pace our work according to the eight-hour workday. If you have twelve hours of work in your IN box, for example, you must compress that work into the eight-hour day. If you have one hour of work in your IN box, you must expand that work to fill the eight-hour day. That was a good question. Feel free to ask questions. Ask too many questions, however, and you may be let go.

That is our receptionist. She is a temp. We go through receptionists here. They quit with alarming frequency. Be polite and civil to the temps. Learn their names, and invite them to lunch occasionally. But don't get close to them, as it only makes it more difficult when they leave. And they always leave. You can be sure of that.

The men's room is over there. The women's room is over there. John LaFountaine, who sits over there, uses the women's room occasionally. He says it is accidental. We know better, but we let it pass. John LaFountaine is harmless, his forays into the forbidden territory of the women's room simply a benign thrill, a faint blip on the dull flat line of his life.

Russell Nash, who sits in the cubicle to your left, is in love with Amanda Pierce, who sits in the cubicle to your right. They ride the same bus together after work. For Amanda Pierce, it is just a tedious bus ride made less tedious by the idle nattering of Russell Nash. But for Russell Nash, it is the highlight of his day. It is the highlight of his life. Russell Nash has put on forty pounds, and grows fatter with each passing month, nibbling on chips and cookies while peeking glumly over the partitions at Amanda Pierce, and gorging himself at home on cold pizza and ice cream while watching adult videos on TV.

Amanda Pierce, in the cubicle to your right, has a six-year-old son named Jamie, who is autistic. Her cubicle is plastered from top to bottom with the boy's crayon artwork—sheet after sheet of precisely drawn concentric circles and ellipses, in black and yellow. She rotates them every other Friday. Be sure to comment on them. Amanda Pierce also has a husband, who is a lawyer. He subjects her to an escalating array of painful and humiliating sex games, to which Amanda Pierce reluctantly submits. She comes to work exhausted and freshly wounded each morning, wincing from the abrasions on her breasts, or the bruises on her abdomen, or the second-degree burns on the backs of her thighs.

But we're not supposed to know any of this. Do not let on. If you let on, you may be let go.

Amanda Pierce, who tolerates Russell Nash, is in love with Albert Bosch, whose office is over there. Albert Bosch, who only dimly registers Amanda Pierce's existence, has eyes only for Ellie Tapper, who sits over there. Ellie Tapper, who hates Albert Bosch, would walk through fire for Curtis Lance. But Curtis Lance hates Ellie Tapper. Isn't the world a funny place? Not in the ha-ha sense, of course.

Anika Bloom sits in that cubicle. Last year, while reviewing quarterly reports in a meeting with Barry Hacker, Anika Bloom's left palm began to bleed. She fell into a trance, stared into her hand, and told Barry Hacker when and how his wife would die. We laughed it off. She was, after all, a new employee. But Barry Hacker's wife is dead. So unless you want to know exactly when and how you'll die, never talk to Anika Bloom.

Colin Heavey sits in that cubicle over there. He was new once, just like you. We warned him about Anika Bloom. But at last year's Christmas Potluck, he felt sorry for her when he saw that no one was talking to her. Colin Heavey brought her a drink. He hasn't been himself since. Colin Heavey is doomed. There's nothing he can do about it, and we are powerless to help him. Stay away from Colin Heavey. Never give any of your work to him. If he asks to do something, tell him you have to check with me. If he asks again, tell him I haven't gotten back to you.

This is the Fire Exit. There are several on this floor, and they are marked accordingly. We have a Floor Evacuation Review every three months, and an Escape Route Quiz once a month. We have our Biannual Fire Drill twice a year, and our Annual Earthquake Drill once a year. These are precautions only. These things never happen.

For your information, we have a comprehensive health plan. Any catastrophic illness, any unforeseen tragedy is completely covered. All dependents are completely covered. Larry Bagdikian, who sits over there, has six daughters. If anything were to happen to any of his girls, or to all of them, if all six were to simultaneously fall victim to illness or injury—stricken with a hideous degenerative muscle disease or some rare toxic blood disorder, sprayed with semiautomatic gunfire while on a class field trip, or attacked in their bunk beds by some prowling nocturnal lunatic—if any of this were to pass, Larry's girls would all be taken care of. Larry Bagdikian would not have to pay one dime. He would have nothing to worry about.

We also have a generous vacation and sick leave policy. We have an excellent disability insurance plan. We have a stable and profitable pension fund. We get group discounts for the symphony, and block seating at the ballpark. We get commuter ticket books for the bridge. We have Direct Deposit. We are all members of Costco.

This is our kitchenette. And this, this is our Mr. Coffee. We have a coffee pool, into which we each pay two dollars a week for coffee, filters, sugar, and CoffeeMate. If you prefer Cremora or half-and-half to CoffeeMate, there is a special pool for three dollars a week. If you prefer Sweet'n Low to sugar, there is a special pool for two-fifty a week. We do not do decaf. You are allowed to join the coffee pool of your choice, but you are not allowed to touch the Mr. Coffee.

This is the microwave oven. You are allowed to *heat* food in the microwave oven. You are not, however, allowed to *cook* food in the microwave oven.

We get one hour for lunch. We also get one fifteen-minute break in the morning, and one fifteen-minute break in the afternoon. Always take your breaks. If you skip a break, it is gone forever. For your information, your break is a privilege, not a right. If you abuse the break policy, we are authorized to rescind your breaks. Lunch, however, is a right, not a privilege. If you abuse the lunch policy, our hands will be tied, and we will be forced to look the other way. We will not enjoy that.

This is the refrigerator. You may put your lunch in it. Barry Hacker, who sits over there, steals food from this refrigerator. His petty theft is an outlet for his grief. Last New Year's Eve, while kissing his wife, a blood vessel burst in her brain. Barry Hacker's wife was two months pregnant at the time, and lingered in a coma for half a year before dying. It was a tragic loss for Barry Hacker. He hasn't been himself since. Barry Hacker's wife was a beautiful woman. She was also completely covered. Barry Hacker did not have to pay one dime. But his dead wife haunts him. She haunts all of us. We have seen her, reflected in the monitors of our computers, moving past our cubicles. We have seen the dim shadow of her face in our photocopies. She pencils herself in in the receptionist's appointment book, with the notation: To see Barry Hacker. She has left messages in the receptionist's Voicemail box, messages garbled by the electronic chirrups and buzzes in the phone line, her voice echoing from an immense distance within the ambient hum. But the voice is hers. And beneath her voice, beneath the tidal *whoosh* of static and hiss, the gurgling and crying of a baby can be heard.

In any case, if you bring a lunch, put a little something extra in the bag for Barry Hacker. We have four Barrys in this office. Isn't that a coincidence?

This is Matthew Payne's office. He is our Unit Manager, and his door is always closed. We have never seen him, and you will never see him. But he is here. You can be sure of that. He is all around us.

This is the Custodian's Closet. You have no business in the Custodian's Closet.

And this, this is our Supplies Cabinet. If you need supplies, see Curtis Lance. He will log you in on the Supplies Cabinet Authorization Log, then give you a Supplies Authorization Slip. Present your pink copy of the Supplies Authorization Slip to Ellie Tapper. She will log you in on the Supplies Cabinet Key Log, then give you the key. Because the Supplies Cabinet is located outside the Unit Manager's office, you must be very quiet. Gather your supplies quietly. The Supplies Cabinet is divided into four sections. Section One contains letterhead stationery, blank paper and envelopes, memo and note pads, and so on. Section Two contains pens and pencils and typewriter and printer ribbons, and the like. In Section Three we have erasers, correction fluids, transparent tapes, glue sticks, et cetera. And in Section Four we have paper clips and push pins and scissors and razor blades. And here are the spare blades for the shredder. Do not touch the shredder, which is located over there. The shredder is of no concern to you.

Gwendolyn Stich sits in that office there. She is crazy about penguins, and collects penguin knickknacks: penguin posters and coffee mugs and stationery, penguin stuffed animals, penguin jewelry, penguin sweaters and T-shirts and socks. She has a pair of penguin fuzzy slippers she wears when working late at the office. She has a tape cassette of penguin sounds which she listens to for relaxation. Her favorite colors are black and white. She has personalized license plates that read PEN GWEN. Every morning, she passes through all the cubicles to wish each of us a *good* morning. She brings Danish on Wednesdays for Hump Day morning break, and doughnuts on Fridays for TGIF afternoon break. She organizes the Annual Christmas Potluck, and is in charge of the Birthday List. Gwendolyn Stich's door is always open to all of us. She will always lend an ear, and put in a good word for you; she will always give you a hand, or the shirt off her back, or a shoulder to cry on. Because her door is always open, she hides and cries in a stall in the women's room. And John LaFountaine—who, enthralled when a woman enters, sits quietly in his stall with his knees to his chest—John LaFountaine has heard her vomiting in there. We have come upon Gwendolyn Stich huddled in the stairwell, shivering in the updraft, sipping a Diet Mr. Pibb and hugging her knees. She does not let any of this interfere with her work. If it interfered with her work, she might have to be let go.

Kevin Howard sits in that cubicle over there. He is a serial killer, the one they call the Carpet Cutter, responsible for the mutilations across town. We're not supposed to know that, so do not let on. Don't worry. His compulsion inflicts itself on strangers only, and the routine established is elaborate and unwavering. The victim must be a white male, a young adult no older than thirty, heavyset, with dark hair and eyes, and the like. The victim must be chosen at random, before sunset, from a public place; the victim is followed home, and must put up a struggle; et cetera. The carnage inflicted is precise: the angle and direction of the incisions; the layering of skin and muscle tissue; the rearrangement of the visceral organs; and so on. Kevin Howard does not let any of this interfere with his work. He is, in fact, our fastest typist. He types as if he were on fire. He has a secret crush on Gwendolyn Stich, and leaves a red-foil-wrapped Hershey's Kiss on her desk every afternoon. But he hates Anika Bloom, and keeps well away from her. In his presence, she has uncontrollable fits of shaking and trembling. Her left palm does not stop bleeding.

In any case, when Kevin Howard gets caught, act surprised. Say that he seemed like a nice person, a bit of a loner, perhaps, but always quiet and polite.

This is the photocopier room. And this, this is our view. It faces southwest. West is down there, toward the water. North is back there. Because we are on the seventeenth floor, we are afforded a magnificent view. Isn't it beautiful? It overlooks the park, where the tops of those trees are. You can see a segment of the bay between those two buildings there. You can see the sun set in the gap between those two buildings over there. You can see this building reflected in the glass panels of that building across the way. There. See? That's you, waving. And look there. There's Anika Bloom in the kitchenette, waving back.

Enjoy this view while photocopying. If you have problems with the photocopier, see Russell Nash. If you have any questions, ask your supervisor. If you can't find your supervisor, ask Phillip Spiers. He sits over there. He'll check with Clarissa Nicks. She sits over there. If you can't find them, feel free to ask me. That's my cubicle. I sit in there.

Pilgrims

Julie Orringer

It was Thanksgiving Day and hot, because this was New Orleans; they were driving uptown to have dinner with strangers. Ella pushed at her loose tooth with the tip of her tongue and fanned her legs with the hem of her velvet dress. On the seat beside her, Benjamin fidgeted with his shirt buttons. He had worn his Pilgrim costume, brown shorts and a white shirt and yellow paper buckles taped to his shoes. In the front seat their father drove without a word, while their mother dozed against the window glass. She wore a blue dress and a strand of jade beads and a knit cotton hat beneath which she was bald.

Three months earlier, Ella's father had explained what chemotherapy was and how it would make her mother better. He had even taken Ella to the hospital once when her mother had a treatment. She remembered it like a filmstrip from school, a series of connected images she wished she didn't have to watch: her mother with an IV needle in her arm, the steady drip from the bag of orange liquid, her father speaking softly to himself as he paced the room, her mother shaking so hard she had to be tied down.

At night Ella and her brother tapped a secret code against the wall that separated their rooms: one knock, I'm afraid; two knocks, Don't worry; three knocks, Are you still awake? four, Come quick. And then there was the Emergency Signal, a stream of knocks that kept on coming, which meant her brother could hear their mother and father crying in their bedroom. If it went on for more than a minute, Ella would give four knocks and her brother would run to her room and crawl under the covers.

There were changes in the house, healing rituals that required Ella's mother to go outside and embrace trees or lie face-down on the grass. Sometimes she did a kind of Asian dance that looked like karate. She ate bean paste and Japanese vegetables, or sticky brown rice wrapped in seaweed. And now they were going to have dinner with people they had never met, people who ate seaweed and brown rice every day of their lives.

They drove through the Garden District, where Spanish moss hung like beards from the trees. Once during Mardi Gras, Ella had ridden a trolley here with her brother and grandmother, down to the French Quarter, where they'd eaten beignets at Café du Monde. She wished she were sitting in one of those wrought-iron chairs and shaking powdered sugar onto a beignet. How much better than to be surrounded by strangers, eating food that tasted like the bottom of the sea.

They turned onto a side street, and her father studied the directions. "It should be at the end of this block," he said.

Ella's mother shifted in her seat. "Where are we?" she asked, her voice dreamy with painkillers.

"Almost there," said Ella's father.

They pulled to the curb in front of a white house with sagging porches and a trampled lawn. Vines covered the walls and moss grew thick and green between the roof slates. Under the porte-cochere stood a beat-up Honda and a Volkswagen with mismatched side panels. A faded bigwheel lay on its side on the walk.

"Come on," their father said, and gave them a tired smile. "Time for fun." He got out of the car and opened the doors for Ella and Ben and their mother, sweeping his arm chauffeur-like as they climbed out.

Beside the front door was a tarnished doorbell in the shape of a lion's head. "Push it," her father said. Ella pushed. A sound like church bells echoed inside the house.

Then the door swung open and there was Mister Kaplan, a tall man with wiry orange hair and big dry-looking teeth. He shook hands with Ella's parents, so long and vigorously it seemed to Ella he might as well say *Congratulations.*

"And you must be Ben and Ella," he said, bending down.

Ella gave a mute nod. Her brother kicked at the doorjamb.

"Well, come on in," he said. "I have a tree castle out back."

Benjamin's face came up, twisted with skepticism. "A what?"

"The kids are back there. They'll show you."

"What an interesting foyer," their mother said. She bent down to look at the brass animals on the floor, a turtle and a jackal and a llama. Next to the animals stood a blue vase full of rusty metal flowers. A crystal chandelier dangled from the ceiling, its arms hung with dozens of God's-eyes and tiny plastic babies from Mardi Gras king cakes. On a low wooden shelf against the wall, pair after pair of canvas sandals and sneakers and Birkenstocks were piled in a heap. A crayoned sign above it said SHOES OFF NOW!

Ella looked down at her feet. She was wearing her new patent-leather Mary Janes.

"Your socks are nice too," her father said, and touched her shoulder. He stepped out of his own brown loafers and set them on top of the pile. Then he knelt before Ella's mother and removed her pumps. "Shoes off," he said to Ella and Ben.

"Even me?" Ben said. He looked down at his paper buckles.

Their father took off Ben's shoes and removed the paper buckles, tape intact. Then he pressed one buckle onto each of Ben's socks. "There," he said.

Ben looked as if he might cry.

"Everyone's in the kitchen," Mister Kaplan said. "We're all cooking."

"Marvelous," said Ella's mother. "We love to cook."

They followed him down a cavern of a hall, its walls decorated with sepia-toned photographs of children and parents, all of them staring stone-faced from their gilt frames. They passed a sweep of stairs and a room with nothing in it but straw mats and pictures of blue Indian goddesses sitting on beds of cloud.

"What's that room?" Benjamin asked.

"Meditation room," Mister Kaplan said, as if it were as commonplace as a den.

The kitchen smelled of roasting squash and baked apples and spices. There was an old brick oven and a stove with so many burners it looked as if it had been stolen from a restaurant. At the kitchen table, men and women with long hair and loose clothes sliced vegetables or stirred things into bowls. Some of them wore knitted hats like her mother, their skin dull-gray, their eyes purple-shaded underneath. To Ella it seemed they could be relatives of her mother's, shameful cousins recently discovered.

A tall woman with a green scarf around her waist came over and embraced Ella's mother, then bent down to hug Ella and Benjamin. She smelled of smoky perfume. Her wide eyes skewed in different directions, as if she were watching two movies projected into opposite corners of the room. Ella did not know how to look at her.

"We're so happy you decided to come," the woman said. "I'm Delilah, Eddy's sister."

"Who's Eddy?" said Ben.

"Mister Kaplan," their father said.

"We use our real names here," Delilah said. "No one is a mister."

She led their parents over to the long table and put utensils into their hands. Their mother was to mix oats into a pastry crust, and their father to chop carrots, something Ella had never seen him do. He looked around in panic, then hunched over and began cutting a carrot into clumsy pieces. He kept glancing at the man to his left, a bearded man with a shaved head, as if to make sure he was doing it right.

Delilah gave Ella and Benjamin hard cookies that tasted like burnt rice. It seemed Ella would have to chew forever. Her loose tooth waggled in its socket.

"The kids are all out back," Delilah said. "There's plenty of time to play before dinner."

"What kids?" Benjamin asked.

"You'll see," said Delilah. She tilted her head at Ella, one of her eyes moving over Ella's velvet dress. "Here's a little trick I learned when I was a girl," she said. In one swift movement she took the back hem of the dress, brought it up between Ella's knees, and tucked it into the sash. "Now you're wearing shorts," she said.

Ella didn't feel like she was wearing shorts. As soon as Delilah turned away, she pulled her skirt out of her sash and let it fall around her legs.

The wooden deck outside was cluttered with Tinkertoys and clay flowerpots and Little Golden Books. Ella heard children screaming and laughing nearby. As she and Benjamin moved to the edge of the deck, there was a rustle in the bushes and a skinny boy leaped out and pointed a suction-cup arrow at them. He stood there breathing hard, his hair full of leaves, his chest bare. "You're on duty," he said.

"Me?" Benjamin said.

"Yes, you. Both of you." The boy motioned them off the porch with his arrow and took them around the side of the house. There, built into the side of a sprawling oak, was the biggest, most sophisticated tree house Ella had ever seen. There were tiny rooms of sagging plywood, and rope ladders hanging down from doors, and a telescope and a fireman's pole and a red net full of leaves. From one wide platform—almost as high as the top of the house—it seemed you could jump down onto a huge trampoline. Even higher was a kind of crow's nest, a little circular platform built around the trunk. A red-painted sign on the railing read DAGNER! Ella could hear the other children screaming but she couldn't see them. A collie dog barked crazily, staring up at the tree.

"Take off your socks! That's an order," the skinny boy said.

Benjamin glanced at Ella. Ella shrugged. It seemed ridiculous to walk around outside in socks. She bent and peeled off her anklets. Benjamin carefully removed his Pilgrim buckles and put them in his pocket, then sat down and took off his socks. The skinny boy grabbed the socks from their hands and tucked them into the waistband of his shorts.

The mud was thick and cold between Ella's toes, and pecan shells bit her feet as the boy herded them toward the tree house. He prodded Ella toward a ladder of prickly-looking rope. When she stepped onto the first rung, the ladder swung toward the tree and her toes banged against the trunk. The skinny boy laughed.

"Go on," he said. "Hurry up. And no whining."

The rope burned her hands and feet as she ascended. The ladder seemed to go on forever. Ben followed below, making the rope buck and sway as they climbed. At the top there was a small square opening, and Ella thrust both her arms inside and pulled herself into a dark coop. As she stood, her head knocked against something dangling from the ceiling on a length of string. It was a bird's skull, no bigger than a walnut. Dozens of others hung from the ceiling around her. Benjamin huddled at her side.

"Sick," he said.

"Don't look," Ella said.

The suction-cup arrow came up through the hole in the floor.

"Keep going," said the boy. "You're not there yet."

"Go where?" Ella said.

"Through the wall."

Ella brushed the skulls out of her way and leveled her shoulder against one of the walls. It creaked open like a door. Outside, a tree limb as thick as her torso extended up to another plywood box, this one much larger than the first. Ella dropped to her knees and crawled upward. Benjamin followed.

Apparently this was the hostage room. Four kids stood in the semidarkness, wide-eyed and still as sculptures, each bound at the ankles and wrists with vine handcuffs. Two of the kids, a boy and a girl, were so skinny that Ella could see the outlines of bones in their arms and legs. Their hair was patchy and ragged, their eyes black and almond-shaped. In the corner, a white-haired boy in purple overalls whimpered softly to himself. And at the center of the room a girl Benjamin's age stood tied to the tree trunk with brown string. She had the same wild gray eyes and leafy hair as the boy with the arrow.

"It's mine, it's *my* tree house," she said as Ella stared at her.

"Is Mister Kaplan your dad?" Benjamin said.

"My dat-*tee,*" the girl corrected him.

"Where's your mom?"

"She died," said the girl, and looked him fiercely in the eye.

Benjamin sucked in his breath and glanced at Ella.

Ella wanted to hit this girl. She bent down close to the girl's face, making her eyes small and mean. "If this is so your tree house," Ella said, "then how come you're tied up?"

"It's *jail,*" the girl spat. "In jail you get tied up."

"We could untie you," said Benjamin. He tugged at one of her bonds.

The girl opened her mouth and let out a scream so shrill Ella's eardrums buzzed. Once, as her father had pulled into the driveway at night, he had trapped a rabbit by the leg beneath the wheel of his car; the rabbit had made a sound like that. Benjamin dropped the string and moved against Ella, and the children with ragged hair laughed and jumped on the platform until it crackled and groaned. The boy in purple overalls cried in his corner.

Benjamin put his lips to Ella's ear. "I don't understand it here," he whispered.

There was a scuffle at the door, and the skinny boy stepped into the hostage room. "All right," he said. "Who gets killed?"

"Kill those kids, Peter," the girl said, pointing at Benjamin and Ella.

"Us?" Benjamin said.

"Who do you think?" said the boy.

He poked them in the back with his suction-cup arrow and moved them toward the tree trunk, where rough boards formed a ladder to the next level. Ella and Benjamin climbed until they had reached a narrow platform, and then Peter pushed them to the edge. Ella looked down at the trampoline. It was a longer drop than the high dive at the public pool. She looked over her shoulder and Peter glared at her. Down below the collie barked and barked, his black nose pointed up at them.

Benjamin took Ella's hand and closed his eyes. Then Peter shoved them from behind, and they stumbled forward into space.

There was a moment of terrifying emptiness, nothing but air beneath Ella's feet. She could hear the collie's bark getting closer as she fell. She slammed into the trampoline knees first, then flew, shrieking, back up into the air. When she hit the trampoline a second time, Benjamin's head knocked against her chin. He stood up rubbing his head, and Ella tasted salt in her mouth. Her loose tooth had slipped its roots. She spat it into her palm and studied its jagged edge.

"Move," Peter called from above. The boy in purple overalls was just climbing up onto the platform. Peter pulled him forward until his toes curled over the edge.

"I lost my tooth!" Ella yelled.

"Get off!"

Benjamin scrambled off the trampoline. Ella crawled to the edge, the tooth gleaming and red-rimmed between her fingers, and then the trampoline lurched with the weight of the boy in purple overalls. The tooth flew from her hand and into the bushes, too small to make a sound when it hit.

When she burst into the house crying, blood streaming from her mouth, the longhaired men and women dropped their mixing spoons and went to her. She twisted away from them, looking frantically for her mother and father, but they were nowhere to be seen. There was no way to explain that she wasn't hurt, that she was upset because her tooth was gone and because everything about that house made her want to run away and hide. The adults, their faces creased with worry, pulled her to the sink and held her mouth open. The woman with skewed eyes, Delilah, pressed a tissue against the space where her tooth had been. Ella could smell onions and apples on her hands.

"The time was right," she said. "The new tooth's already coming in."

"Whose is she?" one of the men asked.

Delilah told him the names of Ella's parents. It was strange to hear those familiar words, *Ann* and *Gary,* in the mouths of these longhaired strangers.

"Your mother is upstairs," Delilah said, her eyes swiveling toward some distant hidden room. "She felt a little swimmy-headed. Your dad just took her some special tea. Maybe we should let her rest, hmm?"

Ella slipped out from beneath Delilah's hand and ran to the hall, remembering the stairway she'd seen earlier. There it was before her, a curve of glossy steps leading to nowhere she knew. Her mother's cough drifted down from one of the bedroom doors. Ella put a foot onto the first stair, feeling the eyes of the adults on her back. No one said anything to stop her. After a moment, she began to climb.

In the upstairs hallway, toys and kids' shoes were strewn across the floor, and crumpled pants and shirts and dresses lay in a musty-smelling heap. Two naked Barbies sprawled in a frying pan. A record player sat in the middle of the hall, its vacant turntable spinning. Ella stepped over the cord and went into the first room, a small room with a sleeping bag on the bare mattress ticking. In a cage on the nightstand, a white rat scrabbled at a cardboard tube. A finger-painted sign above the bed said CLARIES ROOM. Her mother's cough rose again from down the hall, and she turned and ran toward the sound.

In a room whose blue walls and curtains made everything look as if it were underwater, her mother lay pale and coughing on a bed piled high with pillows. Her father sat on the edge of the bed, his hands raised in the air, thumbs hooked together and palms spread wide. For a moment Ella had no idea what he was doing. Then she saw the shadow of her father's hands against the wall, in the light of a blue-shaded lamp. A shock of relief went through her.

"Tweet-tweet," Ella said.

"Right," her father said. "A birdy."

Ella's mother turned toward her and smiled, more awake, more like her real self than earlier. "Do another one, Gary."

Ella's father twisted his hands into a new shape in the air.

"A dog?" Ella guessed.

"A fish!" said her mother.

"No," he said, and adjusted his hands. "It's a horsie, see?"

"A horsie?" said Ella's mother. "With fins?"

That made Ella laugh a little.

"Hey," her mother said. "Come here, you. Smile again."

Ella did as she was told.

"You lost your tooth!"

"It's gone," Ella said. She climbed onto the bed to explain, but as she flopped down on the mattress her mother's face contracted with pain.

"Please don't bounce," her mother said. She touched the place where her surgery had been.

Ella's father gave her a stern look and lifted her off the bed. "Your mom's sleepy. You should run back downstairs now."

"She's always sleepy," Ella said, looking down at her muddy feet. She thought of her tooth lying out in the weeds, and how she'd have nothing to put under her pillow for the tooth fairy.

Her mother began to cry.

Ella's father went to the window and stared down into the yard, his breath fogging the glass. "Go ahead, Ella," he said. "We just need a few minutes."

"My tooth," Ella said. She knew she should leave, but couldn't.

"It'll grow back bigger and stronger," her father said.

She could see he didn't understand what had happened. If only her mother would stop crying she could explain everything. In the blue light her mother looked cold and far away, pressed under the weight of tons of water.

"I'll be down soon," her mother said, sniffling. "Go out and play."

Ella opened her mouth to form some protest, but no words came out.

"Go on, now," her father said.

"It fell in a bush!" she wailed, then turned and ran downstairs.

The other children had come in by then. Her brother stood in line at the downstairs bathroom to wash before dinner, comparing fingernail dirt with the boy in purple overalls. Hands deep in the pockets of her velvet dress, Ella wandered through the echoing hall into a room lined from floor to ceiling with books. Many of the titles were in other languages, some even written in different alphabets. She recognized *D'Aulaires' Book of Greek Myths* and *The Riverside Shakespeare* and *Grimm's Fairy Tales.* Scattered around on small tables and decorative stands were tiny human figurines with animal heads: horse-man, giraffe-man, panther-man. On one table sat an Egyptian beetle made of milky green stone, and beside him a real beetle, shiny as metal, who flew at Ella's face when she reached to touch his shell. She batted him away with the back of her hand.

And then, just above where the beetle had fallen, Ella saw a shelf without any books at all. It was low, the height of her knees, with a frayed blue scarf pinned against its back wall. Burnt-down candles stood on either side of a black lacquer box, and on top of this box stood a glass filled with red water.

Ella reached for the glass, and someone behind her screamed.

She turned around. Clarie stood in the doorway, dress unbuttoned at one shoulder, face smeared with mud.

"Don't touch that," she said.

Ella took a step back. "I wasn't going to."

Clarie's eyes seemed to ignite as she bent down and took the glass in both hands. She held it near a lamp, so the light shone through it and cast a wavering red oval upon the wall.

"It's my mother," she said.

For dinner there was a roasted dome of something that looked like meat but wasn't. It was springy and steaming, and when Mister Kaplan cut it open Ella could see that it was stuffed with rice and yams. Benjamin tried to hide under the table, but their father pulled him up by the arms and set him in his place. He prodded his wedge of roast until it slid onto the tablecloth. Then he began to cry quietly.

"The kids aren't vegetarian," their father said, in apology to the men and women at the table. He picked up the slice of roast with his fingers and put it back on Ben's plate. The other men and women held their forks motionless above their own plates, looking at Ella's mother and father with pity.

"Look, Ben," said Delilah. "It's called seitan. Wheat gluten. The other kids love it."

The boy and girl with almond-shaped eyes and ragged hair stopped in mid-chew. The girl looked at Benjamin and narrowed her eyes.

"I don't eat gluten," Benjamin said.

"Come on, now," their father said. "It's great."

Ella's mother pressed her fingers against her temples. She hadn't touched her own dinner. Ella, sitting beside her, took a bite of wheat gluten. It was almost like meat, firm and savory, and the stuffing was flavored with forest-smelling spices. As she glanced around the table she thought of the picture of the First Thanksgiving on the bulletin board at school: the smiling Pilgrims eating turkey and squash, the stern-faced Native Americans looking as if they knew the worst was yet to come. Who among them that night were the Native Americans? Who were the Pilgrims? The dark old house was like a wilderness around them, the wind sighing through its rooms.

"I jumped on the trampoline," said the boy with ragged hair, pulling on the sleeve of the woman next to him. "That boy did a flip." He pointed at Peter, who was smashing rice against his plate with his thumb. "He tied his sister to the tree."

Mister Kaplan set down his fork. He looked sideways at Peter, his mouth pressed into a stern line. "I told you never to do that again," he said. He sounded angry, but his voice was quiet, almost a whisper.

"She made me!" Peter said, and plunged a spoon into his baked squash.

Mister Kaplan's eyes went glossy and faraway. He stared off at the blank wall above Ella's mother's head, drifting away from the noise and chatter of the dinner table. Next to him Delilah shuttled her mismatched eyes back and forth.

Ella's mother straightened in her chair. "Ed," she called softly.

Mister Kaplan blinked hard and looked at her.

"Tell us about your Tai Chi class."

"What?" he said.

"Your Tai Chi class."

"You know, I don't really want to talk right now." He pushed back his chair and went into the kitchen. There was the sound of water and then the clink of dishes in the sink. Delilah shook her head. The other adults looked down at their plates. Ella's mother wiped the corners of her mouth with her napkin and crossed her arms over her chest.

"Does anyone want more rice?" Ella's father asked.

"I think we're all thinking about Lena," said the man with the shaved head.

"I know I am," said Delilah.

"Infinity to infinity," said the man. "Dust into star."

The men and women looked at each other, their eyes carrying some message Ella couldn't understand. They clasped each other's hands and bent their heads. "Infinity to infinity," they repeated. "Dust into star."

"Matter into energy," said the man. "Identity into oneness."

"Matter into energy," everyone said. Ella glanced at her father, whose jaw was set hard, unmoving. Her mother's lips formed the words, but no sound came out. Ella thought of the usual Thanksgivings at her Uncle Bon's, where everyone talked and laughed at the table and they ate turkey and dressing and sweet potatoes with marshmallows melted on top. She closed her eyes and held her breath, filling her chest with a tightness that felt like magic power. If she tried hard enough could she transport them all, her mother and father, Benjamin and herself, to that other time? She held her breath until it seemed she would explode, then let it out in a rush. She opened her eyes. Nothing had changed. Peter kicked the table leg, and the collie, crouched beside Clarie's chair, whimpered his unease. Ella could see Clarie's hand on his collar, her knuckles bloodless as stones.

Mister Kaplan returned with a platter of baked apples. He cleared his throat, and everyone turned to look at him. "Guess what we forgot," he said. "I spent nearly an hour peeling these things." He held the platter aloft, waiting.

"Who wants some nice baked apples?" he said. "Baked apples. I peeled them."

No one said a word.

After dinner the adults drifted into the room with the straw mats and Indian goddesses. Ella understood that the children were not invited, but she lingered in the doorway to see what would happen. Mister Kaplan bent over a tiny brass dish and held a match to a black cone. A wisp of smoke curled toward the ceiling, and after a moment Ella smelled a dusty, flowery scent. Her mother and father and the rest of the adults sat cross-legged on the floor, not touching each other. A low hum began to fill the room like something with weight and substance. Ella saw her father raise an eyebrow at her mother, as if to ask if these people were serious. But her mother's shoulders were bent in meditation, her mouth open with the drone of the mantra, and Ella's father sighed and let his head fall forward.

Someone pinched Ella's shoulder and she turned around. Peter stood behind her, his eyes small and cold. "Come on," he said. "You're supposed to help clean up."

In the kitchen the children stacked dirty dishes on the counter and ran water in the sink. The boy and girl with almond eyes climbed up onto a wide wooden stepstool and began to scrub dishes. Peter scraped all the scraps into an aluminum pan and gave it to Clarie, who set it on the floor near the dog's water dish. The collie fell at the leftover food with sounds that made Ella sick to her stomach. Clarie stood next to him and stroked his tail.

Then Benjamin came into the kitchen carrying the glass of red water. "Somebody forgot this under the table," he said.

Again there was the dying-rabbit screech. Clarie batted her palms against the sides of her head. "No!" she shrieked. "Put it down!"

Benjamin's eyes went wide, and he set the glass on the kitchen counter. "I don't want it," he said.

The boy in purple overalls squinted at the glass. "Looks like Kool-Aid."

"She gets all crazy," said Peter. "Watch." Peter lifted the glass high into the air, and Clarie ran toward him. "You can't have it," he said.

Clarie jumped up and down in fury, her hands flapping like limp rags. Her mouth opened but no sound came out. Then she curled her fingers into claws and scratched at Peter's arms and chest until he twisted away. He ran across the kitchen and onto the deck, holding the glass in the air, and Clarie followed him, screaming.

The ragged-haired brother and sister looked at each other, arms gloved in white bubbles. In one quick movement they were off the stool, shaking suds around the kitchen. "Come on!" said the boy. "Let's go watch!"

Benjamin grabbed Ella's hand and pulled her toward the screen door. The children pushed out onto the deck and then ran toward the tree castle, where Clarie and her brother were climbing the first rope ladder. It was dark now, and floodlights on the roof of the house illuminated the entire castle, its rooms silver-gray and ghostly, its ropes and nets swaying in a rising breeze. The children gathered on the grass near the trampoline.

Peter held the glass as he climbed, the red water sloshing against its sides. "Come and get it," he crooned. He reached the first room, and they heard the wall-door scrape against the trunk as he pushed it open. Then he moved out onto the oak limb, agile as the spider monkeys Ella had seen at the zoo. He might as well have had a tail.

Clarie crawled behind him, her hands scrabbling at the bark. Peter howled at the sky as he reached the hostage room.

Benjamin moved toward Ella and pressed his head against her arm. "I want to go home," he said.

"Shh," Ella said. "We can't."

High above, Peter climbed onto the platform from which they had jumped earlier. Still holding the glass, he pulled himself up the tree trunk to the crow's nest. High up on that small railed platform, where the tree branches became thin and sparse, he stopped. Below him Clarie scrambled onto the jumping platform. She looked out across the yard as if unsure of where he had gone. "Up here," Peter said, holding the glass high.

Ella could hear Clarie grunting as she pulled herself up into the crow's nest. She stood and reached for the glass, her face a small moon in the dark. A few acorns scuttled off the crow's-nest platform.

"Give it!" she cried.

Peter stood looking at her for a moment in the dark. "You really want it?"

"Peter!"

He swept the glass through the air. The water flew out in an arc, ruby-colored against the glare of the floodlights. Clarie leaned out as if to catch it between her fingers, and with a splintering crack she broke through the railing. Her dress fluttered silently as she fell, and her white hands grasped at the air. There was a quiet instant, the soft sound of water falling on grass. Then, with a shock Ella felt in the soles of her feet, Clarie hit the ground. The girl with the ragged hair screamed.

Clarie lay beside the trampoline, still as sleep, her neck bent at an impossible angle. Ella wanted to look away, but couldn't. The other children, even Benjamin, moved to where Clarie lay and circled around, some calling her name, some just looking. Peter slid down the fireman's pole and stumbled across the lawn toward his sister. He pushed Benjamin aside. With one toe he nudged Clarie's shoulder, then knelt and rolled her over. A bare bone glistened from her wrist. The boy in purple overalls threw up on the grass.

Ella turned and ran toward the house. She banged the screen door open and skidded across the kitchen floor into the hall. At the doorway of the meditation room she stopped, breathing hard. The parents sat just as she had left them, eyes closed, mouths open slightly, their sound beating like a living thing, their thumbs and forefingers circled into perfect O's. She could smell the heat of them rising in the room and mingling with the scent of the incense. Her father's chin rested on his chest as if he had fallen asleep. Beside him her mother looked drained of blood, her skin so white she seemed almost holy.

"Mom," Ella whispered. "Mom."

Ella's mother turned slightly and opened her eyes. For a moment she seemed between two worlds, her eyes unfocused and distant. Then she blinked and looked at Ella. She shook her head no.

"Please," Ella said, but her mother closed her eyes again. Ella stood there for a long time watching her, but she didn't move or speak. Finally Ella turned and went back outside.

By the time she reached the tree castle Peter had dragged Clarie halfway across the lawn. He turned his eyes on Ella, and she stared back at him. The sound of the mantra continued unbroken from the house. Peter hoisted Clarie again under the arms and dragged her to the bushes, her bare feet bumping over the grass. Then he rolled her over until she was hidden in shadow. He pulled her dress down so it covered her thighs, and turned her head toward the fence that bordered the backyard.

"Get some leaves and stuff," he said. "We have to cover her."

Ella would not move. She took Benjamin's hand, but he pulled away from her and wandered across the lawn, pulling up handfuls of grass. She watched the children pick up twigs, Spanish moss, leaves, anything they could find. The boy in purple overalls gathered cedar bark from a flower bed, and Peter dragged fallen branches out of the underbrush near the fence. They scattered everything they found over Clarie's body. In five minutes they had covered her entirely.

"Go back inside," Peter said. "If anyone cries or says anything, I'll kill them."

Ella turned to go, and that was when she saw her tooth, a tiny white pebble in the weeds. She picked it up and rubbed it clean. Then she knelt beside Clarie, clearing away moss and leaves until she found Clarie's hand. She dropped the tooth into the palm and closed the fingers around it. A shiver spread through her chest, and she covered the hand again. Then she put her arm around Benjamin and they all went back inside. Drawn by the sound of the chanting, they wandered into the hall. All around them hung the yellow photographs, the stony men and women and children looking down at them with sad and knowing eyes. In an oval of black velvet one girl in a white dress held the string of a wooden duck, her lips open as if she were about to speak. Her eyes had the wildness of Clarie's eyes, her legs the same bowed curve.

At last there was a rustle from the meditation room, and the adults drifted out into the hall. They blinked at the light and rubbed their elbows and knees. Ella's mother and father linked arms and moved toward their children. Benjamin gave a hiccup. His eyes looked strange, the pupils huge, the whites flat and dry. Their mother noticed right away. "We'd better get going," she said to Ella's father. "Ben's tired."

She went into the foyer and pulled their shoes from the pile. Mister Kaplan followed, looking around in bewilderment, as if he could not believe people were leaving. He patted Benjamin on the head and asked Ella's mother if she wanted to take some leftover food. Ella's mother shook her head no. Her father thanked Mister Kaplan for his hospitality. Somewhere toward the back of the house the dog began to bark. Ella pulled Benjamin through the front door, barefoot, and her parents followed them to the car.

All the way past the rows of live oaks, past the cemetery where the little tombs stood like grounded boats, past the low flat shotgun houses with their flaking roofs, Benjamin sat rigid on the back seat and cried without a sound. Ella felt the sobs leaving his chest in waves of hot air. She closed her eyes and followed the car in her mind down the streets that led to their house, until it seemed they had driven past their house long ago and were moving on to a place where strange beds awaited them, where they would fall asleep thinking of dark forests and wake to the lives of strangers.

Drinking Coffee Elsewhere

ZZ Packer

Orientation games began the day I arrived at Yale from Baltimore. In my group we played heady, frustrating games for smart people. One game appeared to be charades reinterpreted by existentialists; another involved listening to rocks. Then a freshman counselor made everyone play Trust. The idea was that if you had the faith to fall backward and wait for four scrawny former high school geniuses to catch you, just before your head cracked on the slate sidewalk, then you might learn to trust your fellow students. Russian roulette sounded like a better way to go.

"No way," I said. The white boys were waiting for me to fall, holding their arms out for me, sincerely, gallantly. "No fucking way."

"It's all cool, it's all cool," the counselor said. Her hair was a shade of blond I'd seen only on *Playboy* covers, and she raised her hands as though backing away from a growling dog. "Sister," she said, in an I'm-down-with-the-struggle voice, "you don't have to play this game. As a person of color, you shouldn't have to fit into any white, patriarchal system."

I said, "It's a bit too late for that."

In the next game, all I had to do was wait in a circle until it was my turn to say what inanimate object I wanted to be. One guy said he'd like to be a gadfly, like Socrates. "Stop me if I wax Platonic," he said. I didn't bother mentioning that gadflies weren't inanimate—it didn't seem to make a difference. The girl next to him was eating a rice cake. She wanted to be the Earth, she said. Earth with a capital E.

There was one other black person in the circle. He wore an Exeter T-shirt and his overly elastic expressions resembled a series of facial exercises. At the end of each person's turn, he smiled and bobbed his head with unfettered enthusiasm. "Oh, that was good," he said, as if the game were an experiment he'd set up and the results were turning out better than he'd expected. "Good, good, good!"

When it was my turn I said, "My name is Dina, and if I had to be any object, I guess I'd be a revolver." The sunlight dulled as if on cue. Clouds passed rapidly overhead, presaging rain. I don't know why I said it. Until that moment I'd been good in all the ways that were meant to matter. I was an honor roll student—though I'd learned long ago not to mention it in the part of Baltimore where I lived. Suddenly I was hard-bitten and recalcitrant, the kind of kid who took pleasure in sticking pins into cats; the kind who chased down smart kids to spray them with Mace.

"A revolver," a counselor said, stroking his chin, as if it had grown a rabbinical beard. "Could you please elaborate?"

The black guy cocked his head and frowned, as if the beakers and Erlenmeyer flasks of his experiment had grown legs and scurried off.

"You were just kidding," the dean said, "about wiping out all of mankind. That, I suppose, was a joke." She squinted at me. One of her hands curved atop the other to form a pink, freckled molehill on her desk.

"Well," I said, "maybe I meant it at the time." I quickly saw that this was not the answer she wanted. "I don't know. I think it's the architecture."

Through the dimming light of the dean's office window, I could see the fortress of the old campus. On my ride from the bus station to the campus, I'd barely glimpsed New Haven—a flash of crumpled building here, a trio of straggly kids there. A lot like Baltimore. But everything had changed when we reached those streets hooded by gothic buildings. I imagined how the college must have looked when it was founded, when most of the students owned slaves. I pictured men wearing tights and knickers, smoking pipes.

"The architecture," the dean repeated. She bit her lip and seemed to be making a calculation of some sort. I noticed that she blinked less often than most people. I sat there, intrigued, waiting to see how long it would be before she blinked again.

My revolver comment won me a year's worth of psychiatric counseling, weekly meetings with Dean Guest, and—since the parents of the roommate I'd never met weren't too hip on the idea of their Amy sharing a bunk bed with a budding homicidal loony—my very own room.

Shortly after getting my first C ever, I also received the first knock on my door. The female counselors never knocked. The dean had spoken to them; I was a priority. Every other day, right before dinnertime, they'd look in on me, unannounced. "Just checking up," a counselor would say. It was the voice of a suburban mother in training. By the second week, I had made a point of sitting in a chair in front of the door, just when I expected a counselor to pop her head around. This was intended to startle them. I also made a point of being naked. The unannounced visits ended.

The knocking persisted. Through the peephole I saw a white face, distorted and balloonish.

"Let me in." The person looked like a boy but it sounded like a girl. "Let me in," the voice repeated.

"Not a chance," I said. I had a suicide single, and I wanted to keep it that way. No roommates, no visitors.

Then the person began to sob, and I heard a back slump against the door. If I hadn't known the person was white from the peephole, I'd have known it from a display like this. Black people didn't knock on strangers' doors, crying. Not that I understood the black people at Yale. Most of them were from New York and tried hard to pretend that they hadn't gone to prep schools. And there was something pitiful in how cool they were. Occasionally one would reach out to me with missionary zeal, but I'd rebuff the person with haughty silence.

"I don't have anyone to talk to!" the person on the other side of the door cried.

"That is correct."

"When I was a child," the person said, "I played by myself in a corner of the schoolyard all alone. I hated dolls and I hated games, animals were not friendly and birds flew away. If anyone was looking for me I hid behind a tree and cried out 'I am an orphan—' "

I opened the door. It was a she.

"Plagiarist!" I yelled. She had just recited a Frank O'Hara poem as though she'd thought it up herself. I knew the poem because it was one of the few things I'd been forced to read that I wished I'd written myself.

The girl turned to face me, smiling weakly, as though her triumph was not in getting me to open the door but in the fact that she was able to smile at all when she was so accustomed to crying. She was large but not obese, and crying had turned her face the color of raw chicken. She blew her nose into the waist end of her T-shirt, revealing a pale belly.

"How do you know that poem?"

She sniffed. "I'm in your Contemporary Poetry class."

She said she was Canadian and her name was Heidi, although she said she wanted people to call her Henrik. "That's a guy's name," I said. "What do you want? A sex change?"

She looked at me with so little surprise that I suspected she hadn't discounted this as an option. Then her story came out in teary, hiccup-like bursts. She had sucked some "cute guy's dick" and he'd told everybody and now people thought she was "a slut."

"Why'd you suck his dick? Aren't you a lesbian?"

She fit the bill. Short hair, hard, roach-stomping shoes. Dressed like an aspiring plumber. And then there was the name Henrik. The lesbians I'd seen on TV were wiry, thin strips of muscle, but Heidi was round and soft and had a moonlike face. Drab henna-colored hair. And lesbians had cats. "Do you have a cat?" I asked.

Her eyes turned glossy with new tears. "No," she said, her voice quavering, "and I'm not a lesbian. Are you?"

"Do I look like one?" I said.

She didn't answer.

"O.K.," I said. "I could suck a guy's dick, too, if I wanted. But I don't. The human penis is one of the most germ-ridden objects there is." Heidi looked at me, unconvinced. "What I meant to say," I began again, "is that I don't like anybody. Period. Guys or girls. I'm a misanthrope."

"I am, too."

"No," I said, guiding her back through my door and out into the hallway. "You're not."

"Have you had dinner?" she asked. "Let's go to Commons."

I pointed to a pyramid of ramen noodle packages on my windowsill. "See that? That means I never have to go to Commons. Aside from class, I have contact with no one."

"I hate it here, too," she said. "I should have gone to McGill, eh."

"The way to feel better," I said, "is to get some ramen and lock yourself in your room. Everyone will forget about you and that guy's dick and you won't have to see anyone ever again. If anyone looks for you—"

"I'll hide behind a tree."

"A revolver?" Dr. Raeburn said, flipping through a manila folder. He looked up at me as if to ask another question, but he didn't.

Dr. Raeburn was the psychiatrist. He had the gray hair and whiskers of a Civil War general. He was also a chain smoker with beige teeth and a navy wool jacket smeared with ash. He asked about the revolver at the beginning of my first visit. When I was unable to explain myself, he smiled, as if this were perfectly reasonable.

"Tell me about your parents."

I wondered what he already had on file. The folder was thick, though I hadn't said a thing of significance since Day One.

"My father was a dick and my mother seemed to like him."

He patted his pockets for his cigarettes. "That's some heavy stuff," he said. "How do you feel about Dad?" The man couldn't say the word "father." "Is Dad someone you see often?"

"I hate my father almost as much as I hate the word 'Dad.'"

He started tapping his cigarette.

"You can't smoke in here."

"That's right," he said, and slipped the cigarette back into the packet. He smiled, widening his eyes brightly. "Don't ever start."

I thought that that first encounter would be the last of Heidi or Henrik, or whatever, but then her head appeared in a window of Linsly-Chit during my Chaucer class. A few days later, she swooped down a flight of stairs in Harkness, following me. She hailed me from across Elm Street and found me in the Sterling Library stacks. After one of my meetings with Dr. Raeburn, she was waiting for me outside Health Services, legs crossed, cleaning her fingernails.

"You know," she said, as we walked through Old Campus, "you've got to stop eating ramen. Not only does it lack a single nutrient but it's full of MSG."

I wondered why she even bothered, and was vaguely flattered she cared, but I said, "I like eating chemicals. It keeps the skin radiant."

"There's also hepatitis." She knew how to get my attention—mention a disease.

"You get hepatitis from unwashed lettuce," I said. "If there's anything safe from the perils of the food chain, it's ramen."

"But do you refrigerate what you don't eat? Each time you reheat it, you're killing good bacteria, which then can't keep the bad bacteria in check. A guy got sick from reheating Chinese noodles, and his son died from it. I read it in the *Times*." With this, she put a jovial arm around my neck. I continued walking, a little stunned. Then, just as quickly, she dropped her arm and stopped walking. I stopped, too.

"Did you notice that I put my arm around you?"

"Yes," I said. "Next time, I'll have to chop it off."

"I don't want you to get sick," she said. "Let's eat at Commons."

In the cold air, her arm had felt good.

The problem with Commons was that it was too big; its ceiling was as high as a cathedral's, but below it there were no awestruck worshippers, only eighteen-year-olds at heavy wooden tables, chatting over veal patties and Jell-O.

We got our food, tacos stuffed with meat substitute, and made our way through the maze of tables. The Koreans had a table. Each singing group had a table. The crew team sat at a long table of its own. We passed the black table. Heidi was so plump and moonfaced that the sheer quantity of her flesh accentuated just how white she was. The black students gave me a long, hard stare.

"How you doing, sista?" a guy asked, his voice full of accusation, eyeballing me as though I were clad in a Klansman's sheet and hood. "I guess we won't see you till graduation."

"If," I said, "you graduate."

The remark was not well received. As I walked past, I heard protests, angry and loud as if they'd discovered a cheat at their poker game. Heidi and I found an unoccupied table along the periphery, which was isolated and dark. We sat down. Heidi prayed over her tacos.

"I thought you didn't believe in God," I said.

"Not in the God depicted in the Judeo-Christian Bible, but I do believe that nature's essence is a spirit that—"

"All right," I said. I had begun to eat, and cubes of diced tomato fell from my mouth when I spoke. "Stop right there. Tacos and spirits don't mix."

"You've always got to be so flip," she said. "I'm going to apply for another friend."

"There's always Mr. Dick," I said. "Slurp, slurp."

"You are so lame. So unbelievably lame. I'm going out with Mr. Dick. Thursday night at Atticus. His name is Keith."

Heidi hadn't mentioned Mr. Dick since the day I'd met her. That was more than a month ago and we'd spent a lot of that time together. I checked for signs that she was lying; her habit of smiling too much, her eyes bright and cheeks full so that she looked like a chipmunk. But she looked normal. Pleased, even, to see me so flustered.

"You're insane! What are you going to do this time?" I asked. "Sleep with him? Then when he makes fun of you, what? Come pound your head on my door reciting the collected poems of Sylvia Plath?"

"He's going to apologize for before. And don't call me insane. You're the one going to the psychiatrist."

"Well, I'm not going to suck his dick, that's for sure."

She put her arm around me in mock comfort, but I pushed it off, and ignored her. She touched my shoulder again, and I turned, annoyed, but it wasn't Heidi after all; a sepia-toned boy dressed in khakis and a crisp plaid shirt was standing behind me. He thrust a hot-pink square of paper toward me without a word, then briskly made his way toward the other end of Commons, where the crowds blossomed. Heidi leaned over and read it: "Wear Black Leather—the Less, the Better."

"It's a gay party," I said, crumpling the card. "He thinks we're fucking gay."

Heidi and I signed on to work at the Saybrook dining hall as dishwashers. The job consisted of dumping food from plates and trays into a vat of rushing water. It seemed straightforward, but then I learned better. You wouldn't believe what people could do with food until you worked in a dish room. Lettuce and crackers and soup would be bullied into a pulp in the bowl of some bored anorexic; ziti would be mixed with honey and granola; trays would appear heaped with mashed potato snow women with melted chocolate ice cream for hair. Frat boys arrived at the dish-room window, en masse. They liked to fill glasses with food, then seal them, airtight, onto their trays. If you tried to prize them off, milk, Worcestershire sauce, peas, chunks of bread vomited onto your dish-room uniform.

When this happened one day in the middle of the lunch rush, for what seemed like the hundredth time, I tipped the tray toward one of the frat boys as he turned to walk away, popping the glasses off so that the mess spurted onto his Shetland sweater.

He looked down at his sweater. "Lesbo bitch!"

"No," I said, "that would be your mother."

Heidi, next to me, clenched my arm in support, but I remained motionless, waiting to see what the frat boy would do. He glared at me for a minute, then walked away.

"Let's take a smoke break," Heidi said.

I didn't smoke, but Heidi had begun to, because she thought it would help her lose weight. As I hefted a stack of glasses through the steamer, she lit up.

"Soft packs remind me of you," she said. "Just when you've smoked them all and you think there's none left, there's always one more, hiding in that little crushed corner." Before I could respond she said, "Oh, God. Not another mouse. You know whose job that is."

By the end of the rush, the floor mats got full and slippery with food. This was when mice tended to appear, scurrying over our shoes; more often than not, a mouse got caught in the grating that covered the drains in the floor. Sometimes the mouse was already dead by the time we noticed it. This one was alive.

"No way," I said. "This time you're going to help. Get some gloves and a trash bag."

"That's all I'm getting. I'm not getting that mouse out of there."

"Put on the gloves," I ordered. She winced, but put them on. "Reach down," I said. "At an angle, so you get at its middle. Otherwise, if you try to get it by its tail, the tail will break off."

"This is filthy, eh."

"That's why we're here," I said. "To clean up filth. Eh."

She reached down, but would not touch the mouse. I put my hand around her arm and pushed it till her hand made contact. The cries from the mouse were soft, songlike. "Oh, my God," she said. "Oh, my God, ohmigod." She wrestled it out of the grating and turned her head away.

"Don't you let it go," I said.

"Where's the food bag? It'll smother itself if I drop it in the food bag. Quick," she said, her head still turned away, her eyes closed. "Lead me to it."

"No. We are not going to smother this mouse. We've got to break its neck."

"You're one heartless bitch."

I wondered how to explain that if death is unavoidable it should be quick and painless. My mother had died slowly. At the hospital, they'd said it was kidney failure, but I knew, in the end, it was my father. He made her so scared to live in her own home that she was finally driven away from it in an ambulance.

"Breaking its neck will save it the pain of smothering," I said. "Breaking its neck is more humane. Take the trash bag and cover it so you won't get any blood on you, then crush."

The loud jets of the steamer had shut off automatically and the dish room grew quiet. Heidi breathed in deeply, then crushed the mouse. She shuddered, disgusted. "Now what?"

"What do you mean, 'now what?' Throw the little bastard in the trash."

At our third session, I told Dr. Raeburn I didn't mind if he smoked. He sat on the sill of his open window, smoking behind a jungle screen of office plants.

We spent the first ten minutes discussing the Iliad, and whether or not the text actually states that Achilles had been dipped in the River Styx. He said it did, and I said it didn't. After we'd finished with the Iliad, and with my new job in what he called "the scullery," he asked questions about my parents. I told him nothing. It was none of his business. Instead, I talked about Heidi. I told him about that day in Commons, Heidi's plan to go on a date with Mr. Dick, and the invitation we'd been given to the gay party.

"You seem preoccupied by this soirée." He arched his eyebrows at the word "soirée."

"Wouldn't you be?"

"Dina," he said slowly, in a way that made my name seem like a song title, "have you ever had a romantic interest?"

"You want to know if I've ever had a boyfriend?" I said. "Just go ahead and ask if I've ever fucked anybody."

This appeared to surprise him. "I think that you are having a crisis of identity," he said.

"Oh, is that what this is?"

His profession had taught him not to roll his eyes. Instead, his exasperation revealed itself in a tiny pursing of his lips, as though he'd just tasted something awful and was trying very hard not to offend the cook.

"It doesn't have to be, as you say, someone you've fucked, it doesn't have to be a boyfriend," he said.

"Well, what are you trying to say? If it's not a boy, then you're saying it's a girl—"

"Calm down. It could be a crush, Dina." He lit one cigarette off another. "A crush on a male teacher, a crush on a dog, for heaven's sake. An interest. Not necessarily a relationship."

It was sacrifice time. If I could spend the next half hour talking about some boy, then I'd have given him what he wanted.

So I told him about the boy with the nice shoes.

I was sixteen and had spent the last few coins in my pocket on bus fare to buy groceries. I didn't like going to the Super Fresh two blocks away from my house, plunking government food stamps into the hands of the cashiers.

"There she go reading," one of them once said, even though I was only carrying a book. "Don't your eyes get tired?"

On Greenmount Avenue you could read schoolbooks—that was understandable. The government and your teachers forced you to read them. But anything else was antisocial. It meant you'd rather submit to the words of some white dude than shoot the breeze with your neighbors.

I hated those cashiers, and I hated them seeing me with food stamps, so I took the bus and shopped elsewhere. That day, I got off the bus at Govans, and though the neighborhood was black like my own—hair salon after hair salon of airbrushed signs promising arabesque hair styles and inch-long fingernails—the houses were neat and orderly, nothing at all like Greenmount, where every other house had at least one shattered window. The store was well swept, and people quietly checked long grocery lists—no screaming kids, no loud cashier-customer altercations. I got the groceries and left the store.

I decided to walk back. It was a fall day, and I walked for blocks. Then I sensed someone following me. I walked more quickly, my arms around the sack, the leafy lettuce tickling my nose. I didn't want to hold the sack so close that it would break the eggs or squash the hamburger buns, but it was slipping, and as I looked behind me a boy my age, maybe older, rushed toward me.

"Let me help you," he said.

"That's all right." I set the bag on the sidewalk. Maybe I saw his face, maybe it was handsome enough, but what I noticed first, splayed on either side of the bag, were his shoes. They were nice shoes, real leather, a stitched design like a widow's peak on each one, or like birds' wings, and for the first time in my life I understood what people meant when they said "wing-tip shoes."

"I watched you carry them groceries out that store, then you look around, like you're lost, but like you liked being lost, then you walk down the sidewalk for blocks and blocks. Rearranging that bag, it almost gone to slip, then hefting it back up again."

"Uh-huh," I said.

"And then I passed my own house and was still following you. And then your bag really look like it was gone crash and everything. So I just thought

I'd help." He sucked in his bottom lip, as if to keep it from making a smile. "What's your name?" When I told him, he said, "Dina, my name is Cecil." Then he said, "D comes right after C."

"Yes," I said, "it does, doesn't it."

Then, half question, half statement, he said, "I could carry your groceries for you? And walk you home?"

I stopped the story there. Dr. Raeburn kept looking at me. "Then what happened?"

I couldn't tell him the rest: that I had not wanted the boy to walk me home, that I didn't want someone with such nice shoes to see where I lived.

Dr. Raeburn would only have pitied me if I'd told him that I ran down the sidewalk after I told the boy no, that I fell, the bag slipped, and the eggs cracked, their yolks running all over the lettuce. Clear amniotic fluid coated the can of cinnamon rolls. I left the bag there on the sidewalk, the groceries spilled out randomly like cards loosed from a deck. When I returned home, I told my mother that I'd lost the food stamps.

"Lost?" she said. I'd expected her to get angry, I'd wanted her to get angry, but she hadn't. "Lost?" she repeated. Why had I been so clumsy and nervous around a harmless boy? I could have brought the groceries home and washed off the egg yolk, but instead I'd just left them there. "Come on," Mama said, snuffing her tears, pulling my arm, trying to get me to join her and start yanking cushions off the couch. "We'll find enough change here. We got to get something for dinner before your father gets back."

We'd already searched the couch for money the previous week, and I knew there'd be nothing now, but I began to push my fingers into the couch's boniest corners, pretending that it was only a matter of time before I'd find some change or a lost watch or an earring. Something pawnable, perhaps.

"What happened next?" Dr. Raeburn asked again. "Did you let the boy walk you home?"

"My house was far, so we went to his house instead." Though I was sure Dr. Raeburn knew that I was making this part up, I continued. "We made out on his sofa. He kissed me."

Dr. Raeburn lit his next cigarette like a detective. Cool, suspicious. "How did it feel?"

"You know," I said. "Like a kiss feels. It felt nice. The kiss felt very, very nice."

Raeburn smiled gently, though he seemed unconvinced. When he called time on our session, his cigarette had become one long pole of ash. I left his office, walking quickly down the corridor, afraid to look back. It would be like him to trot after me, his navy blazer flapping, just to get the truth out of me. *You never kissed anyone.* The words slid from my brain, and knotted in my stomach.

When I reached my dorm, I found an old record player blocking my door and a Charles Mingus LP propped beside it. I carried them inside and then, lying on the floor, I played the Mingus over and over again until I fell asleep.

I slept feeling as though Dr. Raeburn had attached electrodes to my head, willing into my mind a dream about my mother. I saw the lemon meringue of her skin, the long bone of her arm as she reached down to clip her toenails. I'd come home from a school trip to an aquarium, and I was explaining the differences between baleen and sperm whales according to the size of their heads, the range of their habitats, their feeding patterns.

I awoke remembering the expression on her face after I'd finished my dizzying whale lecture. She looked like a tourist who'd asked for directions to a place she thought was simple enough to get to only to hear a series of hypothetical turns, alleys, one-way streets. Her response was to nod politely at the perilous elaborateness of it all; to nod and save herself from the knowledge that she would never be able to get where she wanted to go.

The dishwashers always closed down the dining hall. One night, after everyone else had punched out, Heidi and I took a break, and though I wasn't a smoker, we set two milk crates upside down on the floor and smoked cigarettes.

The dishwashing machines were off, but steam still rose from them like a jungle mist. Outside in the winter air, students were singing carols in their groomed and tailored singing-group voices. The Whiffenpoofs were back in New Haven after a tour around the world, and I guess their return was a huge deal. Heidi and I craned our necks to watch the year's first snow through an open window.

"What are you going to do when you're finished?" Heidi asked. Sexy question marks of smoke drifted up to the windows before vanishing.

"Take a bath."

She swatted me with her free hand. "No, silly. Three years from now. When you leave Yale."

"I don't know. Open up a library. Somewhere where no one comes in for books. A library in a desert."

She looked at me as though she'd expected this sort of answer and didn't know why she'd asked in the first place.

"What are you going to do?" I asked her.

"Open up a psych clinic. In a desert. And my only patient will be some wacko who runs a library."

"Ha," I said. "Whatever you do, don't work in a dish room ever again. You're no good." I got up from the crate. "C'mon. Let's hose the place down."

We put out our cigarettes on the floor, since it was our job to clean it anyway. We held squirt guns in one hand and used the other to douse the floors with the standard-issue, eye-burning cleaning solution. We hosed the dish room, the kitchen, the serving line, sending the water and crud and suds into the drains. Then we hosed them again so the solution wouldn't eat holes in our shoes as we left. Then I had an idea. I unbuckled my belt.

"What the hell are you doing?" Heidi said.

"Listen, it's too cold to go outside with our uniforms all wet. We could just take a shower right here. There's nobody but us."

"What the fuck, eh?"

I let my pants drop, then took off my shirt and panties. I didn't wear a bra, since I didn't have much to fill one. I took off my shoes and hung my clothes on the stepladder.

"You've flipped," Heidi said. "I mean, really, psych-ward flipped."

I soaped up with the liquid hand soap until I felt as glazed as a ham. "Stand back and spray me."

"Oh, my God," she said. I didn't know whether she was confused or delighted, but she picked up the squirt gun and sprayed me. She was laughing. Then she got too close and the water started to sting.

"God damn it!" I said. "That hurt!"

"I was wondering what it would take to make you say that."

When all the soap had been rinsed off, I put on my regular clothes and said, "O.K. You're up next."

"No way," she said.

"Yes way."

She started to take off her uniform shirt, then stopped.

"What?"

"I'm too fat."

"You goddam right." She always said she was fat. One time I'd told her that she should shut up about it, that large black women wore their fat like mink coats. "You're big as a house," I said now. "Frozen yogurt may be low in calories, but not if you eat five tubs of it. Take your clothes off. I want to get out of here."

She began taking off her uniform, then stood there, hands cupped over her breasts, crouching at the pubic bone.

"Open up," I said, "or we'll never get done."

Her hands remained where they were. I threw the bottle of liquid soap at her, and she had to catch it, revealing herself as she did.

I turned on the squirt gun, and she stood there, stiff, arms at her side, eyes closed, as though awaiting mummification. I began with the water on low, and she turned around in a full circle, hesitantly, letting the droplets from the spray fall on her as if she were submitting to a death by stoning.

When I increased the water pressure, she slipped and fell on the sudsy floor. She stood up and then slipped again. This time she laughed and remained on the floor, rolling around on it as I sprayed.

I think I began to love Heidi that night in the dish room, but who is to say that I hadn't begun to love her the first time I met her? I sprayed her and sprayed her, and she turned over and over like a large beautiful dolphin, lolling about in the sun.

Heidi started sleeping at my place. Sometimes she slept on the floor; sometimes we slept sardinelike, my feet at her head, until she complained that my feet were "taunting" her. When we finally slept head to head, she said, "Much better." She was so close I could smell her toothpaste. "I like your hair," she told me, touching it through the darkness. "You should wear it out more often."

"White people always say that about black people's hair. The worse it looks, the more they say they like it."

I'd expected her to disagree, but she kept touching my hair, her hands passing through it till my scalp tingled. When she began to touch the hair around the edge of my face, I felt myself quake. Her fingertips stopped for a moment, as if checking my pulse, then resumed.

"I like how it feels right here. See, mine just starts with the same old texture as the rest of my hair." She found my hand under the blanket and brought it to her hairline. "See," she said.

It was dark. As I touched her hair, it seemed as though I could smell it, too. Not a shampoo smell. Something richer, murkier. A bit dead, but sweet, like the decaying wood of a ship. She guided my hand.

"I see," I said. The record she'd given me was playing in my mind, and I kept trying to shut it off. I could also hear my mother saying that this is what happens when you've been around white people: things get weird. So weird I could hear the stylus etching its way into the flat vinyl of the record. "Listen," I said finally, when the bass and saxes started up. I heard Heidi breathe deeply, but she said nothing.

We spent the winter and some of the spring in my room—never hers—missing tests, listening to music, looking out my window to comment on people who wouldn't have given us a second thought. We read books related to none of our classes. I got riled up by *The Autobiography of Malcolm X* and *The Chomsky Reader*; Heidi read aloud passages from *The Anxiety of Influence.* We guiltily read mysteries and *Clan of the Cave Bear,* then immediately threw them away. Once we looked up from our books at exactly the same moment, as though trapped at a dinner table with nothing to say. A pleasant trap of silence.

Then one weekend I went back to Baltimore and stayed with my father. He asked me how school was going, but besides that, we didn't talk much. He knew what I thought of him. I stopped by the Enoch Pratt Library, where my favorite librarian, Mrs. Ardelia, cornered me into giving a little talk to the after-school kids, telling them to stay in school. They just looked at me like I was crazy; they were only nine or ten, and it hadn't even occurred to them to bail.

When I returned to Yale—to a sleepy, tree-scented spring—a group of students were holding what was called "Coming Out Day." I watched it from my room.

The emcee was the sepia boy who'd given us the invitation months back. His speech was strident but still smooth and peppered with jokes. There was a speech about AIDS, with lots of statistics: nothing that seemed to make "coming out" worth it. Then the women spoke. One girl pronounced herself "out" as casually as if she'd announced the time. Another said nothing at all: she came to the microphone with a woman who began cutting off her waist-length, bleached-blond hair. The woman doing the cutting tossed the shorn hair in every direction as she cut. People were clapping and cheering and catching the locks of hair.

And then there was Heidi. She was proud that she liked girls, she said when she reached the microphone. She loved them, wanted to sleep with them. She was a dyke, she said repeatedly, stabbing her finger to her chest in case anyone was unsure to whom she was referring. She could not have seen me. I was across the street, three stories up. And yet, when everyone clapped for her, she seemed to be looking straight at me.

Heidi knocked. "Let me in."

It was like the first time I met her. The tears, the raw pink of her face.

We hadn't spoken in weeks. Outside, pink-and-white blossoms hung from the Old Campus trees. Students played Hacky Sack in T-shirts and shorts. Though I was the one who'd broken away after she went up to that podium, I still half expected her to poke her head out a window in Linsly-Chit, or tap on my back in Harkness, or even join me in the Commons dining hall, where I'd asked for my dish-room shift to be transferred. She did none of these.

"Well," I said, "what is it?"

She looked at me. "My mother," she said.

She continued to cry, but seemed to have grown so silent in my room I wondered if I could hear the numbers change on my digital clock.

"When my parents were getting divorced," she said, "my mother bought a car. A used one. An El Dorado. It was filthy. It looked like a huge crushed can coming up the street. She kept trying to clean it out. I mean—"

I nodded and tried to think what to say in the pause she left behind. Finally I said, "We had one of those," though I was sure ours was an Impala.

She looked at me, eyes steely from trying not to cry. "Anyway, she'd drive me around in it and although she didn't like me to eat in it, I always did. One day I was eating cantaloupe slices, spitting the seeds on the floor. Maybe a month later, I saw this little sprout, growing right up from the car floor. I just started laughing and she kept saying what, what? I was laughing and then I saw she was so—"

She didn't finish. So what? So sad? So awful? Heidi looked at me with what seemed to be a renewed vigor. "We could have gotten a better car, eh?"

"It's all right. It's not a big deal," I said.

Of course, that was the wrong thing to say. And I really didn't mean it to sound the way it had come out.

I told Dr. Raeburn about Heidi's mother having cancer and how I'd said it wasn't a big deal, though I'd wanted to say the opposite. I told Dr. Raeburn how I meant to tell Heidi that my mother had died, that I knew how one eventually accustoms oneself to the physical world's lack of sympathy: the buses that are still running late, the kids who still play in the street, the clocks that won't stop ticking for the person who's gone.

"You're pretending," Dr. Raeburn said, not sage or professional, but a little shocked by the discovery, as if I'd been trying to hide a pack of his cigarettes behind my back.

"I'm pretending?" I shook my head. "All those years of psych grad," I said. "And to tell me *that*?"

"What I mean is that you construct stories about yourself and dish them out—one for you, one for you—" Here he reenacted this process, showing me handing out lies as if they were apples.

"Pretending. I believe the professional name for it might be denial," I said. "Are you calling me gay?"

He pursed his lips noncommittally, then finally said, "No, Dina. I don't think you're gay."

I checked his eyes. I couldn't read them.

"No. Not at all," he said, sounding as if he were telling a subtle joke. "But maybe you'll finally understand."

"Understand what?"

"Oh, just that constantly saying what one doesn't mean accustoms the mouth to meaningless phrases." His eyes narrowed. "Maybe you'll understand that when you finally need to express something truly significant your mouth will revert to the insignificant nonsense it knows so well." He looked at me, his hands sputtering in the air in a gesture of defeat. "Who knows?" he asked with a glib, psychiatric smile I'd never seen before. "Maybe it's your survival mechanism. Black living in a white world."

I heard him, but only vaguely. I'd hooked on to that one word, pretending. Dr. Raeburn would never realize that "pretending" was what had got me this far. I remembered the morning of my mother's funeral. I'd been given milk to settle my stomach; I'd pretended it was coffee. I imagined I was drinking coffee elsewhere. Some Arabic-speaking country where the thick coffee served in little cups was so strong it could keep you awake for days.

Heidi wanted me to go with her to the funeral. She'd sent this message through the dean. "We'll pay for your ticket to Vancouver," the dean said.

These people wanted you to owe them for everything. "What about my return ticket?" I asked the dean. "Maybe the shrink will chip in for that."

The dean looked at me as though I were an insect she'd like to squash. "We'll pay for the whole thing. We might even pay for some lessons in manners."

So I packed my suitcase and walked from my suicide single dorm to Heidi's room. A thin wispy girl in ragged cutoffs and a shirt that read "LSBN!" answered the door. A group of short-haired girls in thick black leather jackets, bundled up despite the summer heat, encircled Heidi in a protective fairy ring. They looked at me critically, clearly wondering if Heidi was too fragile for my company.

"You've got our numbers," one said, holding on to Heidi's shoulder. "And Vancouver's got a great gay community."

"Oh, God," I said. "She's going to a funeral, not a Save the Dykes rally."

One of the girls stepped in front of me.

"It's O.K., Cynthia," Heidi said. Then she ushered me into her bedroom and closed the door. A suitcase was on her bed, half packed.

"I could just uninvite you," Heidi said. "How about that? You want that?" She folded a polka-dotted T-shirt that was wrong for any occasion and put it in her suitcase. "Why haven't you talked to me?" she said, looking at the shirt instead of me. "Why haven't you talked to me in two months?"

"I don't know," I said.

"You don't know," she said, each syllable steeped in sarcasm. "You don't know. Well, *I* know. You thought I was going to try to sleep with you."

"Try to? We slept together all winter!"

"If you call smelling your feet sleeping together, you've got a lot to learn." She seemed thinner and meaner; every line of her body held me at bay.

"So tell me," I said. "What can you show me that I need to learn?" But as soon as I said it I somehow knew she still hadn't slept with anyone. "Am I supposed to come over there and sweep your enraged self into my arms?" I said. "Like in the movies? Is this the part where we're both so mad we kiss each other?"

She shook her head and smiled weakly. "You don't get it," she said. "My mother is dead." She closed her suitcase, clicking shut the old-fashioned locks. "My mother is dead," she said again, this time reminding herself. She set her suitcase upright on the floor and sat on it. She looked like someone waiting for a train.

"Fine," I said. "And she's going to be dead for a long time." Though it sounded stupid, I felt good saying it. As though I had my own locks to click shut.

Heidi went to Vancouver for her mother's funeral. I didn't go with her. Instead, I went back to Baltimore and moved in with an aunt I barely knew. Every day was the same: I read and smoked outside my aunt's apartment, studying the row of hair salons across the street, where girls in denim cutoffs and tank tops would troop in and come out hours later, a flash of neon nails, coifs the color and sheen of patent leather. And every day I imagined Heidi's house in Vancouver. Her place would not be large, but it would be clean. Flowery shrubs would line the walks. The Canadian wind would whip us about like pennants. I'd be visiting her in some vague time in the future, deliberately vague, for people like me, who realign past events to suit themselves. In that future time, you always have a chance to catch the groceries before they fall; your words can always be rewound and erased, rewritten and revised.

Then I'd imagine Heidi visiting me. There are no psychiatrists or deans, no boys with nice shoes or flip cashiers. Just me in my single room. She knocks on the door and says, "Open up."

A Conversation with My Father

Grace Paley

My father is eighty-six years old and in bed. His heart, that bloody motor, is equally old and will not do certain jobs any more. It still floods his head with brainy light. But it won't let his legs carry the weight of his body around the house. Despite my metaphors, this muscle failure is not due to his old heart, he says, but to a potassium shortage. Sitting on one pillow, leaning on three, he offers last-minute advice and makes a request.

"I would like you to write a simple story just once more," he says, "the kind de Maupassant wrote, or Chekhov, the kind you used to write. Just recognizable people and then write down what happened to them next."

I say, "Yes, why not? That's possible." I want to please him, though I don't remember writing that way. I *would* like to try to tell such a story, if he means the kind that begins: "There was a woman . . ." followed by plot, the absolute line between two points which I've always despised. Not for literary reasons, but because it takes all hope away. Everyone, real or invented, deserves the open destiny of life.

Finally I thought of a story that had been happening for a couple of years right across the street. I wrote it down, then read it aloud. "Pa," I said, "how about this? Do you mean something like this?"

> Once in my time there was a woman and she had a son. They lived nicely, in a small apartment in Manhattan. This boy at about fifteen became a junkie, which is not unusual in our neighborhood. In order to maintain her close friendship with him, she became a junkie too. She said it was part of the youth culture, with which she felt very much at home. After a while, for a number or reasons, the boy gave it all up and left the city and his mother in disgust. Hopeless and alone, she grieved. We all visit her.

"O.K., Pa, that's it," I said, "an unadorned and miserable tale."

"But that's not what I mean," my father said. "You misunderstood me on purpose. You know there's a lot more to it. You know that. You left everything out. Turgenev wouldn't do that. Chekhov wouldn't do that. There are in fact Russian writers you never heard of, you don't have an inkling of, as good as anyone, who can write a plain ordinary story, who would not leave out what you have left out. I object not to facts but to people sitting in trees talking senselessly, voices from who knows where . . ."

"Forget that one, Pa, what have I left out now? In this one?"

"Her looks, for instance."

"Oh. Quite handsome, I think. Yes."

"Her hair?"

"Dark, with heavy braids, as though she were a girl or a foreigner."

"What were her parents like, her stock? That she became such a person. It's interesting, you know."

"From out of town. Professional people. The first to be divorced in their county. How's that? Enough?" I asked.

"With you, it's all a joke," he said. "What about the boy's father? Why didn't you mention him? Who was he? Or was the boy born out of wedlock?"

"Yes," I said. "He was born out of wedlock."

"For Godsakes, doesn't anyone in your stories get married? Doesn't anyone have the time to run down to City Hall before they jump into bed?"

"No," I said. "In real life, yes. But in my stories, no."

"Why do you answer me like that?"

"Oh, Pa, this is a simple story about a smart woman who came to N.Y.C. full of interest, love, trust, excitement, very up to date, and about her son, what a hard time she had in this world. Married or not, it's of small consequence."

"It is of great consequence," he said.

"O.K.," I said.

"O.K. O.K. yourself," he said, "but listen. I believe you that she's good-looking, but I don't think she was so smart."

"That's true," I said. "Actually that's the trouble with stories. People start out fantastic. You think they're extraordinary, but it turns out as the work goes along, they're just average with a good education. Sometimes the other way around, the person's a kind of dumb innocent, but he outwits you and you can't even think of an ending good enough."

"What do you do then?" he asked. He had been a doctor for a couple of decades and then an artist for a couple of decades and he's still interested in details, craft, technique.

"Well, you just have to let the story lie around till some agreement can be reached between you and the stubborn hero."

"Aren't you talking silly, now?" he asked. "Start again," he said. "It so happens I'm not going out this evening. Tell the story again. See what you can do this time."

"O.K.," I said. "But it's not a five-minute job." Second attempt:

> Once, across the street from us, there was a fine handsome woman, our neighbor. She had a son whom she loved because she'd known him since birth (in helpless chubby infancy, and in the wrestling, hugging ages, seven to ten, as well as earlier and later). This boy, when he fell into the fist of adolescence, became a junkie. He was not a hopeless one. He was in fact hopeful, an ideologue and successful converter. With his busy brilliance, he wrote persuasive articles for his high-school newspaper. Seeking a wider audience, using important connections, he drummed into Lower Manhattan newsstand distribution a periodical called *Oh! Golden Horse!*
>
> In order to keep him from feeling guilty (because guilt is the stony heart of nine-tenths of all clinically diagnosed cancers in America today, she said), and because she had always believed in giving bad habits room at

home where one could keep an eye on them, she too became a junkie. Her kitchen was famous for a while—a center for intellectual addicts who knew what they were doing. A few felt artistic like Coleridge and others were scientific and revolutionary like Leary. Although she was often high herself, certain good mothering reflexes remained, and she saw to it that there was lots of orange juice around and honey and milk and vitamin pills. However, she never cooked anything but chili, and that no more than once a week. She explained, when we talked to her, seriously, with neighborly concern, that it was her part in the youth culture and she would rather be with the young, it was an honor, than with her own generation.

One week, while nodding through an Antonioni film, this boy was severely jabbed by the elbow of a stern and proselytizing girl, sitting beside him. She offered immediate apricots and nuts for his sugar level, spoke to him sharply, and took him home.

She had heard of him and his work and she herself published, edited, and wrote a competitive journal called *Man Does Live By Bread Alone.* In the organic heat of her continuous presence he could not help but become interested once more in his muscles, his arteries, and nerve connections. In fact he began to love them, treasure them, praise them with funny little songs in *Man Does Live* . . .

the fingers of my flesh transcend
my transcendental soul
the tightness in my shoulders end
my teeth have made me whole

To the mouth of his head (that glory of will and determination) he brought hard apples, nuts, wheat germ, and soybean oil. He said to his old friends, "From now on, I guess I'll keep my wits about me. I'm going on the natch." He said he was about to begin a spiritual deep-breathing journey. "How about you too, Mom?" he asked kindly.

His conversion was so radiant, splendid, that neighborhood kids his age began to say that he had never been a real addict at all, only a journalist along for the smell of the story. The mother tried several times to give up what had become without her son and his friends a lonely habit. This effort only brought it to supportable levels. The boy and his girl took their electronic mimeograph and moved to the bushy edge of another borough. They were very strict. They said they would not see her again until she had been off drugs for sixty days.

At home alone in the evening, weeping, the mother read and reread the seven issues of *Oh! Golden Horse!* They seemed to her as truthful as ever. We often crossed the street to visit and console. But if we mentioned any of our children who were at college or in the hospital or dropouts at home, she would cry out, "My baby! My baby!" and burst into terrible, face-scarring, time-consuming tears. The End.

First my father was silent, then he said, "Number One: You have a nice sense of humor. Number Two: I see you can't tell a plain story. So don't waste time." Then he said sadly, "Number Three: I suppose that means she was alone, she was left like that, his mother. Alone. Probably sick?"

I said, "Yes."

"Poor woman. Poor girl, to be born in a time of fools, to live among fools. The end. The end. You were right to put that down. The end."

I didn't want to argue, but I had to say, "Well, it is not necessarily the end, Pa."

"Yes," he said, "what a tragedy. The end of a person."

"No, Pa," I begged him. "It doesn't have to be. She's only about forty. She could be a hundred different things in this world as time goes on. A teacher or a social worker. An ex-junkie! Sometimes it's better than having a master's in education."

"Jokes," he said. "As a writer that's your main trouble. You don't want to recognize it. Tragedy! Plain tragedy! Historical tragedy! No hope. The end."

"Oh, Pa," I said. "She could change."

"In your own life, too, you have to look it in the face." He took a couple of nitroglycerin. "Turn to five," he said, pointing to the dial on the oxygen tank. He inserted the tubes into his nostrils and breathed deep. He closed his eyes and said, "No."

I had promised the family to always let him have the last word when arguing, but in this case I had a different responsibility. That woman lives across the street. She's my knowledge and my invention. I'm sorry for her. I'm not going to leave her there in that house crying. (Actually neither would Life, which unlike me has no pity.)

Therefore: She did change. Of course her son never came home again. But right now, she's the receptionist in a storefront community clinic in the East Village. Most of the customers are young people, some old friends. The head doctor has said to her, "If we only had three people in this clinic with your experiences . . ."

"The doctor said that?" My father took the oxygen tubes out of his nostrils and said, "Jokes. Jokes again."

"No, Pa, it could really happen that way, it's a funny world nowadays."

"No," he said. "Truth first. She will slide back. A person must have character. She does not."

"No, Pa," I said. "That's it. She's got a job. Forget it. She's in that storefront working."

"How long will it be?" he asked. "Tragedy! You too. When will you look it in the face?"

Photograph of Luisa

Melissa Pritchard

Since there are no phone booths in a ghost town, I wrote a postcard. The postcard was white, which bothered me, so I colored it. On top of the red smear, with a black crayon, I printed:

> dear rattlesnake killer,
> please come right away.
> luisa
> p.s. we have money this time

It was two weeks or more before he came and he wasn't even the same man as before. Maybe he was his son, that's what I thought at the time. But before you hear about that, I want to tell you about Luisa.

Luisa's hair pushes out from the underside of her skull, then splits into two branches, or better yet, black forks. Her mouth, it is wide, her fingers tell me that it is wide. She is blind so she must not use her fingers. Poor blind Luisa. I'm fooling you, hah, I'm not blind. But sometimes I would like to turn in the direction of my mother and be prevented from seeing her. My mother, who is quite old, sits in a chair on the porch, near the railing. She whispers that because of me she breathes in red dust all day. Since the photographs came, I have neglected her. I have stopped wondering if she will punish me forever. Carelessly now, I tend my mother. She is too choked up with that dust to thank me.

We live in this ghost town which is a very phony ghost town. It is an old movie set where Henry Fonda used to make westerns. Mr. Sanchez, whose head is yellow-empty like a dried gourd, sighs. "Maybe they'll come back some day and make another movie." And then he shakes his head at me. "Maybe they'll have a part in the movie for you, Luisa." He is quite serious. Hah, I say to him. Hah.

I wrote the rattlesnake killer because they are all over the place this summer. I see and hear one every day. My mother is not especially worried; she boasts that they have many times hiked up her legs to warm themselves in her stone of a lap. Mr. Sanchez even left me a shotgun, but I don't remember how to use it. Have you ever held a rifle every which way and then put it away for good?

In the mornings I'm up in the dark, up when it's still cool. I shake out my hair and go tend the animals, pouring water for them. I don't wear clothes then, I don't wear boots. I am careful not to step on anything living. To step on a living thing, to harm a life, is to have that life and maybe other lives follow you around to the end of your days, that's what my mother believes.

And when it's still so dark and I am with the animals, I can watch my reflection pouring out in the hard dark water. It is the time when ghosts matter least.

After swinging shut the corral gate, I climb up on the rail and face the peak, the Cabezon, watching for the sun which jumps up from behind it. A spit of river circles the base of the mesa, and it's all the water we have here, for the animals, for my mother who thirsts, for the tourists who come. Mr. Sanchez calls them tourists so I do too, because that is my job. When they drive up here lost, I quietly tell them that this is a ghost town and for fifty cents, even though I am blind, I can give them a pretty good tour. And they're hot and tired and curious because a minute ago they were lost and bad tempered, and now they're in a ghost town with a girl with hair split in two and eyes that see everything.

To fence up a desert is to make a dry pasture. Fencing is almost all there is here. Down the road is an abandoned house, red adobe, tin roof, no glass in the windows, no door in the doorway, and an old white washer tipped against one wall. Mr. Sanchez keeps a herd of spotted horses near here. That's all there is, that's it, besides a certain ghost town which, before the sunlight has a chance at it, is cold and blue.

I gulp coffee, spitting out the grounds, and watch my town lose its blue coldness. When the sun is up, the wood buildings are bleached and warped loose; the street, rutted red clay. (I have wiped such reddish stuff off my brother's face and fastened it like a mask, with guilty fingers, over my own. In dreams, my mother saw death approach our house through a different door. Over and over, in her dreams, death had both of us.)

I must go inside and dress before my mother wakes up.

Each day I have expected him. Each day nothing. This morning I wake up and go outside, and I know when my feet hit the ground that someone is approaching the ghost town. I hear no car on the road, but I can feel the clay shaking gently beneath me. I water the animals—the chickens, the goats, and the donkey—then I go back and get dressed right away and sit out on the steps, waiting. I wait for hours, until the blue wood is bleached and warped loose and I hear my mother's bare feet whispering behind me on the porch.

He does not come as a speck of horizon getting larger and larger. He is quietly there, at the end of the street, on his horse. As I said in the beginning, I am surprised because he is not the one I remember from last time. Maybe, I think, this is his son. He leans down to me over his sweating horse. He sweats too. He is fat, very loose around the belly. He wears a holy medallion around his neck and a dirty leather vest. A black cowboy hat with a short dyed feather shades his face. There is a bag for collecting the snakes in. I see his belt is made of the snakeskin.

He says something, and I point to all the places where I have seen them lately. I turn a little and point into one dark house, then another. He nods, slides off his horse and ties it to a weak railing. I go to fetch water. The horse drinks, the man drinks. Loosely holding his rifle, he hooks the sack to his belt, nods at me again, and heads around the back of the street. He has much work to do, so I creep up the steps and sit by my mother. I rest my head on her knee and her hand smooths my hair. The first shot is fired. Her hand stops forever, then continues.

Later he sits on the steps, rubbing his forehead with a red cloth. Even when there is no dampness left, he keeps wiping, slowly, across his forehead. His horse stands in a finger of shade, flies marching around its eyes and muzzle. I am standing here in the doorway of my house and I think of looking for the sack. It is slumped in clay by the feet of the man. It is not even half full. Maybe he is not finished. Maybe he is not so good a shot as the other man. Maybe he doesn't guess where they hide by day as well as I do.

He looks into the wetness on the red cloth and says, "Weren't as many as I'd expected to find." Now he is turned, looking at me through his square dark glasses. He keeps watching me. I am breaking off bits of wood from the doorway with my fingers. I am not used to people. I am not accustomed to anything living. His watching, his not saying anything while he watches, reminds me of that.

He asks my name.

"Luisa Jaramillo."

"Luisa, I'd like to ask you a favor."

"Sure," I say, meaning no. You can have water, that's all. "Sure," I say.

He pauses, looks over at his horse. "I'm a photographer, Luisa, not a snake killer. An amateur snake killer, a professional photographer. I am also a tourist, not from here."

My fingers peel off a sliver of wood that catches and jabs under my nail. Even my mother is quiet but awake.

"I asked the old man who usually comes out here to help you if I could do the job for him. You see, he's been sick since this past winter and I thought I'd help him out and me at the same time." He points to the sack. "Rotten work."

I am looking at him fearfully, wondering if he got them all.

"When he told me about this ghost town and about you living out here, taking care of this place . . ."

The place takes care of itself. I take care of my mother and water the animals.

". . . I got interested. Maybe some great pictures, I thought. Anyway, Luisa . . ." Now he's looking at me, he has taken off his glasses and his eyes are light gray, ghost rock. He knows nothing about me.

"I would like to ask your permission to shoot some pictures."

"Of what?" I ask. My voice comes from the sliver of wood under my nail, slight but painful.

"Of you, in this town."

"There are only ghosts here," I insist in a quiet voice.

"Well yes, it must seem so by now." He sounds surprised but not curious.

"Will you let me, Luisa?"

I answer him.

He gets to his feet as if he has already forgotten me and goes to his horse, to the saddlebag. I come out to the steps, following him that far.

"I've never had my picture taken," I say loudly. He is not far off, but his back is to me, so I yell.

"It won't hurt," he hollers back. He is getting out some kind of camera equipment; he brings it back to the porch and sits on the steps, working with it.

"What's your name?" I ask.

He looks at me. "I'll be ready for you in a minute."

I look away and wait.

By sunset he is finished. I am glad at first, but after he gets up from the steps where we have sat together and goes over to his horse, I feel the connection of film between us breaking. His camera, full of me and my mother, is in the saddlebag.

He lifts the sack and ties it to the saddle. I can see curves through the burlap sacking, long cold coils. I am certain he didn't get them all. I feel very unsafe, very frightened, unable to speak.

He is on his horse, which I imagine is white, then brown grows over many parts of what I have imagined, and he is on his spotted horse, leaning down to me. His hand reaches out and smooths my hair the way my mother's did while he was killing those snakes with his gun.

"The old man tells me that people have grown afraid for you."

I am looking at the horse's red-rimmed hooves, at the tail switching drily between the two back legs. I want this man to know that ghost town pictures will disappoint him.

"Luisa, it was not your fault, what happened. You are no longer blamed." He runs his hand down my face, around my eyes.

"You cannot bury yourself here."

I am sure it is wind or dream and not a human gesture.

I sit on the railing of the corral; the donkey nudges her dry nose against my leg. I am facing Cabezon, the large head, I told him, that's what it means. Large head. He took a picture of me standing in front of it.

I am here for a long time. The light that is left is so brief. There is no moon to cover the stars. The points of the stars which can pierce holes in my skin are beauty. Cabezon is beauty.

"It was not your fault . . . the people have grown afraid for you . . ."

I am among ghosts, where I belong.

Mr. Sanchez's pickup is coming up the road from town. I stop sweeping to watch. Red dust already blows back onto the porch and into the house, but I like the temporary cleanness. His truck stops a few feet from me. I drop the broom and run down to look inside the bags in the back of the pickup. The truck is bright blue. I'd like to tease Mr. Sanchez that he is trying to be an Indian driving around in his turquoise truck. That's what they all buy, those Indians, that color of truck.

"Well here you are, Luisa." He is helping carry the paper sacks into the house, into the kitchen, which is in back. He is listing off everything he bought, his old man's voice like dried seeds inside his throat, rattling. "Bread, cheese, meat, tortillas, chillies, pastries, coffee," and then he rummages around in one smaller bag until he brings it out and waves the small package cheerfully.

"Ballpoint pens, this time, Luisa, no crayons. You're too old for those crayons. Yah, you are, so I brought you some ballpointed pens and maybe now you can write some of your family, Luisa. They miss you, you know." And to hide his embarrassment or whatever, he reaches into another bag sitting on the sink and "Here," he waves this around too, "a box of real stationery." He is so pleased by his gifts that I almost smile too.

He remembers something. "Mail, Luisa. You got a package in the mail."

As he goes out of the kitchen I put away the cans and bottles and jars and noisy plastic packages. I have set aside the ballpoint pens and the box of stationery. Oh, this has happened before. He has tried this change before. I hear the truck door open and slam shut. I stand still and look around at the kitchen wall, thickly blotted with squares of paper. Every space of wall has a crayon drawing taped to it. One wall is for my mother's slow, careful drawings; the rest of it is all for me. We color in the evenings, sorting through the crayons on the table; my mother makes shapes of guns and boy figures lying flat with red snakes crawling off them onto the black wavy line that means earth to her, then she colors everything she remembers back over with white. Me, I rub one color on top of another. It helps to use red. Many of my papers are colored over with various reds, but I have never found the perfect shade or shape. And Mr. Sanchez brings us ballpoint pens and stationery.

I look at this old man with suspicion as he hands me a thick brown envelope. He leaves me alone with it. Perhaps he understands that if you never receive mail from anybody, a large brown envelope with your name all over it should not be fussed over.

He has gone out to the porch to talk with my mother. I never know what they find to talk about or even if she answers him with anything but her monotonous whispers. But Mr. Sanchez is a respectful man.

I go outside, not letting go of my envelope. It feels like a rock through its covering. And on the porch now, he and I talk about the animals, the carrying of water from the river, and the rattlesnakes. I try to say that they are mostly gone, that I have seen only one in all the time since the man left. But all that Mr. Sanchez hears is how frightened I am of them, of how unsafe I feel.

"Hey, it's the end of the summer now," he reassures me. "They'll soon feel sleepy and crawl underground," and he talks about the piñon and the cedar firewood that he has already brought in great bundles down from the mountains.

After he climbs into his truck, I ask about his family, his wife and children, whom I have never met. He quietly answers that they are fine, all fine. Polite, I ask nothing more. I thank him then for the groceries, oh, and for the pens and writing paper too.

"That's ok, Luisa, that's ok." Now it is his turn to say what he says to me each time. "The day you can forgive yourself, Luisa, that day you will come away from here."

A statue of an all-embracing Jesus stands on the dashboard of his truck; rosary beads hang from the mirror.

"It is bad, Luisa, to live like you do, seeing no one."

I wait until I see his speck of turquoise stopped by the pasture down the road. I decide where to sit to open my package. I go out by the corral and sit on the ground in a bit of shade. I face Cabezon. The spotted horses are grazing down by the river, their tails dipping like brushes into the muddy water. My hair falls forward, its two black branches shelter my face.

A Mexican woman sits on a painted chair inside her simple adobe house. Behind her are geranium plants on the windowsill, bursting out of coffee cans. Her hands are folded in her rutted lap. *Families,* this book is called. I open it tenderly, the spine cracks. I turn cool pages, watching photographs go by. I care nothing about these people, these mesas, these ranches outside of town. I see low mud houses, narrow streets, sly faces, wondering faces, but they are uninvited in my memory. I turn pages, or maybe breath from Cabezon, from the large head, helps turn them for me. I see my sister, my pretty little sister; she is crouched against the white stucco wall of our old house. The way her face looks, the way her hands are not childlike but are pressed behind her into the wall, hurts me. The pages are lifted from my fingers by the wind from Cabezon. It is not a large book, nearly finished.

Then I see this one page and lean close to it, rocking back and forth. Mamma's chair is on the ghost porch, near the rail, but it does not hold Mamma in its lap. In this photograph the chair is brimming with air and dust. Oh, I might have told him, ghost town pictures would disappoint him with their nothingness.

Now I am wrong. For here is a photograph of Luisa against the town. Luisa's hair, Luisa's blind eyes, the old clay-spotted shirt of Luisa's.

See, Mamma. I am visible. I am in a photograph. You are not in a photograph. You stop now, stop whispering behind me. I should be forgiven.

This book disappears into its envelope. Sometime I will look at it again. I had meant to tell that man with the sweating belly that ghost town pictures would show him nothing. Poor blind Luisa, he would have said. For in this book of his, what breathes red dust in Mamma's chair, what will not forgive, is shown as nothing, and what is visible in a clay-spotted blouse is me.

I aimed your rifle foolishly; it gave such a little warning, and, as Mamma knew, dreams are dangerous. Dreams will come after you.

Perhaps the people of the town should not be afraid for Luisa. Perhaps the part of Luisa that exists in photographs and is blameless will walk along the black wavy line that means earth, towards home.

And the part of Luisa which must remain, in Mamma's dream, dead alongside the dead, will open wide her eyes, and with Mr. Sanchez's old rifle frighten those snakes underground, before winter. Hah.

The Fence Party

Elizabeth Tallent

With the sound of the river forcing him to lift his voice and pitch it for her ears, Hart is holding forth to a woman with doctored auburn hair on the eccentricities of his father-in-law, a Nicaraguan refugee. She inclines her head, an angle that mimics, and in a shady way pretends to predict, intimacy. She has such a small, guarded face, crowned with the absurd hair, that he wants her to come closer. As a subject, fathers-in-law are a little poignant: Hart knows that this woman has had at least two. Acknowledging his own father-in-law proves that Hart is a family man. He likes to establish that at once and let his amused account, falling into the gentlest irritation, suggest that he might be a slightly disappointed family man. That is the second thing Hart likes to make known. He likes to present the fact and the subtle hint of its contradiction together, a knot.

All afternoon, from a distance, Hart followed the auburn head among his guests, who had been invited to mend the old fence on the steep slope above the house. He watched her swinging a hammer, riding forward on its strokes with a carpenter's grace, her tanned, barefoot daughter handing her tenpenny nails, and fell in love. The party is a reward for the fence's menders, and a housewarming as well, because Hart and his second wife, Caro, bought the house last winter, less than a month after they were married. He is lucky in the weather, as he knew he would be. Only last week, the evening would have been too cold for people to stand around drinking on the lawn. But not tonight, not when everyone feels flushed and high with work. Tonight could almost be summer.

Hart puts his hand on the woman's arm, then knows that was a mistake, and pretends, working thumb and forefinger, to rub out a mosquito. He does voices well and has caught the Nicaraguan lilt exactly, more exactly than the auburn head can take in. Hart's brother-in-law works in a windowless Washington cubicle, and once Hart tricked him, long distance, into believing that he was a desperate, but definitely Nicaraguan, refugee. It was too bad he did that, because Caro found out. She interpreted it to mean that he didn't believe in the serious nature of her brother's work; that he took the entire Dominguez family far too lightly; that she should pack and go before she was ever so shamed in her family's eyes again. If she happened to overhear him now, she would guess exactly what he was up to. Hart glances over his shoulder. Caro is standing on the reedy bank, out of earshot, stripping a willow twig and letting the leaves wing down into the current, fast with snowmelt. Beside her, an elderly guest in baggy trousers scans the river for teal with Caro's binoculars; Caro must have told him what to search for. It's a good thing that in birdwatching Caro has found something she likes. Hart hadn't known how she would handle the solitude of the house in the gorge. He teaches mathematics three days a week, fifty miles each way, and those nights it's easiest for him to sleep on the couch in his office. But in the intense, close Dominguez clan of brothers, sisters, god-parents, and cousins, no one is ever by himself, and at first Caro was frightened of the house's remoteness—of the way that up and down the canyon at night there were no lights that were not stars. Lately, though, Hart has almost ceased to worry about her. Last month when the river began to rise, she spent the days dragging and stacking sandbags into a wall that now protects the house, tapering away along the lawn's undercut, somewhat treacherous bank. Because they were meant to hold wheat for famine relief, the hundreds of dun sandbags had DONATED BY THE PEOPLE OF THE U.S.A. printed on them, and, for longshoremen, USE NO HOOKS. Caro had even been in the paper—a grainy, dramatic photograph of a young woman, her arms streaked with mud, fortifying her house against the rising Rio Grande.

No one knows how badly Hart wanted this house on the river. Not Caro, and not Kevin, Hart's fifteen-year-old son, who reads his father's emotions with uncanny and troubling accuracy. But Caro and Kevin would never have suspected Hart of such single-mindedness, though in fact he was intent on having the house as soon as he saw it, from the intaglio Moorish cross on the granite threshold, through each of the quiet, cobwebbed rooms, to the chicken coop on the slope. He felt a sharp nostalgia when the door rocked open at the real estate agent's prodding to reveal the downy floor of the abandoned coop, with rays of light smoking in between the warped pine planks. Silent with covetousness, back in the shadowy living room, Hart let the agent run through her pitch, but nothing she said mattered to him. He was already sold.

To his surprise, Caro was game. She adapted. Slugging leaden sandbags into place, she had had lots of time to feel furious regret at being tied to an old house in danger of washing away, but she'd been uncomplaining, even stoic. She deserves her picture in the paper; yes, she does.

While he deserves this guest, and with a flirting dance step moves a little nearer. Her daughter looks something like her, only new-minted. The daughter's hair must be the original, brushed away from the brown forehead and falling down her back in a long mare's-tail mass, the kind of hair that would snap when brushed and has a glossy warmth that the mother, twice divorced, still tries for. This is the girl that his son has been courting all afternoon with an awkwardness that makes Hart catch his breath, he recalls so much when he sees it. Kevin pursued the girl across the lawn, along the cobbled-together fence, which they pretended to inspect, and up the river into the cottonwoods. Watching them go, Hart felt all of his amused detachment from Kevin vanish. He has Kevin all summer, but throughout the school year Kevin lives with his mother, and Hart wishes he could keep him longer, for some of the changes in Kevin are disturbing—a kind of vague depression, yet a cockiness, a screwed-up *some*thing. Kevin carries a Skoal can in a back pocket of his Levi's, where it has worn a little halo of lightness in the denim; Hart wonders if there is really chewing tobacco in the can. When he talks to Kevin lately, he feels Kevin's attention shy away, glance back, and swing toward opposition. Recently, Kevin informed Hart that he wanted to change his name to Cisco. Caro laughed, and adopted it at once. That is pure Caro, to turn against Hart in a way that seems to ally her with Kevin but actually doesn't have Kevin's best interests at heart at all. Hart has been critical of her: she doesn't lift a finger to interrupt the wary arguments.

"We're not used to each other," Caro said. "I can't be strict with him, Hart. It makes me feel like an idiot. Discipline, that's your business, if you want to act that way with him. From me he can count on empathy. That's how it goes in my family—the men for strictness, the women for empathy. Who needs it more than a fifteen-year-old kid with this strange imported stepmother?"

"It's not empathy if you just give without thinking what's good," Hart said.

"I don't understand why even little things about Kevin drive you so crazy. He doesn't do anything wrong, Hart. He even remembers your birthday." That was so: there, on the living-room wall, was the painting Kevin did when his father turned forty-three, of a tall, Kevin-like punk rocker in a funereal black suit, with skinny legs, bronze hair, and pointy sunglasses. "See, Kev has a sense of humor about himself. About you, too."

"If you're my wife, you have to begin to act like his mother," Hart snapped. For which he got what he had expected, a longish Caro stare.

Now Caro works her way through the party: an instinctive hostess, she clearly adores each guest. After all, these friends had turned up when needed, to help mend the fence; they have the rare sensation of feeling that they are people who can be counted on. Caro tends that mood, carrying a bottle of Spanish champagne to some stragglers, flushing a little laughter from them. Hart feels an abrupt, cherishing regard for his wife. What more can he ask for?

The answer to that is standing beside him, and he keeps talking.

"See, Spanish is so strange that a vital insult can sometimes be an endearment. Like *'cabrón'*—a very bad word that means 'goat.' That can be mortal. But my father-in-law, he calls me *cabrito*."

"Little goat," the auburn-haired guest says.

"Except when he calls me *chico. Chico* this, *chico* that, because *'chico'* is basically an all-purpose word, a pleasant way of ending sentences."

"My daughter had a boyfriend who called her *chica.* I was kind of worried about that. That went on for a while."

"Worried because he was Spanish?"

"And for other reasons." She touches a diamond earring. "They broke up and she just, she just didn't handle it too well. But I think he was mean to her."

Somehow, he is losing her attention. "How was he mean?"

"In little ways. You know." She turns. "Hart, *look.* In the water." But he's gazing at her, and she does a curious thing: she takes his chin and faces his eyes at the river. On the dark surface, not thirty feet out, there is a floating scrap he slowly recognizes as a forehead. The forehead of a stricken face, a woman's, and then a second face, a man's, turning in slow motion to stare at the party on the lawn. An overturned canoe bucks below their arms, and seems to grind against them. Hart is sure he sees the woman flinch. Her thin arms rest on the canoe's underside, which threatens to throw her off. Hart thinks, she wishes she could just lay her head down and go to sleep, turning her cheek to the slick wood and holding on until she lets go. He thinks, she could die. She is just so tired she could die. Behind him, a guest calls out, "Can't you swim?"

The sound carries across the water.

The man's face, with its drenched hair, lifts, and he calls back, "No."

Hart doesn't feel as frightened for him as for the woman. He hands his wineglass to the auburn-haired guest, who says, "Go on. *Go!*"

On the torn bank, with the familiar muck squishing under his sneakers and a tier of submerged sandbags before him, Hart tries to judge the best way of diving in among the sharp underwater boulders, fallen long ago from the gorge's walls. He knows what the boulders are like near the bank, because except when the river is this high they're exposed. There is a conversation going on between the canoe, still upriver, and the lawn, but Hart can't make it out. The man in the water has roused himself, and is doing all the talking for the couple. Hart can see the woman's glistening head, her cheek lying against the russet wood now. The man begins to resist, according to the instructions of a guest on the lawn, who is calling, "Bring it around! Bring it around!" trying to brake the canoe's speed by kicking against it. The canoe wobbles, and the woman looks up, scared to death.

Then, with a father's alertness to the shape of his son, Hart sees a half-naked Kevin launch himself from a steep boulder so surely that his back, flat over the water, branches with muscle, and his extended arms sweep forward, hiding his face. The river takes him with slapped-up light. An amazing shock—not a stillness but a live shock—startles Hart's chest. Kevin went in thirty feet upstream from the canted canoe. Hart forgets the rocks and dives. His body knows that it wasn't a good dive, and his outstretched hands pat down the plush side of an old boulder that looms up too near his forehead. There is a dappled, wavering radiance that is the river's surface; below that, everything is a thousand shades of brown. Hart strokes strongly through the moving cold. A small voice in the back of his skull is calling, *Kevin Kevin Kevin.* Another, rational voice is reasoning that Kevin is safe. Desperate to breathe, Hart feels the mistakes his son could make. Hart remembers, from long ago, his son's impossibly clumsy adoration of the girl. He's a child, and the water is so strong. Hart strains to believe what he knows—that Kevin isn't safe, that he is somewhere in the river. Hart pushes himself against the current, and when he comes up, a window shatters. He shakes his head harshly, flinging water from his eyes, sucking air. A kind of gold-shot dusk from the river lies over everything. His gut is all springy and young with panic, and he feels very strange. He turns around in a circle. There is no canoe.

There is no Kevin. A voice calls, *Kev Kev Kev.* The wall of the gorge tilts very slowly—slowly but definitely, it rocks forward and back. Hart knows that the gorge's wall is eternal, but he saw it tilt. That dazzle in the corner of his vision is the river wrinkling around reeds. The bitterness in his mouth is the licked-clamshell taste of river water. On a gust of adrenaline, he kicks himself through another complete, more careful circle, because logic dictates that the canoe is either before him or behind him, and that he has missed it. There are some guests on the bank, still holding their glasses. The violence of his emotions buoys him up, but he is sliding rapidly downstream, away from the party.

With a rush of relief, he finds the canoe—and Kevin towing it in to the bank, almost home. The man and the woman are still clinging to the canoe, not helping. Hart hopes they're at least not hurting. Kevin's face has the awed expression of profound exertion. Kevin catches a firm hold near the bank, hooking an elbow around a willow trunk and snugging himself in, out of the full force of the current, drawing the canoe after him only when he's safe, and there. *Good boy,* Hart thinks. The man, then the woman begin to push themselves up thinly, having got their footing. Neither of them helps Kevin with the canoe, but someone on the bank is thinking and comes down to steady it while Kevin shoves. Then several other guests stride down, and there is a kind of choreographed silent-movie struggle to draw the canoeists and canoe from the water. Kevin lurches shyly out, six feet of bare-backed, bright-white boy, and Hart could sing.

He treads through another cold circle, for joy. The shadows of the cottonwoods, thrown across the river's bronze-brown, are almost touching him now. His wet head draws a haze of gnats, so close that when he blinks several are caught in his eyelashes. He dives and strokes in the direction of the lawn. When he surfaces again, he knows Kevin is looking for him among the partygoers and, not finding him there, is frightened that his father hadn't—somehow hadn't—seen the rescue. When Kevin faces the water, Hart is already wading up through the muck below the bank he dived from. His left foot is bare; between his toes, the mud is velvet. Hart hugs himself and slaps his rib cage on either side.

He climbs the stepped sandbags, then labors up the bank, patting the canoe as he passes it. He knows that the canoeists will be shepherded through the party to Caro, and that she will be very good at comforting them, and that there will be a story in it to be relayed from Dominguez to Dominguez across North America. Exultant, Hart moves through what's left of the party. The nearly drowned look awkward, like absurdly late guests. The man rather delicately cracks a can of Dos Equis, and is forced to laugh at himself for the sheer ordinariness of the thing he has just done. He has opened a beer. He could have drowned.

Caro brings a brandy for the woman, who is already feathering her spiky hair away from her face, life and vanity returning, though there are exhausted smudges under her eyes. Hart wants her to look at him, and she does. He guesses she feels a lot of things: embarrassment, pleasure in recognizing him, gratitude, anxious relief, and shock—still, prominently, shock, with shock's cold simplicity. He remembers her cheek laid against the rocking wood. He feels too close to her to try to talk to her. Caro seems to be teaching her how to drink, anyway. The woman takes the brandy in slow, breathy sips.

Hart sees the auburn-haired guest from the corner of his eye, and she gives him a big melancholy grin and swoons backward into the arms of a tennis pro, who catches her neatly. The near-drowning has brought out a rising hilarity in the guests. They are cautious about intruding on the canoeists, yet no one looks away from them, either. The canoeists are so wet they might as well be naked, but it's a charmed, neutral nakedness: no one could make them feel it. No one wishes to be very far from them. They're a little magic.

Before the banalities begin, the harmless things everyone is going to feel compelled to say, Caro catches up with Hart and says softly, "Just because *I* had *my* picture in the paper," and pounds her fist gently against his slick chest. She picks the sodden T-shirt away from his skin, but it sticks again, and she kisses his chest through it, whispering, "O.K., you're a hero now. A hero. Was it worth it?"

He's not a hero. He's abashed, and somehow banished from grace, like all of the others who didn't go in. Twenty feet away, in a clearing among the guests, Kevin is lying on his back in the grass, the wet jeans gleaming on his legs. The girl kneeling beside him is drying his face with her hair.

Hart can taste it, himself saying to his son, "Jesus, Kev, I thought I'd lost you."

Caro hits him. "Oh, no, you don't," she says. "You just leave them alone."

Powder

Tobias Wolff

Just before Christmas my father took me skiing at Mount Baker. He'd had to fight for the privilege of my company, because my mother was still angry with him for sneaking me into a nightclub during his last visit, to see Thelonious Monk.

He wouldn't give up. He promised, hand on heart, to take good care of me and have me home for dinner on Christmas Eve, and she relented. But as we were checking out of the lodge that morning it began to snow, and in this snow he observed some rare quality that made it necessary for us to get in one last run. We got in several last runs. He was indifferent to my fretting. Snow whirled around us in bitter, blinding squalls, hissing like sand, and still we skied. As the lift bore us to the peak yet again, my father looked at his watch and said, "Criminy. This'll have to be a fast one."

By now I couldn't see the trail. There was no point in trying. I stuck to him like white on rice and did what he did and somehow made it to the bottom without sailing off a cliff. We returned our skis and my father put chains on the Austin-Healey while I swayed from foot to foot, clapping my mittens and wishing I was home. I could see everything. The green tablecloth, the plates with the holly pattern, the red candles waiting to be lit.

We passed a diner on our way out. "You want some soup?" my father asked. I shook my head. "Buck up," he said. "I'll get you there. Right, doctor?"

I was supposed to say, "Right, doctor," but I didn't say anything.

A state trooper waved us down outside the resort. A pair of sawhorses were blocking the road. The trooper came up to our car and bent down to my father's window. His face was bleached by the cold. Snowflakes clung to his eyebrows and to the fur trim of his jacket and cap.

"Don't tell me," my father said.

The trooper told him. The road was closed. It might get cleared, it might not. Storm took everyone by surprise. So much, so fast. Hard to get people moving. Christmas Eve. What can you do.

My father said, "Look. We're talking about five, six inches. I've taken this car through worse than that."

The trooper straightened up. His face was out of sight but I could hear him. "The road is closed."

My father sat with both hands on the wheel, rubbing the wood with his thumbs. He looked at the barricade for a long time. He seemed to be trying to master the idea of it. Then he thanked the trooper, and with a weird, old-maidy show of caution turned the car around. "Your mother will never forgive me for this," he said.

"We should have left before," I said. "Doctor."

He didn't speak to me again until we were in a booth at the diner, waiting for our burgers. "She won't forgive me," he said. "Do you understand? Never."

"I guess," I said, but no guesswork was required; she wouldn't forgive him.

"I can't let that happen." He bent toward me. "I'll tell you what I want. I want us all to be together again. Is that what you want?"

"Yes, sir."

He bumped my chin with his knuckles. "That's all I needed to hear."

When we finished eating he went to the pay phone in the back of the diner, then joined me in the booth again. I figured he'd called my mother, but he didn't give a report. He sipped at his coffee and stared out the window at the empty road. "Come on, come on," he said, though not to me. A little while later he said it again. When the trooper's car went past, lights flashing, he got up and dropped some money on the check. "Okay. Vamanos."

The wind had died. The snow was falling straight down, less of it now and lighter. We drove away from the resort, right up to the barricade. "Move it," my father told me. When I looked at him he said, "What are you waiting for?" I got out and dragged one of the sawhorses aside, then put it back after he drove through. He pushed the door open for me. "Now you're an accomplice," he said. "We go down together." He put the car into gear and gave me a look. "Joke, son."

Down the first long stretch I watched the road behind us, to see if the trooper was on our tail. The barricade vanished. Then there was nothing but snow: snow on the road, snow kicking up from the chains, snow on the trees, snow in the sky; and our trail in the snow. Then I faced forward and had a shock. The lay of the road behind us had been marked by our own tracks, but there were no tracks ahead of us. My father was breaking virgin snow between a line of tall trees. He was humming "Stars Fell on Alabama." I felt snow brush along the floorboards under my feet. To keep my hands from shaking I clamped them between my knees.

My father grunted in a thoughtful way and said, "Don't ever try this yourself."

"I won't."

"That's what you say now, but someday you'll get your license and then you'll think you can do anything. Only you won't be able to do this. You need, I don't know—a certain instinct."

"Maybe I have it."

"You don't. You have your strong points, but not this. I only mention it because I don't want you to get the idea this is something just anybody can do. I'm a great driver. That's not a virtue, okay? It's just a fact, and one you should be aware of. Of course you have to give the old heap some credit, too. There aren't many cars I'd try this with. Listen!"

I did listen. I heard the slap of the chains, the stiff, jerky rasp of the wipers, the purr of the engine. It really did purr. The old heap was almost new. My father couldn't afford it, and kept promising to sell it, but here it was.

I said, "Where do you think that policeman went to?"

"Are you warm enough?" He reached over and cranked up the blower. Then he turned off the wipers. We didn't need them. The clouds had brightened. A few sparse, feathery flakes drifted into our slipstream and were swept away. We left the trees and entered a broad field of snow that ran level for a while and then tilted sharply downward. Orange stakes had been planted at intervals in two parallel lines and my father steered a course between them, though they were far enough apart to leave considerable doubt in my mind as to exactly where the road lay. He was humming again, doing little scat riffs around the melody.

"Okay then. What are my strong points?"

"Don't get me started," he said. "It'd take all day."

"Oh, right. Name one."

"Easy. You always think ahead."

True. I always thought ahead. I was a boy who kept his clothes on numbered hangers to insure proper rotation. I bothered my teachers for homework assignments far ahead of their due dates so I could draw up schedules. I thought ahead, and that was why I knew that there would be other troopers waiting for us at the end of our ride, if we even got there. What I did not know was that my father would wheedle and plead his way past them—he didn't sing "O Tannenbaum," but just about—and get me home for dinner, buying a little more time before my mother decided to make the split final. I knew we'd get caught; I was resigned to it. And maybe for this reason I stopped moping and began to enjoy myself.

Why not? This was one for the books. Like being in a speedboat, only better. You can't go downhill in a boat. And it was all ours. And it kept coming, the laden trees, the unbroken surface of snow, the sudden white vistas. Here and there I saw hints of the road, ditches, fences, stakes, but not so many that I could have found my way. But then I didn't have to. My father was driving. My father in his forty-eighth year, rumpled, kind, bankrupt of honor, flushed with certainty. He was a great driver. All persuasion, no coercion. Such subtlety at the wheel, such tactful pedalwork. I actually trusted him. And the best was yet to come—switchbacks and hairpins impossible to describe. Except maybe to say this: if you haven't driven fresh powder, you haven't driven.

PART THREE

The Writing Process and the Writing Life

Talent and Habit

Writers often speak of "talent" as if it were a single quality, the size and nature of which is determined at birth. This is one of the major myths about writing. Actually, creating fiction involves a constellation of talents, including intuition, an ability with language, a strong interest in people, a knack for telling stories, an ability to learn from criticism without being crushed, and such a hunger to write that we will persist through all kinds of disappointments or difficulties. Every writer has different levels of each.

We can augment all of the talents through prolonged work. We can develop the ability to face up to our own weaknesses and absorb criticism without being overwhelmed. We can strengthen our sentences by studying, experimenting, and pushing against our limits. Our work habits, in the end, matter more than our initial gifts. For this reason, it's futile to try to guess how much talent we have, to get assurances from teachers or friends, or to judge our early work against the published stories and novels of the greatest writers. Writers who start out with strong abilities in storytelling or language often gain early attention from teachers, prize committees, or editors. Teachers are baffled when these "most talented" students often give up, while others, less visibly gifted, continue on to do substantial work. But over the long haul of a life of (usually) little money and dubious external rewards, the ability to take criticism and the hunger to write are actually the most essential traits.

Another myth is that it's enough just to write, that it doesn't matter what we're writing, as long as we're writing something. While it's normal to produce "shitty first drafts," as Anne Lamott calls them, it's important that we intend these drafts to become stories. Some advice to writers seems to encourage a happy sense of accomplishment, however false, by counting journal writing, freewriting, or even e-mailing as work. Some writers do use journaling to warm up, but if this replaces time working on a story, we've gone off course. Research and note-taking, although vital, don't substitute for the daily effort to imagine people and their lives.

Some days we feel inspired, electric with ideas, and work pours out of us. Our characters seem alive, the world of our story full of possibility and connections. Other days, we sit wretchedly at the desk, desperate to cough up a sentence, realizing that our whole last draft was in error. Yet our feelings are seldom an accurate guide to the quality or potential of a work; the writing we produce when we're "inspired" is just as likely to need revision as the writing that takes great effort. It's hard and even scary to go on working when ideas don't come easily, when everything we write seems idiotic. But on many days that *is* writing, for college students and Nobel Prize winners alike. When our favorite writers started, they produced some atrocious prose; their first drafts may still be atrocious, but we're grateful that they didn't give up. For the sake of our future readers, we need to stop procrastinating, worrying about whether we have talent, and squandering time in endless journaling,

Web surfing, and chat room visiting. We offer—for support, consolation, and further information—the words of other writers, followed by strategies for establishing work routines and habits that develop our various talents.

ADVICE AND EXPERIENCE FROM THE COMMUNITY

Octavia Butler and Michael Cunningham, in the passages below, let us know why it matters that we write regularly, and how it might be possible to do so:

> First forget *inspiration*. Habit is more dependable. Habit will sustain you whether you're inspired or not. Habit will help you finish and polish your stories. Inspiration won't. Habit is persistence in practice.
>
> Forget *talent*. If you have it, fine. Use it. If you don't have it, it doesn't matter. As habit is more dependable than inspiration, continued learning is more dependable than talent.
>
> —Octavia Butler, "Furor Scribendi," *Bloodchild and Other Stories*

> Marilyn Monroe once said, "I wasn't the prettiest. I wasn't the most talented. I simply wanted it more than anyone else." And I sometimes think that I'm just one of the people who comes here every day and does it, even though I don't feel like it, even though it's difficult and I feel stupid and brain-dead and unequal to the task. I have days that are complete losses. It's awful. I just sit and stare at the screen and nothing happens; hours go by and I write down a line and delete it, then write down another line and save it to delete tomorrow. And that's it. That was the writing day. It happens, with a degree of frequency.
>
> . . . I have known writers over the years, enormously talented, who are so self-conscious about it, who are so terrified of ever writing a bad sentence, that they can't write anything at all. I think a certain fearlessness in the face of your own ineptitude is a useful tool.
>
> —Michael Cunningham, "The Difference a Day Makes: After *Hours* with Michael Cunningham," *Poets & Writers* interview

Both Butler and Cunningham emphasize writing regularly: their advice is essential in getting over the idea that we can only write when we're inspired, when our work seems good to us, when we *feel* like writing. Writing daily is not an absolute rule. Sometimes we need to take a week or two off to think, to give ourselves new perspective on a problem in our work. A workshop or our own rereading of our work can make us examine some key aspect of our writing. If we find, yet again, that our characters spend too much time thinking, or that we don't have enough detail, we might want to immerse ourselves in the work of writers who successfully focus on characters' thoughts, or who make stories come to life despite a spare use of description. Perhaps we need to read five or six books, or a dozen stories, by writers we love (or writers recommended by a knowledgeable friend or teacher). How do they solve the artistic/craft problem we're struggling with? What ideas do their approaches give us that we can translate into our own style and fiction?

Unfortunately, no infallible guide exists to let us know when we need a break from our work in order to deepen it, to keep from going stale, and when we're just procrastinating and avoiding some problem that we can solve only by writing our way through it. If we believe it's legitimate to sometimes substitute intensive, focused reading in place of writing time, we may be able to release our anxiety about not writing, to discern what's appropriate. Most days, though, we will need to actually write on our current project, even when we don't understand what we're doing and even when what we're writing looks awful to us.

Deborah Eisenberg, George Leonard, and Robert Boswell give a sense of why it is that we need to revise so often, what happens as we write and rewrite, how our culture's rhythms and values can interfere with the long, slow process of writing, and how we can feel our way into our stories:

> It's quite usual when writing to discover that what seemed to be an inspiration is actually a platitude, to watch an idea degrade just as it unfolds, to have to write something ten, twenty, thirty times before all the clinging stupidities and excesses are purged from it and something bright and substantial emerges. Since I do a certain amount of teaching, I encounter young writers of real ability who, being unfamiliar with the amount of labor that writing something worthwhile requires from most of us, expect to be able to sit down and just . . . write something worthwhile.
>
> —Deborah Eisenberg, "Resistance," *The Eleventh Draft: Craft and the Writing Life from the Iowa Writers' Workshop*

> . . . We are told to get good grades so that we'll graduate from high school and get into college . . . to graduate from high school and get into college so that we'll get a good job . . . to get a good job so that we can buy a house and a car. Again and again we are told to do one thing only so that we can get something else. . . .
>
> . . . The achievement of goals is important. But the real juice of life, whether it be sweet or bitter, is to be found not nearly so much in the products of our efforts as in the process of living itself, in how it feels to be alive. We are taught in countless ways to value the product, the prize, the climactic moment. But even after we've just caught the winning pass in the Superbowl, there's always tomorrow and tomorrow and tomorrow. If our life is a good one, a life of mastery, most of it will be spent on the plateau. If not, a large part of it may well be spent in restless, distracted, ultimately self-destructive attempts to escape the plateau . . . Where . . . are we explicitly taught to value, to enjoy, even to love the plateau, the long stretch of diligent effort with no seeming progress?
>
> —George Leonard, *Mastery*

> I have grown to understand narrative as a form of contemplation, a complex and contradictory way of thinking. I come to know my stories by writing my way into them. I focus on the characters without trying to attach significance to their actions. I do not look for symbols. For as long as I can, I remain purposefully blind to the machinery of the story and only partially cognizant of the world the story creates. I work from a kind of half-knowledge.
>
> In the drafts that follow, I listen to what has made it to the page. Invariably, things have arrived that I did not invite, and they are often the most interesting things in the story. By refusing to fully know the world, I hope to discover unusual formations in the landscape, and strange desires in the characters. By declining to analyze the story, I hope to keep it open to surprise. Each new draft revises the world but does not explain or define it. I work through many drafts, progressively abandoning the familiar. What I can see is always dwarfed by what I cannot know. What the characters come to understand never surpasses that which they cannot grasp. The world remains half-known. In such a world, insight is only valuable if it produces an equal share of mystery.
>
> Writing fiction, for me, is the practice of remaining in the dark.
>
> —Robert Boswell, *The Story Behind the Story*

Deborah Eisenberg's words help us to realize that our first ideas are not necessarily our best ideas. Our excitement about them may come from a sense of freshness, rather than from the ideas themselves. The problem with writing something "ten, twenty, thirty" times is that we don't know how many drafts a project will take, and until the last few, we may be constantly tempted to throw it out and start over. Or those we show an unfinished project to may not fall in love with it, distracted by all its problems. We get sick of working on it. That's when the advice from George Leonard becomes germane, when we begin to value the process itself. This doesn't mean rewriting a single project for the rest of our lives but giving each project its due, discovering whether we are the sort of writers who can carry out several projects at once or need to focus on one, not racing to finish the piece we're working on.

And the passage by Robert Boswell shows us writing and rewriting as discovery. Even if we write numerous drafts and learn to love the work of revising, we may settle too early into a false sense that we know what a story is about, in a way that limits its meaning. The task is not only to keep reworking, but to do so with an open awareness and willingness to change. In the strategies below, we offer some suggestions for carrying out the ideas in this section.

STRATEGIES FOR DEVELOPING AND MAINTAINING WORK HABITS

Different strategies will work for different writers. If a strategy seems promising, it's best to try it for at least three weeks, to give the habit time to settle in. "Writer's Block" and "Rejection, Publication, and Endurance" also have related strategies that may be helpful.

1. The most important strategy is to work for at least one to four hours a day, five to six days a week, on current fiction-writing projects. As much as possible, the work should be writing, but sometimes it may be research, note-taking, writing in journals about the story, or even reading related works to deepen our ideas. In general, we need to work consistently whether we feel like it or not, are well or ill, happy or sad, frantically busy or slothfully resting, recovering from a vicious rejection or inflated with praise, detesting our writing or convinced of our genius. Some people are "binge writers" when they start, saving it all up for open stretches of time. Over the long haul, this isn't sustainable. Life gets busier and busier, our wrists and backs wear out, and then we find ourselves spending all our time trying to get to writers' colonies. If we work today, it will be easier to work tomorrow.
2. Many people find that it helps to write at the same time most days. Writers tend, physiologically, to do their best work at a particular time. Morning writers can find extra time by going to bed an hour earlier and getting up an hour earlier. Evening writers can get up an hour later or take an early evening nap and stay up an hour later. Once writers find their best time, they often arrange their lives and jobs around it. However, it's best not to get so attached to a particular time or place that we don't write at all if our schedule changes.
3. Most of us will get more done if we keep distractions to a minimum. Many of us have to unhook our computers from the Internet until the day's writing is done. Some writers don't have Internet access at home, but use a library computer and so avoid the addiction altogether. Some writers turn off the TV until they've completed their day's writing stint; others give up on TV altogether. The phone can be another temptation. Often, just when we think we don't have enough "brainpower" or we're overcome by the restless desire to do anything else but write, we're on the verge of uncovering valuable and uncomfortable new material. If we keep a notepad handy during our writing time, we can jot down any urgent errands, tasks, or ideas for other projects that come to us. We can note research ideas to follow up on later, when we hook our computer back up. All our tasks and problems will wait. It may help to imagine solid walls surrounding our writing area: inside, we're alone with our story.
4. One of the best ways to keep ourselves accountable and to stay open to seeing our work with fresh eyes is to get into a writers' group or community. We can put an ad in the newspaper, post a notice in a local bookstore, take a class and continue to meet with some of the writers, attend writers' conferences, and go to graduate school. If the first group doesn't work out, we can keep trying until we find one that does. Nonwriters may consider writing self-indulgent; our writer friends understand that it's essential to us and to our future

readers. A group can provide deadlines, criticism, support, and accountability. Once we start publishing, our group supports us through the ups and downs of publicity, reviews, neglect, and attention. Some writers' groups meet weekly, some biweekly, some monthly. Some groups have a weekly e-mail check-in, in which each group member reports on what they've written (and sometimes read) during the week, and makes a commitment for the week to come. This helps us move our writing off the back burner and make it a top priority.

Writer's Block

Few states are more wretched for writers than the one in which we long to write yet find ourselves unable to. The bad news about writer's block is that almost all of us struggle with it at some point, early or late. The good news is that it doesn't need to be the fearsome killer of talent it's sometimes presented as. As writers, we're good at making up dramatic stories—it's what we do. So the trick is to avoid making a five-act production out of our block, and instead to identify exactly where this block is coming from and what it's asking of us.

Sometimes our "writer's block" is actually a necessary fallow time: a refilling of the well, the inner writing mechanism adjusting to the needs of a particular story or book. We may have misconceived some major aspect of plot or character, and the stoppage is a sign to wait, listen, and be ready to make major changes. Some work may be happening underground and will suddenly emerge in a new burst of activity. Or we may be trying to finish a piece too quickly, to suit our schedule rather than the story's. We imagine that we should be able to pop out five or ten pages in a day. Even if at some point, on some project, we could work that quickly, that's not where our writing is now. The mechanism then balks or shuts down.

Sometimes we say, "I have writer's block," when we haven't given ourselves space in our life to write. We attend to everyone and everything else, go for three weeks without looking at our story, and then expect to sit down and get right to work. But the mechanism becomes rusty; our relationship with our work becomes attenuated. By then, we may even have a deadline hanging over us. While some writers do acceptable work under deadline pressure, others freeze up. Sometimes we mistake the ordinary difficulties of writing (see "Talent and Habit") for writer's block.

But if we've really been working regularly, have no specific artistic or technical difficulties with the project, and just can't move forward, we may have a block we need to deal with. We can then examine the usual sources of blocks to see what we need to alter. Our blocks may be external, internal, or some combination of the two.

External sources for blocks include full-time work, heavy course loads, family pressures, or the lack of education or skills to carry out a particular writing project. People in our life may be less than supportive of our writing, of the time it takes, and of everything we or they sacrifice for it. We may have illnesses or injuries that get in our way. Or we may have no private place to work, or no time when we can be sure of being uninterrupted.

Internal sources for blocks include self-doubt about our work; envy of writers who seem to be unjustifiably successful; excessive self-consciousness caused by either a memorably scathing criticism of our work or too much praise; a perfectionism that causes us to despair when we read our early, lousy drafts; a fear that all ideas have been used and no originality is possible; a concern that we've been writing the same story over and over; or an unduly grand idea of ourselves as great writers that keeps us from doing the work we *can* do. Another common source is censorship or self-censorship on topics, or approaches to topics, that could be unacceptable to our family, friends, or other members of our religious or ethnic group. We may be unwilling to accept our own interests, style, and subject matter because we think they're trivial, despicable, unsalable, or too far from our ideals of great writing. We may fear that we're wasting our time, that no one will ever publish or read our work, that we're spending our life on a fool's task when we could be living in a nice house, driving a functional car, buying our clothes in stores instead of thrift shops, eating out in nice places, and going on real vacations.

The truth is that most of us have these thoughts and problems, to one degree or another, *all* the time. They're the ordinary demons of the writing life. So how do we keep them from overwhelming us and putting a stop to our work? One writer we know has a wooden box that she uses as a footrest under her desk. Whenever these thoughts and fears occur to her, she imagines dropping them in the box. When they all get too noisy, she gives the box a good kick. A really malignant block, though, may require more than this. Therefore we're providing experience and ideas from a number of other writers, as well as some strategies that can be helpful in overcoming blocks.

ADVICE AND EXPERIENCE FROM THE COMMUNITY

The following passages by William Stafford, Victoria Nelson, and Annie Dillard help to shake up our traditional ideas of what writer's block may be. Some blocks might disappear, if we abandon our fantasies of perfection, and others may be providing valuable information about our project:

> I believe that the so-called "writing block" is a product of some kind of disproportion between your standards and your performance. I can imagine a person beginning to feel that he's not able to write up to that standard he imagines the world has set for him. But to me that's surrealistic. The only standard I can rationally have is the standard I'm meeting right now. Of course I can write. Anybody can write. People might think that their product is not worthy of the person they assume they are. But it is.
>
> —William Stafford, *Writing the Australian Crawl*

> Writers, when they are not writing, tend to think of themselves in a number of ways, all bad. They are—so they think—lazy, undisciplined shirkers, failures, cowardly frauds, good-for-nothings; the list of negatives stretches into cold infinity. Being temporarily unable to write, however—or, for that matter, to

perform any creative endeavor—is not a bad thing in itself. Properly interpreted, a block is the best thing that can happen to a writer. . . .

. . . The truth is that [writer's block] is no passive condition; it is an aggressive reaction, a loud shout from the unconscious calling attention to the fact that something is out of adjustment. *The block itself is not the problem;* it is a signal to adjust the way we approach our work. By accepting and responding to the message of the block, a writer matures and receives the blessing of the unconscious self, that side of the psyche not directly accessible to us. . . .

—Victoria Nelson, *On Writer's Block*

When you are stuck in a book; when you are well into writing it, and know what comes next, and yet cannot go on; when every morning for a week or a month you enter its room and turn your back on it; then the trouble is either of two things. Either the structure has forked, so the narrative, or the logic, has developed a hairline fracture that will shortly split it up the middle—or you are approaching a fatal mistake. What you had planned will not do. If you pursue your present course, the book will explode or collapse, and you do not know about it yet, quite. . . .

What do you do? Acknowledge, first, that you cannot do nothing. Lay out the structure you already have, x-ray it for a hairline fracture, find it, and think about it for a week or a year; solve the insoluble problem. Or subject the next part, the part at which the worker balks, to harsh tests. It harbors an unexamined and wrong premise. Something completely necessary is false or fatal. Once you find it, and if you can accept the finding, of course it will mean starting again.

—Annie Dillard, *The Writing Life*

When we read these three writers, we can see how useless it is to try to write perfect drafts, to push ourselves into being some other kind of writer, to call ourselves names, and to try to drive forward with a project that needs rethinking before we can proceed. Stafford's words are famous among writers. But what does it mean to lower our standards? Stafford didn't mean that we should publish slapdash work, or abandon the effort to improve: his advice encourages us to allow ourselves to do exactly the work we're capable of without judging it when we're writing a draft. Sometimes, though, as Nelson and Dillard point out, we have to listen to the message from the block or the "worker" inside. (The advice from "Talent and Habit" addresses the pain of having to substantially revise some work that we hoped was nearly finished.)

Sometimes, the block comes not from the work itself, but from the struggle against the limitations of the world around us, as Margaret Walker points out, or from our own psychological barriers, as Bonnie Friedman and Anne Lamott make clear:

. . . phony writers pretending to take us into a more humanistic century are . . . promoted with super-HYPE. Do I sound bitter? A Black Woman Writer who is free? Free to do what? To publish? To be promoted? Of what value is freedom in a money-mad society? . . .

I am a black woman living in a male-oriented and male-dominated white world. Moreover, I live in an American Empire where the financial tentacles of the American Octopus in the business-banking world extend around the globe, with the multinationals and international conglomerates encircling everybody. . . . What then are my problems? They are the pressures of a sexist, racist, violent, and most materialistic society. . . . The entire world of the press, whether broadcast or print journalism, must acquiesce and render service or be eliminated. And what have I to do with this? . . . How long can I live under fear before I too am blown to bits and must crumble into anonymous dust and nonentity?

. . . I wish I could live the years all over. I am sure I would make the same mistakes and do all the things again exactly the same way. But perhaps I might succeed a little more; and wistfully I hope, too, I might have written more books.

—Margaret Walker, *On Being Female, Black, and Free*

As adults, we may project onto others—editors, other writers—a great awareness of what we imagine to be our own disempowerment. We may project onto others the possession of a perfect, delightful, hoarded life. We may project the power ultimately to judge our talent. We may project the power to decide if we should be happy or not, whether we should accept or reject our own work—even, perhaps, whether we should accept or reject our own selves.

Of course, if you're going to give that much power away, you're going to resent like hell whomever you give it to. Envy has projection at its core. One becomes two: you give away part of yourself, then feel lean and hungry, and you long for what you've given away. If praise comes, it satisfies only briefly. How could it be otherwise? The praise comes from outside you; the prize is given by a man or woman who is not you. You long for something—a sign, an unequivocal sign—that you are a good writer, that what you write is worthwhile. . . . What one longs to take into oneself is what one has given away: the power to say yes.

—Bonnie Friedman, *Writing Past Dark: Envy, Fear, Distraction, and Other Dilemmas in the Writer's Life*

What I've learned to do when I sit down to work on a shitty first draft is to quiet the voices in my head. First there's the vinegar-lipped Reader Lady, who says primly, "Well, *that's* not very interesting, is it?" And there's the emaciated German male who writes these Orwellian memos detailing your thought crimes. And there are your parents, agonizing over your lack of loyalty and discretion; and there's William Burroughs, dozing off or shooting up because he finds you as bold and articulate as a houseplant; and so on. And there are also the dogs: let's not forget the dogs, the dogs in their pen who will surely hurtle and snarl their way out if you ever *stop* writing, because writing is, for some of us, the latch that keeps the door of the pen closed, keeps those crazy ravenous dogs contained.

Quieting these voices is at least half the battle I fight daily. . . .

—Anne Lamott, *Bird by Bird: Some Instructions on Writing and Life*

After reading Margaret Walker, we may want to spend some time writing and thinking about the kinds of pain and limitation that come from the outside world. Where do they stop each of us? How can we acknowledge them truthfully without letting them silence us or ruin our work? In their books, Bonnie Friedman and Anne Lamott give names to the torturous inner chatter and psychological quirks that most writers share, that we can learn to deal with. It helps to know that others share these problems; Friedman's honesty and Lamott's brilliant humor can help give us some perspective. If Friedman's or Lamott's passages strike a chord, we can write a list of the people to whom we have given power over our work, or a list of the voices in our head. Why have we given each one this power? What would happen if we took it back? Where do the voices come from? Sometimes an increased level of awareness is enough to tame some of the demons. Other times writers turn to a therapist or coach, often one who specializes in artists' difficulties, to get through a particularly virulent block. The strategies below offer additional solutions.

STRATEGIES FOR OVERCOMING WRITER'S BLOCK

Different strategies will work for different writers. "Talent and Habit" and "Rejection, Publication, and Endurance" also have related strategies that may be helpful.

1. Sometimes we confuse writer's block with the normal difficulty of writing, and then head into a downward spiral of panic and self-blame that does, in fact, lead to a block. If we can accept that painstaking, almost imperceptible work may actually be normal progress, then we may be able to give ourselves permission to continue. The first and most basic permission we have to give ourselves is the permission to write slowly and badly; if we believe that every word has to be a jewel, or that we must get our story almost right in the first draft, we may be unable to write at all. If it helps, we can write quickly by hand, or turn off the computer monitor, in order to keep ourselves from judging our work as we write. We can give ourselves permission to write, whether or not we end up producing great art.
2. If our block stems from a particularly toxic criticism or rejection of our work, we can enlist the help of our friends to figure out what part of it is useful and what can be discarded. Some criticism is simply wrongheaded and should be ignored. Other criticism may be valuable, but badly phrased. Someone we trust, who knows our work, can help us think through what it means when someone says

our central character is "simply dull." Is our character reacting passively or predictably? Do we need a more complicated and contradictory set of traits to define that character? Do we need more at stake in that character's plot line? Much criticism can be broken apart and examined for possible helpfulness. Our writers' group can help us interpret unusually painful criticism. Of course, if our writers' group is giving us damaging criticism, there may be unacknowledged envy or simply a misunderstanding of the kind of work we're trying to do. The best option is to find another group. And if the sharp remark comes from some unknown editor or reviewer, we have to avoid changing our life or giving up on writing because of it. For all we know, that person was coming down with the flu, hates all stories with more than one viewpoint character, or is, in general, a jerk.

3. Taking 10 or 20 minutes for a walk outdoors before a writing session can be energizing, and if we concentrate on watching what's going on around us, we may see or hear something that jumpstarts the creative mechanism. At the very least, we'll notice that there are other people in the world, with their own problems and issues. Observing the world can help us sidestep the melodrama and self-importance that can contribute to writer's block.
4. Some writers try working in 15-minute blocks of time; the knowledge that they can stop soon diminishes the agony. Others break a huge project into manageable stages. Still others keep handy a box of little slips of paper on which they've written vivid nouns and verbs, so that when they are stuck they can pick three words at random to spark a scene. We can look through our unfinished story fragments or ideas; something we tried years ago and set aside may finally make sense. Writing exercises can give us something to start with if the blank page becomes menacing, even if (perhaps especially if) we generally hold writing exercises in disdain.
5. If deadline pressure is holding us back, we can sometimes change the deadline, allowing more time, or we can reduce the scope of the project. Or we can decide to turn the work in to our class or workshop even though it is less than perfectly polished. Sometimes, when we're trying to push our writing, the ability to write at all disappears. And if we have been suffering from writer's block for a long time, we need to be especially kind and reasonable with ourselves. Many writers in this position feel an increasingly desperate pressure, followed by hopelessness. We need to reestablish regular work habits, bad writing or good, until we are once again in accord with our writing mechanism. It helps not to use our (evidently substantial) creative powers to envision dark futures for ourselves based on our current inability to write.

6. Reading the books we love can reconnect us to our sense of purpose as writers, our excitement about writing, and our ideas of what we want our own writing to do.
7. Members of our writers' group and writing community can help by telling their own stories of the blocks they've recovered from, by asking us questions that help us move forward in our work, by giving us deadlines and people to write for, by providing us with a chance to help out other writers even when our own writing isn't flowing smoothly, and in a dozen other ways. (See "Talent and Habit.")

Rejection, Publication, and Endurance

Two primary misconceptions about rejection and publication are that rejection is an entirely bad thing, and other writers are our competitors in the publishing arena. No one likes getting rejections, but they're a useful part of developing our stories, learning how to *finish* a piece of fiction, and finding our most sympathetic magazines, editors, and presses—the ones that draw the kinds of readers who will like our work. And we aren't in competition with our fellows because each writer is looking for his or her own ways to reach readers; we don't all need the same editors or magazines, any more than we all need to marry the same person. Other writers give us comfort, information, and help; they are our community, our colleagues in the endeavor of making meaningful fiction.

Too often, writers send a story to one or two magazines, get their first rejections, and then give up, using this experience as evidence to bolster their usual self-doubt. This self-defeating practice comes from the assumption that our writing can't get much better than it already is (see "Talent and Habit" for help on this) or that everyone would love our writing instantly if it were any good. This practice is the equivalent of going on a couple of blind dates and then giving up. Maybe we went out with someone who only likes blondes, was in a bad mood that night, or has diametrically opposed political views to our own. Why take it personally? Submitting, receiving rejections, and submitting again is a process of looking for partners—for both sides. In a sense, we've already rejected every magazine that we didn't submit to, so when we send a story out, it's the editor's turn to decide whether or not to dance. At any given moment, thousands of magazines, contests, and editors are looking for writers. We can shorten the time it takes to find a match for our writing by reworking our stories until every word is right. Our other obligation, a pleasurable one, is to discover who publishes the writers we love, our literary kin, so that we're not sending our stories out randomly.

We've named a number of first-rate literary magazines in "Suggestions for Further Reading," but our list is only a beginning. Many libraries, particularly college or university libraries, carry a variety of literary magazines, and *The International Directory of Little Magazines & Small Presses* lists thousands more.

Reading a couple of issues of a magazine will give us a far better sense of its flavor than scanning a capsule description in a directory. What are we trying to do as writers? Which magazines have stories that resonate with our own work? A lyrical, imagistic, experimental writer who focuses most often on family dynamics will be at home with different magazines and publishers than a character-oriented realist writing stories about large-scale political events. We should avoid fixing our hopes on a few high-profile glossy magazines, where most writers will never be published, even when they've been writing for a decade or two. Most of us are more likely to publish our writing in smaller literary magazines.

Some writers naturally do the kind of work that will appeal to a large audience; others, with quirkier sensibilities, may reach a devoted group, more limited in size. Publishing, particularly commercial publishing, is a business. Commercial publishers need to examine fiction for market appeal and to keep track of sales, measuring readers by the bushel and the "success" of a work by the money it brings in (although individual editors more often than not will measure a work's success as writers do, by its power and shapeliness, its truth, and the way it meets its own artistic goals).

Writing is an art form; if we try to judge ourselves by the standards of a celebrity-mad society, we'll be miserable, no matter how "successful" we are. In fact, highly visible writers, even if they earn enough to work full-time at their writing, have a heavy workload—juggling speaking engagements, judging contests, writing back-of-book quotes, and otherwise helping newer writers. They also frequently find themselves the object of envy and subject to attacks, both verbally and in print. Since writers don't change their personalities or concerns just because they become successful, they often feel that their success is undeserved, or that perhaps they wrote something decent once, but all their good ideas have disappeared. In either case, they're waiting for what Charles Baxter calls the "Fraud Police" to show up and expose them as impostors; any bad review becomes ammunition for these fears. Success is no protection against anxiety.

Although most of us wish we could have some definitive proof that our writing is worthwhile, it's just as well that we never get it. Those who do believe that their writing is wonderful can become smug, revise less, ignore criticism, and stop improving. The true satisfactions of writing are available to us at any stage of our process: the sudden connection between ideas, an exact metaphor, insight into a character, the companionship of other writers. It's wonderful to have strangers telling us how they love our story or book, at a book signing or by e-mail, but it's also wonderful when someone in our writers' group is excited about our story. If we weren't writing for readers, we'd stick to journal entries. So part of the endurance process of the writer is to find some readers, whether or not we're getting published.

Our "Advice and Experience from the Community" section includes advice from editors, because editors (and reviewers) are part of the writing community, not enemies. Many of them write themselves, even more have studied literature in school, and most live overworked, underpaid lives because of their devotion to books. The least we can do is to be as courteous to them as we wish they would always be to us. One of the greatest kinds of luck we can have is to find editors we adore and reviewers who understand everything we're trying to do; like happy marriages, these relationships are more common than one would guess from the literature.

ADVICE AND EXPERIENCE FROM THE COMMUNITY

Betsy Lerner and Ted Solotaroff, who are both writers and editors, understand how writers respond to rejection. In the following passages, Lerner gives some advice on how *not* to respond to individual rejections, and Solotaroff discusses the whole process of rejection and its effects on writers over time:

> Just as you shouldn't take a polite letter for an encouraging one, don't let a harsh letter do more damage than necessary. Maybe the editor writing it was just dumped by his wife, or acquired more than her share of projects, or lost the office football pool. It's hard not to focus too deeply on a rejection letter, or any correspondence from an editor, because it's often the only feedback you have, but I beg you not to spend more time with rejection letters than the time it takes to read and file them away. Do not paper your bathroom walls with them, as one woman I went to writing school with did; do not wear them down to fine talc with your worrying fingers. Do not study them like the *I Ching,* hoping to draw symbolic meaning from the arrangement of letters on the page. Trying to figure out what the editor or agent *really* meant or felt is not useful unless she has offered some specific constructive criticism that resonates with you.
>
> —Betsy Lerner, *The Forest for the Trees: An Editor's Advice to Writers*

> The gifted young writer has to learn through adversity to separate rejection of one's work from self-rejection, and with respect to the latter, self-criticism . . . from self-distrust. For the inexperienced writer, a year or two of rejection or a major rejection—say, of a novel—can lead all too easily to self-distrust, and from there to a disabling distrust of the writing process itself. Anxious, depressed, defensive, the writer who is suffering this distrust, whether temporarily or chronically or terminally, gives up her most fundamental and enabling right: the right to write uncertainly, roughly, even badly. A garden in the early stage is not a pleasant or compelling place: it's a lot of arduous, messy, noisome work. . . .
>
> . . . the gifted writer is likely to be vulnerable to rejection from without and within, and how well he copes with them is likely to determine whether he has a genuine literary vocation or just a literary flair. To put the matter as directly as I can, rejection and uncertainty and disappointment are as much a part of a writer's life as snow and cold are of an Eskimo's: they are conditions one has to learn not only to live with but also to make use of.
>
> —Ted Solotaroff, "Writing in the Cold: The First Ten Years," *A Few Good Voices in My Head: Occasional Pieces on Writing, Editing, and Reading My Contemporaries*

Lerner and Solotaroff help us gain perspective by giving a sense of the universality of the rejection process and the emotional nature of writers' responses. Almost no writer is optimistic enough to think that it's possible to get published without rejections, but almost no writer is secure enough to regard any given rejection calmly, as an integral part of the process rather than a shattering blow to our self-worth.

When we receive rejections, especially nasty rejections, or bad reviews, we're bound to feel wounded. Sometimes the response is purely mean; sometimes it's useful advice, tactlessly or harshly put. We're probably not going to be able to decide which it is on the day we receive it. Best to put it away (perhaps first sharing it with someone who can be counted on to sympathize). It's information: the story wasn't what the editor or reviewer was looking for. A day or so of self-indulgence and self-pity is probably warranted if it helps. Some writers learn to take rejection and bad reviews in stride and hardly mind the harsh words. Others, even after ten books, will still be calling their friends in tears or eating entire pints of ice cream. Rejection is everyone's least favorite part of the job, and a condition shared with every other writer who ever lived. Some writers are comforted by the quotation books that show the rejections famous books received along the way (see "Suggestions for Further Reading"). When writers' groups share rejections and reviews, each person has a chance to see beautiful work misunderstood. This helps us take it less personally.

Dorothy Allison and Bharati Mukherjee, each in her own way, address the question of what we may or may not be able to expect from readers:

> A few years ago I gave a copy of a piece of "fiction" I had written about incest and adult sexual desire to a friend of mine, a respected feminist editor and activist. "What," she asked me, "do you want from me about this? An editorial response, a personal one, literary or political?" I did not know what to say to her, never having thought about sorting out reading in that way. Certainly, I wanted my story to move her, to show her something about incest survivors, something previously unimaginable and astounding—and not actually just one thing either, as I did not want one thing from her. The piece had not been easy for me, not simple to write or think about afterward. It had walked so close to my own personal history, my nightsweats, shame, and stubborn endurance. What did I want? I wanted the thing all writers want—for the world to break open in response to my story. I wanted to be understood finally for who I believe myself to be, for the difficulty and grief of using my own pain to be justified. I wanted my story to be unique and yet part of something greater than myself. I wanted to be seen for who I am and still appreciated—not denied, not simplified, not lied about or refused or minimized. The same thing I have always wanted.
>
> —Dorothy Allison, "Believing in Literature,"
> *Skin: Talking About Sex, Class, & Literature*

> I think an awful lot of minority writers and expatriate writers complain that their books don't get into bookstores, that they may get reviews, or the same few will get reviews, but that there really isn't any kind of cross-fertilization of readers.

> I think there are two kinds of writers and I'm not saying that it's only about exilic writers or immigrant writers but all writers: those who reinforce what the public thinks, the conventional values, and those who constantly interrogate the conventional values. An awful lot of the exilic writers, the expatriate writers, are providing the kinds of portraits, moods, positions, and problems with which the readership, the publishing industry, and the scholars—or critics anyway—are familiar and comfortable. The few who are obliterating that particular kind of discourse between Third World and First World, margin and center, or minority and mainstream, have a much harder time being understood or being recognized.
>
> —Bharati Mukherjee, "Holders of the Word: An Interview with Bharati Mukherjee," in *Jouvert: A Journal of Postcolonial Studies*

Some readers will experience the world breaking open, as Allison and many other writers wish, but no writer reaches everyone. After reading the quote from Allison, we may stop to think of who we imagine as our own readers, and what it is we hope our work will accomplish. Mukherjee's interview brings up the question of reader expectations, and how work that doesn't reinforce "the conventional values" is likely to meet with more difficulty gaining mainstream recognition. We need to develop a realistic sense of where our own work is at a given point, how the publishing world—whether book or magazine—works, and who our natural editors might be. (The books on publishing listed in "Suggestions for Further Reading" demystify the systems and procedures of the publishing world.)

James Baldwin and Richard Bausch describe how we can make use of the difficulties of trying to move our writing out into the world and what to focus on:

> Any writer, I suppose, feels that the world into which he was born is nothing less than a conspiracy against the cultivation of his talent—which attitude certainly has a great deal to support it. On the other hand, it is only because the world looks on his talent with such a frightening indifference that the artist is compelled to make his talent important. So that any writer, looking back over even so short a span of time as I am here forced to assess, finds that the things which hurt him and the things which helped him cannot be divorced from each other; he could be helped in a certain way only because he was hurt in a certain way; and his help is simply to be enabled to move from one conundrum to the next—one is tempted to say that he moves from one disaster to the next.
>
> —James Baldwin, "Autobiographical Notes," *Notes of a Native Son*

> *Don't compare yourself to anyone, and learn to keep from building expectations.*
>
> People develop at different rates, with different results, and luck is also involved. Your only worry for yourself should be *did I work today?* Be happy for the successes of your friends, because good fortune for one of us is good fortune

> for all of us. When a friend or acquaintance has good luck, you may feel envy because envy is a natural human reaction: but, as George Garrett once put it, when that stuff rises to your mind, you must train yourself to *contend* with it there . . . You will never write anything worth keeping if you allow yourself to give in to petty worries over whether you are treated as you think you deserve, or your rewards are commensurate to the work you've done. That will almost never be the case, and the artist who expects great rewards and complete understanding is a fool.
>
> . . . try to remember that what you are aiming to do is a beautiful—even a noble—thing, trying to write, or make, the truth as straightly and honestly and artfully as you can; and that it is also, always, an inherently optimistic act, because it stems from the belief that there will be civilized others whose sensibilities you may affect, if you are lucky and good and faithful to the task at hand.
>
> —Richard Bausch, *Letters to a Fiction Writer*

Baldwin's and Bausch's advice will apply at any point of our writing lives or career, and help us to survive all the ups and downs of that life. At some point, we're likely to get published, and it will undoubtedly go to our heads. Our published story/book seems to us like the first story or book in the history of the world, and we'll be unable to stop thinking and talking about it. If our work should happen to get a lot of attention, and we feel that all our dreams are finally coming true, we're likely to become particularly hard to live with, at least for a while. We can become somewhat addicted to the phone calls, faxes, reviews, praise, constant conversations with our editor and agent, interviews, and discussions of movie rights. But if we've been training ourselves, right along, to complain to as few people as possible, we can apply the same strategy to boasting and self-congratulation. We'll keep more of our friends that way. And we'll be more ready for the moment when all the attention dies down, so that we're less like overexcited children on the day after Christmas, strung-out, with too much sugar in our systems.

On the other hand, if we don't get published, or if our publications seem unsatisfactory, we may become bitter, unpleasant, and hard to live with. We might pay inordinate attention to the successes of others, develop angry, paranoid theories about the literary world, and adopt a belligerent or apologetic manner of relating to the world.

In either case, the cure is to return our focus to the satisfaction of doing our work. In the great scale of things, the question of whether one is a "real" writer has nothing to do with publication. If we write, we're writers. We have the opportunity to make up worlds, to invent people who never existed until we thought of them, and to be friends with the other peculiar people engaged in this bizarre life. Writing is actually worth everything we give up for it, as long as we love it for its own sake, and keep working to make it more vivid, honest, memorable, rich, and alive.

STRATEGIES FOR FLOURISHING IN THE WRITER'S LIFE

Different strategies will work for different kinds of writers, at different times in their lives. Try any of these that seem potentially useful and ignore whatever doesn't work for you. And, for difficulties that don't seem to be addressed in these strategies, try reading "Talent and Habit" or "Writer's Block."

1. When we submit stories to publications, we'll usually give them the best chance with a fairly standard, unobtrusive format. Stories with fancy fonts, handwritten text, or single spacing very likely won't be read. Adding a copyright notice also appears amateurish. Submissions should be cleanly typed or printed on a high-quality printer with a functioning toner cartridge, double-spaced, on one side of an 8½-by-11-inch sheet of paper. Margins should be at least 1 inch, but 1½ inches is probably even better—the white space makes it easier for those who are reading hundreds of pages a week. For the same reason, a standard serif font (12 point Times Roman, for example) works best, as does a ragged right (rather than justified) margin. Manuscripts are usually paper-clipped, rather than stapled. The first page of the manuscript contains the writer's name, address, phone number, and perhaps an e-mail address, often in the top left corner. A third of the way down the page, the title appears (usually centered and all caps), then another double-space before the story starts. The beginnings of paragraphs are indented five spaces. White space between paragraphs should only be used to signal some shift in the story (see Chapter 5 for more on white space). Otherwise one paragraph follows another with nothing in between. The top of each page after the first should have the writer's last name, a word or so from the title, and a page number.

   A cover letter is a polite gesture toward the human being who will be reading our manuscript. These letters, addressed to a specific editor (by name, correctly spelled), are usually short, naming the story and indicating why we're sending the story to this particular magazine (a good reason would be that we liked some specific story or stories in recent issues, which lets the editor know that we've done our research and haven't just picked their name from some list). We can *briefly* list any relevant publication credits, or, if we have no credits, perhaps a couple of lines about the background for writing the story (not a synopsis, not our own life story or a plea for publication, but a note that we ourselves worked in a nursing home for five years, or come from the Ozarks, or spent two years studying medieval monasteries). We should let the editor know whether this is a simultaneous submission (see Strategy 2), and close with some pleasant remark like, "I look forward to hearing from you," or

"Thank you for your time and attention." A cover letter can only do so much—if it's professional and shows an awareness of the magazine, it can get the story read with more attention. Over time, if an editor shows any interest in our writing and asks to see more, we'll begin to develop a relationship. Again, editors are very overworked, and many literary magazine editors are volunteers. If we keep this in mind, we'll avoid the temptation to send cranky notes, call them up to yell when they take months to read our work, and generally make their lives even harder than they already are.

2. The usual advice on simultaneous submissions is to keep several copies of each story circulating, to notify all other editors immediately when the story is taken, and to put a rejected story in the mail again to a new magazine as soon as we get it back. (Some magazines don't take simultaneous submissions, and their market listings—see "Suggestions for Further Reading"—specify this.) However, submitting stories takes a lot of time and postage: writers at the beginning of their careers might be better off spending that time on revision. In any case, before sending a story out, it makes sense to put it aside for two or three weeks after we think it's done. If, on rereading it, we still can't find any way to change or improve it, we can check it with our writing group (or instructors, if we're taking a class). Editors have piles of stories to choose from and don't have time to waste on unfinished work, no matter how interesting or promising it may be. When the story is really finished, we send it to a journal or two. When a story comes back, we can read it over and think about it for a few days or a week, to consider whether it could still use more revising before we send it out again.

   It may take longer to get published this way, but we won't give editors a bad impression of our work; we won't depress ourselves with an endless series of rejections of stories that are unfinished or underdeveloped; and we won't have to be embarrassed in later years by stories that prematurely found their way into print. (Later on, writers more often regret the work they did publish than the work they didn't.) And we'll spend our time and energy on writing. Our first years of experiment and growth will be happier if we allow ourselves to work steadily without trying to rush into publication.

3. For many writers, graduate school is one of the best ways to develop our writing and enter into the community of serious writers, those who are in this for the long haul. For this reason, the first consideration in choosing an MFA program is not scholarships, prestige, convenience, location, or even the fame of its graduates (the program may have changed substantially over the years). Graduate school is a great opportunity to study with writers whose work we love. Those who choose their programs for the teachers tend to

be happiest with their choice. The Associated Writing Programs publishes a guide to creative writing programs: *The AWP Official Guide to Writing Programs.* This book describes MA and MFA programs and lists faculty and their publications. It also includes information about conferences and colonies, along with an essay on choosing a graduate program. Ph.D. programs, which train scholars rather than writers, are still of interest to some writers, but are a different kind of study. According to AWP, the MFA is the appropriate "terminal" degree for writers. Residential programs may involve moving to a new place and immersing oneself in the program for two to three years. Nonresidential programs, increasingly popular, often involve 10 days of intensive workshop, lectures, and readings twice a year, followed by individual, long-distance study with different faculty members.

We strongly recommend allowing a substantial amount of time to pass between undergraduate and graduate work: time to have a variety of jobs, to develop material, to be part of writers' groups and conferences, and to discover which graduate programs might be most suitable. Spending time outside academia first helps protect writers against the potential downsides of writing programs, which can include tendencies to emphasize technique at the expense of substance and to internalize numerous critical voices in an attempt to please them all. Nonetheless, the best graduate programs, residential and nonresidential, expand our understanding of literature and our reading and writing abilities. They teach us about the writing world, give us a chance to make long-term writing friends, and help us withstand differences of opinion and criticism in a way that makes rejection just a little more bearable.

4. Sometimes writers make the mistake of thinking that spacious writing comes out of a spacious life—that great writers do nothing but write—but everyone, no matter how successful, has to juggle life and writing. On the other hand, we have to make some choices. If we want time to write, we can't enroll in every group or cause we're interested in, we'll probably have to learn how to live cheaply, and we'll need to cut down on time-wasting amusements. The writer's life is actually more fabulous and rewarding than most writers like to admit in public, but it takes courage and stamina. The older we get, the more we become aware that we have a certain well of energy. Exercise, including yoga or Tai Chi/Qi Gong, good food, and supportive relationships fill it up. Emotional dramas, drugs, alcohol, lack of sleep, and stress empty it out. If we're going to sustain this life, we might want to keep an eye on the extent to which we're draining our well or refilling it.

   We need to have a life outside our writing. If our writing, or publishing, is going badly, and sometimes it will be, it seems more disastrous if we have made writing the entire emotional focus of our lives than if we also "count" our accomplishments and joys in our other communities: with our family and friends, our jobs and volunteer work, perhaps our religious/spiritual community. If we're writing 15 hours a day, after a while, we won't have much to write about, and we will undoubtedly have neglected the people who count on us, as well as our obligations as members of a community, city, state, and country. Many writers keep learning, and find great joy, by teaching and helping other writers grow in their work.

APPENDIX

A

A Writer's Glossary

We have defined and explained a number of essential concepts, such as scene, summary, setting, plot, and POV (point of view), in the appropriate chapters: they're listed in the table of contents and index. The glossary focuses on essential terms not explained in the text.

Absurdism A worldview, originating in the early twentieth century with the existential philosophers, that asserts that life is absurd or meaningless. Absurdist writers grapple with the pain caused by the apparent irrationality of life, often using black humor or farce. Absurdism usually reflects this sense of irrationality by defying conventions of character, plot, and dialogue. Writers known for existentialism or absurdism include Jean-Paul Sartre, Albert Camus, Franz Kafka, Samuel Beckett, Eugene Ionesco, and Daniil Kharms.

Active Voice Verb form indicating that the subject of the sentence is acting rather than being acted upon. "Sam betrayed Hyun" is more informative, direct, and vivid than "Hyun was betrayed." *See also* **Passive Voice.**

Aesthetic Distance The degree to which a story invites readers either to identify and sympathize with the characters and their predicaments, or to judge them coolly. The writer can control the aesthetic distance via tone, authorial commentary, point of view, characters' actions, characters' response to events, and description.

Allegory A type of story or play popular in the medieval ages through the eighteenth century. Allegory contains two specific and continuous levels of meaning: each character represents a specific historical or political entity, abstract concept, or religious ideal. The purpose can be satirical or didactic. George Orwell's *Animal Farm* and John Bunyan's *A Pilgrim's Progress* are allegories for the totalitarian state and the process of Christian redemption, respectively. Modern fiction may use layers of symbolic complexity, but almost never features the one-to-one correlations of allegory.

Authorial Objectivity The degree of perspective an author has on a character. Writers sometimes base characters on themselves, friends, family members, enemies, or even ideals. The challenge is to avoid letting personal biases distort the presentation of characters. A writer may want readers to like or admire a character who bears a striking resemblance to the author, or want to show how awful a particular job was, but a personal agenda usually shows through and breaks the fictional dream for the reader.

Backstory Events that happened before the beginning of the story's plot. Backstory can be revealed in exposition, dialogue, flashback, or documents such as letters or newspaper clippings. A story may begin with several paragraphs of backstory, but writers more commonly reveal backstory in pieces throughout the course of the story. *See also* **Exposition.**

Dramatic Irony *See* **Irony.**

Epiphany In Christian theology, the Feast

of the Epiphany celebrates the moment when the resurrected Christ revealed himself to his apostles. In modernist and contemporary fiction, the term describes any moment of meaningful or life-changing insight, or a new vision of the world. Literary fiction often presents the epiphany as the climax or resolution of a story. James Joyce originated the modern usage, which has become so common as to verge on the cliché, especially when an epiphany substitutes for significant events. Having an epiphany is different from intellectually realizing a moral lesson: at their most powerful, specific events or actions embody the epiphany (the Greek word epiphany means "a showing forth"). For an illuminating discussion of epiphany, read Charles Baxter's "Against Epiphany" in *Burning Down the House.*

Exposition The revealing of information, usually in summary form. Exposition is sometimes used as a synonym for backstory, the information about the characters' past that we need to understand the present story. Unlike backstory, however, exposition can also include historical, technical, and psychological information not directly linked to particular events. Contemporary writers often look for ways to break up large chunks of exposition, distributing necessary information throughout the story.

The Fantastic Fiction incorporating events that are supernatural or otherwise go against the laws of time and space as we know them. A strong work of fantasy establishes its own rules and boundaries and then works within them. The fantastic has a long tradition—those interested in exploring its history might read *Beowulf,* Jonathan Swift's *Gulliver's Travels,* Virginia Woolf's *Orlando,* and the works of writers as diverse as George MacDonald, J. R. R. Tolkien, Jorge Luis Borges, and Russell Edson.

Ground Situation The prevailing conditions, underlying tensions, and nature of the characters' lives at the beginning of a work of fiction.

Irony A contradiction between the apparent meaning and the actual meaning, including *verbal irony, structural irony,* and *dramatic irony,* among others. In verbal irony, the narrator or a character uses words to deliberately convey a double meaning or the opposite of a stated meeting. In structural irony, the author uses a narrator with limited awareness (a mad, unreliable, or innocent narrator). In this case, the irony comes from the difference between the narrator's and the reader's understanding of events. A related but slightly different form of irony is dramatic or tragic irony, most often used in fiction that draws on historical events or well-known stories, or in stories with a narrator who tells the reader what will happen in advance; in either case, the reader knows information that the characters do not about their eventual fate. If a couple on the Titanic are drinking champagne and planning a wedding, they may be cheerful and full of hope; our emotion in reading about them will be much more complicated. Structural irony gives us characters who have all the information we do, but not the ability to interpret it; dramatic irony gives us characters who cannot know what we know about their future.

Magic Realism A hybrid of the realistic and the fantastic, which combines the domestic, political, or everyday with the mythical, magical, or surreal. Writers known for magic realism include Gabriel García Márquez, Milan Kundera, Salman Rushdie, Isabel Allende, Jeanette Winterson, Alice Hoffman, and Thaisa Frank.

Melodrama A narrative with emotionally simplistic characters and/or sensational events. The characters are uncomplicated heroes, victims, or villains. In contemporary fiction, melodramatic elements are usually used only for comic effect. Writers also use the term melodrama informally to describe scenes in which the author depicts a situation with a level of emotion that seems excessive for the circumstances.

Metafiction A style of writing that intentionally calls attention to and comments on the conventions and techniques of constructing fiction. These comments are often directly addressed to the reader. Well-known practitioners include Laurence Sterne, John Barth, Italo Calvino, and Robert Coover.

Minimalism A style of writing that strips away everything the writer regards as inessential. Details tend to be sparse; dramatic events tend to be underplayed; and the narrator gives us little information about the characters' histories, interests, thoughts, and feelings. Some minimalists have used the style to portray people living at a survival level, others have been influenced by the elliptical aesthetic of Japanese art and writing. Well-known practitioners include Raymond Carver, Ann Beattie, Mary Robison, Bobbie Ann Mason, Yasunari Kawabata, and Haruki Murakami. Ernest Hemingway is sometimes considered a precursor of American minimalism.

Narrative Drive The incidents, questions, or concerns that create the readers' desire to know what happens next or what will be revealed next. Narrative drive keeps readers turning the pages. Some works of fiction rely mainly on narrative drive for their power; others give more weight to character exploration or inventiveness of language and imagery.

Narrator The story's teller. In a first-person story, the narrator is a character in the story, often the protagonist. In a third-person story, the narrator is a voice invented by the author to tell the story from the outside. The narrator may simply chronicle events and details or may have a more assertive presence or voice, adding opinions and information about the characters and events.

Objective Correlative A term T. S. Eliot used in his essay "Hamlet and His Problems" to urge that thoughts and emotions be expressed tangibly, through the creation of events or objects (objective correlatives) that embody those states of mind. Although the idea is limiting when taken to its extreme, fiction writers look for opportunities to make the abstract tangible when appropriate to the story.

Passive Voice Verb form indicating that the subject of the sentence is being acted upon. Passive voice uses "to be" as an auxiliary verb with the past participle to focus attention not on who did something, but on what happened to the subject: "Tuition and fees are being raised," "The president was shot." The overall effect tends to be inert or even shifty. Writers generally avoid passive voice under most circumstances. Note that not all occurrences of the verb "to be" signal passive voice: "Susan is cold" is in the active voice. Writers often try to use more dynamic verbs than "to be," but this is a separate issue. *See also* **Active Voice.**

Science Fiction Fiction set in alternate realities, including other planets and imagined futures. For years science-fiction writers were more preoccupied by technology and ideas than by creating complicated characters or vivid language. In recent decades, many writers have written literary work that is also science fiction, including Samuel R. Delaney, Thomas Pynchon, Doris Lessing, William Gibson, Octavia Butler, Ursula K. Le Guin, and Kurt Vonnegut.

Sentimentality The quality of a scene or work that uses clichéd and simplistic language, characters, and situations to manipulate the reader into feeling a predetermined, uncomplicated emotion. To provoke happy relief, a work shows a benevolent protagonist triumph completely over evil. Or to inspire grief, a scene shows a fragile but golden-hearted child destroyed by a wicked character. Strong literary works have portrayed goodness rewarded or destroyed without sentimentality by presenting complex outcomes—not every aspect turns out well for everyone, and the characters have a mixture of flaws and virtues.

Stream of Consciousness A style of writing that plunges the reader into a character's experience by mimicking the fragmentary, associative flow of thoughts, memories, feelings, and sensory perceptions as they pass through the mind. Some literary critics use the term "interior monologue" to describe a stream of consciousness with no presence of an intervening narrator.

> Stream of consciousness: "At last a cab pulled up and he stepped in. Stains on the seat. Just like that cab ride in London."
>
> Interior monologue: "At last here's a cab. Amazing it bothered to stop. Stains on the seat. Just like that cab ride in London."

Writers can apply stream-of-consciousness and interior monologue techniques in any point of view.

Structural Irony *See* **Irony.**

Surrealism An artistic movement, founded by poet André Breton in 1920s France, that thumbed its nose at reason and logic, flouted conventions and morality, and explored dreams and the unconscious, often using experimental literary techniques such as the "exquisite corpse" and automatic writing. Surrealism contributed to the later development of both **Absurdism** and **Magic Realism.** Fiction writers known for surrealist approaches or influences include Leonora Carrington, Angela Carter, and Barry Yourgrau.

Suspension of Disbelief The reader's ability to forget the outside world and the invented nature of the work. Writers can help readers enter this state by checking plots for gaps in logic (including emotional logic), by embodying scenes through exact actions and sensory details, and by paying attention to complicating and layering their characters.

Verbal Irony *See* **Irony.**

APPENDIX

B

Suggestions for Further Reading

For Intermediate and Advanced Writers

Books about writing expand our sense of possibility and keep us company. Some of these books help us become better artists, some of them remind us of what we're doing when we write, and some give us courage to keep going through the hard times. The following list contains a few of our favorites for intermediate and advanced writers in each of these categories; we have quoted from many of these in *Deepening Fiction.*

The books on the art and craft of writing include both collections of essays, which help us rethink the endeavor of writing, and craft-oriented books, which expand our technical possibilities. We've also listed several of our favorite anthologies of fiction. They contain a wide range of excellent, international stories: long, short, and short-short. When we find a story we love in an anthology, we often get a collection of that writer's work, or even several books by that writer. This is a way to follow the thinking of one mind over time as it explores a variety of subjects, and to let that mind educate us, by example, about story-writing.

Books about the writing life give us a sense of our community and of what it is to be a writer, assuring us that others share our peculiar writerly ways of thinking. Books on publication give insight into the process by which writing reaches readers. And literary magazines provide good stories, great stories, and stories we may not like (very useful for thinking through how we would write them differently), as well as reviews and interviews.

Intermediate/Advanced Books on the Art and Craft of Writing

Andrea Barrett and Peter Turchi, Eds., *The Story Behind the Story: 26 Stories by Contemporary Writers and How They Work* (W. W. Norton & Company).

Charles Baxter, *Burning Down the House: Essays on Fiction* (Graywolf Press).

Charles Baxter and Peter Turchi, Eds., *Bringing the Devil to His Knees: The Craft of Fiction and the Writing Life* (University of Michigan Press).

Julie Checkoway, Ed., *Creating Fiction: Instruction and Insights from Teachers of the Associated Writing Programs* (Story Press).

Nicholas Delbanco, *The Lost Suitcase: Reflections on the Literary Life* (Columbia University Press).

E. M. Forster, *Aspects of the Novel* (Harcourt Brace Jovanovich).

David Michael Kaplan, *Revision: A Creative Approach to Writing and Rewriting Fiction* (Story Press).

David Madden, *Revising Fiction: A Handbook for Writers* (Penguin Group).

Jerome Stern, *Making Shapely Fiction* (W. W. Norton & Company).

Peter Turchi, *Maps of the Imagination: The Writer as Cartographer* (Trinity University Press).

Fiction Anthologies

R. V. Cassill and Richard Bausch, Eds., *The Norton Anthology of Short Fiction, Sixth Edition* (W. W. Norton & Company).

Paula Geyh, Fred. G. Lebron, and Andrew Levy, Eds., *Postmodern American Fiction: A Norton Anthology* (W. W. Norton & Company).

Ron Hansen and Jim Shepard, Eds., *You've Got to Read This: Contemporary American Writers Introduce Stories That Held Them in Awe* (HarperCollins).

Daniel Halpern, Ed., *The Art of the Story* (Viking).

Daniel Halpern, Ed., *The Art of the Tale* (Viking Penguin Inc.).

B. Minh Nguyen and Porter Shreve, Eds., *The Contemporary American Short Story* (Longman).

Robert Shapard and James Thomas, Eds., *Sudden Fiction: American Short-Short Stories* (Peregrine Smith Books).

Robert Shapard and James Thomas, Eds., *Sudden Fiction International* (W. W. Norton & Company).

Books on the Writing Life

Frederick Busch, Ed., *Letters to a Fiction Writer* (W. W. Norton & Company).

Annie Dillard, *Living By Fiction* (Harper & Row).

Lewis Hyde, *The Gift: Imagination and the Erotic Life of Property* (Vintage Books).

Anton Chekhov, *Anton Chekhov's Life and Thoughts: Selected Letters and Commentary*; Translated by Michael Henry Heim in collaboration with Simon Karlinsky; selection, commentary, and introduction by Simon Karlinsky (Northwestern University Press; Reprint edition).

Anne Lamott, *Bird by Bird: Some Instructions on Writing and Life* (Pantheon).

Victoria Nelson, *On Writer's Block: A New Approach to Creativity* (Houghton Mifflin Company).

George Plimpton, Ed., *The Paris Review Interviews Writers at Work* series.

Ted Solotaroff, *A Few Good Voices in My Head: Occasional Pieces on Writing, Editing, and Reading My Contemporaries* (Harper & Row).

Eudora Welty, *One Writer's Beginnings* (Harvard Press).

Books on Publishing

Judith Appelbaum, *How to Get Happily Published, Fifth Edition: A Complete and Candid Guide* (Harper Resource).

Richard Balkin (Nick Bakalar, Contributor) *A Writer's Guide to Book Publishing, Third Edition* (Plume).

André Bernard, *Rotten Rejections: A Literary Companion* (Viking Penguin).

Len Fulton, Ed., *The International Directory of Little Magazines & Small Presses* (Dustbooks, updated yearly).

Betsy Lerner, *The Forest for the Trees: An Editor's Advice to Writers* (Riverhead Books).

Writer's Market (Writer's Digest Books, updated yearly).

Literary Magazines

Here are a few of the many terrific literary magazines available to fiction writers: *Alaska Quarterly Review, The Antioch Review, Black Warrior Review, Boulevard, Conjunctions, Epoch, Fiction, The Gettysburg Review, The Georgia Review, Glimmer Train, Granta, Indiana Review, The Iowa Review, The Kenyon Review, McSweeney's, Michigan Quarterly Review, Mississippi Review, The Missouri Review, Northwest Review, The North American Review, Ontario Review, The Paris Review, Ploughshares, Prairie Schooner, Puerto del Sol, Quarterly West, The Southern Review, StoryQuarterly, The Threepenny Review, Tin House, Witness,* and *Zoetrope: All-Story.*

Most of these journals have Web sites; others have addresses and other information in the market directories. They have quite different styles and tastes—order at least one sample copy before submitting, to save your own and the editors' time. Many of these appear at larger newsstands or independent bookstores. Do subscribe to as many of your favorites as you can afford. Subscribing is a great way to keep up on the variety of what's happening in contemporary writing, and the writing community is the main audience for these essential magazines; even the most established ones won't survive without us. Reading them gives us a chance to know about, and to find our place in, the contemporary writing life, not as depicted in the movies or as we imagine it from reading about literary stars, but as lived by actual writers.

APPENDIX C

Author Biographies

Chinua Achebe, born Albert Chinualumogu Achebe in Ogidi, Nigeria, has written more than 20 books of fiction and poetry, including *Things Fall Apart, The Sacrificial Egg and Other Stories, Arrow of God, A Man of the People, Anthills of the Savannah,* and *Collected Poems.* His essay collections include *Morning Yet On Creation Day, Hopes and Impediments,* and *The Trouble With Nigeria.* He has worked for the Nigerian Broadcasting Company, in the Biafran government service, and as a teacher in Nigeria; in the United States he has taught at the University of Massachusetts, Amherst, and at Bard College. His awards include the New Statesman-Jock Campbell Award, Margaret Wrong Prize, and the first Commonwealth Prize (cowinner). He has also been a finalist for England's Booker Prize. He is married and has four children.

Isaac Babel was born in 1894 in Odessa and was homeschooled until he was 12 years old. Despite the restrictions on educational and living opportunities for a Jewish boy, he managed to study Russian, Hebrew, English, French, and German. He lived in Petrograd (later Leningrad) after college, using forged papers since it was illegal for Jews to live in the capital. Maxim Gorky mentored Isaac Babel's writing from its early stages. His stories became wildly popular with the appearance of *Odessa Tales* and later *Red Cavalry,* a book about his time with the Cavalry Corps of the Red Army. He was also attacked for both his style and his honesty about military life. His frankness in writing about sex led to a trial for pornography. He spent long periods of time in Italy and in France, where his wife had moved with their daughter in 1925, but always returned to the Soviet Union. In later years, he gave up publishing fiction because of increasing Soviet censorship and turned to writing screenplays and newspaper articles, heavily censored. His late stories and plays particularly show the effects of censorship. He was arrested in 1939 and disappeared. His family received a death certificate in 1941, but the cause of his death was not specified.

Andrea Barrett, born in 1954, grew up on Cape Cod, received her B.S. in biology at Union College in Schenectady, NY, and then, after a very brief stint in a graduate zoology program, realized she wasn't meant to be a scientist after all. For the next decade she worked at odd jobs while she began trying to learn to write. Her first novel was published in 1988, while she was working as a freelance editor of medical and nursing textbooks. Since then she's written four other novels, most recently *The Voyage of the Narwhal,* and two collections of short fiction, *Ship Fever,* which received the National Book Award, and *Servants of the Map,* a finalist for the Pulitzer Prize. She lives in Rochester, New York with her husband, scientist and photographer Barry Goldstein, and she teaches in the MFA Program for Writers at Warren Wilson College and at the Bread Loaf Writers' Conference.

Charles Baxter grew up in Minnesota and attended Macalester College. After teaching elementary school in Pinconning, Michigan, he entered the SUNY at Buffalo graduate program in English. After receiving his Ph.D. there, he taught at Wayne State University in Detroit, the University of Michigan, and now teaches at the University of Minnesota. He is the author of four books of stories, including *A Relative Stranger* and *Believers,* and four novels, the most recent being *The Feast of Love* (a finalist for the National Book Award) and *Saul and Patsy,* both published by Pantheon in hardback and Vintage in paperback. He is also the author of a book of essays, *Burning Down the House,* published by Graywolf, and a book of poems, *Imaginary Paintings.* He has received the award in literature from the American Academy of Arts and Letters. He is married and has one son. He lives with his wife in Minneapolis.

Jorge Luis Borges was born in Buenos Aires in 1899 and educated largely in Europe. He published numerous essays and poems and more than 100 stories, including parables, metaphysical detective stories, and reviews of imaginary books. His more than two dozen books of poetry, fiction, and nonfiction include *Ficciones, A Personal Anthology, Labyrinths, The Book of Imaginary Beings, The Book of Sand, The Aleph and Other Stories, Collected Poems,* and *Collected Fictions.* He was an honorary member of The American Academy of Arts and Letters and the National Institute of Arts and Letters. He served as Director of the Argentine National Library from 1955 until 1973. He tended to be slyly self-deprecating and contradictory in his accounts of his work as a writer. In an *Agni* interview, he said about his story-writing, ". . . as to my writing short pieces, there are two reasons I can give you. The first is my invincible laziness. The second is that I've always been fond of short stories, and it always took me some trouble to get through a novel, except in the case of such books as, well, *The Pickwick Papers, Huckleberry Finn, Don Quixote,* Conrad's *Lord Jim,* and so on. Besides, I'm very interested in Kipling, and found out that at the end of his life he could pack into a short story as many people, or, indeed, more than most can in a novel. And I thought, maybe I would try my hand at that game, writing very closely packed short stories. Although I'm very lazy when it comes to writing, I'm not that lazy when it comes to thinking. I like to develop the plan of a short story, then cut it as short as possible, try to evolve all the necessary details. I know far more about the characters than what actually comes out of the writing." He married twice and remained close to his mother all her life. He went blind in 1955 but continued writing until his death in 1986.

Willa Cather was born in Virginia in 1873, moved with her family to the Nebraska prairies when she was about 9 years old, and grew up among Scandinavian, French, and Bohemian immigrants struggling to farm in difficult terrain. After graduating from the University of Nebraska in 1895, she worked for a newspaper for several years before moving to New York City to become an editor at *McClure's Magazine.* Her first short story collection, *The Troll Garden,* appeared in 1905. She published her first novel, *Alexander's Bridge,* in 1912 and subsequently quit *McClure's* to write full time. While *Alexander's Bridge* took place in New York City, Cather is most known for her novels set in Nebraska and on the western frontier, including *O Pioneers!, My Ántonia, The Song of the Lark,* and *Death Comes for the Archbishop.* She won the Pulitzer in 1923 and died in 1947. For the last 40 years of her life, she lived with her companion, Edith Lewis.

Lan Samantha Chang writes, "I've recently finished my first novel, *Inheritance,* in which a Chinese immigrant to America relates the story of a long quarrel in her parents' generation and examines the inheritance of memory.

"Writing this novel took me seven years, during which I moved from Menlo Park, California to Iowa City, Iowa, then to Princeton, New Jersey, then to Cambridge, Massachusetts, then back to Iowa City, then back to Cambridge. For a month my official residence was in Wyoming at an artist's colony and working cattle ranch, the Ucross Foundation.

"I currently live in Cambridge, Massachusetts, and teach creative writing at Harvard University and the Warren Wilson MFA Program for Writers."

Anton Chekhov was born in 1860 in Taganrog, Russia, the son of a shopkeeper. When he was 16, his father went bankrupt and fled with the rest of the family to Moscow to escape debtor's prison—leaving Chekhov behind. He lived by tutoring until he entered medical school in Moscow in 1879. While in college, to support the family, he wrote comic stories and light sketches for magazines. Gradually he grew more serious about his writing. In 1888, his story collection *In the Twilight* received the Pushkin Prize. He never finished his dissertation, *The History of Medicine in Russia,* though he traveled to the penal colony of Sakhalin to do medical research. Instead he wrote a nonfiction book, *The Island of Sakhalin,* to expose the conditions under which the prisoners lived and the destruction of the local peoples. His plays include *The Seagull, Uncle Vanya, The Three Sisters,* and *The Cherry Orchard.* He was always struggling to balance his literary work with his exhausting medical work, his efforts against cholera, and his increasing load of tubercular patients. He married the actress Olga Knipper in 1901 and died three years later of tuberculosis.

Julio Cortázar was born in Brussels in 1914 and raised in Argentina. He lived in Paris from 1952 to his death in 1984. In addition to writing novels, short stories, and poems, he was a translator and an amateur jazz musician. In a Center for Book Culture interview, he said, "I, myself, would like to be a kind of synthesis . . . even for a day, for one day of my life, creator and critic. When I say creator, it is always with some embarrassment because it is a word loaded with Romantic significance from the nineteenth century; that is, the creator is a sort of minor god. I no longer believe that. The creator is a laborer like many others. There is no scale of values that places the creator above the critic. A great critic and a great author are absolutely on the same level." Some of his works translated into English include the novels *Hopscotch* and *62: A Model Kit* and the short story collections *Blow-Up and Other Stories, A Change of Light,* and *We Love Glenda So Much.* His essays have been collected in *Around the Day in Eighty Worlds.*

Adam Johnson has published fiction in *Esquire, Harper's, Missouri Review, New England Review,* and the *Paris Review,* and other magazines and anthologies, including *Best New American Voices* four years running. He was born in Arizona and after a short career as an industrial carpenter he attended Arizona State University where he earned his degree in journalism and studied fiction writing with Ron Carlson. He studied writing with Robert Olen Butler in Lake Charles, Louisiana, then earned a Ph.D. in English from Florida State University. He was awarded the Wallace Stegner Fellowship at Stanford University, where he is now a Jones Teaching Fellow. Johnson's debut collection of short stories, *Emporium,* was nominated for a Young Lions Award. His novel, *Parasites Like Us,* was published by Viking in August 2003. Adam Johnson and his wife were married five times: in Stuart, Florida; Scottsdale, Arizona; Tallahassee, Florida; Pacifica, California; and Las Vegas. Adam Johnson lives in Palo Alto with his family.

Denis Johnson was born in 1949 in Munich and raised in Tokyo, Manila, and Washington. He has written numerous works of fiction, including *The Name of the World, Resuscitation of a Hanged Man, Fiskadoro,* and *Jesus' Son*; poetry, including *Inner Weather, The Incognito Lounge,* and *The Veil*; plays, including *Hell Hound on My Trail, Shoppers Carried by Escalators into the Flames,* and *Soul of a Whore*; and journalism. His work has been published in the *Paris Review, Epoch, Big Wednesday,* the *New Yorker, McSweeney's,* and other magazines, and he has won a number of awards, including a Lannan Fellowship and a Whiting Writer's Award. In a *San Francisco Reader* interview, he said, "I really enjoy writing novels. It's like the ocean. You can just build a boat and take off. I can't understand why anybody would criticize anything that ends up being a novel because you've arrived to the other shore, you've made it alive. Maybe you started off for Africa and ended up in Spain, but so what? I'm working on a novel now, but I never entirely gave up on verse. My ears tune into it. When I realized that in my plays I was going to write this sort of large stuff, big stuff with tragic overtones, verse seemed to fit." He lives in northern Idaho.

Yasunari Kawabata was born in Osaka, Japan in 1899, the son of a physician. Both his parents died before he reached the age of 3, and he lost the rest of his remaining close relatives by the time he was 14. He received his degree from Tokyo Imperial University in 1924. In the 1920s, Kawabata was a cofounder of *Bungei Jidai,* the journal of the Japanese "New Perception" movement that drew on the ideas of Dadaism and Expressionism. In his work,

Kawabata blended these influences with the traditions of seventeenth-century Japanese prose and fifteenth-century *renga* (linked verse). His novels include *Snow Country, A Thousand Cranes, The Old Capital,* and *The Sound of the Mountain.* His stories, many of them short-shorts, are collected in *Palm-of-the-Hand Stories, The Dancing Girl of Izu and Other Stories,* and *First Snow on Fuji.* For many years he served as president of the Japanese Center of the PEN Club, and championed and mentored young writers including Yukio Mishima. He received the Nobel Prize for literature in 1968. In his Nobel Prize speech, he said that although his writing had been described as "works of emptiness," it was rooted in Zen rather than Western nihilism. In 1972 he took his own life, not long after Mishima's suicide.

John L'Heureux writes, "My father was a civil engineer and my mother a secretary. In his sixties my father began to paint in oils, brilliantly, I think. This is the only autobiographical element in 'Father.'

"I attended public schools, trained as an actor, and performed briefly on stage and television. After two years at Holy Cross College, I entered the Jesuits. Seventeen years later I requested laicization, which was granted in 1971. While still a Jesuit, I worked as a staff editor of *The Atlantic*; afterwards I taught American literature and fiction writing at Tufts, Harvard, and—for over thirty years now—at Stanford.

"I am married to Joan Polston, a teacher and writer. The marriage, if anyone cares, was okayed by Rome and we are both practicing Catholics. I'm practicing; she's good at it.

"My writing extends far back into my Jesuit life. My first four books—poetry—were exercises in working small, taking the metaphor as far as it would go, exorcising anger, desire, desperation, love. My later books, all of them fiction, explore the mysterious and ironic interventions of God in our lives, the range of the supra-rational, the rags and boneyard of the heart. I'm 68 and not dead yet."

Margot Livesey grew up in Scotland at a boys' private school where her father taught mathematics and geography. She attended a nearby girls' school and then went south to the University of York in England where she studied literature and philosophy. After graduation she went traveling in Europe and North Africa for a year during which she wrote a novel so bad that it made her want to try to write a better one. She spent the remainder of her twenties working in restaurants, shops, and factories—the pharmaceutical factory was a particularly low ebb—while gradually writing the stories that would form her collection, *Learning by Heart.* Since then she has gone on to teach in several creative writing programs, including the Warren Wilson MFA program, the Iowa Writers' Workshop, the University of California at Irvine and currently Emerson College. She has won awards from the Canada Council for the Arts and the National Endowment for the Arts. Her work has appeared in, among other places, the *New Yorker, North American Review,* the *Antigonish Review,* the *Kenyon Review,* and *The New Press Anthology: Best Canadian Short Fiction #1.* She is the author of five novels: *Homework, Criminals, The*

Missing World, Eva Moves the Furniture, and *Banishing Verona,* which "The Niece" is excerpted from.

Alice Munro grew up in Wingham, Ontario, and attended the University of Western Ontario. She has published ten collections of stories—including *The Moons of Jupiter*; *The Progress of Love*; *Friend of My Youth*; *Open Secrets; Hateship, Friendship, Courtship, Loveship, Marriage*; and *Selected Stories*—as well as a novel, *Lives of Girls and Women.* Her awards and prizes include three of Canada's Governor General's Literary Awards and its Giller Prize, the Lannan Literary Award, and the National Book Critics Circle Award. Her stories have appeared in the *New Yorker,* the *Atlantic Monthly,* the *Paris Review,* and other publications, and her collections have been translated into thirteen languages. In an *Atlantic Unbound* interview, she said, "So why do I like to write short stories? Well, I certainly didn't intend to. I was going to write a novel. And still! I still come up with ideas for novels. And I even start novels. But something happens to them. They break up. I look at what I really want to do with the material, and it never turns out to be a novel. But when I was younger, it was simply a matter of expediency. I had small children, I didn't have any help. Some of this was before the days of automatic washing machines, if you can actually believe it. There was no way I could get that kind of time. I couldn't look ahead and say, this is going to take me a year, because I thought every moment something might happen that would take all time away from me. So I wrote in bits and pieces with a limited time expectation. Perhaps I got used to thinking of my material in terms of things that worked that way. And then when I got a little more time, I started writing these odder stories, which branch out a lot." Alice Munro and her husband divide their time between Clinton, Ontario, near Lake Huron, and Comox, British Columbia.

Daniel Orozco earned his MFA from the University of Washington. He was a Scowcroft and L'Heureux Fiction Fellow, then a Jones Lecturer in Fiction in the Creative Writing Program at Stanford University. His stories have appeared in the *Best American Short Stories* and *Pushcart Prize* anthologies, and in *Story, Zoetrope: All-Story,* and *Mid-American Review.* He currently teaches in the Creative Writing Program at the University of Idaho in Moscow. He is completing his first collection of stories. Readings of "Orientation" have been produced for public radio by Radio Canada (*Between the Covers*), NPR (*This American Life*), and New York Symphony Space Performing Arts Center (*Selected Shorts*). The story has been translated into Spanish, Japanese, and Hungarian; and has also been published in English-language textbooks in Germany and Denmark. It was adapted as a dance piece by the Pamela Trokanski Dance Theatre in Davis, California, and by Liam Clancy for the Dance Theater Workshop in New York City. It will soon be produced as a short film by Mike Gallay Productions in Toronto.

Julie Orringer is a graduate of the Iowa Writers' Workshop and Cornell University, and was a Stegner Fellow in the Creative Writing Program at Stanford University. Her stories have appeared in the *Paris Review,* the *Yale*

Review, Ploughshares, The Pushcart Prize anthology, and *Zoetrope: All-Story,* among other places. Her story collection *How to Breathe Underwater* (2003) was a New York Times Notable Book and won the Northern California Book Award for Short Fiction. She lives in San Francisco with her husband, fiction writer Ryan Harty.

ZZ Packer has published stories in the *New Yorker* (where she was launched as a debut writer), *Harper's, Ploughshares, Zoetrope: All-Story,* and *Story.* Her works have appeared in *The Best American Short Stories, 2000* (edited by E. L. Doctorow) and 2003 (edited by Walter Mosley) and various anthologies, including *Twenty-Five and Under*; they have also been read on NPR's *Selected Shorts.* Her story collection, *Drinking Coffee Elsewhere,* was a New York Times Notable Book and was picked by John Updike for the Today Show Book Club. Packer is a recipient of a Whiting Writers' Award and a Rona Jaffe Foundation Writers' Award. A graduate of Yale, the Iowa Writers' Workshop, and the Writing Seminar at Johns Hopkins University, she has been a Wallace Stegner-Truman Capote fellow at Stanford University. She has taught at the Iowa Writers' Workshop and been a Jones lecturer at Stanford. She lives in the San Francisco Bay area with her husband and their dog, Punky.

Grace Paley, who has been a member of the War Resisters' League, Resist, and Women's Pentagon Action, was born in the Bronx in 1922. A long-time feminist and antiwar activist, she has described herself, according to her *Collected Stories,* as "a somewhat combative pacifist and cooperative anarchist." She studied at Hunter College and New York University. Ms. Paley's stories have appeared in the *Atlantic, New American Review, Fiction, Harbinger, Heresies, Mother Jones, Ms., New England Review,* the *New Yorker,* and *Threepenny Review,* among other places. Her collections of stories include *The Little Disturbances of Man, Enormous Changes at the Last Minute,* and *Later the Same Day.* She has also written collections of poetry and essays. Grace Paley has taught at Columbia University, Sarah Lawrence, Dartmouth, and City College. Her awards include a Senior Fellowship by the National Endowment for the Arts, the 1994 Jewish Cultural Achievement Award for Literary Arts, the 1993 Vermont Award for Excellence in the Arts, and the 1989 Edith Wharton Award. In 1989, New York Governor Mario Cuomo named her the first official New York State Writer.

Melissa Pritchard is the author of three short story collections, *Spirit Seizures, The Instinct for Bliss,* and *Disappearing Ingenue,* and three novels, *Phoenix, Selene of the Spirits,* and *Late Bloomer.* Her awards include the Flannery O'Connor Award, the Carl Sandburg Award, the James Phelan Award, the Janet Heidinger Kafka Prize, and fellowships from the National Endowment for the Arts. Pritchard's work has appeared in *Story,* the *Southern Review, Boulevard, Open City, Washington Square,* and the *Paris Review.* Her stories have been widely anthologized, appearing in *Prize Stories: The O. Henry Awards*; *Best American Short Stories*; *The Prentice Hall Anthology of Women's Literature*; and *Three Genres: Fiction, Drama and Po-*

etry; among other places. She is currently Director of the MFA Program in Creative Writing at Arizona State University and serves on the faculty at Spalding University. She has two daughters and lives in Tempe, Arizona.

Elizabeth Tallent teaches at Stanford University. Her books include the novel *Museum Pieces*; the short story collections *In Constant Flight, Time with Children,* and *Honey*; and a study of John Updike's fiction, *Married Men and Magic Tricks.* Her work has appeared in the *New Yorker, Esquire, Harper's, Grand Street,* the *Paris Review,* the *Threepenny Review, Zyzzyva, The Best American Short Stories* and the *O. Henry Award* collections. She has also been a recipient of a National Endowment for the Arts grant.

Tobias Wolff lives in Northern California and teaches at Stanford University. He has published the memoirs *This Boy's Life* and *In Pharaoh's Army,* the short story collections *In the Garden of North American Martyrs, Back in the World,* and *The Night in Question,* the novella *The Barracks Thief,* and the novel *Old School.* He has received the Rea Award for excellence in the short story, the Los Angeles Times Book Prize, and the PEN/Faulkner Award. His stories have appeared in the *Atlantic, Esquire, Harper's,* the *New Yorker, TriQuarterly,* and several *Best American Short Stories* anthologies. He is also the editor of *The Vintage Book of American Short Stories* and *A Doctor's Visit: The Short Stories of Anton Chekhov.*

Credits

CHINUA ACHEBE: "Civil Peace" from GIRLS AT WAR AND OTHER STORIES by Chinua Achebe, copyright © 1972, 1973 by Chinua Achebe. Used by permission of Doubleday, a division of Random House, Inc. Reprinted by permission of Harold Ober Associates Incorporated.

ANDREA BARRETT: "The Forest" from SERVANTS OF THE MAP by Andrea Barrett. Copyright © 2002 by Andrea Barrett. Used by permission of W.W. Norton & Company.

CHARLES BAXTER: "The Cures for Love" from BELIEVERS: A NOVELLA AND STORIES by Charles Baxter, copyright © 1997 by Charles Baxter. Used by permission of Pantheon books, a division of Random House, Inc.

JORGE LUIS BORGES: "Inferno I, 32," by Jorge Luis Borges from *A Personal Anthology*, trans. Anthony Kerrigan. Originally published as *Antología Personal*, © 1961 by Editorial Sur, S.A., Buenos Aires. Translation copyright © 1967 by Grove Press. Used by permission of Grove/Atlantic, Inc.

LAN SAMANTHA CHANG: "The Eve of the Spirit Festival" from HUNGER by Lan Samantha Chang. Copyright © 1998 by Lan Samantha Chang. Used by permission of W.W. Norton & Company, Inc.

JULIO CORTÁZAR: "Graffiti" from WE LOVE GLENDA SO MUCH AND OTHER TALES by Julio Cortázar. Translated by Gregory Rabassa, copyright 1983 by Alfred A. Knopf, a division of Random House, Inc. Used by permission of Alfred A. Knopf, a division of Random House, Inc.

ADAM JOHNSON: "Trauma Plate" from EMPORIUM by Adam Johnson, copyright © 2002 by Adam Johnson. Used by permission of Viking Penguin, a division of Penguin Group (USA) Inc.

DENIS JOHNSON: "Car Crash While Hitchhiking," from JESUS' SON by Denis Johnson. Copyright © 1992 by Denis Johnson. Reprinted by permission of Farrar, Straus and Giroux, LLC.

YASUNARI KAWABATA: "The Rooster and the Dancing Girl" from PALM-OF-THE-HAND STORIES by Yasunari Kawabata, translated by Lane Dunlop and J. Martin Holman. Translation copyright ©1988 by Lane Dunlop and J. Martin Holman. Reprinted by permission of North Point Press, a division of Farrar, Straus and Giroux, LLC.

JOHN L'HEUREUX: "Father" from COMEDIANS by John L'Heureux, copyright © 1990 by John L'Heureux. Used by permission of the author.

MARGOT LIVESEY: "The Niece" by Margot Livesey. Copyright © 2003 by Margot Livesey. First published in *The New Yorker*. Reprinted by permission of the author.

ALICE MUNRO: "The Turkey Season" from THE MOONS OF JUPITER AND OTHER STORIES by Alice Munro. Copyright © 1982 by Alice Munro. Used by permission of Alfred A. Knopf, a division of Random House, Inc. Reprinted in Canada by permission of William Morris Agency, Inc. on behalf of the Author.

DANIEL OROZCO: "Orientation" by Daniel Orozco from THE BEST AMERICAN SHORT STORIES, copyright ©1995 by Daniel Orozco, ed., by Jane Smiley (editor) and Katrina Kenison (editor), published by Houghton Mifflin. Used by permission of the author.

FRANK O'HARA: Lines from "Autobiographia Literaria," by Frank O'Hara from COLLECTED POEMS by Frank O'Hara, copyright © 1971 by Maureen Granville-Smith, Administratrix of the Estate of Frank O'Hara. Used by permission of Alfred A. Knopf, a division of Random House, Inc.

JULIE ORRINGER: "Pilgrims" from HOW TO BREATHE UNDERWATER: STORIES by Julie Orringer, copyright © 2003 by Julie Orringer. Used by permission of Alfred A. Knopf, a division of Random House, Inc.

ZZ PACKER: "Drinking Coffee Elsewhere" from DRINKING COFFEE ELSEWHERE by ZZ Packer, copyright © 2003 by ZZ Packer. Used by permission of Riverhead Books, an imprint of Penguin Group (USA) Inc.

GRACE PALEY: "A Conversation with my Father" from ENORMOUS CHANGES AT THE LAST MINUTE by Grace Paley. Copyright © 1971, 1974 by Grace Paley. Reprinted by permission of Farrar, Straus and Giroux, LLC.

MELISSA PRITCHARD: "Photograph of Luisa" from SPIRIT SEIZURES by Melissa Pritchard. Copyright © 1987 by Melissa Pritchard. Reprinted by permission of The University of Georgia Press.

ELIZABETH TALLENT: "The Fence Party" from TIME WITH CHILDREN by Elizabeth Tallent. Copyright 1987 by Elizabeth Tallent. Reprinted by permission of the author.

TOBIAS WOLFF: "Powder" from THE NIGHT IN QUESTION: STORIES by Tobias Wolff, copyright © 1996 by Tobias Wolff. Used by permission of Alfred A. Knopf, a division of Random House, Inc.

Index